THE GOOD
OLD DAYS

WE GUARANTEE

That each and every article in this catalog is exactly as described and illustrated.

We guarantee that any article purchased from us will satisfy you perfectly; that it will give the service you have a right to expect; that it represents full value for the price you pay.

If for any reason whatever you are dissatisfied with any article purchased from us, we expect you to return it to us at our expense.

We will then exchange it for exactly what you want, or will return your money, including any transportation charges you have paid.

SEARS, ROEBUCK AND CO., CHICAGO

SIMPLE INSTRUCTIONS IN MEASURING FOR WEARING APPAREL ARE FOUND ON PAGE 73

THE GOOD OLD DAYS

A History of

American Morals and Manners

as seen through the

Sears Roebuck

Catalogs

By

DAVID L. COHN

with an Introduction by

SINCLAIR LEWIS

and recently edited by

SALLY ZOHN

Reprint Edition 1976 by Arno Press Inc.
Originally published by Simon & Schuster, Inc.
in 1940

Reprinted from a copy in the
State Historical Society of Wisconsin Library

LIBRARY OF CONGRESS CATALOGING IN PUBLICATION DATA

Cohn, David Lewis, 1896-1960.
    The good old days.

    (America in two centuries, an inventory)
    Reprint of the ed. published by Simon and Schuster,
New York.
    1.   United States—Social life and customs—1865-1918.
2.   Sears, Roebuck and Company.   I.   Title.   II.   Series.
E168.C685   1976   973.8   75-22809
ISBN 0-405-07680-0

Manufactured in the United States of America

FOR

THE MOUNTAIN LADY AND THE QUEEN

V

FOREWORD

The superior survival value of novelists to historians may not be altogether in the eloquence with which fictioneers communicate Mildred's agonies over the virile high diving of Peter, or the glories of Kansas City by moonlight. It may be that the permanence of such institutions as Dickens is due to their recording not the dreary magnificences of coronations and battles, but instead the dear diminutive excitements in commonplace characters which make us identify ourselves with them: what they eat, with what weapons, exactly, they kill one another, and the precise wording of the acid pomposity with which a duke or a dustman complains of his breakfast porridge. Mankind is always more interested in living than in Lives.

Mr. David Cohn, though he is also an historian of American racial stocks and of the metaphysics of finance, has in this volume stolen the novelist's tricks complete. He has portrayed the moral and cultural zigzag of America, not by sterile analyses of "the woman movement" or the elephantiasis afflicting pedagogical departments in our universities, but by recalling just what domestic and commercial gadgets we have used in the past fifty years; how they have changed or vanished—and what we paid for them.

What happened to Gertie Perkins's soul, income, and matrimonial prospects, and what happened to the millions of Yankees and Crackers and Japs and Germans and Scotsmen who make their livings by serving Gertie, when she bloomed from cotton leg-armor to silk stockings, and when she mounted from canning preserves to the bliss of taking dicta-

tion about consignments of carburetors? These matters are delicate but important and—Cohn Tells All.

It seems to me that Mr. Cohn has achieved exactly the right tone of accurate yet diverting narration of our evolving trade. He has neither the contemptuous Frigidaire wit of the professional urbanites to whom Gertie Perkins and her tinted stationery are subhuman phenomena of the Peruna Belt, nor yet the trusting naïveté of the patriotic nostalgicist to whom one hundred per cent of Grandma's ways and wares are incontrovertibly examples of pioneer heroism.

During the past twenty years, America has been perceiving that it now has the privilege, and the responsibility, of being no longer a cultural colony of Europe, but a great and adult and individual and slightly lonely nation, that must depend on itself, and that hugely needs to understand the self on which it depends. In history, in fiction, in music, amid the extravagances of the motion pictures, it has been studying its present and future through a surprisingly candid inspection of its past.

In this book there is an important report of such inspection. By your eyebrow pencils, your encyclopedias, and your alarm clocks shall ye be known. The most scrupulous statistics on the increasing acreage of alfalfa and soy beans, the most elevated dissertations on our tendency to chronic philanthropy, could not make us understand that cranky, hysterical, brave, mass-timorous, hard-minded, imaginative Chosen Race, the Americans, half so competently as Mr. Cohn's parade of the wares that we have been buying and paying for and actually lugging into our homes and barns and offices, these past fifty years:

Electric Thermostats, Ladies' Percale Sunbonnets, Birth Control Manuals, Imported Fancy Lily Bulbs, Cambric Bust Confiners, Two-Color Bibles, 1939 Model Air Conditioners, Vest Pocket Revolvers, Brewster Sleigh Bells, Fancy Colored Mummy Effect Worsted Round Cut Sack Suits, Clarion Harmonicas in Red Leatherette Cases, phonograph records of Uncle Josh in a Chinese Laundry and of the Flogging

Scene from Uncle Tom's Cabin *with Incidental Music Effects, copies of* From Eden to Calvary *by Grandpa Reuben Prescott, of* A Guide to Successful Auctioneering *and of the* Lovers' Guide and Manual, *linen automobile dusters with wristlets, the New Acme Queen Cathedral Gong Clock, Dr. Echol's Australian Auricolo—the Wonder Heart Cure, the Great Chinese Corn, Bunion and Wart Remover, the Handiman R-T Four Wheel Riding Tractor—a mad bazaar with ten times ten thousand magic tokens.*

The political and religious protestations that we and our parents have made, at cocktail parties or prayer meetings, this past half century, have cost us nothing beyond an occasional imputation that we were liars or nihilists. But in these trade goods, these dreams realized in gold and steel and limp leather, we have shown our real faith, by paying for them the money that is our heart's treasure . . . just as, of course, it is also the tender treasure of the English, the Germans, and the Maoris.

Here then, in Mr. Cohn's treatise, equally serious and ribald, is the Proper Study of that portion of Mankind which every day becomes more important to us as the other nations whirl off in the dance of death and leave us sitting, chilly and alone and extremely grateful for it, in the terrestrial chaperones' box.

SINCLAIR LEWIS

New Orleans
December 26, 1939

TABLE OF CONTENTS

Part Two

LADIES

Part Three

GENTLEMEN

TABLE OF CONTENTS

Part Four

EVERYBODY'S BUSINESS

GRAPHOPHONE DEPARTMENT.

OUR $5.00 GRAPHOPHONE TALKING MACHINE.

THIS IS A GENUINE TYPE A Q COLUMBIA GRAPHOPHONE, made by the Columbia Phonograph Co., of New York and London, and uses the regular Columbia Phonograph Co.'s standard size wax cylinder records.

THIS GRAPHOPHONE, as shown in the illustration, is one of the latest 1905 styles, made with clockwork spring motor enclosed in a dustproof metal barrel. It is provided with a speed regulator and leveling screw and has a high grade governor for maintaining a

UNIFORM SPEED,

just the same as furnished with the highest grade talking machines.

A NEW AND IMPROVED FEED SCREW DEVICE carries the reproducer along over the surface of the record, holding it firmly in place and preventing it from slipping or injuring the record.

THE LARGE SIZE ALUMINUM REPRODUCER, made with mica diaphragm, is securely attached to the 10-inch japanned amplifying horn, and will reproduce standard size wax cylinder records with the most wonderful clearness and fidelity. Uses any standard size wax cylinder records.

No. 21C102 Price, complete, without records.....................$5.00

A Q GRAPHOPHONE AND SIX COLUMBIA RECORDS $5.90

No. 21C103 When sorting out our enormous stock of standard size genuine Columbia records to make up into collections of twelve, twenty-five and fifty, as explained on page 382, we made up a large quantity into collections of six, little assortments of extra nice records, and we now offer the A Q Graphophone, as shown above, together with one of these extra good collections of six records, for only $5.90, thus presenting an exceptional opportunity for you to get a complete outfit for very little money.

Remember, the outfit is complete, the A Q Graphophone and six genuine Columbia records, all different. Price.....................$5.90

THE COLUMBIA TYPE Q GRAPHOPHONE AT $7.50.

THIS IS THE COLUMBIA PHONOGRAPH CO.'S GENUINE TYPE

$7.50

Q MACHINE, one of the most perfectly constructed talking machines ever placed on the market for so low a price.

THIS MACHINE will run the regular standard size wax cylinder records just as perfectly as the higher priced machines and it is especially well suited for home entertainment purposes.

THE CAREFULLY CONSTRUCTED SPRING MOTOR which operates this graphophone is encased in a dustproof barrel, and the high grade governor, with latest style speed regulator, insures perfect uniformity of speed.

THE REPRODUCER, made with best mica diaphragm and sapphire reproducing point, is detachable and reproduces the musical and talking records as perfectly as many machines costing two and three times as much. We particularly recommend this graphophone to anyone desiring a strictly high grade instrument for home amusement at a very moderate price. We call your special attention to the possibility of making up a very moderate priced graphophone outfit by purchasing this little machine and an assortment of twelve, twenty-five or fifty of the Columbia Phonograph Co.'s records, which we are now selling in lots of 50 at 15 cents each, as explained on page 382.

No. 21C110 Type Q Graphophone, complete with 10-inch japanned horn and high grade aluminum reproducer, but without records. Price.....................$7.50

RECORDS MUST BE PURCHASED EXTRA, and this machine will use either the XP records, illustrated and described on pages 380 and 381, or the Columbia records, which we are now offering, while they last, in lots of 50 at 15 cents each, as explained on page 382.

A LARGE AMPLIFYING HORN makes a wonderful difference in the effect produced with a graphophone. By attaching a large amplifying horn to a graphophone, you increase its efficiency 50 per cent. If you buy either the $7.50, $8.60 or $20.00 graphophone, we would suggest in addition that you order an amplifying horn, of which we give a selection on page 378. You can hardly appreciate what a difference in the volume of sound an amplifying horn produces until you have made the trial. It is the cheapest way of making a high grade graphophone out of a cheap machine.

$8.60 BUYS OUR SPECIAL HOME TALKING MACHINE.

THIS BEAUTIFULLY FINISHED and thoroughly practicable home entertainment graphophone is made expressly for us by the Columbia Phonograph Co., of New York and London, and we offer it to our customers as a talking machine which is more brilliant in its reproduction and in every way better than any other low priced machine on the market today.

$8.60

CAREFULLY MADE THROUGHOUT, with powerful clockwork spring motor, perfectly adjusted governor for maintaining an absolutely uniform speed of reproduction, and high grade aluminum reproducer with French diaphragm glass.

THE HEAVILY NICKEL PLATED horn, finished in the natural silvery color of aluminum, and the large 14-inch aluminum amplifying horn, make this machine in every respect a little beauty, a machine that will brighten the home, entertain yourself, your family and your friends and keep you in touch with the best and latest music of the finest bands and orchestras and the most celebrated public singers. Uses standard size wax cylinder records.

No. 21C115 The Home Graphophone, complete with nickel plated ornamental metal base, 14-inch aluminum amplifying horn and reproducer, just as shown in our illustration, but without records. $8.60

As a machine for home amusement or parlor entertainment, where a low priced graphophone is desired, there is no talking machine that will answer the purpose better or give better satisfaction than this, our special $8.60 Home Talking Machine. In the first place, it is a strictly high grade machine, well made, perfectly constructed, with all improvements, and with the 14-inch aluminum amplifying horn which is included, gives a wonderful volume of sound. In the second place, it is a very handsome machine, and will prove an ornament as well as a source of entertainment in any home.

When you consider that you can buy 50 different records and selections, the very best musical and talking records, for only $7.50, 15 cents each in lots of 50, and when you can get a full sized, substantial, perfectly operating graphophone from $5.00 up, there seems to be no reason why everyone should not take advantage of these offerings.

See page 382 for our wonderful offer on the regular Columbia records.

THE TYPE A T COLUMBIA GRAPHOPHONE FOR $20.00

RUNS STANDARD SIZE WAX CYLINDER RECORDS.

THIS HIGH GRADE COLUMBIA GRAPHOPHONE is an ideal machine for home entertainment, made with all the latest improvements, constructed with a view to strength and durability, and at the same time with a view to beauty and elegance of design, which makes it an ornament to any parlor.

THE REPRODUCER furnished with this A T Graphophone is the Columbia Phonograph Co.'s latest production, the D reproducer, with indestructible diaphragm, made of built-up mica, 1¾ inches in diameter, furnished with highest grade genuine sapphire reproducing point. In volume, sweetness and naturalness of tone, this machine exceeds any wax cylinder talking machine made.

An extra powerful tandem motor is furnished with this machine, made with the most perfect governor and speed regulating device, insuring perfect reproduction, and it runs five records with one winding. The cabinet is constructed from solid quarter sawed oak, of elegant design and beautifully finished.

YOU CAN MAKE YOUR OWN RECORDS with this machine, as we furnish with each one the latest improved recorder, and half the pleasure in owning a graphophone is derived from record making. Successful record making cannot be accomplished without a machine that is as perfect in its operation as a watch, and this graphophone fulfills all requirements.

With this A T Columbia Graphophone you have an additional opportunity for entertainment and instruction, for the reason that you can make your own records. You can put on a blank record and have any one sing or talk into the machine, and then keep this record indefinitely and reproduce it as often as you care to. Just think of preserving the voices of each and every one in the family, and what a pleasure it would be to listen to these voices and reproduce these records in after years.

If you are willing to invest as much as $20.00 in a graphophone, we especially recommend the purchase of this machine. It is a strictly high grade graphophone, beautifully built in a handsome, solid quarter sawed oak cabinet, with a beautiful bent oak cover to protect it from dust and dirt when the machine is not in use. All of the operating parts are thoroughly protected, the machine throughout is built extra strong and durable and runs five records with one winding. With each machine we include a D reproducer, the latest improved recorder for making records, and a 14-inch aluminum horn, exactly as illustrated.

No. 21C120 Columbia A T Graphophone, complete with D reproducer, recorder and 14-inch aluminum horn, but without records. Price.....................$20.00

For list of XP records suitable for this machine see pages 380 and 381. For price of blank records see No. 21C875, page 378.

INTRODUCTION

SOME years ago, when I was employed by Sears, Roebuck & Company, I used to pass a few minutes occasionally by running aimlessly and dreamily through the collection of catalogs that record the Company's mail-order business from its beginning in 1886 to date. At first, I was merely amused as the buggies, stoves, organs, revolvers, clothes, patent medicines, and cosmetics of another time poured through my fingers in a dun stream already antique. And my amusement was composed largely of that complacency and condescension which a member of one generation feels as he looks back upon the manners, wearables, follies, and foibles of recent generations. Complacency and condescension fell away from me, however, when I suddenly realized that this was not some faraway and long-ago period that the catalog's pages were illuminating, but *my* time—the only time in which I shall ever walk the earth, savor salt, and talk with my fellows; a time, therefore, infinitely more precious to me than all the centuries that have gone before, however broidered with gold they were or immanent with light.

Here, for example, were the buggies of a day already mistily remote, but a day in which I had lived. As a student at the University of Virginia in 1915, I had driven in just such a buggy as this, a young lady at my side, up the mountain to Mr. Thomas Jefferson's home. This is the shotgun with which I killed my first rabbit when I was a boy; these are the shoes I wore to Court School; that is the middy blouse worn by the golden girl who sat across the aisle. (Where is she now?) Here is a graphophone like the one we had in our home, with the blue horn flowering over the parlor and casting a sickly light upon a white, stuffed baby seal (the gift of a Newfoundland relative) that lay upon the floor. I put an Edison record on the talking machine, the cylinder turns, and the strains of "Everybody Works But Father" bring Lucy from the kitchen. There she stands, black and smiling, until the song is ended.

A horseless buggy of 1909, "guaranteed to go 100 miles in 24 hours if good care is taken of it," brightens a catalog page with the red of its body's paint. Seeing it, I become a child again. On a hot summer's day, I am watering with a garden hose the dusty street that runs along our home in Greenville, Mississippi. My bare feet are cooled by the mud of my own making; I turn the nozzle of the hose until it emits a fine spray, point it at the eye of the sun, and hold a trembling rainbow at arm's length. Then suddenly Leroy Wall, a pioneer automobilist of our town, comes thundering across my horizon at twelve miles an hour. Will Butler, the Negro blacksmith in the shop across the way, drops the hoof of the mule he is shoeing and runs to the door to see this latest and most terrifying example of white folks' madness. (He does not dream that it will ever transform him, a skilled craftsman, into a common laborer.) A flock of chickens, dust-bathing in the road, flies squawking in panic; a two-mule team, bringing a load of firewood to town, skitters into a ditch; while I retreat for safety behind the big cottonwoods that line the sidewalk and, with thumping heart, watch Leroy Wall disappear in a cloud of dust and glory.

"This pretty shirtwaist suit," and this "Very nobby suit, nicely tailored"—these are like the clothes worn by my mother and the mothers of my playmates. I see again long-familiar faces down the corridors of time, calm and framed in the windows of Coovert's Photograph Studio, as I loiter lazily before them homeward bound from school.

Here is the mail-order wig (toupee it was called by the elegant) of old man Huntly—a patch of hair more famous in our town than the tresses of Lilith or Lorelei. For once, long ago, in the heat and passion of the ninth inning of the second game of a double-header between Greenville and Pine Bluff,

OUR BOSTON BEAUTY RUNABOUT.

$29.75

DON'T FAIL TO STATE WIDTH OF TRACK

No. 11C155

BODY—Piano body, 23x54 inches; convex panels with concave seat risers; body glued, clamped, screwed and plugged, and finished hardwood seat frame, seat posts and step strips gained into sills.

GEAR—Axles, 1⅛ inch, dust and mudproof, long distance, fantailed, with axle beds clipped; all wood parts are second growth hickory, sand finished. Full circle fifth wheel. Three and four-plate, 36-inch sweep, oil tempered springs, clipped to Bailey body loops. Gear ironed and braced throughout with best Norway iron.

WHEELS—Sarven's patent, screwed rims, 40 inches front and 44 inches rear; rims, ⅞ inch, fitted with oval edge steel tires, bolted between each spoke. Can furnish 38 inches front and 42 inches rear if ordered.

PAINTING—Body, jet black; gear, New York red, neatly striped with black. Can furnish blood carmine or Brewster gear green if ordered.

TRIMMINGS—Seat and back upholstered with No. 1 whipcord, light color; box spring cushion, 10-inch bent panel back, carpet, high patent leather dash; double braced shafts, leather trimmed; quick shifting shaft couplers, wrench and storm apron.

TRACK—4 feet 8 inches or 5 feet 2 inches.

No. 11C155 Price, complete, with double braced shafts and steel tires..$29.75
Price, fitted with ¾-inch rubber tires..................... 40.50
Price, fitted with ⅞-inch rubber tires..................... 41.50

EXTRAS.

Pole in place of shafts............................ $1.60
Both pole and shafts.............................. 3.75
Leather upholstering.............................. 1.65
Weight, crated under 30 inches, 400 pounds. Shipped from factory.

OUR PHAETON RUNABOUT.

$31.00

DON'T FAIL TO STATE WIDTH OF TRACK

No. 11C209

BODY—Bracket front, phaeton buggy body, 25x54 inches; steel rocker plates, hardwood strips gained into sills, glued, screwed and plugged. Carefully selected material used. Roomy phaeton seat.

GEAR—Axles, 1⅛ inch, bell collar, dust and mudproof; long distance spindles, wood caps, cemented and clipped to axles; double reach, fully ironed and braced; three and four-plate 36-inch sweep elliptic oil tempered springs, clipped to Bailey body loops; full bearing fifth wheel.

WHEELS—Sarven's patent, 38 inches front and 42 inches rear; ⅞-inch screwed rims, fitted with oval edge steel tires, full bolted between each spoke. Can furnish 40 inches front and 44 inches rear if ordered, also ¾-inch rims.

PAINTING—Body, plain black, with neat design on seat risers. Gear, Brewster gear green, nicely striped. Can furnish blood carmine or New York red gear if ordered. All striped to match.

TRIMMINGS—Dark green body cloth, springs in cushion and back, solid jet black, padded and lined seat ends, leather dash, carpet, storm apron, quick shifting shaft couplers, wrench and double braced shafts, leather trimmed. Leather in place of cloth if ordered. See extras.

TRACK—4 feet 8 inches or 5 feet 2 inches.

No. 11C209 Complete, with double braced shafts and steel tires....$31.00
Price, fitted with ¾-inch rubber tires..................... 41.75
Price, fitted with ⅞-inch rubber tires..................... 42.75

EXTRAS.

Pole in place of shafts............................ $1.60
Both pole and shafts.............................. 3.75
Genuine leather upholstering in place of cloth......... 2.00
Weight, crated under 30 inches, 380 pounds. Shipped from factory.

THIS CUSTOMER SAVED $40.00 ON A No. 11C2400
RUNABOUT.

Whittier, Cal.

Sears, Roebuck & Co., Chicago, Ill.

Dear Sirs:—I take pleasure in giving you the following statement in regard to the Rubber Tire Runabout No. 11C2400 I ordered from you: I am satisfied with the rig. I examined the same style of vehicle here that I ordered and obtained the lowest cash price. After paying the freight from factory to my railroad station, I saved $40.00 on my purchase.
Yours respectfully,
JOHN WOOD.

THREE-PERCH CONCORD RUNABOUT.

$39.95

DON'T FAIL TO STATE WIDTH OF TRACK

No. 11C225

BODY—27 inches wide by 56 inches long, making it very roomy. Body is extra well made of selected material, with hardwood sills, beams and seat frames, ironed and braced; seat is extra wide and deep, with a high, solid panel spring back.

GEAR—Full Concord gear, with three reaches made of carefully selected second growth hickory, ironed and braced; 1-inch long distance axles, fitted with dust and mudproof bell collars. The axle caps are selected hickory, cemented and clipped to the axles; four-plate springs, hung on equalizers, both front and rear; an extra strong gear throughout.

WHEELS—Sarven's patent, second growth hickory spokes, ⅞-inch screwed rims, fitted with oval edge steel tires, 38 inches front and 42 inches rear. If ordered, we can furnish compressed band wood hubs, also 40-inch front and 44-inch rear wheels.

PAINTING—Body and seat panels, black, nicely striped, shutter work on the seat risers being painted carmine to harmonize with the gear. Gear, blood carmine, neatly striped. Can furnish Brewster green gear if ordered, with shutter work on the seat risers to correspond.

TRIMMINGS—Seat cushion and back upholstered in dark green broadcloth over solid panel spring back and box spring cushion, nicely tufted. Can furnish whipcord upholstering if ordered. Body carpet, handsome patent leather dash, quick shifting shaft couplers, double braced shafts, leather trimmed.

TRACK—4 feet 8 inches or 5 feet 2 inches.
No. 11C225 Price, complete, with shafts and steel tires....$39.95
Price, fitted with ⅞-inch rubber tires..................... 51.70
Price, fitted with 1-inch rubber tires..................... 53.20

EXTRAS.

Genuine leather upholstering....................... $2.00
Pole in place of shafts............................ 1.60
Both pole and shafts.............................. 3.75
Can furnish with a three-bow leather quarter top for.. 11.25
Weight, crated under 30 inches, 400 pounds. Shipped from factory.

THE POPULAR RUNABOUT.

$38.75

No. 11C2400

BODY—23x54 inches, convex panels with concave seat risers; body is glued, clamped, screwed and plugged and fitted with oval edge irons on top and at corners; hardwood step strips gained into sills; hardwood seat frame and corner posts.

GEAR—Naked axles, 1⅛ inch, best steel, swedged top and bottom; 3½-inch arch, dust and mudproof bell collars; self oiling, long distance spindles; reach heels and fifth wheel are riveted and brazed to axles: reaches are selected second growth hickory, ironed full length; open head, full bright, oil tempered springs, 36-inch sweep, clipped to Bailey body loops.

WHEELS—Sarven's patent, 36 inches front and 38 inches rear; low wheel, on account of high arch axle, makes body regulation height from the ground; screwed rims, ⅞ inch, fitted with oval edge steel tires, full bolted between each spoke.

PAINTING—Body, jet black; gear, carmine, neatly striped with black. Gear, black, New York red, Brewster gear green or canary yellow if ordered.

TRIMMINGS—Seat and back upholstered in light colored Bedford cord; box spring cushion and 10-inch bent panel back fancy stick seat; full length velvet carpet; Stanhope seat fenders, 13-inch patent leather padded dash, storm apron, wrench, and shafts trimmed with leather 36 inches from point; round shaft straps; Bradley shaft couplers.

TRACK—4 feet 6 inches only. Not built in wide track.

No. 11C2400 Price, complete, with double braced shafts and steel tires..$38.75
Price, fitted with ¾-inch rubber tires..................... 49.50
Price, fitted with ⅞-inch rubber tires..................... 50.50

EXTRAS.

Pole in place of shafts, Bradley couplings............ $1.90
Both pole and shafts, Bradley couplings.............. 4.25
Genuine leather upholstering....................... 1.50
Weight, crated under 30 inches, 400 pounds. Shipped from factory.

BETTER VEHICLES = LOWER PRICES

All the Vehicles in Our 1915 Line and Especially Our New American Beauty Buggies Represent the Greatest Values We Have Ever Offered

Better Vehicles for 1915 at Lower Prices, Due to Increasing Sales

Year by year we have patiently and persistently labored to improve the quality of our vehicles, always making prices as close as possible to manufacturing cost and insuring the greatest values. That our efforts have been appreciated is proved by the tremendous success of the factory that manufactures our buggies at Evansville, Ind., which now has an annual output of more than 85,000 vehicles and is steadily increasing, putting us far in the lead in the vehicle business of this country. So large is the output that we have been able during the past year to add a number of marked improvements in design and construction, at the same time shading down the cost still further. As usual, we are giving you the full benefit of the saving. We take great pride in the fact that our thoroughness in vehicle construction is being freely acknowledged everywhere throughout the country and we have every confidence that our sales for 1915 will show a marked increase over all former years.

Our New Line of American Beauty Buggies

On pages 1384 to 1387 we show a new line of buggies which we call our "American Beauty" line. There are no better buggies built today than American Beauty buggies. They are up to date in style, well finished, easy riding and so strongly made that they will outwear two ordinary standard buggies. To establish the name and identify these splendid buggies we are marking each with a delicate American beauty rose under each seat riser. This will protect our customers against deception, as it has come to our attention that certain factories, unable to meet our competition, have put out through their agents an inferior grade of buggies designed to look like ours and at prices about the same as ours which they were able to do at a handsome profit because of the cheaper materials used. Customers thus

deceived later found that they could have purchased the same grade of buggies from us at much lower prices; or could have secured a better buggy at the same price.

Each American Beauty Buggy Has a Small American Beauty Rose on the Seat Risers Under the Seat

In order to protect our customers every American Beauty Buggy will have an American beauty rose painted on the side of the seat risers. Do not let anyone else tell you that they can furnish you an American Beauty Buggy; this line of vehicles can be purchased only through us and it represents the highest type of vehicle offered to the user today, at prices that are from 25 to 35 per cent lower than vehicles of equal grade could be purchased through the ordinary dealer.

We Show a Complete Line

On the following pages you will find a complete line of horse drawn vehicles, consisting of runabouts, top buggies, surreys, spring wagons, road carts, standard business wagons, farm wagons, farm trucks and extra farm wagon boxes, all of which are quoted at money saving prices.

Every Vehicle Quoted Is Guaranteed

We guarantee not only to save you money but we guarantee absolutely to satisfy you. If you purchase any kind of a vehicle from us, you can use it as long as you want at your own work and if at any time you do not feel that you have received full value for the money invested, in fact, if you do not feel that you have made a saving by having purchased a vehicle from us, you have the privilege of returning it to us at our expense and we will return your money together with any freight charges you paid. You are the judge as to whether or not we can save you money and give you a high grade vehicle.

our star catcher, Reisinger, dropped the ball, and old man Huntly lost his wig as Pine Bluff scored the winning run. Despite the laughter of the fans, he did not discover his loss until he had gone home for supper. Then his wife, Miss Alice, accused him of drunkenness, and made him go back to the ball park and rescue his wig. Years later I learn from the catalog how he had got it, by sending a lock of his hair to Sears, along with the ingenious measurements required by the mail-order wigmaker, and a money order for $10 plus 42 cents for a tube of Toupee Paste.

In the catalog's pages, one finds how men lived, and what they lived by, for nearly fifty years. Here are the clothes they wore; the books they read; the medicines they used; the organs they played; the songs they sang; the plows they followed. Here also are the games that amused them; the furniture that stood in their homes; the diapers that initiate civilized man into his lifelong bondage to clothing; the clocks that tick men's lives away, and the tombstones that mark the end. These are the kettles that sang upon the stove; the rods that took the trout; the traps that snared the mink; the seeds that blew as flowers in rural gardens; the Bibles in which the sorrowful took refuge; the veils worn by brides; the iron heaters that glowed red in the parlor. Here, even, are the pistols that American men not so long ago wore as casually as their handle-bar mustaches.

As my now-fascinated eyes stared longer and longer at the catalog pages, and as I delved deeper and deeper into them, it seemed to me that they constituted an invaluable record of American life; that they were a diary of the times created by the people; a measure of the desires and ambitions of millions. I thought, moreover, that if all the records of the catalog's years should be lost, and only the catalog preserved, a scholar stumbling upon it in the remote future could recreate from its pages the way in which men had lived in America for fifty years. It was, therefore, with a shock of pleased surprise that I found my point of view had been anticipated by an English visitor to America more than a quarter century ago.

In 1911, Arnold Bennett visited Chicago and made this entry in his *Journal*:

Friday, November 17th

Went to Sears Roebuck & Co., in their auto. Got on very well with Murkland, head of book and china dept.

8 million dollars business last month.

Over 7,000 employees. Over 4,000 women. 5½ millons of large catalogs sold. Big bill-typing room. 600 clickers.

Gradually on to car-yard, where cars being filled up. This yard of cars sent out every day.

But most interesting thing was glimpses of real life of these outlying communities everywhere, as seen in ugly common simple stuff they ordered. Thousands of cheap violins. In one basket, ready for packing, all sorts of little cooking utensils and two mugs (fearfully ugly) labelled 'father' and 'mother.' 4 cents curling iron. Most startlingly realistic glimpse of home life. *All the life (cheap music, chairs etc.) of these communities could be deduced from this establishment.* [My italics.]

The catalogs, however, afford even more than "startlingly realistic glimpses of home life." Just as the concentric rings of California's giant redwood trees reveal years of drought and rainfall through the centuries, the pages of the catalog mark the economic booms and depressions of our times. The catalog for fall, 1915, swells to 1,600 pages from the 1,100 pages of the preceding season. Why? The World War is in its second year; Europe clamors for the produce of American farms and factories; farmers prosper almost overnight; their desires increase, and the catalog dealing with millions of families becomes a heavy, chunky book.

The same process operates also in reverse. As depressions descend on the land, as commodities drop to bankrupt prices and farmers patch their last year's overalls, the catalog suddenly omits several hundred pages, reduces its prices, and begins to adjust itself to hard times.

Year after year, it records the progress of invention and technological change in the United States. Thus, shortly after the turn of the century the great mechanic-revolutionists, White, Duryea, Ford, Olds, and others were beginning to change American manners, morals, ways of living, and business almost beyond comparison with earlier periods. Just as the horses of Cortez burst with terrifying impact upon the Indians of Mexico and cleared the path for the Conquest, while uprooting an ancient culture and diverting the people from their centuries' old course, so did the automobile burst upon the American people, to effect a bloodless conquest in some ways not less profound than that wrought by the conquistadors upon Mexico. Even the allegedly astute gentlemen of finance failed at first to understand the significance of the new vehicle. At the moment when the catalog, expressing not the hopes but the wants of the people, was picturing an automobile, that once famous cosmopolitan financier, Chauncey M. Depew, told his nephew that the horseless carriage would never supplant the horse, and kept the young man from investing $5,000 in the business of a visionary mechanic named Henry Ford. A little later, page after page of tires, oil, and automobile accessories come into the catalog. Simultaneously the buggy begins to disappear, and finally vanishes altogether from the catalog, to survive only in a few rural sections, in the collections of museums, and in the property warehouses of Hollywood.

Buggy whips, too, slowly go out of the catalog. On the day when the last buggy-whip manufacturer closed his factory doors and walked out into the blinding light of a new world where he was lost, no bells were tolled and no dirges sung.

What social historian has marked his passing in a learned study, or assessed the importance of his disappearance? Yet who shall deny that he closed his doors not only upon an empty factory but also upon a long era of American history; that the day when he walked into the street was a day fraught with greater significance for the country than the whole administration, say, of President Van Buren, which is noted in all the histories of America?

The life span of the catalog itself is contemporaneous with

perhaps the most dynamic fifty years in American life. It begins in 1886 when the United States was just emerging from the Civil War and Reconstruction into a period of agricultural and industrial expansion unparalleled in the world for breadth and vigor. It continues through the years of the centralization of business into giant combines, trusts, and monopolies; embraces the feverish dream era of "manifest destiny" before and after the Spanish-American War; goes on to the time when Kansas boys died in Flanders fields; stumbles into the darkness of the economic depression of the 1930's from which we have not yet emerged, and the fall catalog of 1939–40 appeared precisely at the moment when German troops were marching into Poland.

Two pages in the 1905 edition might almost be taken as a short socioeconomic history of the United States, because they embody much of the essence of that history and vividly contrast the old America that was passing with the new America that was emerging. Page 338 contains a sketch of a covered wagon and a description of "White Duck Emigrant Wagon Covers" tailored to fit many sizes of wagons. Page 339 is devoted to a lusty, bitter denunciation of alleged monopoly practices on the part of a giant camera-manufacturing corporation. On the one page the symbol of *laissez faire* and individualism in their most extreme forms; on the other page one of the instruments of the death of *laissez faire* and individualism.

It is an astonishing mark, too, of the newness of America that emigrant wagon covers did not disappear from the catalog until 1924. Throughout the pages of the catalog, as in the pages of American history generally, one is awestruck by the swiftness of change, by the youth of the country, and by the spectacle of men, who were boys in a pioneer society, contributing in their maturity to urbanized, industrialized America. A startling example of this is the life of Paul J. Starrett who built many of the great skyscrapers and some of the subways of New York.

"My brothers and sisters and I," he writes, "were all born in Lawrence [Kansas]. Our early life was lived in an America now completely gone. Through the vista of the years I look back to the prairies which the Indians, with their squaws and papooses were still crossing on their single-file trails. I remember standing one morning with a group of scared children in the city jail yard, where the six Sioux chiefs captured after the Custer massacre were incarcerated. As clearly as I can see the aeroplane overhead today, I can see the long trains loaded with buffalo hides going through to the East."

The boy Starrett watching Indians crossing the Kansas prairies; the man Starrett erecting the world's tallest building —the Empire State Building in New York. That is America and it is the America whose life span is the catalog's.

The catalog reveals American life changing as we turn its pages. Technology walks into the home to transform it and to transfigure the housewife. In edition after edition, we note the liberation of the housewife through the coming of labor-saving devices; we observe the drudgery once done by her hands transferred to machines; we see the means by which even the servantless woman in the United States has come to have a higher degree of leisure than any other woman of her kind in the world. At the same time, the catalog records the progress of technology on the farm. Wood is sawed by hand, and then by power saws; water is hand-pumped or carried to the hogs, and then it is driven by electric pumps; men follow horses down turnrows for centuries, and suddenly they are riding the steel saddles of gasoline-powered tractors.

If the catalog is rich in revelations of economic life and struggle in the United States, if it is a series of endlessly changing pictures of changing America, it is also a social barometer. Here we find the development of countless new attitudes—toward reading, the use of cosmetics, the virtues of fresh air and of bathing, and the pleasures of sports. We note how the luxuries of one generation become the necessaries of the next generation, and how the clothing of the middle class tends to approximate that of the rich in fashion and materials, even if inferior in design and workmanship.

The catalog as a chronicle of change and a panorama of

American life through fifty dynamic years reveals directly, and by implication, countless forces of many kinds that are constantly at work in a virile, restless civilization such as ours. We glimpse something of the age-long struggle against monopoly and price-fixing; the rise of new attitudes toward private debt; changing parent-child relationships, and a radically different conception of sex. The catalog's pages are starred with changes, but among them I can find none more startling than this: in the past few years they list and describe a great number of contraceptives. On the face of it this fact is not at all startling because contraception is nothing new in America. But let us look below the surface. The catalog, it must be remembered, goes to farmers, rural dwellers, and the economic middle classes and lower middle classes of the towns. These folk are the remnant, yet large, of the godly left in America. Evangelism still surges in their souls; their lips are fluent to hymn-singing; their allegiance is to fundamentalism. Here, if anywhere, we should expect the catalog, in the role of Eros bringing gifts of concupiscence, to be ejected from the rural threshold. But, on the contrary, it is welcomed. What strange ferment must then be at work in the souls of the American people if this large group, who are the defenders of the faith and of the old-time religion, now emulates its city brothers and sisters in the use of contraceptives?

The catalog, however, is revelatory of more than social and economic change in this country. It reveals also esthetic change. No one turning its pages can fail to be struck by the tremendous improvement they show in the design of category after category of goods for the person and for the home. And this improvement is highly significant because it reveals the tastes, wants, and desires not of a few wealthy women in the cities, but of millions of simple women living in the small towns and on the farms of America. For—it must be borne in mind—things in the catalog are things people want. They are not things that Sears thinks they ought to have or hopes to sell them.

Flowing out of this is the one fact indispensable to an understanding of this book: the catalog is based not upon hope but upon experience. There is no room in it for guessing, wishing, or, save occasionally and conservatively, experimenting. It does not attempt to cram down the throats of the public its own ideas of taste or merchandise. The catalog never leads; never crusades. It is based purely upon public acceptance of the goods it offers, and not until the public has clearly signified that it wants a thing does that thing appear in its pages. We know, therefore, beyond all doubt, that the catalog's pictures of American life are drawn not from the imagination but from the living model.

The catalog occupies a unique place in American life. It is more than an instrument of business, although it was designed and is maintained solely as an instrument of business. It has become the best-known book in the United States, a part of American folklore, and, passing strange for a tool of business, it has also become the object of widespread affection.

Wherever the traveler goes in the United States, he will find the catalog. It lies dog-eared and finger-smudged on the log-hewn tables of cabins high in the Great Smokies; it is found in the ranch houses of Montana, the cabins of cotton growers in Alabama, the homes of fruit farmers in California, and even in the mansions of the rich. But wherever it is found, a curious affection surrounds it, an expression that arises perhaps out of a subconscious longing for an America which is vanishing but which still continues to be exemplified by the catalog. America is a once pioneer country now approaching maturity, and it is characteristic of such a country, at this stage of its progress, that it look back to its past. And the past—in a dynamic, fast-moving land such as this—may be no more than twenty-five or fifty years removed from the present. The United States, moreover, has been in breathless transition ever since 1914; it has been lifted up and thrown down; it is staggered by change; worried and harassed. It is certain that it is going somewhere, but no man can say with the slightest pretense to accuracy where it is going. Under these circumstances, it is natural that the people of a hurrying, scurrying, industrialized, worried country should look back wistfully to a more leisurely and serene day when—such is the power of the retrospective imagination—every man in America sat content beneath his vine. The catalog is the symbol of that day, and, as such, it has come to be surrounded with the affection that men lavish on the symbols of happier days.

It must be remembered, too, that millions of city dwellers were born in the country where, as likely as not, the catalog was part of their childhood. It has been the half dreamworld of millions of children as they looked with wonder through its enchanting, picture-starred pages. The following scene described by Marietta Minnigerode Andrews, in her *Memoirs of a Poor Relation* (page 169), is one that must have been repeated with endless variations everywhere in the country for nearly fifty years. It is, in reality, a vignette of American life; the stuff of which a painter might have made a typical *Portrait of An American Mother with Her Children*. Here Mrs. Andrews is speaking of herself and her children:

> Mary Lord Andrews the third is engaged in building a card house of souvenir postcards. Helen Tucker the second is inspecting a large catalogue of Sears, Roebuck & Company, in which a large number of legs with no ladies attached, as advertisements of beautiful silk stockings, cover one page, and lovely ladies without legs, advertising hats and blouses, adorn another page. Helen Tucker . . . being not quite two years old expresses no astonishment at these mutilations, but Mary Lord . . . says it is sad to see these pieces of people, and where are the ladies that belong to these legs? She is interested in the Sears, Roebuck catalogue, and I feel her active little brain is at work upon some scheme to defraud Helen Tucker of it without interference from me.

The catalog is widely known as The Farmer's Bible, The Nation's Wishbook, and, in Texas, as The Panhandle Wishbook. And a wishbook it is. No one will ever know how many thousands of worn farm women have thumbed its pages, their eyes lingering with desire upon the picture of a new stove that the family badly needs but cannot afford to buy, upon a new dress to wear to church, or a washing machine to relieve the back-breaking labor of the tub. Often, however, dreams come true. For months a boy feasts his eyes upon a shiny .22-caliber rifle in the catalog, hoping someday to carry it under his arm as he hunts game in near-by pastures. Then strawberrytime comes and he earns enough picking berries to enable him to make out an order, count out the hard-won dimes over the counter of the post office, get a postal money order, and mail both to Chicago. A day or two later there is a package in his family's mailbox—how often did he look down the road for the carrier's buggy!—and he opens it with trembling hands to find the steel beauty inside. From one season to the next, thousands of farm families pore over the catalog. They discuss the wisdom of buying this or that; finally decide upon what they want, and then, as the crops come in and are sold, are at last able to buy the things they have dreamed of having. To such families the catalog is indeed a wishbook. and, as wishes are crystallized into reality, and long-hoped-for things are at last transferred from the catalog's pages into the possession of Sears' customers, it becomes surrounded with an aura of affection.

The catalog thus has a hold on a vast group of Americans that suave public-relations counsel, for all their wiles and expenditures, cannot ever achieve for their clients. The catalog grew up without a press agent; it has none in its maturity. The function of the corporation press agent is, too often, to present his client not as he is but as he would like to have the public think he is. The catalog, on the contrary, sticks strictly to the business of presenting Sears and its merchandise as they are.

In addition to its other qualities the catalog is, of course, a charming, sometimes picturesque, naïve, and often moving, account of how millions of plain folk have lived for five decades. It is a vast archeological museum containing thousands of exhibits labeled and minutely described. Here one finds such items as goat sulkies for children, stereoscopes and pyrography equipment, flageolets, mourning handkerchiefs, the mustache cup, Prince Albert suits, the solid-gold toothpick with ear spoon combined, the fur derby hat, umbrella stands, hall hatracks, and leather Turkish rockers. Posterity with this record in its possession will not have to send out expeditions to the sites of buried towns of the Middle West, as we now send them to Ur of the Chaldees to learn how the Chaldeans lived and to determine the instruments they used at home and in the fields.

The Greeks, transcendently wise, knew the human and poetic values of the trivia of living; they understood the significance of the simple things by which men lived. In their obituary poetry there appear again and again the youth's hound, the fowler's snare, the fisherman's net, the farmer's plow. These values, too, are in the catalog, and they are not the less poignant because they belong to our times rather than to antiquity. In this spirit the late Julius Rosenwald, the genius of Sears, saw the catalog as more than an instrument of business.

During the World War, the late Newton D. Baker, Secretary of War, telephoned Mr. Rosenwald and asked him to come to Hoboken a day or two later and sail with him for France. Mr. Rosenwald arrived at the ship's dock carrying a small suitcase containing his personal effects. He was followed by a large number of porters struggling with four huge wooden cases which they moved with difficulty. Mr. Baker asked him what they contained. "You'll see," Mr. Rosenwald replied.

Later in the journey, when Mr. Baker was making a tour of American hospitals in France, he asked several hospital librarians what book was requested most often by wounded soldiers. To his astonishment he was told that it was the Sears catalog. It then occurred to Mr. Baker that Mr. Rosenwald must have distributed the catalogs. These were the contents of the heavy cases he had put aboard ship at Hoboken. A few days later the two men met in Paris and Mr. Baker asked his companion why he had taken the catalogs to the hospital.

"I'll tell you why," Mr. Rosenwald said. "This is the reason. Here is a sick or wounded American boy lying in a hospital. Where did he come from? What kind of a home did he have? The chances are that he is a farm boy, or a small-town boy. And that means he is a boy who once hunted, fished, trapped, or played baseball. There is a pretty good chance that his parents kept our catalog around the house. Now here the boy is in a strange country where people talk a strange language. He is thousands of miles from home. He is both sick and homesick.

"I give that boy a catalog. He turns the pages. He sees the shotgun that right now is standing in his room back home in Illinois. He recalls the day when he killed a rabbit in the pasture or shot a lot of crows in the corn. A few pages farther on the boy runs into fishing tackle. From that second it is no longer cold, rainy weather in France, but warm springtime at home. He digs worms behind the barn, puts them in a can, and pretty soon he is pulling fish out of the creek as fast as he drops his line. In other words, the catalog helps our soldier boys to escape the miseries of war and live happily again, if only for a little while, amid the scenes of their childhood at home."

"I see," said Mr. Baker.

Now the astonishing fact is—and it is this that moved me to write this book—that hitherto the catalog has been the subject of little more than a few magazine articles and a great many backhouse jokes. It has been, to my knowledge, almost completely neglected by social historians and students of American life and manners; it has not been paid even the dubious honor of being the subject of a thesis for a doctor's degree. Yet the Library of Congress, acutely aware of its high importance as an American document, mourns the fact that it does not possess a complete catalog collection; and, at the other extreme, Hollywood uses it as an indispensable source book.

I have, therefore, undertaken the joyous task not of rescuing the catalog from oblivion—a book with an annual circulation of millions needs no discoverer—but of selecting, arranging, commenting upon, and interpreting certain portions of it that reveal in relatively brief compass some of the extraordinary changes in manners, morals, and ways of living that have occurred in America within the lifetime of most people now alive.

For this purpose I have restricted my inquiry in general to the years 1905–1935, deviating only when necessary to illustrate my thesis. Sears, Roebuck & Company began business as a small mail-order jewelry firm in 1886, but I have devoted little space here to an account of its early beginnings, struggles, or the personalities who made it successful. By 1905—twenty years after its inception—the catalog was already offering not only jewelry but complete lines of merchandise. And as evidence of its maturity it proudly displayed a letter from the First National Bank of Chicago, stating that "They [Sears] show a fully paid up surplus and capital of over Two Million Dollars, and are one of the largest mercantile institutions in Chicago." For the sake of brevity and sharpness of picture, I have elected to consider change as recorded by the catalog not from year to year but in decades.

In conclusion, I want to add that the considerations which apply to the Sears catalog apply with equal force to the catalog of Montgomery Ward & Company. I have chosen the Sears catalog as the vehicle of my exposition because of the familiarity I acquired with it while working for Sears, and out of my friendship with the men who make it and who have placed at my disposal both the catalog collection and their remembrances of times past.

I am particularly indebted to Messrs. Donald M. Nelson and N. W. Jeran of Sears, Roebuck & Company for advice and counsel; to Mr. Lessing J. Rosenwald, I owe thanks for the loan of letters. I wish also to express my gratitude to Mrs. Gerel Rubien and Miss Barbara Heggie for their assistance in research.

DAVID L. COHN

September 30, 1939

Part One

LADIES AND GENTLEMEN

This book is divided into four sections and an appendix. The first three sections deal with the stuff of which the catalog is made—merchandise. The fourth section is concerned with the origins of Sears, the manner in which the catalog is manufactured, the hostility of small-town merchants to mail-order houses, and a general discussion of advertising and installment selling. The appendix contains a collection of letters written to Sears by some of its customers.

All the chapters in this book are bound together by a single thread running through them—the thread of change. Every chapter makes its own contribution to the whole picture of American manners and morals for fifty years as seen through the eyes of the catalog. But each chapter—whether it is read consecutively and in relation to the entire book or merely at random—is a self-contained entity which tells its own complete story.

Since it would be an interminably tedious task to consider change from year to year, it is here considered in terms of decades. It is, of course, an extraordinary fact of our national life that even so short a period as ten years is sufficient to mark emphatic and sometimes startling change. Thus, our story begins with the quiet, agrarian, easygoing America of 1905, but it moves rapidly into the turbulent, industrialized America of 1915. A mere decade had passed but the face of the country had been radically altered. In 1915, the World War had reached its second year, and America was growing rich selling goods to the peoples of warring continents, while its Government simultaneously protested to the combatants who were interfering with its sea-borne commerce, and its

President was soon to be re-elected on a platform of "He kept us out of war."

By the beginning of the next decade—1925–1935—we had made, in some respects, a complete break with the continuity of tradition that dated back to the founding of the republic. Abroad, American soldiers had fought on foreign battlefields. At home, agrarian America had become industrialized; rural America had become urbanized. These were stupendous changes of immeasurably potent consequences.

The sharp deflation of 1920–21 had been all but forgotten by 1925. The so-called "new era" was at hand: the era of limitless prosperity, characterized by pots overflowing with chickens and garages bursting with cars. Four years later, however, came the catastrophic economic crash of 1929; the beginning of the misery and bleakness of the long depression years from which we now seem, in 1940, to be timidly emerging.

Such is the too-brief economic background of the period with which this book deals. It is marked by equally dramatic changes in other departments of men's activities, and these are duly noted as they occur in the barometric catalog. Even the necessarily incomplete picture of America that is presented here would be impossible if this book did not shuttle back and forth between the centuries; if it did not sometimes consider other lands and other peoples. For America is not only an inheritor of the ages; it is also a composite of the peoples of the earth.

In this, the first section, the following fields of merchandise are surveyed, and varying deductions are drawn from them:

Music, radio, the stereoscope, books, automobiles, watches, clocks, patent medicines, and—without suggesting any inevitability of causation—tombstones.

1·PROFUSE STRAINS OF UNPREMEDITATED ART

ON April 7, 1880, *The New York Times* announced that $600,000 had been subscribed toward the building of the Metropolitan Opera House by a group including "the two Roosevelts, the three Vanderbilts," and numerous Iselins, Goelets, and others. This group was soon joined by the multimillionaires, Ogden Mills, Cyrus Fields, John D. Rockefeller, and Jay Gould. In Europe opera had long been subsidized by the state. In America it was underwritten by the rich.

An opera house was built according to what were probably the most extraordinary architectural specifications ever laid down for one. Although its function was the projection of music, the structure was not laid out according to the necessities of acoustics, the stage, and the orchestra pit. It was constructed around the boxes, and bore, therefore, the same relation to functional architecture that a suit would bear to tailoring if one gave a tailor a dozen buttons and told him to surround them with clothes. But the Metropolitan was the creation of the new rich of a prodigally wealthy new continent who were responding to the powerful impulse noted by Veblen in his *Theory of the Leisure Class*:

"In order to gain and hold the esteem of men it is not sufficient merely to possess wealth or power. The wealth or power must be put in evidence, for esteem is awarded only on evidence. And not only does the evidence of wealth serve to impress one's importance on others and to keep their sense of his importance alive and alert, but it is of scarcely less use in building up and preserving one's self-complacency."

If "esteem is awarded only on evidence," the rich supporters of the opera saw to it that they would be much in evidence.

—3—

The Vanderbilts, for example, bought boxes wholesale. They owned no fewer than five and occupied them on the Metropolitan's opening night, March 22, 1883, along with a glittering host of Gerrys, Bakers, Drexels, Rhinelanders, and other plutocrats of the times. Their tiers of boxes—soon dubbed the Golden, or the Diamond, Horseshoe—were as conspicuous as the prisoner at a hanging. But almost before the building had been completed, the same criticism of it was heard that is still echoed today by architects and music lovers. In 1883, *The New York Evening Post* said that "From an artistic and musical point of view, the large number of boxes is a decided mistake. But as the house was avowedly built for social purposes rather than artistic it is useless to complain about this."

After the opening performance at the Metropolitan, New York newspapers made more popeyed comment on the fact that the opera's box holders represented $540,000,000 of wealth than on the quality of the performance. *The Dramatic Mirror,* however, in slightly irreverent mood, said: "The Goulds, the Vanderbilts, and people of their ilk perfumed the air with the odor of crisp greenbacks. The tiers of boxes looked like cages of monopolists."

Mrs. Astor's Gift to Music

The final success of the Metropolitan was assured on the night of March 6, 1884 (one year after it opened), not within the portals of the opera house, but in the home of Mrs. William K. Vanderbilt. There she gave on this evening a fancy-dress ball. It was notable for the fact that it marked the first time that the Astors (beaver fur and tenement houses) had ever crossed the Vanderbilt (railroads and ferryboats) threshold. And as the champagne of the up-to-that-moment plebeian Vanderbilts slid down the patrician Astor throats, the social position of the Vanderbilts, and the success of the opera based upon social prestige, was secure. The country, therefore, if not the Vanderbilts, owes the Astors a debt of gratitude for their democratic gesture of more than fifty years ago.

The years 1884–91 mark one of the most distinguished

periods of opera in America. Magnificent performances of the German masterpieces were given at the Metropolitan, and the house was crowded not only by the wealthy but also by many of New York's 250,000 simple citizens of German descent. One hurdle remained to be taken. It seems that however brilliant the performance on the stage it could not compete successfully with the rattling of tongues in the boxes. This moved the Metropolitan's Board of Directors to issue a stilted notice which, in effect, said, "Aw, go hire a hall." It read: "Many complaints having been made to the directors . . . of the annoyance produced by talking in the boxes during the performance, the Board requests it will be discontinued." Thereafter, the incipient Wildes and Whistlers let the performance go its willful way undisturbed.

New York (population then 1,900,000) was alive with music fifty years ago. Ever since 1853, opera had been presented at the Academy of Music, but its boxes were insufficient to accommodate the growing hordes of millionaires, so that it closed in 1886. By that time, however, the city had the Metropolitan, the New York Symphony Orchestra, the Casino devoted to comic opera, and concert halls where such artists as Adelina Patti and Ignace Paderewski appeared. During the opera season 1884–85, a young man named Walter Damrosch, then twenty-three years of age, was appointed second conductor of the Metropolitan orchestra. Years later, in the machine age of music, he was to be among the first to sense the possibilities for music in the new field of radio and to spread its gospel in millions of homes.

A lively interest in music was not, however, confined to New York in the 1880's and 1890's. New Orleans had had opera long before the Civil War, and in 1859 built its famous French Opera House. "The opera became the focus of social life in New Orleans—'a scene of costly jewels, elaborate costumes, lovely women, gallant gentlemen and magnificent music.' . . . People of all walks of life attended the opera, even those who wished solitude. For these persons the *loges grillés,* or boxes enclosed with lattice work, were intended, being occupied chiefly by those in mourning and *femmes enceintes*. A favorite New Orleans anecdote is that of the Creole belle who was almost born in the opera house. For it was not until the middle of *Faust* that her mother, Mme. Blanque, turned to M. Blanque and said, 'Pierre, I do not think I can wait for the ballet!' " *

At the other end of the country, Boston had its famous symphony orchestra; choral societies flourished in such cities as Cincinnati where there were large German populations; Reginald de Koven's opera *Robin Hood*—probably the most popular American opera ever composed—was nationally famous for years; and the names of John Philip Sousa and Victor Herbert were known to almost every man, woman, and child in the land.

At the same time, if there was no tradition of music in a pioneer country, there had long been an enormous spread of musical education. Thus a United States Bureau of Education "Information Circular" of 1886 reports that seven out of eight pupils in the public schools were taught singing and music reading.

In the West, where the Union Pacific Railroad put up signs requesting passengers not to shoot game from the car windows, there was apparently a veritable lust for music. In 1882, L. P. Brockett of San Francisco wrote: †

> As to musicians and teachers of music, vocal and instrumental, there is no calling in greater demand. Nowhere is the performance of a really excellent brass band more thoroughly appreciated than in any of these western towns. The best opera singers receive a far more enthusiastic reception in the towns and cities of the Western region, than awaits them in the great cities of the East. Every church and hall has its choir, and every town of 3,000 has its music association.
>
> A gentleman went to Leadville, Colorado, when it was in the formative plastic condition in 1878. There were few even frame buildings . . . the majority were living

* *New Orleans City Guide*, American Guide Series, p. 134.
† Brockett, *Our Western Empire, or The New West.*

in tents. The nearest accessible railroad station was 130 miles distant and the roads leading to it were horrible. A young woman asked the visitor to go home and dine with her if he could put up with "canned vittles." As she arranged the table in the tent the visitor was astonished to see a Chickering Grand Piano . . . brought piece meal on the backs of pack mules which had cost nearly $200 to transport.

The diffusion of music and musical knowledge after the Civil War, and until the beginning of the World War, received constant impetus from two sources. The one was the long-lingering tradition that well-brought-up young women should have certain "accomplishments," such as the ability to recite verses in parlors, paint china, and play some musical instrument—preferably the piano or the organ. The other was the invention of the phonograph.

Mr. Edison, the inventor, did not think highly of the possibilities of the phonograph as a musical instrument in its early days and first used it for recording dictation. He thought that it might have some use, too, as a toy, and be valuable in fixing on wax the last words of dying persons. But by 1889, *The Atlantic Monthly* said that "Those persons who smile incredulously when it is said that the perfected phonograph . . . will sing and play for us . . . at almost no cost, and become a constant source of amusement and instruction . . . have forgotten the ridicule they heaped upon the rumor that an American inventor proposed to talk from New York to Chicago. Mr. Edison says that by the beginning of 1890 the phonograph will be far less of a curiosity than the telephone is now. . . . Just at present there is needed a funnel for so magnifying the sound that if the instrument is placed in the center of a table, all the persons sitting around can hear."

By the turn of the century, the phonograph was recording some of the noblest of the world's music, as well as typical American musical-comedy songs and scores, and millions of men and women remote from the cities were able to enjoy, in however narrow and diluted a form, the music heard on the

New York stage, at the Opera, and in the great concert halls. Throughout the land, music teachers struggled with little girls in pigtails and little boys in knee pants, or beamed with satisfaction as their advanced pupils played *Poet and Peasant* or Rubinstein's *Melody in F* at the annual recital for parents and friends. And on the farms and in the towns, men and boys strummed guitars and banjos, sawed on violins, tinkled jew's-harps, or played the auto-zither. Against this background, rich in possibilities for the sale of musical instruments, Sears made up its catalogs.

The Home Favorite

> Amateur performers upon the piano should thoroughly commit to memory a few pieces to play independently of notes, as to take sheet-music to a party is a hint that they expect to be invited to play. If possible, have the voice in good condition also, so as not to be obliged to complain of a cold. To eat a small amount of horse-radish just previous to reading, singing or speaking, will quite effectually remove hoarseness. *

In 1905, when a home was not a home without an organ or a piano, Sears offered four kinds of pianos in its general catalog. These ranged from The Beckwith Home Favorite—"a most wonderful bargain"—at $89 (shipping weight, 750 pounds) to The Beckwith Acme Cabinet Grand Concert Piano at $165.

The advertising copy for The Home Favorite clearly reveals the mental torture of the man who wrote it. He wanted to tell the truth about this parlor ornament, but not in such a way as to cause the prickly heat of sales resistance to break out on the skins of the customers. He invites the rural Paderewskis to come live with him and be his love, but he does not want The Home Favorite to seem a confection of kirtles and posies with no thorns in its make-up. And as the writer tries to serve two masters, the copy dives and soars.

"The Home Favorite," says he, "is a most wonderful bargain, but it is not so large as some of our other pianos and

* Hill, *Manual of Social and Business Forms.*

THE BECKWITH HOME FAVORITE PIANO

A FULL SIZE GUARANTEED PIANO.

WE OFFER OUR HOME FAVORITE PIANO AT	$89.00	TO SHOW HOW GOOD A PIANO CAN BE FURNISHED AT A PRICE NEVER BEFORE HEARD OF.

IT COSTS THE REGULAR RETAIL DEALER OR AGENT MORE TO BUY ONE OF HIS PIANOS THAN WE ARE ASKING YOU TO PAY FOR THE INSTRUMENT AT THE FACTORY.....

OUR HOME FAVORITE PIANO IS A FULL SIZE INSTRUMENT, SUBSTANTIALLY BUILT, AND IS A MOST REMARKABLE INSTRUMENT AT THE PRICE.

Agents and Dealers cannot sell you an instrument the equal of this for less than $200.00.

See our Special $1.00 Deposit and 30-Day Free Trial Plan Offer on Page 110.

No. 4601 OUR $89.00 HOME FAVORITE PIANO. ORDER BY NUMBER.

WE GUARANTEE THE PIANO for only 5 years. It is the greatest value ever seen or heard of; in fact, such an instrument cannot be duplicated elsewhere at anything like the price at which we offer it; but it is not an instrument that we can guarantee as we do our other higher grade pianos, which are all guaranteed for 25 years. It will prove a serviceable instrument and should stand the test of from five to ten years' use.

THE MANDOLIN ATTACHMENT furnished in this piano enables the performer to faithfully reproduce the tones of harp, mandolin, guitar, etc., and for this patent attachment we make no extra charge. If this is not desired we will, with no extra cost, place in instead the Muffler or Practice Pedal.

SIZE OF PIANO. Height, 4 feet 6 inches; width, 2 feet 2 inches; length, 61 inches. Weight, boxed for shipment, 750 pounds.

THE CASE of this piano is made of solid wood, finished in mahogany or burled walnut. Extreme cold or other climatic changes are liable to cause the finish to check or peel in the course of time. We, therefore, cannot guarantee the finish on these cheaper pianos to stand, but otherwise this has no effect upon the tone or durability of the instrument.

WE WISH TO CALL YOUR ATTENTION TO THE HANDSOME NEW PIANO LAMP which we are illustrating on page 117 of this catalogue. This lamp will prove a fine addition to your and, at the price which we fix on it, $3.25, is certainly a bargain. It fills a long felt want, and avoids the purchase of a piano lamp, for which you will have to give from $10.00 to $25.00 at your local dealers.

THIS PIANO IS A MOST WONDERFUL BARGAIN

But it is not so large as our other pianos, hence has not the same volume of tone. The tone is, however, very strong for the size of the piano. To enable us to offer a piano at this price, it is necessary to save wherever possible, hence the sounding board, while very strong, is not so large as in our other pianos; the metal plate is smaller, the strings are not so long, nor is the hammer so heavy, but it is EQUAL to pianos sold by MUSIC DEALERS for about $200.00.

THE ACTION is well made and a very good quality of material is used throughout. The action in this piano is as good as will be found in pianos sold by other dealers at $150.00 to $200.00.

THE SCALE is 7⅓ octaves and has overstrung bass.

THE TONE is always a matter of taste, and in this piano we endeavor to produce a tone which we believe will please most anyone. It is sweet and melodious and of ample power for all ordinary requirements.

WE SEND FREE WITH EACH PIANO a complete instruction book and a good piano stool, and if you favor us with your order and are not entirely satisfied with the instrument after you have tried it for 30 DAYS IN YOUR OWN HOME, we will cheerfully refund your money in full. You certainly cannot afford to purchase elsewhere until you have seen and tried one of our pianos when you are assured that you will not be out one cent in the transaction if everything does not prove entirely satisfactory.

BUYING FROM THE DEALER.

IF A DEALER OFFERS YOU A PIANO which he claims is as good as the Beckwith and attempts to offer it to you at prices anywhere near as low as we are making, you can very easily ascertain what the quality of the piano is by a few judicious questions. The case of his piano may look very fine and may be highly finished, but you should always remember that in a piano, at least, a little veneer covers a multitude of sins. Ask him if the case of his piano is veneered with genuine sawed veneer. Ask him if it is cross banded and veneered both inside and out. In case he evades these questions you can easily ascertain for yourself by examining the bottom edge of the music desk or the lower front panel of the piano. If you do not find two layers of veneer plainly shown, you can make up your mind that they are not there.

Ask him if the piano is a three-string unison in the treble and two-string unison in the bass. If he tells you that it is, just simply raise the top of the piano and look inside and if you do not find each hammer in the treble striking three strings at once and each hammer in the bass striking two strings, you can make up your mind that what he has told you is not true. Ask him if the bass strings of his piano are copper wound, and if they are the best grade of imported piano strings. Ask him if all the felts in the piano are the genuine Dolge piano felts.

Ask him if the wrest plank or pin block, in which the tuning pins are set, is composed of five layers of maple running in opposite directions. If he says it is not do not buy the piano under any consideration. Ask him if the action of the piano will repeat properly. You can easily ascertain this by striking several sharp blows in quick succession on one of the keys. If the piano is fitted with repeating action you will hear every note strike clear and distinct, and if it is not fitted with this action you will get nothing but a succession of blurred tones.

Ask him if his piano is a full size concert grand, and up to the musical standard in every way. If he answers all of the above questions in the affirmative then ask him if he will put it in your home for a full thirty days trial and allow you to return it at any time within one year and receive your money back with all freight charges paid in case it should prove unsatisfactory for any reason. If he agrees to this, then ask him if he will give you a written, binding 25 years guarantee to protect you against any defect in material or workmanship which may appear in the piano at any time within that period. If he refuses to give you this guarantee or to allow you the thirty days trial or to give you permission to return the piano at any time within one year, you may be sure that he has no faith in the instrument, and as he certainly knows more about the piano than you do, you cannot afford to purchase it. If he will not guarantee the instrument, he has no right to ask you to take any chances.

If he agrees to give you the 25 years guarantee and the thirty days trial then ask him if he will sell you the piano for $165.00 cash. If he refuses to sell you the piano at this figure he is simply asking you to pay him not only his large profit, but also the profits and selling expenses of the different dealers through whose hands the piano passed before it came to him. We have had many instances where dealers have offered to sell pianos to our customers at from $165.00 to $200.00 which they claimed were equal to the Beckwith, but in every instance we have found that the piano was lacking in many of the essentials which go to make up a fine instrument. As a matter of fact it is absolutely impossible for a local dealer to sell a piano of the same high grade as the Beckwith for less than from $350.00 to $400.00. The local dealer cannot purchase a piano of this grade from his jobber or manufacturer at as low a price as we can sell it to you. No concern in this country possesses so great an advantage in buying as we do, and we are thus able to purchase these pianos at prices away below what any other concern can obtain. We give our customers all of this great advantage, as we base our prices upon the manufacturing cost with but one small margin of profit added.

A WORD ABOUT FREIGHT CHARGES.

Most of our friends hesitate to purchase pianos from us, because they believe that the freight charges will be so very high that it will make the piano too expensive. This is certainly a great mistake. In the first place the local dealer has to pay the freight upon any piano which he ships to your town, and in making up the price on the piano he has to include the freight charges which he has paid, and when you purchase the piano you not only pay the freight charges, but you pay his large profit as well. By comparing our prices on pianos with those asked you by local dealers, and then comparing the freight charges which you will have to pay with the amount which we can save you on your purchase, you will see at once that the freight charge is but a very small amount in comparison with the amount you will save on your purchase. Another advantage is, that in purchasing a piano from us you know exactly what the instrument costs you at the factory, and you know exactly what you pay in freight charges, while on the other hand, in purchasing from the local dealer you know what the piano costs you, but do not know how much of it is his profit and how much the freight charge. As a general thing the railroad companies are very reasonable in freight charges, and when you consider the fact that you have to pay the freight charges whether you buy from us or from the local dealer, we believe that you should not hesitate in giving us an opportunity to send you one of our splendid instruments under our great Thirty Days Free Trial Offer. We are always willing to tell our customers the exact cost of freight on a piano laid down at their town, and where parties wish us to do so, gladly prepay the freight where the amount of the charges is enclosed with the order. This guarantees that the freight charges will not be over the figures quoted by us. Do not let the small amount of freight charges which you will have to pay prove any obstacle to your purchasing one of these pianos, as we ship each one under our express promise to save you from $50.00 to $200.00, according to the grade of piano which you purchase.

A NEW PIANO LAMP.

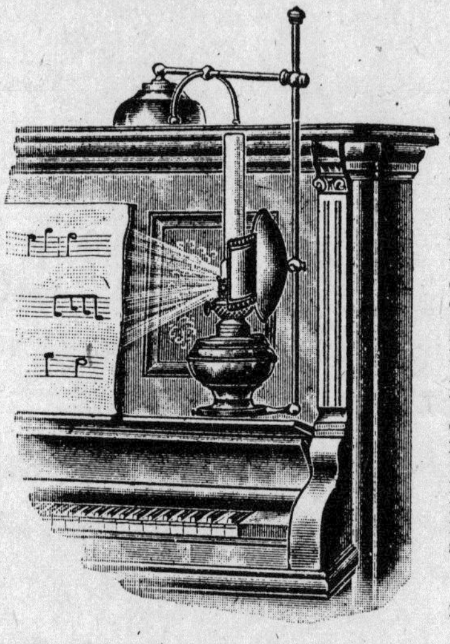

We are giving an illustration of a new idea in a piano lamp, which we are sure will be welcomed by all performers on the piano. This piano lamp is so constructed that the base can be set upon the top of the instrument and the lamp regulated by thumb screws and rods so that it throws the light in any direction. The illustration shows the method of placing it on the instrument. The base is weighted so as to sustain the weight of the lamp. It has adjustable shades which not only throw the light squarely upon the music page, but also screen it from the eyes of the performer. The lamp can be detached from the frame, to be filled or cleaned, and the entire outfit can be removed from the piano by simply lifting it with the hand. It is handsomely nickel plated throughout, is very ornamental and carefully and substantially made. It is fitted with a circular wick and throws a strong brilliant light.

No. 46C102 Price, complete.. **$3.25**

Weight, boxed and packed for shipment, 15 pounds.

WHAT OUR FRIENDS SAY ABOUT THE MAGNIFICENT VALUES WHICH WE ARE GIVING IN PIANOS.

Voluntary Testimonials From Just a Few of Those Who Have Purchased Pianos From Us in the Last Year.

What Our Customers Say About Our Pianos is the Best Evidence of Their Splendid Finish and Magnificent Tone.

The following testimonials will establish in the mind of any candid man, the fact that everything that we have said in regard to the great saving which we can make the purchasers of our pianos is true in every respect. It has been our aim in selling these pianos to make the customer the sole judge as to whether or not the instrument is perfectly satisfactory, and give him every opportunity to thoroughly test and try the instrument before finally deciding to accept it. When a customer purchases a piano from us under our great 30 Days Free Trial Offer we do not ask him to promise us anything or to put himself under any obligation in any way. The only thing we ask from a customer is to give us an opportunity to place the instrument in his home for trial, and give the instrument a thorough test and examination without prejudice or partiality. We are publishing just a few of the hundreds of testimonials we receive, as our space in this catalogue is very limited, and while we do not ask you to take our word for anything we say in regard to the qualities of our pianos, we believe that you will take the opinions of your friends and neighbors who have ordered pianos from us and find them satisfactory in every respect.

We will be glad to have you write to anyone of the customers mentioned on these pages and ask them their unbiased opinion of the pianos they purchased from us. We are willing to risk our reputation and the reputation of the pianos upon what they tell you in their letters. Should you desire to write to one of these persons we suggest that you enclose a two-cent stamp for reply, as it would hardly be fair to ask them to pay their own postage on the letter they send you in reply.

We fully appreciate the difficulties under which we labor in selling these pianos by mail. It is natural that the local dealer and agent who cannot afford to sell a piano at the same low price which we make should feel some hostility toward us. This makes it doubly difficult for us to make sales on our pianos, because it establishes a prejudice in the minds of the customers, which is very difficult to remove. The fact that we are prepared to place the entire matter in the customer's hands at our expense and protect him for 25 years after he purchases the instrument, and refund his money with freight charges added in case he is not in every way satisfied, has done a great deal toward satisfying the public in regard to our instruments. We ask you to read the testimonials which we are giving on this page, as they come from customers widely separated and in different parts of the country, and are purely voluntary in every respect.

AS GOOD AS HIS NEIGHBOR'S PIANO WHICH COST $450.00.

The customer whose testimonial appears below took advantage of our great 30 Days Free Trial Offer, which gave him a splendid opportunity to compare his piano with the $450.00 instrument owned by his neighbor, and by reading the testimonial you will see that he found his piano in every way equal to the one purchased by his neighbor at $450.00.

Sears, Roebuck & Co., Chicago, Ill. Sterling, Nebraska.

Dear Sirs:—The Beckwith piano I received of you in January has given good satisfaction so far. We are well pleased with the same. We cannot see but that it is as good as our neighbor's, that cost $450.00. We are well pleased with the mandolin attachment. My neighbor's has no attachments. C. B. SMITH.

EQUAL TO PIANOS SOLD BY AGENTS AT FROM $350.00 TO $400.00.

Below we give a testimonial from another party, who after comparison and trial of our piano is willing to say that the piano we sold him is equal to those generally sold by agents at from $350.00 to $400.00. Such testimonials as these ought to convince any unprejudiced person that what we say in regard to the great saving which we can make is absolutely true in every respect.

Sears, Roebuck & Co., Chicago, Ill. Elco, Penn.

Dear Sirs:—The piano which I purchased from you reached me on June 1st, and after giving it a thorough test, both myself and friends, I am pleased to inform you that it gives satisfaction in every respect and is equal to pianos sold here by agents at $350.00 and $400.00. I would recommend it to anyone as being all that you say it is and would be pleased to have anyone who is going to purchase a piano refer to me either by letter or personally and I will gladly do what I can to aid you in making a sale. Thanking you for your past favors, I remain, yours truly, JAMES L. MOMETAIN.

EQUAL TO PIANOS SOLD BY DEALERS AT $350.00 AND BETTER TONED.

Below we give another testimonial from a customer who says that the piano we shipped him is equal to pianos sold by dealers at $350.00 and is much better in tone. Bear in mind, that the customer writes this letter entirely of his own accord and without any dictation from us in any respect. We would be glad to have you write to the writer of any one of these testimonials and get his opinion of the merits of our instruments.

Sears, Roebuck & Co., Chicago, Ill. Three Rivers, Mich.

Dear Sirs:—I received the piano April 6th, all O. K. In appearance it is equal to a $350.00 Wellington, sold by a dealer here and better toned.

Yours respectfully, G. W. BARTO.

WOULD NOT PART WITH IT FOR ANY $300.00 PIANO IN TOWN.

It is the universal verdict of our customers as gleaned from the numerous voluntary letters which we receive that, they would not exchange the pianos which we have sold them for other pianos in the neighborhood which have cost much more in price.

Sears, Roebuck & Co., Chicago, Ill. St. Cloud, Minn.

Dear Sirs:—We received our piano and must say that we are more than pleased with it. I would not part with it for any $300.00 piano in town. In fact, we are well pleased with all our goods. I wish to thank you very much. I'll advise everybody to get their goods from Sears, Roebuck & Co.

Yours very truly, MISS M. STUCKE.

hence has not the same volume of sound." Well, what do you want for $89? The pipe organ of St. Sulpice? If it is not as big as other pianos, its tone is nonetheless "very strong for the size of the piano." But, alas. There are other things about The Home Favorite that destine it to linger in a limbo of imperfection, and the copywriter, biting his cigar, bravely points them out. "To enable us to offer a piano at this price, it is necessary to save wherever possible, hence the sounding board, while very strong, is not so large as in some of our other instruments; the metal plate is smaller, the strings are not so long, but"—sound now the trumpets of triumph—"it is EQUAL to pianos sold by MUSIC DEALERS for about $200.00."

At this point, the catalog, so sure of itself when confronting the puny claims of music dealers, wavers when facing the soul of the piano itself—the tone—and weakly lays down a dubious canon of beauty. "The tone," it says in a thin, white voice drained of assurance, "is always a matter of taste, and in this piano we endeavor to produce a tone which we believe will please most anyone. It is sweet and melodious and of ample power for all ordinary requirements." We shall see later, however, that nothing is immutable in a changing mail-order world, and how, under other circumstances, this canon is abruptly thrown overboard.

A piano is more than a musical instrument: it is also a piece of furniture. In 1905, it was what might be termed significant furniture: the pivot upon which the all-important parlor turned. And the piano as furniture was the piano case. Here the catalog, essaying the "Vanity of vanities, all is vanity" role of Ecclesiastes, points out that the case of The Home Favorite was subject to the corruption of everything below heaven, made even as it was of "solid wood, finished in mahogany or burled walnut. Extreme cold or other climatic changes are liable to cause the finish to check or peel in the course of time. We, therefore, cannot guarantee the finish on these cheaper pianos to stand, but otherwise this has no effect upon the *tone or durability of the instrument.*" But what matter if the body falters when the spirit stands erect?

At the other end of the scale from The Home Favorite was The Beckwith Acme Cabinet Grand Concert Piano, price $165. Now all is for the best in the best of all possible merchandise worlds, and the catalog is so certain of the virtues of this instrument that it takes chance out of the buying. The customer may have it on "Our Great Thirty Day Trial Offer. This enables you to fully examine and test this beautiful instrument in your home before you decide to accept it. . . . We will be glad to have you call in any musician who is unbiased and will give his honest opinion of the instrument." And, after the doctors have consulted in a grove of musical academe, "If you, together with your friends do not decide that this is the greatest bargain in a piano you ever saw and fully equal to the instruments which are being sold at $350.00 to $400.00 in your community, then you are at liberty to return the instrument, we will cheerfully refund your money in full and pay the entire expenses of transportation both ways." Inasmuch as the return of an Acme Cabinet Grand (shipping weight, 825 pounds) might involve moving nearly half a ton of wood and metal six or seven thousand miles, the catalog's confidence could hardly go farther.

This grand piano was not what is now called a grand, but an upright. But whatever it lacked in grandness was compensated for by decoration. "The Music Desk," says the catalog, "is elaborately carved with finest raised carvings in the most artistic designs. The background of the carving is dull finish, while the other space is very highly polished, producing the grand effect found only in instruments for which you would pay a city dealer $350.00 to $400.00." The case, moreover, had "that smooth, glassy appearance so much admired in fine furniture." Supporting the keyboard were four Grand Rapids caryatides in the form of elaborately carved wood columns.

At $89 for The Home Favorite, the catalog, as we have seen, made tone the plaything of the gods. It laid down no stern, immutable canons; tone, at that modest price, was "only a matter of taste." But when the catalog speaks of The Acme

Cabinet Grand at $165—a very different matter—it ascends the lonely hill of the absolute and lays down the dictum that tone is "the most important feature in a piano and can be only appreciated after a thorough test of the instrument."

It is not to be expected of an age which abhorred simplicity of line and decoration, when plush simulated cracked marble, and so utilitarian an object as a buggy lap robe was "a handsome reproduction (in plush) of a beautiful picture showing two horses fleeing before an electric storm, with handsome flowered border," that the piano player should be content to derive only piano music from his instrument. Ah, no. With every piano of whatever price Sears offered:

> THE MANDOLIN ATTACHMENT furnished free with each Beckwith piano, perfectly reproduces the tones of the mandolin, harp, zither, guitar, banjo, etc., and which is so widely advertised by other houses who charge $50.00 to $75.00 extra for placing it in their pianos. . . . Many, however, do not care for the Mandolin Attachment and we will, if desired, with no extra cost, place in its stead the Muffler Attachment or Practice Pedal, an attachment of great utility as it deadens sound at the will of the performer, a desirable feature during the hours of practice.

The buyer, therefore, of a Sears piano in 1905, got not only a piano but also the equivalent of a stringed orchestra; he was master of a bagful of sound effects in an instrument that had a fluidity never dreamed of by Beethoven. And when he tired of these, he could, by throwing a lever that disconnected the Mandolin Attachment, retire to the austerities of piano music unadorned. He might have embraced still another choice (at no extra cost) and availed himself of the merciful anesthesia offered by the Muffler Attachment.

Heavenly Diapasons

While the 1905 catalog offered only four kinds of pianos, it presented a bewildering choice of organs. There were fifteen varieties at more than fifty prices. It took thirteen precious pages to illustrate and describe them. A budding Bach of the times could let his fancy (and purse) range from "This Genuine Beckwith Co's Large, Handsome, Beautifully Finished, GOLDEN OAK PARLOR ORGAN at $19.90, to the Beckwith IMPERIAL GRAND ORGAN, Action D, Six Octaves, at $51.95, The Handsomest Organ We Have To Offer."

But Sears, not content with this distinguished achievement, labored and brought forth a very miracle of music. It produced an organ (" 'This is the way,' laugh'd the great god Pan") as easy to carry as reeds that were plucked by the river. And there were many who yearned for such an instrument in the America of 1905. For that was the very heyday of the evangelist who moved from town to town preaching the old-time religion to crowds in a tent or an empty store; preaching the doctrine of brimstone and hell-fire; calling upon men to repent, believe, and be baptized before it was too late; bidding them come up the sawdust trail and be washed forever free of their sins in the blood of the Lamb. But how evoke the reluctant, sinful soul without music? How create rapture without bloodcurdling hymns? Where find an organ so light that it could be carried under the arm, and moved one day to Babylon and the next day to Rome?

Sears had the answer to this anguished cry. It built an organ suitable for the peripatetic purposes of troubadour or evangelist. It was "THE BECKWITH UNIVERSAL FOLDING ORGAN, for Schoolrooms, Evangelistic Work, And In Your Home. Wherever Music is Wanted. The Beckwith Folding Organ is adapted for use under all circumstances and in places where there is no instrument or where portability is desired. . . . It is endorsed by Sunday schools and leading evangelists throughout the country. . . . Actual weight, 29 pounds. Price: $27.50."

Once upon a time an American's home was not only his castle but also his music conservatory. The parlor—not the bathroom—of the 1905 home was where men invited their souls while Mama played "Silver Threads Among The Gold" on the organ. In that distant day, the country possessed more

$25.95 BUYS THE CELEBRATED ACME QUEEN PARLOR ORGAN
OF THE GENUINE BECKWITH MAKE.

Made by the Beckwith Organ Company.

$25.95 Makers of the HIGHEST GRADE PARLOR ORGANS made in the World.

$25.95 MEANS ANOTHER BIG REDUCTION IN PRICE, MEANS THAT EVERY PENNY'S ADVANTAGE WE HAVE GAINED WE HAVE GIVEN TO OUR CUSTOMERS. AS WE HAVE REDUCED

THE COST OF MANUFACTURE at the Beckwith works by increasing the output, increasing the number of organs we make daily, we have reduced our selling prices accordingly, until we are now offering this ACME QUEEN PARLOR ORGAN FOR ONLY $25.95.

REMEMBER, it is covered by our 25-year binding guarantee, and we will gladly send you the instrument with the understanding and agreement that you can give it thirty days' trial, during which time you can put it to every test, compare it with organs that sell at $10.00 to $20.00 more money, and if you are not perfectly satisfied with your purchase you can return the organ to us at our expense, and we will immediately return your money, together with any freight charges paid by you.

WHILE THIS IS A THOROUGHLY HIGH GRADE INSTRUMENT, and worth two of the cheap stenciled organs that are being widely advertised, for it bears the name of the maker, the genuine BECKWITH ORGAN CO.'S make, in selecting an organ we would specially recommend that you select the highest grade parlor organ made, THE BECKWITH IMPERIAL GRAND, which we now offer at $39.95, a $5.00 reduction in price, reduced from $44.95 to $39.95.

IF YOU DO NOT FEEL that you can afford to buy the finest instrument made, we would recommend that you select the next in order, the ROYAL GRAND now offered at $36.75, also a big reduction in price; or, if you do not feel like investing this much, then select the 6-octave Beckwith Cottage Organ, which we are now offering at the cut price of $32.50, as shown on the following page. We especially recommend one of these high grade instruments, the three highest grade instruments the Beckwith Company make, since they are such instruments as go out of no other factory in the country. However, if you feel like making a smaller investment you will find this, our ACME QUEEN, at $25.95, a thoroughly reliable organ, and we guarantee it superior to any instrument you can buy elsewhere, even at $10.00 to $15.00 more money, the equal of organs that are sold generally at $40.00 to $50.00.

THIS ORGAN, OFFERED AT $25.95, is made to combine all of the good qualities found in instruments that sell at $15.00 to $25.00 more money. A special feature of this organ is the Vox Humana stop, which is not found on any other organ, at anywhere near the price. This stop gives it that beautiful wavy, vibrating tone effect. It is an exact imitation of the singing voice. No organ is really complete without this stop, and the Acme Queen is the only organ at anywhere near this price upon which it will be found.

This is a large, full size parlor organ. The instrument is standard in every way. It stands feet high, 42 inches long and 23 inches wide.

THE CASE. The case of this organ is substantially made and comes in solid oak, very finely finished. The design is neat and attractive. In this grade of instrument it is so arranged as to provide for two pretty bric-a-brac shelves, one on each side of the 10x14 inch French bevel plate mirror, with which the top is fitted. The music desk covers a large receptacle for music and on each side is arranged a very nice lamp stand. It is so arranged as to provide for a tone amplifying chamber, which gives the reeds of the organ that fine, pipe like quality of tone so much sought after in reed organs. The pedals are covered with Brussels carpet, and have handsome metal frames, finely nickel plated.

THE TONE. The tone is the important feature of an organ and this has been well provided for in the Acme Queen. The combination of reeds and stops with which this instrument is fitted, guarantees innumerable harmonious combinations. It has great bellows capacity, being fitted with the well known Beckwith bellows, which is constructed of three-ply built up stock and warranted not to warp or split. The cloth used in these bellows is the finest wool silk rubber cloth, manufactured specially for this purpose and guaranteed not to leak. The bellows is fitted with a large reservoir which forms the vacuum for the organ and guarantees a steady stream of air to the reeds, and avoids the jerky, spasmodic effect noticed on most reed organs when the pedals are pumped violently.

WHILE THIS ORGAN, LIKE OUR $39.95 BECKWITH, is covered by our binding 25 years' guarantee, and is sure to please, and we give you the privilege of returning it to us if it isn't perfectly satisfactory, and agree to send your money back, since we have been able to so greatly reduce the cost of manufacture on the finest parlor organs made in the world, the very highest grade instruments we have yet produced in the Beckwith organ plant, the Imperial Grand reduced to $39.95, the Royal Grand at $36.75, in ordering we would especially urge that you select the best that it is possible to build, one of the two highest grade instruments we make, either the Imperial Grand at $39.95 or the Royal Grand at $36.75. Weight, boxed and packed for shipment, 400 pounds.

This organ can be furnished in walnut finish without extra charge. Be sure and specify in your order WHETHER YOU DESIRE OAK OR WALNUT FINISH. ORDER BY NUMBER. See page 120 for description of action.

No. 46C22 The Beckwith Acme Queen Parlor Organ, Action A, Five Octaves. Price........................ **$25.95**

READ the interesting account on page 119 of the BECKWITH ORGAN EXHIBIT at the great ST. LOUIS WORLD'S FAIR.

DID YOU VISIT THE WORLD'S FAIR AT ST. LOUIS?

Thousands of visitors who attended the World's Fair at St. Louis last year will remember the beautiful exhibit of Beckwith Organs in the Manufacturers' building, which exhibit was in charge of the Adler Organ Company. The remarkable thing about this exhibit was not only that the booth was the handsomest in the building, its decorations the most beautiful, and that it was one of the most extensive exhibits of this character at the Fair, but that the prices placed upon the instruments were more than half than those offered by any other exhibit of the character on the grounds. This naturally attracted the attention of the thousands of people who were interested either as purchasers, manufacturers or dealers. This exhibit established a record in the organ trade which has never been equaled by any other concern in the organ trade and we predict that it will be a long time before any other concern will ever approach this standard, because this immense trade which we have established in organs has given us such a prestige that we have now a greater buying advantage than any other concern in the country.

But the **most astonishing thing** in connection with this exhibit was the high quality of the instruments there shown. Musical experts from all over the world, attracted to our exhibit by the remarkably low prices quoted and the unusually high quality possessed by the instruments, were loud in their praise of this splendid line of reed organs. The fact that the Adler Organ Company, in charge of the exhibit, secured many diplomas and medals of honor from the judges at the fair, establishes the fact beyond dispute that the Beckwith Organs are superior to any on the market. The engraving which we show of the exhibit gives a very poor idea of the beautiful design of the booth and its handsome trimmings. This exhibit was conducted at great expense, with the hope that the thousands of our friends who might visit the fair could examine and see for themselves the high quality of organs which we are offering at extremely low prices. As the judges who passed on the merits of the different exhibits at the fair were men of discrimination and judgment, absolutely impartial and unprejudiced, the fact is established beyond any doubt that **the Beckwith Organs are today the very best reed organs which can be manufactured.** Of those who have already purchased organs from us we had this fact proven to them beyond a doubt, but to those who are hesitating in regard to the purchase of one of these instruments, we will simply say that the judgment of the judges at the fair should be sufficient to remove all of your doubts. It has always been our policy to ask the customer to take our word for anything we claim in regard to the merits of the instruments, but to give him opportunity to prove to him by actual trial and examination that the instruments are everything that we claim for them and that we can save him from $25.00 to $50.00, according to the grade of instrument which he purchases. Following out this policy we have from time to time printed testimonials from purchasers all over the country who have bought these organs and have expressed themselves as being more than delighted with the quality of the instruments and fully satisfied of the fact that we saved them the amount we promised on their purchase.

We now call attention, as a further proof of the quality of the instruments and the amount we can save the purchaser, to the **diplomas and medals of honor** which these organs received from the board of judges at the World's exhibit held in St. Louis last year. **The fact that the Beckwith Organs were on exhibition** at this Fair, the fact that they occupied one of the handsomest booths in the building, says nothing whatever as to their quality and the extremely low prices which we place on them, but the fact that they received from the board of judges, composed of eminent musicians from all over the country, the highest **diplomas of merit and medals of honor,** forever settles the fact in this country as to their extremely high quality.

If you are thinking of purchasing an organ, these are facts you should consider, as the voluntary testimonials of your friends and neighbors, and the **diplomas of merit and medals of honor** awarded by the board of judges at the World's Fair are the best evidence of the superiority of the instruments.

EXHIBIT OF BECKWITH ORGANS AT THE WORLD'S FAIR.

BECKWITH ORGAN FACTORY.

WEST VIEW OF THE BECKWITH ORGAN FACTORY AT LOUISVILLE, KENTUCKY.

The illustration above shows one of the two immense factories in which we manufactured the splendid Beckwith Organs. These two factories are devoted entirely to the manufacture of Beckwith Organs and are fitted throughout with the most modern labor saving machinery. The immense capacity of these two factories enables us to keep constantly on hand a large reserve stock of these organs, enabling us to make immediate shipment upon every order received. As we control the entire output of both of these factories, and guarantee to them a market for every organ they turn out, we are able to secure the very lowest possible manufacturing prices. As we place our orders with these factories for hundreds of organs at a time we enable them to purchase large quantities of lumber and material for use in building the organs, and they are thus enabled to take advantage of every depression in the market to purchase at the lowest possible prices. The great saving which is thus made in manufacturing cost, together with the large amount which we save in selling expense, guarantees to our customers prices on our entire line of organs, which are away below what the local dealer or agent can obtain from his jobber or manufacturer upon the same grade of instruments. These organ factories are entirely new plants, which have been built with the distinct object of reducing the manufacturing cost of organs without in any way sacrificing their quality.

Another important point in this connection is that these organ factories have been established at Louisville, Ky., and St. Paul, Minn., these two points are admirably located in regard to shipping facilities. By making our northern and western shipments from our St. Paul factory, and our southern and eastern shipments from our Louisville factory, we can place these organs in the hands or our customers at the very least possible expense in freight charges. This is a great advantage to our customers, because it enables us to make the freight charges on each shipment from $1.00 to $5.00 lower than they would otherwise have to pay. It will pay you to consider these facts when you are ready to purchase an organ.

pianos and organs than bathtubs, just as it now has half as many automobiles as toothbrushes. Later, these conditions were to be changed: the parlor was to become just another room in the house where people ate and slept; the organ was to vanish into the darkness that shelters the spinning wheel; while the bathroom was to emerge as the central altar and pride of the home. But in 1905, no home could afford to be without an organ, and few people were so poor that they could not afford one. Sears, the Largest Music Dealers, saw to that.

The Golden Oak Case Parlor Organ, for example, cost only $19.90—far less than the price of many of today's radios. Yet one got a great deal of lumber, craftsmanship, and music for one's money. The case was made of "selected solid oak, finished golden. . . . The upper part is handsome in appearance, with heavy rail-top of fancy shape, and neatly hand-carved; has a good size bevel mirror, has carved panels in sides, full-length shelf underneath, ornamented with turned knobs; large music desk with carved panels and covers. . . . Pedals are full-size, covered with Brussels carpet, nickel trimmed."

Even today one shares the joy that must have suffused the heart of the copywriter who described the instrument that was the pride of Sears' heart and the desire of all organ lovers: "The Beckwith Imperial Grand, the Handsomest Organ We Have to Offer." It obviously summed up all the genius of the cabinet and organ makers of the times, and the copywriter, every doubt vanishing in the presence of its polished perfection, pulls out the stops and goes to town. "The tone," he cries exultantly, "is full, round and resonant, and is susceptible of the most delicate variations." And the design! It was evidently created by some Midwestern Fra Lippo Lippi whose name unhappily is lost, but there is little doubt that it was the work of the perfect painter in tone, wood, and metal. "The design," says the catalog, "is the finest ever conceived by the mind of the organ designer, and the splendid way in which it has been worked out, together with the brilliant and powerful tone, makes this organ the highest achievement of the organ builder's art." Then the catalog, fearful lest the customer should get the impression that Sears loves art more than living, makes a dizzy turnabout, which would have produced a severe psychological wrench in an age less sturdy, and hurls a challenge into the clenched teeth of the local music dealer. "The case of this organ," it says mockingly through its drooping mustaches, "could not be made in your town for the price we are asking for the organ complete."

The case was so beautiful that the copywriter broke down and blubbered. Here was loveliness so tenuous that "no engraving can do justice to the beauty of finish and elegance for which this instrument is remarkable." But the catalog, faltering for a moment, recovers its voice and tells us that The Imperial Grand had not only "pretty bric-a-brac shelves"—a feature common even to the coarser organs—but also "a beautiful canopy top, ornamented with hand carvings and supported by two graceful pillars." Then finally (a touch of Chartres and Carcassonne brought into the parlors of the prairies): "Supporting the keyboard on each end of the organ are two handsomely carved griffins which give the organ a medieval effect not possessed by another organ." And, as though this were not enough for $51.95, Sears, snuffing out all sales resistance in a burst of Medicean magnificence, offered:

FREE WITH EACH OF THESE ORGANS a fine stool, made in wood to match the case of the organ, with handsome turned legs, brass claws and glass balls.

The catalog's organ section ends with a quiet statement that sharply illuminates the tone deafness in which the present generation has sunk. We creatures of the machine age, who can but dial the radio or push the button of a phonograph, are musical dullards by comparison with Americans of the early years of this century. Hundreds of thousands of them played musical instruments, and those who could not play, yearned to do so. Apparently they did not need a teacher, for with each piano and organ Sears offered "a complete instruction book, by the aid of which one can learn to play the instrument without the aid of a teacher." 1905 was the golden age of music in the American home.

Village Violinists

Before a tent near the river a violin makes lively music; in another quarter, a flute gives its mellow and melancholy notes to the still night air, which, as they float over the quiet water, seem a lament for the past rather than a a hope for the future. *

Seeking coolness in the shadows of barns, throwing corn to hogs in sleety rain, milking cows in green meadows, measuring gingham in country stores, there were once myriads of Americans who not only formed the economic backbone of the country but who also preserved its musical soul. And the hand that rocked the churner as often as not scraped the bow. The 1905 catalog, aware of all this, listed nineteen kinds of violins and violin outfits, and spread illustrations and descriptions of them over eleven pages. For the violinist of that day was as common as caricatures of Teddy Roosevelt's teeth.

No village Paganini, however poor, was condemned to silence because he could not raise the money for a fiddle. If he had had only $1.95 it would have been enough to buy "Our Stradivarius Model. . . . They possess a tone seldom found in instruments of this price and are equal in every way to violins generally sold at twice the price." But pitfalls lay in the path of the unwary customer—particularly if he traded elsewhere—and Sears is determined that its clients shall not stumble into them, $1.95 and all. The catalog tells us that "No musical instruments are so susceptible of false valuations as violins"; and, having warned the customer, it threw a mantle of protection around his shoulders. Sears evidently adhered to the Cartesian doctrine that it is immoral to believe in the truth of a proposition which cannot be demonstrated. Every instrument, therefore, was sold on "Our Ten Days' Trial Offer. Order one of the violins listed, use it ten days and if you do

* Jesse Applegate, *A Day With the Cow Column in 1843.*

not find it satisfactory you may return it to us. We will pay express charges both ways and refund your money in full." The violinist could then, with this assurance before him, freely roam among enchanting pages describing dozens of models, including those two favorites:

> OUR GENUINE MAGGINI VIOLIN, An Exact Of The Well Known Maggini Violins Made by One of the Greatest Italian Makers. $10.00 Violin for $4.35.
> OUR PAGANINI GUARNERIUS VIOLIN, An Exact Copy of the Violin Used by That Marvelous Player, $5.45.

The prospective customer of the most expensive violin offered by Sears in 1905, "Our Genuine Heberlein, the Most Wonderful Value Offered In a Violin, $23.45," saw in it, through the eyes of the prophetic catalog, an opportunity to acquire "a wonderful value" for himself, and at the same time do something for his children or grandchildren. The Heberlein was a violin whose selling price, according to the laws of probability, might increase a thousandfold with the passing of time. The catalog tells us why. "The varnish used on these instruments," it says, "is of such a quality that the colors will blend and soften with years of use and the varnish will so harden and become part of the wood that the resonance of the instrument will be wonderfully increased and the tone will become more brilliant and powerful with continued use. If the violins which the original Stradivarius made and sold for an amount that would about equal $25.00 in our money, can now be sold for from $5,000.00 to $10,000.00, is it not reasonable to suppose that the purchase of one of these violins from us at this time will mean a marvelously profitable investment in the coming years."

Nothing, in the light of experience, could be more reasonable. Has not time turned to gold the white marble of the Athenian temple of Theseus? But the catalog, content with having torn a nasty hole in the veil of the future, does not look back but presses grimly forward, determined that the descendants of a Heberlein owner shall have no trouble cashing in on grandpa's foresight: "With each of these violins we issue a certificate showing that the violin is a genuine Heberlein violin, carefully made by this celebrated maker."

These Heberlein violins that once lay on many a parlor table flanked by the Bible and *The Last Days of Pompeii*—where are they now? Are they lost in attics long unexplored? And if they have miraculously survived, and stored up tone distilled from the wine of time so that they sing like the very harps of heaven, who shall play them? The hands of the children to whom they have descended grip the steering wheel; their ears ring with the strident clamor of the radio. Who shall come forward with a crumbling certificate and a mellowed Heberlein to claim the heritage that his ancestor laid up for him long ago?

Anybody Can Play a Violin

Although Sears gave away an instruction book with each violin, it also sold books to those who already owned violins but felt the need for brushing up on their technique. Thus for thirty-seven cents one could have purchased:

"BENJAMIN'S ILLUSTRATED VIOLIN METHOD (If by mail, postage extra, 5 cents). This is the latest publication in the way of a violin instructor. . . . It is profusely illustrated; also contains a collection of popular music. . . ."

Naturally Sears, The World's Largest Music Dealer, sold music. One of the best-selling books was "The Young Violinist's Gigantic Collection. 350 pieces of the best music. Price 25 cents." But, unfortunately, the Gigantic Collection was in fact so gigantic that the postage on it, in the days before the parcel post, amounted to twenty-five cents, almost doubling the cost of this invaluable folio and making the delivered price forty-eight cents.

Guitars

On a night of cold and blowing rain, a ragged Negro, accompanied by a girl, shuffled into the Bridal Wreath plantation store. His toes stuck out of the remnants of shoes that clung to his feet. "Boss man," he said to the clerk, "I wants me a pair of rubber boots." But the clerk was busy with other duties, and while the prospective buyer waited, he saw suspended from the ceiling among the lanterns, hams, and accordions, a guitar. He asked if he "could set down and pick that gi-tar," and having been given permission, removed it and ran his calloused black fingers lovingly over the strings. Then he sat down, shivering, and began quietly to play to himself, the girl snuggling for warmth close to his side.

"How much is it, white folks?" he inquired of the clerk who had finally come to sell him boots. "Four and a half," replied the clerk. "Den I'll take it," the musician replied. He wearily stood up, counted out four dollars and fifty cents in nickels and dimes won in a dice game, and moved slowly to the door clutching the guitar close to his body. Outside on the store gallery, as though fortifying himself to go out into the cold rain, he stopped to sing and play "I Woke Up This Morning With Jesus On My Mind."

"Niggers are crazy," mumbled the clerk as he prepared to close up for the night.

In 1905, the United States reeked with bucolic and small-town guitarists. In the catfish parlors and on the plantations of the South, Negroes "picked" guitars; in the Middle West and the Far West and in the lonely mountains of Virginia and Carolina, guitar music relieved the pain of living and gave forth a joyous affirmation of the goodness of life.

Sears, conscious of the great number of actual or potential guitarists in the land, laid the benison of music smack down on the bargain counter. The Abou Ben Adhem of the pack, not only leading all the rest, but away out in front with a full catalog page devoted to it, was "OUR $2.95 EDGEMERE GUITAR OUTFIT (shipping weight 12 pounds)."

Other guitars were named for American colleges, and one wonders whether the head of Sears' music department, when he priced and named his guitars, was not at the same time passing judgment upon the merits of the universities according to some secret or unconscious criteria of his own. Note the valuations:

OUR PAGANINI GUARNERIUS VIOLIN, $5.45.

An Exact Copy of the Violin Used by That Marvelous Player.

A BEAUTIFUL MODEL AND A SPLENDID TONE. ACCURATELY MADE AND FINELY FINISHED.

THIS IS A SPLENDID INSTRUMENT in every respect and is an exact copy of the Guarnerius violin used by the celebrated Paganini during his life. This model has never been offered to violinists at this price before and we are giving you an opportunity to purchase a copy of this celebrated violin at an extremely low price. The back, sides and neck are made of pieces of figured maple and the top of choice selected, seasoned silver spruce. The entire instrument is coated with beautiful transparent varnish, finely shaded and polished. The instrument is trimmed throughout with solid ebony, finely polished and its entire appearance is fine in the extreme.

THIS INSTRUMENT is especially desirable for those who desire to purchase a good violin at a low price. It has a full, sweet tone of great carrying power and has never failed to give satisfaction. We furnish this instrument, complete with bow, case, strings, etc., so that it is ready for use when you receive it. We desire to recommend it to all who desire to purchase a fine violin at a low price and upon receipt of $1.00 we will ship it C. O. D. to any part of the country. If it does not prove satisfactory it may be returned to us and the money will be cheerfully refunded.

THE ENGRAVING which accompanies this description shows the front and back of this beautiful violin, but no engraving, however good, will be adequate to carry to your mind any of the several points in beauty of appearance and excellence of workmanship which the instrument possesses. The back and sides are beautifully and evenly flamed and the varnish, with which the instrument is coated, brings out the grain of the wood in a perfect manner.

AT $5.45 we furnish the violin complete with case, fine Brazilwood bow, extra set of strings, rosin, fingerboard chart and instruction book.

THE PRICE which we ask you for this instrument represents but a very small part of its real value, as we do not charge you any fancy price for its excellent quality of tone, but the price we fix on it simply represents the cost of material and the amount paid out by the manufacturer for labor. We are selling you the instrument at the same small margin of profit at which we sell our groceries, dry goods, etc. We know it is the custom for dealers to fix fancy prices upon violins according to the excellent quality of their tone, but we are not dealing in violin tones, and we simply charge you the cost of material and labor with one small margin of profit added. We, however, wish you to remember that we fully guarantee the tone of every instrument which we sell. We are enabled to do this from the fact that all our violins are made by one of the best makers and the care and thoroughness exercised in their construction fully justifies us in guaranteeing the tone.

No. 12C219 Our Paganini Guarnerius Violin. Price.................................**$5.45**

NO. 12C219

ORDER BY NUMBER

BACK VIEW
No. 12C219 PAGANINI VIOLIN. Price. $5.45.

FRONT VIEW

PAGANINI

OUR $6.10 STRADIVARIUS MODEL VIOLIN.

A Violin in Which the Greatest Work of this Most Celebrated of All Makers is Accurately Copied.

ONE OF OUR BEST BARGAINS, $6.10

Complete With Brazilwood Bow, Rosin, Extra Set of Strings, Fingerboard Chart and Instruction Book.

THESE VIOLINS are made especially for us by one of the most celebrated violin makers of Europe, and are patterned accurately after the violins of the celebrated Antonious Stradivarius, who was probably the most celebrated violin maker that ever lived. The model has been strictly followed by the maker and we guarantee the instrument to possess all of the characteristics of the genuine Stradivarius violins. It has a two-piece maple back beautifully flamed, as shown in the illustration. The top is of resonant spruce, especially selected, and the entire instrument is coated with a reddish brown transparent varnish beautifully shaded in imitation of an old violin. **The neck and scroll are made of curly maple, corresponding with the back and side. The fingerboard, tailpiece and pegs are of the best quality selected ebony.** As each one of these instruments is carefully examined to see that it conforms exactly to the model after which it is patterned, the purchaser may

No. 12C222

ORDER BY NUMBER.

assured he is getting a perfectly correct copy of the violins of this Italian violin maker. purchase of one of these instruments will mean an investment which will increase in value each succeeding year, as the effect of the tone vibrations and the constant hardening [th]rough which the vegetable matter in the wood goes, will finally result in producing [re]sonance for which old violins are famous. We have sold many of these violins upon the [recom]mendations of violin teachers to their pupils and we have yet to receive one complaint [re]gard to their quality. **May we not have an opportunity of shipping you one of these** [sple]ndid instruments with the understanding that if you do not find it equal to any $10.00 [or $1]2.00 instrument which you can purchase in your own town you can return it to us and [we w]ill cheerfully refund your money and pay the express charges both ways?

THE ACCOMPANYING ENGRAVING is photographed directly from the instrument and shows both the [fr]ont and the back view very nicely. It will give you some idea of the beautiful [de]tails of the model and the fine proportions of the instrument. [Of] course it can give you no idea of the beauty of appearance, fineness [of fin]ish and excellence of tone quality which is one of the character[istic]s of this entire line. If you desire an instrument which will give [you] good service, upon which it will be a pleasure to play and which [will] have the appearance of a $15.00 or $20.00 instrument, you cannot do [bette]r than give us an order for one of these splendid violins. When [you] purchase a violin at $6.10 from your dealer you are purchasing an [instr]ument which probably costs less than $3.00 to manufacture, the bal[ance] of the price being made up of intermediate dealers' profits and sell[ing] [ex]penses which you have to pay when you purchase the instrument.

THE PRICE which we make on this instrument, $6.10, simply [r]epresents the price we pay the manufacturer, with [o]ne small percentage of profit added to pay us for handling and [selli]ng the instrument. We do not ask you to pay three or four differ[ent] [dea]lers' profits and we do not add anything extra to the price to [pay f]or imaginary qualities in the instrument. All we charge you for [one] of these violins is exactly what the instrument is worth, no more [no] less. You cannot afford to purchase an instrument elsewhere, [with]out considering carefully our line of violins and giving us an op[portu]nity to send you one for examination and comparison with the [instru]ments offered by other dealers.

REMEMBER, that we allow you to return, at our expense, any [ ] instrument which does not prove satisfactory and [we ag]ree to cheerfully refund the money you have paid. Under these [libera]l terms of shipment you do not run any risk whatever, in giving [us yo]ur order for one of these splendid violins.

No. 12C222 Our Stradivarius Model Violin. Price..... $6.10

FRONT VIEW

BACK VIEW
No. 12C222 STRADIVARIUS VIOLIN. Price, $6.10.

OUR $5.75 CHALLENGE BANJO.

Thirty-nine Brackets, Beautifully Made and Finished, Finest Construction Throughout, Beautiful in Tone and Tune, Offered Under Our Binding Guarantee to Prove Perfectly Satisfactory or Money Refunded, and the Equal in Every Way of Banjos that Sell Usually at Double the Price.

DESCRIPTION OF OUR CHALLENGE BANJO.

THE INSTRUMENT WE OFFER as the leader of our banjo line, to show for how little money we can offer a strictly high grade instrument, how much value it is possible to put into a banjo at this price. This splendid instrument has a brass shell, heavily nickel plated, lined with wood, finished in imitation mahogany and has double overspun wired edges. It has thirty-nine nickel plated hexagon brackets and a very fine quality of calfskin head. The diameter of the head is 11 inches. The neck is made of birch, highly finished in imitation of mahogany and highly polished. It has an ebony fingerboard, with pearl position dots and raised frets accurately placed, making the scale perfect. It is fitted with the very latest style nickel plated tailpiece and is thoroughly and carefully constructed throughout. From the illustration you can get a very good idea of the appearance of this instrument, but you must see it to really appreciate the details of design and ornamentation and especially to get a good idea of its splendid tone.

No. 12C822

ORDER BY NUMBER

THE FREE OUTFIT WITH THE CHALLENGE BANJO

With every Challenge Banjo at $5.75 we furnish, free, an outfit consisting of an extra set of strings, instruction book, fingerboard chart, which outfit adds greatly to the value of the instrument.

FREE GLENDON STRINGS. In addition to the strings already on the banjo, we furnish in the free outfit one set of Glendon strings of fine quality, strings that would cost 25 cents at retail.

FREE INSTRUCTION BOOK. In the outfit sent free with every Challenge Banjo, we furnish a complete instruction book for the banjo by which anyone can learn to play the instrument without the assistance of a teacher. A splendid book furnished free only by us.

GUCKERT'S CHORD BOOK BANJO SEARS ROEBUCK & CO.

FREE FINGERBOARD CHART. In the outfit furnished free with every Challenge Banjo, we include a copyrighted lettered fingerboard chart which can be pasted on the fingerboard under the strings and is of the greatest assistance in finding the different positions. All of these items are furnished free with the Challenge Banjo and help to form a value that has never been equaled.

OUR QUALITY GUARANTEE.

EVERY CHALLENGE BANJO that we ship is covered by our binding guarantee for quality by which we guarantee each and every part that enters into the construction of the instrument, guarantee it to be perfect in every respect, in make, material, finish, tone and if the Challenge Banjo you get from us does not exhibit the best standard of quality, you can return it to us at our expense and we will return your money.

OUR $1.00 OFFER.

WHILE NEARLY EVERYONE of our customers send the full amount of money with their order, and we recommend this method, as it will save you the charges on the return of money to us that are always asked on a C. O. D. shipment, nevertheless, if you prefer, you need only send us $1.00 deposit, and we will send this banjo to you by express, C. O. D., subject to examination. You can examine it carefully at the express office and if you find it in every way as represented and consider it a bargain at that price, then pay the express agent the balance of $4.75 and express charges. We recommend that you send the full amount of money with your order as you run no risk whatever and will save the 25 to 40 cents extra charge on the C. O. D. shipment.

IN CONSIDERING THIS BANJO AT $5.75, please do not compare it in your mind with the instruments offered by retail dealers at $5.00 to $6.00. It would be a great injustice to our Challenge Banjo to look at the instrument offered by retail dealers at $5.00 or $6.00 and consider that that is what you are going to get in the Challenge Banjo. Our Challenge Banjo is far superior in quality, tone and finish to instruments sold at the same price by other dealers and if you want to get a fair idea of this instrument, you must look at the banjos sold by retailers at $8.00 and $10.00. Better still, order our Challenge Banjo at $5.75 and order any other banjo from any other dealers at the same price, let them both come together for comparison and if you do this, we are sure you will recognize the superiority of our instrument and it will be the one you buy.

HOW WE CAN MAKE THE $5.75 PRICE ON A BANJO OF THIS QUALITY. We have just made a special contract with one of the largest banjo manufacturers in this country. We have contracted for an immense number of this special instrument which we call our Challenge Banjo. This manufacturer makes nothing but banjos, our order taking a large part of the product of his entire factory. All expenses for selling, such as salesmen's commission, traveling expenses, etc., are eliminated in this transaction. The manufacturer is willing to accept a very low price in consideration of this big order, as it gives him greater buying facilities in the raw materials and helps him to make his other orders to much better advantages. In other words, the prices to us from the manufacturer represents practically the bare cost of material and labor alone and to this original first cost of material and labor, we add our uniform and narrow margin of profit and we are thus able to offer this Challenge Banjo at the remarkable price of $5.75. When you buy this banjo from us at $5.75 you are paying just a little more than actual cost of material and labor and enables you to buy this instrument at about the same price that retail dealers pay in the largest quantities for such banjos. You are getting the benefit of our enormous buying facilities, the willingness of the manufacturer to accept our order at practically his cost, simply for the advantages it gives him in getting down his factory cost on other orders and our customers get the benefit of all of these advantages. When we sell the instrument to you we do not figure any middlemen's profits whatever. We need not consider salesmen's salaries, traveling expenses, any of the expenses known to wholesalers and jobbers, nor must we even consider the expense that the retail dealer must figure. Our musical goods department is only one of the fifty merchandise department in our establishment and must stand only its one-fiftieth of our small selling expense, such as cost of catalogues, rent, light, etc.

$5.75 FOR THIS BANJO is truly a wonder price. It will astonish dealers as well as consumers. If you show this banjo to a dealer, he will hardly believe that you bought it at $5.75. It represents a value in banjos heretofore unheard of.

DO YOU WANT A BANJO? If you think of buying a banjo, don't overlook this opportunity. If you want to invest only a small amount in an instrument, you will never have a better chance. You will be getting a fine instrument at a price that, offered by any other dealer, would secure for you the cheapest kind of a banjo. Bear in mind this is an instrument that we guarantee in every respect, a high class, high grade, beautiful and full toned banjo, not a cheap, unreliable instrument, but one that you will be proud to own and play on. Remember, you get the banjo and entire outfit as described, including the extra set of strings, instruction book and fingerboard chart, all for $5.75.

WE EXPECT every Challenge Banjo we sell to prove a big advertisement for us. We believe that this instrument will make friends for us wherever it goes. We know it will make everyone realize the wonderful value we furnish in musical instruments. Everyone who sees this banjo, will be inclined to ask the price and, learning the price, will surely write to us or look in our catalogue before buying anything in this line elsewhere. In this way we will receive the greatest possible benefit by reason of our low prices and more orders are sure to follow from every neighborhood where we send one of these instruments.

OUR TEN DAYS' FREE TRIAL OFFER.

AS A FURTHER INDUCEMENT and as a further guarantee, that the instrument that you get from us will prove perfectly satisfactory, and to show the great confidence that we have in this banjo, as well as all other musical instruments we show in this catalogue, we give you the further privilege of using this banjo ten days after you have received it, and if you find it in any way unsatisfactory during that time, you can return it to us and we will return your money and pay express charges both ways. Ten days will give you ample time to test the instrument, to compare the banjo with those sold by others and we are sure will only prove to you the great value we have furnished in this instrument at the price. In ordering this banjo, therefore, you are not taking the slightest risk for we stand ready to return your money immediately and pay express charges both ways if you are not perfectly satisfied in every way.

FRONT VIEW
CHALLENGE BANJO. No. 12C822. Price, $5.75.

BACK VIEW

No. 12C822 Our Challenge Banjo. Price, $5.75.

The Stanford	$ 4.25
The Cambridge	$ 8.95
The Cornell	$11.35
The Princeton	$13.75
The Yale	$16.95
The Harvard	$21.45

The Harvard, at $21.45, was nothing short of "The Handsomest Guitar Ever Offered." In this case Sears shot the works.

"In selecting this instrument," says the catalog with quiet satisfaction, "we have instructed the manufacturers to put us up the finest instrument that could be made. . . . It is certainly a work of art in every respect, because the superb finish and the handsome inlaying which is characteristic of the instrument gives it a rich appearance possessed by no other instrument of its kind. It is an excellent instrument for presentation purposes and will compare favorably with any $75.00 guitar that any other dealer has to offer you."

Singing Mandolins

If the guitar was a popular musical instrument of 1905, what shall be said of the even more popular mandolin? What made the demand for them so great that the catalog listed eleven kinds?

One of Sears' mandolins was named with refreshing frankness, "OUR COMPETITION MANDOLIN, at $2.35." "This instrument," we learn, "is giving universal satisfaction, and the sales on it have been immense, owing, undoubtedly, to the great value which we are offering."

In the affairs of men—and mandolins—some things are accepted as the ultimate. Arbitrary ultimates, if you will, merely because men do not at the moment know how to approach nearer to perfection, but acceptable currency nonetheless in the goods and spiritual markets of the world. To this category belonged "The Campanello at $19.95, Sold Generally By Dealers from $35.00 to $40.00." You could not go beyond it "as nothing better is made at any price. It is not only a strictly high-grade instrument from a musical standpoint, but represents also the highest achievement of the mandolin maker's art." The Campanello was guaranteed to go singing down through the years for gentlemen troubadours, or their "money was cheerfully refunded."

Variations on a Theme

In Sears' large company of stringed instruments, in 1905, were ten kinds (and prices) of banjos, plus four variations on the theme: a Mandolinetto, a Professional Banjourine, a Piccolo Banjo, and Banjo-Mandolin.

Many years after 1905, an American advertiser spread over the land the slogan: "What a Whale of a Difference a Few Cents Make." Sears did not put it that way, but looking backward, one sees the White Whale of a Few Cents Difference furiously churning up a page of the catalog with a mail-order Ahab in hot pursuit. "In the past," says the copywriter with a calm that does not betray his inner struggle, "it has been our custom to quote prices on banjos as low as $1.75, but we have found that we cannot furnish a banjo which will give entire satisfaction at this price." This ominous sentence might well have alarmed the banjoists of the day who could feel the ground giving way under them, but they were soon reassured. The difference between cacophony and music, it seems, was only twenty cents. What Sears could not do for $1.75 it could (and did) do for $1.95. At this price it offered "Our Special Banjo with a genuine nickel shell, wood lined; neck stained in imitation cherry."

If faith moves mountains, why won't low prices move mountains of merchandise? Acting on this assumption in its usual forthright and vigorous manner, Sears addressed the banjoists of the country not in the terminology of music but in the language of the market place. In a breathless nonstop sentence, the catalog presented "Our $5.75 Challenge Banjo, Thirty-Nine Brackets, Beautifully Made and Finished, Offered Under Our Binding Guarantee to Prove Perfectly Satisfactory or Money Refunded, and the Equal in Every Way of Banjos that Sell Usually at Double the Price. THIS INSTRUMENT WE OFFER as the leader of our banjo line, to show for how little money we can offer a strictly high-grade instrument, how much value it is possible to put into a banjo at this price."

The catalog, however, was not content merely to convince the prospective customer that it had placed the music of the spheres and of banjos on the bargain counter. It had to take a shot at the local music dealer who, as we shall later show, shot back whenever he could. "$5.75 for this banjo," crows the copywriter, "is truly a wonder price. It will astonish dealers as well as consumers. If you show this banjo to a dealer, he will hardly believe that you bought it for $5.75. It represents a value hitherto undreamed of."

Alpine Music on the Farm

MUSIC BOX MENDER—Joseph Bornand, a French-Swiss by birth, is the only man left in this part of the world, or so we're told, who can mend music boxes. He learned the art as a boy in Switzerland. Now he's living out in Pelham. . . . *

If you played no musical instrument and yet wanted music in your home, the catalog could still provide it. The medium was Swiss Music Boxes at prices ranging from $1.65 to $24.45. It is true that the musical selections offered in the boxes were painfully limited, but the music was genteel, the cabinets were ornamental, and there was something beguiling in the fact that they were imported. The catalog went to some pains to assure cracker-barrel skeptics that its Swiss Music Boxes were indeed—Swiss.

"These boxes," it tells us, "were made by the best manufacturers in Switzerland, the home of the music box. It is a recognized fact that the originators and best makers of musical boxes are the Swiss people. Each box is made with the greatest care . . . to bring forth the best quality of tone—that sweet, delightful tone so peculiar to the Swiss box."

* *Harper's Bazaar,* June, 1939.

There was a great demand for music boxes in 1905. This is evident not only from the numbers listed in the catalog, but also from their prices, which were high in relation to other musical instruments. Several of them sold for more than organs or most of the current phonographs, violins, or banjos. Yet the catalog—which apportioned space not according to hope but experience—gave music boxes nearly a full page. We may therefore conclude that thousands of farmers and small-town men dug deep to place these instruments on the parlor table.

Every Man His Own Musician

One would seem to be on safe ground in dividing musical instruments into two categories: one, those played by hand and demanding instruction and practice, and two, those played by a mechanical device of some kind. Yet such a classification, if made in 1905, would have been inaccurate. There was still another category exemplified by a hand-manipulated stringed instrument that, we are told, anybody could play without instruction. This triumph of ingenuity was called THE AUTO-HARP and its sole demand upon the would-be player was that he should not be paralyzed in both hands. The demand for it was so great among a passionately musical people that Sears offered it at five different prices enumerated upon a whole catalog page.

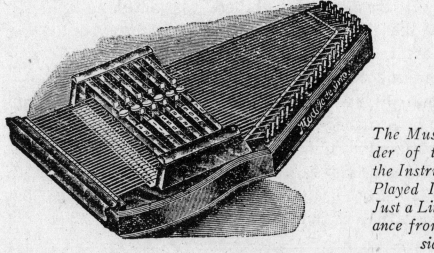

The Musical Wonder of the Age— the Instrument that Played Itself with Just a Little Assistance from the Musician

What was this marvel of another age? THE AUTOHARP, we learn, had "no complicated parts, no mechanism that requires the skilled hand to operate. Anyone—whether he has musical ability or not, can play it with very little practice, and play it well. Thousands testify to its sweetness of tone, which equals that of the highest grade piano. The most difficult productions can be played on it, while as an accompaniment for the voice it has no superior. Never before has it been possible for the house to be graced with high class music at so small an expense. The prices which we name enable the poorest to possess an instrument which will produce the sweetest music and give just as much pleasure as would a high priced piano."

It is interesting to note from this paragraph that while the 1905 period freely used euphemisms in the so-called moral sphere—as "limb" for "leg"—it spoke bluntly in the economic sphere and used the word "poorest" without blushing or apology. Nowadays the poor are the "underprivileged" and the dole, or the old-fashioned poor relief, is simply "relief."

Music Miscellany

Catering to America's insatiable love of music in 1905, Sears' listing of musical instruments went on for page after page. The standard instruments were present, of course, in great profusion but there were also a number of musical exotica. The Zitho-Harp, for example, a "New Overstrung Instrument of Extraordinary Beauty and Elegance, Producing a Tone Which For Sweetness, Purity and Resonance Far Excels Any And All Instruments Of Its Class. Prices: $1.95 and $3.15."

And the Guitar Zither, "an improved and simplified German zither, upon which may be rendered the most difficult music without the aid of a teacher. Prices: $1.65 to $3.95."

At the same time the brittle twanging of that most primitive of musical instruments—the jew's-harp—was heard throughout the land. Sears was proud of the fact that the genius of our own manufacturers was competent to struggle with the difficulties of producing this instrument. The catalog tells us that "The Jews' Harps which we list are made by the best maker in America, and are known as the genuine E. L. American Jews' Harps and are not to be confused with the many inferior harps on the market."

Harmonicas

Joe Moss is a harp-blowing black man. When he bears down hard on his two-bit harmonica he can make trouble leave your weary mind, set your tired feet to stomping, bring Sweet Jesus to your backsliding soul. Joe Moss is a one-harp, two-harp, three-harp-blowing man. Sometimes on hot nights in summer when folks are sitting out on the front porch catching air, talking, or sleeping on a mattress stuck in the front doorway to get the benefit of the draft blowing through the open back door and at the same time to keep the dog from leaving the house, Joe takes a stand on the corner of Redbud Street and Cately Avenue. He draws a harp out of the belt that holds up his red corduroy trousers and slowly eases up on the blues just like a lonesome man sidling up to talk to a lady who has a mean and jealous husband. *

In the golden age of American music, millions of harmonicas trilled their native wood-notes wild, and Sears, as handmaiden to the muse, stood ready with twenty-five varieties in its cornucopia of marbleized pasteboard highly polished. In that happy time, all that the musician needed was the will to music and powerful lungs. Harmonicas were cheap. If you lost one, or broke it, the loss was trivial. Sears sold one kind for only nine cents, and at that it was a "Genuine Bohm." The lordliest variety, "the very latest harmonicas produced by the celebrated maker, Ch. Weiss," sold for $1.15. Strangely enough—and it is maddening not to know why—The Angel's Clarion, went for a mere sixty cents.

We have seen that the piano was forcibly invested with qualities it did not possess in a true state of nature. The harmonica, too, was compelled to blossom with strange foliage

* David L. Cohn, "Black Troubadour," *The Atlantic Monthly*, June, 1939.

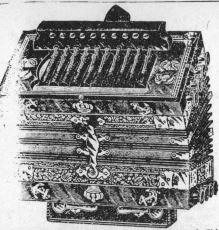

No. 12C1022 The Empress Professional Instrument. This accordion, being 14½ inches high by 9 inches wide, is of mahogany moulded frame, mahogany panels and the frame and panels are ornamented with handsome nickel ornaments. Clasps and corners fully nickel, sunken open keyboard, double ribbed bellows, ten keys, four stops, four sets of reeds, tuned in chords. Complete instruction book free. Price.................$6.45
Weight, packed for shipment, 18 pounds.

THE CELEBRATED PITZSCHLER ACCORDIONS.

Pitzschler is recognized as one of the best manufacturers of Accordions in Germany, the home of this instrument. In presenting our line of Pitzschler accordions we have selected five of the very large number of instruments made by this celebrated maker, and by special arrangement and by contracting for a large quantity, we are able to list them at prices representing the very greatest value ever quoted in instruments of this kind.

Anyone desiring to purchase an accordion should first try our Pitzschler's before deciding to purchase elsewhere. Most remarkably superior in richness and purity of tone, ease of action, as well as details of construction.

No. 12C1080 This Accordion is 6½x7½x13 inches. Is beautifully made and highly finished; has nine folds in the bellows with nickel corners; two stops and two sets of reeds; open action; two basses. The keys are mounted with mother of pearl buttons, making them easily operated and especially adapted to the touch of the fingers. This instrument is beautifully decorated and a handsomer accordion cannot be found except at a much higher price than we ask. We include with each accordion a complete instruction book. Every instrument is carefully packed. Shipping weight, 10 pounds.
No. 12C1080 Price.................$3.90

No. 12C1082 This Accordion measures 7x8½x13½ inches; is of ebony finish, the mouldings highly polished; has 9-fold triple bellows, with metal corners; three sets of reeds and open keyboard; two stops. This is an exceptionally powerful accordion and a great bargain. We include with each accordion a complete instruction book. Every instrument is carefully packed.
No. 12C1082 Price.................$4.95
Shipping weight, 10 pounds.

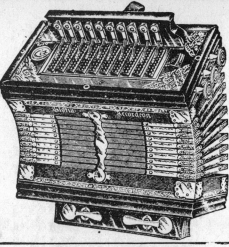

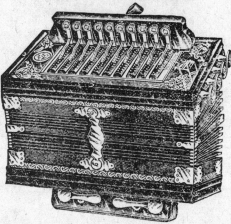

No. 12C1086 This instrument is one of the best of the Pitzschler make. It measures 7¾x7½x13¾ inches. The mouldings are all made in imitation ebony, highly polished and decorated. Has 10-fold, double, very powerful bellows protected with nickel corners; four stops, four sets of reeds and two basses. Sunken keyboard, open action. The keys are fitted with mother of pearl buttons, making the accordion easy to play. The tone of this instrument is especially powerful and of excellent quality. It is in great demand by expert accordion players. We include with each instrument a complete instruction book. Every instrument is carefully packed.
No. 12C1086 Price.................$6.45
Shipping weight, 11 pounds.

Wonderful Value.

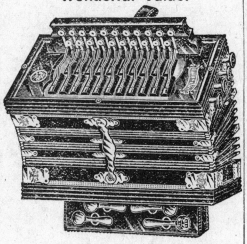

This is the finest Pitzschler Accordion we handle. It has fine fluted mouldings in imitation mahogany; panels genuine mahogany; all wood work finely polished and finished; sunken open action keyboard; double row, nineteen nickel keys; heavy double bellows, with nickel protectors; nickel plated corners and clasps; four stops; four fine sets of reeds. Size, 14 inches by 8 inches. A complete instruction book free.
No. 12C1088 Price.................$7.45
Weight, packed, about 20 pounds.
Genuine Pitzschler Accordion, is just the same in every way as No. 12C1088, described above, but has twenty-one nickel plated keys, as shown in the illustration.
No. 12C1090 Price.................$7.95
Weight, packed, about 20 pounds.

OUR $5.85 ACCORDION.

WONDERFUL VALUE.

No. 12C1084 This Accordion is one of the latest designs; measures 7x9x13½ inches. The mouldings are all finished in imitation ebony, highly polished and beautifully decorated. Has 10-fold extra broad single bellows. The ends of the bellows are entirely covered with nickel and the corners are mounted with beautiful fancy brass caps, making this one of the handsomest accordions ever offered by any music dealer. This instrument has a sunken keyboard, with open action. The keys are all mounted with mother of pearl buttons. This accordion has three sets of reeds, three stops and two basses and produces a beautiful and powerful tone. We include with each accordion a complete instruction book. Every instrument is carefully packed.
No. 12C1084 Price.................$5.85
Shipping weight, 11 pounds.

KALBE ACCORDIONS.

The name Imperial, together with the "double anchor" trade mark, on an accordion is a guarantee of its being of the very highest grade. While the price of these goods may be a trifle higher than others, the satisfaction derived from them, on account of the perfect workmanship and wearing qualities, will amply repay for the difference in price, and they will be found much the cheapest in the end. We guarantee every one to arrive in perfect playing condition. You cannot make a mistake in buying a Kalbe Imperial, for you get the very best article of the kind that is made. Attention is especially called to the patent simplex keys, which are made of heavy metal, in one piece, and are extremely durable. All of the styles of Imperial Accordions that we carry are supplied with patent metal bellows corners and patent folding clasps. Every part of these instruments is of the very best material and workmanship.

No. 12C1100 This is a splendid Kalbe instrument with an ebonized maple frame very handsomely finished. It is very highly polished and is ornamented with fluted molding. It has a powerful double bellows of nine folds with nickel plated corner protectors.

Highly polished nickel trimmings and clasps, two sets of reeds and two stops. This accordion is fitted with a tremolo or vox humana attachment, which gives the tone a wavy and undulating effect in imitation of the human voice. This tremolo can be thrown in and out of action at the will of the player by means of a lever, operated by the thumb of the right hand. The instrument is splendidly fitted throughout and will be sure to satisfy all players upon the accordion. Price.................$3.25
Weight, boxed for shipment, about 10 pounds.

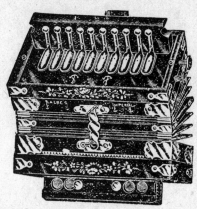

No. 12C1104 Kalbe's Imperial Miniature. Beautifully polished ebonized frame, open action, patent simplex keys, which are very durable; double bellows, with hand painted artistic design on bellows frame, patent nickel plated corners on bellows, thus protecting the weakest part of the accordion. Ten keys, two stops, two sets of reeds, and patent clasps. The size of this accordion is 10¼ inches high by 6¼ inches wide. Price.................$3.45
Weight, boxed, about 10 pounds.

$7.00 a month

The Marquis has proved its merits as a SILVERTONE of finest quality. The excellence of its musical tone delights every listener. The true to life reproduction of all makes of records is due to the perfection of its mechanical parts and to the numerous SILVERTONE features. You will also like the graceful design of the cabinet. The workmanship is of the highest quality, while the selected woods and the splendid finish cannot fail to satisfy the most critical. Notice the tasteful decorations and the spacious record compartment. The door protecting the grill can be conveniently dropped down while playing and pushed back out of sight.

It is 35 inches wide, 34¼ inches high and 21 inches deep. Silvertone reproducer and tone arm. Powerful double spring motor. 12-inch felt covered turntable. Nickel plated metal parts. Shipping weight, 170 pounds. **Shipped from our factory in SOUTHERN INDIANA or PHILADELPHIA STORE.** Price includes five Silvertone records (our selection) and an assortment of steel needles.

46D4836—In mahogany. $98.00
46D4837—In walnut.
46D4838—In golden oak.

$5.00 with order, $7.00 a month. Use Order Blank on page 1100.

Silvertone
BRINGS THE FINEST MUSIC TO YOUR HOME

The MARQUIS

2 WEEKS TRIAL

The GLENFORD

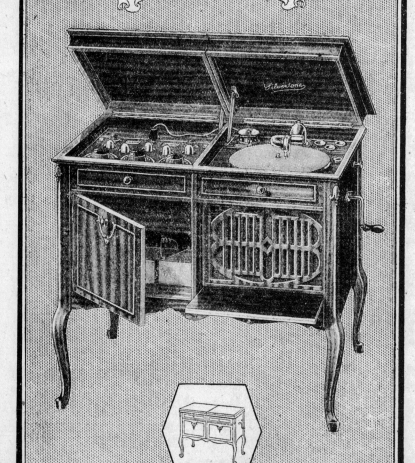

$25.00 a month

Two great instruments have been combined to create this modern and remarkably satisfactory combination phonograph and radio. In its field, the SILVERTONE Phonograph has long been supreme. And the carefully checked performance of the Five-Tube Silvertone Neutrodyne demonstrates that it is the most satisfactory, most convenient and economical receiver manufactured.

The radio unit is specially designed and built into the console. It has an unusual range of distance and a natural quality of tone, and the balanced neutralized circuit gives a distortionless reproduction of both speech and music. It has a matched dial setting and stations can be logged accurately. It does not squeal and cannot interfere with neighboring sets no matter how handled. Adjacent to the Neutrodyne radio, the SILVERTONE Phonograph is installed. It is equipped with Silvertone reproducer and tone arm that will play all disc records except Edison. It has a tone modulator and powerful silent running double spring motor. 12-inch felt covered turntable. All metal parts nickel plated. On the right side of the cabinet is our scientifically constructed amplifying chamber, which is particularly adapted to radio reproduction. The radio loud speaker unit is attached to a separate tone arm extending to the horn. To change from phonograph to radio, or vice versa, you simply move a lever. No disconnecting or changing of reproducer is necessary. This insures maximum tone quality and simplicity of operation.

The console cabinet is a beautiful piece of work. Queen Anne in style, it is made by master craftsmen from selected mahogany or walnut veneers, which are hand rubbed to a fine piano finish. It is 35 inches wide, 34¼ inches high, 21 inches deep.

Sold for dry battery operation only. Cabinet **shipped from factory in SOUTHERN INDIANA.** Accessories **shipped from CHICAGO and PHILADELPHIA STORES.** Price, including five phonograph records (our selection), 5 tubes, 6 dry "A" batteries, 2 45-volt "B" batteries, 1 "C" battery, aerial and ground equipment and loud speaker unit. Shipping weight, 250 pounds.

46D4840—In Mahogany or Walnut (state choice).............. $195.00

Payable $45.00 with order, balance $25.00 a month

Price for cabinet including radio panel, loud speaker unit and five phonograph records, but without tubes, batteries, aerial and ground equipment. Shipping weight, 200 pounds.

46D4841—In Mahogany or Walnut (state choice)............. $165.00

Payable $45.00 with order, balance $20.00 a month

We Guarantee Safe Delivery of All Our Shipments

and bear alien fruit. Thus, "The Brass Band Bell Harmonica is fitted with tuned bells, which can be used with wonderful effect in connection with the instrument. That it is a favorite with all harmonica players is fully proved by the enormous number we sell."

This, however, was but a beginning. Ingenious as the belled harmonica may seem to us who are spoon-fed with radio music, it scarcely tapped the inventive genius of those days. When a harmonica maker of 1905 really got into a frenzy of creation, the walls came tumbling down. The most magnificent achievement of the period was a tiny instrument which made every man his own portable orchestra:

Combination Pipe Organ and Brass Band for Fifty Cents—a Monarch of Music

"The Clarion Brass Brand Harmonica. A new invention. The new idea or invention is in the organ pipes which are placed over the reeds. By means of these pipes, the performer is able to change the tune at will, giving imitations of the flute, church organ or trumpet calls." The price of this monarch of instruments, "Packed In Heavy Red Leatherette Case Having Substantial Hinge and Nickel-Plated Fastener," was more modest than even a catalog customer had a right to expect. It was only 50 cents (if by mail, postage extra, 8 cents).

Accordions

Sears, mother of music, neglected none of her children. She behaved with especial generosity toward our own gypsies of the mountains, the swamps, and the prairies, who yearned to pour out their melancholy souls upon the accordion. And they must have been numerous because the 1905 catalog lists twenty-five kinds, beginning with "a very fine instrument with ebonized highly polished frame and fancy fluted mould-ings," price $1.65, and ending with "Kalb's Imperial," at $11.65.

The man who played an accordion or harmonica in the United States thirty years ago played more than music. He also played a neat economic trick. For these instruments were practically a monopoly of Germany who at the time was one of America's largest buyers of agricultural products, and the farmer who bought a five-dollar accordion or a fifty-cent harmonica really paid for it with meat, wheat, or lard. This was a trade not only valuable to both countries economically, but was also revelatory of the soul of man in a state of nature. At bottom it represented the exchange of bread for beauty: what man lives by in return for what man lives for.

Graphophones

The horns of elfland, oxidized, highly polished, and brass-rimmed, blow more than faintly through the graphophone pages of the catalog. One can still hear them down the long corridors of the years: the nasal voice of the announcer say-ing, "Edison record"; the scratching of the needle; the hum-ming of the motor and the gurgling in the throat of the instru-ment as the motor ran down in the middle of a song.

The graphophones of 1905 shared certain qualities in com-mon. All were equipped with horns; all were run by hand-wound springs; all were fitted for playing either flat or cylin-der disks. Beyond this, nature herself scarcely displayed greater variety. The present American passion for uniformity was then but an idea in the mind of a young man in Detroit—Henry Ford.

There were lower-priced graphophones in the catalog than The Home at $8.60—one popular number sold at $5—but if you wanted something for "home amusement or popular en-tertainment," The Home was your dish. It was obviously a gay, friendly little thing and pleasant to have around the house. In the words of the copywriter who had seen it shining plain, it was "a little beauty, a machine that will brighten the home, entertain yourself, your friends and your family and keep you in touch with the latest and best music of the finest bands and orchestras and the most celebrated public singers."

If, however, you were not precisely a homebody, but were touched with exhibitionism, you passed up The Home, and for $30 (the equivalent of 60 bushels of wheat) bought the AH Disc Graphophone. It would enable you to show off in your neighborhood in a refined and elegant way. The catalog, which seems to have known instinctively much that Freud was later to teach, is conscious of the streak of the show-off in the best of us and, because its business was not teaching but selling, effectively uses it as a sales argument. "IF YOU WANT A TALKING MACHINE," it says straight from the shoulder, "which will create a sensation in your locality, A Machine Which People Will Come Miles to Hear, Order This AH Machine and a Selection of 10-inch records."

The AH was calculated to make a sensation with its "fine black and gold horn," surmounting "The Cabinet Extra Fine and Heavy of a Very Handsome and Ornamental Design, made from solid quarter-sawed oak and very finely finished throughout." It was a phonograph-peacock among crows.

Let us now choose a Genuine Harvard Disk Record (30 cents each), put it on the AH, crank the motor, and take a seat. As from the grave, but preserved for a life beyond life, we hear "An Address by the late President McKinley at the Pan-American Exposition." The parlor is beginning to be crowded now with "People Who Have Come Miles to Hear," and we want to give them something to remember us by. We dip into our selection of records and come up with that masterpiece of music, sound effects, acting, drama, and excitement known as "Cummings' Indian Congress at Coney Island." It was "Descriptive. Grand entree of the Indians and Mexicans, preceded by the Carlisle Indian Band, Princess Wininah, the champion rifle-shot of the world. Indian sham battle and realistic scene introducing the war-song, the attack of the Mexicans who are routed amidst the yells and whoops of the Indians who celebrate by their battle cry of victory. A record of thrilling interest."

Then we rapidly crank the AH again and, before the last war cry has died away, we are magically transferred to the New York water front, where we attend the "Departure of a Hamburg-American liner. The big whistle sounds *All ashore going ashore*. The band plays popular airs, friends shout fare-wells, the giant liner backs into midstream and the music is drowned in the cheering."

Famous Graphophone Musicians

The graphophone records sold by Sears in 1905 reveal some-thing of the musical taste of the people of the time; illuminate their sense of humor; show their devotion to hymns and sacred music, and give us a glimpse of the contemporary operatic and musical-comedy stages.

Orchestra and band selections led all the rest. John Philip Sousa was then in his prime, and his theme song (to antici-pate the radio era), "Stars and Stripes Forever March," was whistled by everybody. (The composer, incidentally, sold his rights to it for ninety dollars.) The 1905 catalog lists fifty Sousa's Band records at twenty-five and fifty cents each. For more than two generations, Americans marched to the blood-tingling strains of such Sousa marches as "Hail To The Spirit of Liberty," "Imperial Edward Coronation March," "Liberty Bell March" (bell effect), "Semper Fidelis March," and the ever popular "Stars and Stripes Forever."

Only one bandmaster has ever been as popular as Sousa. He was the great P. S. Gilmore. So famous, indeed, was he that in 1872, at an enormous music benefit given for him in the Boston Coliseum, Europe as well as America did him honor. The band of the Grenadier Guards played a Grand Potpourri of Irish Melodies; the Garde républicaine band gave the Andante and Marche Nuptiale from *Lohengrin,* and the band of the Kaiser Franz Grenadier Regiment performed the Overture from Mendelssohn's *Athalie.* More astonishingly, there appeared among the band conductors of the great day:

> A man of low stature, dark complexion, large full head, broad shoulders, slender limbs, black hair reached back to his forehead, side whiskers that descend in heavy masses to the angles of the chin and moustache that connects the two as with an arch. He stood before us while leading the Grand Concert Waltz the very incarnation of musical genius.

This musician was none other than Johann Strauss.

The America of thirty years ago never tired of hearing Gilmore's Band playing on the phonograph such favorites as:

> *Bohemian Girl,* Selections from
> *Cavalleria rusticana,* Intermezzo
> "*Die Wacht am Rhein*"
> "Nearer, My God, To Thee" (with cornet solo)
> "Rocked in the Cradle of the Deep" (with saxhorn solo)
> *Tannhäuser,* Grand March from
> "The Vacant Chair" (trombone solo)
> *William Tell,* Overture to

In 1905, the Civil War had been ended only forty years. Thousands of Union veterans, pensioned and reminiscent, were still alive. *Gone With the Wind* had not yet flickered in the mind of a little girl in Atlanta. The phonograph-record manufacturers of the times—all Yankees and not content to let bygones be bygones—fired one last shot at the dispersed Confederate ranks in a disk called "He Laid Away A Suit Of Gray To Wear The Union Blue." (Hisses from Southern catalog customers.) But despite the laying away, the wearing of the blue and all that, the song writers of that day, like their fellows of the present, would have had to go to work if it had not been for sure-fire Dixie themes: Mammy and the Mississippi river; magnolias and the Alabama moon; the mockingbird, listen to; ole Virginia and New Awleens, and the ever-reliable levee, horse-belly deep in nostalgia, guitar music, and starlight.

The levee is now a fifteen-hundred-mile-long rampart maintained by an amiable government as background for local-color writers and as a rostrum from which guitar-strumming Negroes may explain (for the benefit of New York's song writers) to passers-by, respectfully and in syncopated time, just why darkies were born. In 1905, too, its main purpose seems to have been to afford a place where happy blacks, but recently out of slavery, could celebrate their freedom by remembering their slavery in song, and breaking into a sudden buck and wing whenever they saw their former Ole Massa come riding up to brood over his lost fortunes amid the dying rays of the setting sun.

A whole group of records was called Negro Shouts:

> Songs with laughing and whistling choruses. A characteristic representation of the Alabama negro of the old slave days.

Strangely, these records depicting the alleged happiness of the Negro in slavery were sold by thousands to Northern men and women who had fought to abolish slavery, and must have been played in many a parlor that contained a copy of *Uncle Tom's Cabin*.

The Negro, moreover, of the 1905 catalog was a negro. (The battle for the use of the capital "N" in the word Negro was still to be fought.) Frequently he was not even a negro but a "coon" or "darky." Coon songs, so called, were extremely popular in the United States in 1905, and the catalog, faithfully reflecting the tastes of the people, lists many favorites such as:

> "Coon, Coon, Coon (I Wish My Color Would Fade)"
> "Wouldn't It Make You Hungry?" (plaintive coon song)
> "Every Morn I Bring Her Chicken"
> "My Starlight Queen" (the Rogers Brothers' big coon song hit in their latest farce, *In Harvard*)

Most of the coon, or Negro, songs of that period, like those of today, were distinctly false in their understanding of the

Negro whom they purported to picture, but the legend of the Negro—as opposed to his reality—will not die. A pragmatic country takes note of the fact that legends sell goods and services; facts molder on the shelves or are thrown into garbage cans to be picked up centuries later by historians.

Extremely popular were "descriptive disks." These—but let the catalog speak for itself:

> "Clarence the Copper." Clarence leaves his beat to call on his best girl. The sergeant appears and Clarence is transferred.
>
> "Flogging Scene from *Uncle Tom's Cabin*." With incidental music effects.
>
> "Leander and Lulu." Leander attempts to propose while riding downtown on the elevated railway. Charlie Onthespot, his hated rival, is on the spot as usual.
>
> "Arkansaw Traveler." Descriptive of a native sitting in front of his hut scraping his fiddle and answering the interruptions of the stranger with witty sallies. Record is full of jokes and laughter.
>
> "Blazing Rag Concert Hall." Introducing the bouncer, the tipsy soubrette, the professor, and the fight— very realistic.
>
> "Night Alarm." With all the familiar descriptive effects, representing a fire alarm at night—fire bells, cries, horses' hoofs, winding of hose reel, whistle of engine, ending with firemen's chorus.

The farmers of 1905—judging from the records they bought from the catalog—liked to laugh at themselves. They had not yet fallen into the decadence so eloquently reported by *Variety* in a recent headline: "HIX NIX STIX PIX." Records about the sticks were good enough for those who lived in the sticks, and many a mail order contained a requisition for one or more of "Uncle Josh Weathersby's Laughing Stories." The farmer who wanted to see himself as others saw him could choose from:

> "Uncle Josh on a Bicycle"
> "Uncle Josh in a Chinese Laundry"
> "Uncle Josh on a Fifth Avenue Bus"

"Uncle Josh on Jim Lawson's Horse Trade"
"Uncle Josh and the Lightning Rod Agent"
"Political Meeting at Pumpkin Center" (introducing
    speech by Uncle Josh, national airs by county band
    and the Pumpkin Center Glee Club)

Sears' collection of records contained something to suit almost every taste, with the single proviso that that taste be "elegant and refined." The risqué song, the smutty joke, the *double-entendre,* were ruled out. Fun had to be good and clean; entertainment wholesome; amusement the kind you would not mind telling your mother or sister about. All this, of course, for home consumption. What happened outside the home is another story.

One of the oldest forms of the American theater—now dead—is the minstrel. In 1905, it was going strong. Its ritual was highly stylized, with blackface end men, elegant interlocutor, white-voiced tenor, ballad-singing baritone, clog dancers, banjo, trumpet, and cornet soloists, tambourines, and jokes singularly free from smut. The minstrels traveled from town to town, usually giving a resplendent, high-stepping parade up Main Street on the morning of the performance, and to hundreds of thousands of Americans, remote from the great cities, they brought gaiety, color, and music, and were correspondingly popular. The catalog lists:

"AN EVENING WITH THE MINSTRELS. This series of twelve records constitutes a complete minstrel performance. Each record, however, is complete in itself, and is entirely suitable to be purchased separately if desired."

Introductory Overture by the entire company.
Our Land of Dreams, Ballad. Baritone solo by W. J.
    Myers, with chorus by entire company.
End Man Stories by George Graham.
End Man Song, "I'm a Nigger That's Living High," by
    Billy Golden.
Jokes Between Interlocutor and End Man.
I'm Wearing My Heart Away for You. Tenor solo by
    George J. Gaskin, with chorus by entire company.

Jokes Between Interlocutor and End Man.

End Man Song, "My Friend from Home" (coon song), by Len Spencer, with chorus by entire company. Orchestra accompaniment.

Finale, "Black Hussars March." Baritone solo by J. W. Myers, with chorus by entire company.

Musical Specialty, by Albert Bodes. Trumpet solo.

Monologue by George Graham.

Banjo Solo, "Yankee Doodle," by Vess L. Ossman, with orchestra accompaniment.

"Vocal Solos with Piano Accompaniment" are endless. It is striking to observe how many of the phonograph records deal sentimentally and tearfully with old age, as contrasted with our own period in which persons over sixty try to keep themselves young through the devices of the beauty parlor and the Florida sun, and achieve economic security through old-age pensions. And it is equally striking to note how many records of the earlier period display an almost morbid predilection toward death that is now found only in Negro spirituals and cowboy songs. Whether this indicates a decline in formal religionism, churchgoing, and a belief in immortality, as compared with the early years of the century, with a consequent transference of interest to living in the present, is an interesting speculation. In any event, records such as these were popular in 1905:

The Mansion of Aching Hearts
The Letter Edged in Black
Safe in the Arms of Jesus
Face to Face (with violin obbligato)
Hello, Central; Give Me Heaven
Rock of Ages

The light touch was achieved in:

Mc Manus and the Parrot (comic Irish song)
The Mother of the Girl I Love
Whoa, Bill (a trombone extravaganza)
If You Love Your Baby, Make the Goo-Goo Eyes

It Takes The Irish to Beat The Dutch
The Village Choir (illustrating an amusing and charac-
    teristic country choir rehearsal. Imitation of four
    different voices. Baritone.)
You Didn't Tell Me That Before We Married
The Fatal Rose of Red
I Like You, Lil, For Fair (tough song from *Peggy from
    Paris)*
Meet Me in St. Louis, Louis
Mc Ginty at the Living Pictures

Contemporary history was given a waxen immortality:

Hymns and Prayer from the Funeral Service Over Presi-
    dent McKinley
On Board the Oregon Before Santiago
Bugle Call of the Rough Riders in Their Charge Up San
    Juan Hill
Bugle Calls of the United States Army

Millions of immigrants poured into the United States during the period 1870–1914, and the catalog of 1905, issued
when the flood was at its tide, tells us that among its "Foreign
selections are some splendid old German songs, weirdly sweet
Hungarian music, Swedish and Norwegian airs that remind
one of the far away Northland, vivacious French selections,
comical Hebrew songs that make you laugh, patriotic Polish
airs, harmonious Russian selections, beautiful Italian songs
that carry one's thoughts to the sunny Mediterranean, and
Spanish love songs.

"Understand, these are strictly high grade, first quality,
genuine, Columbia Records, just as good as any other records
sold by any other dealer at 50 cents each. We are closing them
out at 10 cents each."

Twilight of the Musician

The decline in the sales and use of hand-played musical
instruments from 1905 to 1935 may be easily traced in ten-
year periods through the catalog, and, simultaneous with their

decline, the improvement of the phonograph and the phenomenal rise of the radio.

It is particularly saddening to students of the American home to note the extinction of the organ. A household pet and parlor ornament in thousands of homes shortly after the turn of the century, it was still extremely popular in 1915. But even then it was allotted but half the space given it in the catalog of 1905. In the next decade a great revolution occurred. The United States went into the World War. Millions of men became soldiers and millions of women workers. The country was gripped for a while in a mad prosperity, until the terrifying deflation of 1920–21; women got the right to vote and to be equals of men (whatever that means); liquor went out and bootleggers came in; skirts began to go up and sexual standards to go down, and in the midst of the uproar, the organ passed quietly from the scene like the last member of a dying species of birds tumbling unseen from the bough of a tree in a secret forest. *The 1925 catalog does not list a single organ.*

The final ignominy to be heaped upon the corpse of a once noble instrument is that the 1925 catalog, which lists no organs, devotes a whole page to "Supertone Ukuleles" and "Banjo Ukes." Mama playing "Just A Song At Twilight" on The Home Favorite, with the *vox humana* stop pulled all the way out, recedes into the mists and is succeeded by her rolled-stocking flapper daughter playing "Honolulu Love" on a ukulele in a parked car.

Where are the Ysayes once so thick on the farms and in the little towns of America in 1905? Are their nimble hands catching swiftly moving parts as they pass by on the assembly line? It took eleven pages to list the catalog's violins in 1905; three pages in 1925, and only two in 1935.

And the guitarists? Who shall say where they are gone? Once they walked the moonlight lanes of the country in gallant hosts, giving cry to love and beauty on guitars that illuminated six pages of the 1905 catalog. But their day was upon them although they knew it not. For by 1925, so decimated had their ranks become, they were represented by but one page, and there they remain in 1935 clinging to the pale ghost of their once passionate life.

Grievously thinned, too, are the ranks of those who plucked mandolins, strummed guitars, and played the Autoharp; while the million hands that cupped a million harmonicas are shrunken to a pitiful few.

But this story—being in part the story of a young and virile land that hates "sad" endings—is not entirely one of crushing defeat. Strange flowers blossom amid the ashes of the burning and of these the strangest is the accordion. In 1905, it was but a simple thing and relatively unadorned; the price for the finest model was only $11.65, and the instrument reflected the stolid simplicities of the *gemütlich* German craftsmen who made it. But both craftsmen and accordion were to pass through a flaming world before 1935 and neither thereafter would be the same.

In 1925, accordions were still "Made in Germany" but the price of the luxury model—$36.95—was three times the price of the luxury model of 1905. Their virgin simplicity is now gone and the mark of Latin corruption is upon them in the legends, "Milan Organetto" and "Hohner Italian styles." The soft South is conquering the hard North.

The chrysalis was complete by 1935. The brown German worm is about to emerge as a multicolored Italian butterfly. We are now told that:

"Italian accordions are famous the world over and Castelfidardo where our G. Fidardo and S. Mariono accordions are made, produces the finest in all Italy." And the finest of the fine was the "G. Fidardo Super De Luxe Professional." This complicated engine of music, its "Celluloid Gallery Set With Rhinestones . . . responsive . . . flexible . . . from the merest whisper of sweet-toned harmony to the most intricate chromatic runs and arpeggios, snapped out with the utmost brilliance and power," was prominently displayed in the 1935 catalog. Its price by comparison with the accordions of 1905 is terrifying. It was $325.

Afternoon of the Faun

Decade by decade, phonograph manufacturers, working in strange ways their mutations to perform, change the instrument while the catalog, chronicler as well as purveyor, records the changes. The flowering horns of the 1905 machine have vanished by 1915, but Sears' models are still hand-cranked. The "descriptive records" dear to an earlier decade are gone, but Uncle Josh Weathersby is stronger than ever with a widened repertoire, and new dance music with strange names appears on the scene: the fox trot, one step, tango, hesitation, and waltz-canter. America has gone into a long afternoon of the faun. "Your library of music," the catalog warns us, "is not complete until you have included some bright, catchy dance records. Our list has been carefully selected to cover all the modern dances; sparkling melodies which set even the non-dancer's foot tap-tapping the floor, and which swing the dance lover off in a joyful whirl. Learn the new dance steps with the help of these wonderful records . . . they truly represent the spirit of the dance."

Calvin and Wesley tumble from their thrones in the farm and small-town homes, while cloven-footed Pan, piping madly to the spirit ditties of no tone, sets the churn to rattling and leads the farmer's pretty daughter in the mazes of the fox trot.

Music As You Go

Before ten more years elapse, something new appears—the portable phonograph. America, for the first time since the founding of the republic, is confronted with the desperate problem of how to employ its leisure. The portable phonograph will be useful in fighting this demon. "It is suitable for the home," we learn, "but so light and compact that it will furnish music anywhere." Melody will follow it like the lamb that followed Mary. The 1925 catalog blossoms with table- and cabinet-model phonographs, some of which are "Louis the sixteenth period," while "The Marquis" is a "modern and remarkably satisfactory combination of phonograph and radio." But this achievement would not have astonished the customer of 1905 half so much as the price of The Marquis— $195.

No one seems to notice or care that dear old Uncle Josh, the rustic comedian of an earlier day, is now on his last legs. He is represented by but four records, and we know that his doom is approaching because it is no longer "Uncle Josh on a Bicycle" but "Uncle Josh Buys An Automobile." He was a hard man to kill.

There are no more coon, or darky, songs by 1925. The negro of 1905 has not only become the Negro of 1925 but there are special "Race Records by Negro Artists."

Seeking perhaps to evoke again the spirit of a lost age of innocence, the catalog offers a number of "Little Tots' Records, Songs, Games, Stories," including the old favorites such as Jack and Jill, Old King Cole, and Simple Simon. But once these were tales told and jingles recited by mothers to children and by children themselves; now they are monotonously unvarying repetitions ground out by machine.

An alien music creeps into the wreck of what was once the organ-sonorous parlor. Mingling with the sound of the wind in the corn are the soft ululations of Hawaiian stringed music. The beach at Waikiki stretches from Polynesia to thousands of American farms.

The Machine Age of the Piano

Although more than once threatened with almost complete extinction, pianos have managed to survive the years. It is true that their once glassy finish and baroque ornamentation have been stripped away in an age impatient of furniture frills, and some of them were submitted to the shame of having their interiors stuffed with machinery, but throughout they have manifested what is perhaps the highest genius of men or pianos—the genius for survival.

In 1915, two catalog pages announced THE IMPROVED BECKWITH PLAYER PIANO SOLD ON EASY PAYMENTS. By comparison with its marvels, the wonder Mandolin Attachment of 1905 seems grotesquely absurd, even if it took some knowledge of music to operate, for all that one needs now is electric current. The player piano, we are told, is A Beautiful Piece of Furniture—a Great Entertainer For Yourself and Friends—a Great Educator For Your Children—Sing, Dance and be Happy, All in Your Own Home.

America has an avid and almost pathetic eagerness for education, and, by some strange and perhaps puritanical quirk of reasoning, many things which might logically be interpreted as fulfilling the high function of the pleasurable are labeled "educational." Thus travel is educational; lectures, the movies, museums, the radio, and the movies are educational. So, too, music.

Music is not only educational but it is one of the "advantages" that can freely be offered children. America is a land filled with first-generation Americanized immigrants and older stock who were too busy or too poor to acquire "advantages" in their youth. But what Papa and Mama could not get they passionately want for their children.

The next logical step, of course, is to make it easy for the children to acquire "advantages" by smoothing the rocky road to knowledge and enabling the young pilgrims to roll along it at sixty miles an hour. In the sphere of music the player piano will do the job neatly. The catalog tells us:

"The Educational Influence of the Beckwith is keenly felt in the homes of all our customers, especially where there are children in the family, as they can play not only the popular songs and dances of the day, but can become familiar with the best compositions of all the different composers. This is an education in itself."

Even education and advantages have an economic aspect. The price of the Beckwith Player Piano with twenty rolls of music and silk-plush scarf is $397. But you can play while you pay. It is available for monthly payments of $8.

Ten years later, in 1925, the catalog beseeches us in giant

print to BUY DIRECT FROM THE FACTORY AND SAVE 1/3. Piano prices rise again. They are higher than they were in 1913, and light-years away from the prices of 1905 pianos. The cheapest nonmechanical instrument is $295. The highest is $549. The installment plan comes, however, to the rescue. One can buy a piano for "$10.00 with order, balance $8.00 a month." Milton's "Linkèd sweetness long drawn out" is given a modern twist.

At the same time, the catalog, wearily aware of the decadence of music in America, rouses itself to rout the forces of apathy and shake the nation out of its slumber. In one full page it begs Americans to:

LEARN TO PLAY BY MAIL FOR LESS THAN 10¢ A LESSON.

"Hundreds of thousands of Sears customers have learned to play musical instruments this low cost, easy way . . . and YOU can, too. Sears have made arrangements with the National Academy of Music in Chicago—most famous organization of its kind—to give the purchaser of a Sears instrument a Special 12-Lesson Course for $1, a fraction of the regular price."

Thirty years ago, Sears thought a music teacher about as necessary to music as the mumps to happiness. In that far day, before education and enlightenment struck their fangs into the nation's jugular vein, all that a man needed to learn violin playing was a book of instructions. But now that we hear more music than ever over the radio and the phonograph, we are becoming tone-deaf and wooden-handed. Modern sissies evidently need the services of music teachers and Sears will provide them.

There's Money in Music

The catalog, however, has no faith, in the hard-boiled, unsentimental year 1935, in the value of music as an indispensable part of a man's or a nation's culture. It makes no appeal for music playing as a source of personal happiness. It plainly sees the ability to play a musical instrument as a ladder to success and success as fame and fame as dollars.

This realistic point of view is extraordinarily illuminating. A favorite theme song of American historians and writers about America is that the hard-pressed pioneer hacking a home out of the wilderness had no time for the amenities; that a civilized culture derives in part from leisure; that when we have leisure we shall have a greater interest in the arts. Yet, so far as music is concerned, we have seen that more people played more instruments in the earlier years of the twentieth century than in the later years, and with the growth of leisure the capacity of the people for self-amusement seems to have diminished. This is not to deny that more people *heard* music via the radio in 1935 than in 1905, but this is comparable to the situation in college athletics in England and the United States. In England nearly all students play one game or another. Here thousands of students sit in stadiums and watch twenty-two star players perform.

The catalog, however, bent upon increasing the sale of musical instruments, goes about it in a matter-of-fact way that will accomplish its purpose. It begins by the familiar and usually successful tactic of you-can-do-what-others-have-done. In this case the others are FAMOUS RADIO MUSICIANS—Ben Bernie, Abe Lyman, Fred Waring, Wayne King, Ted Weems —all of them looking happy and prosperous as they garland the catalog page. They look immortal enough in the arrogance of their youth, but the catalog which has seen men and things come and go, and which, like Pater's Mona Lisa, has "trafficked for strange webs with Eastern merchants," knows that all must pass and knowing, asks:

WILL YOUR CHILDREN TAKE THEIR PLACES?

"New stars must be made to shine on when these sterling maestros have retired. That is where your children should come in." Music is not the pullulating moon shining on the cobweb roofs of an insubstantial world. Music is real and earnest and "full of opportunities . . . it offers Big Money,

Fame, Education, Travel, Popularity, Business and Social Prestige—a thousand advantages not offered by any other profession."

This is a vision alluring enough, it would seem, to bring all the youth of the land a-running to learn music but the catalog breathes life into it and makes it talk with the tongues of angels and—of cash:

$25,000 to $100,000 a Year
And More Made by Many Musicians.
There's BIG Money in Music . . . and more musicians
are needed than ever before. Just think—many musicians
are making $25,000 to $100,000 a year!

And then follows a sentence profoundly revelatory of the processes of our national life. A young man aspiring to be a professional musician might once have been laughed out of court by his parents as a silly dreamer, or have run the risk of having his sexual virility called into question by his friends. But that day is gone. If he should now tell Mama and Papa he would like to be a cornettist, pointing out that Ben Bernie and Ignace Paderewski earn "from $25,000 to $100,000 a year," in all probability he would get the parental blessing and a bus ticket to the nearest conservatory. Music lies no longer in the sphere of the mere ornamentally cultural. It is business and big business at that. And the catalog, a Chicago Confucius, points the moral:

"Why that's more than the presidents of many big corporations earn. Many of these BIG MONEY MAKERS come from the farms and small towns . . . lived in modest homes . . . never had a personal teacher. They realized the Value of Music . . . its possibilities . . . its popularity."

It is to be hoped that many young Americans will join bands and while seeing the world grow rich, famous, and wallow in popularity. And certainly all earnest men will desire that they stand ready to pick up the batons that must some day fall from the magic-making hands of Kyser and

Bernie and Waring. For where there are no maestros the people perish.

NUMBER OF CATALOG PAGES BY DECADES DEVOTED TO MUSICAL INSTRUMENTS

1905	1915	1925	1935
60	27	12	8

2 · WHAT ARE THE WILD WAVES SAYING?

Often I find myself wishing that Signor Marconi
Had become a vendor of spumoni
And that Nikola Tesla
Had decided to be a wrestler
Or that both of them had opened a beauty shop
    and experimented with hair-waves
Instead of fooling around with air-waves
But they had to be so ingenious and tireless
That they wound up by inventing the wireless.
Here's a good rule of thumb:
Too clever is dumb.

THESE eloquent words of Ogden Nash in his *Happy Days* wring a hearty amen from manufacturers of musical instruments whose business was so cruelly mangled by the invention that stemmed from Signor Marconi's wireless. It was primarily the radio that rotten-egged Apollo out of the American home, and so swift was its rise that the dazed god barely had time to pull his bespattered robes around him and make an escape ungodly in its haste. Telephony by Hertzian waves—the thing we call radio—was first achieved by Fessenden in 1900; on Christmas Eve of 1906, he broadcast music, and the next year, speech over a distance of 200 miles. De Forest at the same time broadcast Caruso singing, and the music of the telharmonium. But although Fessenden discussed the uses of point-to-point wireless telephony, he did not mention broadcasting, and nobody seems to have thought much about it until the opening of the first broadcast station— Pittsburgh's KDKA—in 1920 by Westinghouse. Only two

Grows 10 Times as Big!

Eighteen months ago Radio Station W-L-S, owned and operated by the World's Largest Store, was presented to the American Public. It was so well received and met with such instant approval that almost immediately steps were made to increase its volume. Our correspondence and field investigations show W-L-S to be one of the most popular stations in the world.

Popular demand made expansion necessary and today finds W-L-S a super-power station of 5,000 watts which can be heard in all corners of the country. The listeners-in with their hearty support have made this improvement possible and it is to them that this new station—the latest word in Radio Science—is affectionately dedicated as our free-will offering to our people.

W-L-S Staff

Standing, Left to Right
E. Warren K. Howe, *Opera.*
George D. Hay, *"Solemn Old Judge," Chief Announcer.*
Ford Rush, *"Big Ford."*
Grace Viall Gray, *Home Makers.*
Edgar L. Bill, *Director.*

Seated, Left to Right
Anthony Wons, *Drama.*
George C. Biggar, *Farm and Markets.*
Glenn Rowell, *"Little Glenn."*
Martha Meier, *Pianiste and Vocalist.*

STUDIOS

That we may better serve our listeners-in Station W-L-S is broadcasting from the following studios:

HOTEL SHERMAN STUDIO
SEARS-ROEBUCK TOWER STUDIO
BARTON STUDIO

Write us! W-L-S is your station. We want to know what YOU like

Above—"Little Glenn" and His Cornhuskers

LULLABY TIME

—*"there's a pause in the day's occupation that is known as the Children's Hour."*

Sandman time—the time between daylight and dusk when thousands of kiddies the country over nestle down before the radio and listen in on Ford and Glenn's "Now I Lay Me Down to Sleep."

LITTLE RED SCHOOLHOUSE

—*"still sits the schoolhouse by the road."*

The march of progress fails to still within us recollections of happy days in the little red schoolhouse. Every Friday afternoon the old program is given in a new way. Hundreds of schools all over the country accept this Friday afternoon feature as part of their regular curriculum. And every Friday morning the bigger girls and boys have W-L-S High School.

R.F.D. CLUB

—*"and farm homes scattered wide and far are wedded—not through union but through separation."*

The Radio Farmers' Democracy, with 15,000 members in forty states, has presented 350 agricultural authorities. R. F. D. Club programs are broadcast at noon from Monday to Friday, and on Tuesday, Wednesday and Friday evenings. Market and weather reports are on the air five times each day. Music that appeals to farm folks is arranged. If you are a farm radio owner a letter containing a farm program suggestion will enroll you in the R. F. D. Club.

LITTLE BROWN CHURCH

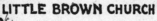

—*"for where two or three are gathered together in My name, there am I in the midst of them."*
—*Matthew 18:20.*

The Little Brown Church is a laymen's community church, organized with the approval of the executive committee of the Community Church Workers of the U. S. A. Non-denominational, non-sectarian, without creed, race or color, the Little Brown Church ministers to the human heart. It is your church. You can become a member by listening in on Sunday evening from 7 to 8 o'clock.

W.L.S. THEATRE

—*"all the world's a stage."*

W-L-S has created a position of its own in Radio Theatricals. Under the direction of an accomplished producer, Shakespearean drama, playlets and readings have been vested with a new interest. Thousands crowd into our theatre. Tickets free.

HOMEMAKERS' CLUB

—*"and national strength lies in the homes we live in."*

Our Homemakers' Hour is the housewife's own. We give her home advice and counsel and enable her to take advantage of association with America's foremost home and club authorities without leaving her easy chair.

LONE SCOUT TRIBE

—*"and the tribes shall be brought together by Manitou's mighty hand."*

The old smoke signals of the scout have given way to a more effective method. News of the tribe flashes across the country and back again in less time than the fire could have been built in the olden days. The active interest of W-L-S in the Lone Scout Tribe is responsible in a large measure for the national unity.

W.L.S. OPERA CO

—*"and the night shall be filled with music."*

To the strains of our Barton Organ, W-L-S opera comes over the air and into thousands of homes. In keeping with our entire policy, we have tried to give the best of opera and our listeners' approval convinces us that we have not failed.

"My Radio Has Made Me $500.00"

Lee Mosher
De Kalb, Ill.

Lee Mosher's radio was the best investment he ever made for his farm! Mr. Mosher said so himself in a letter to W-L-S. His actual additional profit in one year, because he was a radio owner, was over $500 in the marketing of his live stock.

We have all heard a great deal about the advantages of radio from its entertainment and educational aspects. But it is about the profits from radio that we would tell now.

Mr. Mosher's experience is not an unusual one. Radio has found a place in marketing the products of the farm that is invaluable. No grain elevator, no co-operative creamery, no farm organization would consider today giving up their radio for any one other necessity in their business.

And Why?

Because radio makes instantly available the very things that the farmer needs to know to properly buy and sell. Shall I market the hogs today? Radio will supply the answer. Will there be a killing frost tonight? Radio gives the warning!

Shall I plant wheat, feed corn or sell it? Shall I raise cattle for beef or for butter? The advice and counsel of leaders of agricultural thought in America is available over radio because these men know the value of radio.

Are You Sharing in the Profit?

Have you realized that you can no longer get along without radio any more than you can without the threshing machine, the tractor, the silo, the telephone, the automobile, the rural free delivery?

Consider, then, the radio—the instrument which permits you to farm and market the products of your farm in an intelligent manner. Place it with the inventions and improvements which have changed the fabric of farming from the days of the scythe to the present time.

Here Are Some Proofs!

Lee Mosher at DeKalb, Ill., gives radio credit for making $500 for him; Otto H. Nan, Hillsboro, Iowa, tells of profits that paid for his five-tube radio set more than twice; W. W. Hedstrom, Victoria, Ill., of $110 more on one shipment of hogs because radio told him when to market; L. William Rowe, Elburn, Ill., of a saving of $120 on the purchase of cotton seed meal because radio told him the right market price; Baumgartner Bros., Wrightstown, Wis., say the weather reports alone are "worth hundreds of dollars to us each year;" Donald P. Zollars, Beason, Ill., says "Last fall I heeded your advice regarding picking seed corn just before the first cold snap forecast. That sure was a money saving bit of information for me." And so it goes.

There's a Profit to Be Made Out of Radio

Can you afford to ignore it? Get your set now and cash in on this profit!

SEARS, ROEBUCK AND CO.

The Kind of Radio to Buy

A crystal set in some cases will give satisfaction. It will receive within twenty-five miles of a powerful station and the only way you can "listen in" is with the head phones.

The next step is a Two-Tube Set. Our Crescent is a very successful receiver of this type. If you are willing to listen with head phones you will find hours of entertainment within a radius of 500 miles.

Our Three-Tube Meteor Receiver is next. It will permit you to entertain your family and friends on the loud speaker from stations 500 miles away or more. Reception on the head phones can be had over a distance of 1,000 miles or more.

Five-Tube Radio Frequency Sets, such as our Clarion and Veritone, are next in order in performance. Loud speaker reception can be had from stations approximately 1,000 miles away; by using head phones, 1,800 miles should be a frequent accomplishment.

The W-L-S Silvertone Neutrodyne, however, is the peer of all receiving sets. It has a coast to coast range. The W-L-S Silvertone embodies not only the original principles conceived by Prof. L. A. Hazeltine, one of America's greatest radio engineers and inventor of the famous Neutrodyne circuit, but many later refinements resulting from conscientious study and research on the part of our own engineering staff. For maximum results in quality of reception, range, selectivity, power and ease of operation the Silvertone Neutrodyne is the receiver we recommend.

The range given for our various types of sets is estimated conservatively. Under favorable atmospheric conditions and in good locations for radio reception, greater distances can be obtained than those we quote; on the other hand conditions frequently exist where it is not possible to get the results expected.

We Guarantee All of Our Radio Receivers to Perform Equal to Any Similar Type of Receiver on the Market.

STORAGE BATTERIES OR DRY CELLS?

For those who do not have public service power or electric lights in their homes or who are located at some distant point and cannot conveniently have their storage battery charged, we unhesitatingly recommend the dry battery sets. In quality of reproduction, range and dependability, dry battery sets are almost equal to the storage battery types, being extensively used and entirely successful.

Why YOU SHOULD BUY *!* YOUR RADIO FROM US

1 Because we sell direct from factory to consumer with but one profit added. Were you to pay more than the price we ask, you could not buy better quality.

2 Because our radio sets are equal in performance to any similar sets on the market, regardless of name, make or price.

3 Because we can save you from $10.00 to $100.00 on your radio set, depending upon the type you prefer.

4 Because every set in our catalog is laboratory tested, and its range and performance approved before it goes into our catalog.

5 Because the World's Largest Store, with all its resources stands back of every set with a full guarantee to do whatever is proper to insure satisfaction.

years later, however, the Secretary of Commerce released this statement:

> The Department estimates that today over 600,000 persons possess wireless telephone receiving sets, whereas there were only 50,000 such sets a year ago.

Sears' interest in radio jumped from listing the primitive earphone apparatus in its catalog of 1920 to owning its own radio station, WLS, in 1923. By 1925, "Popular demand has made expansion necessary and today finds WLS a superstation of 5,000 watts which can be heard in all parts of the country." The station had three studios and a number of groups organized by it: the R.F.D. Club, The Little Brown Church, The Homemaker's Club, and so on. It was bringing not only music and other entertainment to the farm but also money-making information.

"MY RADIO HAS MADE ME $500.00, says Lee Mosher of De Kalb, Illinois. Mr. Mosher said so himself in a letter to W-L-S. His actual additional profits in one year, because he was a radio owner, was over $500 in the marketing of his live stock."

So enthusiastic in 1925 were farmers over the profits and potentialities of radio that it seemed almost the final solution of the eternal farm problem and the happy transfiguration into a contented citizen of The Man with the Woe. Farmers wrote to WLS and the catalog repeats their words. "Otto H. Nan, Hillsboro, Iowa, tells of profits that paid for his five-tube radio set more than twice; W. H. Hedstrom, Victoria, Illinois, of $110 more on one shipment of hogs because radio told him when to market. Donald P. Zellars, Beason, Illinois, says: 'Last Fall I heeded your advice regarding picking seed corn just before the first cold snap. That sure was a money-saving bit of information.'"

A new day had come to the farm and the farmer. All he had to do then was to sit before the radio and wait until a far-off friendly expert told him when to send his pigs to market or crate his string beans. Nobody seemed to realize that all farmers would be listening at the same time and consequently all would ship to market simultaneously with disastrous effects on prices; that farmers cannot market at their own sweet will, because many products are perishable and others must be sold when money is needed, and, finally, that the farmer's woes came as much from the high prices he paid for merchandise as from the low prices he received for farm products.

The farmer, nonetheless, has never lacked friends full of advice about the beauties of farm life and admonitions that he remain on the land. "The farmer," they say, "can't starve. His children get plenty of fresh air plus rhubarb and whey in season. He can't be fired because he's his own boss. And farm life is beautiful. Think of Autumn. Shocks of golden wheat and heaps of golden pumpkins; pools of maple syrup; hams and bacon in the smokehouse; apples and potatoes in the cellar; a roaring wood fire in the grate; fat cows munching sweet hay and dripping cream while they munch, and nowadays a radio in the parlor, movies in the near-by town, and a Ford in the stable."

But the farmer seems strangely untouched by the Phyllis and Corydon raptures of country life as imagined by his city friends. As stubborn as one of his own mules, he continues to leave the pastures for the pavements. In 1900, the rural population made up 57.4 per cent of the total population of this country. Twenty years later, the phlegmatic Bureau of the Census announced that a stupendous revolution had quietly occurred in America. For the first time since the founding of the republic, so many farm boys and girls had dropped the hoe and the milk pail for the assembly line and the business machine that the rural population was less than the urban population, or 48.6 per cent of the total. In that year, station KDKA of Pittsburgh was opened.

The coming of the radio moved some of our profound urban thinkers to the belief that it would keep the farmer walking the straight and narrow turnrow behind old Beck. In 1925, General Harbord, then president of the Radio Corporation of

America, and a onetime farm boy himself, told the Advertising Club of New York (most of whose members had come from farms or small towns) just why the radio would make the farmer love the land described in his mortgage.

"It has not been the physical hardships," he said, "but the dullness of life, the utter monotony and lack of recreation that have caused the farm boy or girl, as well as the paid farm laborer, to desert the old farm and seek the city. Through radio the farmer receives the advice of agricultural authorities. . . . The great men of the nation, the President himself, will speak in the farmer's home."

By 1933, the President was speaking in the farmers' homes. He did not beg them to stay on the land. He merely told them that he would help them keep their farms—which they were doing by waving shotguns in the faces of mortgage-foreclosing sheriffs.

But to go back to 1925. "In the long run," continued the prescient General, "perhaps the greatest utility of radio to the farmer is in tying in with the extension work of agricultural schools. . . . It will enable the college student whose course has often been interrupted to continue it, often with the same instructors."

Scientific education, in fifteen-minute courses, taken three times a week while seated in your own rocker, is not enough to keep the farmer contented. The heart of the farm problem, according to the General, was lack of entertainment—not cash—on the farm. Consequently, he added:

"Of all that may be said of radio the best is that it will tend to keep the young people on the farm. There is the true independence of the American sovereign. Entertainment, culture and the throbbing life of the metropolis, carried to the farm by radio . . . will sustain that class which is the very backbone of our national existence."

After the pronouncement of this sonorous peroration, the General sat down to applause. Even the hard-boiled members of the Advertising Club of New York, who appraise families in terms of purchasing power and sales resistance, must have been moved by his tribute to the "American sovereign." From the Declaration of Independence to the Emancipation Proclamation, and from the Emancipation Proclamation to the Sherman Antitrust Act (which was the result in large part of farmers' complaints against monopoly), the independent, noble, conservative, hard-working farmer, sending his wheat to town and buying shoes in exchange, has been regarded as the ideal American. One hundred years ago in the play *Fashion,* a song was sung which characterized this feeling:

> *Let sailors sing of ocean deep,*
> *Let soldiers praise their armor.*
> *But in my heart this toast I'll keep—*
> *The Independent Farmer.*
>
> *He cares not how the world may move,*
> *No doubts or fears confound him.*
> *His little flock is linked in love*
> *As household angels round him.*
>
> *The gray old barn whose doors enfold*
> *His ample store in measure*
> *More rich than heaps of hoarded gold,*
> *A precious blessed treasure.*
>
> CHORUS:
>
> *He loves his country and his friends,*
> *His honesty's his armor.*
> *He's Nature's nobleman in life—*
> *The Independent Farmer.*
> *He is Nature's nobleman in life,*
> *The Independent Farmer.*

Another oracle of the early days of radio, and a friend to Nature's nobleman, was Mr. M. H. Aylesworth. In 1927, as president of the National Broadcasting Corporation, he offered his company's services in keeping the Independent Farmer on his mortgaged and eroded throne. "The NBC," said Mr. Aylesworth, "proposes to make an intensive study of the farmer's needs in-so far as broadcasting service is concerned. To the city dweller radio may be almost wholly an entertainment feature. . . . To the farmer, however, radio is both a vital service to the home and the farming industry." Then the NBC inaugurated the Farmer's Network and set out to teach the farmer how to farm and at the same time amuse him with songs and jokes. This was undoubtedly an improvement over the crude days of 1900, when, as two radio enthusiasts tell us, "they [farmers] used to play a wheezy old organ or drive 18 miles to a camp meeting to participate in the singing."

It was estimated that, in 1931, nearly 16 million American families owned receiving sets valued at over $300,000,000. It will be illuminating then to review an actual broadcast of 1931 and see how radio was fulfilling General Harbord's prophecy that it would bring the "throbbing life of the metropolis to the farm," and render, in Mr. Aylesworth's sparkling phrase, "a vital service to the home."

MAXWELL HOUSE PROGRAM

9:30-10 P.M.   Thursday
                         April 30, 1931

ANNOUNCER: Ladies and gentlemen—MAXWELL HOUSE COFFEE—"Good to the Last Drop." . . . If your taste is attuned to modern luxury, you, also, will find complete satisfaction in MAXWELL HOUSE COFFEE.

(There is some doubt whether the taste of the farmer in 1931 was attuned to "modern luxury." In 1929—the year of our great prosperity—huge percentages of American farm homes lacked electric lights, bathtubs, and running water. These deficiencies were to be compensated for, however, by radio music piped into the farmhouse.)

ANNOUNCER: Tonight we present not only a distinguished artist . . . but also . . . the beloved "Old Colonel" of MAXWELL HOUSE FAME. Anna Case . . . will sing for you immediately after our first orchestral program. . . . How many thousands of you have reveled in the beauty of her voice, in opera and concert!

(There is some question about the number of thousands who "reveled in the beauty of her voice, in opera and concerts." It seems that too many millions of Americans were too busy scratching for a living to have much time for reveling at the opera. In 1929, when nearly everybody was either in Paris or playing polo at Aiken, one sixth of all nonfarm families spent $350 a year—less than $1 a day for food. The income of 72 per cent of the same families was under $2,500 a year.)

ANNOUNCER: Again we present . . . ANNA CASE. . . . She weaves a spell of mystic charm in a composition by Pearl Curran. . . .

(Things now begin to move fast. Time is money on the radio. Music, song, and even Miss Case have to shuffle off the stage. They are, in fact, but a hasty prelude to the great event of the evening that is about to occur: the unveiling of an electric sign in New York. A ray of light that left Aldebaran on the day that Pontius Pilate was appointed Procurator of Judea will reach the earth tonight only to be ingloriously outshone by a sign blazing above Broadway. Progress, here we come!)

ANNOUNCER: Tonight MAXWELL HOUSE COFFEE literally brings a new light to American skies. [*Oh, say can you see?*] Within a few minutes a dazzling electrical spectacle will spring to life in the heart of New York. . . . It is fitting that this great beacon of friendship should be dedicated by the gentleman who first gave us MAXWELL HOUSE COFFEE. Millions know him affectionately as "The Old Colonel," the living spirit of those gracious days of the South where MAXWELL HOUSE was born. . . . Permit us to present Joel Cheek, MAXWELL'S famous "Old Colonel," who will address you from . . . Nashville, Tennessee.

(Here we note history in the making and the transformation of a legend. Southern colonels in fact and fiction have performed strange wonders. Some of them have even been accused of being "lit up like an electric sign." This seems, however, to be the first time that a colonel has lighted a sign. The colonel of legend, too, sat on the veranda of his white-columned home sipping mint juleps and mowing down regiments of Yankees, suh, as he sipped. Now he craves coffee. Whether this indicates that the South has progressed or retrograded is a matter of speculation.)

COLONEL CHEEK'S ADDRESS: . . . In a moment I shall

give a signal . . . and far away in New York a bright message will flash from the skies. . . . I would like to think of this bright display as an emblem of hospitality. . . . I hope it will always be that to you and that the coffee it represents will always bring you contentment and comfort. Thank you—God Bless You All and Good Night.

(Southern hospitality is keeping pace with the country. It is now on a mass-production basis. Contrast this with the puny methods of the old days. "My friends," said Colonel McCrea of Kentucky in 1871, "I'm opposed to a hotel going up in this town. If a man gets off a train and he is a gentleman he will be welcome in my home. If he isn't a gentleman we don't want him stopping here.")

ANNOUNCER: And now you are to hear a description of New York's newest wonder. . . . We turn you over to Graham McNamee in TIMES SQUARE.

(The long-promised "throbbing heart of the metropolis" is at last to be brought into the farm home and laid on the parlor table. Left ventricle and right, aorta, capillaries, and pulsing blood, it will be poetically described by Graham McNamee as he stands, a radio François Villon, in the gutters of Broadway.)

GRAHAM McNAMEE: . . . They tell me this is the biggest electric display on Broadway—and that's easy to believe, too. [*In the excitement Mr. McNamee seems to have lost his usual attitude of scientific skepticism.*] . . . Takes enough current to light up two thousand ordinary homes. . . . All this huge river of people . . . it looks as if every blessed one of them is going to spend the evening gazing at this electric display. [*Electric signs are the opium of the people.*] . . . More than a million people a day will see this new MAXWELL HOUSE SIGN. [*Even the Praxitelean Hermes did not draw a fraction of this number.*] . . . It's worth staying here to see—a better show [*folksy touch*] than some of the best fires we've had here lately.

(This was a valuable contribution to the solving of the farm problem. The temptation to farmers sitting in homes without electric light must have been great to move to cities where one electric sign required "as much current as two thousand ordinary homes." The removal of farmers from the farms would automatically solve the farm problem.)

. . . It fairly dazzles you—in addition to seven thousand electric lights . . . there's three huge flashlights playing on the sign. . . . [*Progress again. All the light that Paul Revere had with which to save a country was a lantern.*]

What a crowd there is in Times Square tonight. [*Waiting for Steel common to touch 200 once more.*] Well, I suppose this will go on every night now. . . . This is Graham McNamee speaking and returning you to your studio. . . .

The Well-Educated Farmer

In 1930, the farmer—according to sellers of radio equipment and radio time—had become a changed man. It was the radio that had changed him. Mr. Alfred N. Goldsmith and Mr. Austin C. Lescarboura tell us of the new farmer in *This Thing Called Broadcasting:*

He [the farmer] makes more money and has more leisure to spend it. The news of the world and its entertainment is his for the turning of a knob. Business-like, well-informed, educated, the farmer of 1930 comes to town to attend the conference of grain growers. He attends the concert by the same orchestra that he hears weekly in his home. . . . He stays at the foremost hotels, listening while at dinner to the same fine orchestras that broadcast daily. He talks of the stock market, discusses the grain exports for the coming year, the latest developments in farm machinery. . . .

And now, as the farmer walks down the street of the city, smooth-shaven, neatly dressed, self-possessed—nobody turns to stare. He is no different from anyone else. His hands are clean. The style of his clothes is no different from that of the city. . . . His broad interests, his business acumen and knowledge, his wealth, his education, make him no longer a Rube but a man of the world. . . . No longer is the farmer a man apart. Due in part to the automobile and the movie, due as much to the widespread influence of radio . . . he is truly a citizen of the world.

But this is not all. It appears that the American farmer has been so transformed by the automobile, the movies, and the radio that:

(1) "The farmer makes more money and has more leisure to spend it." Consequently, a farmer who rides in to Evansville to see Hoot Gibson in a horse opera and comes back home to listen to a Wheatena broadcast will make bigger crops and sell them for more money than if he did not possess these soil-building, crop-making, marketing agencies. Leisure, we learn, is not something to be pleasurably employed in making love, growing guppies, or playing pool. It is a device to enable a man to spend more money. The first duty of the citizen is to be a Good Consumer.

"Unless you become a good consumer," wrote an American to a Russian *émigrée* resident in New York, "you will be told to go back to Russia, because the first duty of a good American . . . is to consume even unto death. You must spend your days consuming: buying clothes, getting your hair waved, sending flowers and books (if you haven't a friend who likes flowers and books, the florists will provide one anywhere in the United States), exchanging the old radio for a new one, drinking milk to reduce, and drinking more milk to fatten. In your leisure moments you may play bridge, ski, travel, skate, go to the six-day bicycle races . . . or take a metabolism test. At night . . . you may relax. Then all you have to do is go to the theater or the movies. The movies are our third largest industry and you couldn't let them down. While you consume for Shirley Temple by Eastern standard time, she sleeps; but when you sleep she awakens and consumes for you by Pacific time. Thus, like the True Church, you 'sleep and graze at once.' . . . And what's the result? The highest standard of living in the world!"

(2) By some undisclosed miracle—the internal evidence points to the radio—the farmer in 1930 had become "business-like, well-informed, and educated." Let's see. The South is the most predominantly agricultural section of the country. What miracle had been achieved in Dixie?

In 1929, the per capita of retail sales in the South was

$245. In the rest of the country where there were fewer farmers and more industrialists, the per capita of retail sales was almost twice as great, or $445.

Let's look at the state of Mississippi. It is 83 per cent agricultural. Presumably it reeked with well-to-do, educated farmers. What is the fact? In 1932, this whole state, with a population of two millions, paid in individual federal income taxes the prodigious sum of $134,000. This was less than the tax paid by some individuals elsewhere.

Suppose we extend the inquiry to the ten great cotton states. In 1932, they paid in individual federal income taxes about $17,000,000. The New England states at the same time paid $30,000,000. This section lets the other fellow grow cotton and corn. It is content to run punch presses and lathes.

And education. These are the figures of Southern illiteracy. (An illiterate is defined as a person of ten years of age or over who cannot write in any language.)

South Carolina	14.9 per cent
Louisiana	13.5 " "
Mississippi	13.1 " "
Alabama	12.6 " "
North Carolina	10.0 " "
Georgia	9.4 " "
Tennessee	7.2 " "
Texas	6.8 " "

The average rate of illiteracy in 1930 for the country as a whole was 4.3 per cent. This was exceeded in every one of the cotton states, and sometimes doubled and tripled.

(3) What does the "smooth-shaven, neatly dressed, self-possessed farmer" do when he goes to the city? He certainly does not go to town for so vulgar a reason as to pick up a good brood sow at a stock show or sell a dozen calves with which to pay taxes or the installment on a tractor. Far from it. "He attends the concert by the same orchestra that he hears weekly in his home." We can see him taking a small suite in the Hotel Blackstone in Chicago and finding out what orchestra is playing that night at Symphony Hall. At the concert when he

—54—

hears Debussy's *L'Après-midi d'un faune,* he chuckles with delight. It is as familiar to him—via the radio—as the wrinkles on the teats of Nellie, the brindle-brown cow that he has been milking twice daily for five years. But the composition that really floors him is Stravinsky's *L'Oiseau de feu.* The Clicquot Club Eskimos played it last fall when he and the boys were shucking corn, and that little old radio they had hooked up in the corncrib certainly did make time pass fast.

The next morning, our well-educated, well-informed farmer does not go out to the stockyards or even try to sell the 480 bushels of wheat that he has at home. He attends a "grain conference." There he makes a speech. "Gentlemen," he says, "I see that there is a deficiency of moisture in the Southern Hemisphere. The Russian kulaks are rebelling against the collective economy of Stalin and are sabotaging their wheat areas. The seeded area in Australia is the smallest since 1903. It appears that the wheat surplus, not counting tonnage afloat and in secondary hands, will be less than eighty million bushels while the conversion rate of haikwan taels into Danubian currencies is so unfavorable as to prohibit exports from Asia to that section. I'm willing, therefore, to hold my four hundred and eighty bushels if you gentlemen will hold yours."

The group of well-educated farmers, whom the radio has instructed, heartily applaud. Our farmer stays in Chicago a few days more to brush up on his music, but takes the precaution after leaving the grain conference to wire his daughter in West Branch, Iowa, to be sure and set those hen eggs he left in the cellar.

Thus does radio realize the prophecies made for it by General Harbord and Mr. Aylesworth as an agency that will transform the farmer. The prophecy in short—noting the high civilization, happiness, and prosperity of our cities—that it will make him indistinguishable from city folk.

The farmer, meanwhile, was doing that himself by going to the city where he would be nearer the broadcasting stations and get culture hot off the griddle. By 1930, the rural population had slumped to 43.8 per cent of the total population.

Women also will be benefited by radio, we are told by Messrs. Goldsmith and Lescarboura. The country will soon glitter with the radio-inspired conversations of *salons* conducted by millions of Madames de Staël. And their language will be French. This is how it is done without benefit of mirrors, according to these gentlemen of the radio industry:

"The most hard-working woman, spending her day over the tubs and the kitchen sink (though most of them have been taught by radio to accept the economies of the electric washer and the automatic cooker) has now a chance to catch up with the events of the world. Turning on the radio while she irons the sheets or boils the potatoes she learns French by air, brushes up her games, listens to the same concert or recital as her once more fortunate sister who is free from household duties, and in a dozen other ways relaxes, learns, broadens the scope of her activities and interests."

The radio, it seems, is capable not only of cultural and economic miracles but also biological miracles. It will, according to our expert informants, raise the birth rate. Give a woman a radio, they say, and she will give you back children. There is some subtle affinity between Fallopian and neutrodyne tubes.

"Of recent years," we learn, "the modern girl, longing for the luxuries of single life, or a childless home, fearing the burdens and drudgeries of home making has approved a marked lowering of the birth rate. Unfortunately, most of these women were of the wealthy class, who could best afford to rear a family. But they knew nothing of housekeeping, cared less, and felt they would be cut off from the many activities to which they were accustomed. Now it is largely changed. Anyone can learn to keep house by radio; doing so has become a fascinating endeavor; it no longer means the foregoing of all the interests and pleasures of pre-marital days. Realizing this, thoughtful women are considering marriage, the bearing of children, and the maintaining of a home as less a step to obscurity and drudgery than ever before."

With the realization then on the part of the American people that the radio will amuse, educate, and content them; that it will induce marriage and a higher birth rate; teach French and warn of approaching grasshoppers; we may see what kind of machines were offered by the catalog to serve these high purposes.

The radios of 1925 were marked by two features: high price and low receiving power. The radio user of that day was enchanted, not by the quality of the programs he heard, but by the distance from which they came to him. And manufacturers and distributors of radio described their machines in terms of spatial allure. Thus, "The W-L-S Neutrodyne

They Used to Sit up All Night Trying to Get San Francisco with Sets Like This

Enables You to Easily and Quickly Locate Distant Stations. One thousand miles and over is common on the loud speaker under favorable atmospheric conditions. On the headphones, under the right conditions, coast-to-coast reception is possible."

The lowest-price storage-battery radio sold for $65. The highest-price machine sold for $150.

The catalog listed pages of radio accessories: such things as loud-speakers, headphones, phonograph units, ear pads, batteries, and dry cells.

In 1925, thousands of men built their own radios and Sears supplied the makings. "Enjoy the fun of building and save the cost of construction," the catalog tells us. "Every problem has been worked out in our laboratories and the parts tested to insure success."

Men were proud of their accomplishment in hearing distant stations over the radio, and it was a common boast in 1925 to say "I got Chicago at three o'clock this morning, and

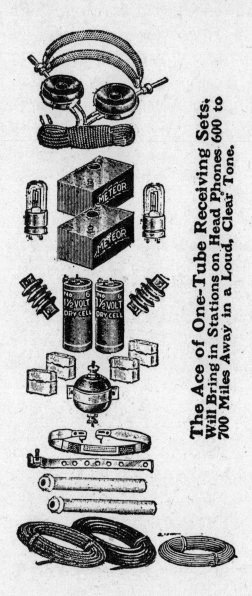

The Ace of One-Tube Receiving Sets.
Will Bring in Stations on Head Phones 600 to
700 Miles Away in a Loud, Clear Tone.

*Radio Makings for Men Who
Made Their Own Sets*

that's going some because it's thirteen hundred miles from here." Sears provided a method to keep the record clear and permanent in a "Broadcasting Station Stamp Album. A convenient, permanent and authentic means of recording the stations you hear. . . . Contains a complete list of stations and a convenient log. Price $1.49."

The catalog also made it easy for radio fans to say what they felt through the use of RADIOPLAUSE CARDS. "Express your appreciation of the programs you hear. Every station wants your comments. Package of 24 cards for 25¢."

Europe Comes into the Parlor

The years 1935–36 were ones of political convulsion throughout the world. Germany, Italy, and Japan were on the march. So far had the radio advanced since 1925 that now a farmer home from a day in the fields, by turning the dial of his "Silvertone AC Electric Radio," could, through its "amazing reception of foreign programs," hear Big Ben tolling in London, Hitler screaming in Berlin, or Mussolini bellowing in Rome.

Radio turned overseas in 1935. "One of the most marvelous developments in Radio," says the catalog, "is Foreign Reception. Think of jumping oceans, mountains and prairies and listening to new music, new speeches, etc. in the most interesting and distinctive manner of that particular country, whether in Europe or South America." Enthusiastic customers write Sears to tell how pleased they are that the world now comes into their parlors.

"I am extremely pleased with my All-Wave Silvertone," says Mr. Fred Weaver of Mattoon, Illinois. "On my old radio I was limited to the central states. Now I listen easily to German, French, English, and South American stations. It is the greatest of modern thrills. . . ."

By the autumn of 1939, Americans were listening in on the second world war, and in order that no broadcast words from Europe might be lost in his town, a radio-service dealer of the Middle West ran the following advertisement in his local newspaper:

"Hitler sounds like the devil, we admit. But we can fix your radio so that you can hear just what he is saying."

Millions of radio sets are now in American homes, and they are regarded as being almost as essential as beds. Mass production has sharply reduced prices. In 1935, they were less than half the prices of 1925. And men were no longer building their own sets. Radio construction materials have vanished from the catalog.

Radio Progress— This Machine Will Bring Hitler into Your Own Home for a Fireside Spat

"Inventions enter the world like new-born babes," wrote R. M. McIver in the University of Toronto *Quarterly.* "Their power to change the modes of life and thoughts of men does not appear until they are grown up."

Radio has grown up but it is still growing. Its powers for good and evil are prodigious. It is now standard equipment in millions of farm homes. And there can be little doubt that many sets have been paid for out of the proceeds of Federal agricultural subsidies which reflect the failure of agriculture that farmers were once told the radio would go far to prevent.

3 · FUN AND LAUGHTER WITH THE STEREOSCOPE

THE stereoscope, through which one could look at colored cards depicting the buildings of the St. Louis Exposition, American battleships, or the life of Christ, was essential to the parlor of 1905. It was an instrument low in price —Sears sold the simplest model for twelve cents—it could be used by a child or an adult, and continuous production of cards to be employed with it brought within the ken of the 1905 home something of the color, variety, and excitement of the remote outside world. The family might gather around the table on Sabbath evenings to look through the stereoscope at the "Life of Christ Set. Twelve splendid views portraying in the most vivid manner the story of our Savior's life before and after cucifixion (plain 48¢, colored 60¢)." Or the patriotic father, at that time so soon after the Spanish-American War, might show his children "Battleships, a very popular series consisting of a fine collection of views of the battleships of our navy," accompanying the pictures with a running recital of the prowess of our navy and omitting the unpatriotic detail that the ships missed ninety-eight per cent of the shots fired at the enemy's vessels in Manila Bay.

The stereoscope, in brief, was a cheap, flexible, useful instrument which provided pleasure and amusement for thousands of American homes in the preautomobile and preradio-moving-picture days. It was listed at prices ranging from twelve cents for a stereoscope made of wood and strawboard to "our imported graphoscope at $3.10," an imposing-looking machine with batteries of mirrors.

Through the Stereoscope

The catalog offers "100 comic views for 85¢," and in this instance, as in so many others, is at pains to assure the prospective customer that his purity will not be sullied by what he sees.

A Parlor Pet and Picture Show of 1905

". . . There is not a vulgar picture in the entire set, not a picture to which the most refined could possibly object. . . . Everybody likes a good laugh and every picture in this set is good for one, big, hearty laugh. Laughable kissing and hugging scenes, humorous scenes of domestic tribulations, amusing bathing scenes, photographs of childish occupations. . . ."

But living is not all laughter; then, as now, it was, in part, "educational and cultural." Hence the "Foreign Picturesque" series of cards, "illustrating the most beautiful and striking scenery and points of interest throughout Europe (per dozen, all different 36¢)"; the "Ruins and Antiquities" series, and "Views in Sweden."

Coming Events

The same pages which describe Sears' stereoscopes list a more sophisticated instrument which in many a darkened

STEREOSCOPIC VIEW DEPARTMENT

SEEN THROUGH THE STEREOSCOPE, a stereoscopic view brings before us in a way that seems almost like magic, so wonderful is the effect of distance, depth, relief and solidity. The marvelously true to life appearance, everything seemingly of full natural life size, the wonderful detail, the perspective,

SEEN FOR THE FIRST TIME, the effect is almost startling, and if you have never looked through the scope at one of these wonderful pictures you have still before you one of the real pleasures of life.

HOW STEREOSCOPIC PICTURES ARE MADE. At first thought a stereoscopic view seems to be simply a double photograph, two photographs mounted side by side on one card. Apparently the two photographs are just alike, but in reality there is a wonderful difference in these two pictures, these two photographs that form the stereoscopic view, and the whole secret of the superiority of a stereoscopic picture over any other form of photograph lies in this fact—that the two pictures are not exactly alike.

STEREOSCOPIC VIEWS ARE MADE WITH A DOUBLE CAMERA, a special camera fitted with two lenses, which makes two simultaneous pictures of the same subject side by side on the same plate, these two pictures differing from each other, because the two lenses are about three inches apart, and therefore the picture which one lens makes is from a slightly different view point than the picture made by the other lens. One lens sees, or takes a little more of the right hand side of the subject, the other lens a little more of the left hand side. When these two pictures are combined by the prismatic lenses of the stereoscope we get that wonderful stereoscopic effect, that effect of reality, of distance, of perspective and of relief which has puzzled the scientists and excited the admiration of everyone since the day of the discovery of the stereoscope by Prof. Wheatstone and Sir David Brewster, away back in the first half of the 19th century.

THE STEREOSCOPE IS AN OPTICAL INSTRUMENT for viewing stereoscopic pictures. It is provided with two powerful prismatic magnifying lenses. When the stereoscopic view is looked at through the stereoscope the prismatic lenses of the instrument combine the two pictures into one and at the same time cause a wonderful transformation in the appearance of the view. The two ordinary looking photographs, the two pictures, apparently just alike, become, when seen through the stereoscope, a single picture, life size, with everything standing out in relief, just exactly as though you were looking at the object itself instead of a picture.

THE EDUCATIONAL VALUE OF OUR STEREOSCOPIC VIEWS

COMPLETE DESCRIPTIONS WITH EVERY VIEW. Ours is the only line of colored stereoscopic views on the market in which each and every view is accompanied by a full description, complete information regarding every picture in our big line of 1,260 subjects.

THIS DESCRIPTIVE FEATURE DOUBLES THE VALUE OF OUR VIEWS. Views sold by other dealers, without descriptive matter of any kind, or simply with the name of the view printed at the bottom, may be interesting for a time. The pictures may be beautiful, may prove a source of amusement, but to be of real value, to be of lasting interest, every stereoscopic view should be accompanied by a complete, accurate and carefully written description.

LET US SELECT AT RANDOM one of the pictures from our big set of 100 views of the World, say, for example, No. 287, which is entitled, "**Interior of the Coliseum, Rome Italy.**" Seen through the stereoscope this is a beautiful picture. As we look at it we seem to be actually in Rome, looking at this most famous of ancient Roman buildings, but no matter how perfect this picture may be, no matter how natural in appearance it is, no matter how true an idea it gives us of the exact appearance of the Coliseum, our interest is very greatly increased and the picture assumes a new and greater value when we turn it over and read on the back that the Coliseum is the largest and most magnificent stone amphitheater ever built, that its erection was commenced by Vespasian, A. D. 72, that it was opened during the reign of Titus, but not completed until the time of Domitian, that 12,000 captive Jews were the workmen and that the Christian martyr Gaudentius was the architect; that this wonderful amphitheater was used for gladiatorial combats and fights of slaves and Christians with wild beasts; that St. Ignatius was the first martyr that was here devoured by lions, and that a cross in the arena now marks the spot where the early Christians suffered. We read that outwardly the building shows four stories, supported respectively by Doric, Ionic and Corinthian columns, on which the arches of each story rested. We learn that five elliptic, massive walls carried spaces for the spectators in the interior, and we learn of the marvelous ingenuity in the arrangement of the passages through which the multitudes reached the 87,000 seats; we learn how the name Coliseum is derived from the Italian word Colosseo, that it was first used in the eighth century, and probably derived from the colossal statue of Apollo-Nero, located near by.

WITH THIS FUND OF INFORMATION BEFORE US, the picture takes on new interest, and when you remember that each and every one of the 1,260 views, constituting our great Educational Series, comes with full and complete descriptive matter, some idea of the genuine and lasting value of this series of views may be gained.

ABOUT POSTAGE, EXPRESS OR FREIGHT on stereoscopic views. If sent by mail, the postage on one set of 100 views and stereoscope is 35 cents, or on the views alone, 20 cents. If more than one outfit is ordered it is cheaper to ship by express, and to most points within 500 miles of Chicago it is cheaper to ship even one outfit by express. If you include with your order for views goods from other departments sufficient to make a freight shipment, the cost of transportation on the views will be so small that it is not worth considering.

This Standard Stereoscope, 28 Cents.

No. 20K2500 This Standard Stereoscope is a first class instrument, guaranteed to give perfect satisfaction, and is exactly the same quality that is sold all over the country by dealers and agents at from 75 cents to $1.00.
The lenses are large, measuring 1 3-16 by 1⅜ inches; specially ground from a fine quality of pure, clear, optical glass accurately adjusted and firmly mounted.
The frame is made from selected hardwood; the lens board is composed of five pieces carefully mortised together to prevent warping, and the hood is of three-ply hardwood veneer, nicely finished and varnished.
Price, each........................$0.28
Per dozen......................3.25
If by mail, postage extra, each, 19 cents.

28c

Our Large Lens Walnut Stereoscope for 60 Cents.

No. 20K2506 This Stereoscope is made from solid black walnut throughout, varnished walnut hood, brass trimmings and patent folding handle. The lenses in this walnut stereoscope are extra large; the very highest grade stereoscopic lenses made, specially ground from the best clear optical glass and accurately adjusted. Best workmanship and carefully selected materials throughout; an extra good stereoscope.
Price, each....$0.60
Per dozen.....6.95
If by mail, postage extra, each, 19 cents.

60c

Our Special Aluminum Stereoscope for 49 Cents.

No. 20K2503 This elegant Stereoscope is made with fine aluminum hood, beautifully engraved and bound with dark red velvet. The frame is of cherry wood, carefully finished and varnished, with patent folding handle. The lenses are extra quality, of good size, carefully ground from the highest grade of fine, clear glass, accurately adjusted and firmly held in place by latest patented aluminum lens lock. Our Special Aluminum Stereoscope is a universal favorite with canvassers, who find that the elegant appearance and sterling good qualities which it possesses, make it a very ready seller. The very low price which we quote on this stereoscope is made possible only by the fact that we have contracted for the largest quantity of high grade stereoscopes ever handled by any one dealer, and have thus been enabled to reduce the manufacturing cost to the lowest possible figure. Price, per dozen. $5.64; each 49c
If by mail postage extra, each, 19 cents.

VARNISHED CHERRY FRAME.
ENGRAVED ALUMINUM HOOD.
PATENT LENS LOCK.

Greatly Reduced Prices on Stereo-Graphoscopes

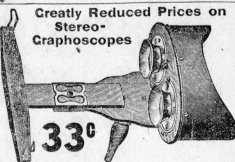

The Stereo-Graphoscope is an instrument made upon a new principle by means of which it can be adjusted for either regular stereoscopic views or single photographs and other pictures by simply reversing the lenses. The manner in which the lenses are mounted and the shape of the hood shuts out all light, making a dark chamber around the eyes and giving a very clear, beautiful effect to the picture.

33c

No. 20K2510 Stereo-Graphoscope, cherry frame, varnished cherry hood, brass trimmings and wood screw handle. Medium size lenses of best quality.
Price, per dozen, $3.80; each.........................33c
If by mail, postage extra, each, 25 cents.
No. 20K2511 Stereo-Graphoscope, cherry frame, varnished mahogany hood, brass trimmings and patent folding handle. Best grade lenses of large size, a first class instrument throughout. Price, per dozen. $5.20; each.........................45c
If by mail, postage extra, each, 25 cents.
No. 20K2512 Our Best Stereo-Graphoscope, made with oiled cherry frame, fine varnished mahogany hood, all trimmings nickled plated and highly polished, patent folding handle, first quality materials and best workmanship throughout. Extra large lenses of very highest quality. Price, per dozen. $7.50; each.........................65c
If by mail, postage extra, each, 25 cents.

A TOUR OF THE WORLD WITH THE STEREOSCOPE.

100 Views of the World and scope 95¢

THIS OUTFIT consists of one hundred magnificent colored reproductions of original photographic stereoscopic views. The original photographs from which these views are reproduced were especially selected for this set, the greatest care being exercised to obtain only views of particular interest, unusual beauty and the most perfect stereoscopic effect.

THIS SET illustrates some of the most noted places in the world—mountain scenery both in America and Europe—waterfalls and other famous natural phenomena, some of the world's most famous buildings, places of historical interest and places famous for beautiful architecture or beautiful natural scenery. **This set is of the greatest educational value,** presenting, as it does, such realistic likenesses of scenes and places that we all should know about.

THERE ARE ONE HUNDRED VIEWS IN THE SET, all different and every one good. All are finished in natural colors, made by a new and secret process, which enables us to offer these colored, high grade stereoscopic views at a price heretofore impossible. **Understand,** these views are reproductions in natural colors, made from

ORIGINAL RETOUCHED PHOTOGRAPHS

by a recently perfected secret process, combining the principles of halftone photography and lithography.

THE STEREOSCOPE which we furnish with this set of pictures, is made with hardwood frame, wood screw handle, fair quality lenses and varnished pressed board hood. While it is not the best stereoscope made, it is a very serviceable instrument, and, if you prefer

ONE OF OUR HIGHEST GRADE STEREOSCOPES,

you can order this set of views alone at 85 cents and make your own selection of stereoscope from page 366.

No. 55C1360 Complete Outfit, 100 Views of the World and Stereoscope. Price.................**95c**

If by mail, postage extra, 44 cents.

No. 55C1361 Views of the World, without Stereoscope. Price.................**85c**

If by mail, postage extra, 24 cents.

FUN, LAUGHTER AND AMUSEMENT WITH THE STEREOSCOPE.

THIS SPLENDID SET OF PICTURES consists of one hundred exquisitely colored stereoscopic pictures, made by our new secret process which, by a combination of well known lithographic and halftone processes, enables us to reproduce with photographic fidelity in all their natural colors these genuine photographic views, and enables us to sell them at one-tenth the actual cost of stereoscopic views made by the old process.

THESE ONE HUNDRED PICTURES ARE ALL PHOTOGRAPHED FROM LIFE. There are no copies of paintings or drawings, but every picture is made with a camera direct from life. The coloring in these comic views is exceptionally good and our new process has enabled us to bring out the details and present the subjects in the most realistically lifelike manner. Great care has been exercised in selecting the subjects for this set so that only unusually good views are included. There is not a vulgar picture in the entire set, not a picture to which the most refined could possibly object, but at the same time every picture in the set is interesting, and they will be looked at over and over again, forming a never failing source of pleasure and relaxation.

EVERYBODY LIKES A GOOD LAUGH, and every picture in this big set is good for one big, hearty laugh. Laughable hugging and kissing scenes, humorous scenes of domestic tribulations, amusing bathing scenes, photographs of children engaged in childish occupations—

FUNNY, ENTERTAINING AND LAUGHABLE PICTURES.

They will amuse you and help to entertain your friends. Understand, this big set consists of one hundred comic colored views, every picture a good one, and our special hardwood, pressed board hood, wood screw handle, stereoscope, all complete, scope and pictures, for 95 cents. If you want a better stereoscope, just order the views alone and pick out your scope from page 366.

No. 55C1364 Complete Outfit, 100 Comic Views and Stereoscope. Price.................**95c**

If by mail, postage extra, 44 cents.

No. 55C1365 Comic Views, without Stereoscope. Price.................**85c**

If by mail, postage extra, 24 cents.

100 Comic Views and scope 95¢

A TRIP TO THE FAIR WITH THE STEREOSCOPE.

100 ST. LOUIS EXPOSITION VIEWS AND SCOPE 95¢

THIS SET OF ONE HUNDRED BEAUTIFUL COLORED STEREOSCOPIC VIEWS of the St. Louis Exposition were all made from original photographs taken on the fair grounds by our special photographer, reproduced in natural colors by our new lithographic halftone process. This set of views is particularly interesting, not only to those who have visited St. Louis, but by particularly to those who have not been fortunate enough to see the beautiful buildings magnificent grounds, fountains, cascades, drives and lagoons of this great exposition.

THE LOUISIANA PURCHASE EXPOSITION IN ST. LOUIS is considered one of the most beautiful Expositions of the World. The naturally picturesque surroundings have been developed and turned to the best possible account by famous architects and celebrated landscape gardeners, and this realistic set of colored stereoscopic pictures will serve to perpetuate the memory of

THE MOST BEAUTIFUL EXPOSITION BUILDINGS AND GROUNDS EVER DESIGNED.

REMEMBER, these views are all reproduced from genuine original photographs. No copies, no paintings or drawings were used—

NOTHING BUT ORIGINAL PHOTOGRAPHS MADE ON THE GROUNDS BY OUR SPECIAL PHOTOGRAPHER.

OUR PRICE FOR THIS SET of one hundred colored stereoscopic pictures all complete with our hardwood screw handle stereoscope is 95 cents, but, if you prefer a better stereoscope, one of our highest grade stereoscopes as shown on page 366, you can buy the views alone for 85 cents and select any style of scope that you prefer.

No. 55C1372 Complete Outfit, 100 World's Fair Views and Stereoscope. Price.................**95c**

If by mail, postage extra, 44 cents.

No. 55C1373 World's Fair Views, without Stereoscope. Price.................**85c**

If by mail, postage extra, 24 cents.

parlor of the 1900's cast that strange thrill which was soon to merge into the greater, universally experienced thrill of the moving pictures. This was the Magic Lantern. A magic lantern, a darkened room, a suspended sheet, a few slides, and an earlier generation was ready for an exciting evening at home.

The catalog rarely departs from its function of selling goods. It seldom lectures or philosophizes or talks out of the corner of its mouth merely to be sociable. Its business is to get business and, in so doing, it must sometimes seize upon what it deems to be characteristics of American behavior, manners, morals, desires, or ambitions, and exploit them to sell goods. In the specific instance it calls upon the desire to make money in selling an instrument designed to give pleasure:

"The young people not only derive great pleasure from giving Magic Lantern Exhibitions, but the business training which they gain in all the various details connected with the management of an entertainment, putting up advertising posters, selling tickets, etc., gives them ideas of the rudiments of money making which starts them on the highway to business success. . . ."

Thus Junior, by saving as little as 59 cents, or as much as $5.80, and buying a magic lantern, could at the same time amuse himself and his friends and "acquire the rudiments of money making." This is literally learning to lisp in numbers, but the catalog is not responsible for the business precocity of the nation's youngsters or the anxiety of parents to foster it. It merely employs the money-making instinct for its own purposes in the same way that an explorer in the tropics floats down the river instead of hacking his way through the jungle.

Through the Magic Lantern

Junior has taken one of Mama's best "company" sheets and stretched it against the parlor wall; brought in extra chairs from the dining room; darkened the parlor, and locked Spot in the henhouse so that he will not walk in at the wrong moment. At the back of the room he stands by his Gloria Magic

Lantern, watching the audience file in, and wondering perhaps, whether, as the catalog said, he will "easily make the original cost of the outfit in your first exhibition." Now that the audience is seated, he lights the kerosene-soaked wick of the lamp, a bright shaft of light appears on the sheet, and the show is about to begin. Everybody is talking about the Russo-Japanese War which is now going on, and Junior, who is an up-to-date showman, projects his slides showing "portraits of prominent officers, pictures of the Japanese and Russian battleships, soldiers in camp and on the march, views in Manchuria, Corea and Japan." The audience applauds the Japanese soldiers who are extremely popular in the United States and is silent when slides showing the Russians are thrown on the screen.

A Bed Sheet, Some Slides, the Magic Lantern, and They Saw the Russo-Japanese War at Home in 1906

The Russo-Japanese War is in the news but we have just had our own little war with Spain; men are using strange terms such as "manifest destiny," and talking of our duty to "our little Filipino brother," of building a canal at the Isthmus of Panama, and expanding all over the world. Rounds of applause therefore roll up in the parlor as Junior's slides of the Spanish-American War flash on the screen, and the audience sees "portraits of prominent officers, battleships, camp life, and battle scenes," while the horrors and glories of war are lightened by Junior's stumbling over words in the written lectures that Sears sends out with each set of slides.

Post Card Projectors

THE MODERN MAGIC LANTERNS

No Glass Slides Necessary
Uses Any Kind of Picture
Pleases the Whole Family

THE PICTURES ON THE SCREEN are large, brilliant and clearly defined, just like stereopticon or magic lantern views, but the expensive glass slides which are necessary with the old style magic lantern are not required. These new projectors use any photograph or post card, any picture cut from a magazine or newspaper, your own drawings, or any small flat object, such as a butterfly, a leaf, a pressed flower or a watch, and the object or picture is accurately projected on to the screen greatly enlarged, sharp and clear in all its details and in all its own natural colors.

Very simple and easily operated instruments which project a brilliantly illuminated and greatly enlarged image of any post card, photograph, clipping or small object of any kind on a white screen or wall.

DO NOT JUDGE these scientifically designed machines by any other post card projectors you may have seen. There are many projectors on the market which will not give satisfactory results, but these new projectors are made right in every way, the optical features are scientifically correct, the mechanical construction is perfect, the finish throughout is beyond criticism, and every detail of design and construction has had the painstaking attention of experts in projection apparatus.

THE REMARKABLY GOOD RESULTS obtained with these machines are largely due to the optically perfect parabolic reflectors together with a more scientific adjustment of reflectors and light. We absolutely guarantee at least double the illumination possible with any other projector on the market. The great illumination, in combination with the specially ground double lenses and curved picture holders, results in larger, brighter and sharper images on the screen than we believe is possible with any other machine.

Model 1 Projector, $2.25

Size of machine, 9 inches wide, 10 inches high.
Finish. Glossy red enamel, handsomely decorated in white, gilt and black.
Single lens, 2⅞ inches in diameter.
Detachable back, with curved picture holder, not reversible. Takes 3½x5½-inch cards horizontally.
Multiplane reflectors.
Size of picture, 4 feet across at 8 feet from screen.
No. 20V2884 For Electricity. 105-115 Volts. Shipping weight, 4 pounds 1 ounce. Price..........$2.25
No. 20V2885 For Acetylene. Shipping weight, 4⅓ pounds. Price..........$2.25
No. 20V2886 For City Gas. Shipping weight, 3⅞ pounds. Price..........$2.25

Model 2 Projector, $4.50

Size of machine, 9¾ inches wide, 10¼ inches high.
Finish. Polished oxidized copper plate with bright copper bands.
Double lens, 2⅞ inches in diameter.
Hinged back, with curved revolving picture holder for either horizontal or vertical cards, 3½x5½ inches.
Parabolic reflectors, 6 inches in diameter.
Size of picture, 4½ feet across at 9 feet from screen.
No. 20V2887 For Electricity. 105-115 Volts. Shipping weight, 5¾ pounds. Price..........$4.50
No. 20V2888 For Acetylene. Shipping weight, 7 lbs. Price..........$4.50
No. 20V2889 For City Gas. Shipping weight, 6¼ pounds. Price..........$4.50

Model 3 Projector, $6.75

Size of machine, 11¾ inches wide, 10¾ inches high.
Finish. Polished oxidized copper plate with bright copper bands.
Double lens, 3⅜ inches in diameter.
Hinged back, with curved revolving picture holder for either horizontal or vertical cards, 3½x5½ inches.
Parabolic reflectors, 7½ inches in diameter.
Size of picture, 5½ feet across at 11 feet from screen.
No. 20V2890 For Electricity. 105-115 Volts. Shipping weight, 7¼ pounds. Price..........$6.75
No. 20V2891 For Acetylene. Shipping weight, 10½ pounds. Price..........$6.75
No. 20V2892 For City Gas. Shipping weight, 9 pounds. Price..........$6.75

Model 4 Projector, $9.00

Size of machine, 11¾ inches wide, 13¼ inches high.
Finish. Polished oxidized copper plate with bright copper bands.
Double lens, 3⅜ inches in diameter.
Two detachable sliding backs with adjustable curved revolving picture holders, which take any size of picture from 3¼x6½ up to 4½x6½ inches.
Parabolic reflectors, 7½ inches in diameter.
Size of picture, 6½ feet across at 12 feet from screen.
No. 20V2893 For Electricity. 105-115 Volts. Shipping weight, 10½ pounds. Price..........$9.00
No. 20V2894 For Acetylene. Shipping weight, 12½ pounds. Price..........$9.00
No. 20V2895 For City Gas. Shipping weight, 11½ pounds. Price..........$9.00

SIZE OF PICTURES ON THE SCREEN

The size of picture thrown on the screen by any of our projectors depends upon the distance of the projector from the screen. The greater the distance the larger the picture will be. Moving the projector closer to the screen results in a smaller but brighter picture; moving it farther away produces a larger but less brilliant picture. The distance at which the most satisfactory results are obtained is largely a matter of personal opinion. In our descriptions we state the size of picture at the distance which we consider most satisfactory.

ABOUT THE LIGHT

Electric models are equipped with two high candle power incandescent electric lamps, 6 feet of double conductor electric cord, and socket for attaching to any electric light fixture. Unless otherwise requested we always send lamps suitable for 105 to 115-volt current.

Acetylene models are equipped with two high candle power acetylene burners, a large generator and connections. Carbide is not included, owing to insurance regulations which prevent us from carrying it in stock. It is easily obtained at any place where bicycle or automobile supplies are sold, or at hardware or drug stores.

City gas models are equipped with two high candle power gas burners with mantles, 6 feet of special gas tubing, and connections for attaching to any gas fixture.

We recommend electric light or city gas where it can be used, because it is a little handier than acetylene, but acetylene gives just as good a picture as electric light or city gas. With our improved generator, which is guaranteed to be absolutely safe, it is only necessary to put in a little carbide, pour in a little water, and the projector is ready to light immediately.

Model 5 Projector, $13.00

Size of machine, 13 inches wide, 14½ inches high.
Finish. Polished oxidized copper plate, hand curled, with bright copper bands.
Double lens, 3¾ inches in diameter.
Two sliding backs with adjustable self centering revolving picture holders, taking any size of picture from 3¼x7½ up to 5⅝x7½ inches.
Parabolic reflectors, 8½ inches in diameter.
Size of picture, 7 feet across at 16 feet from screen.
No. 20V2896 For Electricity. 105-115 Volts. Shipping weight, 13 pounds. Price..........$13.00
No. 20V2897 For Acetylene. Shipping weight, 14½ pounds. Price..........$13.00

NOTE—Models 4 and 5 are provided with two backs. While one is in position the other can be loaded, sliding smoothly into position as the first one is removed, so that one picture follows another without the undesirable interval of a blank and brilliantly lighted screen between pictures.

For Parcel Post Shipments Include Amount of Charges Extra. See Page 754.   SEARS, ROEBUCK AND CO., CHICAGO, ILL.

The performance concludes with "Comic slides, each good for a laugh"; the lantern is darkened; the lamps are lighted; the children talk excitedly, and the friends of Junior's parents tell him what a great big man he is getting to be.

The Greater Magic of the Magic Lantern

By 1915, the stereoscope of 1905 had become a legend of American antiquity; its aluminum frame was corroded, its plush handle moth-eaten, its lenses dust-covered. But the magic lantern has become bigger and better; grown to man's estate, it occupies a whole page in the catalog.

It is now a lordly instrument selling for as much as $11.25 and is operated not by an ancient kerosene lamp but by electricity, "city gas," or acetylene. No longer is the magic-lantern operator limited to glass slides made by manufacturers for the new machine:

"Uses any kind of picture. Pleases the whole family. These new projectors use any photograph or postcard, any picture cut from a magazine or newspaper, your own drawings, or any small flat object such as a butterfly, a leaf, a pressed flower . . . and the object or picture is accurately projected on to the screen greatly enlarged, sharp and clear in all its details and in all its own natural colors."

The home is making its last stand for home entertainment.

Ten years later—1925—the magic lantern has gone into eternal darkness and vanished from the catalog. The family is at the picture show.

4 · READING MAKETH A FULL MAN

In the days before the coming of industry, before the time of the mad awakening, the towns of the Middle West were sleepy places devoted to the practice of the old trades. In the morning the old men of the towns went forth to work in the fields or to the practice of carpentry, horse-shoeing, wagon-making, harness repairing, and the making of suits of clothing. They read books and believed in a God born in the brains of men who came out of a civilization much like their own. . . . *

THE books read by that enormous group of Americans who were (and are) Sears' customers afford rich and endless clues to their character, their ambitions, their ways of thinking, their habits and customs. The old maxim, "Tell me what you read and I'll tell you what you are," may be faulty in that it is perhaps too broad. It can hardly be denied, however, that what a man or a nation reads is an important factor in assessing the character of that man or nation. For these reasons, the books bought by Sears' customers over a period of thirty years, the changing reading habits of this large group, and the criteria by which books were judged are considered at some length.

When the general catalog of 1905 apportions the enormous space of sixteen pages to books, and Sears issues in addition a special book catalog, the inevitable conclusion is that thousands of families bought hundreds of thousands of books by mail.

The times were favorable for readers and mail-order book-

* Sherwood Anderson, *Poor White*.

The Famous "READERS LIBRARY"

Any 5 Books 55¢ Any 10 Books $1.00

Bound in rich red cloth, with beautiful ornamental design stamped in full gilt on side and back. Each book measures 4½x6¾ inches and contains 225 to 300 pages.

Never before has anyone offered such wonderfully well made, good looking books at so low a price. These books are printed from **brand new** plates, with large, easily read black face type on a fine quality of white paper. Each book has fancy pictorial end sheets in the front and in the back.

At **25 cents** each they would be an exceptional value. We believe they are just as good, and just as well made as a very famous library of fiction and classics, extensively advertised, which sells for 60 cents a volume. We daily receive letters from purchasers, teachers, schools, public libraries, etc., saying what good looking books these are, and asking how it is possible for us to sell them so cheap. **The answer is**, an enormous printing order, and an extremely small profit to us—only a fraction of a cent on each volume.

These books will make a fine appearance on your table or in your bookcase.

There are now forty-one books in this library, the forty-one books upon which time has set its approval, and which the reading public has decided are the forty-one best books to read. In the Readers' Library are books to suit all tastes—there are books for young people and books for grownups. If you like adventure, you will find here the most interesting romances; if you like love stories, here are books that have been read and treasured by millions.

Here is a wonderful opportunity to start a library if you do not already have one, or to add to your present library these great books at so low a price.

Inez.	*Augusta J. Evans*
Ishmael.	*Mrs. Southworth*
Ivanhoe. Vol. I.	*Sir Walter Scott*
Ivanhoe. Vol. II.	*Sir Walter Scott*
Last Days of Pompeii.	*Bulwer Lytton*
Self-Raised.	*Mrs. Southworth*
Thelma.	*Marie Corelli*
The Spy.	*J. Fenimore Cooper*
Andersen's Fairy Tales.	*Andersen*
Grimms' Fairy Tales.	*Grimms*
Hans Brinker.	*M. Mapes Dodge*
Lena Rivers.	*Mary J. Holmes*
Jane Eyre.	*Charlotte Bronte*
Tempest and Sunshine.	*Mary J. Holmes*
Treasure Island.	*Robert Louis Stevenson*
Deerslayer.	*James Fenimore Cooper*
Dr. Jekyll and Mr. Hyde and Kidnapped.	*Robert Louis Stevenson*
Homestead on the Hillside.	*Mary J. Holmes*
The Three Musketeers. Vol. I.	*Alex. Dumas*
The Three Musketeers. Vol. II.	*Alex. Dumas*
Sherlock Holmes Detective Stories.	*Doyle*
Alice in Wonderland and Alice Through the Looking Glass.	*Lewis Carrol*
In His Steps.	*Charles M. Sheldon*
Thorns and Orange Blossoms.	*Bertha M. Clay*
Last of the Mohicans.	*J. Fenimore Cooper*
Black Rock.	*Ralph Connor*
Uncle Tom's Cabin.	*Harriet Beecher Stowe*
Plain Tales From the Hills.	*Rudyard Kipling*
File No. 113.	*Emile Gaboridu*
Murders in the Rue Morgue.	*Edgar Allan Poe*
Little Minister.	*John M. Barrie*
English Orphans.	*Mary J. Holmes*
Capitola's Peril.	*Mrs. E. D. E. N. Southworth*
Black Beauty.	*Anna Sewell*
Robinson Crusoe.	*Daniel Defoe*
Scarlet Letter.	*Nathaniel Hawthorne*
Under Two Flags.	*"Ouida"*
Marion Grey.	*Mary J. Holmes*
Pilgrim's Progress.	*John Bunyan*
Tom Brown's School Days.	*Thomas Hughes*
Tanglewood Tales.	*Nathaniel Hawthorne*

Shipping weight, each, 12 ounces.

3V1622—Any five..**55c** | Any ten..**$1.00**

The Six Best Sellers

Here are six of the most popular new fiction titles. Bound in cloth. Average 300 pages. Size, 5½x7¾ in. Shpg. wt., each, 1¼ lbs.

3V1119 — **The Thundering Herd.** Zane Grey. A breathless story of bravery, battle, courage and daring........**$1.65**

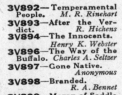

3V186 — **The Midlander.** Booth Tarkington..**$1.65**

The Enchanted Hill.
By Peter B. Kyne.

This story is laid in the great Southwest. As always with his books this one is peopled with big men and wonderful women. This story begins with a thrilling mystery and a girl and from these two elements springs one of the most gorgeous novels the author has written.

3V126..........................**$1.65**

A Gentleman of Courage.
By Jas. O. Curwood.

This story is laid in the Lake Superior region. With this book, as with his others, he has filled that great northern wilderness with romance, heroism and loyalty. Here you find Curwood with a mood of tenderness, a strain of beautiful sentiment. A Curwood who will delight all his old readers as well as fascinate a host of new ones.

3V127..............................**$1.65**

3V555 — **The Clouded Pearl.** Berta Ruck. Full of sparkling wit and rush of incident.
$1.65

3V643—**Rugged Water.** Joseph C. Lincoln. A sunny tale of the old Cape Cod days.
$1.65

Latest Fiction

$1.65 EACH

Bound in cloth. Average 350 pages. Size, 5½x7¼ in. Shipping weight, each, 1½ pounds.

3V892—Temperamental People. *M. R. Rinehart*
3V893—After the Verdict. *R. Hichens*
3V894—The Innocents. *Henry K. Webster*
3V896—The Way of the Buffalo. *Charles A. Seltzer*
3V897—Gone Native. *Anonymous*
3V898—Branded. *R. A. Bennet*
3V899—Moran of Saddle Butte. *L. Gunnison*
3V901—The Glory Hole. *S. E. White*
3V902—Red of the Redfields. *G. S. Richmond*
3V647—Saint Martin's. *R. Sabatini*
3V648—The Passing of Charles Lanson. *Louis Tracy*
3V659—At the Foot of the Rainbow. *J. B. Hendryx*
3V660—Love and Learn. *H. C. Witwer*
3V661—The Fourteenth Key. *Carolyn Wells*
3V663—The Unknown Quality. *E. M. Dell*
3V664—The Locked Book. *F. L. Packard*
3V665—The Needle's Eye. *Arthur Train*
3V678—The Red Riders. *Thomas Nelson*
3V679—Keeping the Peace. *Gouveneur Morris*
3V643—Rugged Water. *C. Lincoln*
3V637—Sackcloth and Scarlet. *Gibbs*
3V1179—The Golden Journey of Mr. Paradyne. *Wm. J. Locke*
3V1180—Grey Face. *Sax Rohner*
3V1181—The Slave Ship. *Mary Johnston*
3V517—The Priceless Pearl. *Alice Duer Miller*
3V554—The Coming of Amos. *Wm. J. Locke*
3V555—The Clouded Pearl. *Berta Ruck*
3V588—Prillilgirl. *C. Wells*
3V589—Rose of the World. *K. Norris*
3V595—The Dancer of Tuloom. *Mary E. Ryan*
3V1262—Queen Calafia. *Blasco Ibanez*
3V183—The City of the Sun. *Edwin L. Sabin*

Any book listed above, $1.65

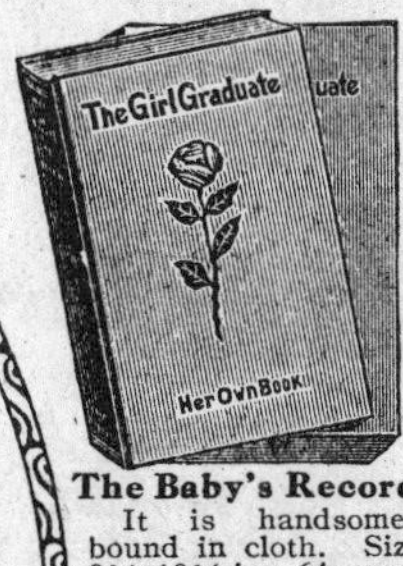

The Girl Graduate.

An artistic arrangement of pages so that the girl graduate can record the school events that are dear to her. Neatly boxed. Size, 5⅝x9 inches. Contains 200 pages. Shipping weight, 1¼ pounds.

3V2592.....**69c**

My Golden School Days.

A memory book for boys and girls in which to record all important events of school life with appropriate verses and poems. Printed in colors, 93 pages. Cover in colors and gold. Sizes, 5½x8 inches. Boxed. Shipping weight, 1⅛ pounds.

3V3188.......**87c**

The Baby's Record.

It is handsomely bound in cloth. Size, 8¼x10¼ in. 64 pages. Every page embellished and decorated with fully colored ornaments and illustrations. Shpg. wt., each, 1⅛ lbs.

3V3049 Pink Binding for Girls..........**$1.38**

3V3048 Blue Binding for Boys..........**$1.38**

My Graduation Journal

A new loose leaf graduation record book, that can be used for a complete record all through school years. Beautifully printed in color on heavy de luxe paper, with ample space allowed for inserting all records and photographs. 96 pages. Size, 9x8 inches. Cloth, cover stamped in gold and color. Shpg. wt., 1½ lbs.

3V2820................................**$1.89**

Dainty Birthday Books.

Printed on a superior quality paper with carefully selected, appropriate text for each day of the year arranged with the utmost care and discrimination. Bound in oriental glazed leather. Full gilt edges. Size, 3½x4¾ inches. Shipping wt., each, 4 oz.

3V3053—**Tennyson's Birthday Book**..............................**68c**

3V3054—**Longfellow's Birthday Book**..............................**68c**

The White Flag.

By Gene Stratton Porter. A special purchase enables us to offer to our customers this regular $2.00 book for only 89c. A book by this author needs no description, but it is sure to be the most popular with the millions of her readers. **Buy it to read. Buy it to give as gifts.** Bound in cloth. Size, 5¼x7⅝ inches. 483 pages. Shipping wt., 1½ lbs.

3V1130—Special price........**89c**

Ingersoll's 44 Great Lectures. Complete.

Gives the complete text of forty-four of Ingersoll's greatest masterpiece orations. Bound in cloth. Size, 6x8¾ inches. 403 pages. Shpg. wt., 1½ lbs.

3V2591..............**89c**

sellers. Only thirty years ago this country still preserved its early pattern of an agrarian economy, despite the stupendous growth of industrialism and urbanism after the Civil War. At the beginning of the twentieth century, there were still far more people in the country than in the cities: 46 millions living in rural territory as against 30 millions in urban territory. And country folk were evidently readers of books.

One reason, perhaps, that reading played an important part in their lives was because men and women stayed or had to stay largely at home and limit their activities to a narrow compass. In 1900, there were only 8,000 registered automobiles in the United States as opposed to millions of bicycles and buggies on the roads. Both the bicycle and the buggy are vehicles of limited range and they could not go far on the roads that were often mule-belly deep in mud during winter and almost axle deep in dust during summer. It was not uncommon in many parts of the country for wagons to become bogged down in December and remain stuck in the mud until spring. Nobody facing the hazards and difficulties of these roads could jump into his buggy or mount his horse or bicycle, and dash off for a quick visit to a town fifty miles away. Such trips required preparation, a train journey, and a considerable length of time, with the result that men tended to stay close to home. And for millions living in the back country, there was often no choice at all—they simply could not go out for weeks at a time. Living was not, so to speak, centralized as it is now, but decentralized; it was intensely regional and local, with the village as the circle, the home as the center of the circle, and the city far out on the periphery.

So, too, in the early years of the century, motion pictures still led a crude and almost furtive existence as nickelodeons operating in ill-smelling, uncomfortable store buildings in down-at-heel neighborhoods of cities; automobiles were the luxury of the rich or the eccentric, and the wireless, out of which the radio was later to emerge, was in an experimental state. In the absence of these elements that later were to play with centrifugal force on the reading habit, men depended upon their own resources for amusement, and reading was one of the most popular forms of entertainment.

It must be remembered, also, that farmers, and small-town dwellers who depend upon farmers for their livelihood, have a large amount of leisure. By 1905, the back-breaking labor of pioneer days had almost disappeared. Land clearing, principally in the South, was still to go on for many years, but it was not the land clearing of early pioneer days when one man and his family, alone in the midst of a wilderness, hacked out a small area for growing corn before the coming of winter and erected a crude hut. It was now done without great hurry, with the use of good tools, with settled communities near by, and often by large lumber companies who sold the cut-over lands to farmers when they did not abandon them as deserts. Labor-saving devices such as the harvester, the reaper, and the horse-drawn rake had long been in use. The farmer, therefore, shortly after the turn of the century, although his work was hard, was not subjected to the almost superhuman labors that faced the nineteenth-century pioneer. And whether or not leisure flows from the use of machinery, the fact is that a large amount of leisure is forced upon the farmer by the very nature of his occupation. A man cannot work in the fields during rains nor plow when the soil is wet or frozen; it is unnecessary to labor when crops are laid by to await the maturity that immediately precedes the harvest. Consequently, while there are always chores to be done about the well-conducted farm, the farmer, nevertheless, has more leisure than the factory worker, the day laborer, or even the business executive. It is estimated, for example, that only one hundred and thirty days of labor are necessary for the making of a cotton crop.

So, too, the tasks of rural and small-town women were less severe than those of pioneer women. By 1905, they no longer made soap for washing or rendered tallow for lighting; canned goods were abundant; home weaving was a lost art and, while there was still a great deal of home sewing, ready-made clothing was finding an ever-increasing market; the carpet sweeper was replacing the broom, and the general tasks of the household were being lightened by labor-saving devices.

In 1905, therefore, the rural population, with leisure before them, and with few facilities for dissipating it, spent part of it reading books. What they read is told us by the catalog.

The World's Best Seller

The best-selling book in the world has always been the Bible. Church attendance may decline, preachers may thunder that the days of Sodom and Gomorrah are at hand, scientists may demolish Adam and Eve, and scholars prove that the Bible is no more the product of divine inspiration than the cookbook, but Bibles continue to lead all other books in annual volume of sales. If this is true now, it was certainly true in 1905, and, as proof, we find the catalog of that year listing seventy-five kinds of Bibles and, for good measure, ten books about the Bible.

Nearly every home had, in addition to smaller Bibles, one big family Bible that was at once the repository of family history and the central altar of the home. It often lay on the parlor table flanked by Longfellow's *Poems* and the mail-order catalog.

OUR LEADER IN FAMILY BIBLES was a huge, cumbersome, dreary-looking book that seems as durable as Plymouth Rock and as austere as the manners and religion of the Old Testament-bred Pilgrims. It contained not only the conventional text, but a number of maps upon which devout parents pointed out to their children the Lake of Galilee, the Dead Sea, and Jerusalem; traced the journeys of Jesus and of Paul, and located the spot on Ararat where the Ark had come to rest. It was also the repository of the family's vital statistics: a registry of births, marriages, and deaths, and the place where men and children sworn to fight the demon rum recorded their pledge to temperance.

The Family Bible was not a book in which to dip; it was not designed for dilettantish reading or bedside skimming. When one read Our Leader, one had to be serious in the service of the Lord, and enlist the services of a table, because it weighed seven pounds. But whatever its spiritual content may be, the Bible is, from a merchant's point of view, an article of merchandise, and the catalog, which was no respecter of books or

A Seven-Pound Chunk of the Rock of Ages for Eighty Cents—Plus Pictures of the Holy Land, a Family Register, and the Temperance Pledge

persons when prices were concerned, gets right down to brass tacks. Our Leader was a "$3.50 retail value. . . . Price 80 cents." On a poundage basis, if no other, it was a bargain at slightly more than ten cents a pound.

The Protestant Sunday of forty to thirty years ago was not one of joy, of dancing under the vine, or celebrating gaily the day ordained by the Lord as a day of rest for man and beast. It was somber, austere, and grim. And for the pious, it was scarcely even a day of rest, with church services morning and night, Sunday school, choir singing, prayers, and Bible reading. In the little towns, blue laws and the conventions of the community laid heavy hands on unseemly activities —that is, any activity which promised pleasure. Sports were barred; dancing was taboo; gambling and drinking unspeakable, and reading Ouida's novels or Nick Carter impossible, except in the seclusion of the barn or the locked bedroom. On the arid Protestant Sabbath one could do only three things: attend church, think higher thoughts, or read the Bible.

Many must have read OUR $12.00 FAMILY BIBLE ONLY $4.89, if not for its text then for the extracurricular course in the appendix. Here one found "10 multi-colored plates, 4 superb half-tone engravings in gold and colors; Jewish Worships, Tabernacles and Vestments, Holy Apostles with descriptions, 8 pages of maps of the Holy Land, and 32 full page Doré engravings."

These were Protestant Bibles, but the religious needs of Roman Catholics were not neglected by the universal catalog. Catholic Bibles were more expensive than those of the Protestants, working out on a poundage basis at about forty cents a pound as compared with ten to twenty cents charged the Dissenters. The Catholic Bibles omit the vital statistics that were standard equipment for the Protestants, and, of course, the temperance pledge, because the temperance movement in this country has largely been Protestant in conception and execution.

I'd Believe It Even If It Ain't True

The catalog of 1905 lists a number of books about the Bible, but none of them reveals the teachings and discoveries of evolutionists, psychologists, anthropologists, or astrophysicists whose words might throw doubt upon the conception of God as the creator of the universe and the father of mankind. Even Renan's *Life of Jesus* is ignored by the catalog and its customers, although as long ago as 1863, such was the fame of this book and its author in Europe that a girl of the Paris Opera ballet asked a young man: "Tell me, who is this Monsieur Renan that everybody is talking about? Is he a member of the Jockey Club?"

The attitude of millions of Americans toward the Bible, before and shortly after the turn of the century, was summed up by the preacher who said, "I'd believe every word of it even if it ain't true." And with respect to evolution their attitude was much like the point of view of the wife of an English canon who greeted the announcement of man's alleged descent from monkeys with the remark, "My dear, I trust that it is not true; but, if it is, let us pray that it will not become generally known." These attitudes persisted for years in rural and small-town America—and still persist to some extent—despite Darwin, Wallace, Tyndall, Huxley, and other investigators; despite the findings of archeologists, philologists, and ethnologists denying the divine inspiration of the Bible; despite, even, the acceptance of the theory of evolution by liberal clergymen. But although the Bible long ago began to be treated as any other book, and was dissected and analyzed in the cold light of scientific inquiry, great numbers of Americans would have nothing to do with the inquirers or their inquiries. Thus, the late William Louis Poteat, for many years president of Wake Forest College, a Baptist institution in North Carolina, wrote of his student years at Wake Forest: *

"... *The Origin of Species* had been out eighteen years when my Bachelor's diploma was handed to me but I do not remember having heard of it. Certainly no reverberations of the fierce fight which evolution had fought and won disturbed our cloistral seclusion. With us religion was not challenging science. Science was not dragging religion into court to answer for its superstitions. There was no intellectual crisis."

Farther down in the scale of fundamentalism, we have the testimony of the great merchant, J. C. Penney. He is writing of the dismissal of his father from his pulpit in 1889: †

"My father," he says, "was a minister of the Primitive Baptists who did not believe in paying their ministers. To earn a living he ran a farm, bought, grazed, and sold cattle. I have seen him and my mother drive in nice weather, and in rough weather have seen him ride on horseback, Sunday after Sunday, year after year, to minister to his people. After all those years of devotion, I saw him read out of church on three counts: he believed in Sunday school; *he believed in educating the ministers* [author's emphasis]; and he believed that ministers should be paid. For his open stand on these tenets he was barred from the church."

How deeply fundamentalism was rooted in America is shown by the fact that while the catalog lists no books critical of the Bible, nonetheless, in the decade before 1905, evolution had seemed to become respectable in many quarters which might be expected to influence rural and small-town America.

* W. L. Poteat in *The American Scholar*, Summer, 1936.
† J. C. Penney, *An Autobiography as Told to Robert W. Bruère*, pp. 4-5.

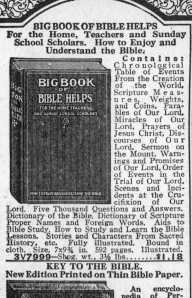

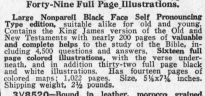

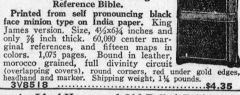
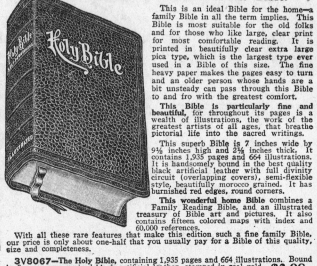

Hand Bibles With Self Pronouncing Text.

No. 3C10150 **Self pronouncing, imitation roan,** red edges, round corners, 6 maps. Minion, 24mo. Price 39c
If by mail, postage extra, 8 cents.

No. 3C10152 **Self pronouncing,** Assyrian levant, divinity circuit, overlapping edges, round corners, red under gold, 6 maps. Minion, 24mo. Price 69c
If by mail, postage extra, 8 cents.

No. 3C10156 **Self pronouncing.** Persian morocco, divinity circuit, overlapping edges, red under gold, 6 maps, silk head bands and marker. Minion, 24mo. Price 95c
If by mail, postage extra, 8 cents.

No. 3C10160 **Gift Bible.** Imitation ivory, gold, silver and illuminated floral sprays, round corners, full gilt, leather backs, gilt edge, rims and clasp. Minion. Retail price, $1.15. Our price....(If by mail, postage extra, 8c).....59c

No. 3C10164 **Large type, self pronouncing text Bibles for old folks, containing six maps without references or teachers' helps. Imitation roan,** limp, red edges, round corners, embossed bands, large clear long primer type. Size, 4⅝x7⅛ inches. Price 69c
If by mail, postage extra, 14 cents.

No. 3C10168 **French morocco,** limp, gold edges, round corners, six maps. Size, 4⅝x7⅛ inches. Long primer. Price 98c
If by mail, postage extra, 14 cents.

Large Type Bible for Old Folks.

Small Pica.

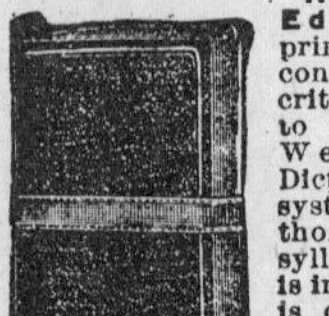

New Self Pronouncing Edition. Very clearly printed. Size, 5½x8½ inches, contains 17 maps, with diacritical markings, according to the latest revision of Webster's International Dictionary. To make the system of pronouncing as thorough as possible, every syllable of the proper name is indicated and every vowel is diacritically marked. Printed from large bold type on especially prepared Bible paper. Size, 6x9 inches.

No. 3C10176 **Imitation roan,** red edges, round corners, embossed bands. Contains family record, etc. Price 79c

No. 3C10180 **Morocco,** limp, gilt edges, round corners, silk head band and marker. Contains family record, etc. Price.....$1.15

No. 3C10184 **Persian levant,** divinity circuit, overlapping edges, round corners, red under gold edges, silk head band and marker, extra grained lining. Price...$1.55
If by mail, postage extra, each, 24 cents.

Testaments.

No. 3C10198 **Bound in linen cloth.** Limp, cut flush, sprinkled edges. Size, 3⅛x5⅛ inches. Retail price, 15 cents. Our price 5c
If by mail, postage extra, 3c.

No. 3C10199 **Bound in leatherette.** Cut flush, round corners, red edges. Size, 2⅞x3⅞ inches. Retail price, 25 cents.
Our price............10c
If by mail, postage extra, 4c.

No. 3C11000 **French seal.** Limp, round corners, red under gold edges. Ruby, 48mo. Size, 2⅜x4 inches. Retail price, 40 cents. Our price............18c
If by mail, postage extra, 3 cents.

No. 3C11004 Same style Testament as No. 3C11000, but with Book of Psalms. Size, 2⅜x4 inches. Price............30c
If by mail, postage extra, 3 cents.

No. 3C11008 **French morocco.** Improved divinity circuit, round corners; red under gold edges. Size, 2¾x4¼ inches. Retail price, 60 cents. Our price............32c
If by mail, postage extra, 3 cents.

No. 3C11010 Same style Testament as No. 3C11008, but with Book of Psalms. Size, 2¾x4¼ inches. Price............40c
If by mail, postage extra, 3 cents.

Largest Type Self Pronouncing Old Folks' New Testament Published.

No. 3C11036 **Imitation roan,** limp, red edges, round corners, embossed bands. Size, 5⅛x7⅛ inches.
Price............39c
Postage extra, 10 cents.

No. 3C11038 Same style as No. 3C11036, but with the Book of Psalms. Size, 5⅛x7⅛ inches.
Price............55c
Postage extra, 11 cents.

No. 3C11040 **Morocco,** limp, gold edges, round corners. Size, 5⅛x7⅛ inches. Price............69c
Postage extra, 10 cents.

Red Letter Testaments.

This beautiful edition of the New Testament is printed in red and black inks. The portions in red being the words uttered by our Saviour while on earth. Beautifully printed on extra quality of thin Bible paper. Handsomely bound. Illustrated with five multi-colored plates. Size, 3¾x4⅞ inches.

No. 3C11060 **Imitation roan,** round corners, gold edges and gold lettering on the side. Price............47c

No. 3C11064 **Leather,** limp, red and gold edges, round corners, gold lettering on side, silk marker. A soft and pliable binding. Price. 64c

No. 3C11068 **Genuine morocco,** soft and flexible, divinity circuit, over lapping edges, round corners, red and gold edges. Price...78c
If by mail, postage extra, any style, 3 cents.

Christian Workers' Testaments.

This testament is marked in red on every subject connected with the theme of Salvation. No Testament has ever been prepared to compare with it in usefulness. Size, 3⅛x5 inches.

No. 3C11072 **Red Russia cloth,** round corners, gilt edges. Retail price, 70 cents.
Our price............47c

No. 3C11076 **Morocco limp,** round corners, red under gold edges. Retail price, $1.00.
Our price............64c

No. 3C11079 **Morocco,** divinity circuit, overlapping edges, round corners. Retail price, $1.25. Our price............78c
If by mail, postage extra, any style, 4 cents.

Dictionary of the Bible.

New Workers' Edition, by Wm. Smith, LL. D.

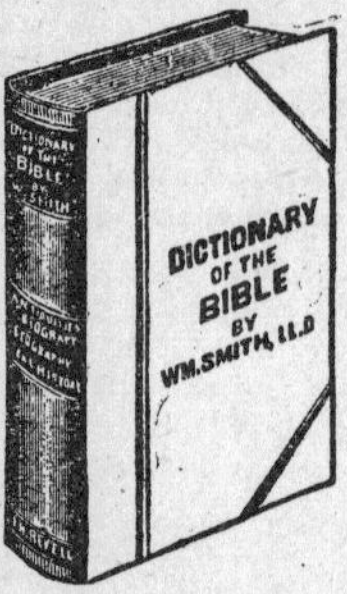

A complete guide to pronunciation and significations of scriptural names; the solution of difficulties of interpretation, authority and harmony. Also a history of and description of Biblical customs, manners, events, places, persons, animals, plants, minerals, etc. Contains over 500 engravings. Cloth. Size, 6⅛x9 inches. Retail price, $1.00.

No. 3C32154
Our price............65c
By mail, postage extra, 25 cents.

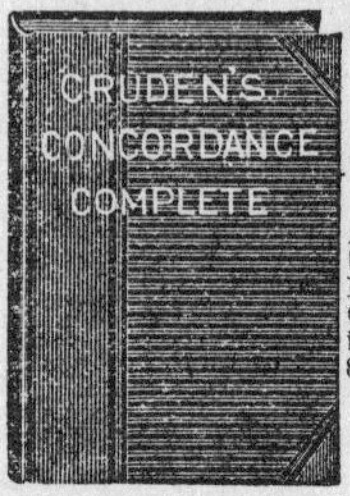

Complete Concordance to the Holy Scriptures.

By Alexander Cruden. A dictionary and alphabetical index to the Bible. New edition. Cloth. Size, 6⅝x9⅜ inches. Retail price $1.00.

No. 3C92237
Our price............65c
If by mail, postage extra, 14 cents.

Episcopal Prayer Books and Hymnals in Sets.

Prayer Books according to the standard. The Hymnals revised and enlarged. Prayers with hymnal. Printed on superior thin white paper. Minion, 48mo. Size, 2⅞x4 inches.

No. 3C11140 **Morocco grain cloth,** enameled cross or I. H. S., square corners, red edges. Retail price, $1.00.
Our price............65c

No. 3C11144 **French morocco,** limp, blind frame, blind cross, round corners, gilt edges. Retail price $1.50. Our price......98c

No. 3C11146 **Venetian morocco,** limp, round, corners red under gold edges. Retail price, $1.75. Our price............$1.35

No. 3C11150 **Seal grain,** limp, gilt cross, round corners, red under gilt edges, gold roll. Retail price, $1.75. Our price............$1.35

No. 3C11152 **French morocco,** limp, gilt I. H. S., blind blocked and gilt continuous border, round corners, red under gold edges. Retail price, $2.00. Our price............$1.60

No. 3C11160 **Persian calf,** limp, round corners, red under gold edges. Illustrated with 12 gravures. Retail price, $2.25.
Our price............$1.80
If by mail, postage extra, any style, 10 cents.

Child's Catholic Prayer Book.

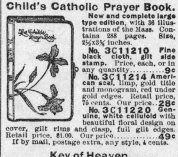

New and complete large type edition, with 36 illustrations of the Mass. Contains 288 pages. Size, 2½x3⅝ inches.

No. 3C11210 **Fine black cloth, gilt side stamp.** Price, each, or in any quantity............9c

No. 3C11214 **American seal,** limp, gold title and monogram, red under gold edges. Retail price, 75 cents. Our price...28c

No. 3C11220 **Genuine, white celluloid** with beautiful floral design on cover, gilt rims and clasp, full gilt edges. Retail price, $1.00. Our price............49c
If by mail, postage extra, any style, 4 cents.

Key of Heaven.

With Epistles and Gospels. 48mo. Size, 2½x3¾ inches. 575 Pages.

No. 3C11242 **Persian calf,** leather padded, gold cross bands, with beautiful parchment picture of St. Anthony and prayer to this great saint, printed in gold inside of both front and back covers, red under gold edges. Retail price, $1.75.
Our price............79c

No. 3C11246 **Pure, white celluloid cover,** beautifully decorated in pearl and gold, celluloid clasp, full gold edges. Retail price, $1.50. Our price............69c

No. 3C11250 **Persian calf,** leather padded, gold crown of thorns on side, beautiful pearl cross and indulgence prayer inside of front cover, red under gold edges. Retail price, $1.75.
Our price............86c
If by mail, postage extra, any style, 6 cents.

FAMILY BIBLES.

SUCH VALUES IN BIBLES WERE NEVER OFFERED BEFORE.

These are really beautiful works, the kind that are usually sold only through agents, and then at double our prices.

Our Leader in Family Bibles.

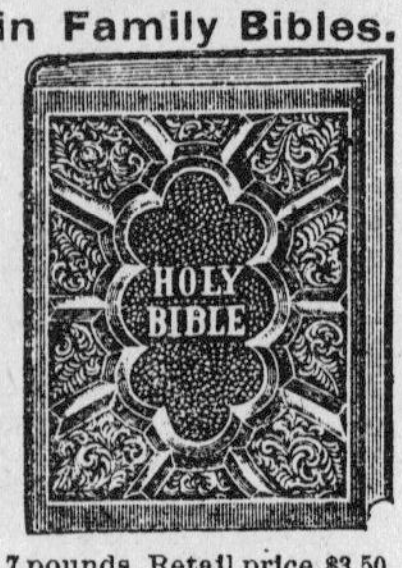

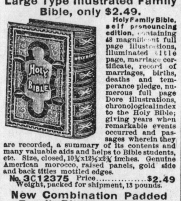

Size, 10x12⅛x3 inches. Contains Old and New Testaments, King James' Text, origin and history of the books of the Bible, pronouncing dictionary of proper names, department of references, with maps and illustrations, marriage certificate and record, temperance pledge and triumphal entry, new Lord's Prayer, etc. Weight, packed for shipment, 7 pounds. Retail price, $3.50,

No. 3C12360 **Imitation leather,** back and side titles stamped in gold, marbled edges.
Price............80c

No. 3C12362 Same style and contents as No. 3C12360, but with full gold edges.
Price............98c

No. 3C12364 Same style and contents as No. 3C12360, but bound in **genuine leather,** with full gold edges. Retail price, $5.00.
Our price............$1.65

Large Type Illustrated Family Bible, only $2.49.

Holy Family Bible, self pronouncing edition, containing 48 magnificent full page illustrations, illuminated title page, marriage certificate, record of marriages, births, deaths and temperance pledge, numerous full page Dore illustrations, chronological index to the Holy Bible; giving years when remarkable events occurred and passages wherein they are recorded, a summary of its contents and many valuable aids and helps to Bible students, etc. Size, closed, 10⅜x12⅛x2⅞ inches. Genuine American morocco, raised panels, gold side and back titles mottled edges.

No. 3C12375 Price............$2.49
Weight, packed for shipment, 13 pounds.

New Combination Padded Family Bible, only $2.79.

Self pronouncing edition, contains illuminated title page, family record of births, marriages and deaths, thousands of halftone and other illustrations. The text is conformable to that of the Universities of Oxford and Cambridge, with a complete concordance of the Psalms of David in meter. This Bible shows also in simple form all changes, additions and omissions made by the revisers of the Old and New Testaments, arranged in parallel columns, etc., enabling the reader to see at a glance wherein the two versions differ. Size, 10x12⅛x2⅛ inches. Genuine padded leather, gold sides and back title, full gold edges.

No. 3C12378 Price............$2.79
Weight, packed for shipment, 13 pounds.

Self Pronouncing Combination Family Bible, $3.69.

New illustrated edition, containing two colored and 24 full page Dore engravings, history of the books of the Bible illustrated with 48 full page engravings, complete concordance of the Holy Scripture, Psalms of David in meter, Chronological index to the Holy Bible, complete history of the Bible with a summary of its contents and many valuable aids and helps to Bible students, illuminated marriage certificate, family record, etc. Size, 9x12x2⅛ inches. American calf, padded sides, round corners, gold title on side and back, full gold edges.

No. 3C12382 Price............$3.69

Family Bible, only $3.89.

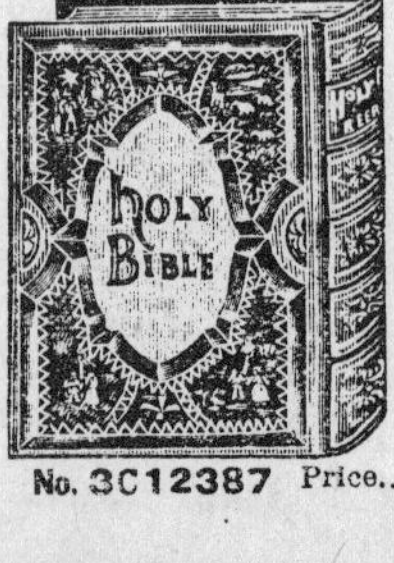

An entirely new Bible, containing all changes, additions and omissions made by the revisers of the Old and New Testaments, and enables readers to see at a glance wherein the two versions differ. This Bible contains in addition to the combination text the following features: Marginal references, many multi-colored plates, including presentation plates, ten colored parable plates, ten commandments and Lord's prayer, family record, family temperance pledge, etc., scenes and incidents in the life of Christ, Proverbs of Solomon, St. Paul's Journeys, Hoffman gallery of original New Testament illustrations, printed in colors with descriptions. Cruden's Complete Concordance, 4,000 questions and answers on the Old and New Testaments, etc. American morocco, calf finish, raised panel sides, embossed in gold with gold edges. Size, 10⅛x12⅛x4 inches.

No. 3C12387 Price............$3.89

A Superb Self Pronouncing Family Bible, only $4.87.

This Family Bible contains the authorized and revised versions of both the Old and New Testaments; arranged in parallel columns, line for line marginal references; marriage certificate and family record; history of the books of the Bible; the ten commandments and our Lord's Prayer, illuminated; a gallery of seventy-two scriptural illustrations and descriptions of the Israelites' Tabernacle; Life of our Lord and Saviour; cities and towns of the Bible; colored maps of Palestine; Ancient and Modern Jerusalem. French morocco, padded sides, round corners, fancy side stamped, full gold edges. Size, 9⅛x12⅛x3⅝ inches.

No. 3C12392 Price $4.87

$12.00 Family Bible only $4.89

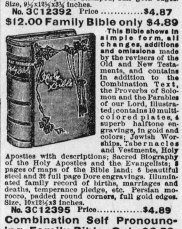

This Bible shows in simple form, all changes, additions and omissions made by the revisers of the Old and New Testaments, and contains in addition to the Combination Text, the Proverbs of Solomon and the Parables of our Lord, illustrated; contains 10 multi-colored plates, 4 superb halftone engravings, in gold and colors; Jewish Worships, Tabernacles and Vestments, Holy Apostles with descriptions; Sacred Biography of the Holy Apostles and the Evangelists; 8 pages of maps of the Bible land; 6 beautiful steel and 32 full page Dore engravings. Illuminated family record of births, marriages and deaths, temperance pledge, etc. Persian morocco, padded round corners, full gold edges. Size, 10x12⅛x3 inches.

No. 3C12395 Price............$4.89

Combination Self Pronouncing Family Bible, Only $6.59.

Magnificent Family Bible, containing illustrated presentation page; parable and ten commandments in colors; marriage certificate; family record of births and deaths; colored temperance pledge; scenes and incidents in the life of Christ; Proverbs of Solomon; path of Jesus; Grecian, Persian and Roman empires; Hoffman's gallery of original New Testament illustrations; Cruden's Complete Concordance and his life. Beautifully bound in genuine Turkey morocco; title stamped on back and side in gold; full gold edges. Size, 10x12⅛x3⅝ inches.

No. 3C12403 Price............$6.59

Holy Catholic Family Bibles.

Holy Catholic Bible, approved by His Eminence, Cardinal Gibbons. Contains the entire canonical scriptures according to the decree of the Council of Trent, translated from the Latin Vulgate, diligently compared with the Hebrew, Greek and other editions of divers languages. Contains also a complete history of the books of the Bible, an illustrated and comprehensive Bible Dictionary; the parables of our Lord and Saviour Jesus Christ, illuminated; life of the blessed Virgin Mary; the stations of the Holy Way of the Cross; portraits of supreme pontiffs, archbishops and bishops; new illustrated plates of the tabernacle, etc. Gallery of full page illustrations by Dore. Weight, packed for shipment, 8 pounds. Retail price, $6.00. Size, 10⅛x12⅛ inches.

No. 3C12412 **American morocco,** crushed paneled sides, combed (mottled) edges.
Our price............$3.65

No. 3C12414 **American morocco,** raised paneled sides, marbled edges. Size, 10⅛x12⅛ inches. Weight, packed for shipment, 11 pounds. Retail price, $9.00. Our price.$4.48

No. 3C12416 **Extra fine imported morocco,** raised paneled sides, full gold edges Size, 10⅛x12⅛ inches. Weight, packed for shipment 14 pounds. Retail price, $15.00.
Our price............$5.98

As early as 1893, the New York Chautauqua had permitted Henry Drummond to lecture on evolution and, inasmuch as his audiences were largely composed of nonurban church-goers, *The Nation* jumped to the conclusion that times were changing:

> Professor Henry Drummond's lectures on Chautauqua are the clearest index yet seen in this country of the silent but sweeping change wrought in the religious world by the teachings of science. . . . Professor Drummond expounding a pretty thorough-going evolution at Chautauqua is a striking phenomenon. . . . Those who flock to the lectures . . . are typical representatives of the church people, to whom, a generation ago, evolution was synonymous with atheism. . . . When therefore Chautauqua managers provide lectures in defense of evolution . . . and audiences . . . hear them with much pious edification and strengthening in their faith, it is a sign of the times. . . .

Little could *The Nation* foresee the antievolution-teaching statutes of later years in America or the Scopes trial in Tennessee in 1925.

Throughout the latter years of the nineteenth century, the struggle between fundamentalists and liberals in religion continued, with, if the catalog is a criterion, little success for the liberals.

In 1897, for example, the influential Dr. Lyman Abbott gave a series of lectures on the Bible as literature—a startling concept at the time—and said in one of them that he did not believe in the truth of the Biblical story of Jonah and the whale. Whereupon came a deluge of sermons from preachers all over the country defending the truth of the story, and much earnest worry on the part of the pious who respected the piety and learning of Dr. Abbott.

Two years later, Rudyard Kipling, who had been living in Vermont and enjoyed an enormous American fame, let loose a fearful blast in his *American Notes*. He wrote:

> Sunday . . . I found a place officially described as a church. It was a circus really . . . fitted up with plush and

stained oak and much luxury. . . . To a congregation of savages a man entered . . . completely in the confidence of their God, whom he treated colloquially and exploited. . . . With a voice of silver and with imagery borrowed from the auction room, he built up for his hearers a heaven on the lines of the Palmer House (but with all the gilding real gold, and all the plate glass diamond) and set in the center of it a loud voiced argumentative and very shrewd creature that he called God. . . .

He was giving them a deity whom they could comprehend, in a gold and jewel heaven. . . .

It was all very well for a high-brow city magazine—*The Nation*—to think that the theory of evolution was being accepted by the people and that times were changing; it was quite all right for a New York divine, Dr. Abbott, to deny the undoubted fact that Jonah was swallowed by the whale, and scoffers, such as Rudyard Kipling, could scorn the church. But at the same time, the people had powerful champions for their beliefs.

There were the great evangelists Moody and Sankey, and, starting in 1895, the famous Billy Sunday who converted more than one hundred thousand people to the true faith in ten years and saved their backsliding souls from the torments of hell. An ex-baseball player, he used the language of the diamond and the streets in snatching souls from perdition; a sound economist, he organized a stock company to finance his revivals and, excelling many more earthy enterprises, generally repaid his stockholders. Billy Sunday "proved" the truth of every word in the Bible in sermons such as this:

"The Devil ain't anybody's fool. Lots of people will tell you there ain't any devil. . . . People who say that—and especially the sneaking, time-serving, hypocritical ministers who say that—are liars! Liars! Liars! They are calling the Holy Bible a lie! I'll believe the Bible before I believe Old Mother Eddy, and a lot of time-serving, tea-drinking, societified, smirking ministers! No, sir! You take God's word for it. There is a devil.

"The devil says to the Saviour: 'Son of God, hey? Are you

the man that's been going up and down the country passing as the Son of God? I'm not as easy as all that. I'm from Missouri. You've got to *show* me! Make good! Turn some of these stones into bread and get a square meal! Produce the goods!' "

American life is perhaps inexplicable if the evangelistic strain that runs through it is omitted from consideration; many of the catalog's books and the attitudes they exemplify are likewise inexplicable save in terms of evangelism. The lengthened shadow of the great and the obscure evangelists lingers upon the land; the orgiastic religionism of the Western and Southern pioneers is still practiced in many parts of the country; everywhere it lies below the surface of the souls of the people capable of being evoked and brought to the top, in times of national stress, by the sonorous voices of eloquent preachers, whether lay, gospel, or political. This accounts in part for the sudden and sometimes cataclysmic changes of the national mood; from mild sunshine in morning to howling tornado by night. It throws some light upon the reason why Americans—as contradistinguished from Europeans—are more easily moved by moral outrage inflicted upon helpless nations or minorities than they are by their coldly logical national interests. Woe unto that foreign power which seeks to interpret the trend of American international policy without taking deeply into consideration the strain of evangelism that surges in the blood of millions of Americans.

Great evangelists such as Moody, Sankey, Torrey, Billy Sunday, Sam Jones, and Gypsy Smith went up and down the land, in the nineties and at the turn of the century, preaching the oldtime religion to multitudes, drawing great numbers up the sawdust trail to repentance and renunciation however short-lived, and winning for themselves national fame. It is not surprising, therefore, that the catalog, which catered to the very people or the friends of the people who were hitting the trail, treated their susceptibilities tenderly, and listed no books about the Bible which might offend them.

It does offer, for example, a life of Christ. But it is not Renan's. It is by Canon Farrar whose "exact scholarship is shown in his valuable notes at the foot of nearly every page, and a large number of fine, truthful engravings make this the best Life of Christ ever written. . . ."

The catalog is conscious of the bleak boredom that affected youngsters after they had attended church in the morning, eaten a heavy meal at noon, and then had nothing to anticipate for the remainder of the day except more Bible reading. It does not offer them for release what was then called a "French novel" or other earthly diversion, but a book whose purpose it frankly says is "to furnish entertainment and instruction for the young people during the long Sabbath afternoons." This sugar-coated morsel—almost profane reading—was *From Eden to Calvary, Or, Through the Bible in a Year,* by Grandpa Reuben Prescott.

After church services, adults, who wanted to sharpen their vision of the delights of heaven that they would someday encounter, peered through chinks in the pearly gates opened for them by the Right Reverend Samuel Fallows, D. D., in *The Home Beyond, Or, View of Heaven,* or dipped into a book written by D. L. Moody, the great evangelist, which contained "several hundred interesting stories about his wonderful works in Europe and America." Such volumes as these were, however, mere spiritual hors d'oeuvres to the genuinely devout When they wanted something substantial upon which to feed their hungry, heaven-yearning souls, they bought forty pounds of Matthew Henry's *Works* (for $7.75), because "Bible students appreciate the unfading freshness, the spiritual force, the quaint humor, and the evangelical richness of Matthew Henry's Exposition of the Old and New Testaments."

The catalog's books—those that it included and those that it omitted—thus accurately reflected the religious mind of rural America in 1905. Twenty years later, as we shall see, the struggle to keep that mind innocent of knowledge was actually to increase in some parts of the country.

He Fell in Love with His Wife

In America, generally speaking, men have been left to

themselves in their choice of reading, except for the attempts of the Comstocks and other censors who sought to save them from the devil. But there have always been shoals of guides to tell children and women what they should read, and the struggle between the readers and their self-appointed mentors is a fascinating chapter of the American mind.

By 1905, however, fiction although decried in the past, had become the best seller after the Bible, and the catalog lists hundreds of novels demanded by its nation-wide audience. This transition was not achieved without a struggle.

In the 1860's, *Godey's Lady's Book* printed an editorial: "On Novel-Reading for Women." "This rage," it said, "for novel-reading pervades our country as well as England. A friend of the *Lady's Book* has just sent us a letter that we give here in place of the words of warning we had intended to write. . . ."

LETTER TO THE EDITRESS:

Will you, dear madam, say something to your young readers on the unhealthy appetite for imaginative literature which increases every day? It is a morbid and exclusive taste for fiction which has nothing to recommend it but its trivial want of the nature of truth . . . the mind is frittered away, and all strength of reasoning and seriousness of reflection gradually deserts the unfortunate student, whose appreciation of the best writers cease, and among authors, *who peppers the highest is sure to please.*

The *Lady's Book* recommended the works of Dr. Cummings for "those who wish to find a worthy literary souvenir for a Christian lady, (old or young) which shall have an impressive interest for the present and be a rich addition to the family library. Let them select from the volumes of Dr. Cummings' works:

The Great Tribulation: or Things Coming on the Earth
The Great Preparation: or Redemption Drawing Nigh
Teach Us To Pray

"These books are wonderful productions, and breathe the pure spirit of Faith, Hope, and Charity."

Perhaps they did, but the ladies persisted in reading novels in which kissing was described as clasping, seducing as beguiling, and the body as a frame. Noting then that they would read novels and neglect Dr. Cummings, the guides sought to steer them toward the more innocuous novels which did not contain a single reference to sex in a carload, and the *Lady's Book* prepared a "list of books for girls who need tales that cheer but do not inebriate."

None of this satisfied the ladies. They did not care about Faith, Hope, and Charity. They wanted books about love, whether it was wedded love or bedded love. And they got them. By the turn of the century, reading, like so many other pursuits, had been turned into an instrument for the broadening of women's minds. *Vogue,* at that time more a family magazine and less a fashion publication than it is today, regretted that women should be fed romantic tales as a preparation for marriage. It said sternly: "Marriage is not elysium or a haven. It is a career fraught with anxiety and responsibility. Out of all the commotion (that is, struggle for women's rights) will come a higher ideal of matrimony, a better appreciation of its grave responsibilities, along with which for the old-time master-and-servant relation between husbands and wives, will be substituted one of equality and reciprocal authority."

In 1900, *Vogue* was roused to fury. A college professor addressing an assemblage of women said that the only romantic love which men are capable of feeling for women is the variety known as sex attraction. This so profoundly agitated the good ladies that they were shaken to the depths of their corsets. But, says *Vogue,* "The fact that women and girls are to be found who fly into a passion over such a statement merely indicates how persistently women accept the conventions in which they are bred without attempting the slightest study of them. . . . If instead of making a foolish exhibition of themselves, these indignant wives or maidens had accepted the professor's contention as a spur to the scientific study of sex, they would have acquired a knowledge of certain facts, which would have taken the heart out of their opposition, and saved them the contempt of the well informed. . . . Coddling illusions of any kind is a silly, nay, a discreditable habit for an adult woman in this country today, when everywhere there is vital work crying out for doers. . . . There is nothing more needful than that scientific fact should replace sentimentality. . . . The phenomena that cluster about sex ought to be among the very first subjects selected for study. . . . Ladies, to books!"

What books? While *Vogue* was urging ladies to read books that might teach them the facts of biology, it was warning them in strong terms not to read the novels and plays of the great realists such as Ibsen, Zola, and Hardy, who were the forerunners of the vast flood of realism that was to swamp the reading public in the twentieth century. These, for example, were what not even the advanced *Vogue* could stomach although it had twenty years to adjust its digestion, to stronger meat. Ibsen's *A Doll's House* was first published in 1879. The institution of marriage is smothering Nora's soul and the only way she can regain her life is to desert her husband and children. He says: "Before all you are a wife and mother." Nora replies: "That I no longer believe. I think before all else I am a human being, or at least I will try to become one."

If this was too strong meat for *Vogue,* then Ibsen's next play, *Ghosts,* was poison. Mrs. Alving leaves her husband when she finds that he has long lived, and is still living, a dissolute life. Her pastor persuades her that law, order, and decency must be upheld by her return. Of this Ibsen speaks scornfully: "That perpetual law and order, that does all the mischief in the world."

Shaw, too, was beyond the pale. He was advocating the specialized breeding of a race of supermen lest democracy destroy us, because the race cannot rise above the material of which voters are made. Marriage delayed the coming of the superman since the best advantages of breeding may be obtained from persons who would not be suitable companions for life. For example: an English squire and an intellectual Jewess. "Thus," says Shaw, "the son of a robust, cheerful ... British squire, with the tastes and range of his class, and of a clever, imaginative, intellectual, highly civilized Jewess might be superior to both his parents but it is not likely that the Jewess would find the squire an interesting companion; or his habits, his friends, his place and mode of life congenial to her."

In *Man and Superman,* Tanner says to Ann: "What we have both done this afternoon is to renounce happiness, renounce tranquillity, above all to renounce the romantic possibilities of an unknown future, for the cares of a household and a family." Shaw adds: "Woman has to repudiate duty altogether," and Samuel Butler chimes in with the all-inclusive mournful cry: "What efforts have not been made to hold together that artificial collection called the family."

In France, Émile Zola wrote a shelf of realistic novels which shocked the fancy-ribbon readers of the world, while in his *The Natural Social History of a Family Under the Second Empire,* he depicts family life as degenerate and undesirable. So strong was the current of realism that swept around the earth that even the romantic, flamboyant literature of the South was torn from its magnolia-tree moorings. Elizabeth Waltz's *Ancient Landmark,* for example, denies that divorce is the greatest disgrace that can come to a Kentucky family. It ridicules the idea that a woman should remain married to a man even if he abuses her, stays drunk, and indulges in promiscuous sexual relations.

Despite all this, *Vogue* editorializes: "All decent people are agreed that the emancipated novelists are not fit reading for the youth of either sex. ... One deplorable effect of the cancerous literature of Ibsen, Zola and other realistic schools of writing is that by unduly emphasizing the baser qualities of the race it develops in the reader a suspicious contempt for humanity."

And it is evidence of the confusion of values in the age of transition and revaluation of values that, while *Vogue* could recommend the scientific study of sex and yet decry the reading of great realists of the novel, it could still publish short stories in which the heroine was described as follows:

"And then her name, Kitty! Could anything be more refreshing than a girl named Kitty? Especially when she was quite as frisky and graceful and fun-loving and tricky, and as altogether entertaining as that same little puff-ball which the name implies."

Is it any wonder, consequently, if such confusions and contradictions existed in the editorial sanctum of a magazine like *Vogue* designed for the upper-class families of the cities, that in the small towns and on the farms, remote from the intellectual currents that were sweeping the world, there should have been little change in the reading habits of the people since the Civil War? The thunderings of European writers on sex, marriage, and the family, the typhoon of literature of protest against the past that blew from the English Channel to the Black Sea, the diminutive storms that passed across America, were almost unheard in the vast stretches of the hinterland. Nowhere in the catalog of 1905 does one find books that reflect the violence of the struggle elsewhere.

Almost the only break with the past was the listing of a large amount of fiction, and a parallel with the present in that then, as now, the "best" novel was likely to be the last novel off the press. Consequently, we find the "best fiction of the day at prices that have no competition. The list given below does not pretend to be a complete record of all the new fiction published, but includes only the more popular and best selling books of the last six months."

Beverly of Graustark	By George Barr McCutcheon
Call of the Wild	By Jack London
The Clansman	By Thomas Dixon
God's Good Man	By Marie Corelli
Lady Rose's Daughter	By Mrs. Humphrey Ward
The Prodigal Son	By Hall Caine

Rebecca of Sunny Brook	
Farm	By Kate D. Wiggins
Sir Mortimer	By Mary Johnston
The Virginian	By Owen Wister

E. P. Roe was in such great demand in 1905 that his contributions to the art of the novel were brought out as "The Works of E. P. Roe in a new uniform edition, at 63¢ a volume." Among his masterpieces were:

He Fell in Love With His Wife
Near to Nature's Heart
Success With Small Fruits
A Young Girl's Wooing
What Can She Do Without a Home?

Augusta J. Evans was a novelist whose popularity remained undiminished for fifty years. The catalog does not exaggerate when it says of her: "The author's genius and fascinating style are as fresh today in her later books as they were in her earlier, which after thirty-six years of constant use still hold their popularity." Mrs. Evans enriched her times, if not posterity, with such novels as:

Speckled Bird
At the Mercy of Tiberius
Vashti
Infelice
Beulah

Pure Authors Write Pure Books

Sir Walter Scott continued to hold, in 1905, the place that he had held for more than half a century in the esteem of American readers. His popularity flowed not only from the fact that he was an expert storyteller, but also because his novels were regarded as being "pure, wholesome, and inspiring," and the author himself one who led a life of noble rectitude. The touchstone, in fact, to popular success in literature over large stretches of America was not the content of a writer's books but the content of his life. If the author drank alcohol in any form, smoked opium, beat his wife, or lived outside the holy bonds of wedlock, then, although he may have been a Shakespeare, a Balzac, and a Dostoevski rolled into one, he and his works were beyond the pale of respectable readers.

This point of view was beautifully expressed in *What Shall I Read: A Confidential Chat on Books,* by J.H.V., published in New York in 1878.

Although this guide appeared nearly thirty years before the publication of the 1905 catalog, its attitudes toward books were substantially reaffirmed by the catalog and continued to dominate it for many years.

"Never read the books of any novelist," says J.H.V., "till you have acquainted yourself with his reputation. The names of some authors are as sure indication of evil as the skull and cross bones with which druggists used to mark their bottles of poison. . . . If you familiarize yourself with the names of good authors you will not make any great mistake. . . ."

Scott was on the approved list. "But I think I am safe in saying that the works of Sir Walter Scott may be read by young and old. It is fair to judge an author *in some degree* by his life and private feelings. A Christian gentleman can scarcely write what is not good. . . . A man who felt and acted sincerely all his life, and died peacefully trusting in his Saviour, can scarcely have been anything but a pure writer. His novels are useful historically, but I will tell you frankly that the first fifty pages are usually dull."

Thackeray, while not entirely pure, also received the approval of J.H.V. "William M. Thackeray," he says, "is another pure writer, although I do not recommend his earliest books to the very young. But *Pendennis, Vanity Fair* . . . are books which may be read with pleasure and profit by all.

" 'What!' some one may say, 'Does not Thackeray tell how a young man fell in love with an actress? How a young woman made her way in the world by her sharp wits, which were not always exercised in the right way? . . .'

" 'Yes! He does all this.'

" 'Then how can you recommend him as a pure writer?'

" 'O, my dear reader, never take a shallow view of a good man's work!'

"Thackeray was gifted by his Maker with a wonderfully clear eye. He saw human nature as it exists every day. . . . He makes a young country boy (Pendennis) fall in love with an actress. Is that a startling fact? Read the book, and see how pure and true it is! In Pendennis we see the career of a young man . . . his temptations, his struggles, his weakness, and his strength. We see purity, mother love, and wise, kind influences, producing their legitimate result. . . . Readers will see the practical working of the fact which they have had dinned into their ears, that to be virtuous is to be happy."

Ouida, a popular novelist of the times, was on the index both of J.H.V. and the catalog. "Her novels," we are told, "are seen frequently in the hands of many a young girl who should blush to be seen reading them. *I unhesitatingly condemn them.*"

The Roosevelt family agreed with J.H.V. on this score. In his *Autobiography,* Theodore Roosevelt wrote:

"I was forbidden to read the only one of Ouida's two books which I wished to read—*Under Two Flags.* I did read it, nevertheless, with greedy and fierce hope of coming on something unhealthy; but as a matter of fact all the parts that might have seemed unhealthy to an older person made no impression on me whatsoever. . . ."

"The Ladies' Home Journal" a Mentor of Reading

J.H.V. wrote in 1878. Twelve years later *The Ladies' Home Journal* laid down criteria that govern the making of a "good book." They constitute a formula by which thousands of books have been written and read in America, and, although enunciated over forty years ago, still influence much of the book and magazine fiction of our times. In 1890, this family magazine said:

What Is A Good Book?

A good book is one that interests you.

One in which the bright rather than the dark side of life is shown.

One that makes you see how mean are the small vices of life and how despicable are the great sins.

One that glorifies virtue in women and honor in man.

One in which the good are rewarded and the wicked are made to suffer. . . .

One which convinces you that the world is filled with good men and women.

One that makes you feel you are meeting real people, people who elevate your thoughts as you associate with them.

A good book is one that you remember with pleasure, that when the dull hours come you can think of with interest and feel that there are people with whom you have a most interesting acquaintance, who are yet only characters of the imagination.

A good book is the one that we want when weary of the people of the world; that we can read out aloud and discuss, that we can hand to our daughters that it may give them pleasure; and which will only be a stepping stone on the road of taste, not only to better and nobler books, but a better and nobler life.

That is a good book—and, my friends, there are hundreds of them.

Virginity and Marriage

Thus, a good book was one written by a pure writer who filled it with noble thoughts. All good books were subject to the iron law that girls must be virgins before marriage and eternally faithful to their husbands after marriage.

At the turn of the century, James Lane Allen's *Summer in Arcady* (first published in 1896) was immensely popular and was recommended in current editorials for reading by young girls. It attracted a great deal of attention and was considered daring, but daring in a wholesome manner, and well may it have been, for it was an excellent and detailed description of how to arouse a man and keep him happy though unsatisfied. Men are regarded as savage and dangerous creatures who must be outwitted and beaten at their own game by young girls, who, if triumphant, would then lead them captive to the altar. This is a point of view, of course, that still survives in much of the magazine fiction of our time: the seducing male turned into the adoring husband by a good woman, with detailed descriptions of trials and titillations en route from the porch swing to the church altar.

The novels of this period—again like much present-day magazine fiction—while containing an ironclad moral, were lush with sensuality and descriptions of what might not be done. As long as the writer prefixed a warm passage with a warning that this is what the young girl should avoid, she could indulge up to the very point where her virginity was in jeopardy and must then retreat.

The hero of *Summer in Arcady* was called Hilary. The heroine is Daphne. This is a description of her:

> She had not reached eighteen, and she was like the red-ripe rose of early summer just where of late were white blossoms. A glance at her lithe round figure, the unusual development of which always attracted secret attention and caused her secret pain, could have made many a mother reflect upon the cruel haste with which Nature sometimes forces a child into maturity and then adds to the peril of its life by covering it with an alluring beauty.

This is Hilary:

> A heavy-limbed, heavy built, handsome young fellow of about 19, with a yellowish mustache just fairly out on a full red lip that had long been impatient for it. . . .

His lip's impatience was doubtless increased sharply for, just at this moment, Hilary sees Daphne pass and "to his gross instinct anything in the shape of a woman was worth gazing after, even at long range—especially a woman alone."

As Daphne passes throughly Hilary's fields, he stops her and kisses her. "There passed through her mind like a scorching flash the remembrance of what she had heard about his ways with girls, and the color began to leave her face. She could not even say, 'how dare you!' He had dared so often already. . . ."

Daphne naturally gets indignant about Hilary's treatment of her, but she finally forgives him and agrees to meet him secretly in the woods because her family does not approve of him. But she, poor thing, "did not dream that she might be crossing the invisible boundary between mortal light and darkness, or that she was advancing gaily toward those wastes of life over which women wander lost and die damned. If she could have known of the countless company of her sisters who have taken their first step toward the central tragedy of the world by doing what she now did—going to the first secret meeting with the men they have loved—if there could have flitted before her the vast pageant of painted butterflies of her race, painted and torn and weary, and drooping all at last into the same foul mire—she might well have recoiled and tottered homeward an old woman, wrinkled with horror, her dark braids turned to snow."

Daphne, however, does not run away immediately. Cruel nature grips her. She is ignorant of the mortal peril in which she stands. But not for long. Suddenly our hero "draws her toward him, unable to resist her beauty. 'Hilary! Hilary!' she cried, resisting him with sudden terror of his advances, his rough tenderness, the torrent of his feelings. Then with one awful thought, and the strength it gave her, she struggled out of his arms to her feet and stood supporting herself with one hand against the tree. . . . Her face seemed cut from marble, and her eyes were full of fright and distress."

Finally, Daphne gets the point and runs home, but Hilary who was not one to be put off lightly, manages to see her again. He is in a bad fix because "Nature had been having her way with him as with an animal," and he tells Daphne he wants to speak to her parents right away about marrying her. She won't let him because they don't like Hilary and have threatened to send her away to a finishing school if she so

much as glimpses his beautiful mustache. She agrees finally
to meet him again beneath the sycamores if he promises to
behave, but when they are once more under the trees that old
tempter, nature, pops up and the author interrupts his story
to read a lecture.

"The young trust themselves alone with Nature who cares
only for life and nothing for the higher things that make life
worth living." Hilary, who doesn't know anything of this,
kisses Daphne again and she breaks down in tears.

Whereupon our hero, for whom things are going nowhere
fast, tells Daphne that she must elope with him now or else
he will punish her by not seeing her again.

" 'Marry me now!' he cried for the last time and without
warning. She stood bending slightly toward him, looking beyond him into the future if she yielded. She saw the unfor-
giveness of her father and mother . . . the uncertainty of getting the marriage ceremony performed that night, and the
necessity of her being left alone with him in a strange place.
To this last thought was linked a new fear of herself and of
him . . . for Nature had stolen treacherously nigh unto them
both, as is her sad wont with her human children. And with
this fear now came again the old torturing doubts of him.
He was no longer even, a member of the church, and to her
mind this was the last thing that made her fear he would
not do what was right."

Daphne was in a desperate position, alone in the woods
with nature and a pagan. Would she ever emerge *vergo in-
tacta*? This is how she went about emerging.

" 'Promise me if I go with you Hilary,' she said very rapidly and incoherently. . . . 'Here on your knees,' she said
shaken by her sobs, 'give me your solemn oath, Hilary, before God who sees us and will judge us for what we do—that
whatever we are together, whatever may happen to us, you
will be *true* to me . . . *true* to me . . . *true* to me. . . .' "

No matter how bad a man may be, there is something in
him that will respond to the tears of a pure woman. And
Hilary responded.

" 'I swear,' he said, his eyes filling. 'God helping me I will be true to you.' "

God having got Daphne out of a jam, she and Hilary elope, get married, and go to a hotel.

"It was all over now—the life of peril and unrest from which they had barely escaped—with its tossing nights and wistful heartsore days, its ungovernable yearnings.

"The hour had come to him when, of all that can ever come to a man . . . he is overwhelmed with some sense of the awful gift that love has brought into his unworthy life,—a pure woman."

Summer in Arcady was recommended as a frank, serious book of great value to young girls, but as it never calls a spade anything like a shovel, it is difficult to see how an ignorant young girl of the proper purity of mind could have understood what it was all about. It seems, however, to teach several lessons. (1) That if you went into the woods alone with a young man and did not let him kiss you, he would eventually propose marriage, but if you did let him kiss you, you were courting "a fate worse than death." (2) That if a girl lost her virginity, she was damned, but she was nevertheless supposed to lead a man on innocently and then at the dangerous moment repulse him. (3) That if a man married a virgin, his whole life would be changed for the better, and uplifted. (4) That girls were not supposed to have any physical desires before marriage and were to be terrified at the evidences of these desires in men. (5) That even in marriage, good women had no sexual desires but merely submitted to the embraces of their husbands as a wifely duty. (6) That nature and natural instincts are always to be deplored.

Mr. Allen dedicated his book "To My Mother."

What Price Virginity and Marriage?

While James Lane Allen's book was being praised by critics as a moral tract for the young, there had appeared shortly before an English novel by Grant Allen called *The British Barbarians: a Hill-top Novel.* The English Allen did not see eye to eye with the American Allen and was condemned on both sides of the ocean. His book was considered blasphemous and immoral and it was carefully kept from young girls, but it enjoyed a certain fashionable popularity since it questioned all the convictions that governed social behavior at the time. Its phraseology seems stilted and ridiculous to this generation, but it was novels like these that caused women to challenge the current mores and to begin to change their points of view toward love.

"What do I mean by a Hill-top Novel?" asks Mr. Allen in his introduction. "Well, of late we have been flooded with stories of evil tendencies; a Hill-top Novel is one which raises a protest in favor of purity. . . ."

The hero of this book is Bertram Ingledew who suddenly and mysteriously appears in the respectable English suburb of Brackenhurst. Naturally he is tall, handsome, and charming. The heroine—a married woman!—is Freda Monteith, wife of Robert Monteith, a dour Scotsman. "She was tall and dark, a beautiful woman. . . . Her eyes were large and lustrous, her lips not too thin but rich and tempting. Her features were clear-cut, rather delicate than regular."

Bertram, who seems to have large means, takes expensive lodgings and announces that he has come to study the taboos of England. He will not say where his own country is. Everyone is annoyed and tells him there are no taboos in England, but he points them out. Sunday, he says, is a taboo. The ownership of land, the sheltering of girls before marriage, and even marriage itself are taboos. This wild talk incenses Robert Monteith and he orders Freda never to see Bertram again.

She, however, goes to his lodgings to tell him good-by but breaks down and confesses that she loves him. Bertram, not to be outdone, says he loves Freda and, since it is wrong for her to stay with her husband, urges her to go away with him. He tells her that the whole of society is ridiculous in its taboos and restrictions.

" 'Oh, Freda, you can't imagine what things—for I know they hide them from you—cruelties of lust and neglect and shame such as you couldn't even dream of; women dying of foul disease in want and dirt deliberately forced upon them by the will of your society; destined beforehand for death ... a death more disgusting than aught you can conceive of—in order that the rest of you may be safely tabooed, each a maid intact for the man who weds her. It's the hatefullest taboo of all the hateful taboos I've seen in my wanderings, the unworthiest of a pure and moral community.' "

He begs Freda to remain with him. She asks him if this would be right, and he replies:

" 'Why Freda, it's right, of course, to go. The thing that's wrong is to stop with that man one minute longer than is absolutely necessary. You don't love him. You never loved him. Or if you ever did, you've long since ceased to do so. Well then it's dishonour to yourself to spend one more day with him. How can you submit to the hateful endearments of a man you don't love or care for? How wrong to yourself, how infinitely more wrong to your still unborn and unbegotten children? ... Nature has given us this divine instinct of love within to tell us with what persons we should spontaneously unite; will you fly in her face and unite with a man whom you feel and know to be unworthy of you? ... Remember, every night you pass under that creature's roof, you commit the vilest crime a woman can commit against her own purity.' "

Freda likes Bertram's ideas and she goes off with him, taking her children along, and they have "four days of happiness."

"She had gone away with Bertram exactly as Bertram himself desired her to do, without one thought of anything on earth except to fulfil the higher law of her own nature; and she was happy in her intercourse with the one man who could understand it, the one man who had worked it to its fullest pitch, and could make it resound sympathetically to his touch in every chord and every fibre. . . ."

Robert, the husband, who is not quite so advanced as Freda, the wife, doesn't see things in the same light. He takes his horse pistol and, surprising the lovers on the moor, flourishes the weapon and threatens Bertram. The brave radical pushes aside the frantic Freda, bares his breast, and is shot by Robert. But no blood can be seen on the wound. Instead "a strange perfume as of violets or of burning incense began by degrees to flood the moor around them." Bertram's voice comes from a great distance saying:

" 'Your husband willed it, Freda, and the customs of your nation. You can come to me but I can never return to you. . . . I forgot with what manner of savages I still had to deal. And now I must go back to the place whence I came—to the *twenty-fifth century.'*

"The voice died away in the dim recesses of the future. The pale blue flame flickered forward and vanished. The shadowy shape melted through an endless vista of tomorrows."

After this startling evaporation of her lover's body, Freda, repulsing her husband's efforts at reconciliation, stalks over the moor, pistol in hand, presumably to shoot herself and join Bertram.

Mr. Allen put his hero too far ahead in the future—the twenty-fifth century—but, however preposterous his novel was, it was read openly or secretly, and illustrates the new ideas that were beginning to nibble at the structure of social ethics and taboos at the turn of the century. (We shall see how the catalog's books, too, were ultimately affected.) His point of view was that (1) a handful of women and girls should not be kept virgins at the expense of an army of prostitutes; (2) women who did not marry should not be condemned to a lifetime of chastity; (3) marriage should be an act of love and not of profit; (4) sex was not to be subdued but heeded; (5) the only sexual sin was to live with one you did not love, with the collateral provision that no one had a legal right of possession of any other person; (6) men were not dangerous creatures from whom girls should shrink but natural parts of their lives, and (7) sex was not something for women to endure but to enjoy.

These attitudes were shining new when Mr. Allen expounded them with such lyric deliriousness, and even he would have been astonished by the rapidity with which they passed into common practice. By 1930, his once radical ideas had become almost staid conventions of both living and fiction, so that it is interesting to speculate on the state of society when Bertram Ingledew returns once more to earth from his twenty-fifth-century retreat.

The Catalog Remains Pure

The battle of conflicting points of view about chastity and marriage and sexual relations is nowhere reflected directly in the 1905 catalog's book section. It offered its readers "the works of standard authors" such as Shakespeare, Oliver Optic, Hugo, Kipling, Robert Louis Stevenson, Washington Irving, and Henty. The disturbing and doubtless immoral Thomas Hardy is absent, along with the wicked English boys of the days of *The Yellow Book,* the infamous Russians, the decadent French, and the vicious Viennese and Germans. GILT TOP LIBRARY BOOKS AT 19 CENTS included such chaste favorites as:

Aunt Diana
Bill Nye's *Sparks*
Black Beauty
Bracebridge Hall
Mrs. Browning's *Poems*
Robert Browning's *Poems*
Bryant's *Poetical Works*
Buffalo Bill
The Cloister and the Hearth
Daily Food For Christians
Drummond's *Addresses*
Idle Thoughts Of An Idle Fellow
Ivanhoe
Little Minister
Prince of the House of David
She Fell in Love with her Husband
Single Heart and Double Face
An Unwilling Bride

Won by Waiting
The Workingman's Wife

Mark Twain Not a Humorist

Although Mark Twain had been practicing the art of letters for many years before 1905, and had achieved fame both at home and abroad as a humorist, he was not represented among the humorists of the catalog. The only reference to him is in a volume called *Hot Stuff,* "A Collection of Witty Writings by Mark Twain, Eli Perkins, Josh Billings, Bill Nye, Alexander Sweet, Bret Harte, De Witt Talmage, and nearly fifty others. Humor, wit, pathos, satire and ridicule, repartee, bulls and blunders, clerical wit and humor, lawyer's wit and humor, anecdotes of great men, puns and conundrums, riddles, puzzles, etc."

The catalog honors another humorist, however, by the inclusion in its pages of Bill Nye's *Remarks*—"the author's greatest and best book." It then adds a devastatingly anticlimactic sentence of appraisal: "It is one that will live for weeks after other books have passed away."

The age-old dislike of country folk for city folk, and their suspicion of the ways of urban dwellers, is pandered to in several volumes. The first is *Jack Henderson Down East,* a book which must have given the farmer-reader much pleasure because it describes the difficulties of the city slicker caught in his own trap; or, more specifically, of the Chicago slicker caught in the toils of the more wily boys of bigger New York.

It was "a story told in a series of letters of a Chicago rounder, who takes a trip down East to burn some money, and incidentally to have a little sport. What he butts into in his travels, is told in his own peculiar style and it loses nothing in the telling. His being cooped up in a Pullman car is laughable."

The second is *Shams, or Uncle Ben's Experience With Hypocrites.* It glorifies the virtues of farmers as contrasted with the vices of city folk. "All who have crossed a farm or halted in front of a country school house, will enjoy its reading. Uncle Ben's trip to the city of Chicago and to California, and his amusing experiences with the shams and sharpers of the metropolitan world."

The third book which employed the same material and used the same sales appeal is *Samantha at Saratoga*. Here the country girl goes among the smart set and brings them down a peg or two. "The funniest book of all. Written amid the whirl of fashion at Saratoga. Take-off on fashion, flirtations, low-neck dresses, dudes, pug dogs, the water craze, toboggans, etc., in the author's inimitable, mirth-provoking style. The 100 illustrations by Opper are 'just killing!' "

Sexology

In 1905, judging from the popular literature and social conventions of the times, one might have come to the conclusion that the rapid growth of the population proceeded not from the unholy contact of vile bodies, but out of pure parthenogenesis. American censorship and American prudery made the circulation and reading of any book difficult for the masses unless it was "wholesome," and the attitude of the country toward realistic literature was still that of Tennyson in "Locksley Hall Sixty Years After":

Authors—atheist, essayist, novelist, realist, rhymaster, play your part,
Paint the mortal shame of nature with the living hues of Art.
Rip your brothers' vices open, strip your own foul passions bare;
Down with Reticence, down with Reverence—forward—naked—let them stare.
Feed the budding rose of boyhood with the drainage of your sewer;
Send the drain into the fountain, lest the stream should issue pure.
Set the maiden fancies wallowing in the troughs of Zolaism,—
Forward, forward, ay and backward, downward too into the abysm.

But there was a large group of books—many of them are listed in the catalog—about sex and its manifestations which escaped the ban because they purported to be "scientific" and at the same time dealt with the question in a "pure" manner.

These books, dragging in God, the Bible, and purity, are obviously the reverse of scientific. They were written and bought primarily for their appeal to the puritan mind as pornography. Pornography indeed of a particularly scabrous kind and dirtier than the writings of jakes on lavatory walls; sootier than the laughter of yokels at a burlesque show; filthier than the talk of boys in a livery stable, because throughout these volumes the voice is allegedly the voice of God, but the tone is the tone of fornication.

Consider, for example, *Science of Life,* by Professor Fowler. "This work treats of Sexual Science, which is simply that great code of natural laws by which the Almighty requires the sexes to be governed in their natural relations. A knowledge of these laws is of the highest importance. It is pure, elevating in tone, eloquent in its denunciation of vice."

And, it may be added, highly piquant. Such a description is as alluring to the prudish American mind as the conventional chandelier of bronze cherubim above the bed of a French demimondaine is to the French mind.

The catalog's Wedekind, contributing a mail-order *Frühlings erwachen,* was Alice B. Stockham. Her *Creative Life* was a medical guide for adolescent girls. This is how she treats that often terrifying and sometimes tragic period of transition from girlhood to womanhood. "Gives high ideals, the knowledge of which leads to a purity of life and thought. It will be a blessing to many in guiding aright the first conscious recognition of the sexual instinct. The author wisely teaches that this impulse should be trained, and directed as a sacred trust, to conserve personal health and morals for service in the world."

In many Moslem countries, a male physician may not attend a woman in childbirth because to do so is to look upon a woman's body plain, the woman of another man. This attitude in highly diluted form has also existed in America, and there was a time when women were too refined to consult even their physicians about sexual matters if the consultation could possibly be avoided. Consequently, the catalog offers two volumes which modest ladies might consult in the privacy of their homes without the necessity of baring their minds or their bodies to vulgar probers of abdomens or mentalities. One was: *What All Married and Those Contemplating Marriage Ought to Know.* "It tells in a matter of fact, easily understood way, the thousand and one questions that occur to the minds of both young and old, but about which they feel a delicacy in consulting their physician."

But,.strangely enough, one book in Sears' shelf of sexology stands out from all the rest. It is a book—whatever its content—of immense importance to the student of the American mind, because the catalog's description tells us in pointed language precisely what was the country's attitude toward sex at the beginning of this century. This daring volume, by an anonymous, mail-order Ellen Key, was *Karezza, or The Ethics of Marriage.* Of it the catalog says: *"She* [the author] *controverts the prevailing idea of baseness and degradation associated with the sexual nature."* [Author's italics.]

Edward Bok—Maxim Gorky—Grover Cleveland

A glance at the world outside the catalog will prove how closely the catalog's books reflected the American mind of 1905.

In 1906, at the suggestion of Lyman Abbott, Edward Bok, the editor of *The Ladies' Home Journal,* began a rather guarded discussion of venereal diseases in his family magazine, with the result that he was overwhelmed with protests from virtuous readers and thousands of subscribers canceled their subscriptions. Bok tells how he "saw his own friends tear the offending pages out of the periodical before it was allowed to find a place on their home tables."

At the same time, the same magazine conducted a court of love in its columns with "A Lady From Philadelphia" as its conductor in the role of Margaret of Navarre. These are typical questions and answers from the column:

> Myrtle: A man has kissed you whom you greatly admire, and you wish to know whether you are in duty

bound to forfeit his friendship in order to maintain your self-respect. No, but you will not risk losing his friendship if you resent familiarity. You may always forgive him you know—on condition that he does not repeat the offense. . . .

Sadie: What to do "When a man persists in holding your hand in spite of all you can say?" No man, who is fit to be welcomed in your home, would refuse to release your hand if you asked him as if you meant it. Indeed it is not at all proper for a man to kiss you good-bye upon seeing you home after an entertainment unless you are engaged to him.

So, too, in *The Ladies' Home Journal* for 1905, there appeared an article by Grover Cleveland, ex-President of the United States. The headline tells the story: "I Am Persuaded that There Are Women's Clubs Whose Objects and Intents are Not Only Harmful, but Harmful in a Way that Directly Menaces the Integrity of our Homes."

Women, in Mr. Cleveland's opinion, should stay in the home. The fact that many women could not find a home does not concern him. "I believe it should be boldly declared," said Mr. Cleveland with a flash of his old fire, "that the best and safest club for a woman to patronize is her home. . . . I would have our wives and mothers . . . happy and contented in following the Divinely appointed paths of true womanhood, though all others may grope in the darkness of their own devices."

The final, and concluding, incident of this period is the visit of Maxim Gorky to the United States in 1906. He and Madame Gorky were given a warm welcome on arrival and the great Russian writer was soon to be the guest of honor at a dinner to be attended by Mark Twain, William Dean Howells, and other famous figures in the American world of literature and politics. But hardly had the Russian couple settled down in their rooms in the Hotel Belleclaire in New York before they were ejected because "the revolutionist was unable to satisfy the proprietor that the mother of Gorky's two children, who is still in Russia, had been divorced and that his present companion is his legal wife."

The Gorkys, it seems, were a menace to the sanctity of the American home, and were hounded from hotel to hotel and forced to deposit their luggage for safekeeping in the unopinionated luggage room of the Grand Central Terminal. Finally, the couple found asylum in the home of a friend on Staten Island. The dinner to Gorky was canceled and Mark Twain gave the following statement to the newspapers:

"Gorky came to this country to lend the influence of his great name—and it is great in the things he has written—to the work of raising funds to carry on the revolution in Russia. By these disclosures he is disabled. It is unfortunate. . . . He is in a measure shorn of his strength. Such things as have been published relate to a condition that might be forgivable in Russia, but which offends against the customs in this country. I would not say that his usefulness has been destroyed but his efficiency as a persuader is certainly destroyed. Every country has its laws of conduct and its customs, and those who visit a country other than their own must expect to conform to the customs of that country."

Here we see Mark Twain applying the criterion of personal "purity" to the person of a revolutionist and writer. He did not even take the trouble to ascertain whether or not the hypocritical charges against Gorky were true. It was enough for America's most distinguished man of letters that the charges had been made.

All over the United States, in newspapers and literary publications and in private conversations, the Gorky scandal was heatedly discussed with what H. G. Wells called "imbecile lying." Finally—God shall we say?—ended the scandal. Shortly after it began came the San Francisco earthquake. The newspapers, the moralists, the good women, and the outraged writers such as Mark Twain turned to doing charity.

Culture and Success by Mail

In a series of "self-teaching" books, the catalog preached

the doctrine that a man could become the master of many languages and the expert practitioner of many trades through a few easy lessons at home. Thus, one could easily make the smooth transition from the language of hog calling to the language of Molière; from drilling with a broom to a commission in the army; from daubing fences with a brush to wagon and carriage painting.

This, of course, is an old American story. The pathetic fallacy that men can grow rich and cultured by reading this or that book was an ancient hoax long before the catalog of 1905 appeared. So-called "how" books are still best sellers whether they are *How to Win Friends and Influence People* or *How to Dance Like Fred Astaire in Six Easy Lessons*. The only difference between our period and the period of 1905 is that the present sales talks are couched in other terms and the cultures and professions are those that appeal to the modern taste, but essentially the argument and the fallacy remain unchanged. Among Sears' self-teaching books were:

Bookkeeping Self Taught
French Without a Master in Six Easy Lessons
Three Roads to a Commission in the United States Army
Carriage and Wagon Painting
A Guide to Successful Auctioneering
Modern Quadrille Book and Complete Dancing Master
First Steps in Photography
Modern Penmanship
One Hundred Lessons in Business

Books for Little Folks

The catalog's list of children's books stresses the fact that those offered will not cloud the purity of the child's mind and will inculcate moral lessons valuable in afterlife. Leading all others are the FAMOUS ELSIE BOOKS FOR GIRLS. "Beautiful books of a high moral order." If the child reader's eyesight lasted, she could journey with Elsie not only from Elsie's girlhood to motherhood, but also from her own childhood to middle age, because Elsie's creator was highly prolific and shook a new volume out of her kimono sleeve every few months.

Let us look at the contents of these "beautiful books of a high moral order." They are revelatory of parent-child relationships in the United States in the latter half of the nineteenth century and the pre-World War part of the twentieth, and of much else besides.

Elsie is unjustly scolded by her teacher over some trifle and "She [Elsie] laid down the geography, and opening her desk, she took out a small pocket Bible, which bore the marks of frequent use. She turned over the leaves as though seeking for some particular passage, and at length she found it and wiping away the blinding tears, she read these words in a low, murmuring tone:

" 'For this is thankworthy, if a man for conscience toward God endure grief, suffering wrongfully. For what glory is it if, when ye be buffeted for your faults, ye shall take it patiently? but if when ye do well, and suffer for it ye take it patiently, this is acceptable with God. For even hereunto were ye called; because Christ also suffered for us, leaving us an example that ye should follow his steps.'

" 'Oh! I have not done it. I did not take it patiently. I am afraid I am not following in his steps,' she cried bursting into an agony of tears."

And then later on.

" 'O mammy, mammy! I've been such a wicked girl today! Oh! I'm afraid I shall never be good. Never be like Jesus. I'm afraid that he is angry with me, for I have disobeyed him today.' "

In another scene, a carriage in which Elsie and Lora are riding is dragged by runaway horses. Elsie is not afraid and afterward Lora says to her:

" 'Oh Elsie! I can't help thinking all the time, what if we had been killed! Where would we all be now? Where would *I* have been? I believe *you* would have gone straight to heaven, Elsie; but *I*—oh! I should have been with the rich man the minister read about this morning, lifting up my eyes in torment.' " (The author of the Elsie books meant that Lora would have been in hell but she was too much the lady to use such language.)

Little Elsie was perhaps an extreme case, and she got on the nerves of her own family, but still the Elsie books were put in the hands of thousands of little girls as models for their behavior. The morbid religious atmosphere and the unwholesome concern with sin and one's afterlife, impressed upon the minds of the young, undoubtedly played their part in the preservation of religious fundamentalism in this country.

It was a long-standing doctrine of parent-child relationships in the United States that the child must render blind and unquestioning obedience to the parent, while the parent is under no obligation to explain anything to the child. This doctrine ran from early colonial days until relatively recently and is, of course, embodied in the Elsie books. Note the Connecticut Code of Laws of 1672:

> If any man have a stubborn or rebellious Son of sufficient understanding and years, viz. 16 years of age, which shall not obey the voice of his Father, or the voice of his Mother, and that when they have chastened him he will not hearken unto them; then may his Father or Mother, being his natural parents lay hold on him and bring him to magistrates assembled in court and testify unto them, that their Son is Stubborn and Rebellious and will not obey their voice and chastisement but lives in sundry notorious crimes, such son shall be put to death.

Thus, there was a time right here in the United States when a father had the power of life and death over his own son, and, although this power was later taken away, it is easy to see how the attitude of an implicit right to authority was firmly planted in the breast of American fathers. And there was the ever-potent Biblical backing for this authority. Not only the commandment to honor thy father and thy mother, but also, "Cursed be he that setteth light by his father and mother," and "The eye that mocketh at his father, the ravens of the valley shall pluck it out, and the young ravens shall eat it."

Elsie's father stood, therefore, upon firm ground in this scene:

" 'Through the meadow?' said Mr. Dinsmore, 'don't you go there again Elsie, unless I give you express permission.'

" 'Why papa?' she asked, looking up at him with some surprise.

" 'Because I forbid it,' he replied sternly; 'that is quite enough for you to know; all you have to do is obey, and you need never ask me why, when I give you an order.'

"Elsie's eyes filled, and a big tear rolled quickly down her cheek.

" 'I did not not mean to be naughty, papa,' she said, struggling to keep down a sob, 'and I will try never to ask why again.' "

Elsie and Love

Since normal sexual relations at the time of which we write were hidden behind a veil of secrecy and shame, children in many cases turned to the emotion of family affection as being uncomplicated by sex, but their natural physical feelings were in this way often perverted, and parental ties sometimes became abnormal in their strength and possessiveness. Elsie's overstressed love for her father appears in this passage:

"How to gain her father's love was the constant subject of her thoughts, and she tried in many ways to win his affection. She always yielded a ready and cheerful obedience to his commands, and strove to anticipate and fulfill all his wishes. But he seldom noticed her, unless to give a command or administer a rebuke. . . . Often Elsie would . . . rush away to her own room to weep and mourn in secret, and pray that her father might someday learn to love her."

In the Elsie books, father and daughter suffer excruciating pain when they are separated by daughter's marriage, yet, because the books had to end somehow and could end only in marriage, the pains must be suffered. This scene is from *Elsie on the Hudson:*

Chester saves Lucilla from a convict and is wounded for his heroism. Lucilla's father says:

" 'I am too grateful to refuse him anything he may ask even to the daughter who is so dear to me that I can scarcely bear the thought of resigning her to another.'

" 'Oh, father, how could I ever endure to be parted from you!' she cried, clinging more closely to him.

" 'Dear child,' he said, holding her close, 'We will make it a condition that you shall not be taken away any distance. And in any event, you are still too young to leave your father. You must remain single and live with me for at least a year or two longer.'

" 'Oh, I am so glad to hear that!' Lucilla said. . . ."

Then Chester proposes marriage.

" 'Will you be mine?' he asked imploringly.

" 'If papa consents and you will never take me far away from him.'

Papa: " 'I cannot give Lucilla entirely to you for a year or two more yet, but you can visit her every day if you like.'

"Captain Raymond did not at all enjoy the thought of even a partial giving up of his daughter to the care of another, but tried to forget that the time was coming when it must be done. . . ."

This was the literature upon which thousands of parents of children, who came of age between 1900 and 1914, were nourished. Is it any wonder that these children set the pendulum swinging so violently that it smashed the clock?

The Rollo Books for Boys

In 1905 the Rollo books for boys were extremely popular, and the adventures of the goody-goody hero were depicted in:

Rollo on the Atlantic
Rollo on the Rhine
Rollo in Naples
Rollo in Scotland

The Rollo books and Rollo, the good boy, were typical of the fiction and the textbooks of the times. Virtue, noble thoughts, obedience to parents, and exemplary conduct in all of the boy's relations were drilled into him in everything he read, with virtue always triumphant over vice. The late Clarence Darrow wrote amusingly of the instruction of his youth: *

If we scholars did not grow up to be exemplary men and women, it surely was not the fault of our teachers or our parents,—or of the school book publishers.

. . . Whether we were learning to read or write, studying grammar or composition, in whatever book we chanced to take, there was the moral precept plain on every page. . . . How these books were crammed with noble thoughts! In them every virtue was extolled and every vice condemned. . . .

I remember the story about the poor widow of Pine Cottage, in the winter, with her five ragged children hovering around the little table. Widows usually had large families then, and most of their boys were lame. This poor widow had at last reached the point where starvation faced her little brood. She had tasted no food for twenty-four hours. Her one small herring was roasting on the dying coals. The prospect was certainly very dark; but she had faith, and somehow felt that in the end she would come out all right. A knock is heard at the back door. A ragged stranger enters and asks for food; the poor widow looks at her five starving children, and then she gives the visitor the one last herring; he eats it, and lo and behold! the stranger is her long-lost son,—probably one that was left over from the time when she was a widow before. The long-lost son came in disguise to find out whether or not his mother really loved him. He was, in fact, rich; but he had borrowed the rags at the tavern, and had just arrived from India with a shipload of gold, which he at once divided among his mother and brothers and sisters. . . . How could any child fail to be generous after this?

* Clarence Darrow, *Farmington.*

—105—

For Want of a Shoe the Rider Is Lost

In 1905, the village blacksmith was no figment of Longfellow's imagination. There were millions of horses and mules in this country, and thousands of men who practiced the now almost lost art of blacksmithing. The blacksmith was then as essential to society as the automobile mechanic is now; his trade was one which offered relative economic security and continually drew upon young men to fill ranks depleted by age or accident. The local smithy supplied shop practice and Sears, theory. It is a measure of the amazing technological transformation of the United States within the past thirty years that a book such as *Practical Horseshoeing* seems almost as archaic to us as the language of Mandeville's *Bees*. This volume was:

"An invaluable treatise on the subject of the humane treatment of the horse, and the scientific treatment of the hoofs, by which the utility and endurance of this invaluable animal are increased two-fold."

Millions of today's children know nothing of wagons—the great instrument of our national expansion—except the milk wagons of the cities. Yet only a short time ago, wagons were indispensable to transport, to commerce, and to the farms. Behind the scenes a large group of men built, repaired, and kept them moving. For them, Sears offered *A Manual of Blacksmithing* by An Expert Blacksmith, whose terminology falls strangely upon ears accustomed to the jargon of automobile mechanics:

"The following subjects are fully treated: Forges and appliances, hand tools, drawing down and upsetting, bending and ring making, miscellaneous examples of forged work, cranks, model work and die forging, home made forges, etc."

How to Be Popular in the Parlor

Elocution, declamation, piano playing, card and coin tricks, mesmerism and hypnotism were once "accomplishments" required of all who would be popular in the parlor. The young man, or woman, who could not recite a poem or ballad, make a card disappear, or retrieve a coin from a glass of water, was a social leper. Through its books of recitations, entertainments, and tricks, Sears stood to the socially popular in the status of a combination gagman, librettist, and magician. In considering these volumes and their contents, it must be remembered that in 1905 people relied largely upon their own resources for entertaining themselves and one another: the job had not yet been delegated to or taken over by Mr. Ford, the NBC, and Metro-Goldwyn-Mayer.

One of the volumes of the times contains an illuminating preface which is an interesting critique of American manners; a plea for gaiety; an expression of rebellion against folded-hands dullness. It was called *The Art of Amusing, Being a Volume Intended To Amuse Everybody, Enabling All To Amuse Everybody Else. A Regular Encyclopaedia of Social Evening Entertainment.*

The preface says: "Perhaps one of the great faults of the American is, that he does not amuse himself enough, at least in a cheerful, innocent manner. We are never jolly. . . . All other nations, the French, the German, the Italians, and even the dull English, have their relaxation, their merry-making; but we—why, a political or prayer-meeting is about the most hilarious affair in which we indulge. . . .

"We should all be so much healthier, so much kinder, so much better Christians, if we would only amuse ourselves and each other a good deal more. We should get infinitely better work out of ourselves, and more of it, so that we should be richer into the bargain."

This preface plays upon two themes repeated over and over by Americans and by foreign visitors to America. (1) That Americans work too much and play too little. (2) That the object of amusement is not sheer joy but a preparation for more and better work.

Typical of the scoldings delivered here on this subject by foreigners is the little lecture of Herbert Spencer, the English sociologist-philosopher, in 1882 at a banquet given him in

New York by two hundred prominent men. He told his hosts that in America "life is too joyless. . . . Work has become your passion. The hair of Americans turns gray ten years earlier than in England. American health is being undermined by stress of business and high-pressure life. The American almost ignores what good the passing day offers him. . . ."

This in 1882—the horse-and-buggy era that we of this generation regard as Arcadian in its leisureliness and simplicity. What would Mr. Spencer have said if he had returned to New York in 1929?

The other theme of the preface, that the object of amusement is to make men healthier, wealthier, and enable them to do more work; is one that is repeated to this day. You do not, for example, play golf because you derive sensory pleasure from the warm sun or the green grass of the golf course or the stinging shower after the game. You play golf, or at least you say you play, because the game keeps you in good shape. Good shape for what? So that if you are an underwear manufacturer you may sell more rayon panties than your competitor, or—in other fields—more buttons, canned salmon, or fly swatters. At the same time—and this is just as important— you make "contacts" on the golf course with buyers of panties, buttons, and fly swatters. Amusement for amusement's sake is taboo.

Similarly, a vacation is valuable because it enables you to return to your desk and do a better job; fishing quiets the nerves; playing tennis makes you a keener competitor. This attitude, in turn, has broader applications. Loafing becomes decadent. Hence the terms of opprobrium: leisure class and the idle rich. The French who are a highly industrious people, with some claims to being civilized, work in order to retire and loaf. But no man can loaf with honor in this country unless he has achieved heart trouble or sixty years of age. The theory of a Southern poet that "it is better to sit under a mango tree and focus one's mind's eye north," is anathema to us. Even upon retiring, many an American, especially if he is rich, feels called upon to exert himself strenuously in doing good works for the lame, the halt, the blind, horses, or dogs. So, too, in the Orient a man may contemplate his navel for a lifetime and die a saint, but, although we have had tree sitters and marathon dancers by the thousands, we have yet to produce a single navel gazer.

Consider the field of the senses and the appetites. We no longer, it appears, even eat and drink for the sheer pleasure of eating and drinking. Thus, you do not eat an apple because you like the apple's taste. You do it because an apple a day keeps the doctor away. Raisins supply iron, spinach gives you sand for your gizzard, and orange juice is everything from an aphrodisiac to an antiseptic. Or travel. No American industrialist or banker ever goes to Paris merely to drink wine and look the girls over. Ah, no! When he takes the ship, it is announced that he has gone "to study conditions." Thus, in such a prosperous year as 1929, the Folies-Bergère and the peep shows of Paris were cluttered with amateur American sociologists and economists studying conditions.

The Boy Stood on the Burning Deck

The widespread clan of elocutionists and declamationists—the passionate troubadours of our 1905 parlors—needed no equipment for the practice of their art save a book of recitations, a few lessons, a good memory, and an audience. The best of them, like the members of the Russian ballet, began their golden flights in youth. Thereafter elocution persisted in their bones, and a superior practitioner could recite "The Face on the Barroom Floor" while sleepwalking. Little boys began early in school by reciting verses such as these:

> *You'd scarce expect one of my age*
> *To speak in public on the stage,*
> *But if I chance to fall below*
> *Demosthenes or Cicero*
> *Don't view me with a critic's eye*
> *But pass my imperfections by.*
> *Large streams from little fountains flow;*
> *Tall oaks from little acorns grow;*

And though I now am small and young,
Yet all great learned men, like me,
Once learned to read their A, B, C.

It may be true that every American boy yearns to become President of the United States. It may also be true that it's

The Teething Ring of American Orators

better to be right than to be President. But boys who recited in 1905 wanted neither to be President nor even to be right: they craved, instead, to be good.

Oh where's the town, go far go near,
That does not find a rival here,
Or where's the boy but three feet high
Who's made improvement more than I?
These thoughts inspire my youthful mind
To be the greatest of mankind;
Great, not like Caesar, stained with blood.
But, like Washington, great in good.

From the context of the one bit of verse, so far as is known, written by the late John D. Rockefeller, it is evident that he was a boy elocutionist filled with noble sentiments. He wrote:

I was early taught to work as well as play;
My life has been one long, happy holiday,
Full of life, full of play—
I dropped the worry on the way—
And God was good to me every day.

Mr. Rockefeller was a devout churchgoer and contributor of millions of dollars to the institution of his creed—the Baptist church. And because good children recited pious verses at school, in Sunday school, and in the parlor, it is not improbable that these lines once fell from the lips of the future founder of the Standard Oil Company:

> *In Adam's fall*
> *We sinnèd all.*
>
> *The Deluge drowned*
> *The earth around.*
>
> *As runs the glass*
> *Our life doth pass.*
>
> *Young Obiedias,*
> *David, Josias,*
> *All were pious.*
>
> *Zaccheus he*
> *Did climb a tree*
> *Our Lord to see.*

Recitations for adults were most successful when they were not only dramatic, enabling the recitalist to display the thousand facets of his art, but also taught a moral lesson. These qualities are perfectly combined in mercifully brief form in "The Captain's Daughter":

We were crowded in the cabin; not a soul would dare to sleep;
It was midnight on the waters, and a storm was on the deep.
'Tis a fearful thing in winter to be shattered by the blast,
And hear the rattling trumpet thunder "cut away the mast!"
So shuddering there in silence; for the stoutest held his breath,
While the angry sea was roaring, the breakers talked of death.
And as thus we sat in darkness, each one busy in his prayers,
"We are lost!" the captain shouted, staggering down the stairs.
But his little daughter whispered, as she took his icy hand,
"Isn't God upon the ocean, just the same as on the land?"
Then we kissed the little maiden, and we spoke in better cheer;
And anchored safe in harbor when the moon was shining clear.

Show Me Your Hand

Long before the Delphian oracle had built up an immense reputation throughout the Ancient World as the champion crystal reader of those times, men had attempted to read the future as it was revealed in the arrangements of the stars in the heavens or in the intestines of a fowl. Sears' customers in 1905 were responding, therefore, to an impulse almost as old as the race when they, too, attempted to peer into the future

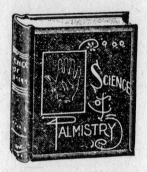

"I See a Tall, Dark, Handsome Man Coming into Your Life"

through the use of fortunetelling books, dream books, and playing cards.

Americans who pride themselves upon being a hard-boiled and skeptical people are, in fact, extremely superstitious. Fortunetellers flourish throughout the land; shopgirls seek their future in tea leaves at lunchtime, and it is not unusual to find New York Stock Market speculators consulting a lady astrologist or numerologist to ascertain whether the stars are propitious for going short of a block of General Motors common. And there are women in America who have made a pilgrimage to Freud, who read Proust and collect Picasso, and yet have their palms read by a Madame Zaza. Rural buyers, therefore, of such catalog volumes as *How to Tell Fortunes by Cards* were merely following in the native tradition.

Once you had learned how to tell fortunes by cards it then became necessary to buy the cards, and the finest were Mme. Le Normand's Gypsy Witch Fortune Telling Cards. This great woman who seems to have performed in her own person the remarkable feat of being at once French, gypsy, and witch, "prophesied to Napoleon I. his future greatness, and the downfall of many princes and great men of France." She seems, however, to have been unconscious of her own impending death, for "the author has left behind her such a

Madame Le Normand's Cards Predict Bryan Will Become President

reputation, the memory of so unusual a talent, that we believe we shall do a favor to the admirers of her system by publishing the cards which were found after her death."

What's Wrong with This Picture?

The French maintain that they and the Chinese are the only civilized peoples in the world, because both possess the two qualities the French consider indispensable to civilization: a cuisine and a code of etiquette. Whatever the deficiencies of our national cuisine, it is no fault of our publishers and writers if we have not achieved a superior etiquette, because each generation for more than a hundred and fifty years has had one or more Emily Posts. And the catalog, in its role of *chef de protocol* to the American people, yearly offers publications on etiquette.

In 1905, it presented two guides to conduct: *Manners: A Book of Etiquette and Social Customs,* and *Practical Etiquette: A Strictly Modern Book On Politeness.* . . . "Hints on politeness and good breeding, sensible talks about etiquette for home, visiting, parties, social intercourse, dress, etc."

Books on etiquette give a picture of the times in which they circulate. They are an invaluable aid to a study of the United States, for they reflect the current codes of behavior. At the same time they must be taken with a grain of salt, because their sternness of tone and frequent lamentations show that the evils they denounce are much in evidence. Throughout our history, rebels have been breaking down old standards of behavior and setting up new ones. The sin of yesterday becomes the custom of today; for example, women smoking or "making-up" in public.

A well-known Chesterfield of the 1880's was Professor G. A. Gaskell, teacher of penmanship and bookkeeping in New Jersey, who published a large volume entitled, *Compendium of Forms; Educational, Social, Legal, and Commercial.* Here the Professor suggests that if you write a letter of condolence write one that makes sense; do not offer vague and unattainable comfort. Thus, if your friend has lost one arm, congratulate him because he did not lose the other. The art of conversation will flourish if you avoid religious or political topics and the use of satire, and do not attempt to speak when your mouth is full.

If you are going on a honeymoon, it is well to buy the tickets in advance so that there will be no delay at the depot. The newlyweds will become better acquainted if friends do not accompany them on their wedding journey.

Professor Gaskell is not the first one to criticize American table manners, and he lays down certain rules of etiquette designed to make things move smoothly at dinner:

> Never carry food away from the table.
> Never smack the lips when eating.
> Never put your finger or your knife into your mouth.
> Never make drawings on the tablecloth.
> Never "ah" or "oh" when the dishes are uncovered and their contents are revealed.
> When fishing with ladies, gentlemen should bait the ladies' hook and remove the fish.

A comparison between old books of etiquette and a new one will illuminate some phases of social change in this country since the Civil War.

Query: Have women brains? If so, should they display them in the presence of men, or sit on them? In 1860, this is how *Miss Leslie's Behavior Book* answered these questions:

"Generally speaking," she said, "it is a mistake for ladies to attempt arguing with gentlemen on political or financial topics. All the information that a woman can possibly acquire or remember on these subjects is so small . . . that the discussion will not elevate them in the opinion of masculine minds. . . . Men are very intolerant towards women who are prone to contradiction and contention when the talk is out of their sphere; but very indulgent towards a modest and attentive listener who only asks questions for the sake of information. Men like to dispense knowledge, but few of them believe that in departments exclusively their own, they profit much by the suggestions of women. . . . Truth is, the female sex is really as inferior to the male in vigor of mind as in strength of body."

In other words, according to Miss Leslie, who seems to have known her way about despite her ladylike manner, the way to get your man is to let him do all the talking. A woman who listens with adoring eyes and closed mouth will be regarded by the male talker as both fascinating and intelligent. Has this attitude changed since she wrote seventy-five years ago?

Let us listen to advice given debutantes by Miss Alice Leone Moats in *No Nice Girl Swears* (1933):

"She [the debutante] needn't make an effort to appear brilliant—brains are a handicap to the debutante, all she has to do is to look vastly interested and amused at everything her neighbor says and keep up a steady flow of adjectives when he pauses for breath."

Query: Should a gentleman drink anything more than a glass of champagne in the presence of a lady? Should he get drunk while with her? Should a lady ever be caught even dead with a man who was not of irreproachable character and conduct?

The answer to all these questions in all the etiquette books from 1860 to 1918 is a flat: *no!* But, in 1933, Miss Moats says:

"When your mothers came out, learning to handle a drunk was not an essential part of a debutante's education. Now every girl has to be capable not only of shifting for herself, but, more often than not, of looking out for her escort as well."

Query: Is the reputation for being a flirt one "to be dreaded by young ladies?" Yes, say the older etiquette books.

And in 1933? Yes, says Miss Moats. "Anyone will admit that in the long run a reputation for being a heavy necker doesn't really add to a girl's popularity. . . . But after all, this whole business is a very personal problem and one that you can scarcely expect someone else to work out for you."

Query: May a girl go anywhere without a chaperon? An etiquette book of 1900 answers the question and tells a story by way of pointing the moral:

"No girl willingly owns that she has been fifty yards from her own door after dark without a chaperon. A chaperon often averts great embarrassment. One night, at a theatre, in a box, were seated two very youthful maids and two older men. The play developed suddenly into an unspeakable situation. The two girls sat crimson, the men were squirming in their chairs. It seemed the lesser of two evils to sit still and be as inconspicuous as possible. A maturer woman would have given the signal for the party to leave the box quietly."

The hard facts of living, the realities of the struggle for existence changed all this for millions of women. Ever since the Civil War, women had been going into industry and commerce; earning their own keep. Economically dependent on no man and far removed from the status of the sheltered women discussed in the etiquette books, they disregarded both man and the books in their conduct. They came and went as they pleased, with or without a man, and certainly without a chaperon. Eventually American women came to enjoy more freedom from this point of view than any other women in the world, and for the bachelor girl with her apartment new books such as *Live Alone and Like It* were written. Working girls actually led girls of social position and wealth down the road to this freedom, and chaperonage now exists only in attenuated form for debutantes.

Query: When you write your current beau should you tell all? Not all, warn the older books. "Avoid all pretty sayings, compliments, or suggestions. Write just such a reply as you would be willing to have read in a room full of strangers."

1933 model (by Miss Moats): "When your latest beau goes to South America, don't try to out-Ethel Miss Dell. . . . If you can't restrain yourself, at least extract a promise from your correspondent that he will tear up the letters as soon as they are read."

Finally: May a woman pursue a man? Unthinkable, answer the lady mentors of the past.

But by 1928 even Emily Post broke down and made this damaging admission: "Catlike, she may do a little stalking."

Standard Library Sets

Sears' serious readers in 1905 bought good books which have long since disappeared from the catalog, just as the kind of men who read them have in general disappeared from

American rural and small-town life. They bought such books as Grote's *History of Greece*:

"New edition. Mr. Grote has illustrated and invested with an entirely new significance a portion of the past history of humanity. He has made great Greeks live again before us and has enabled us to realize Greek modes of thinking. Four volumes, $2.89."

Also listed were Gibbon's *The Decline and Fall of the Roman Empire,* five volumes, price $1.85; Prescott's *Conquest of Peru,* 65 cents; Macaulay's *Works,* five volumes, price per

They Read Books Like This on the Farm and in the Towns Before Colleges Took Over the People's Education

set, 65 cents; Green's *History of the English People,* four volumes, 98 cents, and volumes of Ruskin, Kipling, Stevenson, Shakespeare, Lyall, Dickens, and other "standard" authors, at exceedingly low prices.

The works of General Lew Wallace were incredibly popular—especially *Ben-Hur.* Their success made him rich, and

America Enjoyed Dickens Before It Had Been Overwhelmed by Prosperity. Reading Time: One Year and Three Months

Minister to Turkey. One wonders whether the Department of State had ever read the General's writing. For it was the strange fate of this chronicler of the suffering of Christians of the first centuries of the Christian era to be sent as Min-

Dynamo Tenders' Handbook.

By F. B. Badt. Containing instructions and rules required by practical men, as dynamo tenders, linemen, stationary engineers and operators of all kinds of electric plants. This is the best book of the kind in print. Cloth. Illustrated. Size, 3½x6 inches.

No. 3C34292 Price, 65c
If by mail, postage extra, 4c.

Electricity, Arithmetic of.

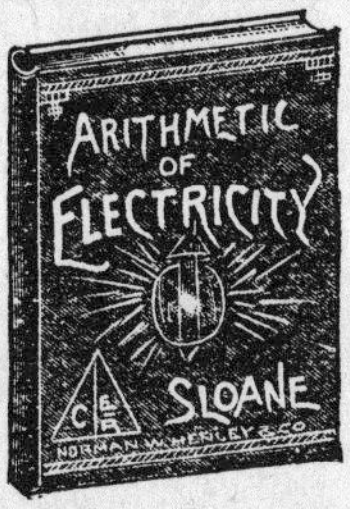

By T. O'Connor Sloane. The latest edition. A practical treatise on electrical calculations of all kinds reduced to a series of rules, all of the simplest forms and involving only ordinary arithmetic. The principal object of this work is to give a practical review of the mathematics of electricity within the scope of those who are not acquainted with algebra and higher mathematics. Illustrated. Cloth. Size, 5¼x7½ inches. Retail price, $1.00.

No. 3C34306 Our price 63c
If by mail, postage extra, 6 cents.

Electrical Experiments, Easy, and How to Make Them.

By L. P. Dickinson. Elementary handbook of lessons, experiments and inventions. Explains in simple and easily understood language everything about galvanometers, batteries, magnets, induction coils, motors, voltometers, dynamos, storage batteries, simple and practical telephones telegraph instruments, rheostat, condensers, electrophorous, resistance, electro plating, electric toy making, etc. Cloth. Illustrated. Size, 4½x6 inches.

No. 3C34326 Price 68c
If by mail, postage extra, 12 cents.

Electricity and Magnetism.

By Sylvanus P. Thompson. A book full of practical information. A book for the beginner; for the advanced student. These lessons in electricity and magnetism are intended to afford to beginners a clear and correct knowledge of the experiments upon which the science of electricity and magnetism are based. Cloth. Illustrated. Size, 5½x7½ inches.

No. 3C34330 Price..................56c
If by mail, postage extra, 12 cents.

Electrician, How to Become a Successful.

By Professor T. O'Connor Sloane. It is the ambition of thousands of young and old to become electrical engineers. Not every one is prepared to spend several thousand dollars upon a college course, but the book is designed to tell how to become a successful electrician without the outlay usually made in acquiring the profession. Illustrated. Cloth. Size, 5¼x7½ inches. Retail price, $1.00.

No. 3C34334 Our price.............60c
If by mail, postage extra, 8 cents.

Electric Toy Making.

By T. O'Connor Sloane. A work especially designed for amateurs and young folks. This work treats of the making at home of electrical toys, electrical apparatus, motors, dynamos and instruments in general, and is designed to bring within the reach of young and old the manufacture of genuine and useful electrical appliances. Cloth. Size, 5¼x7½ inches. Retail price, $1.00.

No. 3C34382 Our price.............60c
If by mail, postage extra, 8 cents.

Electrical Transmission Handbook.

By F. B. Badt. In simple language the author has avoided as much as possible the use of scientific terms. This is a book easily understood, and one that should be in the hands of students, amateurs and professional electricians. Illustrated. Size, 3½x6 inches. Cloth.

No. 3C34384 Price......................65c
If by mail, postage extra, 5 cents.

Horseless Vehicles, Automobiles and Motor Cycles.

By Gardner D. Hiscox, M. E. A practical treatise for automobilists, and everyone interested in the development, care and use of the automobile. This book is written on a broad basis, and comprises in its scope a full description with illustrations and details of the progress and manufacturing of one of the most important innovations of the times. This book is up to date and fully illustrated with various types of horseless carriages, automobiles, and motor cycles. Cloth. 316 illustrations. 460 pages. Size, 6x9½ inches. Retail price, $3.00.

No. 3C34283 Our price $1.98
If by mail, postage extra, 24 cents.

How to Make, Test and Repair Dynamos and Motors.

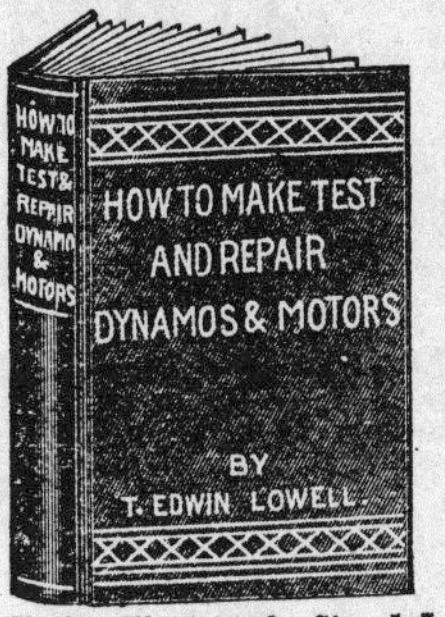

By T. Edwin Lowell. Handbook for electrical amateurs and students, with instructions, working drawings for making small dynamos and motors of various sizes. Chapters on armatures and how to wind them, tables of windings for smal dynamos and motors, valuable hints on testing and repairing, chapter on field magnets, commutator and other details, etc. Cloth. Illustrated. Size, 5x7 inches.

No. 3C34294 Price.....................45c
If by mail, postage extra, 5 cents.

Incandescent Wiring Handbook.

By Lieut. F. B. Badt. Full instructions for incandescent wiring and complete information concerning methods of running wire, location of safety devices and switches, splices, insulation and testing for faults, wire gauges, general electrical data, calculating size of wires, wiring of fixtures, elevators, buildings, isolated and central station plants. Cloth, profusely illustrated. Size, 4x6 inches. Retail price, $1.00.

No. 3C34524 Our price 65c
If by mail, postage extra, 5 cents.

Induction Coils.

How to Make, Repair and Use Them.

By T. E. Lowell. The induction coil has always been a popular piece of apparatus with amateurs and students interested in electrical science, so numerous and fascinating are the experiments that can be performed with it. This is a practical book on the construction and use of induction coils, containing full instructions for making a powerful shocking coil, ½-inch spark coil, and 4-inch spark coil, and other hints on experiments with induction coils. Fully illustrated. Size, 5x7½ inches. Retail price, $1 00.

No. 3C34530 Our price..............45c
If by mail, postage extra, 5 cents.

Telegraphy Self Taught.

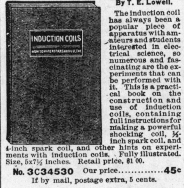

Telegraph operators are always in demand by railroads, corporations, telegraph companies newspaper offices, etc. Explains all about batteries, operating keys, Morse code, block signals, commercial messages, earth as a conductor; how to count the words in a message, order of transmisson; railroad rules for telegraph operators and movements of trains by telegraphic orders, train order form. Cloth. Illustrated. Size, 5¼x7¾ inches.

No. 3C35162 Price.....................58c
If by mail, postage extra, 11 cents.

ENTERTAINMENTS, AMATEUR THEATRICALS, READINGS, ETC.

Embracing Stump Speeches, Comic Lectures. Conundrums and Riddles, Monologues, Vaudeville Jokes, Tricks (Card and Coin), Etc.

American Star Speaker and Modern Elocutionist, The.

By Charles Walter Brown. A book for schools, churches, libraries, societies, lodges, etc. This is unquestionably one of the best books of its kind published in recent years. Contains a treatise on acting, Delsartism, elocution, oratory, and physical and vocal culture, by the late Isaac Hinton Brown, professor of those subjects in the Missouri State University, halftone illustrations. Size, 7x9¾ inches. Cloth. Retail price, $1.50.

No. 3C38125 Our price,..............59c
If by mail, postage extra, 14 cents.

Brudder Gardner's Stump Speeches and Comic Lectures.

Containing some of the best lists of the leading negro delineators of the present day, comprising the most amusing and side splitting contributions of oratorical effusion which have ever been produced. Paper cover. Size, 4½x6½ inches.

No. 3C38158 Price..................14c
If by mail, postage extra, 3 cents.

Card Tricks and How to Do Them.

Principles of Sleight of Hand, by Professor A. Roterberg. Illustrated. This book explains all card tricks, among which are the animated card, dealing five from the bottom, causing a chosen card to appear at any given number in the pack; method of dealing one's self all the trumps in whist; how to palm a card, etc. Size, 4½x6¾ inches.

No. 3C38206 Paper per. Price 14c
No. 3C38207 Cloth, gold titles.
Price...........................27c
If by mail, postage extra, paper, 3c; cloth, 5c.

Choice Dialect and Vaudeville Stage Jokes.

A new collection of readings, recitations, jokes, gags, monologues in Irish, Dutch, Scotch, Yankee, French, Italian, Spanish, Chinese, Negro and other dialects, representing every phase of sentiment, from the keenest humor or the tenderest pathos to that which is strongly dramatic. Size, 4¼x6¾ inches.

No. 3C38218 Paper. Price..........14c
No. 3C38219 Cloth. Price..........27c
If by mail, postage extra, paper 3c; cloth, 5c.

Comic Recitations and Readings.

Contains some of the best efforts of such world renowned humorists as Mark Twain, Josh Billings, Artemus Ward, Ezra Kendall, Brete Harte, Bill Nye, Ben King, George Thatcher, Lew Dockstader, William S. Gilbert, Jame Whitcomb Riley and others. Suitable for recitations in drawing room entertainment and amateur theatricals. Size, 4¼x6½ inches.

No. 3C38238
Paper cover. Price...............14c
No. 3C38239 Cloth. Price.........27c
If by mail, postage extra, paper, 3c; cloth, 5c.

Conundrums and Riddles.

Collected and arranged by John Ray. Containing upward of 4,000 choice, new intellectual conundrums and riddles which will sharpen your wit and lead you to think quickly. They are always a source of great amusement and pleasure, whiling away tedious hours and putting every one in a good humor. Any person with this book may take the lead in entertaining a company and keep them in roars of laughter for hours. 160 pages. Size, 4¼x6½ inches.

No. 3C38242 Paper. Price..........14c
No. 3C38243 Cloth. Price..........27c
If by mail, postage extra, paper, 3c; cloth, 5c.

Dick's Diverting Dialogu[es]

Consisting of twenty comedies and f[arces] by some of the best known authors. Ad[apted] for parlor performance by young ladie[s] youths, and also includes elaborate decora[tions] for exhibiting living pictures, etc. Size, 4[...] inches.

No. 3C38268 Board cover. Price[...]
No. 3C38269 Paper cover. Price[...]
If by mail, postage extra, board, 5c; p[...]

Dutch Dialect.

Jokes and [recita]tions, as told [by the] foremost va[udeville] stars, Webe[r and] Fields, R[ogers] Brothers, Man[n and] Wilder, Ezra [Kendall,] George Fulle[r Golden,] Gus Willi[ams and] others. Every [phase of] German [...] wit and humo[r is sure] to procure a [...] this new and [up to] date book, as [it con]tains the c[hoicest] emanations [of the] most celebra[ted and] renowned Dut[ch come]dians and hum[orists] of the present day. Size, 4¼x6½ inch[es].

No. 3C38290 Paper cover. Price[...]
No. 3C38291 Cloth. Price.......[...]
If by mail, postage extra, paper 3c; clo[th ...]

Debaters' Manual.

By Charles Walter Brown, A. M. This book fills a place occupied by no other. It is not only a manual of parliamentary usages, but a complete guide pertaining to matters of organization. Debating clubs will find this book unequaled. It tells us all about how to start the machinery, how to outline and prepare a debate. It gives full debates, so that the inexperienced speaker may know about what he is expected to say. 160 pages. Size, 4¼x6¾ in[ches].

No. 3C38258 Paper cover. Price[...]
No. 3C38259 Cloth. Price.......[...]
If by mail, postage extra, paper, 3c; clot[h ...]

Little Folks' Dialogues a[nd] Dramas.

A collection of o[riginal] dialogues and dram[as by] various authors. Sp[irited] and sensible, partic[ularly] adapted for little [folks] from 3 to 12 years o[f age;] subjects and ideas fi[t for] their age, and deve[lop] the germs of mimic[ry,] appropriate action, s[...] observed in even c[hildren] of tender age. Size, 4¼[...]

No. 3C38660 P[...]
Price[...]
No. 3C38661 C[...]
Price[...]
If by mail, postage extra, paper, 3c; clo[th ...]

Little Folks' Speaker.

Containing cute and catchy pieces for small children ten years and much younger, including speeches of welcome and short dialogues for opening and closing children's entertainments. The subjects are such as delight the infantile mind, and the language, while childlike, is not childish. Size, 4¼x6¾ inches.

No. 3C38664 Paper. Price......14c
No. 3C38665 Cloth, gold title.
Price...............27c
If by mail, postage extra, paper. 3c; clot[h ...]

Negro Minstrels.

By Jack Haver[ly]. A complete hand[book] written to enco[urage,] help and guide [ama]teurs in their effo[rts to] form troupes and [give] a successful eve[ning's] performance. A [en]tire program i[s ar]ranged with fulldi[rections,] consisting of a [first] part with the bri[ght] dialogue betw[een] Tambo, Bo[nes] and the Middle[man,] the introductio[n of] ballads, songs, [...] conundrums, side[...] ting stump spe[eches,] etc. 150 pages. [Size,] 4¼x6¾ inches.

No. 3C38762 Paper cover. Price....[...]
No. 3C38763 Cloth. Price..........[...]
If by mail, postage extra, paper, 3c; clo[th ...]

Patriotic Recitations and Readings.

For children. This is the choicest, newest and most complete collection of patriotic recitations published, and includes all the best known selections, together with the best utterances of many eminent statesmen. Selections for Decoration Day, Fourth of July, Washington's and Lincoln's Birthday, Arbor Day, Labor Day and all other patriotic occasions. Size, 4¾x6½ ins.

No. 3C38858 Paper cover. Price. 14c
No. 3C38859 Cloth. Price.......[...]
If by mail, postage extra, paper 3c; clo[th ...]

What Tommy Did Series.

A Series of books for boys. Each complete in one volume. Each written by an author of recognized ability. Bound in cloth. Size, 5¼x7½ inches. Retail price, 50 cents.

Black Beauty
Captain George; or the Drummer Boy
Dog of Flanders
J. Cole
Laddie
Miss Toosey's Mission
The Golden Gate
What Tommy Did
Wonder Book for Boys and Girls

No. 3C61318 Our price, per volume..........**28c**
If by mail, postage extra, each, 5 cents.

Young People's Natural History.

By Isaac Thorne Johnson, A. M., forming a popular history of animals, birds, reptiles, fishes and insects, and describing in easy, simple language how wild creatures great and small look, live and act, comprising also many thrilling stories of adventure with them, and amusing anecdotes about them. Illustrated with 200 photos, engravings true to life, showing animals, birds and reptiles.

450 pages. Cloth, lithographed cover. Size, 7¾x9⅞ inches. Retail price, $1.00.
No. 3C61443 Our price..............**54c**
If by mail, postage extra, 24 cents.

Linen Toy Books.

Cosy Corner Series. Printed on genuine linen, untearable. A very interesting collection of rhymes about A B C, in which the domestic animals are introduced for the instruction of very young folks. Each book illustrated and printed on linen cloth. Size, 5⅝x7⅜ inches. Embracing a series of six books, different kinds:

Friends in the Meadow
Little Chicks **On Guard** **Pet Lambs**
Neddy Bray **The Pet Goat**

No. 3C60665 Linen cover, handsomely printed in colors. Price, each..........**6c**
Per dozen..........**68c**
If by mail, postage extra, each, 1 cent; per dozen, 9 cents.

LAW.

Civil and Business Law.

By Prof. Geo. W. Conklin. Most legal difficulties arise from ignorance of the minor points of law. This book furnishes a busy man or woman information on just such points as are likely to arise in every day affairs and forestall them against mental worry and financial loss. How to keep out of trouble, and how to get out if you happen to get in, etc. Don't consult a lawyer. Buy this book.
No. 3C91706 Cloth, colored edges. Retail price, 25 cents. Our price..........**14c**
No. 3C91708 Full leather, gilt edges. Retail price, 50 cents. Our price..........**28c**
If by mail, postage extra, either style, 3 cents.

Law, and How to Keep Out of It.

By Paschal H. Coggins, Esq. Most legal difficulties arise from ignorance of the minor points of law. This book furnishes to the busy man and woman information on just such points as are most likely to arise in every day affairs, and thus forstall them against mental worry and financial loss. Cloth. Size, 4½x6 inches. Retail price, 50 cents.
No. 3C62658 Our price..............**30c**
If by mail, postage extra, 5 cents.

Law at a Glance.

A complete work, embracing every known subject, among which are the following: Affidavits, agents, agreements, arbitration, assignments, power of attorney, bankruptcy, bills of lading, exchange and sale, chattel mortgages, co-partnership, corporations, damages, debts, deeds, frauds, forms of guarantee, injunction, injury, insolvency, insurance, judgment, sales; husband and wife—their relations, divorce, losses, etc. Cloth. Size, 5¼x7½ inches.

No. 3C94606 Price...**58c**
If by mail, postage extra, 12 cents.

LIQUORS.

Including Books on the Art of Compounding Liquors, Wines, Mixing Cocktails, Fancy Drinks, Etc.

Drinks, as They are Mixed.

By a leading buffet manager. A new, up to date guide to the art of mixing fancy beverages, in vest pocket (time saving) size. This is the only complete and practical book on the subject published. It is especially adapted to the home, buffet or club. The recipes are simple, making it possible for the butler or the lady of the house to properly prepare them. Paper cover. Size, 2½x5½ inches.
No. 3C64275 Cloth. Price..............**18c**
No. 3C64276 Leather. Price..........**30c**
If by mail, postage extra, either style, 3 cents.

Independent Liquorist.

By L. Monzert. The art of manufacturing all kinds of syrups, bitters, cordials, champagnes, wines, lager beer, ale, porter, beer, punches, tinctures, extracts, brandies, gin, essences, flavorings, colorings, sauces, catsups, pickles, preserves, etc. Cloth. Size, 5¼x7¼ inches. Retail price, $3.00.
No. 3C64527 Our price..........**$1.98**
If by mail, postage extra, 12 cents.

LOVE AND COURTSHIP.

Comprising Lovers' Guides, Letter Writing, Art of Making Love, How to Write Love Letters, Etc.

Because I Love You.

The Book of Love, Courtship and Marriage. It fully explains how maidens become happy wives, and bachelors become happy husbands in a brief space of time and by easy methods. Also complete directions for declaring intentions, accepting vows and retaining affections. Tells plainly how to begin courting, the way to get over bashfulness, and is just the treatise to be in the hands of every young bachelor or maiden.

200 pages. Size, 4¼x6⅜ inches.
No. 3C66163 Paper cover. Price..........**14c**
No. 3C66164 Cloth. Price..........**27c**
If by mail, postage extra, paper edition, 3 cents; cloth edition, 5 cents.

Lovers' Guide and Manual.

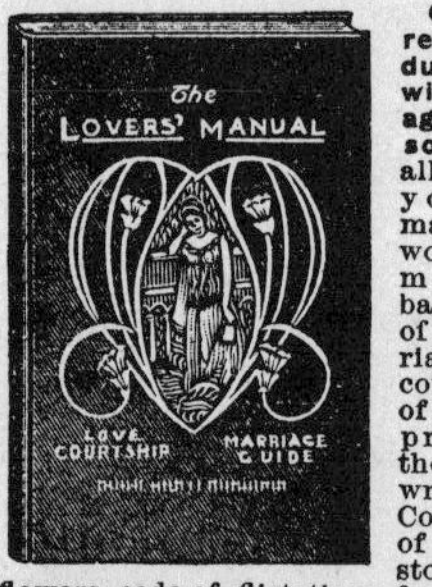

Contains full directions for conducting a courtship with ladies of every age and position in society. Explains all about love, young men and marriage, young women and matrimony, courtship, bachelors, influence of matrimony, marriage, etiquette of courtship, essence of good breeding, proposals, love thoughts of famous writers, love letters. Contains also poems of love, funny love stories, language of flowers, code of flirtations, fortune telling, and character reading, including rules for good society, handkerchief, parasol, fan, hat, postage stamp, cigar, glove, eye, whip, pencil flirtation, and lovemaking. Paper cover. Size, 4¼x6⅜ ins.
No. 3C66676 Price..........**15c**
If by mail, postage extra, 2 cents.

Modern Art of Making Love, The.

A complete manual of etiquette, love, courtship and matrimony. Something every boy and girl, man and woman ought to know. Tells how to begin a courtship, when and whom to marry, the advisability of long and short courtships, points to be observed in the selection of a husband or wife, the secret of pleasing a sweetheart, how to address and win the favor of ladies, etc. Also contains a complete system of love telegraphy, handkerchief flirtation, the language of flowers, precious stones and their signification, etc. Size, 4¼x6⅜ inches.

No. 3C66140 Paper cover. Price..........**18c**
No. 3C66141 Cloth. Price..........**30c**
If by mail, postage extra, paper, 3c; cloth, 6c.

North's Book of Love Letters.

With directions how to write and when to use them. This is a branch of correspondence which fully demands a volume alone to provide for the various phases incident to love, courtship and marriage. Few persons, however otherwise fluent with the pen, are able to express in words the promptings of the first dawn of love. It tells how to follow up a correspondence with the dearest one in the whole world, and how to smooth the way with those who need to be consulted in the matter. It also contains the art of secret writing, the language of love portrayed, and rules in grammar, etc. 160 pages. Size, 4¼x6⅜ inches.
No. 3C66778 Paper cover. Price..**14c**
No. 3C66779 Cloth. Price..........**27c**
If by mail, postage extra, paper, 3c; cloth, 6c.

MECHANICS.

TO MACHINISTS, ENGINEERS, FIREMEN AND MECHANICS, our Book Catalogue will be invaluable, as it describes only the best books, embracing every branch of mechanics, including gun making, die cutting, glass working, mechanical drawing, etc. Best works on mineralogy, metallurgy, mines and mining.

Modern Air Brake Practice. Its Use and Abuse.

By Frank H. Dukesmith. The new airbrake book. Invaluable to trainmen, engineers, firemen, conductors, electric motormen and mechanics. The latest and best 1904 edition. With questions and answers for locomotive engineers and electric motormen. While there have been many air brake books written, we feel safe in saying that never before has the subject been treated in the same lucid, understandable manner. The book is fully indexed and cross-indexed, so that any subject can be turned to immediately, as desired. Cloth. 303 pages; hundreds of illustrations. Size, 5x7 inches. Retail price, $1.50.

No. 3C68118 Our price..........**98c**
If by mail, postage extra, 12 cents.

Catechism, Locomotive.

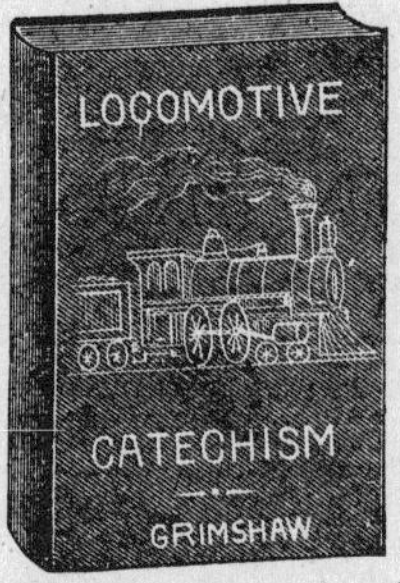

By Robert Grimshaw. A new revised edition. How to run a locomotive. Contains 1,600 questions and gives 1,600 simple, plain and practical answers about the locomotive. Also official form of examination of firemen for promotion and of engineers for employment. 450 pages. 200 illustrations. 12 large folding plates. Cloth. Size, 5¼x7½ inches. Retail price, $2.00.
No. 3C68218 Our price...**$1.29**
If by mail, postage extra, 12 cents.

Catechism, Steam Engine.

By Robert Grimshaw, M. E. A series of direct practical answers to direct practical questions, not only intended for young engineers and for examination questions, but a handy volume for everyone interested in steam. Also contains formulas and worked out answers for all the steam problems that appertain to the operation and management of the steam engine. Illustrations of various valves and valve gear, and how to operate them, etc.

413 pages. Illustrated. Cloth. Size, 4¼x5¾ inches. Retail price, $2.00.
No. 3C68220 Our price..........**$1.29**
If by mail, postage extra, 8 cents.

Combustion of Coal.

By William M. Barr. New edition. Prepared with special reference to the generation of heat by the combustion of the common fuels found in the United States, and particularly with the conditions necessary to the economic, and smokeless combustion of bituminous coal in stationary and locomotive steam boilers. How to make steam. Contains 800 practical questions and answers on the science of steam making. 85 illustrations. 349 pages. Cloth. Size, 5x7 inches. Retail price, $1.50.
No. 3C68237 Our price..........**$1.10**
If by mail, postage extra, 12 cents.

Dies, Their Construction and Use for the Modern Working of Sheet Metals.

By Joseph V. Woodworth. A treatise upon the designing, constructing and use of tools, fixtures and devices, together with the manner in which they should be used in the power press. A book written by a practical man for practical men and one that diemakers, machinists, toolmakers or metal working mechanics cannot afford to be without. Illustrated. Cloth. Size, 7x8½ inches. Retail price, $3.00.
No. 3C68265 Our price..........**$1.98**
If by mail, postage extra, 25 cents.

Engines, Gas, Gasoline and Oil.

By Gardner D. Hiscox, M. E. Simple, instructive and up to date. Tells all about the running and management of gas engines. This book is designed for the general information of everyone interested in this new and popular motive power, and its adaptation to the increasing demand for a cheap and easily managed motor requiring no licensed engineer. 369 pages. 312 illustrations. Cloth. Size, 6¼x9¼ inches. Retail price, $2.50.
No. 3C68325 Our price..........**$1.69**
If by mail, postage extra, 21 cents.

Engine Runners' Catechism.

By Robert Grimshaw, M. E. Latest edition. Tells how to erect the principal steam engines in the United States. To young engineers this catechism will be of great value, especially those who may be preparing to go forward to be examined for certificates of competency, and to engineers generally it will be of no little service, as they will find in this volume more really practical and useful information than is to be found anywhere else within a like compass. 336 pages. Illustrated. Cloth. Size, 4¼x5¾ inches. Retail price $2.00.
No. 3C68330 Our price..........**$1.29**
If by mail, postage extra, 8 cents.

Farm Engines and How to Run Them.

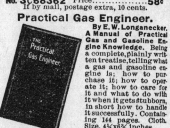

By Stephenson, Maggard and Cody. Revised and enlarged by William L. Webber. This is the only authentic and best book of the kind published. It tells how to successfully operate all farm and traction engines, giving a plain, simple and correct explanation of the different parts. How to set a valve, how to line an engine and other information. Contains 200 questions and answers for engineers, firemen, etc. Cloth. Illustrated. Size, 5¼x8 inches.

No. 3C68362 Price..........**58c**
If by mail, postage extra, 10 cents.

Practical Gas Engineer.

By E. W. Longanecker. A Manual of Practical Gas and Gasoline Engine Knowledge. Being a complete, plainly written treatise, telling what a gas and gasoline engine is; how to purchase it; how to operate it; how to care for it and what to do with it when it gets stubborn, in short how to handle it successfully. Containing 144 pages. Cloth. Size, 4¼x6⅜ inches.
No. 3C68410 Price..........**60c**
If by mail, postage extra, 6 cents.

Locomotive Engineers, Ready Help for.

By Norman Gardenier. Contains matters of the utmost value for locomotive firemen seeking promotion; for the scholar and student, and for the help of the examiner. It comprises a remedy for every conceivable breakdown that may occur to the locomotive. Cloth. Size, 4½x6 inches. Retail price, $1.00.
No. 3C68670 Our price..........**60c**
If by mail, postage extra, 6 cents.

Locomotive Up to Date, The.

By Chas. McShane. An absolute authority on all subjects relating to the locomotive. The greatest accumulation of new and practical matter ever published, treating upon the construction and management of modern locomotives, both simple and compound. More than 100 prominent railway officials and inventors of special railway appliances have furnished practical information about

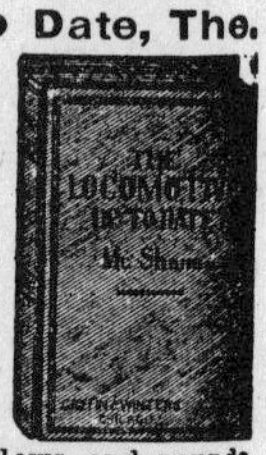

air brakes, break downs, blows and pounds, combustions, link and valve motions, valve setting, steam indicator, injectors and lubricators; examination questions and answers for locomotive firemen and hundreds of other subjects of interest. Contains 736 pages. Cloth. 380 illustrations. Size, 6¾x9 inches.
No. 3C68672 Price..........**$1.89**
If by mail, postage extra, 22 cents.

Motorman's Guide, The.

By G. H. Gayelty. A new, up to date edition. A practical treatise on street railway motors, containing everything a motorman should know about the care and running of electric cars. Cloth. Illustrated. Size, 4¾x6½ inches.
No. 3C68772 Price..........**33c**
If by mail, postage extra, 8 cents.

Railroad Men, Standard Handbook For.

By A. Kilburn. A complete, practical and instructive treatise on the modern railroad locomotive and all its attachments. Contains questions and answers on all points referring to engineering, automatic air brakes, link motion, injector breaks, break downs, signaling, etc. Illustrated with full set of double trip daily time sheets and other illustrations. Cloth. Size, 6¼x4 inches. Retail price, $1.00.

No. 3C68908 Our price..........**59c**
If by mail, postage extra, 8 cents.

ister to Turkey—the Moslem power which, nineteen centuries after the birth of Christianity, ruled over its holiest places in Palestine.

"Good Books Make Short Evenings"

These words introduce the catalog reader—in 1915—to the huge wartime edition listing ten thousand books, or, in numbers alone, what amounts to a fair-sized library. Rich America was growing richer as the result of the first World War. This country was spending more money on education than any other country in the world. Millions of its people had enjoyed the alleged benefits of a high-school or college education. Many of the states were devoting nearly one half of their total revenues to schools, and everywhere the cry arose for greater appropriations. In the period 1906–16, Andrew Carnegie had built one thousand library buildings, and by 1914 the country had 3,000 libraries each possessing more than 5,000 books. Given this background what did the catalog book buyer read? The answer is short but not sweet: trash.

The catalog, be it ever remembered, is no sentimentalist

We Buy 'Em, You Grab 'Em. The Country's Literary Taste
Is Shell-Shocked in the Second Year of the World War

urging the people onward and upward. And because it refrains from attempts at uplift, we can see the people more clearly in their own light.

In 1915, the catalog features three novels. The first is *Ben-Hur,* "The Most Remarkable and Masterly Novel of the Century." It is here in a new edition, "each book covered with an illustrated jacket showing a gorgeous reproduction in colors of the Chariot Race. Price 39¢."

The second featured novel is *Corporal Cameron* by Ralph Connor. What were its components according to the catalog?

GLAMOUR: Soldier service on the frontier.
ROMANCE: Tender romance of a human hero.
SPIRIT: Vigorous and wholesome.
MEN: Strong men who are not afraid.
WOMEN: Tender, pure, ready to meet death for love.
SCENERY: The great outdoors.
PRICE: 39¢

The last of the trilogy is *The Life Everlasting* by Marie Corelli. What did the buyer of this book get for his thirty-nine cents?

LOVE: An overpowering and occult love.
LOCALE: A yacht on northern lochs. Past incarnations in granite Egypt and purple Rome. Finally, a strange monastery amid the eternal snows.
ROMANCE: Highly colored.
WOMAN: Dares all and is rewarded.
PASSION: Mortal and immortal.

These three were catalog favorites in 1915.

Moving-Picture Novels

Here is something new under the publishing sun, and the moving-picture novels reflect the public's taste both in novels and motion pictures. These books pose the old question of which came first: the hen or the egg? Is the procedure to read the book and then see the movie, or vice versa? Sears, perhaps because it did not run movies but sold books, suggests that its customers first read the novels.

The catalog says: "Here are the popular novels, the stories which have been put on the screen as feature reels":

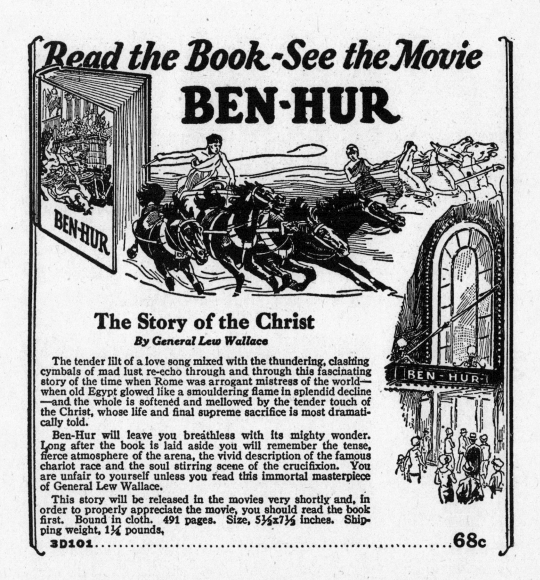

Read the Book - See the Movie
BEN-HUR

The Story of the Christ
By General Lew Wallace

The tender lilt of a love song mixed with the thundering, clashing cymbals of mad lust re-echo through and through this fascinating story of the time when Rome was arrogant mistress of the world—when old Egypt glowed like a smouldering flame in splendid decline—and the whole is softened and mellowed by the tender touch of the Christ, whose life and final supreme sacrifice is most dramatically told.

Ben-Hur will leave you breathless with its mighty wonder. Long after the book is laid aside you will remember the tense, fierce atmosphere of the arena, the vivid description of the famous chariot race and the soul stirring scene of the crucifixion. You are unfair to yourself unless you read this immortal masterpiece of General Lew Wallace.

This story will be released in the movies very shortly and, in order to properly appreciate the movie, you should read the book first. Bound in cloth. 491 pages. Size, 5½x7½ inches. Shipping weight, 1¼ pounds.

3D101..**68c**

Brewster's Millions	By George Barr McCutcheon
Chip of the Flying U	By B. M. Bower
The Goose Girl	By Harold MacGrath
The House of Bondage	By R. W. Kauffman
Lion and the Mouse	By Klein and Hornblow
Port of Missing Men	By Meredith Nicholson
The Squaw Man	By Faversham and Boyle
Soldiers of Fortune	By Richard Harding Davis

Mail-Order Love

In the mail-order world, as in the greater world of which it is a part and which it reflects, many things change with the passing of time, but one thing does not change. It is that love always ends before the altar with "the bride becomingly attired in a white satin dress, carrying a white Bible and lilies-of-the-valley." This world has no patience with past or contemporary Heros and Leanders, Paolos and Francescas, Héloïses and Abélards. It would not swap one marriage license for a trainload of roses and raptures. While Sears is conscious of the potent legend that marriage is made in heaven, it feels that a little tactful guidance on its part toward matrimony could harm neither angels nor men. In this spirit, the 1905 catalog presents a group of books which shows the reader how to make the course of true love flow smoothly toward the altar.

Here, for example, is the catalog's *Ars Amatoria,* for only fifteen cents. It is called *Lovers' Guide and Manual*:

Recipe Book for Love. Satisfaction Guaranteed or Your Money Back

"Contains full descriptions for conducting a courtship with ladies of every age and position in society. Explains all about love, young men and marriage, young women and matrimony, courtship, bachelors, essence of good breeding, proposals, love thoughts of famous writers, love letters. . . . Language of flowers, code of flirtations, character reading, including rules for handkerchief, parasol, fan, hat, postage stamp, cigar, glove, eye, whip, pencil flirtation and lovemaking."

Throughout the ages men have written love letters to women, and even the great Casanova sometimes took quill in hand to supplement more direct methods. And although the woods of America were filled with strong men who could tear a bear limb from limb, or toss a bull into the air like so much confetti, they broke down blubbering and stammering in the presence of a pure woman whom they loved. Sears sets out therefore to give first aid to the inarticulate, and, inasmuch as the mail-order method moved mountains of merchandise, why would not the same method move frail woman's heart? The delicate device provided for the purpose was *North's Book of Love Letters*:

"With directions how to write them and when to use them. . . . Few persons, however otherwise fluent with the pen, are able to express in words the promptings of the first dawn of love. It tells how to follow up a correspondence with the dearest one in the whole world, and how to smooth the way with those who need to be consulted in the matter. It also contains the art of secret writing, the language of love portrayed, and rules in grammar, etc. Price 14¢."

The Renascence of Sex

Sex and sin were synonymous in the 1905 catalog. But by 1915, the tentative conclusion seems to have been reached that sex, whether we liked it or not, was a fact just as typhoid was a fact, and America decided to give the apparatus and the manifestations of human reproduction a belated *de facto* recognition. A sperm, it was at last discovered, need not necessarily be a species of whale. And the catalog, never in advance of, but barely abreast of, the throng, no longer apologizes for the contents of its sex books or sugar-coats them with assurances that they "will not offend the most refined." Flushed with the pagan joy of its new-found freedom, it actually boasts of the fearlessness of its medical authorities. Thus, *Marriage* by Dr. Julia Seaton, "is remarkable for its freedom of expression and fearless in its conclusions."

It was inevitable that we should have a popular literature of the psychology of sex, because few words hold more enchantment for us—a people fascinated by the pseudoscientific

—than the word "psychology." Since we are impatient of pure science and of theory, we insist upon making immediate and "practical" applications of the tentative conclusions of scientists and investigators. Hence, in our common tongue, it is "good psychology" to do this, "bad psychology" to do that. We have a psychology of salesmanship, of interior decorat-

The Mail-Order Havelock Ellis, or, How to Skate on Thin Ice with Roller Skates

ing, of delicatessen management, of tap dancing. What more natural then than a popular psychology of sex? And why not make a delectable dish of it by spicing it with the red pepper of the discoveries being made in Vienna by that fellow called Dr. Freud?

This seemed entirely reasonable. So, turning thought into action, Dr. Seaton cooked up an *olla podrida* called *Psychology of the Solar Plexus and the Subconscious Mind*. We may well take the catalog's word for it that this is "an extraordinary book full of new and interesting statements." It was, in fact, a miracle book. "Invaluable in the cure of mental and nervous diseases, in voice culture and for singers."

And, it might have been added, extremely dangerous to the reader. Just as the country was once flooded with fake medicines purporting to cure all ills from cancer to hoof-and-mouth disease, so now, in 1915, it began to be flooded with books filled with recipes enabling the mental sufferer to cure himself.

Here again the catalog reflects accurately what is happening in America. The misuse and perversion of the incomplete data of psychology, psychiatry, and of the so-called social sciences are confined neither to the catalog's authors nor to its readers.

"A Columbia professor," writes Dr. Abraham Flexner,* "greatly concerned with the personal characteristics of industrial leaders, suggests an interview so framed 'as to bring to light the emotional conditioning of the types of experience which have led one man to become bitter, another pugnacious, another very diplomatic and still another frank and open in a cooperative way. . . .'

"I am inclined to award the palm to a questionnaire research into 'the origin and nature of common annoyances' by Professor Cason of the University of Rochester. Professor Cason read this important paper at the Ninth International Congress of Psychology in Sept. 1929. After several years' work, he compiled a list of 21,000 annoyances, but finding duplication and *many instances of spurious annoyances,* he boiled the list down to 507, which he arranged on a scale marked from 30 to 0. 'To find hair in food I am eating,' is marked 26, 'a dirty bed' 28, 'cockroaches' 24, 'to see baldheaded men' 2, etc.!"

Dr. Flexner concludes: "It would be obviously unfair to call attention to the absurdities I have mentioned but for the fact that they are so numerous as to be representative of a large part of the literature of sociology and education—so large as to imperil the development of a scientific spirit in either field. . . ."

History Is Bunk

"History," said Mr. Henry Ford on a memorable occasion, "is bunk." These words coming from a man so colossally rich

* Abraham Flexner, *Universities: American, English, German,* pp. 108-09.

carry weight, because in our tradition a rich man is more or less an authority on everything. But, whatever the weight of his words or lack of it, many of his countrymen seem to agree with him. Bunk or not, America had had three hundred years of stirring history by 1915, but the catalog's customers seem either to have had no curiosity about it or perhaps satisfied their curiosity elsewhere. Sears' sole contribution to American history in 1915 is Edward Eggleston's *Household History of the United States and Its People.*

Rural and small-town America wanted books about the West, not academic studies like those of Frederick Turner on the frontier, but lusty, coagulated-blood tales of gore, fighting, stampedes, cattle rustling, and derring-do. And the catalog gave them what they wanted in rich abundance.

Typical of the "history" in demand was *Indian Horrors, or Massacres by The Red Men.* Naturally there are no books describing white massacres of Indians, although there are two about Buffalo Bill. But nothing is said of Sitting Bull, the Indian hero of Custer's Last Stand, or of the horrors of white civilization from his point of view. In the summer of 1885, Sitting Bull, the hunted Indian, was a member of a wild West show conducted by Buffalo Bill, the Indian hunter.

"Sitting Bull traveled with the show all summer. In the States he endured with silent dignity the booing and curses and cat-calls of the American crowds, sold his autographed photographs like hot cakes, shook hands with the President, and acquired a taste for oyster stew. . . .

"Sitting Bull made money, most of which, as Annie Oakley bears witness, 'went into the pockets of small, ragged boys. Nor could he understand how so much wealth could go brushing by, unmindful of the poor.' He formed the opinion that the white men would not do much for Indians when they let their own flesh and blood go hungry. Said he, 'The white man knows how to make everything, but he does not know how to distribute it.' "*

As a people we have never been intensely interested in our

* Stanley Vestal, *Sitting Bull,* pp. 256-57.

adventures overseas, whether in the Philippines, Alaska, Cuba, or even in the Argonne. But our interest in the settling and winning of the West never decreases. For it was this achievement, the peculiar institutions derived from it, the men who brought it about, and the backdrop against which it was played, that we think of as uniquely and typically American. The Old South was an Anglo-Saxon squirearchy functioning through slaves, but this was not peculiarly American but rather tropical American. In the West Indies, Brazil, the Argentine, and elsewhere in South America, there were Spanish prototypes of the Southern gentry holding slaves, codes of honor, and conceptions of duty not unlike those to be found at Natchez. New England was much like old England: a land of small farmers, shippers, bankers, craftsmen, and merchants. But the West was *sui generis,* and it is Daniel Boone crossing the wilderness with his long rifle, rather than Paul Revere clattering to alarm the countryside, who beguiles the imagination of our times.

By 1876, the Old West was gone; by 1890, the frontier was practically closed. But as we march farther away from those years the legend of the West grows; a restless people yearns subconsciously for the days when freedom of movement and free lands were unlimited, and the covered wagon seems a golden argosy to a man riding on the 7:57 to his desk in the city.

Out of remembrance of and nostalgia for things past, we try even to recreate some of the characteristics of the vanished West: the buffalo lives again in guarded Federal herds; the Indian population increases mightily in government nurseries, and cowboys wear chaps on dude ranches for the benefit of fat-bottomed women from the East. The movies, that move to the pragmatic doctrine of "giving 'em what they want," find that the horse opera always produces dividends. This peculiarly American form of entertainment has recently been glorified in such films as *Union Pacific* and *Dodge City* in which horsemen make history. Sears' book department, therefore, followed good business practice in offering the public a host of books on the West of which *The Red Blooded Heroes of the Frontier* is typical. The catalog's synopsis of it might be the outline of a Western movie of today:

"Tales of frontier heroes who faced annihilation in the bloody track of the crafty Indians, bad men, outlaws and border bandits. Hair raising adventures of men who were jugglers with death on the outposts of civilization. Thrilling stories of fights with Indians; their attacks on the prairie schooners; and their raids when the Indians left trails red with the blood of many an innocent victim, and gray with the ashes of many a plundered ranch and farmhouse . . . the holding up of the Overland Mail, etc."

Science and Health

A new bible comes into the 1915 catalog: *Science and Health,* for Christian Scientists. It was not mentioned in 1905, and its presence ten years later in the catalog is evidence of the growth and acceptance—after sharp hostility—of this new religion in America.

Havelock Ellis once wrote that men of the East like to sit in coffeehouses spinning new religions and tossing them away just as they export their tawdry vases to the West. Religion spinning is one of our national habits. Some of the religions make sense; others make only wonderful nonsense; but we go on creating them just the same. Among those that make sense for a great number of intelligent people is Christian Science, and its growth was so rapid that, at the time of Mary Baker Eddy's death in 1910, the church had 100,000 members, ample financial backing, and Mrs. Eddy left an estate valued at three million dollars.

Christian Science did not grow, however, without great opposition. Mark Twain attacked it savagely; thousands ridiculed its doctrines of healing, and Mr. Dooley seems to have spoken for the whole people when he wrote: "I think that if the Christian Scientists had some science, and the doctors more Christianity, it wunnen't make any difference which ye called in—if ye had a good nurse." But the new religion con-

The Old Favorites

The American Home Classics.

These volumes are bound in a fine quality of linen weave pattern book cloth in assorted colors set off by gilt stamping on the side and back in a rich and tasteful design. Printed from new plates. Size, 5⅛x4¾ inches. Average 250 pages. Shpg. wt., 1 lb.

3V1774—Each, 27c; 4 for.....................$1.00

Treasure Island. Stevenson
The Little Minister. Barrie
The Scarlet Letter. Hawthorne
Tale of Two Cities. Dickens
The Three Musketeers—Vol. 1. Dumas
The Three Musketeers—Vol. 2. Dumas

Lena Rivers. Holmes
Under Two Flags. Ouida
Plain Tales From the Hills. Kipling
Jane Eyre. Bronte
Last of the Mohicans. Cooper
Ishmael. Southworth
Self-Raised. Southworth

Last Days of Pompeii. Lytton
Tempest and Sunshine. Holmes
Ivanhoe—Vol. 1. Scott
Ivanhoe—Vol. 2. Scott
Dr. Jekyll and Mr. Hyde and Kidnapped. Stevenson
Uncle Tom's Cabin. Stowe
Thorns and Orange Blossoms. Clay
The Spy. Cooper
Homestead on the Hillside. Holmes
Sherlock Holmes' Detective Stories. Doyle
David Copperfield—Vol. 1. Dickens

David Copperfield—Vol. 2. Dickens
Thelma. Corelli
Inez. Evans
Murders in the Rue Morgue. Poe
The Deerslayer. Cooper
The Pilgrim's Progress. Bunyan
In His Steps. Sheldon
Tanglewood Tales. Hawthorne
Robinson Crusoe. Defoe
Tom Brown's School Days. Hughes
Hans Brinker. Dodge
Black Beauty. Sewell
Alice in Wonderland and Through the Looking Glass. Carroll
Marian Grey. Holmes

Grimm's Fairy Tales. Grimm
Andersen's Fairy Tales. Andersen
The Light That Failed. Kipling
Swiss Family Robinson. Wyss
The Master of Ballantrae. Stevenson
The Two Orphans. D'Ennery
The Hunchback of Notre Dame—Vol. 1. Hugo
The Hunchback of Notre Dame—Vol. 2. Hugo
Gulliver's Travels. Swift
The House of the Seven Gables. Hawthorne
A Study in Scarlet. Doyle
Christmas Stories. Dickens

The Royal Blue Library.

These superb volumes attain a degree of beauty, dignity and good taste such as has only been found heretofore in books which sell at twice their price. Bound in artificial leather. Printed on white book paper from new plates. Size, 7¼x5 in. and contains approximately 250 pages each. The books have gold tops, head bands and a ribbon marker. Shipping weight, 1 pound.

3V83—Each.....................65c

Treasure Island. Stevenson
The Little Minister. Barrie
The Scarlet Letter. Hawthorne
Tale of Two Cities. Dickens
The Three Musketeers—Vol. 1. Dumas
The Three Musketeers—Vol. 2. Dumas
Under Two Flags. Ouida
Jane Eyre. Bronte

Plain Tales from the Hills. Kipling
Last of the Mohicans. Cooper
Last Days of Pompeii. Bulwer-Lytton
Dr. Jekyll and Mr. Hyde and Kidnapped. Stevenson
Uncle Tom's Cabin. Stowe
Sherlock Holmes' Detective Stories. Doyle

Thelma. Corelli
Murders in the Rue Morgue. Poe
The Pilgrim's Progress. Bunyan
In His Steps. Sheldon

The Light That Failed. Kipling
The Master of Ballantrae. Stevenson
The Two Orphans. D'Ennery
The Hunchback of Notre

Dame—Vol. 1. Hugo
The Hunchback of Notre Dame—Vol. 2. Hugo
The House of the Seven Gables. Hawthorne
Christmas Stories. Dickens

Standard Fiction

Each 42c   Each 42c

Old Favorite Library.

A library of popular and standard works of some of the world's best authors. Bound in cloth. Size, 5⅛x7⅝ inches. Average 250 pages. Shipping weight, each, 1⅛ pounds.

Aesop's Fables.
Alice in Wonderland. Carroll
Andersen's Fairy Tales.
Beulah. Wilson
Black Beauty. Sewell
Bride's Fate. Southworth
Capitola's Peril. Mrs. Southworth
Count of Monte Cristo. Alexander Dumas
Courtship of Miles Standish. Longfellow
Cruel as the Grave. Mrs. Southworth
David Copperfield. Dickens
Darkness and Daylight. Mary J. Holmes
Deerslayer. J. F. Cooper
Deserted Wife. Southworth
Dora Deane. M. J. Holmes
East Lynne. Mrs. Wood
Edith Lyle's Secret. Holmes
Ethelyn's Mistake. Holmes
Evangeline. Longfellow
Green Mountain Boys. D. P. Thompson
Grimms' Fairy Tales.
Hans Brinker. Dodge
Helen's Babies. Habberton
Hidden Hand. Southworth
How He Won Her. Mrs. Southworth

In His Steps. Sheldon
Inez. Augusta J. Evans
Ishmael. Mrs. Southworth
Ivanhoe. Sir Walter Scott
Jane Eyre. Charlotte Bronte
John Halifax. Miss Mulock
Kenilworth. Sir Walter Scott
Lamplighter. Cummins
Last Days of Pompeii. Lytton
Last of the Mohicans. Cooper
Lena Rivers. Holmes
Little Lame Prince. Mulock
Little Minister. Barrie
Macaria. Augusta J. Evans
Maggie Miller. M. J. Holmes
Mildred. Mary J. Holmes
Millbank. Mary J. Holmes
Missing Bride. Southworth
Mysterious Island. Verne
Mystery of Raven Rocks. Mrs. Southworth
Noble Lord, A. Southworth
Oliver Twist. Dickens
Pathfinder. J. F. Cooper
Pilgrim's Progress. Bunyan
Pioneers, J. F. Cooper
Prince of the House of David. Rev. J. H. Ingraham
Red Rover. Cooper
Robinson Crusoe. Defoe
St. Elmo. Augusta J. Evans
Self-Raised, or From the Depths. Mrs. Southworth

Silas Marner. Eliot
Sketch Book. Irving
Spy, The. J. F. Cooper
Stepping Heavenward. Prentiss
Sweet Girl Graduate. Meade
Swiss Family Robinson. Wyss
Tales From Shakespeare. Charles and Mary Lamb
Tale of Two Cities. Dickens
Tempest and Sunshine. Mary J. Holmes
Thelma. Corelli
Tom Brown's School Days. Thomas Hughes
Treasure Island. Stevenson
Tried for Her Life. Mrs. Southworth
Twenty Thousand Leagues Under the Sea. Jules Verne
Two Orphans. D'Ennery
Uncle Tom's Cabin. Stowe
Victor's Triumph. Mrs. Southworth
We Two. Edna Lyall
Wide, Wide World. Warner
Woman Against Woman. Mary J. Holmes

3V125—Each, 42c; any two.....................83c

Books by Mark Twain.

Cloth. Size, 5½x8 inches. Average 350 pages. Shipping weight, each, 2 pounds.

3V1202—Huckleberry Finn.....$1.95
3V1206—Pudd'nhead Wilson.... 1.95
3V1200—Tom Sawyer 1.95
3V1201—Tom Sawyer Abroad... 1.95
3V3077—Innocents Abroad. Special Edition 63c

Ben Hur.

A Tale of the Christ.
By Gen. Lew Wallace.
The most famous novel of the present day. 560 pages. Bound in cloth. Colored jacket. Size, 5x7½ in. Shipping wt., 1½ lbs.
3V101 ....63c

MEDICAL BOOKS

Husband and Wife.

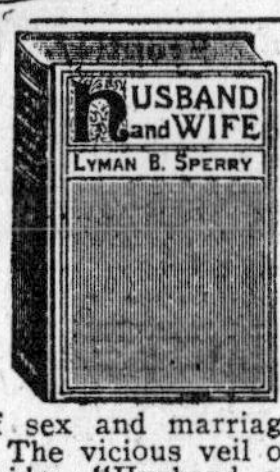

A woman looks forward to the miracle of motherhood. A man plans to be a decent, enlightened husband. But newspapers today are filled with accounts of unhappy marriages, divorces whose predominant cause is ignorance of sex and marriage relations.

The vicious veil of prudery is now torn aside. "Husband and Wife," by Lyman B. Sperry, M. D., gives valuable instructions and suggestions to those who have entered upon the relations of married life. Bound in cloth, 228 pages. Size, 5x7½ inches. Shipping weight, 1⅛ pounds.
3V3752 ....$1.18

Getting Ready to Be a Mother.

By Carolyn C. Van Blarcom, R. N. Formerly assistant superintendent and instructor in obstetrical nursing and the care of infants and children at the Johns Hopkins Hospital Training School for Nurses. A book of information and advice for the young woman who is looking forward to motherhood. If every expectant mother followed the simple, practical advice which this book offers, the rate of injury and death among our mothers and babies would be materially lessened.

Bound in cloth. Size, 5¼x7⅝ inches. 237 pages, 75 illustrations. Shpg. wt., 1 lb.
3V3704 ....98c

The Prospective Mother.

By J. Morris Slemons, M. D. The purpose of this enormously helpful book is to insure the health of the prospective mother during pregnancy. Complete and detailed directions clearly and concisely stated, give her an intelligent understanding of her changing physical condition. Bound in cloth. 343 pages. Size, 5⅝x7⅝ in. Shipping wt., 1¼ lbs.
3V3769 $1.58

Vitality Supreme.

By Bernard Macfadden. This book teaches men and women how to be 100 per cent alive, thus giving them a great advantage over their average competitor in life's conquests. 259 pages. Bound in cloth. Size, 5½x 7⅞ in. Shpg. wt., 1½ lbs.
3V3770 ....$1.85

Books for the Married and the Marriageable.

Is Sex Barring You From Happiness?

"Sex Problems Solved," by Dr. William Lee Howard, is an all revealing, fearless and corrective discussion of sex and the all important part it plays in your life and mine and in the lives of our wives and children. To sex adjustments, say eminent authorities, are due, many mental disorders of the adolescent boy or girl. Bound in cloth. Size, 5¼x7⅝ inches, 161 pages. Shipping weight, 1 pound.

3V3756—Sex Problems Solved 87c

Most Vital of All Books on Marriage Relations.

This book by Dr. William Lee Howard is a discussion of the vital, fearless, plain-speaking personal problems confronting every married couple. Those who are about to enter into the married state will find this book priceless. Bound in cloth. Size, 5⅛x7⅝ in. 161 pages. Shipping wt., 1 lb.

3V3758—Facts for the Married 87c

Help Stamp Out the Great Social Evil.

Here is a book laying bare the appalling devastation of the great social evil that is sapping the manhood and womanhood of the nation. "Plain Facts on Sex Hygiene," by Dr. William Lee Howard, will do much toward preventing childless marriages, subnormal children. Bound in cloth, 171 pages. Size, 5⅛x7⅝ inches. Shpg. wt., 1 lb.

3V3754—Plain Facts on Sex Hygiene 87c

The World's Great Medical Book

A friend in need is a friend indeed. Dr. Evans and his great book represent just such a friend. There is a time—an emergency—in every man's and woman's life when such a book as this is priceless. Such an emergency never gives you warning. Perhaps you or some member of your family will be suddenly stricken—of all times—in the dead of night; it may be hours before you can get a doctor. Perhaps you live miles from a railroad or town and no doctor is available. This great book may mean the difference between life and death.

In it nearly every known disease and ailment to which human beings are subject is frankly and ably discussed. The book contains thousands of questions asked Dr. Evans by thousands of people seeking the road of health, together with the answers by the physician. So varied are the topics covered that without doubt the very question that you want to ask about yourself or some one in your family is here answered authoritatively in Dr. Evans' simple, direct manner.

"HOW TO KEEP WELL" is a great big book, printed in large, easily read type. Bound in cloth. Size, 10x7 inches. It contains 1,040 pages, and over 400 practical and helpful illustrations with complete descriptions. Shipping weight, 3½ pounds.

3V5946—Dr. Evans' How to Keep Well.

Our special low price,

$1.48

A Complete and Authoritative Library on Sex Knowledge.

These three books described above make up the most complete and authoritative library on sex knowledge ever published. We are making a special reduced price combination offer of these three vital books, put up in a set. Shipping weight, 3 pounds.
3V3765—Special reduced price for this 3-volume set.....................$2.50

NEW REVISED MECHANICS' AND BUILDERS' ENCYCLOPEDIAS

STANDARD AMERICAN CYCLOPEDIA OF STEAM ENGINEERING $2.78

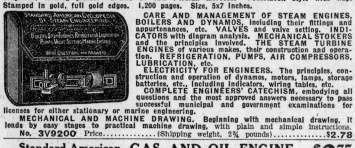

BY CALVIN F. SWINGLE and others. Four volumes in one. 1,000 illustrations. diagrams, folding plates. Bound in full Persian morocco. Pocketbook style with flap. Stamped in gold, full gold edges. 1,200 pages. Size, 5x7 inches.

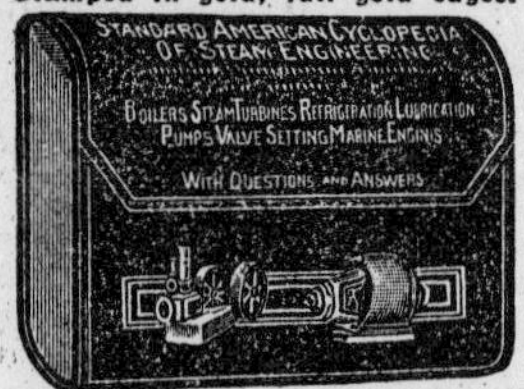

CARE AND MANAGEMENT OF STEAM ENGINES, BOILERS AND DYNAMOS, including their fittings and appurtenances, etc. VALVES and valve setting. INDICATORS with diagram analysis. MECHANICAL STOKERS and the principles involved. THE STEAM TURBINE ENGINES of various makes, their construction and operation. REFRIGERATION, PUMPS, AIR COMPRESSORS, LUBRICATION, etc.

ELECTRICITY FOR ENGINEERS. The principles, construction and operation of dynamos, motors, lamps, storage batteries, etc., including indicators, wiring tables, etc.

COMPLETE ENGINEERS' CATECHISM, embodying all questions and the most approved answers necessary to pass successful municipal and government examinations for licenses for either stationary or marine engineering.

MECHANICAL AND MACHINE DRAWING. Beginning with mechanical drawing, it leads by easy stages to practical machine drawing, with plain and simple instructions.

No. 3V9200 Price..............(Shipping weight, 2¾ pounds)..............$2.78

Standard American LOCOMOTIVE ENGINEERING $2.85

COMPLETE IN ALL ITS BRANCHES

By C. F. SWINGLE AND W. G. WALLACE. Over four volumes in one. 1,250 pages, 1,000 illustrations. Bound in full Persian morocco, pocketbook style, with flap. Stamped in gold. Full gold edges, folding plates, diagrams. Size, 5x7 inches. A VERITABLE ENCYCLOPEDIA of Locomotive Engineering. Special chapters with full illustrations are given on LOCOMOTIVES, their various types, their appliances and equipment; Locomotive Firemen's Duties, etc. BOILERS, including their construction, care and operation. VALVES, including valve gear and valve setting. AUTOMATIC AIR BRAKE PRACTICE. Both the New York and the Westinghouse systems. WALSCHAERT VALVE GEAR AND E. T. LOCOMOTIVE BRAKE EQUIPMENT.

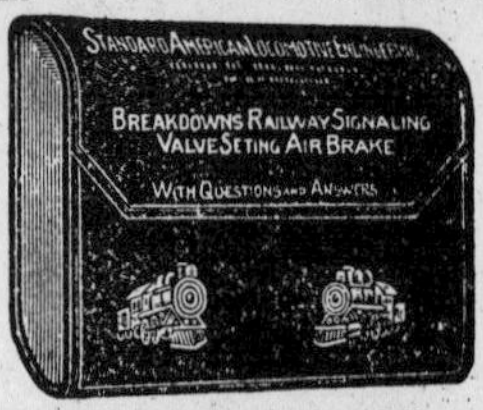

LOCOMOTIVE BREAKDOWNS in the form of Questions and Answers. Engine failures and what to do in case of an emergency, including broken cylinder heads, piston rods, etc.

RAILWAY SIGNALING AND STATION WORK, including Freight, Passenger and Baggage Departments. Block systems, with trainmen's questions and answers on all signals.

QUESTIONS AND ANSWERS are given after each important subject. Also complete first, second and third year mechanical examinations, with standard questions and answers.

No. 3V9210 Price..............(Shipping weight, 2¾ pounds)..............$2.85

Standard American GAS AND OIL ENGINE, AUTOMOBILE AND FARM ENGINE GUIDE $2.75

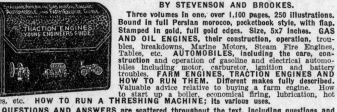

BY STEVENSON AND BROOKES.

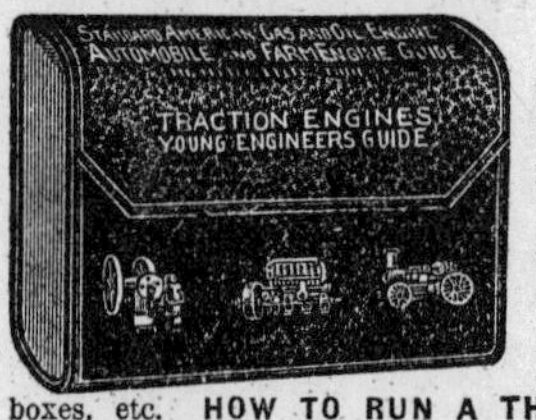

Three volumes in one, over 1,100 pages, 250 illustrations. Bound in full Persian morocco, pocketbook style, with flap. Stamped in gold, full gold edges. Size, 5x7 inches. GAS AND OIL ENGINES, their construction, operation, troubles, breakdowns, Marine Motors, Steam Fire Engines, Tables, etc. AUTOMOBILES, including the care, construction and operation of gasoline and electrical automobiles including motor, carburetor, ignition and battery troubles. FARM ENGINES, TRACTION ENGINES AND HOW TO RUN THEM. Different makes fully described. Valuable advice relative to buying a farm engine. How to start up a boiler, economical firing, lubrication, hot boxes, etc. HOW TO RUN A THRESHING MACHINE; its various uses.

QUESTIONS AND ANSWERS are scattered throughout the text, including questions and answers for examination when applying for engineer's license.

No. 3V9220 Price..............(Shipping weight, 2¾ pounds)..............$2.75

STANDARD AMERICAN ELECTRICIAN $2.88

A Complete Cyclopedia of Electricity

BY SWINGLE, HORSTMANN AND TOUSLEY. Three volumes in one. 350 pages. Profusely illustrated. Bound in full Persian morocco, pocketbook style, with flap. Stamped in gold, full gold edges. Size, 5x7 inches.

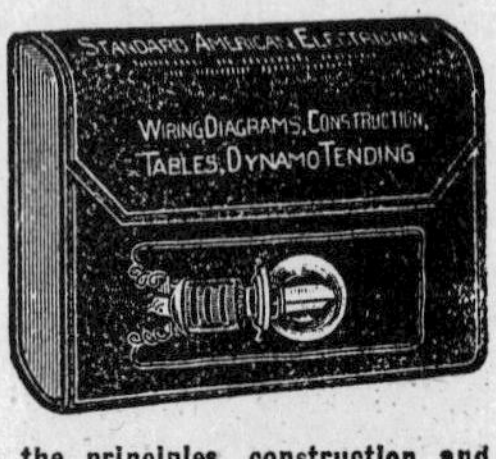

MODERN ELECTRICAL CONSTRUCTION, fundamental principles of electricity and magnetism, dynamos and motors. Latest improved methods of wiring all classes of buildings for light and power, including fittings and materials.

WIRING DIAGRAMS AND DESCRIPTIONS. It explains how to wire for call and alarm bells, for burglar and fire alarms, how to install and manage batteries, how to locate trouble. Explains alternating and direct current, ring out circuits and meters.

ELECTRICAL WIRING TABLES, showing combined carrying capacity of different wires, capacity of conduits and pole line data dimensions, kinds of wires, fittings, etc.

DYNAMO TENDING FOR ENGINEERS. A treatise on the principles, construction and operation of dynamos, motors, lamps, storage batteries, and how to operate a plant.

No. 3V9230 Price..............(Shipping weight, 2½ pounds)..............$2.88

The Dyke Course of Automobile and Gasoline Engine Self Instruction $6.65

Endorsed By Barney Oldfield, Chas. E. Duryea, Splitdorf Co., Etc.

The Dyke course not only teaches you the principle and construction of the automobile, but it teaches you the gasoline engine as well, and when you master the automobile and gasoline engine with the Dyke course you will understand all automobiles and all gasoline engines either for automobile, marine or stationary work If you are really ambitious, there is no quicker, cheaper or better way than this Dyke course. It will surely teach you. The encyclopedia is as simple as A B C, the diagrams and charts are large and clear, and above all the Real Working Models will give you the practical work. If you are an owner of an automobile, if you are a chauffeur or desire to become one, if you are desirous of obtaining a position in an automobile factory, garage or repair shop, you will find this course invaluable. Then there is the field of opening a repair shop of your own in which the opportunity for making a livelihood is unlimited. With the Dyke course you learn the principle and construction of not only one car but you learn the principle and construction of all cars. At the same time you learn how to adjust all the principal parts right on the models and with large clear charts to explain. You learn how to remedy all troubles and how to make repairs. The absolute necessity of working models when studying the automobile and the superiority they give the Dyke course is now universally recognized.

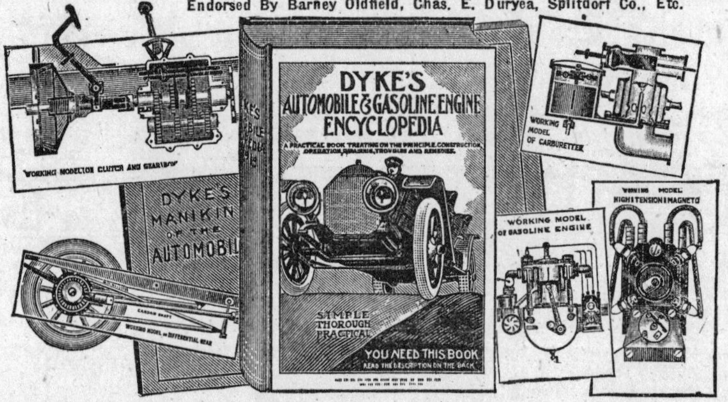

What Dyke's Course of Automobile and Gasoline Engine Self Instruction Contains.

DYKE'S AUTOMOBILE AND GASOLINE ENGINE ENCYCLOPEDIA. Latest edition. Thoroughly practical. Written in simple language so as to be easily understood. Contains 239 big charts, 5½x8 inches. Over 1,000 illustrations. Technical terms are avoided throughout the book, so that anyone who can read will have no trouble in understanding. It progresses in easy steps from one part to another until finally you are taught the operation of this wonderful power plant as a whole, then how to locate, remedy and repair trouble, etc. Each step is carefully explained by specially prepared charts. A complete dictionary giving the meaning of the words and terms used throughout the book will be found at the back. Explains everything you can possibly think of, from the construction of all types of motor vehicles to the setting of valves and tinning of magnetos. Tells how to build a repair shop for the home or business; how to make repairs; how to increase the power of your engine; how to overhaul engines; how to drive twenty-two different makes of cars; how to figure horse power; how to start in the automobile business, etc. With the aid of this book you will be able to keep your car out of the repair shop and increase the life of your car, and will be enabled to get greater value for it when you desire to sell. Contains hundreds of questions and answers on the automobile and its troubles. To this latest edition have been added 36 pages on the principles, construction, operation and care of electric starting, generating and lighting systems. With 107 illustrations and 118 questions. 593 pages. Bound in cloth. Size, 7x10 inches.

THE FIVE WORKING MODELS. Practice Right on the Models.

It is impossible to describe these models so that you will clearly understand what wonderful pieces of mechanism they actually are. They show every detail. All moving parts are made of real metal. These working models represent the connecting link between study and practice. Simple—Thorough—Practical.

Working Model of a Gasoline Engine. Teaches the cycle principle, the principle of the gas engine; how to set valves and time the ignition, etc. Size, 5¼x8½ inches.

Working Model of the Magneto. It seems to spark like a real magneto. Teaches the construction or principle of the magneto and how to set all leading makes. Size, 6x10 inches.

Working Model of the Differential Gear. Turn drive shaft and gears work. Size, 5x10 inches.

Working Model of the Carburetor. Size, 9¾x6 inches. Showing how to adjust any carburetor and gain the maximum power.

Working Model of a Transmission or Gear Box and Clutch. When you have learned the principle of this modern selective type you will understand all.

No. 3V4880 Complete Course of Automobile and Gasoline Engine Self Instruction. (Shipping weight, 5¼ pounds) Price..............$6.65

NOTE—With every order for the complete set we will give, without extra charge, a 16-page manikin chart of the automobile which completely explains the relation of one part of the automobile to the other and shows how the automobile is built from the ground up.

No. 3V4868 Dyke's Automobile and Gasoline Engine Encyclopedia only. (Shipping weight, 3¼ pounds.) Price..............$2.48

The Modern Gasoline Automobile.

Its Construction, Operation, Maintenance and Repair. Latest Edition.

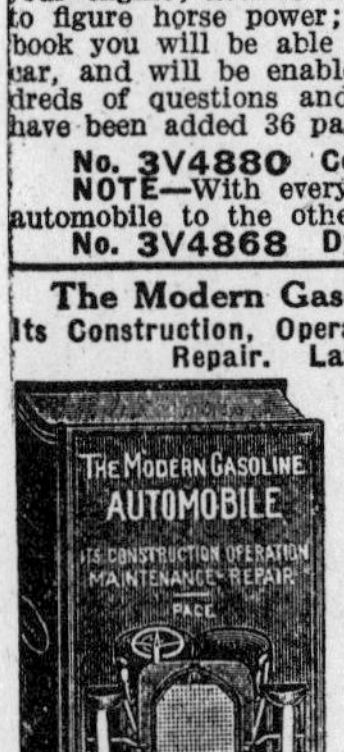

By Victor W. Page, M. E. One of the most practical and complete up to date books on the gasoline automobile ever published. Valuable to motorists, students, mechanics repairmen, designers and engineers. Every phase of the subject is treated in a practical, non-technical manner. Illustrated with 500 specially detailed illustrations and diagrams. 816 pages. Cloth. Size, 6x8¾ inches. Shipping weight, 2¾ pounds.

No. 3V4859 Price..............$1.75

Automobile Catechism and Repair Manual.

By Calvin F. Swingle. A series of questions and answers covering the construction, care and operation of automobiles. Also complete instructions on locating trouble and making adjustments of all kinds. Illustrated. 165 pages. Bound in flexible leather. Size, 4½x6¾ inches. Shipping weight, 8 ounces.

No. 3V4851 Price..............89c

Self Propelled Vehicles.

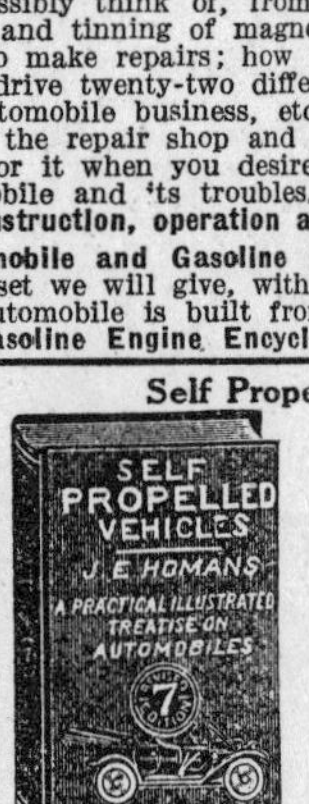

Latest edition. By J. E. Homans, A. M. A practical treatise on the theory, construction, operation, care and management of all forms of automobiles driven by steam, gasoline or electricity. 500 illustrations and diagrams. 667 pages. Cloth. Size, 5⅝x8½ inches. Weight, 3 pounds.

No. 3V4857 Price..............$1.68

Car Troubles.

Their Symptoms and Their Cure.

By H. W. Slauson. Concise, accurate, practical. Troubles are classified alphabetically. Cloth. Size, 6⅞x4⅛ inches. Weight, 3 oz.

No. 3V4875 Price..............23c

Automobile Instructor.

By Clyde H. Pratt. Clear, concise, practical and valuable information in regard to every part of the gasoline automobile, including its mechanism, driving, repair and care. Simple enough for the amateur and thorough enough for the expert. Fully illustrated. 225 pages. Cloth. Size, 8¾x5⅝ inches. Shpg. wt., 1⅜ lbs.

No. 3V4856 Price..............98c

Audel's Answers on Automobiles.

Latest edition. For owners, operators and repairmen. Covers the parts, operation, care, management, road driving, carburetors, wiring, tuning, ignition, motor troubles, lubrication, tires, including chapters on the storage battery, electric vehicles, motorcycles, overhauling the car, and a special chapter on how to run an automobile. Fully illustrated with diagrams and detail drawings, halftones, etc., and fully indexed. Cloth, with leather back. Size, 7x5½ in. Shpg. wt., 1¾ lbs.

No. 3V4858 Price..............$1.18

Gasoline Engines, Their Operation and Care.

By A. H. Verrill. Fully illustrated with 152 original engravings. A comprehensive, simple and practical work on gasoline engines, their construction, management, care, operation, repair and installation. Written especially for the owners and operators who are not familiar with the technicalities and who are not machinists. Contains also a complete table of motor troubles and remedies, and a full glossary of technical gasoline terms. 273 pages. Cloth. Size, 5¼x7⅜ in. Shpg. wt., 14 oz.

No. 3V4572 Price..............98c

BOOKS EVERY FARMER SHOULD OWN.

Traction Farming and Traction Engineering.

Gasoline, Alcohol, Kerosene.

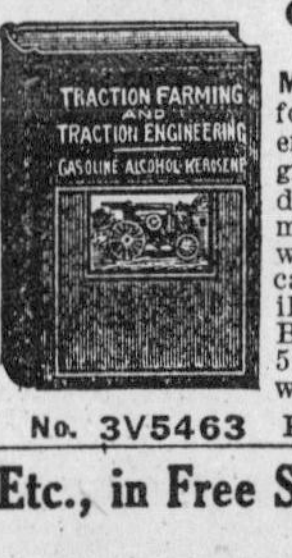

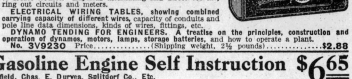

By James H. Stephenson, M. E. A practical book for the owners and operators of gas and oil engines on the farm. A full description of the leading makes of farm tractors with directions for their care and operation. Over 150 illustrations. 400 pages. Bound in cloth. Size, 5¼x7¾ inches. Shipping weight, 1½ pounds.

No. 3V5463 Price..............$1.18

The Gasoline Engine on the Farm.

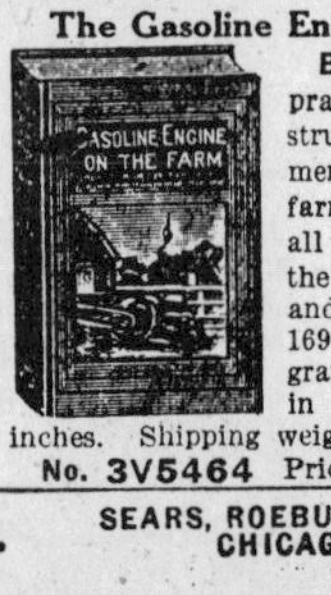

By W. X. Putnam. A practical book on the construction, repair, management and use of this great farm power as applied to all farm machinery, and the farmer's work indoors and out. Illustrated with 169 carefully selected engravings. 527 pages. Bound in cloth. Size, 5⅝x7½ inches. Shipping weight, 1¾ pounds.

No. 3V5464 Price..............$1.88

A Complete Line of Books for Electricians, Engineers, Builders, Etc., in Free Special Book Catalog.

SEARS, ROEBUCK AND CO., CHICAGO, ILL.

tinued to grow and to spread from the cities to the small towns and the country, as is evidenced by the fact that the 1915 catalog lists four varieties of *Science and Health.* Prices ranged from $1.35 to $3.35.

Our Favorite Novelists

The book section of the 1925 catalog is almost oblivious to the extraordinary changes that had taken place in American prose fiction since the beginning of the century. As early as 1900, the change from the romantic idealism of nineteenth-century American novels to the grim realism of the twentieth century had begun with Theodore Dreiser's much-damned *Sister Carrie.* Dreiser flouted the deeply held American belief (at least in books) that virtue always triumphs over vice; refused to accept as either fixed or just the conventional moral codes of society, and acidly sketched the streaks of hypocrisy in the souls of men.

Changing economic conditions, too, began to affect the novel. The closing of the frontier, the concentration of wealth, and the creation of monopolies increased the economic pressure on the average American and found expression in such novel-studies as Upton Sinclair's *The Jungle,* and Dreiser's *The Financier* and *The Titan.* In the face of the hard facts of life and the difficulties of making a living in twentieth-century America, romanticism seemed out of date; a new interest arose in the classes, and the common man against a commonplace background began to emerge as a major character in the new novels.

Immediately after the World War, there ensued in America a period of almost neurotic unrest, of bitter disillusionment, and a sharp revival of nationalism. The enormous popular success of Sinclair Lewis's *Main Street,* in 1920, clearly showed that a new spirit had arisen in this country. Here the heroine, Carol Kennicot, rebels against the dullness of the people and the environment in which she lives; discovers that dullness is not a virtue but a vice, and concludes that the exposure of the mind to dull people is almost as wrong as to expose it to vicious company. The enthusiastic reception of the book proved that thousands of other people in the country must have reached the conclusions arrived at by Carol Kennicot, and dimly resented the increasing tendency to standardize human beings as machine products were being standardized.

Two years later (1922), Lewis shifted his scene in *Babbitt* from the village to the city. Here he portrays a noisy and moderately successful businessman who feels at bottom that he has been cheated of joy in his personal life because he conformed religiously to the conventions of the community, without obeying his own inner impulses, and so achieved merely a life of discontent and frustration.

As the American novel moved from romanticism to realism, and as it painted the contemporary scene and contemporary man in drab colors, it also threw off old attitudes about sex. Affected, too, by the new psychology stirring in the world, it made minute studies of the normal, the subnormal, and the abnormal in man's sexual life, as in Sherwood Anderson's *Winesburg, Ohio* (1919).

In brief, the most striking, if not the most enduring, American novels of the period 1900–25 are those that dealt with discovery, change, and revolt. Yet these novels, typical new expressions of an America in convulsion, are almost entirely absent from the 1925 catalog.

Babbitt is mentioned in small space and, interestingly, it is accurately analyzed: "George F. Babbitt is a prosperous, hustling, real estate broker in a city of about 350,000. Back of his business and clubs and 100 percent activities is a wistful wonder as to what this business of living is all about. *Babbitt* tells the truth to you. *Babbitt* tells the truth about you."

But *Babbitt* stands alone in the catalog as the representative of the new school of realistic fiction that was already a quarter century old when the catalog of 1925 appeared. It features new novels by Harold Bell Wright, Gene Stratton Porter, Peter B. Kyne, and James Oliver Curwood.

Miss Porter turned her searching talents on the tragedies of the World War in *The Keeper of the Bees*. A disciplined artist who permitted herself none of the sprawlings displayed by Tolstoi in *War and Peace*—also a novel about war —she tells "The poignant tale of a war-shattered veteran. The unknown girl who loves him, by a clever ruse and pretended suicide, persuades him to marry her and save her honor."

Harold Bell Wright, whose pure men and women love the great outdoors with claustrophobic passion, delighted his vast audience with a bit of cheesecloth mysticism called *A Son of His Father*. James Oliver Curwood in *The Ancient Highway* took his readers for a ride down "the world of highway of romance." Peter B. Kyne in *The Understanding Heart* wrote "a story of love and broad understanding in California mining camps."

Ben-Hur is back again in 1925, bigger and better than ever before. The catalog advises us to "Read the Book—See the Movie." We are fast approaching the long-dreamed-of synthesis of the arts.

It is dispiriting to find amid this garden of lilies a lush growth of poison ivy dangerous to the spiritual flesh, but it is here and unconcealed. The tiger woman of literature, Elinor Glyn, is represented by five novels, including the once notorious *Three Weeks*. The catalog gives us a glimpse of their contents that makes us thirst for more. "The novels of Elinor Glyn have a keen fascination for old and young alike —dealing as they do with the age-old problems of passion-swayed hearts and restraining conventions."

Learn to Be Popular for 93¢

"Be popular or bust" is not only a truism of American life but also the lifework of thousands of Americans, and the lifeblood of a dozen industries. Thousands of guides to popularity offer the people their services in millions of dollars' worth of advertising. It is, however, a strenuous life that one must lead in order to achieve popularity. You must, for example, speak French; play the piano; know what to say and do on all occasions; have pearly teeth, orderly intestines, that schoolgirl complexion, a smooth-shaven face, a slender figure, a book, no dandruff fringe; own a canoe, and dance well. Anybody may be popular who does or avoids doing these things. Sears, knowing that millions dread unpopularity as they do pyorrhea, taps the rich popularity market with a few homeopathics of its own.

One easy and pleasant way to popularity is to *Dance Well and Be Popular*. The catalog embroiders the theme for us:

> Some people seem to be born good dancers; they are light on their feet and naturally fall into all the new steps. Everyone wants to dance with them and their programs are filled before the evening begins. Do you envy these people? You need not do so. For you can be just as popular. Don't be a wall flower, for good dancing is a magic wand which sweeps you to social popularity.
>
> Get this marvelous, up to the minute book, *Dancing Made Easy*. . . . It sets forth new steps that are being danced, with illustrations and diagram charts. It will teach you the latest variations of jazz which, when danced properly, are pretty and graceful; the toddle; the camel-walk, the canter, the pivot, the one-step, the two-step, waltz, etc. . . . Be the first to introduce in your crowd the new steps.

Does this sound naïve? Does it smack of flora and the country green? Is it only the mail-order millions who aspire to popularity through dancing? Not at all. The cities are filled with dancing schools whose pupils—executives, housewives, clerks, and bartenders—are moved by advertising and the desire for popularity to learn how to dance well. And at least one of these schools—that of Arthur Murray in New York— has achieved a national reputation.

After the popularity aspirant has acquired a canoe, abolished dandruff and body odor, learned to play the piano and speak French, and bought a book, it would seem that he might then relax and lave his tired body in the refreshing waters of popularity. But there is one thing more. Despite all his achievements, he might dwell in a hell of insecurity because he does not know what to say or do on all occasions. For example: (*a*) when he discovers a fly in his soup at a formal dinner; (*b*) when he has taken his guests to the theater and finds that he has left the tickets in the pants of his other suit; (*c*) when he drops in at a bridge party to take his wife home and her best friend says, "Why Harold, what *are* you doing with that lipstick on your shirt collar?" The answers to these questions, it may be assumed, and a host of others equally puzzling, are to be found in *Etiquette—An Encyclopedia of Social Usage.* "With the aid of this book you need never be at a loss to know what to do on all occasions."

The Bible Is Still a Best Seller

Although it was popular to be popular in 1925, and many chose dancing as the road to popularity, the Bible was still the best-selling book in the catalog. And no book, moreover, which was critical of the Bible was listed in the catalog. America clung to fundamentalism in religion, and it was in 1925 that William Jennings Bryan was to die in its defense.

Mr. Bryan, whose scientific attitude was summed up epigrammatically in his statement that he was "not so much interested in the age of rocks as in the Rock of Ages," was a special prosecutor in the famous Tennessee "monkey case." The defendant was a young Dayton schoolteacher, John T. Scopes, who was indicted for breaking the state statute against teaching evolution in the public schools. The late Clarence Darrow appeared as chief attorney for the defense.

Mr. Bryan took the stand as an expert on religion, saying that he was "prepared to defend religion against any infidel." He then stated his personal beliefs which are those of millions of his countrymen: that God first created Adam and then Eve from Adam's rib; that the world was created in 4404 B.C.; that the Flood occurred about 2384 B.C., and that out of the wranglings of the Tower of Babel came the multiplicity of human tongues.

During the course of the trial, thousands of people poured into the little town of Dayton. Clarence Darrow reports that:* "Pop-corn merchants and sleight-of-hand artists vied with evangelists for the favor . . . of the crowds . . . speeches were bawled at street corners under the glare of artificial-lighting arrangements; the venders raised their voices to drown the evangelists . . . and each worked his own side of the street, up and down.

"Then over the river, under the trees, a band of Holy Rollers gathered every night. As they grew excited and shouted and sang and twitched and twirled, the people crowded closer around them in curiosity and wonder. Now and then some one would sidle forward from the dark woods and, seeming to be seized with some inspiration, would rush in amongst the other performers and dance and squirm and shout and stutter with such vigorous contortions that the regulars were put to shame for their mild form of worship. All sorts of weird cults were present in Dayton, all joining forces to put up a strong fight against Satan and his cohorts. . . ."

Amid such scenes died the man who had been candidate three times for the Presidency of the United States, President maker, Secretary of State under Woodrow Wilson, and idol of millions.

Mr. Bryan, the White Knight, was dead, and John T. Scopes, found guilty, was fined one hundred dollars. But fundamentalism was not dead. It still lives in the breasts of millions of Americans, and the catalog, which must seek to please everybody, carefully avoids listing books critical of the Bible.

The Battle of the Books

"They read books," said Sherwood Anderson of the men and women on the farms and in the little towns of America fifty to forty years ago. And, as we have seen, the catalog listed large numbers of good books in 1905. But, by 1935,

* Clarence Darrow, *The Story of My Life,* pp. 261-62.

Sears' mail-order readers were buying fewer and poorer books than they had bought thirty years ago. Yet the population had grown from 84 million to 127 million in this period; there had been a prodigious increase of education, and the annual circulation of the catalog was then about fourteen million. The decline in books listed in the catalog, however, is graphically shown by the number of pages given them:

1905: sixteen pages.

1935: eight pages.

But while the quantity and quality of the books listed by the catalog declined in the period 1905–35, the quantity of good books sold in the United States increased. A. D. Dickinson's survey of the "Best Books of the Decade from 1926 to 1935" is valuable proof not only because of the care with which the survey was made but because it reveals the books America read in a period of golden prosperity and black depression.

Leading the Dickinson list of twenty-five "favorite authors" for the years 1926–35 were James Truslow Adams, Willa Cather, Pearl Buck, and Ellen Glasgow; at the bottom of the list, but still a "favorite author," was Carl Sandburg. Other authors and books in the Dickinson survey of "fifty best books" were:

> Douglas Southall Freeman's *Robert E. Lee*
> Mark Sullivan's *Our Times*
> Stuart Chase's *Men and Machines*
> Walter Lippmann's *Preface to Morals*
> Lewis Corey's *Decline of American Capitalism*
> Vernon Parrington's *Main Currents in American Thought*
> Helen Gardner's *Art Through the Ages*

These "best" books of the period (using the word to mean "selected by a consensus of expert opinion as most worthy the attention of intelligent American readers") were also "favorite" books of large groups of readers. But almost without exception they do not appear in the 1935 catalog. Why?

Mr. Henry Ford, in his *My Life and Work,* unconsciously

gives us a clue to one important reason for the decline of serious reading among the catalog's customers.

After telling us the startling but good news that the struggle for existence grows less, he says that now "we have an opportunity to release some of the finer motives. We think less of the frills of civilization as we grow used to them. Progress, as the world has thus far known it, is accompanied by a great increase in the things of life. There is more gear, more wrought material, in the average American backyard than in the whole domain of an African king. The average American boy has more paraphernalia around him than a whole Eskimo community. The utensils of kitchen, dining room, bedroom, and coal cellar make a list that would have staggered the most luxurious potentate of five hundred years ago. . . ."

More gear in the back yard than in the whole domain of an African king; more paraphernalia in the possession of an American boy than in a whole Eskimo community; more things in the kitchen than in the hands of a potentate of five centuries ago; but—fewer books in the home. Whether more Fords and fewer Shakespeares is advance or retrogression is perhaps debatable; what is one man's progress may be another man's poison.

It is worth noting, in passing, that Mr. Ford's thesis, that the struggle for existence in America grows less, is confirmed by that august institution, *The Encyclopaedia Britannica,* which is owned by Sears. It is highly ironical that its fourteenth edition should have been published in—of all years —1929 with this statement in its article on philanthropy:

"Philanthropic endeavour in America differs from that of other countries in its greater variety and in the larger proportion undertaken through private initiative as compared with that carried on by the State. . . . Moreover, as *little poverty exists and there is no pauper class,* welfare work is carried on in a more confident spirit, with the expectation of making social relief ultimately needless. . . ." (Author's italics.)

In any event, whether Sears' customers in 1935 were riding in their Fords, taking pride in their Frigidaires, listening to Graham McNamee, or merely sitting on their piles of gear and paraphernalia while waiting for a job, they did not buy many books. And if they bought books, they were not those of old-fashioned writers such as Gibbon, Thackeray, Dickens, and the English poets, who figured so largely in the 1905 catalog. Only the Bible, of all the old favorites, remained as popular as it was thirty years ago. What did the citizens of leisurely, paraphernalia-cluttered America select from the catalog library in 1935?

The Fruits of Leisure

Sears does not tell us whether the people enjoyed a voluntary leisure in 1935 because of the beneficence of machines or an involuntary leisure because millions were without jobs. Yet what to do with leisure had become a problem to a worried citizenry and their government. Only last year, a man appeared in a Southern town armed with authority and money from Washington to establish a number of what he called "recreation projects for Negroes." It did not occur to him, or to Washington, that Negroes are perhaps the only large group in America so civilized that they are not bored by leisure and have little difficulty amusing themselves. But white people are suffocated by idle time and, to them, Sears offered a way of escape that was not only pleasant but also offered possibilities of profit. The catalog lists a number of HOBBY BOOKS. "Hobbies sometime become a profitable life work!" While waiting for a job or for your bond coupons to mature, you could amuse yourself today and prepare for a richer future tomorrow through the use of these volumes:

Photography for Fun
Life of the Party
You Can Write
You Can Sell What You Write
Music for Everybody
Tropical Fish

A man out of work has much time for sleep. But even sleep could be profitably employed if you would dream and then seek riches through *Ten Thousand Dreams Interpreted*. Or, if you were not a dreamer but a doer, bought *Complete Courses in Civil Service*.

If, however, your ambitions were in the grand manner, you would employ your leisure studying *How to Develop Your Personality* and "become the person you would like to be!" This is an important book and as American as a two-bagger or a cop bawling out a speeder. In no country of the world, perhaps, is personality so much worshiped as in the United States, and, at the same time, nowhere (until the rise of the totalitarian states of Europe) is there so little of it. We want to be different and yet all alike.

Out of our frenzy for personality come such things as Personality Pies, the Four Personality Sisters, the Car with a Personality, the Personality Brassière. We even have a personality Texas politician who was elected Governor of his state through hillbilly music played by himself and his family and a platform of "Pappy please pass the biscuits."

The object of personality is leadership. Leadership for domination; domination for the purpose of getting the other fellow to eat your pies, hear your singing, wear your brassières, or give you his vote. Mr. Hoover, we are told, was a failure as President because he lacked personality; but Mr. Billy Rose is the American Max Reinhardt because he has personality, and, since more Americans would rather be Billy Rose than Herbert Hoover, there is a wild scramble for personality and for books that tell you how to get it. What with millions of these books circulating, with everybody dripping charm while they fix one another with their glittering eyes, the situation is alarming and the end is not clear. The movement has gone far enough, however, to enable us to answer with confidence a question once asked by the puzzled Mr. Aldous Huxley. He said:*

* Aldous Huxley, Introduction to *Texts and Pretexts*.

> The Ideal Man of the eighteenth century was the Rationalist; of the seventeenth, the Christian stoic; of the Renaissance, the Free Individual; of the Middle Ages, the Contemplative Saint. And what is our Ideal Man? On what grand and luminous mythological figure does contemporary humanity attempt to model itself? The question is embarrassing. Nobody knows.

Ah, but we do know, Mr. Huxley. The question is not at all embarrassing. Speaking for America, the answer is clear. "The grand and luminous mythological figure" on which most of the contemporary United States attempts to model itself is: the Personality Boy or Girl.

Salesman, What of the Night?

The importance of selling had become so overwhelming by 1935 that the catalog did not think it sufficient merely to list a few books on "the art of selling" and let it go at that. In the lesser arts—writing or music—it was enough to offer the student a few "how" books and let him find his way, but for salesmen Sears offered a whole course in salesmanship. The catalog cries lustily down the silent corridors of depression-ridden America bidding men awaken and be of good cheer:

TRAINED SALESMEN ARE IN DEMAND!

"Selling is the foundation of all Business and Social Success. A good salesman is not 'born that way.' He studies. And if he is trained through this valuable spare-time course in 'Effective Salesmanship' he can't be beat! . . . This New course even includes Character Analysis and Memory Training and, of course, the whole selling procedure. A penny postcard will bring you full details. Don't delay!"

Here again Sears is in the American tradition. Under the stupendous impulse of mass production, goods must be moved faster and faster and ever faster from the machines of manufacturers to the shelves of merchants, to the homes of consumers. Let the process falter for a moment, let the machinery become clogged with goods, and mills close, men lose their jobs, misery descends on the land. If the machine is our god, then the salesman is the god of the machine, for it is he who feeds it. And by way of subconscious recognition of his almost religious place in the community, we call those who undertake the sternest tasks of selling—missionaries.

Gentlemen, the King

The Missionary Salesman is the man who takes a new line of, say, Mexican Hairless Depilatory, into Itta Bena, Mississippi, for the first time. He converts the heathen who hitherto have not known this great civilizing agent, or, in the words of the trade, "educates" them; lays out "dealer's helps," and helps the druggist make window displays. Sales go up, hair comes off, employment increases, and a widow in Stonington, Connecticut, who owns stock in General Depilatories, gets an extra dividend, buys a new dress, and sets in motion a new little wave of prosperity of her own.

The salesman, then, is the motor force of American life, leading us out of the desert into the land of plenty, giving food to babes, enabling us to enjoy "the better things of life." It is consequently understandable that there should be an enormous literature about and for him. Its fine essence is a book depicting Christ as a great salesman. This business-age Messiah is Bruce Barton's *The Man Nobody Knows*.

"Surely," says Mr. Barton, "no one will consider us lacking in reverence if we say that every one of the 'principles of modern salesmanship' on which business men so much pride themselves, are brilliantly exemplified in Jesus' talk and work. The first of these and perhaps the most important is the necessity for 'putting yourself in step with your prospect.' "

(A few years after the publication of Mr. Barton's contribution to the spiritual literature of our times, Mr. Dale Carnegie published his enormously successful *How to Win Friends and Influence People*. Academicians still quarrel over the question whether this book is derivative or original, but it is certain that one of its first principles is that you win friends "by putting yourself in step with your prospect.")

In his Epistle to the Salesmen, Mr. Barton tells us that in order to become an executive—the apex of salesmanship—you must have no doubts about anything. Your confidence in yourself must be so great that everybody believes in you and is driven into action by your imperious glance. Or, in the author's words:

"Most of us go through the world mentally divided against ourselves. We wonder whether we are in the right jobs, whether we are making the right investments, whether, after all, anything is as important as it seems to be. . . . Instinctively we wait for a commanding voice, for one who shall say authoritatively, 'I have the truth. This way lies happiness and salvation.' There was in Jesus supremely that quality of conviction."

Convictions in the business world must have practical applications. Idle thoughts, like idle capital, bring no return. Impractical people end by being mere poets, astronomers, botanists, musicians, or even religious visionaries. They will never have to wonder whether "they are making the right investments." But the others? Those who count: practical men, salesmen, executives. How are these men of convictions to proceed? It is simple enough after reading Mr. Barton's book, and hundreds of thousands of men did read it.

You have a profound conviction that the world needs, say,

a better baby's diaper—one that will give baby a better chance to grow up a cultured man or woman, and at the same time give mama more leisure to listen to the radio. You become a Missionary Salesman hearing voices along the road to Detroit, seeing visions of a hunk of government bonds at the end of the rainbow. You call upon lady buyer after lady buyer. Everywhere you are thrown out. You need new shoes for yourself and new tires for your car. Finally, in desperate mood, you corner Miss Mamie Martingale, buyer for Weston's in Indianapolis. As goes Miss Mamie, so goes the trade. Win her and you win all.

Your diapers are on the table and Mr. Barton's words are in your mind. You fix Miss Mamie with your glittering eye. You turn on ten thousand volts of Confidence. She weakens. You hand her her order book and she gives you the largest order for diapers ever placed east of the Mississippi River. You leave her a made man but an unhappy one, because thereafter you will have to worry about your investments.

This nonsense is practiced on a continental scale, inside and outside the universities; so, in its salesmanship course, Sears is accurately reflecting American life. In 1930, about 27,000 students were taking university courses in selling; high schools were turning out junior salesmen; psychiatrists and psychologists were vending nostrums, and an immense "literature" of salesmanship circulated everywhere.

The greatest of our universities turned from Cardinal Newman's *Idea of a University* to Mr. Barton's idea. In 1928, the Harvard Business School awarded a prize for an advertisement entitled "Kill My Cow for an Editor? I should say not!" and, in 1929, for one entitled "The Call That Will Wake any Mother." At the same time, Columbia University, in teaching the psychology of salesmanship, aspired "to present in a *scientific manner* those facts of psychology that bear on the sales process. . . ."

The catalog was therefore in good company when it offered a course in salesmanship.

What the People Like to Read

The future student of our times who appraises the reading habits of depression-chastened America in terms of the catalog's books may conclude that we were a race of children seeking escape from reality in tinsel novels and volumes of lurid adventure. Of all the great novels of the past in all languages, only two or three are in the catalog of 1935. During a period when life was being lived intensely on a political plane, there is not one book—not even the most elementary—on politics. At a moment of severe economic crisis that affected almost everybody in the country, there is nothing at all on economics. When our history was being minutely searched for clues that might throw some light on our present and help us to ascertain the future, history is represented only by a few books of the flourishing "outlines" school of historical writers. The only American poet represented is Edgar Guest. But, as we have said before, the catalog is not a mentor but a merchant. Its job is not to rush in where the high schools and universities evidently fear to tread. Its business is to get business, and that means offering the people the goods they want—including books—at prices they can afford to pay.

What kind of novels did the people want in 1935? Novels about love—love that ended happily; that terminated in a

Faith Baldwin Puts Love in Its Place for Sixty-Three Cents

wedding. Although the divorce rate has risen sharply since 1860, in the mail-order world there is no divorce. When wedlock closed down on a happy couple to the strains of "O, Promise Me," they threw the key away and stayed married until death—in the catalog. And, just as good thrillers have a murder or two in almost every chapter, so some of the catalog's novels have a wedding or two every hundred pages. This was one of the advertised virtues of *Laddie* by Gene Stratton Porter: "Now even the movies are filming Laddie, that bright and cheery tale. There's a wedding midway in the book and a double wedding at the close."

This was tough competition for Miss Porter's rivals, but the ingenious Ruby M. Ayres was equal to it. A wedding in the book is guaranteed in the title: *Come to My Wedding.*

Harold Bell Wright, the Tolstoi of the mesas, also dealt with many a wedding in his career, but in 1935 he turned to the Cinderella theme and, touching it with his genius, turned the fable into an appealing tract for our times. In *Ma Cinderella,* "a boy comes back to the Ozarks and Ma becomes Cinderella." Mr. Wright is also represented in the catalog by three earlier but equally noble books: *God and the Groceryman, Shepherd of the Hills,* and *When a Man's a Man.*

Kathleen Norris, in *Angel in the House,* deals with the difficult question once treated lyrically by James J. Walker, ex-Mayor of New York, in his unforgettable folk song: "Will You Love Me in December as You Do in May?" "Does age make a difference in love?" is the subject matter of Mrs. Norris's book.

Temple Bailey presents a novel composed of elements that have an irresistible appeal: (*a*) a beautiful and charming woman who (*b*) "desperately needs protection," and (*c*) "brings romance to young Dr. Ferry." An undertaker or a plumber may actually be an incorrigible romantic, but a man with the brown tubes of a stethoscope flowering out of his ears seems to be the most beautiful and appealing of all men to American women novel readers. Eros, stricken many times to earth, rises triumphantly again in the form of an obstetrician.

Ethel M. Dell is made of sterner stuff. In her *Donna Celestis,* she comes to grips with reality and throws it for a loss. Here she tells with her accustomed skill, "a gripping story of a ruthless man and what happens to the loving heart that trusted him."

Drop That Gun, You Skunk!

Life, however, is not all loving and marrying. It is also adventure—in books. Americans, a once adventurous people whose adventurousness has come at last to rest on the soft bosom of life insurance and old-age pensions, have an insatiable appetite for books of adventure. The most lawless people in the world, and a people who have not yet resigned themselves to living within the cramped spaces of the law, we are fond of Jesse James who broke the law and equally fond of the men who broke Jesse James.

One of the most skilled caterers to our appetite for adventure was Zane Grey, whose readers made him rich and famous by buying over twenty-four million copies of his books. Fortunately for him and for us, Mr. Grey was a prolific writer, and the 1935 catalog presents twenty-two of his novels. These are typical of his genius:

Drift Fence: "Tenderfoot Jim tumbles in love with pretty Molly Dunn of the no-good Dunns and there's the dickens to pay! A cattle-country thriller!"

Hash Knife Outfit: "A thrilling episode in early-day Arizona history. With Old Traft and his nephew against the ornery Hash Knife outfit."

The adventures, however, of cowboys, cattle thieves, sheriffs, and Indians are mere dishwater by comparison with those of Tarzan, "the orphaned son of a British nobleman." This jungle dweller, with the manners of an English gentleman, a heart of gold beneath a chest-mattress of hair, the strength of an elephant and the agility of an ape, saves young women from the embraces of sex-mad gorillas; roams through buried-treasure cities; consorts with the Ant Men; plunges to the Earth's Core, and, finally, turns up in Hollywood in the person of Johnny Weissmuller. The catalog lists twelve "world famous stories by Edgar Rice Burroughs. The amazing exploits of Tarzan, the ape-man come to you in all their rich detail."

— 145 —

By Wisdom Is a House Builded

As a people, we yearn for wisdom, especially if it is in tabloid form, is "practical," and does not take too much thinking to absorb. This yearning is satisfied by Dr. Frank Crane, the late newspaper Solomon, who gives us the distilled essence of his thoughts in *Every Day Wisdom*. At a time when America was desperately worried, G. L. Watson relieved the country's fears with *Why Worry?* For those eccentrics who insisted on doing their own thinking, the logical French, in the person of Abbé Dimnet, sent us *The Art of Thinking*, and, in *Piloting Your Life*, Joseph Jastrow "clearly and helpfully discusses every-day problems."

But the summation of all wisdom—high, helpful, get-a-job wisdom—is contained in Walter B. Pitkin's best seller, *Life Begins At Forty*. For centuries the problems of forty were no problems at all, because the majority of men evaded them by dying before reaching that age. Nowadays men live longer only to become victims of gallstones, unemployment, or the refusal of employers to hire men who have slumped into the senility of middle age. Happily for this immense group, Mr. Pitkin demonstrates that "no longer is age forty a forbidding barrier in your life's path. Inspiring!" Inspiring, indeed. After all, an unemployed fortyish paperhanger can derive much comfort from reflecting that Titian still managed to paint pretty well at the extreme age of seventy-eight.

Nothing Succeeds Like Sexcess

We have observed the progressive changes in the catalog's attitude toward sex and books about sex. The sterner puritan concepts decay; hypocrisy comes off its high horse; illusion gives way to realism, and, in 1935, as symbol of the great change of three decades, the catalog presents that oft-banned book: *Married Love* by Dr. Marie C. Stopes. It is offered bluntly as "the solution for sex difficulties."

How revolutionary is this change may be measured by a few brief references to the past.

1873: In *Good Morals and Gentle Manners for Schools and Families* by Alex M. Gow, the story is told of a young woman who was hurt in an accident. Well covered in bed, the physician to whom she will not unveil herself asks where she is injured. "One of my limbs is injured," the lady replies. He inquires whether it is an arm or leg. The patient, shocked, does not reply. The surgeon tries again. "Which is it," he asks this time, "the limb you thread a needle with?" "No," responds the sufferer, "it's the limb I wear a garter on."

1903: *Huckleberry Finn* is removed by the librarians of Omaha from their open shelves because it is an immoral book.

1906: *Huckleberry Finn* suffers the same fate in Brooklyn.

1909: "Novels dealing with sex problems in an unconventional manner" were being written all over the country, according to *The New International Year Book,* but the best sellers were "pure and inspiring" books.

1920: The publishers of Cabell's *Jurgen* were indicted for publishing an obscene book.

1927: Boston, the home of Harvard University and New England culture, banned a long list of books which it deemed obscene. Among them were:

Dark Laughter	By Sherwood Anderson
What I Believe	By Bertrand Russell
Black April	By Julia Peterkin
An American Tragedy	By Theodore Dreiser
Mosquitoes	By William Faulkner
Manhattan Transfer	By John Dos Passos
Oil	By Upton Sinclair
Elmer Gantry	By Sinclair Lewis
The Sun Also Rises	By Ernest Hemingway
Nigger Heaven	By Carl Van Vechten

Married Love was barred for a long time in England where it was written, was buffeted about by the censors in this country, and encountered a strange division of opinion in the Federal government. The New York Customs admitted it freely, but once in the country it became an obscene book to the Post Office Department which would not soil its purity by delivering it. But, by 1935, it had become merely one of a long list of books on sex which circulated freely and openly.

It is consequently a measure of the nation's rebellion against earlier attitudes that so frank a book on sex, and one so often banned, should appear in the catalog. For the catalog is not addressed to the small group of so-called "emancipated people," to the intellectual elite, or to the intellectual snobs. It is addressed to millions of the people, and we may conclude from the inclusion of this book in the catalog and from the evidences of change over a period of thirty years that, so far as the people are concerned, the days of hush-hush about sex, if they are not ended, are rapidly approaching their end.

A New Culture

If the catalog is in any degree a measure of the book-buying habits of the nation, two conclusions must be drawn

The Class of '35 Votes for Its Favorite Books

from it: (*a*) that its readers bought fewer books in 1935, and (*b*) they bought books of poorer quality.

Whether this quantitative and qualitative decline in reading is the result of the disappearance of rural isolation, leading farm folk to indulge in the pleasures of the automobile, the moving pictures, and the radio, instead of the pleasures of reading; whether men in depression seek vicarious adventure and romance in novels of escape, or whether greater access to libraries enabled them to borrow more books and buy fewer books is not clear. It is also difficult to measure with exactness the effect upon book-reading habits of the now enormous circulation of newspapers and magazines. Many of the most widely circulated magazines are not designed even to be read but merely to be looked at; their photographs are supposed to tell the story with little textual embellishment. So far as the catalog is concerned, however, it is clear that it now lists books sharply inferior in quality to those listed thirty years ago. Perhaps we are developing a new form of intellectual culture: one that proceeds from the periphery of the eyelids outward.

5 · THE HORSELESS CARRIAGE

NEVER, perhaps, in the history of mankind has any generation had to withstand the successive impacts of so many bewildering inventions altering ways of human living as this one. In the period since 1900, the telephone has come of age, the motion pictures, the radio, and the automobile. In 1900, the automobile was just coming into use, and the newspapers of the times commended Theodore Roosevelt for his "characteristic courage" for riding in one—yet it was a courage tempered by caution, because as late as 1902, when he rode in the new car, he was followed by a horse-drawn carriage in event of breakdown or accident. At the beginning of the century, there were only 8,000 automobiles and 144 miles of paved roads in the United States; clergymen denounced "automobilitis" as deleterious to morals and religion; while the state of Tennessee required a man to advertise publicly, one week in advance, his intention of going upon the public roads with an automobile.

Yet by 1910, the catalog listed FIVE ATTRACTIVE MODELS OF SEARS MOTOR CARS, each of which was "a good hill-climber and excellent performer in mud or sand." Twenty years later, there were 25,000,000 automobiles in this country moving over 750,000 miles of hard-surfaced roads. Speeds up to seventy miles an hour were negotiated with reasonable safety; manufacturing plants, garages, gasoline stations, and tourist camps were scattered throughout the land, and the automobile had become America's largest industry. The social and industrial changes wrought by the motorcar are incalculable, but this invention, like nearly all other important

MODEL J

SEARS 1910 ~ MODEL H.

AUTOMOBILES

—FIVE ATTRACTIVE MODELS—

THE GREAT SUCCESS OF 1909—YOU WILL SEE THEM EVERYWHERE IN 1910

The SEARS Is So Simple That Anyone Can Operate It

It is not necessary to have a demonstrator to teach you how to run the SEARS Motor Cars. We send with each SEARS Motor Car a complete instruction book explaining how to operate it. We have shipped hundreds of them to every state in the Union. We have sent them from New York to California, from Minnesota to Florida, and all of our customers were able to run them after reading our instruction book. Do not be afraid to order a SEARS Motor Car, as it is the simplest car to operate on the market. We have shipped hundreds of cars and we have never found it necessary to send out a man to teach a customer how to operate it. Any lady or child can start and run a SEARS Motor Car.

Tested Out By Our Customers

We build the SEARS for our customers, build it to please and satisfy our customers. It is not an experiment, but has been in use since the summer of 1908, when we started delivering the perfected car to our customers.

Hundreds of customers have tested our SEARS in every state in the Union and all say that we have given them the right car; that it is better than we claim; that it is worth twice what we ask for it; that they were surprised to receive such a good car. Write us for copies of letters from users of the SEARS and read what they say. These letters tell exactly what the car does in the hands of our customers.

The SEARS is not an experiment. It has been thoroughly tested out by actual users the past two years and demonstrated itself a perfect machine.

We are prepared to build thousands of these machines during this year of 1910 and each car sent out will be an important rock in the foundation we are building for our motor car reputation.

Our Strong Guarantee

We guarantee each SEARS Motor Car to be perfect in material and workmanship, and will replace at any time any broken parts showing defective material or workmanship, on condition that the defective or broken parts be returned to us for our inspection. The first SEARS car built has been in use over three years, has run over 20,000 miles and is still giving daily service. While we do not guarantee the SEARS cars to last any definite length of time or run any definite number of miles, as that depends entirely upon the driver and the use given it, we do guarantee that with proper care and careful attention the car will go from 1 to 150 miles daily and last as long as any other motor car built.

Our Liberal Terms

Our only terms are cash; we do not sell on installments or extend credit. Send us your order and enclose our price in the form of a postoffice money order, express money order, bank draft or check. If you don't want the motor car immediately, send us $25.00 as a deposit and we will enter your order in its turn and then later on you can send us the balance when you want us to make shipment.

Prompt Shipment

We can ship any motor car ordered in from one to ten days after order is received.

General Design

Large, roomy, two-passenger, piano box top buggy pattern, moroccoline deck boot covering body back of seat. Three-bow moroccoline auto top, fitted with complete side curtains and storm front. As comfortable in rainy days, stormy or wintry weather as when the sun shines. Body rests on a rigid pressed steel frame which carries motor and mechanism. Four-point full elliptic spring suspension. Easy riding; absorbs road shock without pneumatic tire equipment; 1/4-inch solid square steel axles; heavy drop forged steering knuckles; 36-inch wheels; solid rubber tires.

Strong Features

Fourteen-horse power, weighs only 1,000 pounds, nearly 1½-horse power per 100 pounds; the correct proportion of power and weight to make a good hill climber and excellent performer in sand or mud. Simplest car ever built; easy to operate; most pleasing and attractive pattern ever conceived in high wheeled solid tire type of car. With proper care there should be no expense for repairs, no tire expense. Fuel consumption very small, 15 to 30 miles on 1 gallon of gasoline. The solid tires will wear 3,000 to 5,000 miles; cost of renewal about $25.00. Contact surfaces on friction transmission will wear 3,000 to 4,000 miles; cost of renewal about $5.00.

Our air cooled motor is less liable to overheat than the average water cooled motor. Exhaust valve located in valve chambers where cool intake charge is inhaled, keeping cool and preventing it from burning out. Spark plug located in valve chamber where both intake and exhaust rush by and keep it clean, permitting liberal oiling of motor without danger of smutting plugs.

MODEL H $395.00

See Illustration on Page Below.

Our regular model, as illustrated below, complete equipment as described on page 1143. Black body and a rich dark carmine red gear.

No. 21T333 Model H. Price (F. O. B. Chicago).................$395.00
No. 21T444 Same as above, without top and fenders. Price......$370.00
Our regular construction (see detailed specifications, page 1143), 1⅜-inch solid rubber tires, complete with full equipment, including top, lamps, fenders and storm front. Body, black; gear, rich dark carmine.

MODEL J $410.00

See Illustration on Page Below.

Our regular model, with fenders, as illustrated below, complete as described on page 1143. Black body and a rich carmine red gear.

No. 21T555 Model J. Price (F. O. B. Chicago).:..............$410.00
Our regular construction (see detailed specifications, page 1143), 1¾-inch solid rubber tires, running boards, complete with full equipment, including top, lamps, fenders and storm front. Body, black; gear, rich dark carmine.

See Detailed Specifications on Page 1143.

inventions that preceded it, had to pass through an initial period of skepticism and hostility.

Hostility to Automobiles

The year 1895 was marked by three incidents characteristic of the early struggle of the automobile to achieve a place in American life. At Chicago, Frank Duryea had won a race in his horseless carriage. Leaving the city early in the morning, he had returned at seven o'clock in the evening, after driving to Evanston, Illinois, covering the distance of fifty-five miles in little more than ten hours.

A short while later, at Springfield, Massachusetts, Samuel Bowles II, editor of the Springfield *Republican,* refused to ride in Duryea's car on the ground that it would be incompatible with his dignity and position.

In Detroit, a young man named Henry Ford, after running his first car one thousand miles, sold it for $200 in order to get money with which to build a new one. Aside from the mechanical difficulties it had exhibited, Mr. Ford was so much troubled by curious persons anxious to drive his "gasoline buggy" that he had to chain it to a post whenever he left it.

At New York, in 1897, the *Times* mused sadly and wistfully in an editorial upon the coming change:

> The imagination of Mr. Kipling . . . may in time be lent to the idealization of the new mechanical wagon with the awful name—automobile. For that thing has come to stay . . . sooner or later they will displace the fashionable carriage of the present hour. . . . Sensitive and emotional folk cannot view the impending change without conflicting emotions. Man loves the horse and he is not likely ever to love the automobile . . . nor will he ever get quite used, in this generation, to speeding along the road behind nothing.

Important technological inventions arouse the hostility of interests which they threaten to replace. Thus, the early railroads of the United States were opposed by private and state owners of canals, and, in Pennsylvania, where there were many state canals, tonnage taxes were imposed for many years on the Pennsylvania Railroad.

"The propaganda of vested interests was potent. It was easy to arouse opposition of farmers along the right-of-way, on the grounds that the roaring locomotives would startle the cattle and prevent them from grazing in safety, that the hens would not lay, that the poisoned air from the locomotives would kill the wild birds and destroy vegetation, that farmhouses would be ignited by sparks, and property would deteriorate. Farmers likewise were made apprehensive lest through competition there would be no markets for horses, and that their crops of hay and oats would be worthless. . . . An eloquent divine in the United States went so far as to declare that the introduction of the railroad would require the building of many insane asylums, as people would be driven mad with terror at the sight of locomotives rushing through the country with nothing to draw them. Railroads were likewise denounced as impious because they were not foreseen in the Bible." *

In time, the railroads won their battle against the interests opposing them, only to meet the competition later of automobiles, trucks, and buses; but the automobile, too, was opposed by horse growers, draymen, and livery-stable owners. The last group was effectually forced into silence by the argument that the reduction of the numbers of horses in cities would reduce the flies and consequently communicable diseases carried by flies. But moral arguments against the motorcar continued to be advanced, while the law sought to restrain it as an agent of destruction. The city of New York, for example, barred Central Park to horseless vehicles just before 1900, while New York State passed a law fixing the maximum rate of speed at ten miles an hour in villages and cities, and twenty miles an hour on highways. And the magazine *Life* in 1901, regarding the automobile as a machine which no gentleman

* *Technological Trends and National Policy,* National Resources Committee, June, 1937, p. 41.

would employ, said, "A man who would now win the parvenu's bow must belong to the automobility."

It was argued, too, that the terrifying speeds of automobiles would break down the nerves of automobilists, and warnings by medical men began to appear in the press. In 1904, *The Literary Digest* quoted the following from *The Medical News:*

> Soon physicians will be called on for numerous cases of nervous symptoms traceable to excitement and nervous tension of rapid travelling with the emotional repression necessary to secure a reasonable feeling of enjoyment, while speeding rapidly with risks and dangers constantly at hand. . . . Dr. Paul Magin considers that the indulgence in speed is not unlike in alcohol and tobacco. . . . It is clear that permission to drive such heavy machines should not be accorded to anyone who has ever exhibited signs of mental disequilibrium . . . even healthy persons find it hard enough to keep their balance.

While Dr. Magin indulged in the thoroughly sound speculation that many automobile drivers had no brains—a speculation which is now accepted as axiomatic—the *Review of Reviews* concluded that the automobile was dangerous because it was brainless. Hence the country would be faced with the peril of brainless men driving brainless machines—a prevision of startling accuracy. This magazine said:

> Granted that the horse is not cleanly and that his hoofs make a noise, how about the automobile? The exhaust and cinders from a steam truck, the noisy and evil smelling exhaust of certain gasoline cars, the dripping of oil, the difficulty of cleaning a storage battery . . . these are some of the objections that might be pointed out. . . . The horse is an intelligent animal, the automobile is a brainless machine . . . one will take care of itself if the driver is suddenly smitten down, the other may run amok.

Thirty-five years after these lines were written, the *Scien-*

tific American (September, 1939) in an article called "Insanity At The Wheel," said:

> You smash into the car ahead, dash past the red signal, send pedestrians scurrying for safety as you swing the wheel hard. You may not have contributed to the nation's 32,400 deaths and 1,150,000 non-fatal injuries resulting from automotive mishaps last year, but that's no sign you are sane. Crazy drivers crowd the highways, and their insanity is easily demonstrable. Hell hath no friend like these speeding, swerving, horn-blowing lunatics, and psychology is determined to find them, thus aiding the engineer and the automobile builder in curbing the grim reaper.

Finally, in the early days of automobiles, when their speeds rarely reached twenty miles an hour, it was assumed that while technique would raise the speeds of the cars, the human being would not be able to manage them: In 1901, the *Automobile Magazine* quotes Dr. Winslow Forbes, a brain specialist:

> "When these racing motor cars reach a speed of 80 miles per hour, they must drive themselves, for no human brain is capable of dealing with all the emergencies that may arise should that rate be maintained for any period worth thinking of. The human animal is not designed to travel 80 miles an hour; neither the human brain, nor the human eye can keep pace with it."

William Allen White Defends the Horse

In 1912, Colonel Theodore Roosevelt visited his friend William Allen White in Emporia, Kansas. The visit moved the editor of the *Ottawa* [Kansas] *Herald* to make a few remarks at the expense of the town of Emporia:

> Emporia claims that it can accommodate almost any request in the form of entertainment. Colonel Roosevelt wanted "a day of rest" Sunday, and Emporia proceeded to give him a ride behind Old Tom. Old Tom, by the way is one of the most restful horses you ever saw.

Whereupon Old Tom's owner and Colonel Roosevelt's

MODEL L

SEARS 1910 ~ MODEL K

MODEL K $475.00

See Illustration on Page Above.

Our regular construction (see detailed specifications below) 38x2-inch Swinehart Cushion Tires. Double back twin auto seat and special auto top with dust hood, running board, black enameled lamps, complete with full equipment, including top, lamps, fenders and storm front. We strongly recommend it as the most complete and highly pleasing in every respect. The tire equipment is almost as resilient as pneumatics and is the longest wearing tire on the market. Body, black; gear, Brewster green.

No. 21T666 Model K. Price (F. O. B. Chicago)..............$475.00

MODEL L $495.00

See Illustration on Page Above.

Our regular construction (see detailed specifications below), 34x3-inch double tube, detachable flare back tire, with special auto top cover, running lamps, complete with full equipment, including top, lamps, fenders and leading model. This is the car for those who prefer pneumatic tires. It has light weight soft on the market. Body, black; gear, Brewster green...........$495.00

No. 21T777 Model L. Price (F. O. B. Chicago)..............

DETAILED SPECIFICATIONS

GENERAL DIMENSIONS.

Large, roomy body, 67 inches long, 30 inches wide, 8-inch sides, 16 inches from cushion top to floor, 27 inches from floor to ground; 11½-inch three-panel patent leather dash. Body space in front of seat, 21x30 inches. Space under seat used for gasoline tank, battery box and spark coils. Seat, 37 inches wide; back, 22 inches high.

MOTOR—Two-cylinder, direct opposed, 4⅛-inch bore, 4-inch stroke, 14-horse power (A. L. A. M. rating), four-cycle, air cooled with valve chambers, mechanically operated exhaust, automatic intake, 1⅝-inch nickel steel forged crank shaft, two four-blade fans running twice the speed of crank shaft. Removable cylinder heads, our own patented timer, large 3-inch ball thrust bearing between fly wheel and crank case, 1,800-pound pressure capacity. Priming cocks in each cylinder. All crank shaft and connecting rod bearings accessible and adjustable.

TRANSMISSION—Selective friction type. Contact wheel shifted on countershaft across face of wheel by side lever. Contact effected by slight pressure on foot pedal. No ratchet; the weight of the foot is all that is necessary to connect power to drive wheels.

DIFFERENTIAL—Friction clutch type; coaster brake plan, one on each end of countershaft; pulls on both wheels going straight ahead or back; allows outside or faster wheel to coast freely when rounding a turn. Works backward or forward; simple, light and indestructible. Our own design, covered by U. S. patents.

DRIVE—Double chain from countershaft to each rear wheel. Endless riveted roller chains ½ inch wide, 1-inch pitch.

LUBRICATION—Shooting type, mechanical force feed oiler, delivers oil to crank case cover, dripping it on crank shaft and connecting rod bearings, spattering the oil into the cylinders; also delivers oil to exhaust cam cases, effecting a constant bath for cams, shafts and plungers. Countershaft hanger bearings have oil reservoirs filled from oil can.

IGNITION—Jump spark, double coil, six dry cells, spark plugs mounted in valve chamber.

BRAKE—Internal expanding on each rear wheel. Adjustable.

STEERING—Side lever; left side, the side that runs closest to every vehicle you pass on the road. You steer with your right hand. Quick and handy to get around. Used on the highest priced electric runabouts. Simple, light and direct. Reliable and nothing to get out of order.

Sig. 77—Ed. 1.

CONTROL—Flexible as a steam throttle, with a range of 1 to 25 miles per hour, without shifting contact wheel. Gas throttle to carburetor. Spark control to timer. Both levers convenient at top of side steering post, operated with the left hand.

MUFFLERS—Two silencers, our own design. Exhaust almost entirely silenced.

ACCESSIBILITY—By lifting floor boards in front, the engine, carburetor, oiler, timer, spark plugs, fans, oiler belts and coils are all within easy reach. Cylinder heads can be removed independent of any other part. Intake valves removed by loosening intake pipe. Exhaust valves removed through end of valve chamber. Connecting rod and crank bearings easily adjusted by removing crank case cover.

CARBURETOR—Latest improved carburetor, float feed, auxiliary air inlet. Thoroughly reliable. Only one simple adjustment of needle valve on gasoline. Simple to adjust.

WHEELS—36 inches in diameter, front and rear; selected hickory 1⅛-inch spokes, Sarven's patent metal hub and spoke flange; 1⅛-inch rim, fitted with 1⅜-inch steel channel and 1⅜-inch solid rubber tires.

AXLES—1¼-inch solid square steel anti-friction, self oiling automobile axles, heavy drop forged steering knuckles and steering connections.

SPRINGS—Four oil tempered, resilient, full elliptic 1¼-inch four-leaf 36-inch springs, secured to the angle steel frame and the axles with heavy wrought iron clips. Exceptionally easy riding; absorbs all road shocks without the aid of costly pneumatic tires.

TOP—Three-bow skeleton automobile top of heavy moroccoline; moroccoline leather detachable side curtains. Top held up and tightened by two straps from front bow to dash. A secure and noiseless fastening for driving over rough roads.

STORM FRONT—Complete storm protection, covering dash and reaching back to middle bow, inside of top. Two large mica windows in storm front and two in each side curtain.

PAINTING—Body and seat black. Wheels and chassis rich dark carmine or dark Brewster green, striped with a double fine line.

FRAME—2x1½x3-16-inch pressed angle steel. Heavy corner plates and cross frame all riveted.

BODY—Piano box style, detachable, substantially built, 30 inches wide, 67 inches long. Bolted to the angle steel frame, the strongest possible construction. Rear of body back of seat covered with rainproof rubber deck boot, 11½-inch patent leather dash.

SEAT—Special roomy surrey seat, 22-inch spring back, spring cushion 37 inches wide. Seat sides padded and lined; genuine machine buffed best quality leather.

EQUIPMENT.

Two good oil lamps in front; oil tail lamp in rear, showing white light to right side and red light to rear. Acetylene attachments and generator furnished with oil lamps for $10.95 extra. Complete set of fenders; three-bow top with front straps, side curtains and storm front, completely enclosed for most severe weather; large deep toned horn, floor carpet; set of tools, consisting of an adjustable wrench, manifold wrench, screwdriver, pair of pliers and a copper spring bottom oil can.

We send with each car a booklet giving full instructions for the care and operation of the car; also furnish 1 gallon of lubricating oil.

ROAD CLEARANCE— 13 inches.
WHEEL BASE—72 inches.
TRACK—56 inches.
WIDE TRACK—62 inches, $4.65 extra.
GASOLINE CAPACITY—About 6 gallons.
WEIGHT—1,000 pounds.

Extras listed below are not necessary, but are listed for those who want additional equipment.

EXTRAS, IF WANTED.

Magneto $35.00
Combination Acetylene and Kerosene Front Lamps, with Generator... 10.95
Acetylene Headlights and Generator in place of Oil Lamps 19.75
Speedometer, showing speed and total mileage.... 15.00
Speedometer, showing speed, total mileage and trip mileage 25.00
Extra Switch Key.. .15
Extra Set Six Dry Cells.................................. 1.56
Extra Spark Plug... .69

HOW TO ORDER.

Each of the five models has a catalog number. Give catalog number of the model you choose. Each model is complete. Send money by postoffice money order, express money order or bank draft.

SHIPPING.

We ship the SEARS Motor Car crated or set up, whichever will get the best freight rate. If you want to know what the exact freight charges will be, write us and we will gladly tell you.

host, Mr. White, rushed editorially to the defense of Old Tom, and incidentally made a few bitter remarks about the newfangled automobile: *

> Old Tom, of course, is no Maud S nor Joe Patchen. . . . But he has the same number of legs attached and his heart is true. He makes no claim to speed, but his carburetor always works, and while he has but two cylinders he brings his guests back in one piece and leaves them at home rather than down town at the undertaker's to be assembled by total strangers into their aliquot parts.
>
> What if he isn't speedy; what if his best record is a mile in 15 minutes? . . . Old Tom may not have a windshield or speedometer. But what would he do with them? He is fully equipped with a few kind words and a whalebone whip. Tom, like Spartacus the gladiator, has "faced every form of man or beast the broad empire," could produce. Princes and potentates, fair women and brave men have lolled luxuriously among the $4 springs of the surry behind Old Tom and have seen Emporia and Lyon County whizz by them at four miles an hour without fear or anxiety. They knew they were safe. He will go longer . . . on a forty-cent bale of hay than these new-fangled vessels of wrath fitted unto destruction with a bucket of gasoline and a cord of rubber.
>
> Then, of course, there is this important thing to say of Old Tom: while, of course, it is difficult to get new parts when he breaks, yet after all he is paid for, and there's no ninety-day note turning up every season to make the years a melancholy procession on the other side of the street from the bank. . . . Taken up one side and down the other —Old Tom has his good points.

A few years later, we shall observe, Old Tom is in a horse's heaven and Mr. White is singing a different tune behind the steering wheel.

Automobile Etiquette

As the automobile increased in numbers on the roads of America, there arose a formulated automobile etiquette. As recently as 1921, Emily Holt, in her *Encyclopaedia of Eti-*

* William Allen White, *Forty Years on Main Street.*

quette, laid down rules for the governance of the automobilist and his host, which not only reflect in some degree the manners of the period, but also give us glimpses of the clothes worn by automobilists and the construction of the then current automobiles:

> When a man, driving an automobile, stops his car to take a woman friend into the seat beside him, he dismounts to do so, and remounts from the other side after the lady has gained her place. . . .

Here the writer is talking the language of the horseman, and she points out niceties of difference in the etiquette of the automobilist and the driver of a horse-drawn vehicle:

> . . . Whether driving himself or being driven by a friend of either sex who returns the bows of passing acquaintances, he does not fail to lift his hat each time the person beside him bows. The driver of a horse-drawn trap . . . achieves an effect equally courteous by touching his hat's brim with the stock of his whip. In a motor, he returns or gives a bow with a military salute.

Miss Holt then gives a few "Hints for an Automobile Host":

> Make sure that the wind-shield, top, and side-curtains are so adjusted as to afford your guests the maximum of comfort.
> Provide linen dusters for the summer guests and heavy cloaks, coats, and gloves for those who brave the winter winds in your care. Have goggles at hand for those who care to protect their eyes with them.
> Remember that jolting is most noticeable in the tonneau, where guests are ordinarily seated. Accordingly drive carefully and slowly enough to insure your passengers against discomfort.

Mass Production

John D. Rockefeller was the pioneer of mass production in this country—one of the transcendently revolutionary accomplishments of our times—but it is Henry Ford who is popularly regarded as its god. It is he, more than any other American, who broadcast to the United States and the world the technique of putting a mass of parts onto one end of a moving assembly line and removing the finished product from the other end. By 1908, he had decided to concentrate all his efforts on one model of car—the famous "tin Lizzie" Model T—and to effect economies in production by greater mechanical efficiency resulting from the use of mass-production methods. Charles Merz, in *And Then Came Ford,* describes the early workings of the process that was so deeply to influence American life:

> The idea of the belt was borrowed from the Chicago packers, who used an overhead trolley to swing carcasses of beef down a line of butchers. Ford tried the idea first in assembling a small unit in his motor, the fly-wheel magneto, then in assembling the motor itself, and then in assembling the chassis.
>
> A chassis was hitched to a rope one day, and six workmen, picking up parts along the way and bolting them in place, travelled fifty feet in length as a windlass dragged it through the factory. The experiment worked, but developed one difficulty. God had not made men as accurately as Ford made piston rings. The line was too high for short men and too low for tall men, with a resultant waste in effort.
>
> More experiments were tried. The line was raised; then lowered; then two lines, were tried, etc. . . . In the end, the time allotted for assembly on a chassis was cut from twelve hours and twenty-eight minutes to one hour and thirty-three minutes, the world was promised Model T's in new abundance, and mass production entered a new phase as men were made still more efficient cogs of their machines. . . .

Mass production had come to America and thereafter it was to be a changed country.

Sears and the Automobile

In 1905, the only reference to the automobile in the catalog—the invention that twenty years later was to compel

Sears to abandon its exclusive mail-order policy and open retail stores—is a book called *Horseless Vehicles, Automobiles and Motor Cycles,* by Gardner D. Hiscox, M.E.

"A practical treatise for automobilists, and everyone interested in the development, care and use of the automobile. . . . Comprises in its scope a full description . . . of the . . . manufacturing of one of the most important innovations of the times. . . . Fully illustrated with various types of horseless carriages, automobiles and motorcycles."

But only three years later—in the summer of 1908—Sears began to sell automobiles, and, in the 1910 catalog, lists "five attractive models" and illustrates them with two (then) rare color pages.

MODEL L

Neither Mud nor Sand nor Missing Cylinders Kept This Swift Courier from Making Its Appointed Rounds at Twelve Miles per Hour

It is interesting to note that, while Mr. Ford's standardization of manufacture led him to say in 1909, "Any customer can have a car painted any color that he wants so long as it is black," Sears, actuated perhaps by a wider merchandising knowledge, offered black cars with red or green gear. And eventually Mr. Ford's mania for one style of car made serious difficulties for him.

The catalog's description of the Sears motorcar may stand as a description in general of the cars of the times, of the terms by which they were sold, the wearing qualities of tires, and the performance to be expected of the motors.

In 1910, the automobile as such had not come into being, and the cars of the period are more accurately described as horseless carriages, being, in reality, buggies propelled by motors. The catalog describes the Sears car as follows:

"Large, roomy, two-passenger, piano-box top buggy pattern, moroccoline deck boot covering body back of seat. Three-bow moroccoline auto top, fitted with complete side curtains and storm front. As comfortable in rainy days, stormy or wintry weather as when the sun shines. . . ."

The motor was "fourteen-horse power, weighs only 1,000 pounds, nearly 1½ horse power per 100 pounds; the correct proportion of power and weight to make a good hill climber and excellent performer in sand or mud. . . ."

The tires were generally solid and "will wear 3,000 to 5,000 miles; cost of renewal about $25. Contact surfaces on friction transmission will wear 3,000 to 4,000 miles. . . ."

What performance on the road could the owner of a Sears car expect? The catalog tells us.

"The first SEARS car has been in use over three years, has run over 20,000 miles and is still giving daily service. While we do not guarantee the SEARS cars to last any definite length of time or run any definite number of miles, as that depends entirely upon the driver and the use given it, we do guarantee that with proper care and careful attention the car will go from 1 to 150 miles daily and last as long as any other motor car built. . . . We have shipped hundreds of cars and we have never found it necessary to send out a man to teach a customer how to operate it. Any lady or child can start and run a Sears Motor Car."

The cars were lighted by oil lamps; the gasoline capacity was six gallons; the floor was covered with carpet, and a set of tools, plus one gallon of lubricating oil, came as standard equipment. The prices of the Sears varied between $395 and

$495, but the final prices were higher because of the cost of extra equipment listed as follows:

EXTRAS, IF WANTED

Magneto $35.00
Combination Acetylene and Kerosene front Lamps,
    with Generator 10.95
Acetylene Headlights and Generator in place of
    Oil Lamps............................. 19.75
Speedometer, showing speed and total mileage.... 25.00
Extra Switch Key............................ .15
Extra Set Six Dry Cells...................... 1.56
Extra Spark Plug........................... .69

Only the most expensive model, selling for $495, was equipped with "detachable clincher pneumatic tires."

The terms on which the Sears car was sold were—cash. The great day of installment selling of automobiles—and eventually of everything else—had not yet come.

The Automobile Opens New Markets

While the sole reference, as we have seen, to automobiles in the 1905 catalog was a book about motorcars, the 1910 catalog listed not only Sears automobiles but a wide range of merchandise for motors and motorists. From this time on, automobile accessories are to assume the first rank in Sears' sales activities.

As mariners prepare for rain and storm with oilskins and boots, so the automobilists of 1910 prepared themselves against dust storms arising from the dirt roads. The dust usually came with the heat of summer, but that made no difference to the hardy women pioneers who went out in their cars wearing "traveling or automobile coats made of good quality imitation linen ... the sleeves are provided with wristlets to keep the dust out," and silk veils pulled about their faces. This costume was hot in warm weather, but it was fashionable and dust-resistant, and so commonly worn as to have been a uniform that women donned before getting into an automobile.

The intrepid male automobilist of the same period seems also to have been sensitive to dust, but insensitive to heat, for he wore a linen duster buttoned up high around the throat and a linen or leather automobile cap with "flaps that can be turned down and fastened underneath chin with elastic connecting band, thus protecting sides of face and neck from dust." Thus also making certain that the motorist would stifle with heat if he was not choked with dust, but stifle fashionably.

Sears Drops the Sears Car

Between 1910 and 1915, Sears stopped selling automobiles, and the only reference to them in the catalog of the latter date is: "automobiles, toy." The automobile industry was following the pattern of the telephone industry, and later of the radio, in which the field of a revolutionary invention, at first occupied by a large number of producers, soon narrows under the stress of competition to a few. Already by 1912, more than half the American production of motorcars was produced by seven manufacturers; in 1917, ten makers accounted for seventy-five per cent of the total production, and in 1923, these ten produced ninety per cent of the total. Not only was competition severe, but Sears had no facilities for servicing cars scattered all over America. It therefore went out of the automobile business and into the automobile-accessories business.

First on the list of important accessories for cars is tires. The catalog says: "Justice tires are a famous make standard brand tire sold under our own brand name Justice, direct to the user. We save you 20 percent or more by selling these tires under our own brand name, instead of the widely advertised and popular name, direct to the car owner instead of through the expensive and indirect methods usually employed in selling standard tires. Justice tires are made side by side with a well known brand of standard tires. They duplicate the latter in everything except name and price, neither of which adds to the quality of the tires."

What performance was expected of a 1915 tire? It was a poor performance as measured by present standards. Sears' "liberal guarantee" read:

"We guarantee Justice tires to give you the performance you can reasonably expect from any standard tire. Should any Justice Tire prove defective in material or workmanship we will make an adjustment based on 3,500 miles service." Nowadays a tire has hardly made its debut at this distance, but there have been prodigious advances in tire-making techniques since 1915.

When a man bought a Ford or other car in 1915, his troubles had just begun; thereafter he spent time and money

Gilding the Lizzie

on accessories that would "dress it up," and the catalog offers long lists of gadgets whose job it was to make a Ford roll like a Rolls-Royce or purr like a Packard. Among them were:

> Electric Lighting Outfits.
> Easy Riding Aids—The Little Steersman. "Makes desirable tension between front springs and steering rod, giving driver absolute control over car."
> D. C. Shock Absorbers. "The Shock Absorbers will give your Ford car balance and smoothness in riding usually found only on costly heavy cars."
> Anti-Rattling Devices and Tow Ropes.
> Seat and Top Covers. "Give your Ford the classy appearance of high priced touring cars."

Thousands of Americans habitually leave their agricultural implements to rust in the rain, but few can be found who do not provide shelter for their automobiles. In 1915, however, houses were not being built, as they are now, with attached garages, and sensing a new market, the catalog offers ready-made garages, shipped knock-down, made of steel or wood, for $59.75.

The automobile of 1915 was neither rainproof, dustproof, nor windproof, and this fact opened the door to the sale of other accessories necessary to the comfort of motorists. The catalog's description of a plush automobile robe gives us a clue to what the pioneers faced as they jolted perilously over the face of a continent:

"Green on one side, black on the other; rubber interlined; pinked felt border. A sheet of rubber cloth between the two pieces of plush makes the robe stormproof, windproof and rainproof."

The ladies are still wearing automobile veils and scarfs in 1915, but the more dashing are appearing in their Fords attired in silk poplin caps with visors or the even more desirable Hindu turban made of "silk mull in fancy jacquard designs." Dusters, however, have disappeared to come no more; but roads are being built everywhere in the country; motorcar production reaches new heights year after year, and the ever-increasing pages of the catalog devoted to automobile accessories testify how deeply the car has penetrated into the lives of the people.

Twelve years after his spirited defense of Old Tom, who is now grazing in heaven's pastures, and his indictment of the automobile which he did not then own, William Allen White returns to the columns of the *Gazette* with a discussion of the once maligned motorcar. But he is singing a different song which he calls "Prodigal's Return":

Last evening the White family Dodge turned into Exchange Street after a six weeks' joyous family journey in Kansas. It had covered 2,783 miles. In that time Mr. and Mrs. White and young Bill had been out campaigning. They have covered the state from Lincoln in the northwest to Galena in the southeast, from Anthony in the southwest to Hiawatha in the northeast, speaking at least once in all except three counties of that territory. Mr. White has made 104 speeches and probably addressed 100,000 people.

Mr. White has not slept in the same bed for any two consecutive nights for the last six weeks, though he has been home every Sunday. . . . He is in better shape physically than he has been for years. . . . The six weeks in the open air, in the open car, riding from four to ten hours a day, and speaking three or four hours visiting around the firesides of scores of friends at night, have restored his physical vigor. . . .

Mr. Ford Takes a Lesson and Gives One

Between 1918 and 1922 inclusive, the production of American automobiles exceeded the total of all the previous years; by the end of the first quarter of the twentieth century, there were over 20 million automobiles in a nation of about 25 million families. The motorcar had begun to kill its thousands and wound its hundreds of thousands annually; men met the installment payments on their automobiles even if meant going without bread; cars and the merits of cars were stock topics of daily conversation everywhere; industry looked to the attendance at automobile shows for clues to prosperity or depression in the future, and it was evident that the country had entered upon a new phase of civilization in which the automobile was all important.

The catalog's multiple and ever-growing pages of automobile accessories reflect not only increasing demand but sharply improved quality. In 1915, Justice tires were guaranteed on the basis of 3,500 miles of service, but ten years later, "we guarantee Justice Fabric Tires . . . on the basis of 6,000 miles' service, and Justice Cords on the basis of 10,000 miles' service."

The new balloon-type tire is coming on the market and the catalog announces "Justice Balloon Type Cords. The Latest Development in Tire Construction. They Fit Your Present Wheels and Rims." Men are still tinkering with the "One-Man Top" that twenty men had never been able to maneuver even in calm weather, but the catalog thinks it has the final solution in its "Real One-Man Top." Actually, the motor industry which solved so many difficult problems never succeeded in creating a one-man or a ten-man top that would work, and merely dodged the problem by creating closed cars.

Whatever the failures of the one-man top, the catalog offers other delights for the motorist: "Classy Sun Curtains to protect car occupants from hot sun, blinding headlights at rear"; while esthetes were urged to buy a "De Luxe Flower Vase complete with a small cluster of artificial roses for your coupe or sedan."

At this period all seemed serene and prosperous in the automobile industry. It is no exaggeration to say that no group of industrialists since the beginning of the industrial revolution had enjoyed such unparalleled opportunities as those afforded to American motorcar manufacturers. Here was a vast continent sparsely settled, and, even in the twentieth century, but sketchily linked by railroads, rivers, roads, and canals; a continent that needed, above all things, a cheap and flexible form of transport. In the earth of this continent lay most of the materials necessary for the making of automobiles, while it produced gold and goods to trade abroad for materials not found at home. Here, too, was an abundant supply of skilled and intelligent labor; capital goods of every kind; energy, initiative, and a per capita income—however low—higher than that enjoyed by any other people in the world. Here was a domestic market greater than any on earth and free of trade barriers of any kind, and a nation laying down hard-surface roads with an ease and prodigality that made it appear that they were bought at the ribbon counters of Woolworth's. Beyond our borders were the markets of the world eager to buy American automobiles, because American mass-production methods and the giant domestic market enabled our manufacturers to excel all others in both quality and price. It would seem, therefore, that this industry was capable of almost indefinite expansion, yet events were soon to show that the industry as a whole was to be faced with grave difficulties, while Mr. Ford, the industry's leader, was to encounter a problem created by his own methods and peculiar to himself.

Shortly after the close of the World War, the motor industry, frightened by talk of the saturation of the market, abandoned its policy of selling for cash, and reached out through installment selling to a great group of low-income workers who had not been "saturated." This group, eager to ride in cars but unable to ride for cash, responded by hundreds of thousands when they were permitted to pay as they rode. Lowered prices also brought more thousands of customers, but production moved faster than sales, and, in order to keep the wheels of the factories turning, the industry soon had to adopt another device. This is what the advertising gentlemen call the "theory of obsolescence"; that is, a manufacturer can make consumers vaguely unhappy and disturb their sleep by constantly bringing out new car models differing but little from the old ones except that the new models have new tin whistles and a stylish new finish. The consequence is that the consumer soon becomes dissatisfied with his "old" car and trades it in for a new one. Car models soon began to change, therefore, almost as rapidly as fashions in women's clothes, and consumers, anxious to keep pace with or even be ahead of the times, successively bought new editions of tin whistles attached to the same kind of bodies and engines they had bought before.

The automobile industry continued to forge ahead after the World War by virtue of (a) installment selling; (b) continually finding new buyers in lower and lower income groups; (c) reducing prices, and (d) frequent changes of models. It is estimated that, by 1929, the replacement demand alone had reached 3 million cars a year. All the while Mr. Henry Ford had been undisputed king of the industry, fabulously rich, and better known to the whole world than any man with the possible exception of Charles Chaplin.

It is now 1927, and we are considering the same Mr. Ford who eighteen years before had said with dogmatic complacency: "Any customer can have a car painted any color that he wants so long as it is black." The time has now come when Mr. Ford is to take and to give a lesson.

Long before 1927, American manufacturers had begun to "sell" that concept which has immemorially been the stock in trade of poets and the despair of philosophers—beauty. By 1927, the perils of motoring were over; when a man left home in his car, he was almost certain to return under his own power instead of at the tail end of a pair of mules. The automobile engine would continue to be improved, but it was no longer an awesome thing to behold or to tinker with, and actually it needed little tinkering. What the ugly, skyscraper-high, monotonously black car needed was beauty, and some manufacturers were getting ready to supply it. It was soon to have beauty with the coming of lower-slung bodies, the invention of quick-drying pyroxylin varnishes enabling manufacturers to turn out colored cars cheaply and quickly, and closed bodies that did away with unsightly tops and flapping curtains flying in the wind or drooping like the wings of dead birds.

Mr. Ford, however, who was neither poet, philosopher, nor esthete, but a man with a mania for the mass production that had served him well in the past, stuck to the color black with a passion for this shade found only among the best-dressed women of Paris. Mr. Ford seems to have been oblivious, too, to the fact that, when cars were bought by men on the score of their technical excellence, women, who knew nothing of engine performance, let the men do the buying. But once the time had arrived when all cars of whatever brand were reliable, women took a hand in choosing them and women had become acutely conscious of beauty, color, and style. Mr. Ford, however, continued to say "let 'em have black," and the result of his color blindness and esthetic obliquity was that thousands of men and women chose the new beautiful Chevrolets in colors. The huge Ford plants were closed almost the entire year of 1927, while new models were concocted behind the doors.

What then happened testifies not only to the magic exerted upon the minds of machine-enchanted Americans by the name Ford, the symbol of the incredibly successful Master Mechanic, but also to the motor mania of the nation. During the period when the Ford plants were closed, millions of men asked one another millions of times the same but ever-interesting question: what kind of car will the new Ford be? Newspapers printed endless columns of speculation on the subject; a man who said, "I know a guy that knows a guy that's seen one," attained fleeting prestige in the community; while Ford dealers, with little to sell for the moment, took orders for the new car sight unseen for delivery in the indefinite future, and drew on their savings for living expenses. Finally, the day of days came—December 2, 1927—when the new car would be shown. On that day, reports Charles Merz in *And Then Came Ford,* "one hundred thousand people flocked into the showrooms of the Ford Company in Detroit; mounted police were called out to patrol the crowds in Cleveland; in Kansas City so great a mob stormed Convention Hall that platforms had to be built to lift the new car high enough for everyone to see it."

The miracle car was distinguished by two features: it was painted in colors, and it matched competitors' models mechanically. But, from that time until today, Mr. Ford was never again to be the undisputed king of the motors industry.

Tire Prices Fall While Quality Rises

So great is the dominance of the automobile in American life that, of the 846 pages in the spring and summer catalog of 1935 (Philadelphia Edition), 42 of these pages are devoted to tires and automobile accessories. The brand name "Justice" has, however, been dropped, whether because of the growing cynicism of the people toward the abstract concept from which Sears' tires took their name, or whether it did not sound sufficiently sonorous to the ears of the Company's advertising executives. ALLSTATE is the tire of the 1935 catalog, and both its price and quality reflect changes in American economic life and improvements in manufacturing technique.

In the period 1926–37, the price of a 29 × 4.40 Allstate tire (the size used for Ford, Chevrolet, and other small cars) dropped from $11.25 to $5.65—a reduction of $5.60. What brought about this enormous change in prices?

For one thing, $3 of the lowered cost came from the precipitous drop in the prices of two "controlled" commodities—rubber and cotton. For another thing, improved manufacturing efficiency accounted for $0.42 of the decrease. During the period we are considering, the output of tires per man per day jumped from three tires to six. And the remaining $2 of the difference in price resulted from improved distribution methods and increased competition which lowered selling prices and also cut down profit margins. The consequence was that a tire buyer in 1937 paid about one half the price he had paid in 1926 and got a far better tire than in the earlier period.

We have seen how Sears increased its guarantee on tire mileage from 3,500 miles in 1915 to 6,000-10,000 miles in 1925. The final step was taken in 1935, when mileage as a criterion of measurement was altogether discarded. This is the new guarantee:

18-Month Guarantee

The Allstate Companion 4-Ply Tire is guaranteed to wear for 18 full months. This guarantee includes all road hazards that would render the tire unfit for further service. There are No Exceptions! Should this tire fail within 18 months from date of purchase, return it to our Mail Order House. We will replace it with a *brand new tire,* charging you one-eighteenth of the current price for each month the tire has been in your possession.

The Past Lives and Runs

In a country where publishers permit many books to go out of print sometimes within one year after publication, and where the woman who buys a set of china dishes today from so-called "open stock" cannot replace a broken plate of the same pattern a few months later, it is heartening to observe the care and attention lavished on our old motorcars. The 1935 catalog lists radiators for Model T Fords although their manufacture had ceased in 1927; radiators for Buicks going back fifteen years to 1920, and for Graham Trucks reaching into the distant past of 1917.

The Automobile Revolutionizes Sears

When Sears began to sell automobiles in the prehistoric days of 1908, and, a little while later, when it had stopped selling cars and embarked on the extensive selling of automobile accessories, it does not seem to have occurred to its executives that the motorcar would one day shake the business to its foundations and compel it to abandon its policy of selling exclusively by mail. Yet it was little more than twenty years from the time Sears first started selling automobiles to the time automobiles forced it to begin opening retail stores throughout the country.

The mail-order business at its inception found its economic justification and its opportunity in the twin facts of isolation endured by millions of people living on the land and their inability to satisfy more than a limited range of wants when they succeeded in reaching the nearest small town. In its simplest terms, the mail-order method simply meant taking a large store to the customer, permitting him to make his selections of merchandise at leisure, and then delivering the goods to his door by freight, mail, or express. Upon these terms the mail-order houses flourished and grew great through the latter years of the nineteenth century and the earlier years of the twentieth century.

All this was changed by the automobile. Above everything else, it gave Americans mobility, and they were quick to use it. America literally came out of the mud onto the surfaced highway. Automobiles improved in ease of operation and speed while their prices came sharply down through the years, with the result that passenger cars increased from 458,-

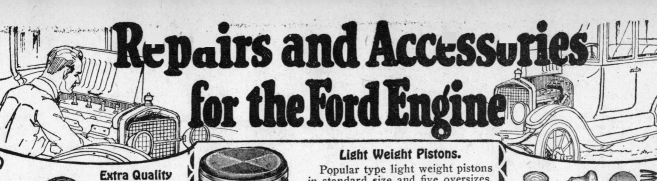

Repairs and Accessories for the Ford Engine

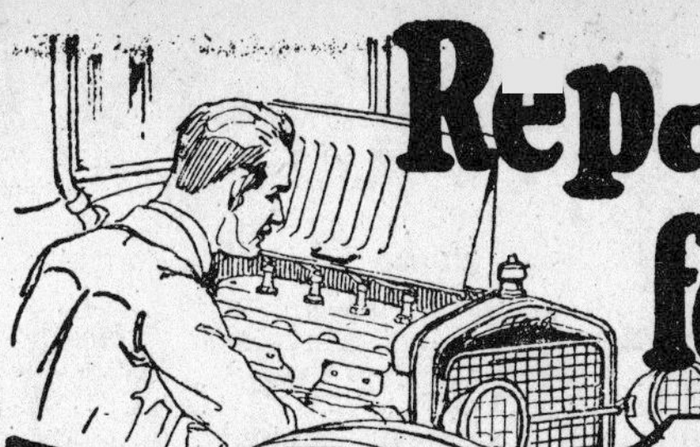
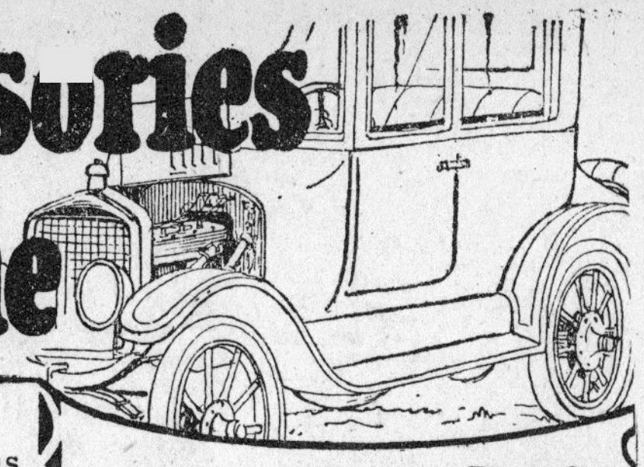

Extra Quality Pistons.

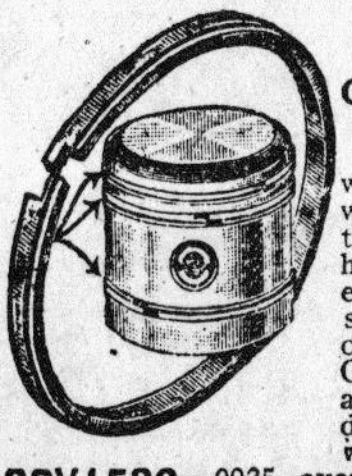

Complete With Quick Seating Oil Rings.

High grade, light weight pistons, fitted with popular type effective step-cut oil rings having correctly designed oil groove and quick seating face. Furnished only as listed below. Complete with bushings and wrist pins. A splendid value. Shipping weight, 3 pounds.

28V1520—.0025 oversize............$1.59
28V1516—.005 oversize............1.59
28V1518—.010 oversize............1.59

Transmission Oiler and Cooler.

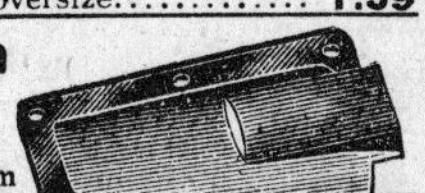

Supplies uniform flow of oil to entire transmission, including clutch yoke. Has important cooling feature, supplying enough oil to prevent drums becoming too hot. Ordinarily little of the oil carried up by flywheel reaches beyond reverse drum. Use of this oiler prevents burned transmission linings, a cause of chattering and grabbing. Install under regular transmission cover. Shpg. wt., 12 oz.
28V7819............48c

Oil Gauge.

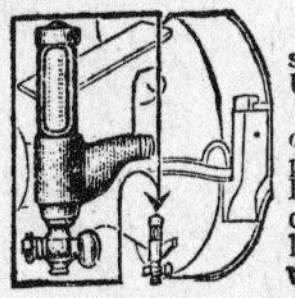

Don't guess at your oil supply. It's often expensive. Use an oil gauge.

A well made gauge with drain cock. Has glass tube protected by metal guard. Heavier construction than ordinary type. Replaces lower pet cock. Shipping weight, 7 ounces.
28V11655............45c

Force Feed Oiling System.

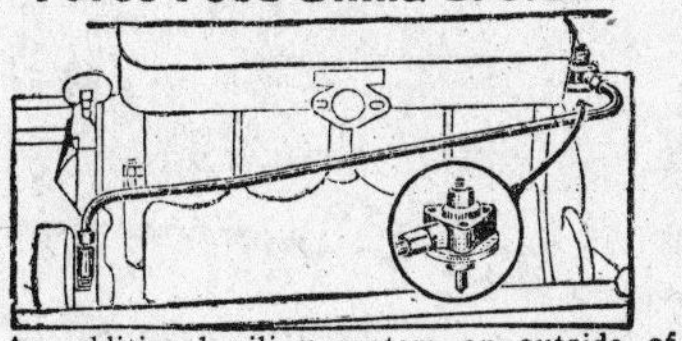

An additional oiling system on outside of motor, insuring oil supply to motor if regular oil line in motor becomes clogged with pieces of transmission lining, etc. Outfit comprises special magneto plug with oil outlet, copper tubing and fitting for attaching at front of motor over timing gears. Insures adequate oil supply at all speeds, up steep hills, etc., having both gravity feed and force feed from flywheel action. Instructions for quickly installing. Shipping weight, 9 ounces.
28V6707............98c

Apco Dash Oil Gauge.

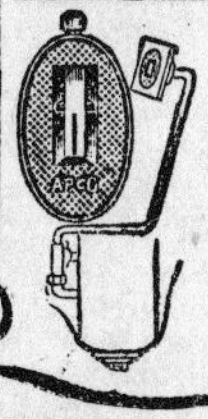

A handy oil gauge, always in sight on dash, where many high priced cars have it. Height of fluid in glass tube is regulated by air pressure in metal tube running from gauge to lower oil petcock to show exact oil supply. Don't guess at your oil supply! Complete with metal tubing and fittings. **About half the usual price.** Shipping wt., 1 pound.
28V9420
$1.28

Light Weight Pistons.

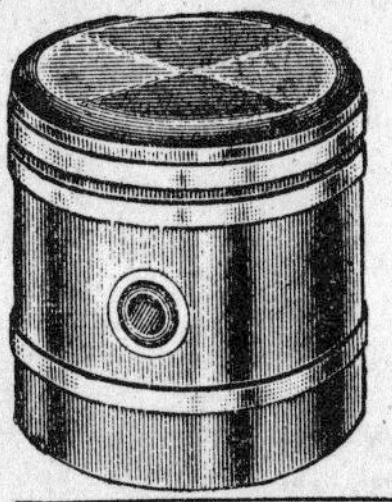

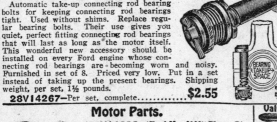

Popular type light weight pistons in standard size and five oversizes. Complete with rings, bushings and wrist pins. An unusual value. Shipping weight, 3⅛ pounds.

28V14029—Light Weight Piston, standard size............$1.25
28V14030—Same, .0025 oversize... 1.25
28V11558—Same, .005 oversize... 1.25
28V11557—Same, .010 oversize... 1.25
28V11556—Same, .025 oversize... 1.25
28V14031—Same, .03125 oversize... 1.25

Kil-Nock Connecting Rod Bearing Bolts.

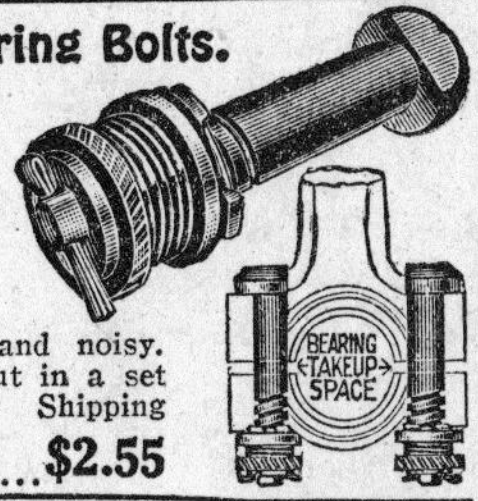

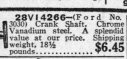

Automatic take-up connecting rod bearing bolts for keeping connecting rod bearings tight. Used without shims. Replace regular bearing bolts. Their use gives you quiet, perfect fitting connecting rod bearings that will last as long as the motor itself. This wonderful new accessory should be installed on every Ford engine whose connecting rod bearings are becoming worn and noisy. Furnished in set of 8. Priced very low. Put in a set instead of taking up the present bearings. Shipping weight, per set, 1½ pounds.
28V14267—Per set, complete............$2.55

Motor Parts.

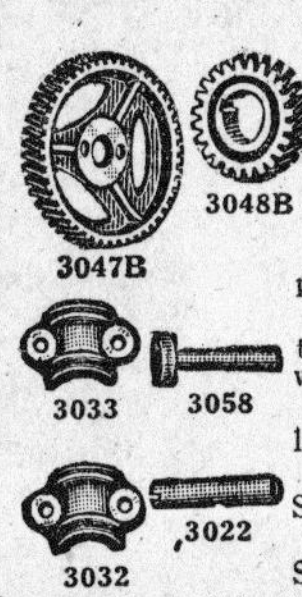

3048B
3047B
3033 3058
3032 3022

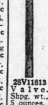

28V14032—(Ford No. 3022) Piston Pin. Shipping weight, 5 oz............17c
28V14255—(Ford No. 3022½) Piston Pin Bushing (pair). (Not illustrated). Shipping wt., 4 oz. Per pair............15c
28V14036—(Ford No. 3032) C. S. Front Bearing Cap. 84% in babbitt. Shipping wt., 12 oz............37c
28V14037—(Ford No. 3033) C. S. Center Bearing Cap. 84% tin babbitt. Shipping weight, 12 ounces............37c
28V1504—(Ford No. 3047B) Time Gear, large. Shipping weight, 2 lbs............63c
28V1506—(Ford No. 3048B) Same, small. Shipping weight, 1 lb............51c
28V14045—(Ford No. 3058) Push Rod. Shipping weight, 3 oz............9c

Valve.

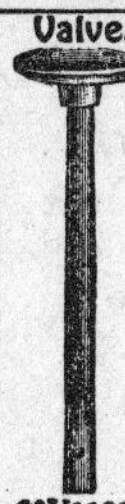

28V11813 Valve. Shpg. wt., 5 ounces. 9c

Crank Shaft.

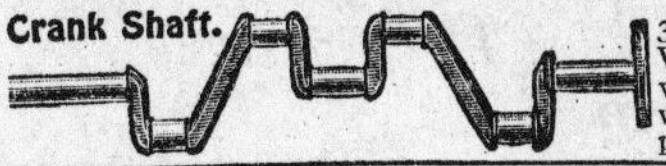

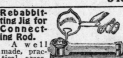

28V14266—(Ford No. 3030) Crank Shaft. Chrome Vanadium steel. A splendid value at our price. Shipping weight, 18½ pounds............$6.45

Counterbalanced Crank Shaft.

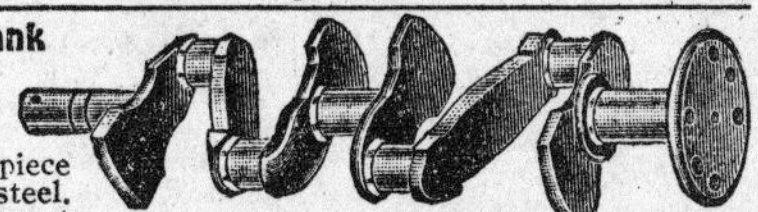

A high grade counterbalanced crankshaft made of one-piece drop forged alloy crank steel. Counterbalances are a part of shaft itself. Has perfect running balance, eliminating motor noise and vibration. Makes your Ford run surprisingly smooth at any engine speed. A splendid value at our price. Shpg. wt., 20 lbs.
28V15056¼............$13.85

Victor Gaskets.

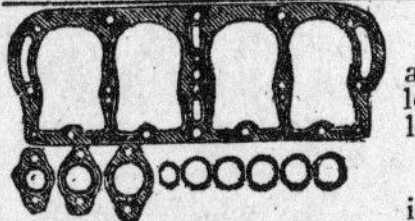

Made in one piece, ready for placing over all engine cylinders at one time, to prevent loss of compression. Copper-brass, asbestos lined. Shpg. wt., 1¼ lbs.
28V11750............22c
Victor Gasket Set, containing eleven gaskets, in all sizes needed around the Ford engine, including cylinder head gasket. Shpg. wt., 1⅜ lbs.
28V11751—Per set............34c

Connecting Rod.

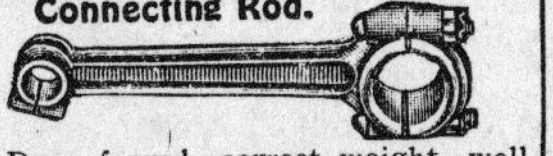

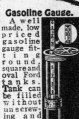

Drop forged, correct weight, well machined. Excellent babbitt bearings. Very low price. Shipping weight, 2 lbs.
28V11010......93c

Rebabbitting Jig for Connecting Rod.

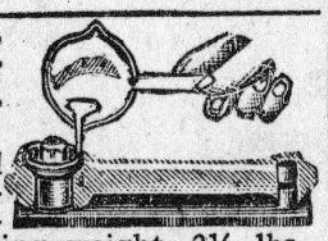

A well made, practical accessory. Shipping weight, 2½ lbs.
28V15035—Rebabbitting Jig only... 78c

Little Sioux Valve Repair Tool Set.

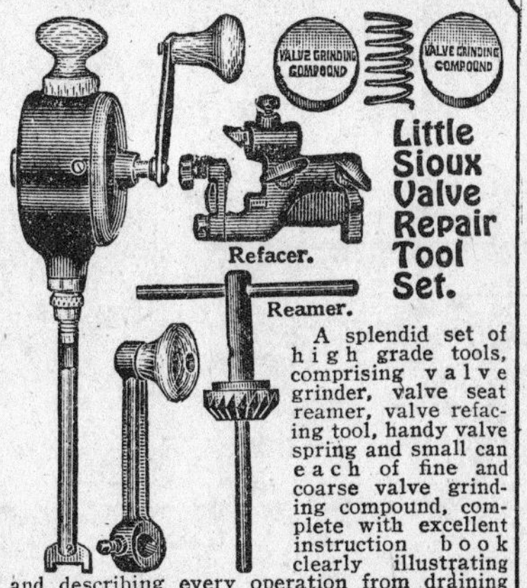

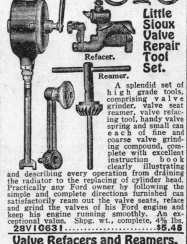

A splendid set of high grade tools, comprising valve grinder, valve seat reamer, valve refacing tool, handy valve spring and small can each of fine and coarse valve grinding compound, complete with excellent instruction book clearly illustrating and describing every operation from draining the radiator to the replacing of cylinder head. Practically any Ford owner by following the simple and complete directions furnished can satisfactorily ream out the valve seats, reface and grind the valves of his Ford engine and keep his engine running smoothly. An exceptional value. Shpg. wt., complete, 4⅝ lbs.
28V10631............$5.45

Valve Refacers and Reamers.

Little Sioux Valve Refacer. Smooths face of valve quickly, working like small lathe. A few turns makes valve fit perfectly to valve seat. Shipping wt., 1¾ lbs.
28V11609............$1.30

Valve Refacer for 1/64-inch oversize stem. Shipping weight, 1¼ lbs.
28V11377............$1.30

Valve Refacer for Fordson tractor engines. (Not illustrated.) Shpg. wt., 1½ lbs.
28V9295............$1.50

Valve Refacer for Fordson tractor engines, for 1/64-inch oversize stem. Shpg. wt., 1½ lbs.
28V11379............$1.50

Little Sioux Valve Seat Reamer. Made at correct angle to seat valve perfectly. Reamer shank keeps reamer perfectly centered and insures accurate cutting. Shipping weight, 9 ounces.
28V9296............$1.30

Valve Seat Reamer for 1/64-inch oversize stem.
28V11373—Shipping weight, 9 ounces............$1.30

Valve Reseater for Fordson tractor engines (Not illustrated.) Shipping weight, 10 ounces.
28V9293............$1.50

Valve Seat Reamer for Fordson tractor engines, for 1/64-inch oversize stem. Shipping weight, 10 ounces.
28V11375............$1.50

Gas-Oil Saver Manifold.

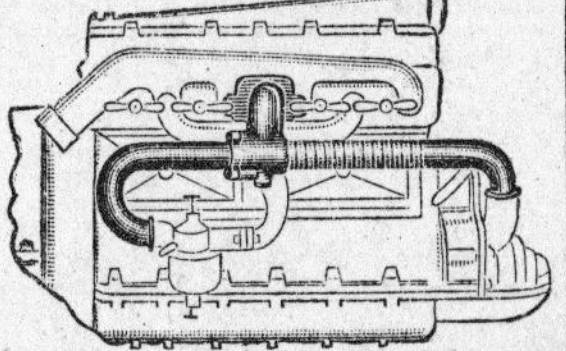

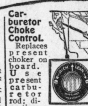

Makes big saving in gas and oil, a smoother running engine, greater motor power and prevents carbon. Draws all oil vapor and unburnt gas from crank case, drawing them into carburetor. Its use prevents waste of fuel and dilution of oil in crank case caused by gas leaking by piston rings. Properly lubricates valves and piston tops, creates partial vacuum in crank case, stopping all oil leaks. Quickly installed without drilling holes, etc. Shpg. wt., 2 lbs.
28V1618
$2.98

De Luxe Accelerator.

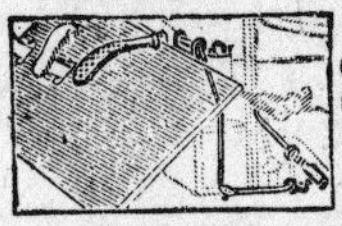

A high grade accelerator at a popular price. Comes complete with handy foot pedal; invaluable for steady, even feeding of gas. Well made, no lost motion or interference with hand throttle. Quickly installed; does not interfere with floor boards. Nickel finish. Instructions for attaching. Shpg. wt., 1¼ lbs.
28V8203 $1.15

Get-A-Way Accelerator.

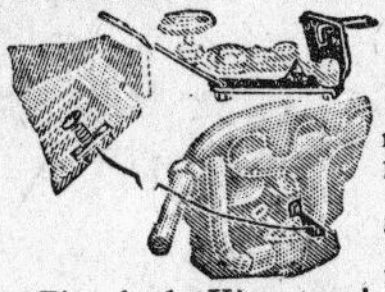

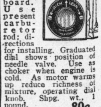

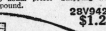

Fits both Kingston and Holly Carburetors. Substantially made, easily attached without bending or shortening pedal pull rod. Does not interfere with ready removal of floor boards. Instructions for installing. A wonderful value in a low priced accelerator. Shipping weight, 1 lb.
28V4624......53c

Gasoline Gauge.

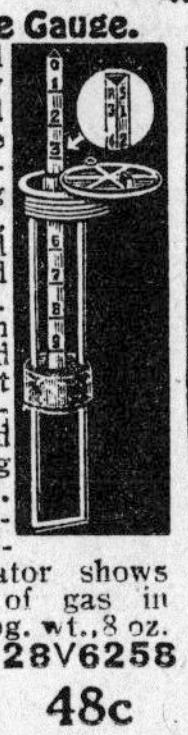

A well made, low priced gasoline gauge fitting round, square and oval Ford tanks. **Tank can be filled without unscrewing and removing gauge.** Triangular shaped indicator shows amount of gas in tank. Shpg. wt., 8 oz.
28V6258
48c

Late Model Kingston Carburetor. With Strainer.

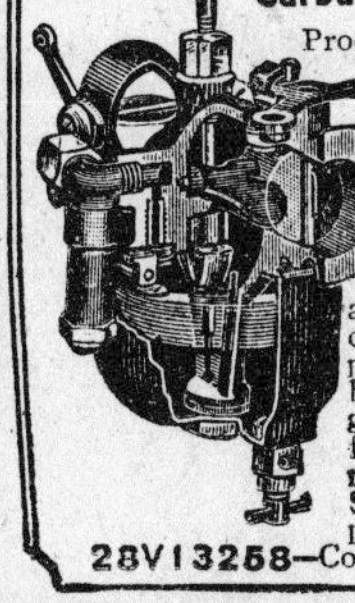

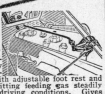

Produces more power, greater gasoline mileage and greater flexibility. Has spray nozzle carburetion principle, insuring quick get away and smooth "idling." Equipped with an improved float, special metal fuel valve, practically indestructible bronze air valve and a good strainer, invaluable for use with the ordinary gasoline available. Shipping weight, 3 pounds.
28V13258—Complete............$4.45

U. & J. Style Accelerator.

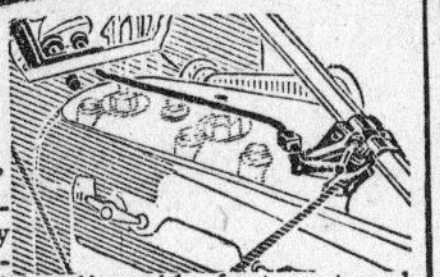

An excellent, widely known accelerator with adjustable foot rest and guide permitting feeding gas steadily under all driving conditions. Gives splendid control of motor. Made with hardened bushings and reinforced joints. Nickel plated. Works without any change of carburetor throttle rod. Easily attached, being clamped to steering column. Note our remarkably low price. Shipping weight, 1⅜ pounds.
28V11726............$1.79

Carburetor Choke Control.

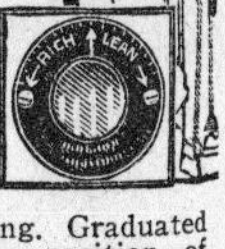

Replaces present choker on board. Use present carburetor rod; directions for installing. Graduated dial shows position of needle valve. Use as choker when engine is cold. As motor warms up reduce richness of mixture, operating dial knob. Shpg. wt., 1 pound.
28V5557....80c

Cylinder Head.

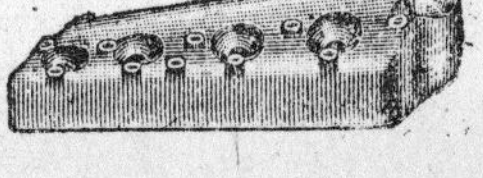

Carefully machined for a perfect fit. Replaces Ford part No. 3001. Cast iron. Head cap screws not furnished. Shipping wt., 30¾ lbs.
28V14265¼......$4.55

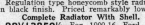

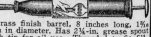

000 in 1913 to 24,250,000 in 1936, and, in addition, thousands of trucks were used to haul men as well as materials.

The car and the roads brought the farmer to town, to the large town as well as to the small town. The small-town merchant, too, began to visit the cities; to inspect the stores, and to come home and improve his own store and stocks. The isolation that had been the source and almost the guarantee of the mail-order business was fast vanishing, and Sears, faced with the alternative of increasing its business through opening retail stores or hanging onto a decreasing mail-order business, chose to open retail stores and at the same time to continue its mail-order method of distributing.

The Apotheosis of the Automobile

In 1937, William Allen White, looking backward over twenty-five years of his life, remembered Old Tom and, remembering, wrote an editorial for the *Gazette* which is an interesting dissertation on the automobile's place in American life:

> We had bought a horse. He cost $125.00. He was hitched to a buggy that cost $325.00. It was a canopy-topped phaeton with a fringe around it and cut under front wheels, a carriage of state and style. Only two other carriages were more expensive. They belonged to bankers and merchant princes and were drawn by two horses. Probably they would cost a thousand dollars each.
>
> Today the swellest private passenger vehicles in this town are Buicks, Packards, Lincolns, and Cadillacs which cost from $2,500 to $5,000. When we bought Old Tom and his equipment for $500 there was a vast difference between my equipage and that of anyone in THE GAZETTE office. When I passed by an employee not more than two or three of them had buggies, they were walking and I was riding—almost a caste distinction. Today everyone of the forty employees of THE GAZETTE has a car that cost more than $500 and three or four of them have a better car than mine. They can whizz by me.
>
> Six years after I bought Old Tom I drove him with Theodore Roosevelt on the backseat. We had a leisurely

gossipy view of Emporia. Leading citizens were ashamed of Old Tom and the canopy-topped phaeton with the fringe in a day when automobiles were coming in, and I was offered my choice of three or four cars that cost more than $5,000. But I preferred Old Tom and I fancy Roosevelt did too, though he laughed about it. Later in the same period when Mrs. J. Pierpont Morgan and her daughter, Anne, came to visit us, the mother took a nervous look at Old Tom who had the sleepy eyes of a camel and asked nervously, before she stepped into the phaeton:

"Is he safe?"

And the ribald laughter of the few townsmen who were at the station to see the great lady, cackled like thunder in the mountain. And Anne Morgan, looking at the sway-backed old charger, put on one of her sweetest grins and assured her mother that she was certain Old Tom would not run away.

$112⁰⁰

Guaranteed for Three Years.

No. 11T1244

6 · TIME, YOU OLD GYPSY MAN

IT IS shortly before six o'clock in the morning, December 25, 1905. In their Iowa farm home Mr. and Mrs. Joe Hutchins are sound asleep. The big double bed sags under their weight and the edge of the blanket touches the floor. The room is silent save for the snoring of Mr. Hutchins and the energetic ticking of a clock that hangs above the mantel. Its hands move rapidly and, when they are perpendicular to the floor beneath, a cuckoo pokes its head out of a bower of carved oak leaves and calls six times. Joe Hutchins groans and rolls over. His wife, Mamie, stirs slightly in her flannelette nightgown. The couple sleep on. Christmas comes but once a year. Again the room is silent, but precisely at fifteen minutes after six, a quail emerges from its little shelter of wooden leaves next to that of the cuckoo and whistles the quarter hour. This time the Hutchins awaken, sleepily murmur "Merry Christmas," and prepare to arise for the happy day.

Above the mantel the faithful clock hurries on to a rendezvous with the year 1906. This is no ordinary timekeeper but a famous, if not uncommon, quail-and-cuckoo clock. Nature has never been able to make these birds work tandem, but the combined ingenuity of Sears and German clockmakers has brought them together to sing for their supper in a clock and earn their keep by whistling and calling the hours for their owners. They are happily housed in "the latest improved and Genuine Black Forest masterpiece, imported especially for us from Germany. The case is hand carved German walnut or oak, as desired. . . . The quail whistles the quarter hours and the cuckoo calls the full hours. Price, $11.80."

—173—

A clock can be ornamental as well as useful, and for centuries the world's clockmakers, as though fascinated by the mysterious qualities of the time-substance marking beginning, transition, and end, have exhausted their ingenuity on instruments beautiful to the eye which record in pitiful min-

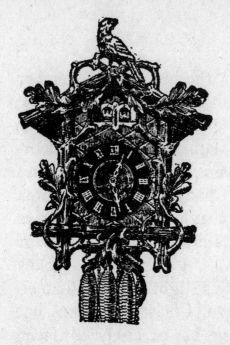

The Iowa Nightingale

utes the immortal marchings of the stars. We may expect to find, therefore, that the catalog, an inveterate traditionalist, will not only continue but even embellish the great tradition. And we shall not be disappointed. In 1905, it gave America "OUR NEW ACME QUEEN CATHEDRAL GONG, Price Cut To $5.55. (Weight, boxed ready for shipment, 25 pounds)."

An Acme Queen, one gathers, is the Queen of Queens, even as Solomon was King of Kings. It is consequently astonishing to find nothing even vaguely feminine about this Queen of clocks. Its "marbleized imitation onyx case which so closely resembles Mexican onyx that it cannot be detected except by an expert," was not, as we might assume from the clock's name, surmounted by a figure of Boadicea or Victoria. There rode instead on its top, "a handsome bronze figure." The figure of a bearded, broad-hatted, Cavalier horseman—the spitting image of Bonnie Prince Charlie thundering silently, if somewhat incongruously, above "lion head bronze ornaments, heavy bronze panel and center ornaments, and handsome mosaic dial in heavy gilt."

In the hierarchy of Sears' clocks there were not only Queens, but also Princes, Countesses, and Ladies. Commoners were not permitted to strike the hours for democrats. Among the more distinguished members of the mail-order nobility was "Our $3.75 Countess Janet Clock," which was in its day, "the most wonderful bargain in the United States," even though its case was not made of Pentelic marble but ordinary wood, "hard enameled in black with marbleized ornamentation." There is something fittingly and beguilingly mysterious about the Countess Janet as there was about the Venetian ladies whose swift gondolas cleaving the midnight waters of the Grand Canal were noted by Casanova. We know, it is true, where the Countess Janet went, but we shall never know from whence she came, because "we cannot divulge the maker's name on account of the low price quoted."

One glance at The Gibson Calendar 8-Day Clock With Thermometer and Barometer told all you needed to know and

*Classic Revival
for $4.95*

whether it would be safe to mow the hay tomorrow. But The Beauty Mantel Clock, "one of the finest clocks we have ever manufactured," was to The Gibson as gold to dross. The Beauty, with its case surmounted by a pensive figure of a sandal-shod goddess, one hand resting on a lyre at her side

—175—

and the other supporting an evidently aching head, had about it something of the melancholy loveliness of the Petit Trianon. It is gratifying, in retrospect, to know that it was not lost upon the desert air, for the demand for it was so great that "we have contracted with the factory to use an immense quantity at a hitherto unheard of price."

Alarming Alarms

There was no foolishness about the alarm clocks of 1905, and it is to the credit of Sears that it made no effort to sell them through half-apologetic advertising which sought to convey the impression of wooing the sleeper awake. It was then the business of an alarm clock to bang on your eardrums and continue banging until they burst or you got out of bed, and the more nearly an alarm clock simulated a boiler factory being run by maniacs, the more it was prized by the hardy men of thirty years ago. They had not been brought up on the debilitating, sugar-teat psychological theory of later years that one ought to be awakened gently. The very names of the clocks indicate their purpose in life without evasion or apology. One popular consciousness-crasher was called The Racket Strike Alarm. Another was a Chinese torture device named The Repeater Intermitting Alarm. A third was The Wasp. If these were not enough to make you wish you had never been born, we may safely assume that The Fly and The Must Get Up would have filled you with the desire to end it all.

These clocks were as austerely utilitarian in design and

The Racket Strike Alarm—Early American Instrument of Torture

purpose as a gallows, but even in a sterner age than ours there were some who craved illusion in the form of the velvet glove concealing the iron hand. For these weaklings,

Sears created its Beautiful Oxidized Alarm Clock. Its case was "finished in oxidized copper, beautifully finished . . . making an ornament that would grace any parlor mantelpiece." It is not to be expected, however, that a country poisonously indoctrinated with the Longfellow creed of "Let us, then, be up and doing," would be satisfied with any clock whose sole reason for existing was beauty. The Oxidized Alarm's handsome exterior concealed, therefore, an inner mechanism which shattered sleep with fifteen minutes of unrelenting ringing. It was, says the catalog complacently, a "clock longed for by thousands."

Cuckoos and Cannon

In the fall of 1915, the British navy was spread across the seas to intercept and destroy German commerce, part of which consisted of cuckoo clocks for the American market. Whether Germany succeeded in sending them through the blockade, or whether Sears, more astute than many a Foreign Office, anticipated the War and stored clocks against The Day, the fact is that a whole page of the 1915 catalog is devoted to IMPORTED BLACK WALNUT CUCKOO CLOCKS. The peasant carvers of the Black Forest, as though fearful that their art might perish in a warring world, seem to have outdone themselves, for the 1915 clocks are more elaborately carved, supercarved, and encrusted than ever before. But war has already brought its burdens to America, for the $11.80 clock of 1905 has become the $19.48 of 1915. This time, however, the instrument has become a miniature zoo inhabited not only by a cuckoo and a quail but also a stag, making it indeed a "clock you will be proud to own."

It is not, however, the mantel clocks but the alarm clocks that show us how much the times have changed since 1905. In 1915, we were growing rich selling our goods to a warring world, and, during those lush days, Sears pictured an alarm clock named THE NATIONAL CALL against a shadowy background of cannon and swords. We actually believed, in 1915, that we could be in the world but not of it, and peace was not only virtuous but profitable. Two years later, Americans were to be dying in Flanders' mud, but at the moment "The National Call is the sentry for the great American army of peaceful industry. He is Father Time's most alert son, trained·to foil every approach of oversleep. Peace is his watchword, so he carries no arms, but with two big hands and a clear ringing voice makes every signal thoroughly understood. . . . Wherever the roll call, on the farm, in the mine, in the factory, at the railroad yards, wherever there's work to do, all answer HERE with a salute to The National Call."

These are brave words, but the cold fact is that the old gray mare ain't what she used to be. Where now are the clocks of 1905—The Wasp, The Must Get Up, and The Racket Strike Alarm? Soft boys sleep now in soft beds and the clocks that purr them awake are innocuous and weak. Their names betray their lack of virility: The Luminous One-Day Nickel Plated Alarm, The Small One-Day Alarm, The Brass Finished Eight-Day Alarm.

Genuinely alarming is the fact that Sears' clocks are now so polite that they do not shout and pound on the ears of sleepers. For example: "Our Musical Alarm Clock; a pleasing novelty. Plays one tune about ten minutes. . . . Musical attachment is so arranged that when clock is set at a certain time a tune is played instead of an alarm." Or—even more alarming—"The Gold Plated One-Day Desk or Dresser Clock. Cupid design." Here the catalog unblushingly makes a shameful admission. "The One-Day Dresser Clock," it says, "does not alarm." An alarm clock that does not alarm! What have we come to? A three-word essay on the degeneration of a nation. As a footnote to the decline of the West, there is a group of French Ivory (grained celluloid) clocks, dripping gentility, which couldn't prod even an early robin to catch the early worm.

The catalog, however, like the America it mirrors, fills one alternately with despair and hope. After a succession of alarm-clock vipers with stingers removed, one's hopes for the recrudescence of our ancient virtues are aroused by "The

Electric Alarm Clock, $5.00." Its design and function remind us that time, far from being a mere metaphysical football of the philosophers, is—money. "The compartment on the right side of case contains the battery and the compartment on the left side contains a savings bank with combination lock. The entire case is nickel plated and polished, making it highly ornamental." Who could lie sleeping or futilely dreaming in bed with this "nickel plated and highly polished" reminder constantly before him that time is a pregnant synonym for dollars?

A New World

1905–1915–1925. The decades pass. The catalog itself, born in 1886, is now graying a bit around the temples. The War has come and gone, and Germany for the moment is crushed, but in the Black Forest, not far from Baden-Baden where international profiteers fondle their wines and their mistresses in the Hotel Stephanie, peasant artisans carve wood into leaves, stags, quail, and cuckoos for the faraway cuckoo-clock fanciers of the United States. Once more the cuckoo calls and the quail whistles while the stag looks on benignly, just as though the sun had not risen and set for four years upon the broken bodies of millions.

In the world of clocks the Greek influence of 1905 is also gone. The Twelve in their broidered garments have gone back to Parnassus and never shall the parlors of the Middle West shelter them again. Ormolu gold (gilt, to the vulgar) still remains, no longer in broad patches, but in mere thumbnail daubs. A few "variegated columns" survive to remind us of an age that has flown, but the majority of the clocks are of plain polished wood.

The National Call is still calling, but business apparently is not so good as it was in the golden days of 1915 when it cheerfully hailed the boys to the factory and the railroad yards. The copywriter knew, of course, that business was not what it used to be, and one glance at the thin 1,000 pages of the 1925 catalog, as opposed to the fat 1,600 pages of the 1915, confirmed his unhappiest convictions. And he—being human—doesn't seem to know why people should now get up at all and is correspondingly vague about it. Note his false briskness and property smile: "On time! Work, school, meals, appointments,—*punctuality is demanded* by modern life and the alert and active family demands a *reliable* alarm clock. . . . America is rising to the clear inviting ring of The National Call for thousands upon thousands of homes depend on this sturdy clock to start their day and keep them punctual."

Sadly enough, while it cost only $2 to be called by The National Call in 1915, when there was something to get up for, it cost $2.50 for a false-alarm call by the same clock in 1925, when there was little reason to get up at all.

The Vogue of the Simple

"Thou wast not born for death, immortal bird!" It is 1935 now, and, after thirty years of wars, revolutions, and panics, the cuckoo and the quail are still calling and whistling through the pages of the catalog. Popular choice, allegedly fickle, has bestowed a temporal immortality upon the quail-and-cuckoo clock.

The bright host of "richly ornamental clocks," that once

Despoiler of the Cuckoo's Nest

illumined the parlors of America with their Third Empire gilt brightness, is now reduced to a sole survivor, and the catalog tempers its description of this baroque beauty with the cold-water word "dignified." Wood clocks are now austerely simple. Planes are not ashamed to be planes, and wood at last is content to be wood, naked and unadorned.

The National Call will call for you now at the same price demanded for its services fifteen years ago, if you are content with the "round style, very popular."

New materials are in vogue: chromium and plastics. New colors, too, are widely used. No longer are alarm clocks merely brass or nickel; they now are black, rose, green, or ivory. And the catalog, scarred veteran of many a fight with manufacturers of nationally advertised brands of merchandise, lists, but without enthusiasm, the well-publicized Big Ben clocks. A new merchandise era is in the making.

As the twentieth century grows older, more and more narrowed becomes the freeborn American's ability to exercise unrestrainedly his individual taste, however exotic or eccentric, in the choice of many lines of mercandise. It may make for lower costs and higher efficiency, as Mr. Herbert Hoover suggested when he was Secretary of Commerce, to produce fewer kinds of monkey wrenches or shades of silk stockings, but it is undeniable that this form of business puritanism tends to wither the lushness of our national life. In 1905, however, when Mr. Hoover was an engineer (but had not yet become the Great Engineer) and American taste had not been constricted into the strait jacket of the assembly line, the consumer who wanted a cow that could jump over the moon could get one, because some enterprising manufacturer would make it for him. The limits of pampering of consumers' tastes were the limits merely of the existing technological abilities of manufacturers. The worm of standardization had not yet begun to canker the rose of individualism. Nowhere were roses flung more riotously with the throng than in the gold- and silver-spangled pages that present Sears' watches for ladies and gents. Here, as in teeming tropical seas, one is confounded by the richness, the coloring, the variety of the species.

Where now, for example, will you find Moon Calendar Watches, at Prices Cut Again? Under their crystal covers framed in base or precious metal, one kept automatic tab of the day of the week, day of the month, day of the year, month of the year, and the changes of the moon. The stupendous solar system, tamed and reduced to miniature, lay in your pocket beating warm and snug against the beatings of your heart. One's admiration for this mechanical marvel is tinctured only with the patriotic regret that it was made not in America but in Switzerland. The price? $6.30.

A few years after the Klondike gold rush and the shooting of Dan McGrew, Sears wrought a metallurgical marvel and commemorative piece in the form of THE ALASKA SILVER ALL AMERICAN OPEN FACE WATCH, $1.98. Alaska silver,

*American Eagle with
Steam Up*

the catalog tells us simply, is no creation of bungling nature working alone and unaided, but is "a composition of several metals giving the watch the appearance of coin silver."

Alaska was much in the public prints in 1905; Seward's Folly was now declaring fabulous dividends, and watchmakers, the catalog clinging to their coattails, swung onto the bandwagon. One of the fine pieces commemorating the history of the times was a watch of "Alaska silver with solid gold inlaid." The case was decorated with an engraving of

The Old 97 thundering across a trestle above a lake, a plume of black smoke trailing from its stack. In the foreground, a sailboat careened to the breeze; in the background, a steamer was hull down on the horizon. A pleasant combination of landscape *cum* trestle and seascape, and a satisfying, ever-present symbol of the gold rush that conquered Alaska.

The country was still rich in giants in 1905. John Henry, "who weighed forty-four pounds when he was born," and built the Yellow Dog Railroad between dawn and dusk, was laughing his gold-toothed laugh up and down the Mississippi River from Cairo to New Orleans. Paul Bunyan was living in the north woods, and he and his playmates were letting daylight into the dense forests of the Middle West and the Pacific slope, or raising thunderous payday hell in the pleasure parlors of Muskegon and Seattle. These bonebreakers and peavy bulls had no use for timepieces of lavender and old lace, however encrusted they might be with sentiment or historical associations. They wanted watches that could not only take it but also dish it out when the going became hard, and the catalog, being all things to all men, offered a watch especially made for oversized giants.

This gargantuan instrument was THE ONLY 4½ OUNCE ALASKA SILVER CASE MANUFACTURED IN THE WORLD. YOU CANNOT FIND THEM ELSEWHERE. And little wonder. Where else but in the catalog's imperial domain could you find men capable of toting a watch whose case alone, without the movement, weighed more than a quarter of a pound? Men who carried such watches were obviously subjected to emotional and physical stresses beyond the ordinary, and Sears, the ever anticipatory, provided for their extraordinary requirements. The catalog tells us that "This case is made to stand 800 pounds strain; your movement is safe no matter what happens."

Amid the manifold designs of watchcases that flowered in heterogeneous catalog profusion, one discerns the working of a certain order which reduced the principal motifs to three. These were: (1) The Noble Stag. He seems to have spent his time either at bay with lowered and threatening horns or in rut with raised and questing antlers. (2) The Little Birds. One finds them nearly always swooning amid the honeysuckle or carrying streamers of ribbons in their gold-filled beaks to the little gray home in the West. (3) The Iron Horse. This monster was generally depicted coming down the

A Combination Watch, Concealed Weapon, and Deck Armor

mountain, a black belching avalanche sweeping everything before it, or gliding on high driving wheels across a lake.

The ingenuity and skill of early twentieth-century American watchcase artists in their avoidance of monotony in treatment seems sometimes to rival the Greek sculptor of the fifth century who gave a deathless exhibition of avoiding monotony by the slightest variations of the postures and draperies repeated twelve times in the Weeping Women. Consider, for instance, The Noble Stag. We see him time after time, and while he is always the same in his forest-primeval nobility and his woodsy staginess, yet he is never quite the same. Sometimes he stands amid gold-plated bulrushes, ears at the alert and antlers brushing a copper-gold sky, in a give-me-liberty-or-give-me-death mood. At other times, he hotfoots, as if in answer to a mating call, across a grassy meadow hedged in by engine turning. Occasionally, we find him alone and forlorn, thinking higher thoughts against a background of dark mountains hanging above a sunny lake. But always, and in

Noble Stag Thinking Higher Thoughts

whatever posture, no one could doubt the congenital nobility of a catalog stag, although one might wish sometimes that he would unbend and stand on his head for joy of living, jump in the lake to avoid the northland mosquitoes, or rip up from head to heels a hunter who is annnoying him, and thus give some evidence of the warming common touch.

St. Francis of Assisi could not have loved birds more than our own watchcase designers. Their love of birds—all of them, of whatever kind or feather—was so deep, indeed, that fearing subconsciously to offend them by depicting members of a particular species, they kept the peace and confounded ornithologists by creating a singular genus: the watchcase bird.

This little symbol of love was usually found in pairs, thereby betraying some earthly relationship with their ancestors of the Ark, although occasionally they appear alone or in threes. On rare occasions, the designers indulge in subtle symbolism and present only the merest evocation of the birds in the form of gold-filled eggs snug in a bower of gun-metal leaves.

The lot of the watchcase bird was an unhappy one. It must have been plagued by the ills of maladjustment and frus-

Gold-Filled Watch Bird Hovering on
Silverine Wings Above
Gun-Metal Flowers

tration, for it seems to have spent much of its time hovering with beating wings above clusters of babies'-breath or Queen Anne's lace which it could never quite reach. When the world is too much with it, it leaves the flowers to get along as best they may and flies on silverine wings toward the westering sun. But the watchcase bird, after all, was American, and its wings, like the clouds among which they fluttered, had a silver lining. In happier mood, we see the birds touch beaks, without apparent sense of modesty, above expectant nests; perch on the doorsills of love-filled cottages in the gloaming; spread their feathers against a blank space that will one day contain someone's initials, or, in a frenzy of joy, dash from bough to bough of a springtime forest bearing streamers of ribbons.

While it is somewhat difficult to understand the decorative popularity of stags and birds in a country whose arts and life have been but little influenced by the Orient, it is immediately apparent why The Iron Horse should appear so often on the watchcases of a continental, restless, machine-enchanted people. So strong indeed is the impact of locomotives and trains upon us that occasionally an able American novelist such as the late Thomas Wolfe actually seemed to be obsessed with them, and in page after page of magical prose, described trains hurtling across America. And Benjamin R. C. Low, knowing that every American boy—certainly in the preairplane age—wanted to be a locomotive engineer, wrote:

THE LITTLE BOY TO THE LOCOMOTIVE

Big iron horse with lifted head,
Panting beneath the station shed,
You are my dearest dream come true;—
I love my Dad; I worship you!

Your noble heart is filled with fire,
For all your toil, you never tire,
And though you're saddled-up in steel,
Somewhere, inside, I know you feel.

All night in dreams when you pass by,
You breathe out stars that fill the sky,
And now, when all my dreams are true,
I hardly dare come close to you.

If the locomotive had a strong appeal to the American imagination, it possessed grave limitations in its decorative possibilities, but our watchcase designers proved that their ingenuity flowed from an inexhaustible well. The Iron Horse, by comparison with The Noble Stag or the The Little Birds, was pretty wooden. It could not strike postures, answer love calls, or make the forest look like the ribbon counter of a department store during a bargain sale. It was not permitted even to venture from the monotonous normal and indulge in the capricious orgy of a wreck. This vagary seems to have been forbidden it by the success-story tradition and the iron law of the happy ending, although, perversely, some locomotives are celebrated in song precisely because they turned on their masters and scalded them to death. In any event, all that The Iron Horse was permitted to do—on watchcases—was to emit smoke. Yet even within the framework of this severe limitation, it is an ever-fascinating gun-metal or gold-filled monster as it rounds curves in darkling mountains, thunders through cavernous night, or steams serenely across sail-studded lakes, and always accompanied, whether steaming or thundering, by a sky-blackening cloud.

In 1905, when the individual was more than an academic theory debated by antiquarians, and individualism expressed itself by demanding a wide choice of merchandise, Sears ransacked the inventor's attics and the artist's ateliers of two continents for things to please its myriad clientele. For precious gents (or ladies) whose souls dwelt in Tempe, although they got their mail on a rural route in South Dakota, the catalog presented OUR NEW GENTLEMEN'S THIN 16-SIZE GERMAN SILVER, GRAY OXIDIZED FINISH, ANTIQUE PATTERN OPEN-FACE NOVELTY WATCH. Its price—$3.15—may seem something of an anticlimax after the sonorous horns of this overture, but we are told that it was a splendid time-keeper and the design proves it to have been an unforgettable souvenir of the grandeur that was Greece. Here a Swiss watchmaker employed his Alpine genius and, with a hand as fluent as that of Giòtto, introduces us into the presence of a well-fleshed goddess wearing a stylish-stout flowing robe, seated on her well-tempered clavichord blowing mad timbrels in the innocent face of a fat, foot-bathing Cupid on the other side of the brook.

Generally the eyes of the intensely pragmatic catalog focused on the present, but occasionally they gazed into the future and we are permitted to see what they beheld. An unhappy revelation of the shape of things to come is found in the catalog's description of BOYS' OR GENTLEMEN'S GENTEEL THIN 17-SIZE GOLD FILLED WATCHES, $7.50. Note the new and ominous word "genteel" occurring in the same pages that proclaimed the quarter-pound watch capable of standing a strain of 800 pounds. We know now that the frontier is passing; the covered wagon is being used for hayrides and picnics. The catalog-Cassandra goes on chanting doom by implication: "A small, thin, genteel, high grade, twenty-year gold filled watch, the coming size, thickness, shape and style for boy or gentleman; the neatest, most perfect watch made."

The death rattle is already in Paul Bunyan's throat; the peavy bull is going out and the drugstore cowboy is coming in; flapjacks and molasses are giving way to tea and crumpets; the enervating running-water bathtub will soon stand in men's homes all over the land to sap their strength with its Roman temptations. For now, alas, the very same watch may be worn by boys or—not men—gentlemen. And what kind of a watch? "A genteel, thin watch," fit for a porcelain-fragile Daughter of the Confederacy living on crusts in refined retirement from the world, but scarcely the thing for men who ripped open the hard belly of a continent and drew forth staggering riches. This microbe, moreover, burrowing into the once vigorous heart of America is, we are told, "the coming size." We shall see with what accuracy the catalog predicted the future.

Anchoring Chains

When a man bought a watch in 1905, he had to buy a chain or fob to hold it down. Consequently, Sears as a purveyor of watches became also a purveyor of watch accessories and, never one to tackle a job without hearty gusto, threw fountains of fobs and intricate traceries of gold-filled chains about the land.

A watch chain, one would think, offers only the most sterile possibilities to the goldfilledsmith, because seemingly the only

A Watch-Anchor Chain of 1905

reasonable variations lie in the shape and the size of the links. But as we have seen before, what might have been a headache for Cellini was all in the day's work for the anonymous artists of the catalog. For example: No. C5560. "Gold Filled Bright

Polish, Extra Strong. Warranted For Twenty Years. Price $4.25." This was an intricate composition of gold-filled horseshoes soldered to metal replicas of men's belts linked together with long staples, from which depended another and smaller-size link chain.

In the previtamin, predietetics days of 1905, when men ate long and often because, paradoxically, the country did not then have Too Much of Everything, mail-order watch chains, embellished by attached charms, flowed smoothly across many an ample belly. A pleasing example of the chain plus charm is No. 4C6308: "Fancy swedged trace links, gold filled, bright polish, warranted 20 years; fancy signet charm for monogram. Two-letter monogram, 25 cents extra. Price

The Dude's Delight—Chain with Charm

$3.00. (If by mail, postage 3 cents)." The "fancy stone set charms," simulating onyx, sardonyx, or opals, were usually engraved with the head of a woman wearing flowers in her hair—a woman, comfortingly, who might just as easily be Pinkham of the pills as Ceres of the fields.

The Great Brotherhood

Many of the chains bore attached emblems of the Masons, the Elks, the Woodmen of the World, the Beavers, the Knights of Columbus, the Moose, the Redmen, and other insignia of that vast fraternity of lodge members which counts its numbers by millions.

In 1921, G. K. Chesterton,* traveling in Oklahoma, saw a "lean, brown man having rather the look of a shabby tropical traveller, with a grey moustache and a lively and alert eye. But the most singular thing about him was that the front of his coat was covered with a multitude of shining metallic emblems made in the shape of stars and crescents. I was well accustomed by this time to Americans adorning the lapels of their coats with little symbols of various societies; it is a part of the American passion for the ritual of comradeship. There is nothing that an American likes so much as to have a secret society and make no secret of it."

Mr. Chesterton, like many another casual traveler to the United States, or, for that matter, like many a city smart aleck holed up in one of the anonymous cells of New York, utterly failed to comprehend the role played in American life by lodges, clubs, and societies. Secret societies did not, for one thing, spring from American soil. They are as ancient as early Egypt; as old as Periclean Greece. The Masonic lodge, for instance, was founded in Britain, and the male members of the British royal family still belong to it and play an important role in it. In this country, as long ago as 1778, George Washington, when he retook Philadelphia, marched with his brothers to a special Masonic service "in full Masonic attire and adorned with all the jewels and insignia of the brotherhood."

Many American lodges and societies, moreover, are primarily insurance organizations. Some of them antedate the insurance companies and offered life insurance to their membership long before there were either accurate vital statistics or actuarial tables based on the statistics. A number of them coat their otherwise dry-as-dust proceedings with ritual and regalia; others have no ritual or regalia. But most of them served—and still serve—a useful and once indispensable function in a country whose devotion to life insurance is little short of religious.

* Gilbert Keith Chesterton, *What I Saw In America*, p. 178.

The point, however, that seems to have escaped Mr. Chesterton and American sneerers at lodges and societies, is this: the United States is a stupendous continent. We have no such expression in our language as the French *petit pays,* which derives at once from living in a small country and a strong sense of local attachment born of age-long association with a definite bit of soil or neighborhood. What Texan, for instance, would speak of Texas, or any part of it, as his *petit pays,* when the state is as large as Germany and France combined; when the Sunset Limited of the Southern Pacific takes almost twenty-four hours to cross it from border to border? Generations of Americans spent their lives moving over the face of this country; many of them lived in little towns remote from other little towns and farther still from cities; men were born and died in homes that were thirty or fifty miles away from the next nearest homes. In small and crowded western Europe, this condition has not existed for centuries. Men felt lonely and lost amid this fertile desolation called America; they huddled together when they could for comfort under the wide sky, and, huddling, formed societies and clubs out of a desire for warm human companionship.

Similarly, there has never been in the United States a normal group life such as that expressed for the Germans by their *Saengerbunds* and *Turnvereins;* for the Czechs by their *Sokols;* for the Swedes by their gymnastic clubs, or, for that matter, for the French by their cafés. We had, it is true, saloons which at least served the purpose—whatever their evils—of supplying a place cool in summer and warm in winter where men whose homes were hot or cold tenements could find a moment of escape, but they expressed neither a group life nor even an approach to the poor man's club atmosphere of the French café. A group life—in the European sense—is perhaps impossible in the United States, because the country is too large and the population too heterogeneous. But searching consciously or unconsciously for such a life, men formed societies which in some degree served the purpose.

— 193 —

These, then, are some of the implications and meanings that lie behind the fraternal charms offered by the catalog, and because there are millions of brothers in the country—black and white—such charms appear in every issue.

Chains for Dudes and Lovers

The United States, despite its he-man tradition, has always had a certain number of dudes, and their scented coin being as sound as that of the catwalking steel worker, the catalog, which plays no favorites, goes after some of it. These biological sports—strange offspring of Paul Bunyan and Daniel Boone—seem to have been satisfied on ordinary occasions with a mere "gold-filled pony vest chain." But when *en fête,* they demanded nothing less than No. 4C5651. "Fancy Woven 3-Strand Hair Vest Guard, 8½ inches long, with very fancy gold plated tips, side bar and swivel."

American men are accused nowadays of lacking those gallantries called Continental; of failing to bring to love those little touches that are at once endearing and exciting. They are, we are told, good providers but poor lovers. They send flowers from the florist. They do not bring a single flower in hand to the lady of their choice. "They always prefer," said a French critic, "the entree before the hors d'oeuvres." Whatever the truth of these assertions, American men were not always like this. The ardent lovers of 1905, the sentimentalists suspiring with love requited or unrequited, expressed themselves fully and prettily through watch fob No. C6498. "Hair Chain Braided To Order, Like Above [illustration]. Price $1.00." How did one go about it? The catalog tells us.

"Requires about 1½ ounces haircombings to braid a chain. Is made in two pieces, and together with mountings is 12½ inches long. When you send in your hair to be braided be sure and write us when you do so and put your name and address on package."

Here, then, is a picture of American love in a time that reaches back to Richard Lovelace when he wrote "To Amarantha, that She Would Dishevel Her Hair":

Amarantha sweet and fair,
Ah, braid no more that shining hair!
As my curious hand or eye
Hovering round thee, let it fly!

War Kills the Watch Bird

In 1915, this advertisement of the Cleveland Automatic Machine Company appeared in the *American Machinist.** It describes a shrapnel-making machine for the use of warring Europe.

The material is high in tensile strength and VERY Special and has a tendency to fracture into small pieces upon the explosion of the shell. The timing of the fuse for this shell is similar to the shrapnel shell, but it differs in that two explosive acids are used to explode the shell in the large cavity. The combination of these two acids causes a terrific explosion, having more power than anything of its kind yet used. Fragments become coated with the acids in exploding and wounds caused by them mean death in terrible agony within four hours if not attended to immediately.

From what we are able to learn of conditions in the trenches, it is not possible to get medical assistance to anyone in time to prevent fatal results. It is necessary to cauterize the wound immediately, if in the body or head, or to amputate the limbs, as there seems to be no antidote that will counteract the poison.

It can be seen from this that this shell is more effective than the regular shrapnel, since the wounds caused by shrapnel balls and fragments in the muscle are not as dangerous, as they have no poisonous element making prompt attention necessary.

At the time when this advertisement appeared—a far-off, mournful New World horn announcing the death of humanitarianism, liberalism, and reason in the Old World—Sears' catalogs, in near-by Chicago, were pouring from the presses in millions and going out to a people whose lives by compari-

* Quoted in Engelbrecht and Hanighen, *Merchants of Death,* p. 182.

son with those of Europeans were like Eden before the Fall.

In the pages of watches for men, we find they have changed but little since 1905, although there are unmistakable signs of coming change. The Little Birds still hover above the flowers, but we know with unhappy prescience that they will soon join the once billion-winged passenger pigeon in limbo, because their nests have disappeared and they will mate no more amid the jack-in-the-pulpit. The Noble Stag—noble to the bitter end—faces us in one model with defiant eyes, but in another turns his rump toward us in tired resignation and gazes wistfully at a never-never land beyond the setting sun. Only one Iron Horse remains of all the splendid company that once shook a continent, and it plunges smoke-enveloped down the mountain in the manner of the old tradition. But it runs now on a track paralleled by a border of fleur-de-lis encroaching on the roadbed, and it is evident that The Iron Horse is on its last wheels.

The watch with the quarter-pound case survives unchanged, but the changing language of the catalog gives us a clue to what is happening in America. In 1905, we were told that the case of this watch was "made to stand 800 pounds strain; your movement is safe no matter what happens." Ten years later the catalog is unable to talk straight from the shoulder. Compare this description of 1915 with that of 1905. "Nickel is known to be much tougher and more durable than solid silver. This combination of metals, nickel and solid silver makes it possible to produce a case with a tensile strength that is simply marvelous." Education—the great American panacea—is evidently getting in its dirty work both at the copywriter's desk of Sears and out in the country among the customers. The precision-tool exactness of the former language of the people is giving way to the mealymouthiness of the educated. American speech is losing its bite.

Hunting-case watches are still popular in 1915, but the cases have become thin and wanly elegant; the rich, baroque *décor* of the preceding decade gives way to plain surfaces unrelieved by anything except deeply engraved Spencerian initials. The massive watch chain is gone. The tender sentiment that decreed the braiding of hair chains is flown. America is growing rich; going to college; building country clubs; playing golf. A new kind of man comes upon the scene: "stylish dressers."

Many of the chains are attached to gold-plated pocket knives. Where now are the steel knives once carried by American men, equally suitable for whittling a stick, drawing a wild duck, or picking the teeth? And in a land where strong men once bit off cigar ends with strong teeth, the chain is sometimes pendant upon a "gold filled cigar cutter, bright polish, engraved."

One wonders whether Count von Bernstorff, the German Ambassador in Washington in 1915, did not with characteristic German thoroughness, survey the catalogs and report to his government that the Americans had become a degenerate people who would not fight.

After the War Is Over

It is 1925. Our boys have been home nearly eight years from the wars overseas. They are growing fat around their bellies and gray around the ears. More and more, as time passes, tee-da-dums take the place of the forgotten words of "Mademoiselle from Armentières." Their conversation seems to harden with their arteries. During the war they had picked up a hitherto sissy innovation—the wrist watch—and, passing it through the fire of battle, made it an instrument worthy of men. But once back in the factory or on the farm, they slumped into old ways and wore again their old-fashioned watches with chain or fob. Although millions of wrist watches enabled American soldiers to keep engagements with the enemy on the battlefield or in Paris with a girl, it is a strange fact that the catalog of 1925 lists only a few.

Watches Go Hollywood

In 1935, the wrist watch takes the center of the stage, and the old-fashioned hunting-case watch retires to the wings to await an infrequent cue from an unreconstructed American. The catalog pictures dozens of slender models bearing now the proud names of Waltham, Bulova, and Elgin. Bulova has done more for time than all the philosophers and physicists who have ever wrestled with it. Bulova, set free by the radio, gave men a new concept and called it "Bulova watch-time."

The industrial revolution, unlike the physical evolution of nature or the political revolutions of men, seems to move forward not in a zigzag but a straight line. And it is not deflected one whit from its course by American William Morrises who go to Mexico and cry out to us from its high air for a return to the crafts era. The Federal government recognized that the American industrial revolution was in full swing long ago, because in 1900, for the first time, it ceased to record crafts production in its business census. The catalog, too, keeps its eye on the ball and, seeing men soaring on wings in the sky, lists the Aero wrist watch for men. Then, turning to the sanctum of the movies where millions of Americans daily turn, it shakes out of its voluminous sleeves THE MICKEY MOUSE WRIST WATCH. MICKEY MOUSE KEEPS TIME FOR OVER 1½ MILLION CHILDREN. TWO MORE MICKEYS IN ENAMELED COLORS ON THE WATCH. But Mickey, for all that he is as much a favorite in Athens, Greece, as he is in Athens, Georgia, is an American mouse and consequently must be useful as well as amusing. Therefore: "Daily, Mickey teaches boys and girls to be on time. Note Sears low price. Regular $2.95 Value, $2.69."

Once, long ago, the heroes of American childhood were Uncas—the Last of the Mohicans—Paul Revere, Dick Merriwell, and Daniel Boone. But they were storybook heroes. You had to read—even buy—a book to get at them. These pioneer hardships have happily been eliminated by the radio, and a new group of ethereal heroes has been created. Among them none was more famous in 1935 than Buck Rogers whose thrilling adventures the children followed while they dribbled on their bibs (thereby creating more sales) the nourishing, rich in vitamins, iron, quinine, ipecac, phosphorus, nicotine, and other character-building properties found only in Bunko, The Breakfast Food of a Nation of Children. The people who erected a tomb for General Grant and an arch for Admiral Dewey made a watch for Buck Rogers. This is how the catalog describes it:

"YOUR OWN BUCK ROGERS. See your hero and Wilma on the dial in brilliant colors. Tiger Man on back. Nickel plated case. Every boy should have one of these popular watches. In attractive colorful box. Shpg. wt., 8 oz, 89¢."

Sears and the Old-Fashioned Girl

As long ago as 1883, Mary A. Livermore, in *What shall we do with our Daughters?,* speaks of a woman engineer at the Philadelphia Centennial Exposition of 1876. She was, says Mrs. Livermore, "a comely maiden with a pleasant face, refined manners, and dainty dress, who, amid the heat, dust, smoke, and noise, preserved her neatness, and yet did all the work from starting the fire in the morning to blowing off the steam at night. The girl herself said that her labor was not so exhausting as taking charge of an ordinary cook-stove, while her pay was twelve dollars a week."

A little later, Emily Faithfull, in her *Three Visits To America,* reported: "I saw American women employed in all kinds of ways—in staining and enamelling glass, cutting ivory, pearl, and tortoise shell, as well as weaving carpets, working the looms for furniture and carriage draperies; they are press feeders as well as type-setters, they make and pack candles, and cut glue in sheets. . . . There are thousands of women tailors in New York, and in the button trade the proportions of women to men is six to one. . . . Girls were packing chewing tobacco in tin-foil . . . and judging from the extent to which this pernicious habit is practiced in America, it must be difficult to keep the supply in due proportion to the demand. . . ."

The golden age of the American woman is evidently in the making. She still has not got the vote, but that will come in time, and she is not waiting for a Lincoln to set her free. She is demanding and getting the privileges hitherto reserved by men for men. Soon she will have the right to work long hours for low wages in dark factories. It is certain that she will never submit to the low status of Chinese and French women who share nothing with their husbands except a home, a profound intimacy, and an integrated family life. But in the 1890's, while the woman's emancipation movement was stronger than ever, doubts arose even among the women. Seven hundred girl students of Stanford University were asked: "What person of whom you have heard would you like most to resemble?" *Vogue* recorded the replies. In nine cases out of the ten, the person the girls most wanted to resemble was—a man.

Despite these alleged evidences of change; despite the fact that women for a long time had been packing chewing tobacco, cutting glue into sheets, and stoking furnaces, the catalog, whether out of sheer gallantry, or whether it considered that its clientele was still made up of old-fashioned girls who painted china, pouted, and swooned, ignored the changes and went blithely on its way. Thus in 1905 it listed:

"No. C45556. Less Money Than Ever Before and Better Than Ever. Genuine French Enameled Chatelaine Watch for $5.00. The case is gold filled, beautifully enameled in either blue, ruby red or green. The chatelaine matches the watch. The movement is an imported one, made in Switzerland, perfectly trued and adjusted. . . . At $5.00 for the complete outfit, case, chatelaine and watch, you have a bargain at least 50 per cent cheaper than any local jeweler could possibly sell it."

The chatelaine watch was worn attached to the shirtwaist, the coat, the sweater, or any outer garment, and, because it was highly conspicuous, designers sought to make it beautiful in a ladylike way. The case of one popular model was "beautifully enameled with various subjects as illustrated," and one may safely guess what the subjects were from the illustration. It depicts a plainly high-minded gentleman walking, stick in hand, some paces ahead of an equally high-minded lady above whose head is poised a little bird in fluttersome flight. Other models had silver fleur-de-lis inlaid upon gun metal or were decorated with handsomely engraved flowers whose delicate convolutions covered the entire case.

The Little Watch Birds, whom we saw at play, at work, at love, and at home, on the cases of men's watches, are at their birdie best on the ladies' watches of 1905. They swoop and swoon; sit upon eggs and leave eggs unsat upon; touch beaks above flower-pierced hearts, and support clusters of "genuine rose diamonds."

We encounter again The Noble Stag. His nobility clings to him like an infatuated tick, but he nonetheless displays a fine sense of the proprieties, for now that he is on the watches of ladies, he modestly hides his rough male body and permits only velvety antlers and soft eyes to appear above the leaves.

The name of a sweetheart may arouse tender sentiments in the breast of a man. And many a man of 1905, when so aroused, could not have been restrained by a team of brewery horses until he had ordered a watch from Sears, with the lady's name spelled out in more or less precious stones. In all cases—be it clearly understood—the ladies were the wives or relatives of the gentleman donors, for, at that time, refined women would not accept precious gifts from gentlemen to whom they stood in the mere relation of friend or acquaintance.

Unfortunately, however, even in that halcyon day, there were ladies who refused to abide by the rules. "Yet we are sorry to say, that there are ladies so rapacious and so mean that they are not ashamed to give broad hints to gentlemen (particularly those gentlemen who are very young or very old) regarding certain beautiful card-cases, bracelets, essence-bottles, and etc. which they have seen and admired, even going so far as to fall in love with elegant shawls, scarfs, splendid fans, and embroidered handkerchiefs. . . . There are ladies who keep themselves supplied with certain articles of finery, (for instance white kid gloves) by laying ridiculous wagers with gentlemen, knowing that, whether winning or losing, the gentlemen out of galantry, always pay. . . .

"Another and highly reprehensible way of extorting a gift is to have what is called a philopena with a gentleman. This very silly joke is when a young lady, in cracking almonds, chances to find two kernels in one shell; she shares them with a beau; and whichever calls out 'philopena' on their next meeting, is entitled to receive a present from the other; and she is to remind him of it till he remembers to comply. . . .

"There is a great want of delicacy and self-respect in philopenaism, and no lady who has a proper sense of her dignity *as a lady* will engage in anything of the sort."

We may accept, therefore, as fact that gentlemen who selected valuable presents from the catalog to give to ladies gave them only to their wives, wives-to-be, or relatives.

Man's Best Friend Is His Watch

"As the years go by," said the catalog in 1915, "you will conceive a genuine affection for your watch, until it comes to seem more a thing alive than an affair of wheels and springs. It becomes endowed with a personality, a boon companion of your daily life; its loss or disability the cause for very real grief; its possession a constant stimulant to effort."

These touching words, which unfortunately by implication hurl the Watch into the midst of the ancient controversy of just who is Man's Best Friend—his Wife, Mother, Horse, or Hound—conclude the introduction to the watch section of the catalog in the second year of the World War. Happy is the country that can afford to lavish affection on watches while men are dying in the mud around Passchendaele.

The wrist watch has almost, but not quite, arrived. It is now called the Bracelet Watch, but the bracelet is detachable and the watch may also be worn attached to the clothes with a "chatelette pin." But one model—foreshadowing the future—is already called Ladies' or Men's Knockabout Wrist Bracelet Watch.

Whatever the future may hold, the watch styles of 1915 were still dominated by the styles of 1905, and The Little Watch Birds, more numerous than ever in a year of rising prices for farm products, soar in genteel abandon.

Plows are now free to break the plains and the plowmen are certain of a rich market. Orders pour into Chicago, and trains go out from Sears heavily freighted. Monogrammed watches are again in demand, but whether gentlemen in the age of suffragettes feel that Soft and Gentle woman is losing her softness and gentleness, or whether the ladies have tired of the fashion, the fact is that the diamond-encrusted B-E-A-T-R-I-C-E watch of 1905 is no more. Instead there is the "Blue Enameled Monogrammed Watch—It Takes Two Weeks To Fill An Order For Colored Enameled Monogrammed Watches." Monograms are no longer in the florid Spencerian manner but are wrought in angular, block letters. Women, the world, and watches are changing.

New Ladies and New Watches

There was little time for sentiment in the year 1925. The index for farm products had been going through awesome gyrations, having risen from 71.5 in 1915 to 150.7 in 1920; fallen to 88.4 in 1921, and slowly risen to 100.0 in 1924. Sears' copywriter no longer sits dreaming and writing pensive essays on the watch as Man's Best Friend. Woman, Gentle Woman, does not sit at home now if she can help it, but is out pounding a typewriter or dipping chocolates. And you cannot pound or dip efficiently if your watch is bobbing into the keys or dropping into the fudge. The copywriter, with these considerations in mind, goes straight to the unhappy heart of things and proclaims: "LADIES' WRIST WATCHES AT BIG SAVINGS."

The ladies now have the vote and the privilege of standing behind Mr. Woolworth's counters, but they have forever lost The Little Birds. Who shall count the cost or assay the gains and losses? We mortals, whose minds are circumscribed by the constricting veil of the mortal flesh, know only that the

Birds have flown to come no more and that something we shall never recapture has gone out of American life. Only wrist watches remain, and, however feminine they may be with encrustations of precious stones or delicate traceries in gold, they somehow suggest flat heels, flat chests, flat voices,

Wrist Watch in Early Stage of Evolution

and that flattest of all things in nature: a woman who does not rely upon a man for protection.

Something seems to have happened also to the codes by which ladies—now become women—were once governed. In language which would have been offensive to a lady or gentleman of 1905, the copywriter of 1925 boldly makes this suggestion:

"Give 'her' a wristwatch. It is a useful gift and will certainly be appreciated. Any of the watches on these pages are acceptable."

Who is this ill-defined, ambiguous "her" of 1925, surrounded by eye-winking quotation marks? Apparently she is anybody. But only twenty years ago she could have been none save wife, relative, or betrothed. Can it be that ladies who stand in none of these relationships to gentlemen now accept precious gifts from them?

Miss America and The Elf

In the 1935 catalog, two American girls—symbolized by wrist watches—face each other on opposite pages, and while they may meet they will never become pals. The first is The Elf:

"Among the dainty, up-to-date wrist watches for women is The Elf. Delicately styled with silvered metal dial and plain black numerals and black hands. Yet strongly built for practical service. The chromium plated embossed case has a perfectly matching Ratchet Band similar to higher priced watches. This watch is a new small size and has a world of style. . . . Price $4.59."

Who does not know The Elf and, knowing her, fails to realize that this is the watch she wears? She is the young woman who as a school child was never tardy, whose report card was always marked "Deportment Excellent," who made the highest grades in the class without impressing the teacher or her fellow pupils, kept her desk and person neat, brought wild flowers to school in spring and pressed them in her geography book in fall. She is the girl who read "inspirational" books during the summer vacation, bound up the broken leg of a chickadee, helped her mother put up pickles and prepare little pillows of sachet for the coming Christmas, and saved money out of her allowance to give it to the missionary fund.

The Elf is now thirty-five years old. Everybody in town has a good word to say of her, and she holds what is called a "responsible position" at Tatums, Your Wholesale Grocer. The younger girls adore her, and whenever they become engaged to marry they run to The Elf's house to tell her, and she, smiling behind her glasses, immediately arranges a linen or kitchen shower for the bride-to-be. The older ladies of the community, too, are deeply fond of The Elf and ask her to meetings of their sewing circles and temperance clubs, and the men of the town are invariably kind and courteous to her. But The Elf never has a beau of her own, although there was considerable talk that winter when Professor Willard, who taught mathematics at the high school, used to call on her two or three evenings a week and once took her to an oyster supper at the Hagar House. He, however, as the *Tocsin* reported, "accepted a position with a New York book company,

and we'll always be glad to see him whenever he comes back."
He never came back.

The years roll on, and more and more old man Tatum relies
on The Elf. Day after day she turns the pages of his ledgers
and each day, almost automatically, glances at her "dainty
wrist watch delicately styled," when the hands approach
twelve, and then goes home to dinner, to return to her desk
at one o'clock.

The Elf and her sisters live in every town of America and
on remote farms. They are the predestined spinsters of the
land, leading conventual lives amid the trappings of the jazz
age.

As remote from her as Handy's "St. Louis Blues" is from
Strauss' "Blue Danube" is Miss America. This is her wrist
watch as described by the catalog:

Dainty Miss America. Bulova's 7-Jewel Radio Star.
"This little Radio Star watch is one of the world's most popular models. It has been described over the radio many times.
Richly embossed 10-Karat White Rolled Gold Plated case
with adjustable safety bracelet to match. Distinct black numerals on attractive dial. A gift any girl would be thrilled to
have. Price $24.75. Postpaid, Cash or Easy Payments. Terms
$4 Down, $4 Monthly."

This is no watch for The Elf or her kind. Here within the
compass of one paragraph designed merely to sell a watch
are obliquely indicated some of the startling changes that
have occurred in American life since 1905. A young lady of
that period, with a chatelaine watch attached to her shirtwaist by a fleur-de-lis pin, did not dream either of the wrist
watch or the radio. She had limbs but no legs and these were
well covered in public. And the very idea that a girl could
ever at any time achieve fame and fortune by appearing almost naked in a bathing-beauty contest, and not only escape
the brand of the scarlet woman but actually receive the accolade of her contemporaries' esteem and envy, would have
caused her to swoon.

Yet by 1935, winners of national bathing-beauty contests

become nationally, if ephemerally, famous. Watches and other things are named for them, and millions of girls would like to step into the winner's beach sandals. For Miss America, immediately after her victory, enters into a heaven of night-club and personal-appearance contracts; recommends (for a price) diets, brassières, toothbrushes, and soaps, and finds, perhaps, at the end of a Broadway rainbow, a rich, handsome husband modestly hiding under a pot of gold. These are not empty, academic honors that "don't get you nothing," but are tangible, cash values and sound currency throughout the forty-eight states, Alaska, and our possessions overseas.

"Miss America," moreover, is the watch that "has been described over the radio many times," and it bears the cachet of New York's fashionable Fifth Avenue, making it more than ever desirable, although it may be worn by a girl who fries hamburgers in the Busy Bee Café on Route 61 outside Hushpuckana, Mississippi. For, as everyone now knows, a road that does not lead either to Hollywood or New York is just a blind alley.

So much for the woman and the watch. But what of the man? It takes two to make a gift. As recently as 1925, the copywriter spurred the timorous cavalier trembling on the verge of giving a girl a present by assuring him that "she will appreciate it." But not in 1935. The noble quality of gratitude seems no longer to have either sales or sex appeal; it is dated and seems stalely *fin de siècle*. The thing to do now—if possible—is to give and get thrills. So the copywriter whispers to the undecided male: "A gift any girl would be thrilled to have."

One more difference between the manners of 1905 and 1935 remains to be noted. In the earlier period, a gentleman who gave a gift to a lady within the permitted degrees of consanguinity or love laid the money on the line. If he did not get gratitude in return, he also got no bills. But in 1935, a guy bought thrills for a gal on the installment plan and hoped they would hold out at least until he had made the last payment.

8 · YOU GET IT—WE CURE IT

FEW CHAPTERS in our national life are filled with as much evidence of brutal disregard of human life and suffering as those that record the disgraceful years when fake medicines were sold to millions of people, and when publishers of newspapers and magazines thrived by printing advertisements of outrageous quackeries. If the health of a nation is an asset of the nation, we treasured ours about as carefully as we conserved our forests and wild life. It is indeed, as the historian Schlesinger has remarked, a tribute to the robustness of Americans that they were not exterminated by the medicines they drank. Yet for long years medical fakers were permitted to pile up fortunes for themselves and misery for their dupes through the sale of nostrums that often caused pain, torture, blindness, paralysis, and even death. They were allowed to swindle the sick and the suffering; to keep them from seeking medical advice until it was too late; to deceive them through devices that would shock the morality of the criminal insane; to do all this openly, or with bribery ill-concealed, and with the apparent consent of an impotent, ignorant, or apathetic country.

How widely these fake nostrums, these preposterous remedies and dangerous "cures," were distributed throughout the country may be deduced from the fact that the catalog of 1905 devotes the enormous space of twenty pages to them; what they were, and what they purported to cure, may readily be gathered from a description of some of those that were offered for sale in these pages. But the story of patent medicines in America begins long before 1905.

DRUG DEPARTMENT

OUR QUALITY GUARANTEE.

EVERY REMEDY, every proprietary medicine put up in our own laboratory or sold by us and prepared at the Seroco Chemical Laboratory is guaranteed absolutely pure, made from the very highest grade ingredients, positively free from any adulteration or alloy, never cheapened in any way at the expense of efficiency, and positively the best known prescription in each case for the ailment for which it is intended; and every patent (or proprietary) medicine of other makes offered in this catalogue, to the best of our knowledge and belief, is of standard quality, made by concerns of established and proven reliability; every drug, every article of merchandise shown in this catalogue is of the highest grade, never cheapened, efficiency never sacrificed for cost.

WITH OUR FACILITIES, with the most skilled chemists, the most skilled pharmacists, with the facilities afforded in our big laboratory, we are in such a position that no retail druggist can possibly be in a better position to thoroughly test, carefully analyze the goods we buy and sell, to know they are strictly pure and of the highest potency. You have our guarantee for this backed by our reputation known everywhere. You are sure of getting not only the highest quality, but you are also sure of getting the lowest price, one-half the price charged by others, and many times even much less.

WHY WE CAN GIVE SO MUCH MORE IN QUALITY.

WITH NEARLY ALL THE EXPENSE common to other dealers eliminated, where it is only necessary to ask our customers to pay a price that barely covers the cost of material and labor in our own laboratory, with but our one small percentage of profit added, there is not the slightest necessity of sacrificing quality for price, since we can make the price attractively low on the highest grade of goods obtainable.

FIRST, our reputation alone will preclude us from using anything but the very best, and secondly, it is very easy with our facilities to give our customers the very best, and then furnish them the goods for at least one-half the price others must get for inferior goods. If in our laboratory the remedy requires any spirits for its preservation, we do not consider price in the purchase. We only look to the quality, the very best obtainable, and the same applies to every ingredient, every formula we have. So, in ordering anything from this catalogue, and particularly remedies put up in our Seroco Chemical Laboratory, by comparison you will find them in every way better, more efficient, more satisfactory, not to mention very much lower in price than any similar remedy or article you can buy from any dealer anywhere.

SPECIAL ADVANTAGES TO AGENTS, DRUGGISTS, MERCHANTS AND HANDLERS OF DRUGS AND PROPRIETARY REMEDIES (PATENT MEDICINES.)

WE HAVE ON OUR BOOKS thousands of customers who make a business of buying goods from this department to sell again, particularly our own special remedies, made in our own laboratory, the Seroco Chemical Laboratory, and make a nice income at this work.

AGENTS MAKE FROM $5.00 TO $10.00 A DAY by devoting their time to selling our Seroco Chemical Laboratory remedies. Druggists, merchants and others often double their income by carrying a stock of these goods, supplying their customers with the highest grade goods made, and at a liberal profit to themselves.

THE ADVANTAGES WE OFFER over any other line of remedies made are many. First, every remedy put up in our own laboratory is put out under the manufacturing name of Seroco Chemical Laboratory, Chicago, and does not bear the name of Sears, Roebuck & Co., in any place, hence you can buy these goods and offer them for sale without any indication on the goods that they were purchased from us and in this way you haven't even the slightest competition from our house.

SECOND, every remedy is plainly priced on the outside of the package (without any reference whatever to our selling price), at the usual price at which similar remedies are retailed. For example, our sarsaparilla, the intrinsic value of one bottle of which is worth two of any other sarsaparilla made, bears the name on the outside of the carton "Seroco Chemical Laboratory, Chicago. Price, $1.00," whereas our price in single bottles is 50 cents or when you order a dozen of remedies together, only 40 cents a bottle. Therefore you can buy a bottle of Dr. Hammond's Sarsaparilla under the name Seroco Chemical Laboratory of which the price is plainly $1.00, for only 40 cents, if included in an order of one dozen or more of the different remedies, whereas any other widely advertised sarsaparilla of one-half the strength or efficiency would cost at least $8.00 per dozen if bought from the largest wholesale drug house, or nearly twice the price at which we sell Dr. Hammond's Sarsaparilla, so the agent, canvasser, druggist or retailer selling Dr. Hammond's Sarsaparilla who can sell it for $1.00 per bottle and make 60 cents, or can cut the price as much as he likes, making for his profit the difference between 40 cents per bottle and the price he chooses to ask for it. The same applies to other of our preparations. The name Sears, Roebuck & Co. appears on no package. Every package bears the name Seroco Chemical Laboratory. You can buy these goods direct from us in quantities of one dozen or more of the different remedies or assorted, at about one-half the price at which wholesale dealers sell inferior goods, you can offer them to your trade at cut prices and make a far bigger profit than on any other line of remedies offered to your trade. You can get the benefit of our dozen prices by ordering six or more packages. You need not order six of one kind, but as long as your order is for six or more packages you can take advantage of the dozen price.

ANOTHER ADVANTAGE.

OUR GOODS ARE PUT OUT IN HANDSOMER, far more attractive, better selling and more satisfactory packages than any other remedy made. Every package is of most convenient size. We use the handsomest, best shaped and most attractive boxes, bottles, cartons, wrappers and general package material that is in any line of remedies made. The packages are in strict keeping with the contents of the same. As a rule, all packages are beautifully lithographed in colors in handsome designs, all bear the name of Seroco Chemical Laboratory, Chicago, and the usual retail selling price is plainly printed on each package. Each package carries with it the laboratory's binding guarantee for quality, a very essential point to the customer buying.

THE BOOK OF INSTRUCTIONS which we furnish with each remedy is far more complete and instructive than is furnished with any other remedy made. It is a complete treatise on the diseases for which the particular remedy is a specific, gives the patient much more information and enables him to use the remedy to far better advantage than if we were to furnish only the stereotyped information that usually goes with the ordinary patent remedy.

THE PRICES ASKED by the manufacturers for most patent medicines make it impossible for us to save you more than from 25 to 50 per cent, whereas, from our own laboratory, the Seroco Chemical Laboratory, we can furnish you higher grade remedies on the basis of the actual cost for the ingredients, compounding, package, etc., with but our one small percentage of profit added. As a rule, the price is from one-third to one-half that charged by retail dealers for inferior goods.

OUR POSITION ON THE PATENT MEDICINE QUESTION.

WE SELL NEARLY ALL OF THE ADVERTISED or so called patent medicines without adding our recommendation to any particular preparation. We simply furnish our customers such advertised patent medicines as they may want and which they would buy anyway, just the same as we supply any other merchandise, giving our patrons, however, the advantage of our buying facilities and supplying this class of goods at from 25 to 40 per cent lower prices than the prices which they would have to pay at any drug store. It must be understood, however, that we know nothing about the formulae or ingredients and we can, therefore, say nothing for or against the merit of such patent medicines.

IN ADDITION we furnish to our customers a selected line of household remedies, not only for the minor ills, but also for chronic diseases, and these remedies, being prepared in our own laboratory, under our own supervision, every ingredient going into these remedies being known to us and the formula itself being in every instance one used by thousands of physicians as the most reliable and efficient for the treatment of symptoms for which they are intended, we do not hesitate to guarantee them absolutely pure and harmless and to highly recommend these remedies, feeling confident that they will meet all reasonable hopes and expectations of the customer.

THESE HOUSEHOLD PREPARATIONS of ours, put up in the Seroco Chemical Laboratory, are preparations that are the result of a great deal of experience and are based on the most successful formulas and prescriptions that are recognized by practitioners as the most successful in the treatment of these certain symptoms and for the relief and cure of the disorders and diseases for which they are intended.

IN ALL CASES OF ACUTE SICKNESS, it is usually necessary, and in many cases of chronic diseases it is advisable, to employ the services of a skilled physician. The patient may not know what is ailing him; he may not be able to judge as to the nature of his symptoms, and a careful diagnosis should be made and the treatment employed should be suitable to his condition as ascertained by the physician's examination and as determined by his judgment. When you know, however, that you are suffering from indigestion or stomach trouble; when it is a question of saving for yourself inconvenience, time and expense; when you know that your ailment is a catarrh trouble which may have become chronic and which neither by treatment of the physician or by the use of so called patent medicines has been benefited, you need not hesitate to give our household remedy for indigestion or for catarrh, as the case may be, a fair test, as it may be just the remedy that covers your condition exactly, affording quick relief and a possible cure within a comparatively short time.

EVERY ONE OF OUR HOUSEHOLD REMEDIES is considered one of the best, if not the best prescription employed by the most successful medical practitioners for the treatment of the condition for which we supply them. Of this fact you may be certain. We also wish to emphasize the fact that these remedies are prepared in our own laboratory, that we know every ingredient that goes into the preparations and we consequently know and can assure you that they are absolutely harmless. You are not taking the slightest risk in giving our household remedies a thorough trial.

WE DO NOT CLAIM that any one of our household remedies is a "Cure All," nor do we wish you to understand that we (or anybody else) can claim that without a diagnosis of your case we know beforehand that our remedy will cure you. This would be unreasonable and you would have a perfect right to question our sincerity. What we do know is that our household remedies comprise the most valuable and highly successful prescriptions for the different ailments which they cover. We know that there is nothing barmful in any single one of our preparations. We know that they have afforded relief and even permanent cure in hundreds and thousands of cases. We know that they are prepared with the greatest care and we know that we are able to and do offer these remedies for a fraction of the cost of what the same prescription would cost put up in any drug store.

YOU CAN EASILY ASCERTAIN whether any one of the household remedies we recommend is suitable for the treatment, relief and cure of your case. You are taking no risk, for we do not ask, nor do we expect that you should risk a single penny when making a test of these remedies. They may be the best remedies made, they may have relieved and cured thousands of men and women, which fact would ordinarily be sufficient to secure your confidence. No matter how good a remedy may be, no matter how much it has done for others, the question for you to determine is "What will it do for me?" Is it at all suitable for your particular case? To learn whether it is or not you have the privilege of ordering the first bottle or package of our household remedies with the understanding that after you have used it you find that it has not benefited your case, upon receipt of your report to that effect and the statement that you have never ordered or used the same remedy before, we will refund you the entire amount you have paid for the first package. We shall not expect you to be put to any expense or to proceed with the treatment, unless you find that the medicine is helping you and seems to be just what you need for obtaining relief and a cure.

PRESCRIPTION DEPARTMENT.

OUR PRESCRIPTION DEPARTMENT is under the direct charge of one of the most able chemists and pharmacists in the country. Every prescription is compounded with the greatest care, only the very best drugs are used, and yet we are able to save our customers in nearly all cases one-half in price. If you send your doctor's prescription, or any other prescription, to us, you can rest assured it will be given professional care. There will not be any substitutions such as local druggists are often compelled to make for want of certain drugs. The prescription will be compounded in the most scientific manner and returned to you immediately and at a saving in price on an average of more than one-half.

REGARDING SPIRITUOUS LIQUORS. We do not deal in spirituous liquors for general use. We do not believe in the traffic and we allow no liquors to go out of our house, except for medicinal purposes and as may be required in our laboratory for compounding remedies that could not be manufactured in any other way. We call the attention of our customers to this fact, for the reason that we constantly receive inquiries with reference to prices on various kinds of liquors, and we wish it to be understood that we can furnish spirituous liquors only when they are to be used for medicinal purposes. Poisonous, inflammable or explosive materials cannot be mailed.

WE ISSUE A SPECIAL CATALOGUE of Surgical Instruments and Physicians' Supplies, which will be mailed to any physician or surgeon, free on application.

SEE INDEX, PINK PAGES 492 TO 499, TO FIND WHAT YOU WANT.

DR. WILDEN'S QUICK CURE FOR INDIGESTION AND DYSPEPSIA.

DO YOU SUFFER FROM INDIGESTION? DO YOU HAVE DYSPEPSIA? DOES YOUR FOOD DISTRESS YOU?

Do you suffer from a stuffed up, choking feeling, a difficulty in breathing, pain in the chest, as if a lump were there, after your meals? These are the easily recognized and sure symptoms of indigestion. Send for Dr. Wilden's Quick Cure for Indigestion and Dyspepsia, the great stomach remedy, the enemy of indigestion in any form.

A GREAT PRESCRIPTION. Put up in the form of plain, easily taken tablets and highly recommended as a cure for dyspepsia. If you suffer from only an occasional attack of indigestion, even though your stomach is out of order but seldom, keep Dr. Wilden's Quick Cure on hand, take a tablet after your meals and you will not be troubled. You can then enjoy your meals and never suffer one particle of distress, you won't know you have such an organ as a stomach.

ONLY 38 CENTS PER BOX CONTAINING 50 DOSES, enough for 50 treatments. For 38 cents we furnish a box of Dr. Wilden's Quick Cure for Indigestion and Dyspepsia containing almost double the number of tablets or treatments, found in boxes of other so called dyspepsia tablets that retail at 50 cents everywhere.

FOR 58 CENTS we furnish a large box containing as much as three small ones and more tablets than are contained in dyspepsia remedies that retail at $1.00. Don't wait until your indigestion or occasional stomach trouble has become chronic. Don't think that because you suffer from distress after meals only once in a while that you should overlook it. With Dr. Wilden's tablets at hand for convenient use, you can check the trouble at once and at the slightest intimation of indigestion, the least fullness, stiffness or uncomfortable feeling after eating, take a tablet (they are small and dissolve easily), and in a short time you will be completely relieved. At the same time the stomach is toned and strengthened, better able to perform its natural functions and you are insuring yourself against after dangerous complications.

ONE TABLET OF DR. WILDEN'S QUICK CURE FOR INDIGESTION AND DYSPEPSIA HELPS THE STOMACH TO DIGEST FOOD. There is wonderful digestive power in a single tablet of this great stomach remedy and yet this splendid remedy does not contain one single particle of opium, calomel or any harmful ingredient, but it digests food, assists the stomach and strengthens the digestive organs.

WE EARNESTLY ASK YOU TO GIVE THIS DYSPEPSIA PREPARATION A FAIR TRIAL. We do not believe there is a preparation on the market that possesses more of the valuable digestive properties found in Dr. Wilden's Quick Cure for Indigestion and Dyspepsia. We are willing that you should send for a box of Dr. Wilden's Quick Cure for Indigestion and Dyspepsia with the understanding that you can give it a trial and if it does not benefit you and you will simply tell us that you received no benefit and that this is the first package you have tried, we will immediately return your money. We have great confidence in this remedy, and we do not want any of our customers to suffer, if we are able to offer them means of relief and cure.

No. 8C1 Price, per dozen boxes, **$3.60**; regular size box.......... **38c**
No. 8C2 Price, per dozen boxes, **$4.80**; large box.......... **58c**
If by mail, postage extra, per small box, 2 cents; large box, 8 cents.

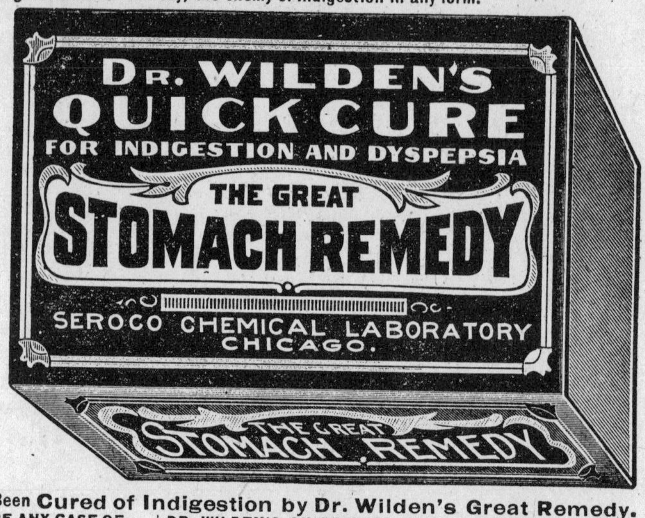

These Letters Are From Only a Very Few of the Great Number Who Have Been Cured of Indigestion by Dr. Wilden's Great Remedy.

THREW THE OTHER MEDICINES AWAY AFTER HE GOT DR. WILDEN'S QUICK CURE, AND HE IS NOW WELL.

Sears, Roebuck & Co., Chicago, Ill. Alexandria, S. D.

Gentlemen: In regard to Dr. Wilden's Quick Cure for Indigestion and Dyspepsia, I believe it to be the best remedy for indigestion on the market today. I had been suffering from indigestion for some time and I was getting worse instead of better under the treatment I was taking. I sent for some of your cure and threw the other medicine away when I received yours. I noticed a decided improvement after I had taken only two or three doses and I continued to improve steadily until I was entirely relieved and I do not suffer or have the least trace of indigestion left. I am very glad that I was able to find a remedy for this dreaded disease before it got so bad or developed into some worse disease that would be impossible to cure.

Yours very truly, WM. OVERMAN.

DR. WILDEN'S QUICK CURE WILL CURE ANY CASE OF INDIGESTION.

Sears, Roebuck & Co., Chicago, Ill. Newark, Ohio.

Gentlemen: Dr. Wilden's Quick Cure for Indigestion and Dyspepsia is indeed as you claim for it, a quick cure, and it not only cures quickly but cures completely any case of indigestion for which it may be taken. This seems like a strong statement, but I know that it is true because I have taken the cure myself and have given it to two of my children and a nephew, all of whom were suffering from stomach trouble and were not able to find relief from the medicines which they were taking. Your wonderful preparation effected a sure and quick cure in every case and you may well believe that we do not fail to give you the proper credit and to recommend your medicine whenever we can. Everything that we have ever received from your store has been the best we had ever bought any place and we have been treated fairly and honorably in all of our transactions with you.

Yours respectfully, JAS. A. PAGELS.

DR. WILDEN'S QUICK CURE MADE IT POSSIBLE FOR MR. ADAMS TO SLEEP, WORK AND ENJOY HIMSELF.

Sears, Roebuck, & Co., Chicago, Ill. Lebanon, Ky.

Gentlemen: I feel that I have been helped more by your Dr. Wilden's Quick Cure for Indigestion and Dyspepsia than I ever have by any other medicine or cure which I have taken for any disease. I suffered so much from indigestion that I was not able to sleep at night and I could not do my work properly in the daytime, and I was so nervous and irritable from my stomach trouble that I was becoming a burden both to myself and to my friends. I sought relief everywhere and took all the medicines and so-called cures that were recommended to me, but none of them did me any good until I took your Dr. Wilden's Quick Cure for Indigestion and Dyspepsia, which I read about in your big catalogue. I speedily began to grow better under your treatment and it was not long before all my suffering was gone and I was able to sleep and work and enjoy myself as I had done before I was afflicted with that awful disease.

Yours truly, THOMAS ADAMS.

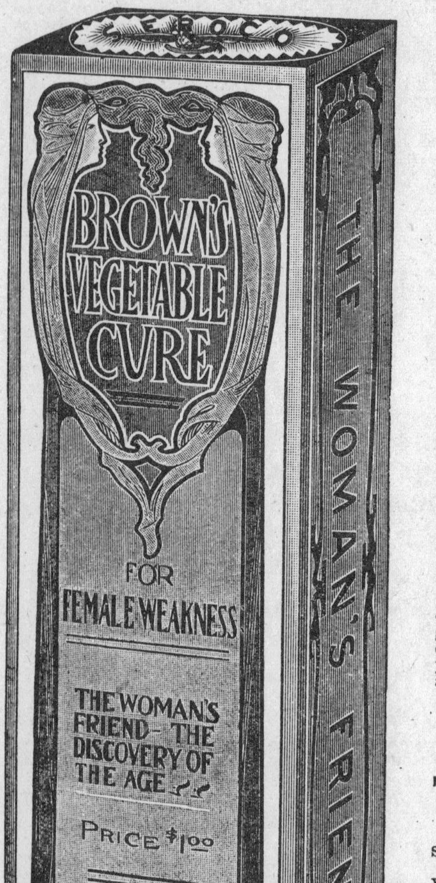

BROWN'S VEGETABLE CURE FOR FEMALE WEAKNESS.

LARGE COMMERCIAL SIZE QUART BOTTLES. RETAIL PRICE $1.00. OUR PRICE, EACH, 55c; PER DOZEN, $5.10.

A Very Effective Vegetable Tonic to be Used in the Treatment of Female Weakness, Falling of the Womb, Leucorrhea, Irregular or Painful Menstruation, Inflammation and Ulceration of the Womb, Flooding and all Female Disorders.

WOMEN, BROWN'S VEGETABLE CURE is most highly recommended for female disorders. If you have any of the following symptoms take this remedy at once, it may afford you an easy and lasting cure: Nausea and bad taste in the mouth, sore feeling in lower part of bowels, an unusual discharge, impaired general health, feeling of languor, sharp pain in region of kidneys, backache, dull pain in small of back, pain in passing water, bearing down feeling, a desire to urinate frequently, a dragging sensation in the groin, courses irregular, timid, nervous and restless feeling, a dread of some impending evil, temper wayward and irritable, a feeling of fullness, sparks before the eyes, gait unsteady, pain in womb, swelling in front, pain in breastbone, pain when courses occur, hysterics, temples and ears throb, sleep short and disturbed, whites, impaired digestion, headache, dizziness, morbid feeling and the blues, palpitation of the heart, nerves weak and sensitive, appetite poor, a craving for unnatural food, spirits depressed, nervous dyspeptic symptoms, a heavy feeling and pain in back upon exertion, fainting spells, difficulty in passing water, habitual constipation, cold extremities. If you have any of these symptoms send for a bottle of Brown's Vegetable Cure and give this preparation a trial. It will be sufficient to show you that Brown's Vegetable Cure is just the remedy you need—the remedy that will bring you not only relief but a cure, as it has in thousands of cases of suffering women who have given this medicine a fair test. Invalids have been made well and strong. Do not delay, one bottle will help and convince you.

UNDER THE GENERAL HEADING OF FEMALE WEAKNESS are included a vast array of systemic troubles, including leucorrhea or whites, prolapsus, or falling of the womb, irregular and painful menstruation, inflammation and ulceration of the womb, kidneys, bowel and liver troubles and ovarian difficulties. The term "female weakness" itself has no specific meaning and covers a multitude of ailments; in fact, given six different women with six different ailments peculiar to their sex, each one of them would be pretty sure to characterize her trouble as female weakness. **Brown's Vegetable Cure is very effective in the treatment of all of these diseases peculiar to women.**

BROWN'S VEGETABLE CURE FOR FEMALE WEAKNESS is a prescription that has proven highly efficient in a very large number of cases. It is one of our household remedies put up in our own laboratory, guaranteed to contain nothing harmful, but made up of those ingredients which are known to have the best effect in cases where the symptoms of female weakness are present. We offer it with every confidence and if you are suffering you can give this remedy a trial. If it affords you no relief, it will positively not harm you, and we will return to you your money if you have not used this remedy before.

Our Booklet, "The Woman's Friend," Valuable and Instructive, Sent Free with Every Bottle of Brown's Vegetable Cure.

No. 8C4 Price, per dozen bottles, **$5.10**; per bottle.......... **55c**
Cannot be mailed on account of weight.

READ THESE LETTERS FROM GRATEFUL WOMEN.

MRS. FULLER ENTIRELY CURED OF FEMALE WEAKNESS BY BROWN'S VEGETABLE CURE.

Emmet, Ark.
Sears, Roebuck & Co., Chicago, Ill.

Gentlemen: I received the Brown's Vegetable Cure which I ordered from you some time ago and I want to tell you that it has been a remarkable cure in my case. I have used it for female weakness and have been entirely cured. I had tried several cures which my friends had recommended before I used Brown's Vegetable Cure, but I did not receive any permanent relief. I think that this is the very best remedy of its kind on the market today and I do not hesitate to tell all of my friends about its remarkable properties. I think Mrs. Jones, who lives about three miles from me, will order some of the cure in a few days.

Yours sincerely,
MRS. CYNTHIAN FULLER.

BROWN'S VEGETABLE CURE IS THE BEST REMEDY OF ITS KIND ON THE MARKET.

Warsaw, Minn.
Sears, Roebuck & Co., Chicago, Ill.

Gentlemen: I feel that it is my duty to write and tell you of the remarkable cure which has been effected in my case by using your Brown's Vegetable Cure. I was a sufferer for a number of years from kidney and bladder troubles, but all of these troubles are now a thing of the past and I am once more a well woman, able to do all of my work and take care of my house as it should be taken care of. I certainly think that Brown's Vegetable Cure is the best remedy of its kind on the market. I had been taking medicine and was, when I received your medicine, taking medicine from a doctor here in Warsaw, but your Cure produced such an immediate and favorable result that I threw away all of the doctor's medicine and used nothing but Brown's Vegetable Cure.

Yours very truly,
MRS. C. C. CLAYTON.

BROWN'S VEGETABLE CURE DOES MORE GOOD THAN ALL OTHER MEDICINE PUT TOGETHER.

Sears, Roebuck & Co., Chicago, Ill. Leon, Iowa.

Gentlemen: It gives me much pleasure to tell you of the great good I have obtained from your excellent remedy, Brown's Vegetable Cure. I used the Cure for female weakness and I have received more help and benefit from it than I have ever received from any other medicine that I have tried. I have been a constant sufferer for a number of years and have tried a great number of remedies and have doctored for all of these years, but did not seem to get any stouter until after using Brown's Vegetable Cure, which is invaluable for female weakness or change of life. I am 46 years of age and have been quite poorly for some time, but since I received such great benefits from your medicine I am stronger than I have been for years. I am going to send to you for some more of your medicine. I was just telling my husband the other day that Brown's Vegetable Cure had done me more good than all of the rest of the medicine I have taken put together. I will continually praise your medicine for the great benefit I have received.

Yours very truly, MRS. W. L. ARNOLD.

Fake Medicines After the Civil War

W. G. Marshall, an English traveler who visited America in the 1880's, gives us this portrait of the American landscape of the period in his *Through America*:

"America is daubed from one end of the country to the other with huge white paint notices of favorite articles of manufacture, with an endless array of advertisements puffing off the medicine of pretentious quacks. . . . It is one of the first things that strike the stranger as soon as he has landed in the New World; he cannot step a mile into the open country . . . without meeting the disfigurements. . . ."

Marshall mentions these advertisements painted in huge white characters on houses, rocks, and fences between New York and Albany:

TARRANT'S SELTZER APERIENT CURES DIARRHOEA
USE CARBOLINE FOR THE HAIR

"The nuisance," he continues, "culminates at Chicago . . . the paradise of whitepaintism. . . ." Here he saw these advertisements:

DR. KING'S NEW DISCOVERY FOR CONSUMPTION, COUGHS, COLDS
WIZARD OIL GOOD FOR NEURALGIA
GARGLING OIL

—probably the most popular advertisement in America, always in huge yellow letters.

Lydia Pinkham

It was Lydia Pinkham of Lynn, Massachusetts, who more perhaps than any other person opened the door to the vast flood of nostrums that poured out all over America from shortly after the Civil War until about 1910. And it was Lydia Pinkham who first used those concepts in advertising which later became so popular and so profitable to their users:

the whispering campaign—the "your best friend won't tell you" copy; the personal touch; the capitalization of the theory that woman is always ill and that the perfidy of men causes their illness—a theory that moved Havelock Ellis to say in his *Man and Woman*: "Quite recently a woman has sought to revive the idea that women are normally in a pathological condition—the cause of which, she finds in some unexplained way, in the brutality of men." It was Mrs. Pinkham, too, who pitched her advertisements to a highly emotional key and addressed her readers as a suffering woman to suffering women.

Her famous Vegetable Compound, first marketed in 1876, bore this label: "A sure Cure for Prolapsus Uteri, or Falling of the Womb. . . . Pleasant to the taste, efficacious and immediate in its effect. It is a great help in pregnancy, and relieves pain during labor." But this was only a beginning, because this wonderful remedy was as good for men as for women. "For all weaknesses of the generative organs of either sex. It is second to no remedy that has ever been before the public; and for all diseases of the kidneys it is the Greatest Remedy in the World."

Every advertisement of the Vegetable Compound carried a picture of Lydia Pinkham, and her popularity soon became so great that, as a writer in *Printer's Ink* puts it: "This was the only portrait of a lady to be found in many newspaper offices, and more than once I have seen Lydia's picture used by the enterprising editor as a timely portrayal—all the way from Queen Victoria to Lilly Langtry." Sometimes editors removed Lydia's comb and made her into Susan B. Anthony or the current President's wife.

Mrs. Pinkham used advertisements describing real or imagined tragedies back of which were suffering women brought to commit crime because they did not take her Vegetable Compound. For example:

"A Fearful Tragedy. Clergyman of Stratford, Mass., Killed By His Own Wife. Tragedy Brought on By 16 Years of Suffering With Female Complaints The Cause. Lydia E. Pinkham's Vegetable Compound The Sure Cure For These

Complaints. Would Have Prevented The Direful Deed."

This "savior of her sex," as she was called by her admirers, diagnosed her correspondents' ills by mail, and annually received thousands of letters from women. But when she died in 1883, rich and famous, many persons refused to believe that she was dead, although her obituary was printed in hundreds of city and small-town newspapers. The Pinkham Company continued for years after her death to run this advertisement:

"Mrs. Pinkham, in her laboratory at Lynn, Mass., is able to do more for the ailing women of America than the family physician. Any woman, therefore, is responsible for her own suffering if she will not take the trouble to write to Mrs. Pinkham for advice."

Women did continue to write Mrs. Pinkham, and *The Ladies' Home Journal,* in 1905, exposed this advertisement as a fraud by printing a photograph of her tombstone showing that she had been dead for twenty-two years. It made no difference. The ladies continued to tell their troubles by mail to Mrs. Pinkham just the same.

Suffering men—that is, men suffering from a thirst they could not openly gratify because they were prohibitionists— also had their saviors. These gentlemen filled the pages of religious periodicals and newspapers with advertisements of "bitters" allegedly good for toning up the digestion, but which were actually almost pure alcohol colored and flavored. So great were the ravages of indigestion among the godly and so insistent the demand for these tonics that one of the most successful proprietors—Colonel Hostetter of Hostetter's Bitters—died leaving a fortune estimated at $18,000,000.

Years later, during prohibition days, a number of churchgoing Mississippi prohibitionists incurred "jake paralysis" as the result of drinking a lot of Jamaica ginger that contained wood alcohol. These outraged citizens petitioned Congress for compensation on the ground that if the Federal governmen had enforced the prohibition laws they would not have become paralyzed!

Traveling Medicine Men

Throughout the latter part of the nineteenth century and the earlier part of the twentieth, medicine shows moved from hamlet to hamlet, from small town to small town, and few hamlets were so obscure or remote that they did not receive at least one annual visit from a traveling cure-all doctor accompanied by his more or less pretentious minstrel show. These shows followed the harvesting of crops, playing, for example, in the Middle West wheat areas in the summer and in cotton towns of the deep South during the fall, for it was only at harvest time that many agriculturists had cash in their pockets.

The medical shows offered color, music, song, and jokes to the mud- or dustbound folk of little towns; spellbinding orations on the ills of the human body and their remedies; plus the glitter of a parade by day and a kerosene-torch-lighted platform at night. Medicine-show doctors, like the medical fraternity of today, tended to specialize in the treatment of certain real or imaginary diseases, the most frequent of which were worm diseases of all kinds, led by the tapeworm. Other doctors, in keeping with the best patent-medicine practice, offered nostrums alleged to cure everything from hangnails to hair lice.

The routine followed by all the shows was the same. The doctor and his retinue would arrive in, say, a small river town of Mississippi; erect a covered platform near the river and usually adjacent to the fish dock (that was where Negroes tended to congregate on Saturdays as they came to buy a catfish or "buffalo"); parade down Main Street, and invite everybody to the big free show to be given that night on Washington Avenue. Handbills, advertising the doctor's nostrums, would be distributed to the crowd, and announcement made of the pie-eating contest to be held every night the show was in town.

Shortly after darkness had fallen, kerosene torches blazing on the medicine-show platform proclaimed that gaiety, music,

OUR OWN COUGH CURE.

SOLD UNDER A POSITIVE GUARANTEE.

Retail price	50c and $1.00
Our price, 50-cent size, each	$0.35
Our price, 50-cent size, per dozen	3.00
Our price, large $1.00 size, each	.59
Our price, large $1.00 size, per dozen	5.40

NEGLIGENCE ON THE PART OF PARENTS, negligence on your own part, very often permits serious sickness to overtake the children or yourself when a little caution, a trifling expense, would have saved all the worry, trouble and not infrequently spared a dear life. We positively believe that there is among household remedies none that can prevent slight indispositions and serious illness so quickly, providing it is kept on hand, not sent for after the trouble has already developed to a certain degree, and also providing you secure the right preparation, a remedy that will not only relieve, but positively cure. We mean OUR OWN COUGH CURE.

WE RECOMMEND OUR OWN COUGH CURE knowing that it is without question the only cough remedy that will act quickly and at the same time is perfectly safe. What we recommend, however, still more is that you under no consideration delay ordering this remedy until you actually need it. Order it at once, see that you have a supply of same always on hand, so that it can be administered the moment the first signs of a cough are apparent. A few doses will then do the work, will prevent the cough from developing into bronchitis, pleurisy, pneumonia and other diseases of the lungs and pulmonary organs.

THERE IS DANGER indicated in the slightest cough. Don't neglect it. You owe it to yourself, to your relatives and friends to have the best means, that is, Our Own Cough Cure, ready at hand as soon as the cough makes its appearance. We cannot express it too strongly. We can't point out the danger too forcibly, and again ask you to consider the consequences of neglecting the first symptoms of a cough, and the necessity of immediate treatment to prevent the cough from developing into something worse, something that cannot be easily cured, something that may finally lead into consumption—incurable.

> There is no city, no town, no hamlet, nor a single household where you cannot sell Our Own Cough Cure. Everyone needs this remedy and will keep it on hand. You will need large quantities of both sizes. Be sure and order enough. . . . . . .

OUR OWN COUGH CURE is not only the best to stop the cough immediately, it is not only the best cough remedy for infants and children, it is practically the only safe and sure cure where a cough has become chronic; and we know of no medicine in existence that will do what Our Own Cough Remedy does in chronic cases, affording relief, always promptly allaying the inflammation of the bronchial tubes, and by its healing influence upon the organs that are always affected in such cases, it will gradually restore them to normal and healthy functions and assist in removing the chronic condition within the shortest possible time.

OUR OWN COUGH CURE is sold under a positive guarantee to be non-poisonous, to possess all the elements necessary for preventing the development of a cough, and where it has already taken hold of the patient, to quickly cure it. We personally guarantee it to be perfectly safe and harmless and to be the only cough remedy in existence that we can conscientiously recommend as being not only the cheapest but the best that can be produced. We supply Our Own Cough Cure in two sizes, the regular 50-cent size for 35 cents, the large $1.00 size for 59 cents.

DO NOT FAIL to include in your next order a supply of Our Own Cough Cure. You should never be without it. It is one of the greatest sickness preventers—a life saver.

No. 8C42 Price, per dozen, regular 50c size, $3.00; each 35c
No. 8C43 Price, per dozen, regular $1.00 size, $5.40; each 59c
Unmailable on account of weight.

Our Twenty-Minute Cold Cure.

NEVER FAILS.

Retail price	$0.25
Our price, per dozen, $1.50; each	17c

OUR TWENTY-MINUTE COLD CURE is not only what its name implies, but a gentle laxative and a powerful tonic. It acts gently on the bowels without griping, induces the liver to healthy action and assists in restoring your general health. It is a splendid tonic for the nervous system, and if once used you will never be without it. It promptly cures colds, la grippe, headache and all the symptoms usually present in a severe cold.

YOU MAY SIT IN A DRAFT, or get your feet wet, may become chilled and soon notice that the pores are stopped up, perhaps a slight fever starts, you begin to snuffle. These are the signs of your getting down with a cold. This is the time to use our Cold Cure. Use one or two doses, follow it up by another dose or two in twenty minutes, and you may have cured your cold in its incipiency.

> Don't forget that Our Twenty-Minute Cold Cure is a good seller. It is an extraordinary low priced remedy and yields you a big profit. It can conveniently be carried by the patient and will always be ready for use.

There is no good reason why you should suffer with a cold for days, for weeks. There is absolutely no reason why you should take any chances of having the cold proceed and perhaps get down with a more serious disease after letting the cold reach a stage where it will require the services of a physician on account of the development of a very dangerous disease.

TWENTY MINUTES' TREATMENT with our Cold Cure will oft times be sufficient to stop the cold, to prevent it from getting any further. A few doses of this grand preparation taken right at the beginning of the first symptoms of a cold will do the work. Don't wait a day or even an hour. Take Our Cold Cure at once. Promptness is the important part.

HAVE OUR COLD CURE in the house and if away from home carry a box with you in your vest pocket. The remedy is supplied in tablet form, in neat boxes, convenient to be carried in that manner. Nothing else will be needed to prevent a cold. Our Twenty-Minute Cold Cure will save all the dangerous results of a cold. All that is necessary is that you take it in time. In cases where the cold has already become seated before our cold cure could be obtained and used, be sure and get same as quickly as possible, use it in accordance with directions supplied with the remedy, and in connection with it Our Own Cough Cure, and you may feel assured that the combination of these two medicines will break up and cure the most severe cold and cough in the very shortest time.

No. 8C45 Our Twenty-Minute Cold Cure. Per dozen, $1.50; each . . . 17c
If by mail, postage extra, per box, 2 cents.

Cure for the Opium and Morphine Habit.

Retail price	$1.50
Our price, each	$0.69
Our price, per dozen	6.80

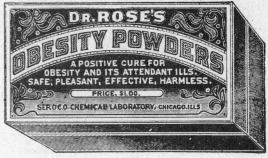

WE HERE OFFER A PERFECTLY SAFE AND RELIABLE CURE to those addicted to the habit of using opium or morphine in any form or manner whatever. We guarantee this preparation to be absolutely harmless, to contain no poisonous narcotics. Can be taken freely without producing any of the deleterious effects on the system, such as are caused by the use of opium and morphia. Soon after taking a dose of this remedy a calming and soothing effect is produced. It acts as a tonic to the nerves; its use will completely destroy that terrible craving for morphine and opium in those who are victims to the deadly habit of taking these poisonous drugs, and free them from their bondage, restoring their health and making them feel like living again. A dose can be taken whenever a craving for morphine or opium exists; it will act at first as a perfect substitute, rendering the patient independent of these poisonous drugs, and after continued use for a short period the nerves will become strong and the general health improved, so that the remedy can be taken at longer intervals and soon altogether discontinued; then the cure is complete.

No. 8C48 Price, per dozen bottles, $6.80; each 69c
Cannot be sent by mail on account of weight.

FAT FOLKS, TAKE Dr. ROSE'S OBESITY POWDERS

THEY REDUCE YOUR WEIGHT 15 TO 40 POUNDS IN A COMPARATIVELY SHORT TIME

Retail price, $1.00. Our price, per dozen, $5.40; each 60c

TOO MUCH FAT IS A DISEASE and a source of great annoyance to those afflicted. It impairs the strength and produces fatty degeneration of the heart, which sometimes leads to a premature death. All people who have obesity are troubled with sluggish circulation and labored action of the heart.

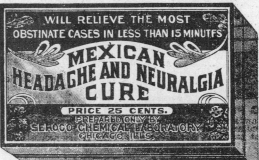

The patient feels lazy and burdensome. There is a

SLUGGISH CONDITION OF THE WHOLE SYSTEM

while they are not exactly sickly, there is a feeling that all is not right. Nervousness, rheumatism, headache, dropsy and kidney diseases are frequent complications of obesity, and, more cause to be alarmed, the heart is always affected.

> A boon to fat people who will be glad to obtain this remedy at home when they know you keep it on hand . . . .

—SEND AT ONCE FOR A BOX OF—
DR. ROSE'S OBESITY CURE

It will reduce corpulency in a safe and agreeable manner, perfectly harmless. No bad results follow its use, as is the case with many other preparations. Explicit directions and valuable information for fat folks enclosed in each box.

No. 8C52 Price, per dozen boxes, $5.40; per box 60c
If by mail, postage extra, per box, 7 cents.

Mexican Headache Cure.

Retail price	25c
Our price, each	$0.19
Our price, per doz.	1.60

A SPLITTING HEADACHE CURED IMMEDIATELY by our positive Headache and Neuralgia Cure. Almost everyone is more or less troubled with a headache at some time or other. Some persons are hardly ever free from them, and suffer martyrdom. We

confidently say to our customers that it is not necessary to suffer longer than the time it takes to get a package of our Mexican Headache Cure. We can promise relief within a short time after the first dose has been taken. A second dose is not required except in very obstinate cases. No matter from what cause, whether a nervous headache, or from the stomach, or a severe case of neuralgia, you will usually obtain complete relief. It is perfectly harmless, no bad results follow its use. Give it a trial when you suffer, and you can easily convince yourself that the Mexican Headache and Neuralgia Cure is the best and most uniformly successful headache remedy in existence.

No. 8C55 Price, per box $0.19
Per dozen boxes 1.60
If by mail, postage extra, per box, 3 cents.

> Who does not suffer from headaches occasionally? You can sell this cure to everybody you meet. Many customers who are now in charge of a distributing point for our remedies are sending twelve dozen orders at one time. . . . . . .

LIQUID IROZONE (FERROUS LIQUID OXYGEN)

A GERM KILLER. AN OXYGEN SUPPLIER.

Cures Germ Diseases. Strengthens, Invigorates and Cures by Furnishing that Great Life Property, Oxygen to the Blood.

No. 8C309 Price, per bottle (commercial pint size)..46c

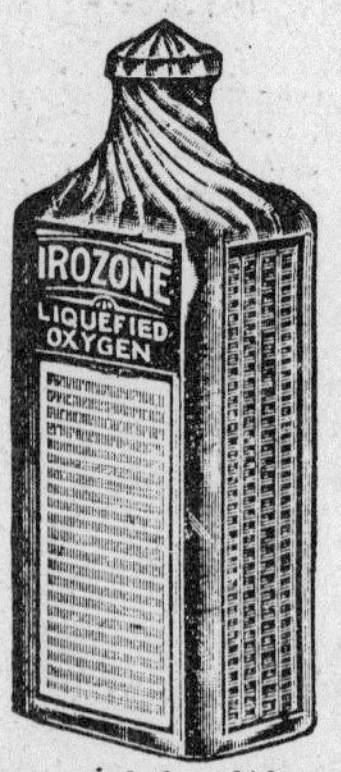

A WONDERFUL DISCOVERY.

LIQUID IROZONE (Ferrous Liquid Oxygen or Ozone Liquefied) is a harmless but powerful preparation for the prompt and effectual cure of all germ diseases. It cures by supplying oxygen (or ozone liquefied) to the blood and thus creating healthy tissue. Germs cannot thrive or live in healthy oxygenized tissue.

MANY DISEASES are directly caused by germ infection. In all such cases Liquid Irozone is an ideal, positive remedy because it kills the germs, it purifies the blood by supplying oxygen and it does all this without harming tissue or organ.

GREAT BENEFIT IS DERIVED by taking Liquid Irozone even if you are not positively sick, because it strengthens, invigorates and purifies the blood by supplying an extra quantity of oxygen, the life-giving principle of the atmosphere. It is perfectly safe, wonderfully effective and positively certain, a complete destruction of all germ life wherever germs may be the real cause of disease. It is nature's own tonic, supplying to the blood that substance that the human body most vitally requires in health and in sickness, namely, oxygen, and it supplies this great life principle in a new and scientific way.

YOU KNOW, OF COURSE, that without oxygen no human being can live. Every second of your life you need oxygen. Nature supplies it to you in every breath of air you inhale. It reaches the blood through the lungs. It is at this stage of the circulation of the blood through the body that the oxygen is taken into the blood, immediately changing the impure dark venous blood (vein blood) into purified, healthy, bright red or arterial blood. The blood after being ozonated with oxygen becomes purified and then passes into the heart and finally into the circulation, supplying to the weakened, impoverished and diseased tissues, cells and organs an abundance of that life sustaining fluid, pure, rich and healthy blood. If the blood is liberally supplied with oxygen, in its travel through the system it destroys germ life and at the same time revitalizes every organ, every part of the body, acting as a stimulative, tonic and invigorator, sustaining life and the healthy condition of the body.

THE NORMAL QUANTITY OF OXYGEN needed is supplied in nature by our breathing pure, fresh air. A lack of fresh air means a diminishing of the supply of oxygen for your body. Those that live constantly in the pure, open air, feed their lungs with all the oxygen needed to maintain life and to protect them against germ diseases, but millions of men, women and children, under the modern system of living, suffer from an insufficient supply of oxygen and therefore their systems are not immune from the attack of germs, and they may already be troubled with a germ disease in some form, or from the lack of pure air, or oxygen, they are unable to resist an attack if exposed to germ infection, no matter in what manner the infection may present itself.

BY TAKING LIQUID IROZONE you fortify your system against sickness, you ward off and cure all germ diseases by furnishing your system with a liberal and greater supply of oxygen. In Ferrous Liquid Oxygen we have the only liquefied oxygen that will destroy germs without destroying the tissues of the body and without creating a disturbing or distressing effect upon the digestive organs. Oxygen, as every one knows, is the vital part of air. It is the very source of vitality, the most essential element of life. **Oxygen is also nature's greatest tonic, the blood food, the nerve food, the scavenger of the blood.** It is oxygen that turns the blue blood to red in the lungs, it is oxygen that eliminates the waste tissue and builds up the new. You can therefore realize what a wonderful and valuable preparation Liquid Irozone is, how important it is that every one should avail himself of this great chemical product, Ferrous Liquid Oxygen or Ozone Liquefied.

LIQUID IROZONE supplies to weakened, exhausted and anemic subjects, a soluble, tasteless and non-constipating form of iron, which is so combined with purified ozone (or concentrated oxygen), as to produce a pleasant and palatable blood and tissue building tonic.

LIQUID IROZONE quickly restores to the impoverished blood an abundance of bright, red, healthy corpuscles.

BY THIS TREATMENT iron and ozone are carried to the tissues and cells, thus, the whole body shares in the benefit from this treatment of Liquid Irozone.

LIQUID IROZONE should be freely used as protection against germ infection and for the treatment and cure of so called germ diseases, especially all diseases of the blood: Anemia, blood poison, erysipelas, impure blood, running sores, skin diseases, scrofula, syphilis, salt rheum, tumors, ulcers; also in catarrh, consumption, cancers, dropsy, hay fever, la grippe, sore throat, tuberculosis, tonsilitis, malaria, pneumonia, pleurisy, bronchitis.

LIQUID IROZONE may be employed with great success in the treatment of all stomach, kidney, liver and bowel complications.

LIQUID IROZONE is exhilarating, vitalizing and purifying. Its effects are immediate. It gives to every organ the needed stimulation and without reaction. It positively purifies the blood. Liquid Irozone should be in every home. It is a universal necessity, applicable to each and every individual. There is no one who will not be benefited by its use.

No. 8C309 Liquid Irozone, commercial pint bottles, dollar size, each........................46c
Not mailable on account of weight.

DEPARTMENT OF
FAMILY REMEDIES AND HOUSEHOLD PREPARATIONS.

Prepared and put up by careful and experienced pharmacists and chemists in our own laboratory and sold under an absolute guarantee of highest strength and purity.

Borax.

The housekeeper's friend; has more uses about the home than even that of common salt. For the laundry, the kitchen, the bath and for various medicinal uses it is indispensable. Chemically pure and finely powdered. We put it up in 1-pound boxes with complete directions for using in **washing, starching, keeping away moths, killing cockroaches, dressing wounds and bruises, arresting fermentation, cleaning clothes, etc.** You can rely on getting from us the pure powdered borax, which will be a source of satisfaction to you, as it is a much adulterated article.

No. 8C420 Price, per 1-pound box..............10c

Laudanum.
(Tinct. Opium.)

U. S. P. Strength. Directions on each bottle for young and old.

No. 8C424 Price
1-ounce bottle..............8c
2-ounce bottle..............15c
4-ounce bottle..............25c
Unmailable.

Paregoric.

Always useful, both for children and adults. One of the best known and most extensively used house remedies. Full directions.

No. 8C426 Price, 2-ounce bottle..10c
Price, 4-oz. bottle..............15c
If by mail, postage and tube extra, small, 12 cents; large, 16 cents.

Sweet Spirits of Nitre.

This article is more liable to adulteration than any other medicine. You seldom can get it pure and full strength from a drug store. It is a valuable medicine when fresh and unadulterated. **We guarantee what we sell to be absolutely pure.**

No. 8C429 2-ounce bottle..........10c
4-ounce bottle..........18c
1-pint bottle..........75c
If by mail, postage and tube extra, 2-oz., 12 cents; 4-oz., 16 cents. Pints unmailable on account of weight.

Essence Peppermint.

Pure and strong. Best quality for medical use.

No. 8C431 Price, 2-ounce bottle..18c
Price, 4-ounce bottle..............30c
If by mail, postage and tube extra, 2 oz., 12 cents; 4 oz., 16 cents.

Essence Jamaica Ginger.

Prepared of great strength from the finest quality of Jamaica ginger, imported by ourselves. Ginger has healing properties peculiar to itself; many preparations are offered for sale which are represented as containing ginger, when generally they owe their hot taste to pepper alone. **Buy our genuine essence and get the full benefit of its valuable properties.**

No. 8C433 Price, 2-oz. bottle..............12c
Price, 4-oz. bottle..............20c
Postage and tube extra, small, 12 cents; large, 16c.

Essence of Pepsin.

A preparation regularly prescribed by physicians, and usually recommended for the treatment of indigestion, and in complications resulting therefrom. A teaspoonful before or after meals will aid digestion and assimilation of food, and affords prompt relief when suffering from indigestion, as well as the distressing attacks to which chronic sufferers of dyspepsia are subject.

No. 8C435 Price, 8-oz. bottles.$0.50
Per dozen..............5.40

Neutralizing Cordial.

A well known household remedy. Useful in treatment of diarrhea, dysentery and cholera morbus. Also a great remedy for dyspepsia, a general corrector of the stomach and bowels.

No. 8C438 Price, 4-ounce bottle..16c
Postage and tube extra, 16 cents.

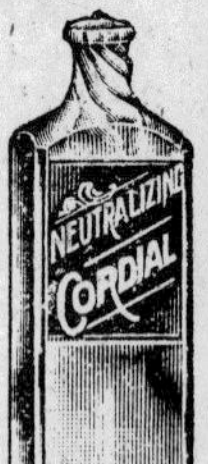

Castor Oil.

Cold pressed and almost tasteless.

No. 8C440 Price, 2-oz. bottle..............8c
Price, 4-oz. bottle..12c
Price, 1-pt. bottle..25c
If by mail, postage and tube extra, 16 cents Pints, unmailable.

Olive Oil (Sweet Oil).

This is a fine domestic oil considered equal to imported olive oil made from olives grown in vineyards of Italy. For either internal or external use. Anyone wishing to use an **absolutely pure olive oil** should send for this.

No. 8C442 Price, 2-oz. bottle.......7c
Price, 4-oz. bottle..............10c
Price, ½-pt. bottle..............17c
If by mail, postage and tube extra, 16c. ½ pints unmailable.

Spirits of Camphor.

Made from pure Gum Camphor, imported by ourselves from Kobe, Japan.

No. 8C444
Price, 2-ounce bottles..............10c
Price, 4-ounce bottles..............16c
Price, 1-pint bottles..............60c
If by mail, postage and tube extra, 2-oz., 12 cents; 4-oz., 16 cents. Pints unmailable on account weight.

Camphorated Oil.

An excellent article for rubbing on children's and grown up persons' chests and throats in cases of croup, difficulty in breathing, sore throat, coughs. A small quantity of pure spirits of turpentine added to it will increase its effectiveness in many cases.

No. 8C446 Price, 4-oz. bottles..............18c
Price, 8-oz. bottles..............28c
Postage and tube extra, 4-ounce bottle, 16 cents. 8-ounce bottle unmailable on account of weight.

Spirits of Turpentine.

Pure, for internal or external use. When you wish to use turpentine as a medicine, whether internally or externally, **always get a pure article.** Never use the common oil of turpentine that is generally sold for mixing with paints. **We sell the pure.**

No. 8C448 Price, 4-ounce bottles, 9c
Price, 8-ounce bottles..............12c
Price, 16-ounce bottles..............20c

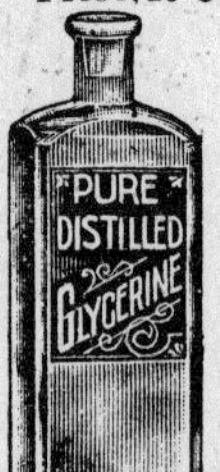

Glycerine.

Warranted absolutely pure. Can be used either externally or internally.

No. 8C450
Price, 2-ounce bottles...7c
Price, 4-ounce bottles..12c
Price, ½-pound bottles17c
Price, 1-pound bottles.28c

Carbolic Acid.

A saturated solution of Carbolic Acid for disinfecting purposes, destroying contagion, cleansing purposes, etc. Excellent for keeping away disease, destroying bad smells. Put up expressly for household use.

No. 8C452 Price, 1-pound bottles, each..............18c
Unmailable on account of weight.

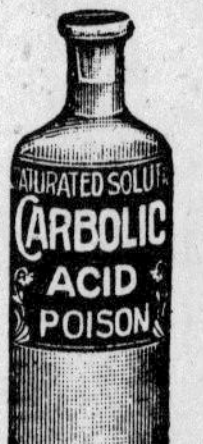

Tincture of Arnica.

We are careful to make this of great strength from recently picked arnica flowers, thereby getting the full virtues of the herb. The value of arnica is well known as an application to bruises, sprains, cuts, swellings, etc., but to secure any benefit it is necessary to have a strong, well prepared tincture **such as ours.**

No. 8C454 Price, 4-oz. bottles$0.12
Price, ½-pint bottles..............20
Price, 1-pint bottles..............35
Price, per gallon..............3.00
If by mail, postage and tube extra, 4-oz. bottle, 16 cents. Larger, unmailable on account of weight.

and song were to be had there free of charge, and soon a crowd, composed largely of Negroes with a sprinkling of whites, would gather for the fun that was to follow. Here the audience saw the doctor, dignified and professionally remote, standing at the rear of the platform talking solemnly with one of his assistants or arranging fearsome-looking jars filled with alcohol-pickled tapeworms and other worms that had "been expelled from the bodies of sufferers by one dose of Dr. Davidson's Kickapoo Snake Oil"; arranging physiological charts of the human body whose functioning the doctor would later explain, and sometimes a skeleton which held the colored audience with fascinated attention. Usually the doctor wore a gray, pointed beard and a Prince Albert coat with shiny satin lapels occasionally bedecked with medals given him "by the crowned heads of Europe, Asia, Africa, and Australia."

At the front of the platform stood the showmen, ordinarily two or three Negroes with tambourines, guitars, or banjos, dressed as blackface minstrels, and occasionally a mock-dignified tramp with a huge putty nose, wearing tattered tails and dirty white tie.

As the crowd gathered, the minstrels played, sang, and clogged. When the song was that old favorite "The Little Red Caboose," the crowd roared with delight as the end man turned his lighted cigar backwards in his mouth, blew streamers of smoke out into the air, and whistled an imitation of The Old 97 coming round a curve. Then the songsters and dancers—doubling now as comedians—brought the audience closer to the platform with conundrums and jokes, most of which were to be found in the immortal collections of Thomas W. Jackson, author of *On A Slow Train Through Arkansaw* and *Through Missouri on A Mule*—books that were once sold by the thousands in rural America and are still being sold. Wisecracks such as these enjoyed unfailing success:

Q: Why do old maids go to church so early on Sunday?

A: So they can be there when the hymns are given out.

—213—

Q: Why does Roosevelt's pictures always show him in a hunting suit with a big stick?

A: That's because he's always hunting to stick some trust with a suit.

Q: Why do old maids wear silk gloves?
A: Because they don't like kids.

Q: When is a hog a tree?
A: When he's rooting.

When the audience had been put into a mellow mood by the minstrels, the doctor would come forward, explain the hells of torture to which the body was subject by virtue of the ravages of "heartburn" or tapeworms—depending upon the kind of medicine he was selling that night—describe the functionings of the heart, liver, lungs, stomach, and all the other organs affected by heartburn or tapeworms, and then extol the virtues of his remedy. Usually medicine-show remedies were snake oils—oils gathered at great danger to human life from deadly poisonous snakes that inhabited the mountain jungles of Abyssinia or lurked in dark African swamps. Every ounce of the oil represented at least one human life lost in gathering it, and great pain and danger incurred in bringing it out of Africa. For some of the snakes were the sacred serpents of the natives who shot at you with poisoned arrows, but "ladies and gentlemen, right there's the secret of this medicine, because it's the hair of the dog that bites you that gives you the cure, and these natives use that poison —you know they don't have doctors over there like me to wait on the sick. And just for tonight, my friends, in order to introduce Dr. Davidson's Kickapoo Snake Oil to you good people of Greenville and Washington County, I'm going to let a limited number of you that come forward first to the platform have a few bottles at one dollar a bottle, and then, folks, we're going to have more fun at the pie-eating contest that will be held right after my assistants here have handed out this great remedy to the first suffering people that come forward."

Then those nearest the platform swarmed forward with silver dollars or small silver coins in their hands, while those at the rear pushed forward to be among "the limited number" permitted to buy a bottle of snake oil at the "introductory price" of one dollar a bottle. Usually, however, the doctor graciously permitted everybody to purchase a bottle whether he came early or late to the platform, but only upon the assurance that "you will tell your friends to be here tomorrow night." After this, the pie-eating contest was held. A dozen or more pies were suspended on strings from the platform roof and dangled at about the level of a boy's head. The pies, liberally smeared with molasses, dripped syrup, and the hands of the Negro boy contestants were tied behind them. All were off at the flourish of a tambourine, and the first boy to finish his pie got the prize—twenty-five cents. Soon twelve black heads, dripping sweat and molasses, were pursuing the dangling pies, while the minstrels added to the excitement by rattling their tambourines. The crowd roared with laughter, and, when the contest was over, reluctantly left the scene of so much free gaiety and amusement. Then the torches were extinguished, the doctor and his company walked to their boarding houses, and the little town, partially cleansed of the evils of tapeworm and heartburn, slept.

Most of the famous medicine-show doctors of the past live now only in the memory of older men, but one of them was to beget a son who was to influence the United States far more than many of our Presidents. In the early part of the nineteenth century, an itinerant pill doctor visited small towns of the Middle West and put up a sign bearing this legend: "Dr. William A. Rockefeller, the Celebrated Cancer Specialist. Here for One Day only. All cases of Cancer Cured unless too far gone and then they can be greatly benefited."

In 1839, a son was born to Dr. and Mrs. William Rockefeller to whom was given the name John.

During his [William Rockefeller's] long absences, his wife had to live on credit at the village shop, but whenever he returned he brought enough money to pay debts and give each of his children a five-dollar piece. He was a big, jolly, vigorous man, who lived at least to the age of 96. . . . He was very proud of his shrewdness, and would boast of his skill in outwitting people. "He trained me in practical ways," said his son John. "He was engaged in different enterprises and he used to tell me about these things and he taught me the principles and methods of business." The father's own description of his teachings and "principles" of business is simpler: "I cheat my boys every chance I get. I want to make 'em sharp. I trade with the boys and skin 'em and I just beat 'em every time I can. I want to make 'em sharp." *

One medicine man thus left his mark indelibly on the American scene, but medicine men, in general, were merely amateurish mountebanks and not businessmen at all; at best they eked out a meager living from their activities, and, however ridiculous their medicines, the customer got at least a laugh for his money. Later, in the great era of the patent-medicine racket, when it was taken over by businessmen, the customer did not get even a laugh, and high-pressure advertising methods enabled the new exploiters to reach a vast audience scarcely touched by the medicine men. These pirates, surveying the market with cold and careful eye, soon saw that the mine offering the greatest gold return was woman's perpetually suffering body.

Female Weakness

A favorite fake medicine was one that purported to cure "female weakness," or "female troubles." Under these headings were gathered all the ills and disorders that proceeded from pregnancy, childbirth, menstruation, the menopause, and the thousand aberrations of the delicate and complex structure of the reproductive apparatus in woman. As though this were not a wide enough field for any medicine to cover, the manufacturer often greedily reached out to an even wider market for his product, by making it cover—on the label—al-

* Bertrand Russell, *Freedom versus Organization, 1814–1914,* p. 313.

—216—

THE NEW IMPROVED RATIONAL BODY BRACE
REDUCED FROM $1.69 to $1.19
SOLD UNDER OUR PERSONAL GURANTEE.

The Highest Grade, Most Perfect Woman's Brace for only $1.19. Guaranteed to be Not Only Equal, but Far Superior to Any Other Body Brace, Regardless of the Price at which they are Sold.

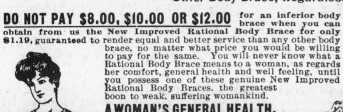

DO NOT PAY $8.00, $10.00 OR $12.00 for an inferior body brace when you can obtain from us the New Improved Rational Body Brace for only $1.19, guaranteed to render equal and better service than any other body brace, no matter what price you would be willing to pay for the same. You will never know what a Rational Body Brace means to a woman, as regards her comfort, general health and well feeling, until you possess one of these genuine New Improved Rational Body Braces, the greatest boon to weak, suffering womankind.

A WOMAN'S GENERAL HEALTH, strength, grace, erectness and beauty of form are regained and retained by wearing a properly adjusted Rational Body Brace. It will, in the most natural and always successful manner, cure the complaints of women. It will meet and remove the cause of weaknesses and organic displacements by applying its strengthening influence and natural support to parts of the body where it is most needed.

THE FRONT PAD, as illustrated, and abdominal supporter is fitted with the new hygienic, sanitary perforated, nickel plated shield, and made of specially prepared scientifically and correctly tempered brass perforated plates, which makes them pliable and strong. They quickly adjust themselves, and fit all figures. The springs used in this brace are silver plated and welded, the recently discovered Bessemer process being employed for this purpose, which makes them practically indestructible. Four nickel plated pads form a joint attachment to these springs, arranged in a manner so as to make the hips the main part upon which the supporting power of the New Improved Rational Brace rests, thus relieving the weakened internal organs, muscles and nerves from all unnatural strain. The effect is an immediate feeling of relief to the wearer, followed by regular and natural functions of every organ of the body involved.

THE IMPROVED RATIONAL BODY BRACE is highly recommended by physicians for all persons suffering from general weakness, to persons whose shoulders droop and whose posture is neither natural nor correct. It is the proper and only comfortable brace for fat people. A large abdomen is often reduced a few inches per month as a result of relief afforded by the brace to the stretched and overloaded muscles.

IT IS THE ONLY APPLIANCE that should be used by women troubled with falling of the womb or other irregularities of the female organism, including unnatural discharges, painful, delayed or profuse menstruation; also for all affections of the bladder. For the removal of pains in the shoulders, backache, headache, pains in the chest and weakness of the lower limbs nothing will equal it.

THE IMPROVED RATIONAL BODY BRACE is an abdominal supporter and shoulder brace combined, constructed so as to form a natural support to every organ of the body, including the spine, ribs, lungs, heart, liver, bowels, womb; in fact, every organ, bone and muscle of the human body. The supporting, strengthening and healing influence of the Rational Body Brace has never been approached by any other appliance. It assures to the wearer comfort, vigor, health, elasticity, ease; all of the utmost importance to women subject to physical changes, in all conditions and in every walk in life. The Improved Rational Body Brace is made of specially prepared material and is adjustable, thus always insuring a perfect fit. The upper portion of belt and shoulder pads consists of strong elastic webbing. The lower belt is non-elastic and as a result you will find in this appliance perfect support, yet absolute freedom for every movement of the body

WHITE MATERIAL is used throughout, which can easily be laundered and kept clean and in a sanitary condition. Every part of the belt and straps is treated by a special process, so as to reduce absorption of perspiration to a minimum.

YOU CAN WEAR the Improved Rational Body Brace to suit your own convenience and as you may prefer, either under corset, over vest, under closed drawers, over open drawers. The adjustable features of this brace make it possible to wear the same appliance at all times; whether before or after confinement will make no difference.

WOMEN SHOULD NOT under any circumstances cease wearing the genuine newly Improved Rational Body Brace before and after confinement. It will not only support them better than anything else, but will preserve their figure, and, what is still more important, it may be the means of saving their life.

HOW TO ORDER. Take measure over vest and drawers; state size around body about two inches below tops of hip bones. Mention if extra large adjustment is desired, giving height and weight at the same time.

An extra set of understraps is furnished with each body brace, free of charge, to be used when the first set is in the laundry, thus enabling the wearer to use the Rational Body Brace without interruption during the time when it is most needed.

No. 8C1260 The Improved Rational Body Brace complete, only $1.19

If by mail, postage extra, 20 cents.

EVERY RATIONAL BODY BRACE IS FURNISHED BY US UNDER OUR PERSONAL GUARANTEE.

THE VENUS OR SANITARY PROTECTOR.
NOW ONLY 23c EACH!

No woman who values comfort, cleanliness and health should be without it. The only practical protector. Perfect in fit. Safe in use.

THE ENORMOUS SALE of this grand protector has enabled us to manufacture it in such immensely large quantities, to reduce the cost of production to such an extent, that we are today in a position to offer this valuable appliance for the never heard of low price of 23 cents each.

THE VENUS PROTECTOR is made of a transparent India rubber sack which is very silky, soft and pliable and also very strong. This sack readily admits a napkin or any other soft substance like cheesecloth or cotton, and will hold it securely in the proper position. The belt is made of the very best lisle, non-elastic. The strap to which the sack is buckled is made of a superior grade of lisle elastic, which gives with the different movements of the body, thus keeping the protector always in the right place.

No. 8C1262 Price, each..............23c

If by mail, postage extra, each, 3 cents.

Absorbing Pads or Napkins for the protector, made of especially prepared muslin and medicated cotton.
No. 8C1264 Price, per dozen.........25c
If by mail, postage extra, 6 cents.

THE VENUS OR SANITARY PROTECTOR will save many times its cost in washing and bleaching. It is absolutely waterproof and thereby positively prevents soiling of the underwear. Each protector comes put up in a neatly finished box with full and explicit directions. With proper use will last a lifetime. After use each month all that is necessary is to clean it with a damp cloth or sponge. In ordering give waist measure.

POINTS OF EXCELLENCE in the Venus or Sanitary Protector. It is perfectly sanitary, comfortable, pliable and non-irritating; easily adjusted and readjusted, and indispensable to women walking, riding or traveling. Always clean and ready for use. Feels cool in summer and protects the wearer from cold in inclement weather. Retail price of the Venus or Sanitary Protector, $1.50 each.

A bottle of Sanative Wash in concentrated form, sufficient for six months' supply, put up especially to be used in connection with the celebrated Venus or Sanitary Protector.
No. 8C1266 Sanative Wash. Price, per bottle.........20c
Unmailable on account of weight.

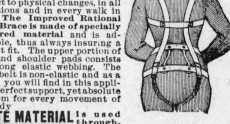

Engraving shows the napkin in place, ready for use.

LADYLINE
ANTISEPTIC SUPPOSITORIES.
THE NEVER FAILING

LOCAL TREATMENT for the cure of inflammation, congestion and falling of the womb, antiversion, retroversion and prolapsus, dropsy of the womb, ulceration, polypus, tumor, leucorrhea (whites), profuse, difficult and delayed menstruation, ovarian tumors, fibroid tumors, inflammation and congestion of the ovaries, and cancers in the early stages. The Ladyline Antiseptic Suppositories are soothing, healing and curing.

Retail Price, $1.50 to $2.00.

No. 8C1268 Our price, regular size box, containing full month's treatment, only..........60c
Additional information and explicit instructions will be sent with each box.
If by mail, postage extra, 6 cents.

ANTI-CONGESTION PLASTIC DRESSING. THE GREAT REMEDY FOR INFLAMMATORY RHEUMATISM, INFLAMMATION, FEVER.

AS RECOMMENDED, USED AND PRESCRIBED TODAY BY EVERY PHYSICIAN IN THE CIVILIZED WORLD, in the treatment of diseases accompanied by external or internal inflammation or congestion.

SOLD UNDER OUR PERSONAL GUARANTEE.

IF USED AND FOUND NOT SATISFACTORY, we will return every cent you have paid us for same. NO HOUSEHOLD, whether rich or poor, should be a single day without a sufficient quantity of ANTI-CONGESTION PLASTIC DRESSING.

Order a supply without a moment's delay. Send for it even before you send for a physician, for it is a real godsend, a remedy for any and all cases, acute or chronic, where superficial or deep seated congestion exists. **DO NOT UNDER ANY CIRCUMSTANCES FAIL TO PROVIDE YOURSELF with a package of ANTI-CONGESTION PLASTIC DRESSING** and keep it in the house ready for instant use. **DO NOT WAIT until you need it and then send for it. IT MAY BE TOO LATE WHEN IT ARRIVES** to give you the protection it would have afforded you if it had been kept for ready use. **ALTHOUGH IN CASES LIKE pneumonia, bronchitis, pleurisy, peritonitis, erysipelas, and poisoned wounds a physician should be called in,** you should have Anti-Congestion Plastic Dressing on hand. In nine cases out of ten he will surely make an immediate application of an Anti-Congestion Plastic Dressing to reduce and remove the inflammation. You will, therefore, save money, worry, and perhaps the life of the patient by having this remedy on hand to meet the emergency without any delay.

BUT THIS IS NOT ALL. Simple instructions are furnished with this remedy and any one can make the application, so that you can in critical cases apply the Plastic Dressing and do for the patient, long before the doctor arrives, the exact thing he would have advised you to do as the first step after his examination of the patient. **In anticipating the action of the physician, you have aided him as much as may lie in your power in making the sufferer comfortable and in saving the life of the sick one.**

WHAT ANTI-CONGESTION PLASTIC DRESSING WILL DO:

It is the only bland and non-irritating remedy which allays and heals inflammation and congestion. It absorbs from the tissues over which it is placed, the moisture resulting from the inflamed condition. **It is applicable in all stages and in all varieties of inflammation.**

It acts as a complete dressing, furnishing compression, support, rest and protection for that part of the body to which it is applied; it acts as a poultice, does all any poultice can do, supplying heat and moisture, but it goes a great deal further, as it is absorbent, antiseptic, anodyne and nutrient, lasting from twelve to forty-eight hours. It does not annoy and irritate the patient, which nearly always is the case where irregular and too frequent poultice applications are made. **Anti-Congestion Plastic Dressing does not interfere with internal remedies of any kind.**

ANTI-CONGESTION PLASTIC DRESSING WILL GIVE INSTANT AND CERTAIN RELIEF IN ALL CASES OF

PNEUMONIA, PELVIC INFLAMMATION, TUMORS, FELONS, BURNS, TONSILITIS, BOILS, POISONED WOUNDS, INFLAMMATORY RHEUMATISM, BRONCHITIS, INFLAMED BREASTS, PERITONITIS, SPRAINS, CHRONIC ULCERS, ERYSIPELAS, PILES, DYSMENORRHOEA, FROSTBITES, SUNBURN AND OPEN WOUNDS IN WHICH INFLAMMATION OR CONGESTION IS A FACTOR. HEED OUR WELL MEANT ADVICE AND KEEP IT ON HAND READY FOR IMMEDIATE USE.

No. 8C177 12-ounce can Anti-Congestion Plastic Dressing. Price $0.22
No. 8C178 1-pound collapsible tubes Anti-Congestion Plastic Dressing. Price .... .32
No. 8C179 5-pound package Anti-Congestion Plastic Dressing. Price 1.20
If by mail, postage extra, 12-ounce package, 22 cents. Larger sizes unmailable on account of weight.

COMPLETE INFORMATION AND INSTRUCTIONS will be furnished with each package.

Our Great Offer. Absolutely Free.

A very handsome, substantially made, cloth covered Medicine Case and our valuable book, "The Family Doctor," absolutely FREE.

WITH EVERY ORDER for twelve of the following 13-cent remedies we will send "The Family Doctor," a book giving full instructions how to use these remedies and containing other valuable information for the cure of the sick, **free.** We also supply these remedies in a well made medicine case for which there will be no extra charge. You can select any twelve of the following named remedies at **13** cents each, and a black cloth covered case will be furnished with the same **without extra cost. For $1.50, covering the price of 12 bottles of the following listed household remedies, we will send the medicine at once, together with medicine case and medicine book free.**

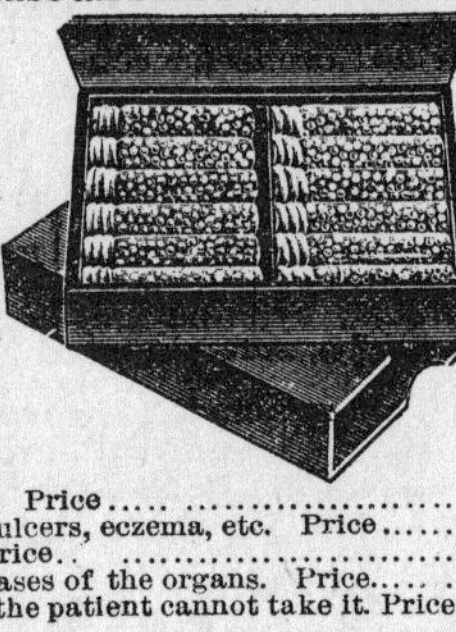

No. 201. **COLD IN THE HEAD.**—Will cure quinsy, tonsilitis, cold in the head, influenza, and many of the milder troubles arising from cold. Price 13c
No. 202. **COLIC**—Very useful for all childish pains, such as cramps, colic, or for the restlessness of teething, diarrhea, etc. Price 13c
No. 203. **COUGH**—Valuable in coughs, bronchitis, hoarseness and any trouble in throat and chest arising from cold. Price 13c
No. 204. **CONSTIPATION**—Will relieve obstinate cases of constipation, which are often the cause of headache, biliousness, offensive breath, etc. Price 13c
No. 205. **DIARRHEA**—Useful and a sure cure for any form of diarrhea, cholera morbus, cholera infantum, sour stomach, etc. Price 13c
No. 206. **HEADACHE**—Good for headache of any sort, fever, cold, nervousness, la grippe, etc. Price 13c
No. 207. **TONIC**—For any weakened condition of the system. Price 13c
No. 208. **ALTERATIVE**—For impure blood, boils, scrofula, ulcers, eczema, etc. Price 13c
No. 209. **DYSPEPSIA**—From any of the ordinary causes. Price 13c
No. 210. **KIDNEY AND LIVER**—To remove or cure all diseases of the organs. Price 13c
No. 211. **MALARIAL**—To be used when quinine fails, or when the patient cannot take it. Price 13c
No. 212. **RHEUMATIC**—A true remedy. Price 13c
No. 213. **NERVOUS TROUBLES**—Calms and soothes; will relieve nervousness in any form. Price 13c
No. 214. **HEART REGULATOR**—A splendid tonic for the heart. Price 13c
No. 215. **LIVER CORRECTOR**—For biliousness, jaundice, sallow complexion, sour stomach, etc. Price 13c
No. 216. **KIDNEY DISORDERS**—Gently stimulates the kidneys and relieves urinary troubles in both old and young. Price 13c
No. 217. **BRONCHIAL**—For difficult breathing, pain in the chest, cold in the bronchial tubes. Price 13c
No. 218. **THROAT**—For hoarseness, tickling in the throat; useful for speakers and singers. Price 13c
No. 219. **NEURALGIA**—For the relief of neuralgia, sciatica, etc. Price 13c
No. 220. **FEVER**—For all kinds of fever, especially that arising from cold. Price 13c
No. 221. **CROUP**—For children; to be given when the first symptom appears. Price 13c
No. 222. **MUMPS**—Give regularly and follow instructions in our Medical Guide. Price 13c
No. 223. **PLEURISY**—For pain in the chest on breathing and coughing. Price 13c
No. 224. **PIMPLES**—For skin blemishes. Price 13c

HANDY POCKET TABLET REMEDIES. Twenty-four different remedies in large glass vials with metal screw top, will keep in every climate for years, a cure for almost every disease for only 13 cents. For 13 cents each, 2 cents extra for postage, we offer twenty-four different remedies, put up in neat tablet form, easy to take and convenient to be carried in vest pocket. These remedies are compounded in our own laboratory, and represent the best prescriptions of the highest medical authorities in the land, **are absolutely harmless, prepared from vegetable tinctures, herbs and roots. No mineral, mercury or poison.** These handy pocket tablet remedies will save you doctor bills and much suffering. **No family can afford to be without a supply of these remedies, and the price has been fixed so low, only 13 cents each vial, that all may be supplied.**

No. 8C199 12 Bottles of any of the above $1.50
Medicine Case and Medical Book free.
No. 8C200 24 Bottles of any of the above 2.50
Medicine Case and Medical Book free.

A Few Handy Pocket Goods in Screw Top, Air Tight Glass Vials.

No. 8C275 **Aromatic Cachou Lozenges,** for perfuming the breath. Make a delicious confection. Price 6c
No. 8C276 **Silver Cachous,** for perfuming the breath, vest pocket size 6c
No. 8C278 **Chlorate Potash Tablets.** 5 grains each. For sore throat, hoarseness, etc. Price 5c
No. 8C280 **Soda Mint Tablets,** for sour stomach, flatulency, nausea, etc. 5c
No. 8C282 **Bronchial Troches,** for coughs, colds, sore throat, hoarseness 5c
No. 8C284 **Licorice Lozenges, pure,** very soothing to the throat and bronchial tubes. Price 5c
No. 8C286 **Slippery Elm Lozenges.** Demulcent, for roughness in the throat and irritating cough. Price 5c
No. 8C288 **Paregoric Tablets.** Each tablet equals 15 drops of paregoric; dose 1 to 4, according to age. Price 5c
No. 8C290 **Pepsin Tablets, made from pure pepsin,** for dyspepsia, indigestion, etc. Price, per bottle 15c
No. 8C292 **Trix,** for the breath. Price, per package 3c
No. 8C294 **Sen-Sen.** Price, per package 3c
If by mail, postage extra, 2 cents.

Our Homeopathic Remedies.

12 bottles of different Homeopathic Remedies, your own selection $1.50
A nice, black cloth covered Medicine Case and Instruction Sheet free.

OUR HOMEOPATHIC SPECIFICS are prepared under the supervision of an old, experienced homeopathic physician. Great care is taken in preparing them according to the rules laid down by the **highest authorities on homeopathy,** and only the purest drugs used. Every one of the following specifics is a **special cure** for the diseases named on it. **Adults take 6 pellets, children from 1 to 3, according to age,** and from two to four doses are to be taken every day, according to the severity of the case. We ask the special attention of all our customers to these **high grade remedies.** If you have them near at hand, we guarantee they **will save you many a doctor's bill,** and what is of more consequence, quickly relieve any suffering member of the family and ward off more serious sickness.

No. 8C230 **12 bottles, any selection $1.50**
No. 8C232 **24 bottles, any selection 2.50**
No. 8C234 **36 bottles, any selection 3.00**
Medicine Case and Instruction Sheet free.

A SPECIAL OFFER. As an inducement to give these remedies a thorough trial, we will allow you to select 12 cures, including the 60-cent ones. Make your own selection, one or more of **any kind, and we will put them in a neat case, such as we represent here,** and only charge you $1.50. **No family can afford to neglect this great offer.**

A 12-Box Case will save you many dollars doctors' bills in a year and may save your life.
No family should be without a case of our Homeopathic Remedies.

No.		Usual Price	Our Price
No. 8C235	Cures rheumatism or rheumatic pains	$0.25	$0.15
No. 8C236	Cures fever and ague, intermittent fever, malaria, etc.	.25	.15
No. 8C237	Cures piles, blind or bleeding, external or internal	.25	.15
No. 8C238	Cures ophthalmia, weak or inflamed eyes	.25	.15
No. 8C239	Cures catarrh, influenza, cold in the head	.25	.15
No. 8C240	Cures whooping cough, spasmodic cough	.25	.15
No. 8C241	Cures asthma, oppressed or difficult breathing	.25	.15
No. 8C242	Cures fevers, congestions, inflammations	.25	.15
No. 8C243	Cures worm fever or worm diseases	.25	.15
No. 8C244	Cures colic, crying and wakefulness of infants teething	.25	.15
No. 8C245	Cures diarrhea of children and adults	.25	.15
No. 8C246	Cures dysentery, griping, bilious colic	.25	.15
No. 8C247	Cures cholera, cholera morbus, vomiting	.25	.15
No. 8C248	Cures coughs, colds, bronchitis	.25	.15
No. 8C249	Cures toothache, faceache, neuralgia	.25	.15
No. 8C250	Cures headache, sick headache, vertigo	.25	.15
No. 8C251	Cures dyspepsia, indigestion, weak stomach	.25	.15
No. 8C252	Cures suppressed or scanty menses	.25	.15
No. 8C253	Cures leucorrhea, or profuse menses	.25	.15
No. 8C254	Cures croup, hoarse cough, difficult breathing, laryngitis	.25	.15
No. 8C255	Cures salt rheum, eruptions, erysipelas	.25	.15
No. 8C256	Cures ear discharge, earache	.25	.15
No. 8C257	Cures scrofula, swellings, ulcers	.25	.15
No. 8C258	Cures general debility, physical weakness, brain fag	.25	.15
No. 8C259	Cures dropsy, fluid accumulations	.25	.15
No. 8C260	Cures seasickness, nausea, vomiting	.25	.15
No. 8C261	Cures kidney disease, gravel, calculi	.25	.15
No. 8C262	Cures nervous debility, vital weakness	1.00	.65
No. 8C263	Cures sore mouth and canker	.25	.15
No. 8C264	Cures urinary incontinence, wetting bed	.25	.15
No. 8C265	Cures painful menses, pruritus	.25	.15
No. 8C266	Cures diseases of the heart, palpitation	1.00	.60
No. 8C267	Cures epilepsy, St. Vitus' dance	1.00	.60
No. 8C268	Cures sore throat, quinsy or ulcerated sore throat	.25	.15
No. 8C269	Cures chronic congestions, headache	.25	.15
No. 8C270	Cures grip and chronic colds	.25	.15

If by mail, postage extra, per case, 26 cents; per bottle, 2 cents.

WE ARE PREPARED TO FURNISH ANYTHING in the line of Homeopathic Supplies, and guarantee them to be full strength and in fresh condition. We mention a few of the more prominent. When ordering the following remedies please specify what form you wish them in—pills, powders, discs or liquid.

Name	Strength	Name	Strength	Name	Strength	Name	Strength
Aconite	3x	Cinna	2x	Hydrastis	1x	Phosphorus	3x
Antimon. crud	3x	Cocculus	3x	Hyoscyamus	3x	Phosphorus aci	3x
Apis mel	3x	Coffea crud	3x	Ignati	3x	Phytolacca	0x
Arnica	3x	Colchicum	3x	Iodium	3x	Podophyllin	3x
Arsenic alb.	3x	Colocynthis	3x	Ipecac	3x	Pulsatilla	3x
Baptisia	1x	Cuprum met	3x	Kali bichr	3x	Rhus tox	3x
Belladonna	3x	Digitalis	2x	Lachesis	6x	Sanguirnaria	2x
Bryonia alba	3x	Drosera	2x	Lycopodium	3x	Secale cor	1x
Calcarea carb	3x	Dulcamara	3x	Mercurius bnod	3x	Sepia	3x
Cantharis	3x	Eupatorium p'r	1x	Mercurius corr	3x	Silicea	6x
Carbo veg	3x	Ferrum phos	3x	Mercurius sol	3x	Spigelia	3x
Caulophyllum	1x	Gelsemium	1x	Mercurius viv	3x	Spongia	3x
Causticum	3x	Glonoine	3x	Natrum mur	6x	Staphysagria	3x
Chamomilla	3x	Graphites	6x	Nitric acid	6x	Sulphur	3x
China	2x	Hamamelis	1x	Nux vomica	3x	Tartar emetic	3x
Chinnin, arsen	2x	Hepar sulph. tr	3x	Opium	3x	Veratrum alb	3x
Cimicifuga	1x						

No. 8C300 ¼-ounce vials, each, 10c; by mail 15c
No. 8C302 ½-ounce vials, each, 15c; by mail 20c
No. 8C304 1-ounce vials, each, 20c; by mail 25c
No. 8C306 2-ounce vials, each, 40c; by mail 45c

most any illness that might attack the human body. Then he clinched the sale by advertising that his nostrum was made of roots, bark, berries, leaves, or vegetables; the Mother Nature touch being particularly appealing to buyers of patent medicines and at the same time carrying a suggestion of the purity of the ingredients. The following examples of the carrot-and-cabbage school of remedies might have been found in 1905 by the hundreds throughout the United States. Here again the catalog reflects contemporary life:

"BROWN'S VEGETABLE CURE FOR FEMALE WEAKNESS. A Very Effective Vegetable Tonic to be Used in the Treatment of Female Weakness, Falling of the Womb, Leucorrhea, Irregular or Painful Menstruation, Inflammation and Ulceration of the Womb, Flooding and all Female Disorders."

This is the headline. But an examination of the descriptive text shows that this remedy was offered as a cure for many other ills, and since, at one time or another, every woman was likely to experience some of the symptoms described, they were sure to be caught in the dragnet.

"Women, Brown's Vegetable Cure is highly recommended for female disorders. If you have any of the following symptoms take this remedy at once, it may afford you an easy and lasting cure."

Note that, although in 1905 a woman's leg was still a "limb" and the time was not far past when a woman had been a "female," the catalog uses language of Elizabethan frankness in describing its medicines.

The ills which Brown's Vegetable Cure would cure are:

Nausea and bad taste in mouth, sore feeling in lower part of bowels, impaired general health, sharp pain in region of kidneys, pain in passing water, bearing down feeling, a desire to urinate frequently, a dragging sensation in the groin, timid, nervous, and restless feeling, a dread of some impending evil, temper wayward and irritable, sparks before the eyes, pain in womb, swelling in front, pain in breastbone, hysterics, temples and ears throb, sleep short and disturbed, whites, headache, dizziness, morbid feeling and the blues, nerves weak and sensitive, appetite poor, a craving for unnatural food, fainting spells, difficulty in passing water, a heavy feeling and pain in back upon exertion, cold extremities.

If you have any of these symptoms send for a bottle of Brown's Vegetable Cure and give this preparation a trial. It will be sufficient to show you that it is just the remedy you need—the remedy that will bring not only relief but a cure, as it has in thousands of cases of suffering women who have given this medicine a fair test. Invalids have been made well and strong. Do not delay, one bottle will help and convince you.

If this did not appear sufficiently convincing, the catalog, and all other vendors of these medicines, used the orthodox method of printing testimonials from satisfied customers. Here the prospective customer is told to READ THESE LETTERS FROM GRATEFUL WOMEN.

One of these grateful women was Mrs. W. L. Arnold, of Leon, Iowa, who wrote the following letter to Sears:

It gives me great pleasure to tell you of the good I have obtained from Brown's Vegetable Cure. I used the Cure for female weakness and I have received more help and benefit from it than I have ever received from any other medicine that I have tried.

I have been a constant sufferer for a number of years and have tried a great number of remedies and have doctored for all of these years, but did not seem to get any stouter until after using Brown's Vegetable Cure, which is invaluable for female weakness or change of life. . . . I was just telling my husband the other day that Brown's Vegetable Cure had done me more good than all the rest of the medicines I have taken put together. . . .

How the ailing woman, torn between the desire to buy Brown's Vegetable Cure and Dr. Worden's Female Pills, was to make her decision, the catalog does not tell us. Each had its virtues and exactly the same virtues; the only difference between them seems to be that Brown's was a liquid selling at fifty cents a bottle while Worden's was in pill form at thirty-eight cents a box. But the catalog—while it does not tell us the basis on which suffering womanhood might resolve

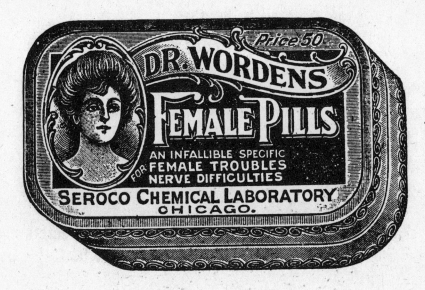

The Woman's Home Companion

the difficult dilemma of choosing between these remedies— does paint an eloquent word picture of woman's ills.

> Female Trouble. What a world of misery is expressed in these two words. What headaches, nausea, weakness, sickness, depression, etc. . . . is the direct result of the derangement of the delicate female organism and nature's regular functions.

It was unfortunate to have female trouble; it was unbearable to be unable to tell one's troubles to the doctor.

> Every woman well understands, far better than pen or words can tell, the suffering her sex must undergo by what is known as female trouble; suffering which is usually borne in silence, because only a woman can be confided in.

Miraculously enough, Worden's "are not cure-alls." They were nothing to take for sore throat, barber's itch, or St. Vitus's dance. They were merely "intended to relieve only the troubles peculiar to women . . . and cure leucorrhea, irregular, suppressed or painful periods, thin blood, nervousness, sleeplessness, sick headache, anemia, chlorosis or green sickness, hysteria, numbing of the hands and feet, ovarian difficulties, etc."

Profits Are Where the Heart Is

Ovaries, among human beings, are confined to women—but everybody has a heart. Hence the heart offered an even richer field for medicine men. The catalog's contribution to the ills of the heart was:

"WONDER HEART CURE or, Dr. Echol's Australian Auriclo." But how is one to know whether one has heart trouble? It was easy enough: merely look up the symptoms in the catalog.

"In order that one may determine if the heart is affected, we ask attention to the following list of symptoms which denote heart disease:

1. Fluttering of the Pulse.
2. Palpitation of the Heart.
3. Shortness of Breath.
4. Tenderness and Sudden, Sharp Pains in the Left Side.
5. Dreaming of Falling From a Height.
6. Inability to Sleep upon the Left Side.
7. Fainting or Smothering Spells.
8. Dropsy.
9. Sudden Starting in the Sleep and Noises in the Ears.

"In the simple descriptions of these symptoms, we have included the facts whereby heart trouble is recognized."

These symptoms might also have been caused by a lumpy mattress, bedbugs, underdone pork chops, an abscessed tooth, or an overdue loan at the bank, but since the Wonder Heart Cure was a "safe, scientific remedy . . . which acts upon the nerves, membraneous linings and valves of nature's life pump, the heart," it was better perhaps to play safe with Australian Auriclo. The purchaser risked nothing but his health, because, if he was not satisfied with the medicine, Sears "would cheerfully refund the purchase price." The no-cure-no-pay formula

YOUR MONEY WILL BE IMMEDIATELY RETURNED TO YOU FOR ANY GOODS NOT PERFECTLY SATISFACTORY.

A CURE FOR WEAK HEARTS

WONDER HEART CURE

DR. ECHOLS' AUSTRALIAN AURICLO,

42 CENTS AND 75 CENTS PER BOX, ACCORDING TO SIZE.

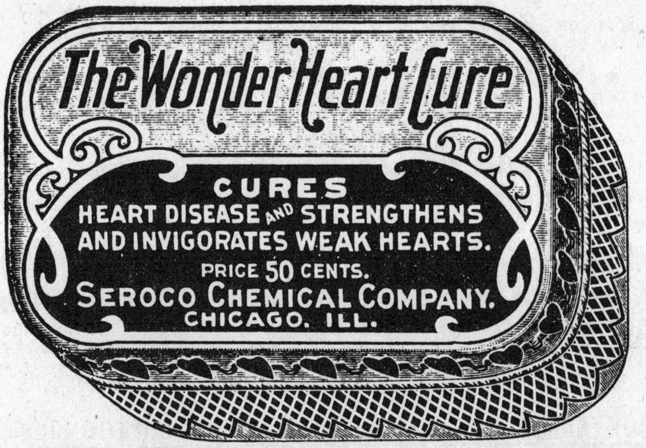

A Most Important Preparation. Recommended for Complications Indicating Heart Trouble.

THE HEALTH OF THE HEART IS MOST IMPORTANT. The heart is the great human pump, that sends the life giving blood to every part of the body. The amount of labor it performs day and night, working incessantly year after year, is almost beyond belief. All this vast amount of work must be done, and done well each day; if not, your health will surely suffer in consequence of the least failure of the heart to properly perform its duties.

SYMPTOMS OF HEART TROUBLE. In order that one may determine if the heart is affected, we ask attention to the following list of symptoms which denote heart disease: Fluttering of the Pulse, Palpitation of the Heart, Shortness of Breath, Tenderness and Sudden, Sharp Pains in the Left Side, Dreaming of Falling from a Height, Inability to Sleep Upon the Left Side, Fainting or Smothering Spells, Unconscious Spells, Dropsy, Sudden Starting in the Sleep and Noises in the Ears. In the simple descriptions of these symptoms, we have included the facts whereby heart trouble is recognized.

If you have the slightest suspicion of heart trouble, it would be advisable to take the Wonder Heart Cure immediately. You cannot make a mistake. The preparation will not harm a well heart and it may relieve and cure a disordered heart. The Wonder Heart Cure is a safe, scientific, carefully prepared remedy which acts upon the nerves, muscular tissues, membraneous linings and valves of nature's life pump, the heart. It is based on a prescription that has relieved hundreds of cases. It may fit your case exactly and you would receive wonderful benefit. If you are suffering from heart trouble, you should not overlook the opportunity of getting relief at a small expense and we are willing that you make a trial of Dr. Echol's Australian Auriclo. If you find that you have not received any benefit, simply write us to that effect and tell us that this is the first package of this remedy that you have tried, and we will cheerfully refund your money. We do not want to sell our customers anything, whether it is a sewing machine or a medical preparation or any other merchandise, unless we know that they get value received for their money; in fact, it is our aim to give them a great deal more value for their money than any other firm does. The price of this household remedy is very small indeed, but that does not mean that it has no efficiency; it means simply that we are willing to sell it on a small margin of profit. If you know that you are a sufferer from heart weakness or other heart complications, we recommend to you giving a trial to the Wonder Heart Cure. It has offered many a sufferer a means for relief and cure, and may accomplish the same for you. Under our liberal terms, you can find out whether the Wonder Heart Cure is suitable for the treatment of your case, without the slightest risk on your part. First, it cannot harm you, for we know the ingredients; and, secondly, if you try this remedy, if it does not help you, you need only notify us that the first box you have used of this remedy has not benefited your condition, and we will return to you every cent you have paid us for same.

WONDER HEART CURE is prepared in the form of a tablet and the remedy can be carried in the pocket without inconvenience. We furnish a box, containing 40 doses, for only 42 cents, larger boxes, containing 100 doses, for 75 cents. The price of the remedy is insignificant compared to its value, and no one who has the least indication of heart trouble should be without a box of this valuable remedy.

No. 8C6 Price, per box, containing 40 doses $0.42
Per dozen boxes 3.90
No. 8C7 Price, per box, containing 100 doses .... .75
Per dozen boxes 6.60
If by mail, postage extra, per small box, 3 cents; large box, 6 cents.

THOSE WHO HAVE TRIED WONDER HEART CURE ARE CERTAINLY THE BEST JUDGES. READ WHAT THEY SAY.

SUFFERED FOR YEARS FROM HEART TROUBLE, BUT WONDER HEART CURE CURED HER.

Sears, Roebuck & Co., Chicago, Ill. Kaufman, Texas.

Gentlemen: I am glad to say that I feel much relieved since taking your Wonder Heart Cure. I do not suffer any more from fluttering of the heart or from shortness of breath. I believe I will soon be completely cured. I have been suffering from heart trouble for a number of years and have tried a number of remedies without success until a neighbor friend of mine, who has bought a great many goods of you, told me of your Wonder Heart Cure. I immediately sent for some of the tablets, and began to feel better within two or three days after I first commenced taking them. I have steadily improved in health and I am now almost cured. Your Wonder Heart Cure is certainly a great remedy. Yours truly, MRS. R. E. SCOTT.

WONDER HEART CURE PRODUCES WONDERFUL RESULTS.

Sears, Roebuck & Co., Chicago, Ill. Five Mile, Ohio.

Gentlemen: I received the box of Wonder Heart Cure Tablets, and I am very much pleased with the results obtained from taking them, and want you to send me another box, for which please find enclosed the money. The tablets have done all you recommend for them, and I am indeed grateful to you for a medicine which has helped me like your Wonder Heart Cure Tablets. I do not have fainting or smothering spells as I used to have, and I now feel better than I have felt for several years. Your Wonder Heart Cure Tablets are certainly a grand remedy for anyone suffering from any kind of heart trouble.
Yours truly, MRS. JOSEPH WARLAIMONT.

OUR WONDER HEART CURE A GODSEND.

Sears, Roebuck & Co., Chicago, Ill. Joppa, Ala.

Gentlemen: Regarding the Wonder Heart Cure which I ordered and received from you some time ago, will say that I have taken it with wonderful results. I was bothered with the palpitation of the heart and had very great pains in the left side. At first your medicine did not seem to help me, but by following the directions closely and taking it just as you advised, I soon began to be better and am now cured. Your Wonder Heart Cure is indeed a godsend to suffering humanity and anyone suffering from palpitation of the heart or troubled with fainting spells will be cured as I have been by using your Wonder Heart Cure. I cannot praise it too highly. Yours respectfully,
JAMES WARREN.

GLAD TO TELL OF THE GOOD RESULTS OBTAINED BY USING OUR WONDER HEART CURE.

Sears, Roebuck & Co., Chicago, Ill. Canon Diablo, Ariz.

Dear Sirs: It gives me great pleasure to tell you of the good results that I have obtained by using your Wonder Heart Cure Tablets. I was in very poor health, due, so my doctor told me, to heart trouble. I had fluttering of the heart and sinking spells at intervals. Reading the description of your Wonder Heart Cure Tablets and thinking that they would help me, I ordered some of them, and am pleased to say that they have cured me and I no longer suffer from heart trouble as I did. Thanking you for what the Wonder Heart Cure has done for me, and trusting that my suffering sisters may be relieved in the same manner, I remain,
Very gratefully yours, MRS. W. L. JONES.

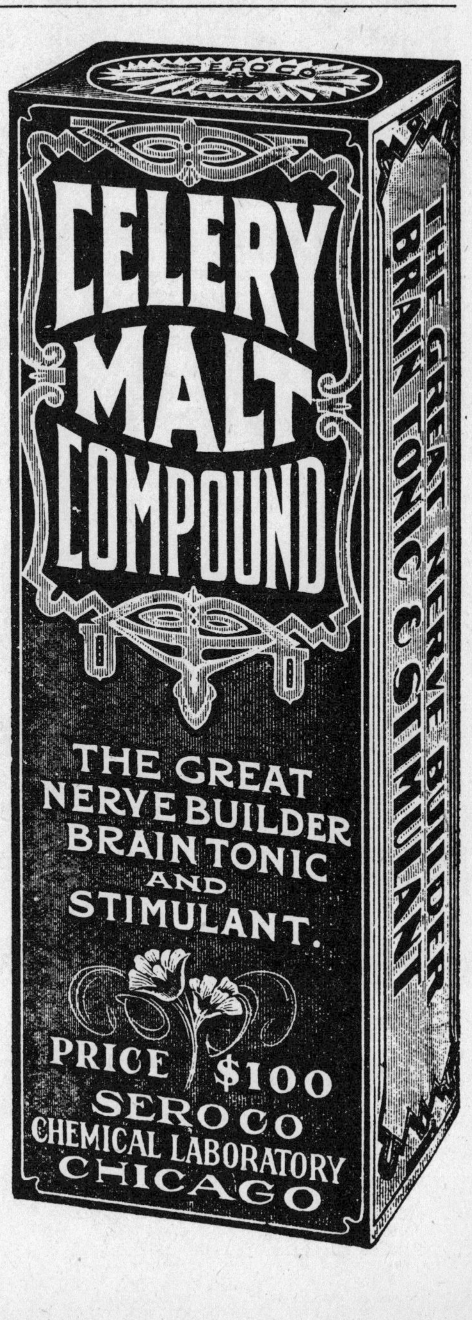

CELERY MALT COMPOUND.

A HIGH CLASS PREPARATION. LARGE REGULAR $1.00 SIZE BOTTLES—COMMERCIAL QUART SIZE— OUR PRICE ONLY 56 CENTS.

THE GREAT NERVE BUILDER, BRAIN TONIC AND STIMULANT.

Celery Compound has for years been recognized as one of the best possible health tonics. Our Celery Compound is improved by the addition of malt, making it far superior to other similar remedies. We guarantee our Celery Malt Compound to be absolutely pure and unadulterated. It is regarded as superior to any other celery compound on the market, regardless of name or price.

IT IS A TRUE NERVE TONIC, a genuine appetizer, a stimulant both for the young and old. We do not claim that Celery Malt Compound is an absolute specific for any chronic disease, but it has a much wider range of usefulness, as it is just the preparation required in hundreds of cases, and where no chronic disease has taken hold, it is very beneficial in hundreds of the ills that flesh is heir to. It is a preparation of such usefulness that in many houses it is regarded as standard and is always kept on hand for immediate use.

CELERY MALT COMPOUND IS A RECOGNIZED NERVE AND BRAIN MEDICINE. It combines the tonic and quieting effects of celery with the nutritive and digestive elements of malt, and thereby gives immediate relief in nearly every form of nerve trouble. This great preparation contains in a concentrated form the active medicinal properties of the Italian celery seed, well known to the physicians as one of the best and most active controlling and strengthening agents for the nerves, also the phosphates in the same state as found in the strong, healthy, vigorous, natural body, and in quantities approved of by the medical profession, the value of which has been so thoroughly demonstrated in all brain and nervous affections and in emaciated conditions. In addition it contains a large percentage of malt, which is very strengthening and fattening. All this makes it an ideal combination, and it is not only a useful tonic and stimulant, but an extremely pleasant tasting preparation as well. As a brain and nerve tonic, appetizer and stimulant it has few equals in the realm of medicine. For insomnia, nervousness, mental or physical exhaustion, loss of appetite, impoverished blood and for that tired feeling that comes from close confinement or sedentary habits, it is very effective and infinitely better than all stimulants of an alcoholic nature.

IF YOU ARE NERVOUS, EXHAUSTED, CANNOT SLEEP, DIGESTION IMPERFECT, or if you are out of sorts generally and in a low physical condition, we earnestly recommend a trial of Celery Malt Compound. As a rule it will give new life and vigor and build up the entire system.

IF YOU ARE SUFFERING, make a trial of this great preparation, Celery Malt Compound, under our liberal offer as explained on the first page of this department. It is likely that this remedy will cover your case exactly and you will be surprised and delighted at the benefit you will receive. You can depend on it that the preparation will not do you a particle of harm. You assume not the slightest risk in making your test as to whether the Celery Malt Compound is the proper remedy indicated for the treatment of your condition.

LARGE SIZE BOTTLES. A big supply of medicine in each bottle. The dose is a teaspoonful, and a bottle will cover about two months' treatment. Considering price, the quantity, and its high efficiency, this preparation is indeed a wonder of value.

WITH EVERY BOTTLE OF CELERY MALT COMPOUND we send free of charge our interesting and instructive booklet, "How to Have Strong Nerves." A practical treatise on nerves and their disorders.

No. 8C8 Price, large bottle, each $0.56
Per dozen .... (Cannot be mailed on account of weight.) 5.10

READ WHAT OTHERS THINK OF CELERY MALT COMPOUND.

CELERY MALT COMPOUND A PERFECT SUCCESS. MR. CHAMPION CURED.

Sears, Roebuck & Co., Chicago, Ill. Forest, Ohio.

Gentlemen: I am going to write to you and tell you what my experience has been and how much good I have received from using your Celery Malt Compound. I have been using this compound for a little over two months now, and I can truthfully say that I am deriving a very great benefit from its use. I have tried several nerve preparations before, but have never been able to obtain the satisfactory results that I have obtained by using your Celery Malt Compound. In additon to toning up my nervous system, it has also aided my digestion wonderfully and has cured my entire system of all its ailments. Anybody suffering from nervousness could not do better than use your Celery Malt Compound. Respectfully yours, C. CHAMPION.

IS VERY THANKFUL FOR SUCH A VALUABLE REMEDY AS CELERY MALT COMPOUND.

Sears, Roebuck & Co., Chicago, Ill. Mt. Vernon, Ark.

Gentlemen: The Celery Malt Compound which I ordered and received from you some time ago, I have taken with very beneficial results. I feel that it has done me a great deal of good, and my health is about 100 per cent better than it has been at any time within the last six years. I was very nervous and could not eat with any degree of satisfaction, but now I do both to perfection. Celery Malt Compound gives perfect satisfaction, and I am very thankful to you for such a valuable remedy.
Yours very truly, A. J. TROBAUGH.

CELERY MALT COMPOUND CURES A NERVOUS CASE OF TEN YEARS' STANDING.

Sears, Roebuck & Co., Chicago, Ill. Mondamin, Ia.

Gentlemen: I want to add my testimony to hundreds of others who have used your valuable remedies, and I want all to know of the valuable and permanent results that I have obtained by using your Celery Malt Compound. My life was almost unbearable on account of my severe nervous disorders and my stomach troubles which came from my nervous condition. I could not do any work around the house and had been in a nervous state almost bordering on collapse for ten years. I used scores of remedies, each one guaranteed to cure me, but none of them produced any permanent effect. Your Celery Malt Compound began to help me after I had taken only half a bottle, and by the time I had taken two bottles, my sleeplessness was a thing of the past and I am now able to sleep well and I feel in excellent condition all of the time. I had not been able to eat or sleep good for ten years before I took your valuable medicine. It is a grand preparation and should be used by all who need a like remedy.
Yours respectfully, MARY J. ROBINSON.

should have gone far toward advancing the spirit of scientific medical inquiry in this country.

Is Your Brain Weak?

Brains, too, are common to all mankind, including women. Some brains are strong; others are weak. But nobody need despair, because we have always had men who could tell us how to make weak brains strong and strong brains stronger. In the days when we were inclined to do things the hard way, the method was to instruct the young in mathematics or Greek; later, when we had softened a bit, we exchanged Euclid and Euripides for haddock and flounder. We found a whole category of foods—especially fish foods—that were good for the brain, and, while boiled cod was nothing to go mad about, it was easier to take than trigonometry. This was progress, but not the end of progress. The cod was beneficial to the brain but troublesome to the body. You had to buy one; cook it; eat it. Whereupon a medical genius arose and invented a "brain tonic" that could be taken from a bottle. This involved only the exertion of shaking the tonic before using. It soon acquired great popularity. Sears kept the brains of its customers alert, vigorous, and growing, through the sale (in quart bottles at fifty cents) of:

"CELERY MALT COMPOUND. A Recognised Nerve and Brain Medicine." This extraordinary remedy combined "the tonic and quieting effects of celery with the nutritive and digestive elements of malt, and thereby gives immediate relief in nearly every form of nerve trouble. . . . As a brain and nerve tonic, appetizer and stimulant it has few equals in the realm of medicine."

Drug Addicts in Our Rural Arcadia

It is with a tremendous shock of surprise that one comes in the catalog upon Sears' Cure for the Opium and Morphine Habit. For the legend is that the user of morphine, opium, and similar narcotics is the decadent city man or woman; that the independent farmer sniffing the sweet air that blows over his fields of blue clover would never sniff cocaine; that the devout dweller in a small, churchgoing town would never puncture his arm with the hypodermic needle charged with morphine. Yet the presence of this cure in the catalog indicates infallibly that rural and small-town America in 1905 had a considerable number of drug addicts; that the taking of drugs is not an urban but a national phenomenon, and that the victims of the drug habit pathetically sought cures through the use of medicines that were of less value for the purpose than soda pop.

The use of narcotics by Americans first became fairly widespread during the Civil War, and after the War, when drug addiction had so become common, it was popularly called "the army disease." Drug addiction in this country seems to have grown slowly but steadily from the Civil War to the World War.

Rural and small-town narcotism is proved not only by the internal evidence of the catalog but also by the external evidence of investigators. As long ago as 1877, it was found that there were about 1,300 addicts in Michigan *outside* the large cities, and, if the rate as determined from the Michigan study is applied to the whole country as of 1874, the total number would be over 250,000. In 1913, Jacksonville, Florida, reported 541 cases of drug addiction, or 0.8 per cent of its population, indicating a total number for the United States of 782,000. By 1918, the Secretary of the Treasury estimated that there were 1,000,000 cases in the country.

It is beyond the province of this book to consider why men use narcotic drugs, but there can be no question that many rural and small-town addicts acquired the habit as the result of the indiscriminate use of morphine by their physicians. Thousands of so-called doctors in the United States were no more qualified to practice medicine than to lead a symphony orchestra. They knew that the patient was in pain because he said he was in pain; what caused the pain was beyond them; the patient wanted to be rid of pain; a shot of morphine was the answer to the patient's prayer and the doctor's dilemma. In rural and small-town areas of the South, Federal narcotic agents checking doctors' consumption of morphine cannot believe that such great quantities are used legally in medical practice. Yet investigation generally proves that they are so used, with the result that white and Negro addicts are turned out by the hundreds at the hands of ignorant and unscrupulous medical men.

But whatever the causes of rural drug addiction were in 1905, Sears offers its Cure and promises that it will:

"Completely destroy that terrible craving for morphine and opium in those who are victims to the deadly habit of taking these poisonous drugs, and free them from their bondage, restoring their health and making them feel like living again. . . ."

Secret Cure for Open Vice

The catalog announces with almost pugnacious virtue that Sears does not sell alcoholic liquors, and, abandoning its attitude of objectivity toward the political issues of American life, takes a flat-footed stand concerning alcohol.

"We do not deal in spirituous liquors for general use. *We do not believe in the traffic and we allow no liquors to* go out of our house, except for medicinal purposes. . . ."

Sears thus stood with the great majority of its customers who were prohibitionists, but it did not blink at the fact that drunkenness was a widespread American phenomenon, and the catalog offers in nearly a half page of space the:

WHITE STAR SECRET LIQUOR CURE. This medicine was sent in a plain, sealed package, with the obvious purpose of preventing the drunkard from knowing that his relatives were trying to cure him of drinking, and all correspondence between the customer and Sears was kept confidential. For the great virtue of this remedy was that it was:

"A treatment to be administered without the knowledge of the drinker. It is claimed that it has saved many from that awful monster, Drink, and has protected thousands against a life of disease, poverty and degradation; that it has the power to release man from the bondage of whiskey, to reform even obstinate drunkards and to prevent the whiskey habit from taking hold on only moderate drinkers."

Drunkenness, we learn, is a disease against which "pledges and prayers often prove powerless after the appetite for intoxicants is once established," and because it "is a disease more than a habit . . . is subject to treatment."

Success in applying this remedy was believed to lie in the fact that it could be given secretly in the drunkard's food and beverages so that he would literally eat and drink his way into sobriety. Out in the kitchen Mama dropped a bit of the Secret Liquor Cure into Papa's coffee; stirred it in with the biscuit dough, or sprinkled the pork chops with it. This was easy to do because:

"The White Star Secret Liquor Cure is odorless, tasteless and colorless; a powder that can be given secretly in tea, coffee, or food, and by its action on the system removes the taste . . . for intoxicating liquors. . . . Can be given to any man, young or old, without his knowledge. . . . The normal health will return, eyes become bright, step elastic, appetite good, sleep sound and natural—*he is a saved man.*"

This is a story with a happy ending, marred only by the fact that Papa's condition after he had taken a bottle or two of the Cure would possibly be worse than it was before he started. In the ordinary case, Papa did his drinking after supper; either curling up with a bottle of booze at home, or, in small towns, going down to Manny's Saloon and getting tanked up with the boys. The Cure, however, kept him at home. It was a strong narcotic sleeping potion, and Papa was likely to fall asleep soon after he had drunk his Cure-tinctured coffee. This meant that he would drink no whisky that night. The danger, of course, was that he would become a narcotic addict instead of a drunkard unless he discovered Mama's little trick and dusted her off with an ax handle.

So, too, if Papa found that he had a tendency to fall asleep after supper and miss the pleasures of Manny's, he might have shifted his drinking from night to afternoon. Or, if Mama doped his breakfast coffee, he would be unable to go down to the sawmill, and so the family would have starved in the days when government relief had not even been imag-

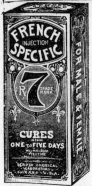

Injection No. 7.

Retail price,..........................$1.00
Our price, each..........................$0.64
Our price, per dozen..........................6.00

CURES IN ONE TO FIVE DAYS. No other medicine required. No fear of stricture. No bad results. A French specific having a great reputation abroad as a reliable cure for all troubles of the urinary organs in either male or female; has a very quick effect and leaves no bad result, no matter how severe the case. Either gonorrhea or gleet quickly and easily cured. Full instructions and valuable information with each package.

No. 8C133 Price, per dozen, $6.00; per bottle....64c
If by mail, postage and mailing case extra, 18 cents.
No. 8C822 Hard Rubber Syringe, to be used with this remedy. Price, 16c

Bromo Vichy.

Retail price........10c and 25c
Our price, 10c size, each..........................$0.08
Our price, 10c size, dozen..........................85
Our price, 25c size, each..........................20
Our price, 25c size, dozen..........................1.60

A Morning Bracer.　A Headache Reliever.
A Brain Clearer.　A Nerve Steadier.

THIS IS BY FAR THE BEST "BROMO" preparation at present offered to the public. One or two teaspoonfuls taken in half a tumbler of cold water will instantly dispel any sickness of the stomach, relieve a severe headache, clear up the brain and steady the nerves. **It is a thirst quencher,** and causes a pleasant feeling to prevail all through the body. It is a quick remedy for nervous headaches, neuralgia, sleeplessness, over brain work, depression following alcoholic excesses, and all nervous troubles. A little should always be on one's bureau table for use in the morning or at night.

No. 8C136　Price, 10c size, per dozen, 85c; each...........8c
　　　　　　Price, 25c size, per dozen, $1.60; each...........20c
If by mail, postage extra, small size, 4 cents; large size, 8 cents.

Corns, Bunions and Warts.

Retail price..........................25c
Our price, each..........................10c
Our price, per dozen..........................90c

THE GREAT CHINESE CORN, Bunion and Wart Remover, never fails to give immediate relief, and a complete cure is certain when directions are faithfully followed. No one suffering from corns, bunions or warts should fail to give our great Chinese Corn, Bunion and Wart Remover a trial. We have tried it ourselves and found relief, therefore can testify knowingly as to its great merits.

No. 8C139　Price, per dozen, 90c; each..........................10c
If by mail, postage extra, 3 cents.

Dr. Walker's Skin Ointment is another preparation that is needed by thousands of sufferers. This remedy is already well known in every section of the country, and those who have tried it will accept no other ointment under any circumstances. You will find a ready sale for this article and it will yield you a good profit.

No. 8C157　Dr. Walker's Skin Ointment. Price, per dozen, $2.70; per box..................(If by mail, postage extra, 3 cents.)..................29c

Angel's Oil.

The Greatest Cure on Earth for Pain.

Retail price..........................50c
Our price, each..........................$0.28
Our price, per dozen..........................2.70

COMPOSED OF VEGETABLE OILS. Offers great relief in cases of bronchitis, rheumatism, neuralgia, gout, sciatica, pleurisy, backache, quinsy, sore throat, stiffness of the neck and joints, sprains, cuts and wounds, lumbago, scalds and burns, headache, toothache, earaches, eruption, sores and swellings, inflammations, chilblains, frostbites, frosted feet, chapped hands and face, bites and stings of poisonous insects, weak ankles and joints, sore feet, pain in the back and limbs, ulcerated sores, or any other bodily pain or ailment.

THIS LINIMENT is worth its weight in gold and well named Angel's Oil, as it seems really a gift from the angels. Its uses are more numerous than we can mention here. Send for a bottle and try it. We are confident that you will never be without a bottle in the house. We make the price very low so that every one of our customers may afford to have a bottle constantly at hand.

No. 8C142　Price, per dozen, $2.70; per bottle..........................28c
If by mail, postage and tube extra, per bottle, 14 cents.

Every Mother Who Has Used It Proclaims Castroline Better than Castoria.

1100 Drops for Only 18 Cents.

Retail price..........................35c
Our price, each..........................$0.18
Our price, per dozen..........................1.80

KEEP YOUR CHILDREN HEALTHY and cheerful by using Castroline only. You need not have any other medicine in the house for your children. It is unquestionably the best thing for infants and children the world has ever known. It is harmless, and children like it. It gives them health and may save their lives. Mothers, keep it beside you, and you will always have something absolutely safe, pleasant to take, and the acme of perfection as a child's medicine for every ailment they are subject to. **CASTROLINE WILL DESTROY WORMS,** allay fever, prevent vomiting, cures diarrhea and wind colic, relieves teething troubles. Cures constipation and flatulency. It assimilates the food, regulates the stomach and bowels, and gives to the child a healthy and natural sleep. When your baby cries give it a dose of CASTROLINE, its effect will be soothing to the baby and pleasant to you. It contains neither morphine nor opium nor any other narcotic properties. It is much superior to the so called soothing syrups which are being advertised daily. It will cause the baby to sleep when fretful, giving the mother her much needed rest. One size bottle only.

No. 8C143　Price, per dozen, $1.80; per bottle..........................18c
If by mail, postage and tube extra, per bottle, 16 cents.

Dr. Walker's Celebrated Skin Ointment.

Retail price..........................50c
Our price, each..........................$0.29
Our price, per dozen..........................2.70

A positive cure for all skin diseases and blemishes and superior to every other skin ointment in the market, and furnished by us at less than one-half its selling value. This skin ointment is guaranteed to cure all eruptive and skin diseases, pimples, blotches, boils, eczema, salt rheum, erysipelas, ringworms or any scaly or scabby eruptions, often healing cracked or rough skin on the hands, face or any part of the body by a single application. We are in a position to furnish this grand cure for skin diseases and blemishes for only 29 cents a box. You could obtain no remedy that is better or can equal it in healing qualities if you were to pay $1.00 per package.

WHITE STAR SECRET LIQUOR CURE.

Drunkards Cured Without their Knowledge.

Regular retail price..........................$2.50
Our price, complete box, 30 treatments..........................$1.10
Our price, complete box, 30 treatments, per dozen..........................9.60

AN EXCEEDINGLY SUCCESSFUL DRINK CURE. A treatment to be administered without the knowledge of the drinker. White Star Secret Liquor Cure, only $1.10 per box, 30 complete treatments. It is claimed that this remedy has saved many from that awful monster, Drink, and has protected thousands against a life of disease, poverty and degradation; that it has the power to release man from the bondage of whiskey, to reform even obstinate drunkards and to prevent the whiskey habit from taking a hold on only moderate drinkers.

WHITE STAR SECRET LIQUOR CURE is odorless, colorless and tasteless; a powder that can be given secretly in tea, coffee or food, and by its action on the system removes the taste, desire or craving for intoxicating liquors. Anyone can give the powder, no preparation required, absolutely no danger. Can be given to any man, young or old, without his knowledge, and whether he is a regular drinker or only a mild tippler it removes the desire for liquor and stops the terrible habit in due time. White Star Secret Liquor Cure stays the weak and flagging nerves, the mind becomes clear, the brain active, the flush of the face subsides, the step becomes steady, new health and strength are imparted, a higher moral tone is upheld; in a word, it makes him a man among men.

DRUNKENNESS IS A DISEASE and must be fought and counteracted by proper medical methods, the same as any other disease. The desire for liquor once established, the system requires its stimulus, and unless this appetite is counteracted it must be satisfied and the victim is powerless against its demands. Pledges and prayers often prove powerless after the appetite for intoxicants is once established. The system craves liquor with an insatiable demand that the average strength of the drinker cannot resist, and every time this desire is satisfied it means that the next time it comes on with redoubled force.

SEND FOR A BOX OF THE WONDERFUL WHITE STAR SECRET LIQUOR CURE, give it according to directions, a small powder in his tea or coffee. He cannot tell any difference, but it will work just the same. The effect will surprise and delight you. You will soon notice the improvement. The remedy will not only stop drinking, but it usually produces a dislike for liquor. The normal health will return, eyes become bright, step elastic, appetite good, sleep sound and natural—he is a saved man.

CAN THERE REALLY BE A CURE FOR DRUNKENNESS, or is it a habit that cannot be shaken off but grows stronger every day? Does it not seem reasonable that drunkenness is curable? Drunkenness is a disease more than a habit and as such is subject to treatment. If the proper medical elements necessary to counteract the effect of liquor and destroy the appetite for it are combined, there is no reason why it is not curable. White Star Secret Liquor Cure is the most successful and considered a perfect secret liquor cure. It is made expressly for us according to the celebrated original formula in our possession and we know just what it is and can offer it to our customers with every assurance that they will receive the genuine Secret Liquor Habit Cure. It is prepared in the form of this odorless and tasteless powder so that it can be given secretly without the patient's knowledge.

MAKE A TRIAL OF THIS REMEDY.

SEND FOR IT ACCORDING TO OUR OFFER AND AFTER GIVING IT A FAIR TRIAL ACCORDING TO DIRECTIONS, IF THERE IS NO BENEFIT DERIVED, WE WILL REFUND YOUR MONEY. If you buy it and do not receive benefit, write us so, state that this is the first box that you have tried and we will promptly refund your money. Remember, the price is only $1.10 per box (30 complete treatments). Full directions sent with each box. Medicine is sent in plain sealed package. All correspondence confidential.

No. 8C151　Price, per dozen boxes, $9.60; per box..........................$1.10
If by mail, postage extra, 12 cents.

The New Ease and Comfort Back Rest.

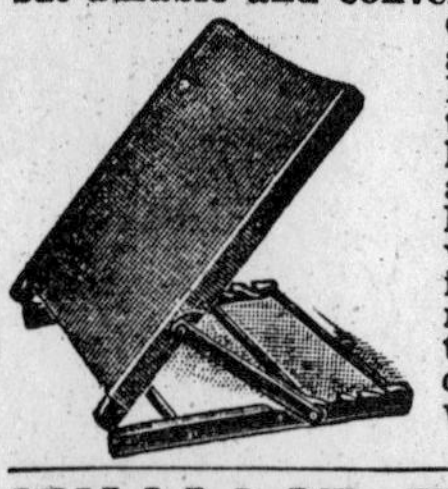

The New Ease and Comfort Back Rest, as illustrated here, is of the most simple construction, but durable and convenient, and should be on hand in every home to be used in the sick room. Others ask from $2.50 to $4.00 for back rests which are not made in as substantial and convenient a manner as the well known Ease and Comfort Back Rest. The Ease and Comfort Back Rest relieves much of the discomfort of persons confined to the bed, and is really indispensable to those who are compelled to endure a prolonged siege of illness, also to invalids who have to spend most of their time in bed, and in addition it will relieve the attendant waiting on the sick, of much arduous labor. The construction of the Ease and Comfort is very simple. Made of a stout wood frame with a ratchet underneath the back, so that the back rest can be placed in any inclined position to make the patient entirely comfortable. The cover is made of stout linen duck, laces in back, so that it can easily be removed and washed thus giving an opportunity to keep the back rest always in a clean and sanitary condition. The new Ease and Comfort Back Rest is cool and elastic, can be used with or without a pillow, or it can be placed under a mattress if preferred.

No. 49C8020 Ease and Comfort Back Rest. Price........................**$1.15**

INVALID RECLINING AND ROLLING CHAIRS

ARE YOU AN INVALID, **or have you a relative or friend who needs a reclining or rolling chair,** built especially for the comfort of invalids? We carry a complete line of standard styles of invalid chairs which are supplied to our customers at about half the prices at which these chairs have heretofore been sold. You need not pay from $40.00 to $60.00 for an invalid chair. We show you below a few styles with prices so low that you might think the chairs must be of inferior quality. We furnish these invalid chairs, however, under a binding guarantee that they are the highest grade of invalid chairs made; that their style, arrangement, adjustment, workmanship and finish is equal to, and **in many cases better** than that of any invalid chairs sold at two and three times our special low prices. We have a special **Invalid Chair Catalogue.** If you care for a larger selection, send for it, it is free.

IF YOU DESIRE **you need not wait to write for this special free catalogue of invalid chairs, for you can send your order direct from this catalogue from the styles illustrated herein** with the assurance that you will get the very best values we have to offer. We show on this page our leading and most popular styles of chairs, representing the very best values in the entire department, and if you find a chair among the following styles that pleases you, send us your order immediately. However, if there is any other style which you want (not shown herein), do not fail to write for the special **Free Catalogue of Invalid Chairs.**

AT OUR NEVER HEARD OF LOW PRICES, **every home that needs one, can afford an invalid chair.** For a comparatively small outlay you can brighten the hours and days of an invalid sufferer, make his condition less burdensome, supplying comforts which cannot be had without these specially designed invalid chairs, and thus contribute in the greatest measure possible to the relief, comfort, contentment and happiness of the patient. **Special Invalid Chair Catalogue free on application.**

Self-Propelling Rolling Chair.

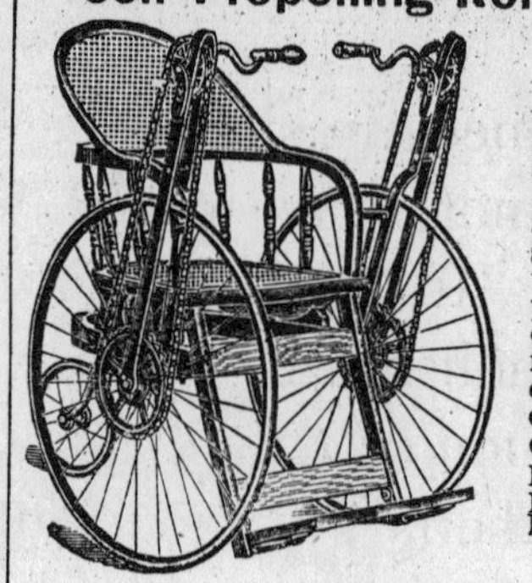

This chair is made in the same style and manner as chair No. 49C14066. But in addition it has the self propelling device which gives the patient greater independence of movement. The chair is propelled easily and it is especially intended for persons who are paralyzed in the lower limbs.

DIMENSIONS.

Height of arms from seat	9¾ inches
Height of back from seat	20½ inches
Height of seat from floor	21 inches
Height of seat from footboard	17¾ inches
Depth of seat	18 inches
Width of seat between arms	18¾ inches
Diameter of front wheels	28 inches
Diameter of rear wheel	10 inches
Width over all	30 inches

No. 49C14063 With oval steel rim wheels, plain bearings........................**$15.95**

No. 49C14064 With ¾-inch cushion tire wheels, front and rear, plain bearings..............**$21.90**

No. 49C14065 With 1-inch cushion tires on front and rear wheels, plain bearings.............**$24.85**

For steel elliptic springs on the above chair, extra........................**$3.00**

Weight, crated for shipment, about 100 pounds.

SEND FOR OUR
SPECIAL INVALID CHAIR CATALOGUE
IF YOU WANT ANY KIND OF AN INVALID CHAIR NOT SHOWN ON THIS PAGE.

Reclining Rolling Chair.

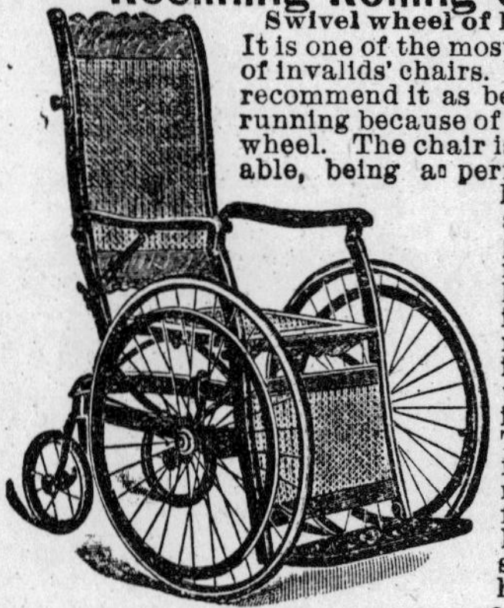

Swivel wheel of large diameter. It is one of the most popular styles of invalids' chairs. We particularly recommend it as being the easiest running because of its large swivel wheel. The chair is very comfortable, being a perfect fit to the human body and well proportioned. It is made of the best hardwood, finished in oak, rubbed and polished, with cane work as shown in illustration. The footboard folds up when not in use. It is furnished regularly with stationary push handle without extra charge.

The above is but one illustration and description of reclining rolling invalids' chairs. We issue a special **Invalid Chair Catalogue,** giving large illustrations, complete descriptions of every up to date, practicable, comfortable invalid's chair, at prices about one-half to one-third what other houses charge for same. If interested send for **special Invalid Chair Catalogue. It will be sent free on application.**

DIMENSIONS.

	Wide	Narrow
Height of back from seat	31 inches	31 inches
Height of seat from floor	22½ inches	22½ inches
Height of seat from footboard	17 inches	17 inches
Height of arms from seat	9½ inches	9½ inches
Depth of seat	20 inches	20 inches
Width of seat	19 inches	17 inches
Diameter of large wheels	28 inches	28 inches
Diameter of small wheel	10 inches	10 inches
Width over all	29 inches	27 inches

No. 49C14012 With oval steel rim and plain bearing wheels. Price..................**$13.95**

No. 49C14014 With ¾-inch cushion rubber tires and plain bearing wheels. Price..............**$18.50**

No. 49C14015 With 1-inch cushion rubber tires and plain bearing wheels. Price..............**$23.20**

Weight, crated for shipment, about 100 pounds.

Ball bearings in both front and rear wheels, extra........................**$2.25**

In determining whether to order the narrow or wide pattern, measure the width of the doorways through which the chair is to pass.

Reclining Rolling Chair.

WITH COMMODE ATTACHMENT.

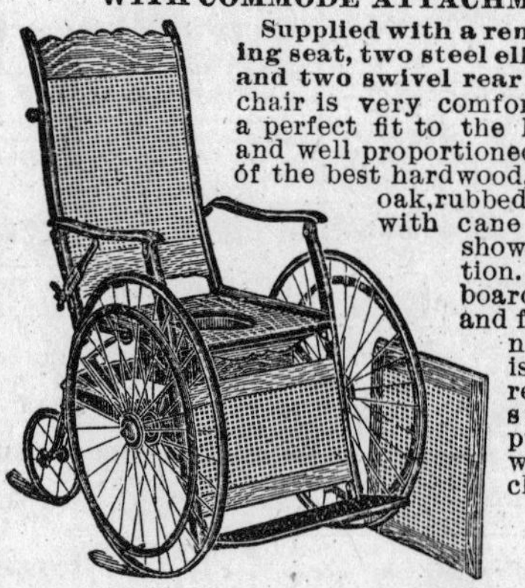

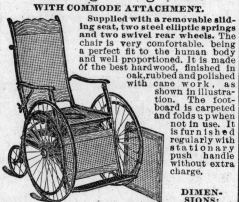

Supplied with a removable sliding seat, two steel elliptic springs and two swivel rear wheels. The chair is very comfortable, being a perfect fit to the human body and well proportioned. It is made of the best hardwood, finished in oak, rubbed and polished with cane work, as shown in illustration. The footboard is carpeted and folds up when not in use. It is furnished regularly with stationary push handle without extra charge.

DIMENSIONS:

	Wide	Narrow
Height of back from seat	31 inches	31 inches
Height of seat from floor	23½ inches	23½ inches
Height of seat from footboard	18 inches	18 inches
Height of arms from seat	9½ inches	9½ inches
Depth of seat	20 inches	20 inches
Width of seat	19 inches	17 inches
Diameter of large wheels	28 inches	28 inches
Diameter of small wheel	10 inches	10 inches
Width over all	29 inches	27 inches

Specify whether wide or narrow is desired.

No. 49C14038 With oval steel rim and plain bearing wheels. Price..................**$17.45**

No. 49C14039 With ¾-inch cushion rubber tires and plain bearing wheels. Price..............**$22.35**

No. 49C14040 Same, with bicycle ball bearing wheels. Price........................**$24.35**

No. 49C14041 With 1-inch cushion rubber tires and plain bearing wheels. Price..............**$26.40**

No. 49C14042 Same with bicycle ball bearing wheels. Price........................**$28.40**

Weight, crated for shipment, about 100 pounds.

In determining whether to order the narrow or wide pattern, measure the width of the doorways through which the chair is to pass.

Rolling Chair.

WITH SPRINGS AND STEEL EXTENSION PUSH HANDLE. REED WORK IS FINISHED, SHELLACED AND VARNISHED.

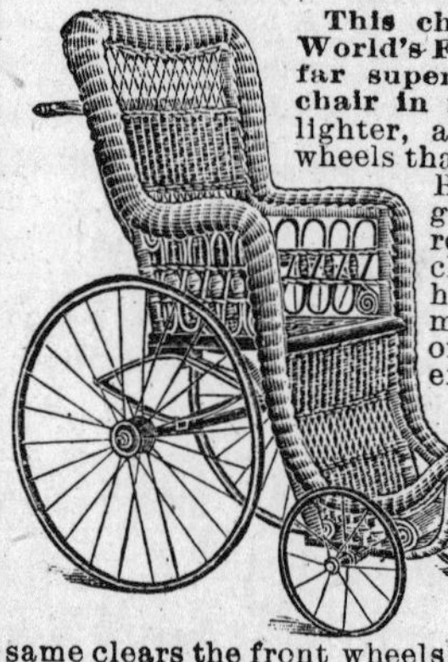

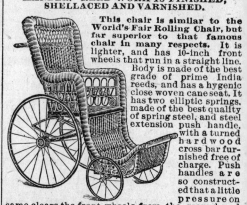

This chair is similar to the World's Fair Rolling Chair, but far superior to that famous chair in many respects. It is lighter, and has 10-inch front wheels that run in a straight line. Body is made of the best grade of prime India reeds, and has a hygenic close woven cane seat. It has two elliptic springs, made of the best quality of spring steel, and steel extension push handle, with a turned hardwood cross bar furnished free of charge. Push handles are so constructed that a little pressure on same clears the front wheels from the ground, and allows the chair to be turned in a very small space and to go over crossings and obstructions very easily.

DIMENSIONS.

	Adult's size, inches	Child's size, inches
Height of back from seat	27	24
Height of seat from floor	22	19
Height of seat from footboard	15½	14
Height of arms from seat	11	9
Depth of seat	17	14½
Width of seat	19	15½
Diameter of rear wheels	26	24
Diameter of front wheels	10	8
Width all over	29	26

ADULT'S SIZE.

No. 49C14092 With oval steel rim wheels. Price........................**$13.70**

No. 49C14093 With ¾-inch cushion rubber tires on rear wheels and ½-inch rubber tires on front, plain bearings. Price..............**$16.90**

No. 49C14096 With ¾-inch cushion rubber tires on rear wheels and ½-inch on front, with bicycle bearings in both front and rear wheels. Price, **$18.70**

Weight, crated for shipment, about 100 pounds.

CHILD'S SIZE.

No. 49C14097 With oval steel wheels. Price........................**$11.50**

No. 49C14098 With ¾-inch cushion rubber tires on rear wheels and ½-inch rubber tires on front wheels, plain bearings. Price..............**$14.90**

No. 49C14099 Same as No. 49C14098, except with bicycle ball bearings in both front and rear wheels. Price........................**$17.20**

Weight, crated for shipment, about 100 pounds.

SEND FOR OUR SPECIAL INVALID CHAIR CATALOGUE.

Fixed Rolling Chair.

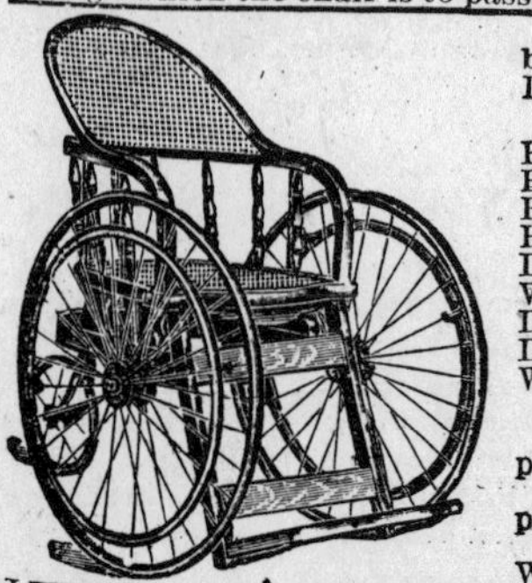

This chair has a bent oak frame filled in with open cane seat and back. The back of the chair is made to fit comfortably to the patient. It is a good substantial non-reclining chair.

DIMENSIONS.

Height of arms from seat	9¾ inches
Height of back from seat	20½ inches
Height of seat from floor	21 inches
Height of seat from footboard	17¾ inches
Depth of seat	18 inches
Width of seat between arms	18¾ inches
Diameter of front wheels	28 inches
Diameter of rear wheel	10 inches
Width over all	29 inches

No. 49C14066 With oval steel rim wheels, plain bearings........**$11.80**

No. 49C14067 With ¾-inch cushion tires on front and rear wheels, plain bearings........................**$17.25**

No. 49C14068 With 1-inch cushion tires on front and rear wheels, plain bearings........................**$18.40**

For steel elliptic springs on the above chair, extra..........**3.00**

Weight, crated for shipment, about 100 pounds.

SEND FOR OUR SPECIAL INVALID CHAIR CATALOGUE.

ined. In short, the White Star Secret Liquor Cure promised more than it could deliver.

In offering this home-administered cure for chronic alcoholism, the catalog, with its usual gallantry, omits any mention of lady drunkards. Whether or not they existed in 1905, the large amount of space devoted to the Secret Cure proves that there was much drunkenness in rural and small-town America—the stronghold of prohibition sentiment—and that the reform of drunkards was not left entirely to the efficacy of prayer.

Blemishes Removed

Cromwell ordered his portrait painter to paint in his wart, but Sears' customers wanted their warts removed. The Great Chinese Corn, Bunion and Wart Remover made "a complete cure certain when directions are faithfully followed." The powers of this remedy are proved not only by letters from satisfied customers but also by the unusual testimony of Sears itself. "We have tried it ourselves and found relief, therefore can testify knowingly as to its merits."

Electrical Healing

Electricity, perhaps because of its mysteriousness and awfulness, its spectacular qualities as seen by the naked eye in the flashing lightning or the sputtering spark, and its ability to produce ligh, heat, and power, was long ago seized upon by medical fakers as a miraculous curative agent. It was felt by the public—or the public was made to feel—that weak humanity could derive strength merely by being brought into contact with electricity. How strong a grip it had on the imagination of the people is shown by the catalog's:

"ELECTRIC LINIMENT. We call this remedy Electric Liniment because its application produces a feeling similar to the feeling produced by a mild charge of electricity."

But medical electricity, as it was called, found its complete expression in a host of mechanical devices of which the supreme example is the ANTI-DOC BATTERY.

This was a dry-cell battery which conveyed mild charges

of electricity to "carrying-handles" that were gripped by the patient, and as the charges coursed through his body he was cured of whatever ailed him. So numerous were devices of this kind that Sears issued a special instruction book called *Medical Electricity at Home.*

The Anti-Doc Battery was a rather cumbersome and expensive device selling for $2.25, but, while more complicated, it was less ingenious than Electric Insoles which sold for only

Electric Insoles Kept Cold Feet Warm and Wet Feet Dry in 1905

eighteen cents. These were placed inside the shoes with the "pure polished metals arranged in such a manner that a mild, pleasant current is produced along the soles of the feet, which stimulates the blood and keeps it circulating constantly."

Electricity came to the aid of suffering womankind in the form of Electric Battery Plasters: big black plasters which were stuck on the patient's back for the relief of rheumatism and kidney troubles. "If used according to instructions, the battery on this plaster will generate a strong galvanic current, which makes the plaster effective."

At little extra expense and with no trouble at all, the rheumatism sufferer who wore a battery plaster on her back could also wear an Electric Ring for Rheumatism on her finger. This was a plain metal finger ring, illustrated in the catalog with showers of sparks flying from its electricity-charged interior, but possessed of mysterious curative powers. Sears is indignant that fakers have invaded the rheumatism-ring market and warns its customers that:

"These are the first rings introduced into the United States, all others being imitations. Their popularity has

The Electric Sparks Kept Rheumatism at Bay

caused many rings to be placed on sale that are without curative properties."

Bleeding America

Bleeding the patient is an ancient medical practice that we might assume had long ago been abandoned in the United States, but the fact is that, as late as 1905, bleeder-surgeons were still buying bleeding instruments from Sears. The catalog lists and illustrates the:

"Spring Bleeding Lance. The only practicable, safe and convenient instrument for bleeding on the market. Used almost exclusively by old school physicians for the purpose."

Are You Ruptured?

The medical market is a market that has produced greater profits than all the Eldorados, Bonanzas, and Mother Lodes of the country combined. Unregulated, unrestricted, requiring almost no plant investment, free from labor troubles, and exacting a fabulous profit per unit of sales, it is typical of the high, wide, and handsome methods of thirty years ago. One of the richest subdivisions of this rich market was that for trusses.

Sears, whatever the volume of its sales and however many its customers, could sell only a fraction of the trusses that were sold in America at the time, but the size of the whole market may be gleaned from the amount of space devoted to trusses and braces in the 1905 catalog—nearly five full pages.

Medical practice then employed trusses as a cure for hernia and what were vaguely called ruptures; often when the physician could not diagnose the patient's illness he prescribed a truss just the same. It was painless, if perhaps uncomfortable, to wear; usually it could do the patient no especial harm, and the employment of trusses was medically fashionable. The market thus became enormous, the profits immense, because trusses cost little to make, and Sears' fighting determination to get its share of the business is shown by its setting up of a truss factory and its lusty language denouncing the allegedly piratical prices charged by local druggists.

In one respect, however, Sears seems to have been handicapped. The truss was generally fitted to the person of the patient by the physician or the druggist. But how could Sears in Chicago fit a truss to the body of a man living in Vermont? This challenge to its ingenuity was easily met in the catalog's instructions:

How to Order: "State Your Height And Weight, How Long You Have Been Ruptured, Whether Rupture Is Large Or Small, also state number of inches around the body on a line with the rupture, say whether rupture is on Right or Left Side, or Both."

This was asking a high degree of confidence toward Sears on the part of the distant sufferer, but the catalog assures him that it can do an even better job than his local physician or druggist:

"The gentleman in charge of this department alone has made the supplying of trusses by mail possible, and by following our rules for measurement he can not only fit you as accurately as you could be fitted by your physician at home, but, different from your physician or druggist, who may not have your exact size or shape, he is able to have the truss made and adjusted to your exact requirements. . . ."

Then the catalog attacks the local druggist, and here again we note the knock-down-and-drag-out language of competition used in a less polite era than ours. Nowadays competition is as bitter—or more bitter—as it was in 1905, but we are politely hypocritical in the language we use toward our competitors. Sears used no polite talk.

"From the limited stock carried by the average druggist a professional man could not honestly fit and adjust a truss for one man in ten, for he would be unable to find the exact size . . . but the druggist, in his eagerness to make the sale and get your money, will furnish you with a truss which he claims is a fit at from $2.00 to $10.00. . . . You are compelled to pay this druggist three or four prices for a truss that *is little better than nothing and very dangerous at the best.*"

Fitting New Legs to Old Bodies

If Sears could measure man at a distance for a truss, it could also take his measure for an artificial leg. The victim of an accident resulting in the loss of a leg is warned not to buy "an artificial leg until you have sent for our Special Artificial Leg Pamphlet." Just because a man has lost a leg it does not follow that he must lose his sense of the value of a dollar. "We can save you from $40 to $60 on the best artificial leg made."

The "French Disease"

In 1905, when *The Ladies' Home Journal* was receiving thousands of cancellations of subscriptions because it had dared to suggest that it was time to discuss openly the dangers of venereal diseases, the catalog blithely and frankly offered a medicine for the treatment of gonorrhea. This was "Injection No. 7. Cures In One To Five Days. . . . A French specific having a great reputation abroad as a reliable cure for all troubles of the urinary organs in either male or female. . . . Either gonorrhea or gleet quickly and easily cured. Price, per dozen, $6.00; per bottle, 64¢. Hard Rubber Syringe, to be used with this remedy, price 16¢."

Here, as in the case of the liquor and narcotic remedies,

the rural population seems to have tacitly admitted that it contained many sufferers from venereal diseases. This tacit admission made it possible to mention these ills frankly in the catalog without arousing the antagonism of its customers who, in all probability, were glad to be able to buy patent remedies by mail without submitting themselves to the embarrassment and possible gossip that might flow from going to the local druggist.

A Revolution Takes Place

In the ten years that elapsed between the publishing of the catalogs of 1905 and 1915, a revolutionary change took place in the field of fake medicines. The 1915 catalog contains only one page of medicines as compared with the multiple pages of 1905, but the change is perhaps greater in the kind of medicines offered than in the shrinkage of the pages. Here are no nostrums held out as remedies for everything from cancer to colic; no cures; no miracles of electric plasters. The catalog now offers only simple medicines such as aspirin and epsom salts, accompanied by the notation that most of them conform to the standards of the United States Pharmacopoeia.

At the very moment when the 1905 catalog was bulging with medical miracles, a series of articles exposing patent medicines began to appear in *The Ladies' Home Journal* in 1904–05, followed by another series written by Samuel Hopkins Adams for *Collier's Weekly* in 1905–06.

These articles made a tremendous impression on the country, and the public outcry that followed them forced Congress in 1906 to pass the Food and Drugs Act which makes it a misdemeanor to ship, or offer to ship, adulterated or misbranded food or drugs in foreign or interstate commerce. The apparently inalienable right of manufacturers to poison the public was somewhat modified through this legislation, and later Congress amended the Act to prevent the placing of misleading curative claims on the labels of medicines.

The catalog, however, complied with the law through the

drastic method of eliminating nearly all patent medicines and nostrums from its pages with the fall edition of 1908. Thus one great source of distribution of patent hokum was closed to the public and a considerable volume of sales was closed to Sears. But the profits in the manufacture of fake medicines are great, the gullibility of the public is still enormous, and the enforcement of the law is lax. A man may no longer order a bottle of rheumatism remedy along with his trace chains from Sears, but it is still available to him through other sources.

Modern manufacturers of fraudulent medicines are more subtle than their earlier prototypes. They do not use the forthright lusty language of the old-timers in describing the disease their remedies will allegedly cure, but achieve almost the same effect through the use of innuendo, euphemisms, and pseudoscientific language. Even when they are compelled by law to state on their labels the contents of their medicines, they state them in terms which the public does not understand. Moreover, by virtue of a powerful lobby aided by many newspaper proprietors greedy for advertising, they have defeated every effort of Congress to enact laws that will effectually control their activities. The country is still safe for many patent-medicine manufacturers.

THE late Clarence Darrow, recalling the village cemetery of his youth, wrote:

> . . . It was long before I realized that even the barred gates of a graveyard could not keep vanity outside. I often heard the neighbors talk about these stones. Sometimes they said it was strange that Farmer Smith could not show enough respect for his wife to put up a finer gravestone. Again, they said it would have been better if Farmer Smith had been kinder to his wife while she lived, than to have put up such a grand monument after she was dead. . . .
>
> . . . All the inscriptions on the stones told of the virtues of the dead, and generally were helped out by a Scriptural text. In the case of children the stone was usually ornamented with a lamb or a dove, which we thought wonderful and fine. Sometimes an angel in the form of a woman was coming down from the clouds to take a happy child away to heaven.

Men have attempted immemorially to achieve immortality on earth for themselves, their families, or the great of their countries through the use of gravestones, mausoleums, or monuments. In memory of the dead, they have erected monuments of breathless beauty such as the Taj Mahal; monuments of stupendous size such as the pyramids, and monuments neither beautiful nor stupendous such as Grant's Tomb in New York or Lenin's in Moscow. Other men—simple, unsung millions of men, their womenfolk, and their children—lie in graves marked by modest stones, and it is members of this group who turn to Sears for markers or monuments to star the graves of those they cherished.

Tombstone Fashions

Most Americans, until about fifty years ago, were content to mark graves with simple slate or limestone slabs modest both in design and size. Such markers sufficed for the wealthy as well as for the moderately wealthy or the poor. Stones of this kind dot historic graveyards of the South and New England, and are familiar to the hurrying thousands of New York's financial district where messengers munch their hot dogs among the simple slabs of Trinity Cemetery. But wealth and Victorian taste inaugurated a long era of marble and granite cut and carved into trumpeting angels, drooping doves, little lambs, gates ajar, weeping angels, and likenesses of the deceased himself, which when repeated hundreds of times in the same cemetery led to an ugliness and a vulgar pretentiousness that afflicted the eyes of the living and assaulted the dignity of the dead.

In 1905, Sears' tombstone business was already so important that its memorial department issued a special tombstone catalog, while grave markers were listed in the general catalog. At that time, Sears offered:

"A FINE SELECTION of handsome headstones or markers at prices ranging from $4.88 to $40.00, with some very choice designs from $5 to $8; a grand variety of monuments at from $8.59 to $173.30, many new and elegant designs in the way of entirely new shapes and finishings. . . ."

The memorial department employed "only the choicest Vermont blue and white Rutland Italian marble," and promised to send a sample piece of marble on receipt of ten cents. As we have often seen on other occasions, the catalog and the local dealer indulge in violent battles, and now we find them wrestling for life in the cemeteries of the dead. "Don't buy a marker . . . or monument of any kind until you see this free catalogue. We will furnish you something handsomer, newer, more stylish and more up to date . . . than you can buy elsewhere. We will guarantee the price in every way, and you can get it at less than one-half the lowest price at which any dealer will furnish you the same size of inferior workmanship and finish."

In 1905, the catalog wasted neither time nor space in sentimental reflections upon death or the dead or the wisdom of commemorating the departed with monuments. It assumed that when a man died his family would erect a marker over his grave, and forthrightly discussed the question of price. Consequently, it tackles the question of buying a tombstone with a flying leap into the matter of price:

OUR SPECIAL $14.38 NEW DESIGN LOW ROLL MONUMENT. Or, "This Beautiful Tombstone with a sleeping lamb on the top is furnished at the hitherto unheard of price of $11.65 in Acme Blue. . . ."

Lettering on the markers called for an added outlay, and it may be assumed led to brevity of epitaphs. "Ordinary sunk inscription letters, 6 cents each." Poetry, however, cost less than prose to engrave on stone, and this may have encouraged an American school of obituary poets. "Sunk verse, 2½ cents each."

The High Cost of Burying

The catalog talks of tombstones in terms not of mawkishness but of merchandise. Long ago men complained of the alleged exorbitant charges of undertakers and monument makers, and said they were ghouls battening upon the susceptibilities of grief-stricken folk. Sears does not attack the alleged ghoulishness of those who deal in the necessaries of the dead, but says that their distribution methods are wasteful and warns the customer against the local dealer in monuments. Its special catalog in 1910, we learn, is:

"A revolution in prices and a revelation to you, telling you how memorials in granite and marble have heretofore been a fat field for profit for those doing business under the old fashioned selling methods, with their large selling expenses and long profits, who for a century past have found the highest of high prices to be essential to their methods. . . ."

Death Is an Industry

All his life man actively consumes; at his death he is a passive consumer for the last time. Burying the million and a half persons who annually die in the United States has resulted in an industry whose sales mount up to $500,000,000 a year, and it is an industry without peaks or depressions, because in good times or bad times men die with astonishing regularity throughout every day and month of the year. Of this huge sum, about $55,000,000 a year goes to monument makers, and it is this large market that Sears seeks to tap through its memorial department.

The markers and monuments listed in the 1935 catalog are, on the whole, simple and lacking in sentimentality, being mere blocks of granite or marble with a minimum of decoration and relying for effect on mass and polished surfaces. The carved-lamb design survives, however, as a marker for children's graves in "The Olivet—the carved lamb and the heart and floral design which is traced on the front only, make this an appropriate tablet for a child's grave." One model is suitable either for children or husband and wife and consists of two stone hearts hewn out of marble. This is "The Heartsease—a graceful and fitting memorial for two children or for a husband and wife."

After the customer has selected a tablet or monument, he is then confronted with the difficult question of the epitaph—a field of writing in which simple Americans have often risen to heights of beauty and dignity—and the catalog, coming to the rescue of the inarticulate, suggests "quotations and verses suitable for inscriptions."

". . . If you have no verse or words of your own that you wish to use, you can, no doubt, find something in the selection below which will express your grief in an appropriate and beautiful way." The following are a few selections from the mail-order *Greek Anthology*:

FOR A CHILD

Our Little One
Entered Into Rest
In Heavenly Love Abiding
Under the Shadow of His Wings
God's Finger Touched Him and He Slept

Let no hopeless tears be shed,
Holy is this narrow bed

FOR AN ADULT

At Rest
Safe Into the Haven Guide

He who dies believing
Dies safely through Thy love

We with Him to life eternal
By His resurrection rise

Someday, some time, but Oh not yet,
For we must wait and not forget

FROM THE SCRIPTURES

Blessed are the dead which die in the Lord
Be thou faithful unto death and I will give thee a crown
of life.

I sought the Lord and He heard me and delivered me
from all my fears

Customers' Testimonials

Sears' customers write glowing testimonial letters to its memorial department. Mr. R. A. Wilson of Kingsley, Michigan, writes:

Your records will show that I purchased from you for cash this summer, memorials to the amount of nearly $200. The material and workmanship are very good indeed. I figure I saved about $120. . . .

Mrs. A. H. Custin of Crown Point, Indiana, says that she commemorated her husband's memory economically:

I purchased a marker from you last August and I am very much pleased with it. I sent in my order and in less than a month my marker was in place at my husband's grave and at a saving of about $25 less than I would have had to pay at the dealers here.

Part Two

LADIES

Here we enter into the large, complex, colorful world tenanted by women. Huge sectors of American manufacturing, retailing, and the services exist only to serve the multifarious demands of women. They constitute not only a huge market for the things that they consume directly, but they also deeply influence the purchasing of things jointly used by the family as, for example, the automobile, and the clothing worn by their men. Women, therefore, indulge in no idle boast when they say that if they stopped buying for only one week they would seriously cripple the economic structure of the country.

In this place, however, woman is not considered as a market but is merely projected against the catalog mart to show her as a flesh-and-blood person in her various roles of consumer, worker, girl, wife, mother, and grandmother. Through the things that she uses and wears, she is related to the social-economic structure. of the times, to the changing place and status of woman in American society, and is seen as a reflector of contemporary manners and morals.

This section deals with: typewriters and contraceptives; cosmetics and fashion; hair, millinery, silk hosiery, corsets, underwear, and bathing suits, labor-saving devices in the home, and gardening.

CARL SANDBURG wrote a poem. It is called "Working Girls":

> The working girls in the morning are going to work—
> long lines of them afoot amid the downtown stores
> and factories, thousands with little brick-shaped
> lunches wrapped in newspapers under their arms.

> Each morning as I move through this river of young-
> woman life I feel a wonder about where it is all go-
> ing, so many with a peach blossom of young years
> on them and laughter of red lips and memories in
> their eyes of dances the night before and plays and
> walks. . . .

And a man employed by Sears wrote a piece of advertising copy:

> The Chicago Typewriter. An Up to Date Typewriter for
> only $35.00. . . . It has 32 keys which print 90 dif-
> ferent characters, the maximum reached by any type-
> writer; is fitted with the universal key board and a
> steel type wheel.

> These type wheels are interchangeable, and in less than a
> minute's time can be changed, not only as to style of
> letter, but also from one language to another, and to
> the medical and mathematical wheels.

This was in 1905, but already the "river of young-woman life" was flowing in ever-greater volume down the streets of the cities, the leafy lanes of small towns aspiring to be cities, and in hamlets that yearned to be small towns. The particles of the river were young women workers; atoms sucked and drawn out of their homes by the forces of industry; disordered parts of a disordered pattern still in process of forming a unified whole. These bodies fluent for reproduction, these hands facile for the coddling of children, and skillful

The Machine that Wrote Woman's Emancipation Proclamation

for the preparing of the evening meal against the homecoming of the breadwinning man, will bend over machines, serve behind counters, dip chocolates, sew up sacks, and tap typewriters. More than any other machine, the typewriter is the symbol of industry; the machine which, above all others perhaps, started women along a new road to living, as it is at the same time the instrument by which business makes itself articulate and, second only to the inventions of writing and printing by movable type, is the most important invention in the history of the machinery of human expression.

In a million buildings of thousands of cities and towns, pothooks flower on notebooks in the morning; at the setting of the sun, they have become the language of business transcribed on letterheads; by night, they are the cargo of lonely airplanes soaring over mountains; of mail trains thundering through sleep-drowned villages. All of this we take for granted and as though it had always been; yet these are recent developments in young America.

Mark Twain Recommends the Typewriter

Shortly after the Civil War, when the United States first began to feel the tremors of prodigious expansion, the

Scientific American said that the pen had become inadequate for the transaction of modern business and that the country needed a better method by which correspondence and book-keeping could be conducted. The new method was soon at hand. By 1868, Christopher Latham Sholes of Milwaukee had obtained a patent for a typewriter that wrote far more rapidly than the pen. Yet it was still a very crude machine, and it was not until 1874 that the Sholes typewriter, renamed the Remington, had been perfected sufficiently to be put on the market. Shortly after its appearance, Mark Twain said of the new typewriter: "I believe it will print faster than I can write. One may lean back in his chair and work it. It piles an awful stack of words on one page. It don't muss things or scatter ink blots around; of course it saves paper."

Mark Twain paid $125 for his typewriter in 1874—or just a little more than the price of today's product. Type-writers were then turned out by the hundreds; they are now manufactured by hundreds of thousands. Is this an instance of the economies of mass production dissipated by the extravagances of modern distribution?

Typewriter Improvements

The first typewriter wrote capital letters only because it had no key-shift mechanism, and the writing was invisible to the operator, who could see what she was typing only by constantly lifting the carriage. These stumbling blocks to perfection were soon cleared away. By 1878, the key-shift machine was invented which permitted the operator to use small or capital letters at will, and a competing typewriter appeared which attempted to solve the same problem with a double keyboard containing twice the number of keys—one for every character, whether capital or small letter. Critics of the latter machine said that it took a deaf Hercules to run it and, according to J. B. Priestley, the English novelist, the objection seems to have been well founded. He decribes it as follows: *

"It had the old double keyboard—typing then was a mus-

* J. B. Priestley, *English Journey,* pp. 122-23.

cular activity. If you were not familiar with those vast keyboards, your hand wandered over them like a child lost in a wood. The noise might have been that of a shipyard on the Clyde. You would no more have thought of carrying about one of those grim structures than you would have thought of travelling with a piano."

While the key-shift and double-keyboard machines were competing for the market, the next great improvement in typewriters came in 1883 with the invention of the visible-writing machine. This speeded up the operation of typing and, as the urgent demands of increasing business called for more and more speed, the "touch method" of typing came into use in the 1890's and rapidly superseded the old hit-or-miss usage. The touch method, in turn, doomed the double-keyboard machine because it was not adapted to the new system of typing. Thereafter the key-shift typewriter enjoyed a monopoly of the field.

Hostility to the Typewriter

The typewriter, however, was destined to meet hostility before it became generally accepted. In the mechanical, as in the socioeconomic and political, worlds, aversion to change is deep-rooted. Many men said that it was silly to pay $125 for a newfangled machine that could merely do the work of a one-cent pen. As the typewriter was improved and became more efficient, questions involving the status of women soon entered into arguments over its utilization.

It had often been said that men and women must not be employed together in industry because this would lead to sexual irregularities and the breakdown of the country's morals. Yet here was the typewriter; it was useful; it could be operated by girls, and girls were not only more efficient typists than men but would work for less. The girl typist thus soon became the symbol of woman's emancipation, and in 1881, when the New York Young Women's Christian Association announced that it would offer typing lessons to girls, strong protests were made on the ground that the delicate female constitution could not endure the hardships of a six-month typing course. The young ladies managed, however, to survive the rigors of the training course and were willing to work for less than men. When Emily Faithfull spoke to Colonel Higginson of Boston in 1883, he told her that "Like Charles Lamb, who atoned for coming so late to his office in the morning by leaving it early in the afternoon, we have in the United States first half educated the women, and then, to restore the balance, only half paid them."

Miss Faithfull, in her travels in America at this period, reports that:

> Shorthand enables many women to make a good living, especially in connection with type-writers, which are found invaluable to stenographers. I visited several offices started by lady stenographers where from six to a dozen girls were busily employed copying legal documents and authors' manuscripts by means of these marvellous machines. Girls quickly learn to use the type-writer, and seem quite to enjoy manipulating the keys. A few months' practice enables them to write with it three times as fast as with a pen, and with perfect neatness and accuracy. It is probable an effort will shortly be made in London to open a well-appointed office for the employment of girls in this direction.

In 1898, S. S. Packard, in *What Women Can Earn,* recites his accomplishments in training girls to be stenographers and says:

> The advent of the typewriter opened a new and limitless field, and I had the great satisfaction of placing the first girl stenographer in business. This line of employment, as is now so well known, was especially adapted to to the clear brain, quick fingers and methodical habits of the resourceful girl, and it is not at all strange that it has grown to be almost exclusively woman's work. . . . It is difficult to find young men willing to undertake stenography . . . and so today one of our chief difficulties is to fill the places that are open. . . . The surest and best means of becoming expert stenographers is through the best

schools, and . . . in all parts of the country . . . there are well-conducted schools . . . where the learner can count upon attaining proficiency. . . .

How much could stenographers earn? Almost as much in 1898 as in 1940, and, measured by real wages, perhaps they earned more forty years ago than they do at present. Mr. Packard continues:

> The rates paid for good stenographers in the best business houses vary from $10 to $20 a week, and there is possibly no line of work in which women engage having a fairer prospect of leading to something better.

There were, however, moral objections to girl stenographers: it was feared both that they would corrupt and be corrupted by their employers. Mary B. Sanford, writing in *What Women Can Earn,* discusses these objections:

> According to the humourous paragrapher, the woman stenographer is commonly regarded as a frivolous, illiterate, and irresponsible young person, who acts the part of the "pretty typewriter" in the domestic drama with the untrustworthy husband and employer and the jealous wife. The squibs appear with wearying frequency and monotony. . . .
> The manners and morals of a small minority offer a slight foundation for such innuendoes. The representative stenographer is a responsible business woman, capable, faithful and thoroughly in earnest. She is often elderly and not always beautiful.
> And as a rule, though the woman in his service be young and attractive, the employer does not misuse his position. He is a busy man . . . and his relations to the stenographer are in general strictly of a business nature. Good principle exists in business offices, despite the paragraphers and the fact that some unprincipled persons are found there. . . .

Typists—and Skeptical Wives

It was all very well for Miss Alice Leone Moats, in *No Nice Girl Swears,* to tell debutantes who might be anticipating a business career that "No man can be on the make twenty-four hours a day." Despite this assurance, there are a considerable number of jealous wives in the United States who are fearful that their businessman-husbands *can* be on the make twenty-four hours a day, and who fear that when George telephones that he is detained at the office he is actually on the town with his attractive typist or secretary. The executives, too, of some firms believe that good-looking stenographers in an office lead sometimes, let us say, to lapses of attention to business on the part of the male staff, and they decree that typists in their employ should physically be on the alkaline side. Other firms make it a rule that no executive may keep a girl typist at work in his office during evenings. But still others, adhering perhaps to the poet's theory that "beauty can do no wrong," employ only the most toothsome-looking, well-dressed young typists they can find, and let the quips fall where they may when they return home to their wives.

The Typewriter and the Typist Triumph

While the moral debates about typists continued, more and more girls prepared themselves to be stenographers, more and more typewriters were bought, and the machine itself moved through many mechanical changes. It continued, however, to be looked upon by many people as a smart-aleck form of affectation on the part of men who owned one—a pretense to literary authorship or professionalism—while others felt that to receive a typed letter was a reflection upon their ability to read. "A short while ago," says Emily Post, "it was considered the height of rudeness to write personal letters to friends on a typewriter. . . . But in the present day, when most people themselves use a typewriter, this objection no longer holds true. . . . A typewritten letter is not only proper but to be preferred in all letter writing of length. . . ."

The typewriter, nonetheless, made its way and the time soon came when the only obstacle to its spread was the lack of competent typists. These were quickly provided by the opening of training schools which are the forerunners of today's business schools, and, as the typewriter opened up new work worlds for women, thousands of other women followed in their paths. By 1900, two hundred and six women out of every thousand in the population over the age of sixteen were gainfully employed in business and the services.

Catalog Typewriters

Typewriters are tucked away in a modest corner of a page of the 1905 catalog. The star of the machines offered was "The Chicago Typewriter. . . . It has 32 keys, which print 90 different characters . . . is fitted with a steel type wheel. These type wheels are interchangeable, and . . . can be changed not only as to style of letter, but also from one language to another, and to the medical and mathematical wheels. Our special price . . . $35.00."

A Pocket Portable

Sears presented in 1905 a portable typewriter so small and so ingeniously contrived that it could be folded and carried in the pocket. This triumph of invention was called "Coffman's

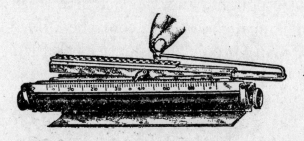

The Machine that Turned Many an Honest Man into an Author

Pocket Typewriter. An ingenious writing machine, 7½ inches long, ½ inch wide and ¾ inch thick. Thoroughly practical, writes 78 characters. . . . Can be folded up and carried in the pocket. It is endorsed and used by traveling men, doctors, lawyers, ministers, etc. Used in restaurants in printing bills of fare. Teachers, students and ministers will find this machine very helpful in preparing examination papers, making weekly announcements, etc. . . . Weight, packed for shipment, 18 ounces. Price . . . $3.90."

Typewriters Ten Years Later

The war-swollen catalog of 1915 devotes one page to the Harris Visible Typewriter and mentions no other kind or brand. We are told that "The Harris Visible Typewriter has been used exclusively in our big Chicago store for several years. The typewritten letters you receive from us are nearly always written on the Harris. If you will visit us you can see hundreds of Harris Typewriters being used to address envelopes, fill in cards . . . make carbon copies, and in fact for every purpose to which a typewriter is adapted."

If the fact that Sears itself used the Harris did not convince the skeptical customer of its quality, the catalog was prepared to break down his skepticism by giving him a chance to use the machine in his own home. "We Will Gladly Send You a Harris on thirty days' trial so you can test it out with your own work and in your own way. If it does not satisfy you completely you can return it to us and we will at once send back all money paid and pay all transportation charges. The Harris has held its own in competition with all the big selling $90.00 to $100.00 machines and we are sure it will please you."

Yet the price of the Harris in 1915 was but little more than that of the Chicago in 1905. It sold for $44.50 as against $35 for the machine of ten years ago.

By 1915, thousands of girls were tapping typewriters in the United States, and other thousands were preparing for typing careers, either to take the places of those who were retired by marriage or old age, or in response to the demands of business that seemed to grow in almost geometrical progression. In hundreds of schools and in homes throughout the nation, girls were learning how to take shorthand dictation and operate typewriters. It would have struck them as absurdly funny had they been told that in 1881 it was feared that the delicate female constitution would break under the rigors of a six-month training course in stenography. For this group, the catalog offered among its "Home Study

Books For Self-Education," three volumes for the aspiring business girl:

> *Boyd's Shorthand Instructor.* . . . Easily learned in one month.
> *The Diagram Short Line to Typewriting.* Self instruction on touch typewriting. . . .
> *Course in Touch Typewriting.* The most modern scientific method, very fully explained and easy to learn, with model business letters on real letterheads, in two colors. . . .

Every Man His Own Typist

The first portable typewriter to attain a market of considerable dimensions appeared in 1912. Small, light, compact, it can be carried by a child and used by anybody who can use his fingers with any degree of facility. Hundreds of thousands are now used by high-school and college students, ministers, lecturers, traveling men, and individuals who find it easier to write letters on the portable typewriter than to use the pen. On ships, trains, and even in airplanes, one hears the tap-tapping of portable machines, but soon this sound will vanish. Noisy America, becoming more sensitive to noise, has invented the noiseless typewriter and reduced to silence both the portable and the standard-size machines.

In 1935, portable typewriters had become so popular that the catalog devoted a full page to them. It featured the Underwood and Remington Noiseless. "So Quiet They Whisper. Typing That Can't Disturb Your Thoughts! . . . Type anywhere with a Noiseless. . . . You won't disturb others in the same room . . . you won't keep the household awake. Light enough to carry easily . . . that's why the portable is the most practical of all machines. . . . Price $67.50."

Underwood standard-size typewriters are introduced to the catalog reader in the following words:

"MORE THAN HALF OFF THE MANUFACTURER'S ORIGINAL PRICE.

"Here's the Underwood You Get From Sears!

"Underwood sturdiness—you've heard of it—you've wanted to own this big substantial machine that costs over $100 when it's new! We've completely rebuilt it in one of the greatest rebuilding plants in the country—and we are selling it as low as $39.95! To put it in brand new shape for you, we did more than recondition it; we actually stripped it to the base, even putting hidden parts in order. . . ."

Sears also rebuilt other famous-brand typewriters: the Remington, L. C. Smith, and Royal; sold typewriter ribbons and supplies, and, for the children of a country in which many mothers raised their daughters to be typists, offered toy typewriters.

"Yours of the Tenth Received"

In 1935, it took 15,000 workers to turn out $34,000,000 worth of typewriters, and the American machine was so efficient that it was being exported all over the world. In this country, thousands of girls in high schools and business schools were preparing to become typists. Salaries were fairly good, the work was distinctly white-collar work, and technology had not yet found a way to do away with the typist entirely or even to enable one girl to operate more than one machine at a time. At the same time, hundreds of thousands of Miss Joneses—anonymous acolytes in the temple of business—were translating pothooks into typewritten letters that form the very fabric of American business:

"Yours of the tenth at hand. We shall expect check by return mail." "Shipped GYX motor yesterday and know that it will work to your entire satisfaction." "We are not interested in any blankets at this time." "How's things out your way? For once, these guys in New York have quit belly-aching."

It was the typewriter, more than any other machine, that enabled American women to enter business in the 1880's, and sixty years later it is the typewriter, more perhaps than any other machine, that calls more women to enter business each year. The early controversy over whether men and women ought to be employed together in industry has long been settled, and the girl typist is now an indispensable part of American business. In million-windowed New York and in sleepy prairie towns, the business day begins with: "Miss Jones take a letter," and ends with: "Mr. Brown, will you sign the mail?"

CROP control and birth control—these mark the amazing economic and social transformation of rural America that has occurred within the past few years. Voluntary sterility on the land and voluntary sterility of the human body—this is the change that has come to the once crop-teeming and population-teeming America. The catalog's customers now accept the listing of birth-control devices without lifting an eyelid in disapproval; more than that, they buy more and more contraceptives, and, as their demand grows, the catalog's pages keep pace with the demand. Contraception has come not only to urban America but also to rural and small-town America, and it has apparently come to stay.

Yet the catalog deals with a great group of men and women who might be expected to regard contraceptives as the devil's invention, and those who sell them, as the devil's agents on earth. Farmers and small-town dwellers make up the larger part of this group, and it was their kind on this continent who made fornication a crime by law and once punished adultery with death. It is they who stood firmly and still stand uncertainly for the prohibition of liquor; who continue to condemn dancing and card playing as sinful; who are churchgoers of every manner of persuasion, from mild liberalism to last-ditch fundamentalism, and who in general represent the last stand of puritanism and the old guard of conservatism. Members of this group in the South shook their heads in pious doubt and shocked unbelief when the Department of Agriculture ordered them in 1933 to plow up one third of a cotton crop that was rapidly approaching fruition. This was "agin God," because it was destroying life or preventing life from coming to maturity. And a Southern planter wise in the ways of his people told Mr. Henry Wallace, Secretary of Agriculture, that they would accept crop prevention without a murmur but not crop destruction, for the one was birth control—the prevention of life *ab initio*—while the other was abortion, or the destruction of life in being, and therefore sinful. Even the mules of the cotton fields were shocked—mules, as any plantation Negro will testify, have sensitive souls—and had to be lashed severely in order to make them turn aside from the ordained turnrow and plow up cotton.

Thousands of farmers and their wives who daily thumb the Bible and regard every word of it as divinely inspired must believe that it is man's duty to multiply his kind. When, therefore, rural groups embrace contraception almost as fervently as the metropolitan groups, when fertile rural America abandons its natural fertility for the voluntary sterility of birth control, it does no violence to truth to say that it marks one of the greatest—if not the greatest—moral transformations of our times.

It is not necessary for proof of the spread of birth control to resort to statistics gathered by social agencies, business, or the Bureau of the Census; the catalog's pages are filled with convincing evidence of the widespread use of contraceptives among country people. And the practice of birth control spread with great rapidity. The 1925 catalog does not mention contraceptive devices at all, but the 1935 catalog contains a whole page devoted to what are called "feminine hygiene needs," while the 1939 catalog emblazons this headline above two pages of contraceptives: "Avoid Embarrassment . . . Order Feminine Hygiene Needs by Mail from Sears."

Yet at least half the states of the Union treat the subject of birth control as part of the general provision against obscenity and lewdness, and forbid by statute the circulation both of information about birth control and contraceptive

devices. The *use,* however, of birth-control apparatus is forbidden only by the state of Connecticut, the other states concluding that to enforce the law it would be necessary to put
a policeman under millions of beds, and while this would
solve the problem of unemployment it might put something
of a strain on the right of privacy. The result is that in most
states contraceptive devices are illegal, and they are, therefore, bootlegged, opening the door to quacks of every kind
and forcing the consumer to get the best article available,
just as he used to buy the best Scotch he could get in the days
of prohibition. The whole traffic is given the appearance of
legal respectability by putting birth-control devices on the
market allegedly for use in preventing disease or for purposes of "feminine hygiene." Thus the demands of everybody, including the law, are satisfied.

The Mississippi statute is typical of those on the books of
many states. It punishes:

"Every person who shall expose for sale, loan, or distribution, any instrument or article, or any drug or medicine
for the prevention of conception . . . or shall write, print,
distribute, or exhibit any card, circular, pamphlet, advertisement, or notice of any kind, stating when, where, how, or of
whom such article or medicine can be obtained . . . or purchased or who manufactures . . . same."

The legislators of Mississippi, moreover, with the lofty
purpose in mind of legislating a becoming modesty into farm
animals (or their owners) passed a law under which a fine
of $25 may be imposed against any person "who shall keep
a stallion or jack . . . in public view of an enclosure bordering on a public highway or nearer thereto than one hundred
yards."

In addition to the state laws, we have the Federal law of
1873 which is still in force, under which the transportation
of contraceptive information or materials by mail is punish-
able with a fine of $5,000 and imprisonment for five years.
Yet, throughout the states, contraceptive devices are openly
sold in drugstores; boxes and bottles of them are piled up on

counters and in shop windows as though they were talcum powder, and almost everywhere in the country the simplest form of contraceptive agent may be obtained in hotels and gasoline filling stations merely by dropping a coin in the slot of a vending machine. Laws or no laws, contraception has come to America.

Sainte-Beuve and Anthony Comstock

Although contraception had long been known to man, it may be said that for the Western World in general it is a nineteenth-century concept which came to full flower in the twentieth century. It spread rapidly from the Old World to the New, despite hostility, prosecution, and persecution. The tale may be told chronologically:

1803: The second edition of Malthus's *Essay on Population* emphasizes the need of prudential checks and late marriage to limit the birth rate.

1821: James Mill writes in England: "The grand practical problem therefore is to find a means of limiting the number of births."

1830: Robert Dale Owen, in New York, advocates scientific and hygienic practice of contraception.

1831: The birth rate begins to decline in France because of artificial contraception.

1842: Bishop Bouvier in the little French town of Le Mans warns Rome that his parishioners are practicing contraception and its classification among the deadly sins is stultifying the confessional and harming the Church. The Curia Sacra Poenitentiaria replies that the confessor need not inquire into individual usage unless his opinion is asked.

1848: The scene shifts again to America. This time, John Humphrey Noyes, head of the Oneida Community at Oneida, New York, writes in his first annual report: "We are not opposed to procreation. But we are opposed to involuntary procreation. We are opposed to excessive and, of course, oppressive procreation, which is almost universal. We are opposed to random procreation. . . . We are in favor of intelligent, well-ordered procreation."

1848: The New York *Herald,* in the same issues which denounce the books of Dickens as immoral, carries advertisements of abortifacients written in the manner of grape-juice advertising during prohibition—that is, "if the lid is left open, the grape juice will not retain its purity but will ferment." The *Herald*'s pill advertisements say they "must not be used during pregnancy as they are certain to produce miscarriage during that period."

1873: Largely through the efforts of Anthony Comstock, Congress passes a statute barring from the mails information and devices concerning contraception, even when sent by the medical profession, and declaring such information illegal and obscene. Ralph Waldo Emerson, on the other hand, says "If government knew how, I should like to see it check, not multiply the population."

1878: The first birth-control clinic in the world is opened in Amsterdam, Holland.

1900: Scientific birth control is endorsed by Dr. Abraham Jacobi in *The Journal of the American Medical Association.*

1904: An article in *The Independent* quotes a physician as follows: "As a rule, the second child is an accident, the third is a misfortune, and the fourth a tragedy. I cannot recall in all my practice a woman who wished for or sought to have a family of five or six."

1906: At Chicago, Moses Harman, editor of *Lucifer,* is condemned at the age of seventy-five to hard labor in Leavenworth Prison for writing an article on birth control.

1912: Sir James Barr endorses hygienic prevention of pregnancy in an address to the British Medical Association.

1914: Margaret Sanger, in New York, issues the first number of *The Woman Rebel.* It is barred from the mails, and the phrase "birth control" is coined to express the purpose of her campaign. She is indicted under the Federal statute prohibiting the dissemination through the mails of birth-control information, and a group of English writers, including H. G. Wells and Arnold Bennett, protest to President Wilson against her prosecution.

1916: The Federal case against Mrs. Sanger is dropped and the first American birth-control clinic is opened in Brooklyn, New York. It results in the arrest of Margaret Sanger and Ethel Byrne. Mrs. Byrne goes on a hunger strike in prison and is released by Governor Whitman after eleven days in jail, while others are arrested for distributing birth-control information. But the movement spreads, and birth-control clinics are soon opened in New York, San Francisco, Cleveland, Boston, and Minneapolis.

1921: The First American Birth-Control Conference is held in New York at the Hotel Plaza and Town Hall. The public meeting in Town Hall is prohibited by the police, and Mrs. Sanger and Miss Mary Windsor are arrested and released.

1922: Birth-control conferences are held in Pennsylvania and Ohio. Mrs. Sanger, touring the world on behalf of birth control, organizes leagues in Honolulu, Peking, and Tokyo.

1929: P. J. Ward of the National Catholic Welfare Conference writes in *The New Republic*: "The Catholic Church teaches that the artificial prevention of conception by chemical, mechanical or other means, is intrinsically evil. The Church does not forbid the limitation of families, under all or any conditions. It does not require child bearing without regard to the health of the mother, or to the family income. It simply teaches that if a limit is placed on the number of children brought into the world, it must be done through abstinence and continence." Catholic spokesmen have made it clear on many occasions that they approve of the restriction of sexual relations to those periods of the month when conception is least likely to occur—that is, if limitation of families is sought—and that the use of any other contraceptive method is "unnatural" and consequently sinful.

1936: The United States Circuit Court of Appeals, in the notable case, *United States of America v. One Package Con-*

taining 120, more or less, Rubber Pessaries to Prevent Conception, practically nullifies the Comstock Federal statute so far as the medical profession is concerned.

1937: The American Medical Association comes out in favor of birth control under medical supervision—thirty-seven years after the advocacy of such action by Dr. Jacobi.

1938: North Carolina, a state with a large rural population, becomes the first state in the Union to establish state-sponsored birth-control clinics. No village in the entire state is more than fifty miles from such a clinic. With less than three per cent of the nation's population, this Southern state has thirteen per cent of the country's birth-control clinics.

But long ago in France, Sainte-Beuve, meditating on contraception, had expressed that fear of it that sometimes haunts sensitive minds everywhere: "How many poets are lost tonight to France."

Birth Control on the Farm

The farm or small-town woman (or man) of 1935 who was in search of contraceptives found a whole page of them in the catalog for that year. Gentility and the need for circumventing the law dictated, however, that they should not be plainly labeled contraceptives but should be called "feminine hygiene needs." Under this general heading, the catalog lists, first of all, a group of vaginal sprays and douches, followed by a long list of contraceptive suppositories, liquids, and jellies. Among them are:

> Liberties—"small greaseless inserts"
> Orthygynol—"an antiseptic vaginal jelly"
> Improvo Douche Powder
> Lysol
> Zonite suppositories
> H. W. Warner's Vaginal Creme

As the knowledge of contraception spread outward from the cities until it penetrated every village and town in the United States, a public eager for birth control bought contraceptives of every kind and description, so that a market with annual sales estimated at $250,000,000 was quickly built. Here, as in the case of patent medicines, the field was soon filled with quacks, fakers, and charlatans selling drugs and devices that at best are harmless and inefficacious, and at worst are harmful and useless. The demand is great, the profits enormous, and the public is ignorant and without protection. Reputable and honest manufacturers are also in this field, but the public has no way in which to distinguish their products from those of the charlatans.

The Unknown Consequences of Contraception

We may take it for granted that birth control is a central fact of life for millions of Americans, although a fact ignored or frowned upon by the laws of the United States and of many of the states. We may also take it for granted that knowledge of birth-control methods will spread to larger and larger groups of the nation, but the ultimate consequences, social and economic, cannot yet be predicted with any degree of accuracy. It may be argued, for example, that the automobile and contraceptive knowledge are among the great social revolutionary agents of our times, enabling men and women to break down age-old taboos against pre-nuptial sexual relations on the part of women. The automobile, because it affords escape from prying eyes; contraceptive knowledge, because it lessens the fear of the consequences of sexual relations in the form of disease or a child born out of wedlock. This is a phenomenon whose effects, whatever they may be, extend to all America. There are other consequences of birth control that relate directly to the farm and indirectly to the whole country.

Rural birth rates are higher than the birth rates for any other major population group, and rural areas are now the source of the nation's net increase in population. (Once, it is said, Frederick the Great stood at the window of his Potsdam palace staring outward into the darkness of a night of iron cold. He turned finally to his courtiers and remarked,

"This night will bring many soldiers to Prussia.") But who are the people in these areas that contribute to the increase? They are, in general, that large section of our people who through ignorance or poverty are either unaware of contraceptive devices or are unable to buy them.

"Birth rates are highest among the half of the farmers who accounted for only 10 to 11 percent of commercial production. This group had lower cash incomes; in general, occupied poorer land, and employed fewer products of science and invention. Their children by and large, have fewer educational opportunities and more reason to leave their homes and communities to seek employment elsewhere." *

If, then, the increase of population among this group is socially undesirable for the country and works misery upon the parents and children most intimately concerned, and if the laws and customs of the country forbid the spreading of contraceptive knowledge among this group and the making available to them of contraceptive devices, it follows that the country is conspiring to increase precisely that part of the population whose increase it most deplores. The studies of the Milbank Memorial Fund made in 1934 show that the poorest families have the greatest number of children. As of 1932 it appeared that:

(a) There were 129 births for each thousand married women between the ages of 15 and 44 in the white-collar class.

(b) Among skilled workers the rate was 150.

(c) Among unskilled workers the rate was 184.

(d) The rate of increase in families without employed workers during 1932 was 48 per cent higher than in those whose breadwinner was employed.

(e) Families receiving relief were having 53 per cent more births than families who were self-sustaining.

At the same time, it must be noted that the birth rate for the United States has been falling for a long time:

*Henry Pratt Fairchild, in *Harper's Magazine,* May, 1938.

In 1875, the rate was 37 children per thousand people a year.

In 1912, the rate was 26 children per thousand people a year.

In 1935, the rate was 17 children per thousand people a year.

What proportion of the decline may be attributed to the practice of contraception is unknown, but there can be little doubt that it is now an important factor in the decrease of the birth rate. The Milbank Fund has shown that it is highly effective in cities, and there is no reason to believe that it is not equally effective when practiced by equally intelligent citizens in rural and small-town America. The Fund made a study of the number of pregnancies among a group of city women habitually using contraceptives and another group among whom contraceptives had not been used. The authors of the study summarized their findings as follows: *

> We can therefore conclude that in all durations of married life and for first, as well as for later pregnancies, the pregnancy rate of this group of women is significantly reduced by their use of contraceptives. . . . These data simply show that for a given exposure to the risk of conception about one-fourth as many pregnancies were observed when contraceptives were used as would be expected if no contraceptives were used.
>
> In this limited sense contraception was about 75 percent effective in preventing pregnancy. However, since these women as a group exhibited a high degree of fertility, and an expressed interest in limiting their families, they may have practiced conception with unusual diligence. Such diligence would tend to make the ratio of effectiveness higher than we should expect to find in the general population.

* Regina K. Stix and Frank W. Notestein: "Effectiveness of Birth Control, a Study of Contraceptive Practice in a Selected Group of New York Women," Milbank Memorial Fund, Quart. Bull., 12 (1934) 57-68

Contraception Changing the Catalog

Contraceptives are now available to everybody in the population who has knowledge of them and the small amount of money necessary to buy them. The increase of population in both rural and urban areas is coming from the most depressed groups in those areas, and the birth rate of the entire country is slowing down.

The use of contraceptives and the decline of the rural birth rate are indicative of the changes that have come into American rural life and attitudes since the turn of the century. We are moving and moving fast; toward what, no man knows. Children who were once an economic asset on the farm in the age of handicrafts may be, as often as not, an economic liability in the age of machines. When a prospective Negro share cropper says nowadays to a Southern cotton farmer, "Boss, I has eight head er chillun," the farmer is no longer impressed. Machines now do much of the work on the farm formerly done by hand. And signs are not lacking that great groups of the population in the future will look to the government rather than to their children to support them in their old age.

Agriculture is no longer the dominant occupation of Americans. There is no assurance that the farm child will have a place on the farm when he grows up; the pattern of rural life is thereby broken, and the farmer becomes concerned with circumventing his own fertility. Country folk, moreover, now demand a higher standard of living, and, where such a standard is impossible for a large family, parents keep the family small by contraception and assure a relatively high standard for a few children. This, too, is an age of wars, revolutions, unemployment, general insecurity, and disorganization, unfavorable to the creating of large families, and, since the North Dakota wheatgrower is as well aware of the state of the world as the Chicago banker, he sells the future short by producing fewer children.

It is impossible to evaluate the social, economic, and political changes that will be wrought in America in the second half of the twentieth century as the result of the constantly falling birth rate. It is quite possible, however, to determine the merchandise trends that will follow from the decline and to foresee their effect on the catalog. Inasmuch as the day will soon come when there will be more older people than younger people in the population, the type, kind, and character of goods offered by the catalog will be more in keeping with the demands of older people. The qualities of style and novelty will give way to those of comfort, utility, durability, warmth or coolness, and economy.

The demand will be for more armchairs and fewer layettes; more walking sticks and fewer tennis rackets; more house slippers and fewer dancing slippers; more woolen underwear and less silk underwear; more lounging clothes and fewer sports clothes.

The catalog now reflects in its pages the demands of the people for contraceptives. Later—and inevitably—its pages will reflect the changes that its contraceptives have helped to bring about.

12 · SAVE THE SURFACE AND YOU SAVE ALL

WOMAN'S search for physical beauty seems almost as old as historical woman, and the authorities are filled with references to the use of perfumes and unguents by women throughout the ages, including those two famous girls, Cleopatra and the Queen of Sheba. The quest was once confined, however, to the small number of women who constituted the nobility and the smart demimondaine who had the time, the money, and pressing need for preserving or accentuating their beauty. Even in modern times, the search for beauty on the part of practically all women did not begin until the twentieth century, when it was proclaimed that the genii of the drugstore could somewhat repair the omissions of the genes.

There is a sharp distinction between the beauty methods of the latter part of the nineteenth century in America and those pursued in the twentieth century. During the former period, women were told that beauty proceeded from within and could not be superimposed upon the body from without; in the latter period, women accepted the doctrine that the paint industry projects in its advertising: save the surface and you save all.

In the 1860's, *Godey's Lady's Book* laid emphasis on manner and expression rather than on the attempted improvement of physical appearance by artificial means. "Be amiable and wear a pleasing expression," it said. "Be graceful and modest in your ways; an erect carriage is also of the utmost importance to the good appearance of females." Women were told, too, "it matters not what is done to the outside so long as all is not well within," and purifying draughts were urged upon those burdened with "blotches and pimples."

If the eyes were not bright, the remedy was not to be found in a drugstore nostrum; it was "to splash the neck, chest, back, and face with cold water." If the hair looked dull and rough, "it should be brushed well with oil, well rubbed into the scalp." The hundred brushes every night and morning was the nineteenth-century recipe for keeping the hair beautiful.

In short, the beauty advice of that century was, when tendered to "good" women, more of a lecture on health and modest amiable behavior than on so-called beauty treatments. The general theme was simple: keep yourself in good condition and you will be attractive. *Godey's Lady's Book,* which was read not only by women of fashion but also by simple housewives, contains no instructions on how to "paint" or any mention of artificial aids to beauty. Today whole issues of some magazines and large sections of others are devoted to this subject alone and are greedily read by anxious housewives everywhere. *Godey's* contented itself with giving the simple suggestions already enumerated, and exhorting women on the value of neatness and the necessity for concealing their curlpapers lest they lose their husband's love.

This does not mean, however, that certain daring ladies—usually exalted leaders of fashion—did not risk the condemnation of their contemporaries by "painting." In 1897, *Eve's Glossary* published *The Guide-book of a Mondaine,* by the Marquise de Fontenoy (whose real name was Marguerite de Godart, Comtesse du Planty et de Sourdis, née Cunlifee-Owen), for the edification of American women. She writes:

A great many society women have adopted the custom of "making up," . . . or painting their faces. . . . It is a mystery to me why women of the world . . . insist on plastering their skins with . . . paints and powders, which . . . deceive nobody and . . . give any woman an appearance of doubtful respectability.

As women are credited with desiring to please the opposite sex, it would seemingly follow that the latter must admire what is commonly called "paint." This is an egregious mistake, for I have always found that men jeer at painted women—not in their presence of course—and seriously object to *maquillage* where their wives, sisters or daughters are concerned. How could it be otherwise?

Do those who redden their cheeks with *rouge,* darken their eyes, and cover their complexion with chalk, verily believe that they will call back the semblance of youth promised them by cosmetic concoctions? Or by constant contemplation of their own artificiality have they become blind to the spectacle they present to the world? It has been charitably alleged that the increase in "painted ladies" is the fault of fashion, the complexions of whose votaries would, but for artificial aid, appear hopelessly washed out by contrast with the brilliant hues of their garments. But as the *rouge* and *blanc de perle* are only too painfully apparent on the wearers of many a white or black gown, the blame cannot consistently be laid at the door of fashion.

Despite the strictures and laments of the Marquise, it appears, however, that at the very moment she was writing the ladies were clamoring ever more loudly for madder rouges and more alluring perfumes. She continues:

No one who has any idea of modern social life can deny that the use of all the adventitious aids to the toilet which have been condemned since the days of Jezebel— paint, powder, enamel, hair-dye, and every other kind of "beautifier"—is enormously on the increase in society. They seem to have attractions for all ages. No longer are girls proud of those skins which have made the name of the American Beauty famous in all parts of the habitable globe. The competition for admiration has become so keen that public attention must be arrested at all costs. The débutante sees with the keen eye of feminine criticism—that visual sense which it is not possible to deceive when the object of its study is another woman's appearance—that the "smart" young married women who are the most surrounded by crowds of admirers—are those who owe the most to the aid above-mentioned; and poor tender little rosebuds that they are, bedaub their clear, fresh, young skins with red, white and blue—very patriotic colors to be sure, but which look far more in place on the silken folds of Uncle Sam's flag than on the cheeks of his daughters.

The Marquise now presents that argument against the use of cosmetics which, as in the case of woman's adornment generally, has always failed—the moral argument.

"Making-up," she concludes, "except when it is done in a very discreet and thoroughly artistic fashion, stamps the most honest woman at least as 'fast,' and this ought certainly be sufficient to deter the fair sex from indulgence in so unladylike a practice. A painted, or worse, an enamelled face [enameled faces were common among the great ladies of the Edwardian period, including the late Queen Alexandra of England, and were produced by applying a mask of white liquid which hardened on the face] loses its individual expression; for the artificial complexion constrains one to avoid any passing emotion. Tears would destroy it, smiles or hearty laughter would crack it, and as to blushes—if *fin-de-siècle* women still blush—these delicate waves of color, so becoming to the feminine countenance, are invisible under a thick crust of *blanc de perle* and *rouge*."

These railings against the use of cosmetics were, of course, useless, but before taking leave of the Marquise de Fontenoy, it is interesting to observe her blasts directed against gentlemen of fashion in the so-called gay nineties:

"There has been of late years," she writes in *Eve's Glossary,* "much talk about the 'mannish' woman, but it is well to remember that she is closely rivalled by the womanish or 'ladylike' man. . . . Many of the toilet shops in New York would have to put up their shutters if deprived of their male customers. Paint, powder, perfumes, dyes, irons for waving and curling their exquisite mustaches, which, by the by, must be dyed to the latest tint of reddish brown, scented sachets to fasten inside their coats . . . all these and many other items of toilet trickery form part of the indispensable 'get-up' of our modern society man."

Morals and Manners Meringue

It is an interesting commentary on the manners and morals of the United States in the latter part of the nineteenth century that, while a woman who "painted" was condemned as an abandoned woman, the New York *Herald* could through its columns act as an accoucheur of love. Such advertisements as these crowded the personal columns of this newspaper during the 1870's and 1880's:

> Fifth Avenue Stage, Thursday Up from Niblos. Will the lady who noticed gentleman with fur cap exchange cards? Address with confidence, Zachary, *Herald* office.

> WILL THE STOUTEST OF THE THREE LADIES who rode down to Fulton ferry in a Fifth Avenue stage yesterday afternoon send her address to Romeo, *Herald* office?

> BROADWAY AND FOURTEENTH STREET CAR THURSDAY EVENING. . . . Gentleman gave seat to lady, afterward waved handkerchief corner Twenty-seventh Street and Broadway, which was returned, desires an interview. Address Eugene, *Herald* office.

> CENTRAL PARK IMPOSSIBLE TODAY. Appoint interview for Saturday or Sunday. Wear red rose.

More than twenty years later, Henry T. Finck, in his *Romantic Love and Personal Beauty* (1902), expressed the prevailing opinion on the use of rouge:

> It is needless to say that women who paint their faces put themselves on a level with savages; for they show thereby that they prefer hideous opaque daubs to the charm of translucent facial tints. Masculine protestation, combined with masculine amorous preference for pure complexions, has at last succeeded in banishing paint from the boudoir of the most refined ladies; and this, combined with compulsory vaccination for smallpox, accounts for the increasing number of fine complexions in the world.

And in the same volume, in which the author condemns the use of rouge by women, he gives instructions on "How to Kiss."

> Kissing comes by instinct, and yet it is an art which few understand properly. A lover should not hold his bride by the ears in kissing her, as appears to have been customary at Scotch weddings of the last century. A more graceful way, and quite as effective in preventing the bride from "getting away," is to put your right arm around her neck, your fingers under her chin, raise the chin, then gently but firmly press your lips on hers. After a few repetitions, she will find out it doesn't hurt, and become as gentle as a lamb.

In the instances, then, of the *Herald*'s advertisements and the laments of the pure in heart over the use of rouge by women, and in the instructions on how to kiss, we have the full flowering of nineteenth-century hypocrisy. We may now consider the use of rouges and cosmetics among the nation-wide group who were (and are) Sears' mail-order customers and, as the story unfolds, we shall see again how the daring acts of one generation become the commonplaces of the next.

The Cosmetiques of 1905

Some curious snobbery seems always to be associated with the sale of toilet preparations in the United States, and even the earthy catalog succumbs, in 1905, to the temptation of calling cosmetics "cosmetiques." The same tendency appears today in the advertisements of national advertisers in which perfumes are always *parfums,* odors are *odeurs,* and bottles are *flacons.* Such terms presumably connote the French origin of the goods offered and titillate the consumer's vanity with the implication that she understands the language of fashion—French.

In recent years, such organizations as the Consumer's Union have come into being whose purpose it is to analyze and test various products for the protection of the consumer against adulteration, misbranding, and other frauds. Yet the catalog is frankness itself when it introduces the reader to its perfumery section with these words: "We can truthfully say that there is hardly another line of goods in which so much adulteration and substitution is practiced as in perfumery." It adds that Sears imports its own perfumes in bulk from France and bottles them in Chicago, thereby preventing adulteration.

In 1905, the catalog offers no so-called standard brands; the odors most in demand are simple flower odors, and the prices are very low, ranging from twenty to thirty cents an ounce. The favorite odors were:

HYACINTH	SHANDON BELLS
TUBEROSE	SWEET CLOVER
CRAB APPLE	YLANG YLANG
VIOLET	NEW MOWN HAY
ROSE GERANIUM	JOCKEY CLUB
WHITE HELIOTROPE	WILD ROSE

Typical of the perfumes offered was "Our Special Violette France Perfume, put up in magnificent 2-ounce cut glass stoppered bottle, for only 60 cents. . . . Contain's society's latest, most exclusive odor. People of fashion and all those usually referred to as 'swell' people prefer Violette France. . . . With a touch of this sweet, elegant and dainty perfume you can make the most simple as well as the most stylish and fascinating toilet complete. Its odor is often recognized as the perfume of gentility and good breeding."

Toilet Waters

In its introduction to Sears' toilet waters, the catalog makes a statement which must have enraged the patriotic toilet-goods makers of the United States; a statement which years later was confirmed by one of the Federal government's unemotional and nonparochial fact-finding bodies, the United States Tariff Commission. The catalog says:

"RECOGNIZING THE FRENCH TOILET PREPARATIONS as the standard and in many cases far superior to the preparations of like kind manufactured in any other country, the United States not excepted, we have at all times carried a very extensive line of French toilet preparations. . . ."

Many years later the Tariff Commission, conscious of the fact that the French had developed a superior technique of making perfumery and had perfected it through centuries of experience, said of perfumes imported into the United States:

"Imports are principally from France, where growing of flowers and plants for oils is an old and highly developed industry. French products also have prestige and their perfumers are leaders in this industry."

The catalog stood then on firm ground in extolling the

A White-Lily-Face-Wash User

virtues of French perfumes, but offering French toilet waters in the catalog was another story. Only a few are listed, and they are not French but American concoctions selling at from five to seven cents an ounce, including that once firmly established favorite, Florida Water. The catalog reserves its greatest amount of space and its most earnest sales arguments for preparations such as OUR WHITE LILY FACE WASH, forty cents per bottle; asks the rhetorical question, "Do You Want To Be Beautiful?" and by implication assures ladies who answer in the affirmative that Our White Lily will work the desired transformation.

One half of a page is given to Floral Massage Cream. The virtues of the massage are lyrically described for the benefit of hard-working housewives and farm women who had curried many a horse and rubbed the sore leg of many a cow, but had never themselves felt the soothing hand of the masseur:

"HAVE YOU EVER TRIED FACE MASSAGE? Do you know that massaging the face is now considered a function which no progressive lady omits in order to produce and preserve that healthy glow, that pink of complexion which makes the beautiful features more beautiful, and adds to irregular ones attractions, the effect of which is really remarkable. . . . It is not surprising that the foremost professional massageurs will use nothing else in their work but Floral Massage Cream, which can be found in every fashionable massage parlor. . . ."

Painted Women in Rural America

In the United States, the masses tend to ape the classes (or, now, Hollywood), in the fields of dress, clothes, and even household furnishings. National advertisers, conscious of this fact, therefore make us privy to the contents of Mrs. Vanderbilt's bedroom distinguished by a Simmons bed; Mr. Pyne of the Princeton Pynes tells us in a paid advertisement that he uses a certain brand of toothpaste, and everybody who is anybody in the feminine world, from the late Queen of Rumania to the latest ornament of café society, has testified to the beauty-procuring qualities of Pond's cold cream. *Ergo:* what is good enough for our betters is the best thing for us.

As we have seen, it was women of fashion who were the American pioneers in the use of rouge toward the end of the nineteenth century, and so far had their influence and example spread, even in the preradio era, that, by 1905, rouge in limited quantities was demanded and used by simple housewives throughout the country. Thus the catalog listed:

"ROUGE DE THEATRE. This is positively the best, giving a natural and lifelike glow. . . ."And here follows a recommendation extraordinary for the times. To say, in 1905, that rouge, a then morally dubious product, is being used by the theatrical profession, a then morally dubious profession, is the equivalent of recommending a bed today because it is the kind used in some bawdyhouse. Yet the catalog states that its Rouge de Theatre "is considered by the theatrical profession the only satisfactory rouge, and used by them almost exclusively owing to the fine distributive qualities which it possesses so that it can never be noticed or detected."

Brunette Today and Blonde Tomorrow

Woman's prerogative of changing the shade of her hair at will was exercised as well in 1905 as in latter days when the country was dazzled by thousands of peroxide blondes. The 1905 catalog offered a bleach that would turn a brunette into a blonde.

"BLONDINE. The Famous Hair Bleach. . . . A preparation that will gradually turn the hair from any color to a beautiful blonde color. . . ."

And for gentlemen and ladies who desired to dye hair or mustaches, the requisite agent was available in "The Perfect Combination Hair Dye. . . . A really perfect dye for dyeing the hair, mustache, or whiskers, quickly, all shades of brown or deep black."

Soap Without Wonders

The catalog lists a whole page of soaps, including such old favorites as Colgate's Cashmere Bouquet, Pears', Cuticura, and many kinds of Castile bars. But the copy does not promise for any of these soaps that their use will:

(*a*) Remove body odor.

(*b*) Procure a rich husband for a girl, or a well-paid position as the head of a foundry for a man.

(*c*) Make a woman beautiful, cultured, and a wit.

(*d*) Act as an aphrodisiac at fifty yards' distance.

It was merely claimed for soap that it would, as in the words of the Negro song, "surely wash you clean." The renascence of wonder in advertising was yet to dawn on America.

Armed to the Teeth

Four out of five might have had it in 1905, but, if they did, Sears said nothing about it in the catalog's listing of dentifrices. The copywriter who described these articles seems to have been innocent of the dread fact dug up by advertising agencies in later years that the purpose of the human mouth in nature's scheme is to serve as a protected reservation for wild germ life. He did not seem to know that, even as he wrote, pyorrhea was secretly gnawing at the gums of four out of five people in the country; that halitosis was keeping thousands of girls in the unhappy condition of being "always a bridesmaid but never a bride," and preventing many a young man from dominating the directors' meetings of United States Steel. Nor did he see even the brighter side of things: "the million dollar smile," "the smile that wins," and similar bits of magic which then languished in the imaginations of boys who would become the copywriters of the 1920's. The time would come when they would arm women to the teeth in the struggle of life and love, but in 1905, Sears' tooth pastes and powders were distinguished from those that later came on the market by two drab factors: they were low in price, some kinds selling for four cents, and it was not promised for them that they could do more than cleanse the teeth.

Toothbrushes were then also only simple devices for brushing teeth; "science" had not yet taken hold of them and converted them into extraordinary curative agents, but apparently, by way of compensation, they were cheap. The Prophylactic toothbrush, for example, sold for twenty cents in 1905, and we shall observe how, years later, the patriotic company who manufactures it, sought to protect the United States against the invasion of cheap toothbrushes made by the wily Japanese, doubtless in an effort to undermine the morals of the West.

Paean to Beauty

The 1910 catalog leaves far behind the nineteenth-century conception that beauty is to be cultivated from within, and preaches the twentieth-century creed that it may be superimposed from without. In five short years, the catalog has passed from self-conscious timidity about cosmetics to a bold, assured position so strong that it ventures a long lecture on beauty. And this means simply that American women on the farm and in the small towns were beginning to reach for the bottles that would beautify. The catalog's paean to beauty begins with a ringing call to arms—at that time, naturally, the husband's:

"WOMEN! BE BEAUTIFUL
LET US SHOW YOU THE WAY
It Is Simple When You Use the Best Beauty Products."

And then completely unperturbed by philosophical or esthetic doubts, and with the obvious purpose of assuring the ladies that to be beautiful is not necessarily to be sinful, Sears' copywriter asks and answers the question:

"WHAT IS BEAUTY? Beauty is one of the greatest blessings that heaven has bestowed upon woman. Let no woman be ashamed of her love for the beautiful, for beauty is adorable, be it in landscape, picture, bird, flower or woman. God would never have filled this world so full of beauty if it were wrong to admire it. Where beauty is of such infinite variety and form, let no woman despair of obtaining it in some degree. Among those we meet there are very few who are hopelessly homely."

This is an enormously comforting statement of faith, because, if beauty is good enough for God, it is good enough for folks living in Iowa. Furthermore, where there is so much of it, every woman has a chance to grab some of it for her own private use. Since the number of those who are "hopelessly homely" is small, it may be presumed, they hide in the old barn where the copywriter cannot meet them.

Having then laid down a general doctrine of beauty, the catalog deserts the lilies of esthetics for the harsh business of life. "A complexion," it tells us, "is admirable when it pleases, like a beauteous flower." But never an instrument of art for art's sake, it points out that (a) a good complexion is handy in getting your man, and (b) in keeping him.

"When A Man Marries, Nine Times Out Of Ten He Chooses The Girl Who Is Careful About Her Personal Appearance, The Girl With The Pretty Complexion." But what about the girl with the ugly complexion? She is doomed to be an old maid.

"You can't blame men for not being attracted to women whose faces are disfigured with pimples, blotches, blackheads, or other unnecessary blemishes. . . . Order some of Mrs. Graham's beauty products and start today."

This world, it appears, is a harsh world for women. Once Mrs. Graham, Sears' beauty specialist, has removed every pimple that is a stumbling block on the road to marriage, and the maid has become a matron, may she relax and enjoy a few blemishes in peace? She may not. Why?

"Because You Are Married Is No Excuse For Neglecting Your Personal Appearance.

" 'Don't care' women make unhappy homes. If you would like the admiration of your husband, children, and friends be even more particular than you were in 'courting days.' . . . Take care of your complexion . . . a skin free from blackheads, pimples, freckles, and wrinkles will make you attractive. . . . Always keep Kosmeo cream in the house to retain and improve your beauty. . . ."

A glance at the world outside the catalog shows that Sears,

in delivering these lectures on beauty and prescribing beauty nostrums, was keeping in tune with the world of fashion. In the same year (1910) that the catalog published its paean to beauty, Mrs. Hubbard's Salon was opened on Fifth Avenue in New York. She published an "Essay on Beauty" with a curriculum of treatments that makes Elizabeth Arden look like a sorority mother telling the girls what to put on their faces before they go to chapel. Mrs. Hubbard's preparations were called Grecian, and included all kinds of muscle oils, powders, rouges, and face enamels. It was still the fashion, however, to strive for a natural effect in the use of rouges, and the Grecian Lip-Pencil was advertised as "imparting a natural color"—precisely the color that no woman now expects or wants a lipstick to impart.

Nonetheless, even at this time, the cheeks of nice young girls were supposed to be "innocent of artifice save nature's own," and the most that was permitted them was a little surreptitious powdering with cornstarch, while great numbers of respectable middle-class women continued to shun "making-up" until the delirious days of the World War period.

After the War Is Over

Long before the 1925 catalog appeared, American girls had abandoned their corsets, rolled their stockings, shortened their skirts, painted their faces and lips, and shocked their elders. (In time the elders would shock their children, but that is another story.) And the War had its effects on perfumes and cosmetics just as it had on almost every department of human behavior.

Thousands of American soldiers in France sent home hundreds of thousands of parcels containing French perfumes and powders, many of which were relatively unknown to the American masses because of their high prices. But as the gifts of soldiers they came in duty-free, and once women had scented the perfumes of France and used the face powders of Paris, they began to demand them thereafter, regardless of price. Thus the catalog of 1925 lists Coty's face powder and rouges and Coty's perfumes. The price of the perfumes in 1925 was $5.79 for two ounces, as compared with two ounces of perfume in 1905 for fifty cents. Subsequently, the French, who are no fools, proceeded on the sound theory that "American ladies like to pay much money for perfume," and began to sell their extracts here in great quantities for as much as thirty dollars an ounce. High-priced perfumes—and according to the testimony of expert French perfume chemists, few of them cost more than seventy-five cents an ounce to manufacture—enjoyed a great success here, both because they represented conspicuous waste in the Veblen sense and because they afforded the women who bought them the intoxicating pleasure of believing that they were not available to women of lesser means. But they were wrong. The millions of women of lesser means demanded precisely the perfumes that were being bought by the rich: Caron's Nuit de Noël, Chanel's No. 5, and Guerlain's Shalimar. But they could not buy them bottled at from $12 to $30 a bottle. Whereupon thousands of stores opened the bottles and sold these perfumes by the dram or fractions of a dram, at an expenditure of fifty cents or a dollar. So the working girl could use these perfumes being worn by the women they read about in the society columns of the newspapers.

The War made another contribution to the American woman in search of physical beauty—a contribution born of pain and suffering. Modern guns made gargoyles of the faces of thousands of men on the battlefields, but plastic surgeons miraculously restored them. Women quickly took advantage of the superior techniques worked out amid blood and pain in war hospitals and, shortly after the War, resorted in great numbers to surgeons to have their noses snipped, clipped, and otherwise reshaped; their faces "lifted"; their legs straightened; their too prodigal breasts reduced. In the meantime, those soldiers whose faces were shrapnel-smashed beyond all hope of repair lay immured in hospitals where they would spend the remainder of their lives, unloved by women and unseen by men.

The Great Toothbrush War

We like to think of ourselves as the best-washed, -tubbed, and -scrubbed people on earth, and indeed it is only with respect to our alleged superior hygienic methods that we are likely to boast of our achievements. This is especially true since the birth of humility in 1929. In the light, therefore, of our sanitary achievements, it is worth while noting some phases of the great toothbrush war that was quietly waged in Washington in 1934. Hostilities began with a letter from Mr. William C. Bird, executive vice-president of the Prophylactic Brush Company, of Florence, Massachusetts, to Representative Treadway of Massachusetts. This company's toothbrush was listed in the 1905 catalog at twenty cents; by 1934 it was selling generally in drugstores at fifty cents. But dread events are in the wind and Mr. Bird warns his Congressman of them:

> It is perhaps in order at this time for me, in behalf of the Pro-Phy-Lac-Tic Brush Co., to bring to your attention how the toothbrush industry of the United States is being affected by foreign imports, mostly from Japan.
>
> We estimate that in 1933 approximately 50,000,000 toothbrushes were sold in this country. Of this amount, approximately 13,000,000 . . . were imported brushes, 95 per cent of which were from Japan. Three-fourths of the balance were made in two Massachusetts plants, namely our own, and the plant of the DuPont Viscoloid Co., at Leominster, Mass.
>
> You can, therefore, see how important it is for the welfare of Massachusetts employees that these imports be prevented. I might also add that these imported toothbrushes were landed in this country at the low cost of 1½ cents each.
>
> Perhaps the above simple facts will aid you in determining what your position should be relative to tariff matters now pending.

The facts and implications of this letter reveal that if four out of five have it they are likely to keep it.

(1) Fifty million toothbrushes were sold in 1933 to a population of about one hundred and twenty-five millions. Some persons buy six or twelve toothbrushes a year. It follows, therefore, that millions of Americans—the allegedly sanitation-mad people—do not own a toothbrush. And it is estimated that only 30 to 40 per cent of the American people ever brush their teeth at all. We are consequently a nation with a higher family ownership of automobiles—or the use of automobiles—than of toothbrushes.

(2) Dental hygiene is now taught to millions of children, and millions of dollars are annually spent by toothbrush and tooth-paste manufacturers assuring the people that the way to beauty, truth, success, culture, love, and the avoidance of pyorrhea is through brushing the teeth. Yet the majority of Americans did not brush their teeth. Why? One of the main reasons was that the price of toothbrushes was too high. When cheap brushes are available people buy them, as Mr. Bird has shown, to the extent of 13,000,000 from Japan in one year.

(3) If, then, (a) the majority of our people do not brush their teeth; if (b) brushing is hygienically valuable, and (c) more people would brush their teeth if they could afford to buy brushes, it follows (d) that the public interest is served when cheap brushes are put in the hands of the people, whether they come from Kobe, Japan, or Florence, Massachusetts.

(4) Such imports might, however, affect the profits and near monopoly of two companies making toothbrushes in this country. Mr. Bird's letter admits that his company and Du-Pont Viscoloid make 75 per cent of the toothbrushes sold in America.

(5) Finally, the United States Tariff Commission reported that Japanese toothbrushes are of a kind not produced in the United States—that is, a very cheap kind—and consequently are used by people who could not afford to buy higher-priced brushes:

Imports (from Japan) are chiefly low-priced tooth-brushes having bamboo handles, a type not produced in the United States. Some bamboo-handle toothbrushes are sold chiefly to prisons, asylums, and other public or charitable institutions; others are marketed in regular trade channels. Bone-handle toothbrushes, the next most important type imported, are produced in small quantities in the United States.

What, then, is the poor but patriotic American to do? Is he to risk pyorrhea by buying no toothbrush at all because he cannot afford to pay the price, or is he to buy a Japanese toothbrush?

Priestesses of Beauty

In the topsy-turvy world of 1939, a photograph of Elizabeth Arden standing on her head appeared in a New York fashion magazine. In the quieter world of 1910, Sears employed its own beauty specialist in the mature person of Mrs. Gervaise Graham. Her catalog clientele would have been shocked to see a photograph of Mrs. Graham standing on her head, even if she could have achieved the feat at her age. For Mrs. Graham was a grandmother, and the catalog went to some pains to assure ladies that the Sears beauty specialist was no brash young thing:

"Would you not feel certain that preparations have great merit if a woman who uses them lived and worked hard for twenty years without perceptibly aging and kept her contour girlish, her flesh firm, and maintained her beautiful, youthful complexion without wrinkles, though she is a grandmother with a grandchild 14 years of age? This is what the preparations have done for Mrs. Graham herself...."

Mrs. Graham, as her catalog photograph shows, was no beauty, but her whole life was "a beautiful ideal."

In the 1935 catalog, customers are told to tell their beauty problems to "Miss Lorraine de Barker, Sears famous beauty adviser.... She will be glad to help you with the problem of correct make-up if you will write her a description of your skin tone, and the color of your hair and eyes."

Hair Switches

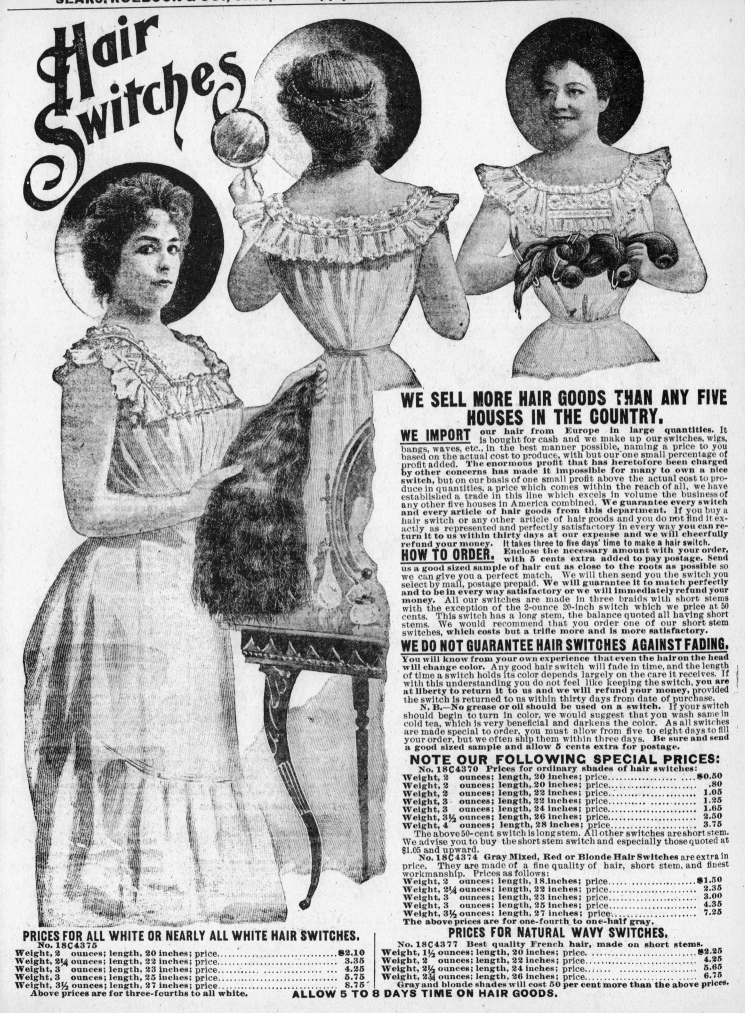

WE SELL MORE HAIR GOODS THAN ANY FIVE HOUSES IN THE COUNTRY.

WE IMPORT our hair from Europe in large quantities. It is bought for cash and we make up our switches, wigs, bangs, waves, etc., in the best manner possible, naming a price to you based on the actual cost to produce, with but our one small percentage of profit added. The enormous profit that has heretofore been charged by other concerns has made it impossible for many to own a nice switch, but on our basis of one small profit above the actual cost to produce in quantities, a price which comes within the reach of all, we have established a trade in this line which excels in volume the business of any other five houses in America combined. We guarantee every switch and every article of hair goods from this department. If you buy a hair switch or any other article of hair goods and you do not find it exactly as represented and perfectly satisfactory in every way you can return it to us within thirty days at our expense and we will cheerfully refund your money. It takes three to five days' time to make a hair switch.

HOW TO ORDER. Enclose the necessary amount with your order, with 5 cents extra added to pay postage. Send us a good sized sample of hair cut as close to the roots as possible so we can give you a perfect match. We will then send you the switch you select by mail, postage prepaid. We will guarantee it to match perfectly and to be in every way satisfactory or we will immediately refund your money. All our switches are made in three braids with short stems with the exception of the 2-ounce 20-inch switch which we price at 50 cents. This switch has a long stem, the balance quoted all having short stems. We would recommend that you order one of our short stem switches, which costs but a trifle more and is more satisfactory.

WE DO NOT GUARANTEE HAIR SWITCHES AGAINST FADING.

You will know from your own experience that even the hair on the head will change color. Any good hair switch will fade in time, and the length of time a switch holds its color depends largely on the care it receives. If with this understanding you do not feel like keeping the switch, you are at liberty to return it to us and we will refund your money, provided the switch is returned to us within thirty days from date of purchase.

N. B.—No grease or oil should be used on a switch. If your switch should begin to turn in color, we would suggest that you wash same in cold tea, which is very beneficial and darkens the color. As all switches are made special to order, you must allow from five to eight days to fill your order, but we often ship them within three days. Be sure and send a good sized sample and allow 5 cents extra for postage.

NOTE OUR FOLLOWING SPECIAL PRICES:

No. 18C4370 Prices for ordinary shades of hair switches:

Weight, 2 ounces; length, 20 inches; price			$0.50
Weight, 2 ounces; length, 20 inches; price			.80
Weight, 2 ounces; length, 22 inches; price			1.05
Weight, 3 ounces; length, 22 inches; price			1.25
Weight, 3 ounces; length, 24 inches; price			1.65
Weight, 3½ ounces; length, 26 inches; price			2.50
Weight, 4 ounces; length, 28 inches; price			3.75

The above 50-cent switch is long stem. All other switches are short stem. We advise you to buy the short stem switch and especially those quoted at $1.05 and upward.

No. 18C4374 **Gray Mixed, Red or Blonde Hair Switches** are extra in price. They are made of a fine quality of hair, short stem, and finest workmanship. Prices as follows:

Weight, 2 ounces; length, 18 inches; price			$1.50
Weight, 2¼ ounces; length, 22 inches; price			2.35
Weight, 3 ounces; length, 23 inches; price			3.00
Weight, 3 ounces; length, 25 inches; price			4.35
Weight, 3½ ounces; length, 27 inches; price			7.25

The above prices are for one-fourth to one-half gray.

PRICES FOR ALL WHITE OR NEARLY ALL WHITE HAIR SWITCHES.

No. 18C4375

Weight, 2 ounces; length, 20 inches; price			$2.10
Weight, 2¼ ounces; length, 22 inches; price			3.35
Weight, 3 ounces; length, 23 inches; price			4.25
Weight, 3 ounces; length, 25 inches; price			5.75
Weight, 3½ ounces; length, 27 inches; price			8.75

Above prices are for three-fourths to all white.

PRICES FOR NATURAL WAVY SWITCHES.

No. 18C4377 Best quality French hair, made on short stems.

Weight, 1½ ounces; length, 20 inches; price			$2.25
Weight, 2 ounces; length, 22 inches; price			4.25
Weight, 2½ ounces; length, 24 inches; price			5.65
Weight, 2¾ ounces; length, 26 inches; price			6.75

Gray and blonde shades will cost 50 per cent more than the above prices.

ALLOW 5 TO 8 DAYS TIME ON HAIR GOODS.

No. 31C3612 THIS HANDSOME WAIST is highly tailored and made of very fine French lawn. Entire front is plaited and richly trimmed with fine embroidery. Detachable crushed collar, large sleeves, plaits on cuffs. Side plaits in back from neck to waist. Color, white only. Price..............$1.48
If by mail, postage extra, 18 cents.

No. 31C3615 THIS ATTRACTIVE WAIST is made of very fine French lawn. Trimmed with very fine buttonhole effect embroidery in front and across the shoulders. Tucked and plaited in front on sleeves and cuffs. Has three clusters of tucks in back, from neck to waist. Detachable collar, trimmed with faggoting. Color, white only. Price..............$1.48
If by mail, postage extra, 18 cents.

No. 31C3618 HANDSOME WAIST. Made of fine French lawn. Entire front is side plaited and trimmed with lace insertion, and center of front is trimmed with beautiful flower design embroidery. This embroidery is very rich and attractive. Side plaits on sleeves and in back, from neck to waist. Color, white only. Price..............$1.48
If by mail, postage extra, 18 cents.

No. 31C3621 THIS ATTRACTIVE WAIST is made of very fine French lawn. Tailor made. Entire front is trimmed with small tucks and side plaits all over. Very rich design in embroidery and Mexican openwork. Large sleeve plaits from shoulder to cuffs. Detachable crushed collar. Two clusters of tucks in back from neck to waist. Color, white only. Price.....$1.75
If by mail, postage extra, 18 cents.

No. 31C3624 LADIES' WAIST. Made of fine French dotted mull. The entire front is side plaited and trimmed with beautiful design in openwork embroidery. Detachable crushed collar. Plaits in back from neck to waist. Very stylish. Color, white only. Price........$1.75
If by mail, postage extra, 18 cents.

No. 31C3627 ENTIRELY NEW STYLE TAILORED WAIST. Made of fine French lawn. Front trimmed with side plaits and buttonhole embroidery in military effect. Detachable crushed collar, large sleeves and side plaits in back from neck to waist. Color, white only. Price.....................$1.48
If by mail, postage extra, 18 cents.

No. 31C3633 THIS PRETTY WAIST is made of fine French lawn. Entire front is tucked. Yoke effect. Lace and embroidered insertion, as shown in picture. Several rows of tucks in sleeves at top and in cuffs. Detachable crushed collar finished with an embroidered buttonhole in front and caught with a white lawn tie, as shown in picture. Two clusters of tucks in back from neck to waist. Color, white only. Price....$1.75
If by mail, postage extra, 18 cents.

No. 31C3630 ELABORATELY TRIMMED WAIST. Made of fine French lawn, pointed yoke effect in front, tucked all over. Openwork embroidery all around yoke and on front piece. Side plaits from yoke down. Similar trimming on large sleeves at the cuffs. Detachable crushed collar. Side plaits in back from neck to waist. Color, white only. Price.......................$1.75
If by mail, postage extra, 18 cents.

No. 31C3636 THIS HIGHLY ATTRACTIVE WAIST is made of very fine imported French lawn, nicely tailored and richly trimmed with beautiful design in openwork embroidery. Plaits from yoke to waist. Large sleeves finished with plaits. Side plaits in back from neck to waist. Color, white only. Price..................$1.89
If by mail, postage extra, 18 cents.

No. 31C3639 THIS VERY FINE LADIES' WAIST is made of imported French lawn. The entire front is beautifully trimmed with tucks, lace insertion and elaborate embroidered designs. Detachable crushed collar, trimmed with lace. Several rows of tucks on the large sleeves and plaits at cuffs. Round yoke in back, trimmed with lace. Tucks from yoke to waist in back. Color, white only. Price........$1.98
If by mail, postage extra, 18 cents.

No. 31C3642 THIS PRETTY WAIST is made of fine imported French lawn, fancy yoke in front trimmed with lace insertion, neat embroidery and buttonhole embroidered circles. Tucks in front from yoke to waist. Entire sleeves tucked as shown in illustration. Detachable crushed collar. Three clusters of tucks in back. Color, white only. Price.....................$1.98
If by mail, postage extra, 18 cents.

No. 31C3645 THIS IS ONE OF THE MOST ATTRACTIVE WAISTS we have ever shown. It is made of good quality organdy, entire front is trimmed with tucks, lace insertion. Detachable crushed collar and a circular yoke in back. Large sleeves trimmed with lace and tucks on cuffs. Has a cape made of white lace reaching all around the back to front. Color, white only. Price....................$1.98
If by mail, postage extra, 18 cents.

No. 31C3648 THIS HIGHLY TAILORED LADIES' WAIST is made of fine imported French lawn. Entire front is made of buttonhole effect embroidery, and two plaits. Quality is the very best. Detachable crushed collar, large sleeves and neat cuffs. Side plaits in back from neck to waist. Color, white only. Price...................$1.98
If by mail, postage extra, 18 cents.

No. 31C3651 THIS HANDSOME WAIST is made of very fine imported French lawn, entire front is tucked and is beautifully trimmed with battenberg work as shown in illustration. Has detachable crushed collar, large sleeves with tucks at the cuffs. The back is tucked all over. This waist buttons in back. Colors, white or tan. State color when ordering. Price..................$2.35
If by mail, postage extra, 18 cents.

No. 31C3654 LADIES' WAIST. Made of fine imported French lawn. The entire front is trimmed with tucks, embroidered medallions, lace insertion and newest design in lapover embroidery, finished with buttons on both sides. Detachable crushed collar, large sleeves tucked at the shoulders, lace cuffs. Three clusters of tucks in back from neck to waist. Color, white only. Price....................$2.75
If by mail, postage extra, 18 cents.

Miss de Barker is evidently not a grandmother with a grandchild of fourteen years, and by 1935, both grandmother and grandchild were dipping powder and rouge out of the same compact, while the accent is on youth and heaven is in Hollywood.

In the catalog for this year, the enormously pervasive Hollywood influence is apparent in the listing of the beauty products of Max Factor of Hollywood and a photograph of "Max Factor Supervising Claudette Colbert's Make-Up." Millions of American girls no longer care what the wealthy debutantes wear at Bailey's Beach in Newport; they do care greatly what the movie stars wear at Malibu Beach.

It now takes ten pages to list Sears' toilet preparations, including such famous names as Coty, Houbigant, Yardley, Bourjois among foreign manufacturers, and Woodbury's, Hudnut, and Harriet Hubbard Ayer among domestic manufacturers. There are dozens of lipsticks in dozens of shades, including "Hawaiian, Coral, Exotic"; there are eyelash growers, eyelash curlers, eyelash cream, eyebrow pencils, and eyebrow pluckers; wrinkle creams, face creams, tissue creams, bleach creams, and all-purpose creams; deodorants and depilatories; hand lotions; wonder-working soaps; bands to hold sagging chins; dozens of hair dyes and tonics; manicure kits; cream rouges and cake rouges; perfumes and perfume atomizers; powder puffs and endless arrays of face powders, including such exotica as "Kissproof powder."

We are now as remote from nineteenth-century America in the field of manners and morals as from seventeenth-century America. Consider the changes in cosmetics chronologically:

(1) In 1820, an English traveler in the United States reports that "Several gentlemen have gone so far as to assure me that when a woman rouges, it is considered in this country *prima facie* evidence that her character is frail."

(2) In 1859, an etiquette book utters a warning: "Avoid saying anything to ladies (while travelling) with showy attire, with painted faces, and white kid gloves. Such persons

have frequently the assurance to try to be very.sociable with a woman who is travelling without a companion. Keep aloof from them always . . . have little to say to a woman whose face is painted, who wears a profusion of long curls about her neck, who has a meretricious expression of eye."

(3) In 1910, a young girl of fifteen who had bright red cheeks was often followed down the streets of Evanston, Illinois, by children chanting: "Her mother lets her pai-ent, her mother lets her pai-ent."

(4) In 1935, thousands of high-school girls used rouge and lipstick as commonly as they used soap and water.

13 · FASHION PARADE

A FEW years ago when Paul Poiret, the Paris dressmaker, was at the height of his fame, he visited and lectured in America. Going home, he wrote about his experiences in this (to him) fabulous country: *

At Chickasha, in Oklahoma, I spoke to 3,000 girls and I said to them:

"It is not from fashion journals that you will learn how to be beautiful. What have you got to do with fashion? Don't bother yourself with it, and simply wear what becomes you. Look at yourselves in the mirror. Observe those tones that enhance the brilliance of your own colors, and those that dim them. Adopt those which are favorable to you, and if blue suits you, don't think you ought to wear green because green is the fashion."

After I had developed this theme for an hour, I asked my audience if anyone had a question to ask.

Little folded papers were passed up to me, on which were written the following questions:

"What will be the fashionable nuance this winter?" Or:

"What color should one wear for a wedding?"

They had understood nothing, or perhaps heard nothing.

To repair this mishap, the girls' Directress gave permission to the pupils of the senior class to parade past me in order to learn from my own mouth which was the color that each ought to adopt. Thus, I saw file by in front of me 1,500 virgins, into whose eyes I stared to discover the color of their irises, and I had to say immediately, like a seer, the tone that suited them. I said: "Blue, green, garnet," and the young ladies withdrew content.

* *King of Fashion*, autobiography of **Paul Poiret**.

You must know that I was fee'd a thousand dollars a lecture. You will agree that it was not too much.

Later M. Poiret, as though unnerved by gazing into the eyes of 1,500 virgins of Chickasha in Oklahoma, and thinking perhaps of all the women of the Western world and all their clothes, put to himself the mournful query: "What can one do against a donkey or a woman's wish?"

He might have asked himself a question equally strange. What is there in the air of America that causes a small Oklahoma town to pay a famous French dressmaker a fee of one thousand dollars for a lecture on fashion to high-school girls? And this in a land where, as Henry Adams lamented, "an American Virgin would never dare command; an American Venus would never exist."

Other questions about fashion clamor for answer. What is fashion? Who originates it? Do women dress to attract men or to arouse the envy and admiration of other women? Do they dress richly out of response to fashion or out of the desire for "conspicuous waste"? Do women, for that matter, have any sense of fashion at all or are they merely puppets of dressmakers? In an attempt to answer these questions, anthropologists, philosophers, economists, laymen (usually bewildered husbands), and lady buyers have delved and probed. At one extreme, Santayana, in terms of reason, concluded that fashion is "that margin of irresponsible variation in manners and thoughts which among a people artificially civilized may easily be larger than the solid core." At the other extreme, working from physical measurements, the anthropologist A. L. Kroeber, using as a test case the length and width of skirts in full-dress toilette from 1844 to 1919, concluded that styles move in cycles of great length, and because of their time duration are obviously beyond the influence of any one dressmaker or designer. This conclusion is confirmed by the observations of the fashion reporter, Lois Long, who wrote in *The New Yorker* (October, 1939) as follows:

Fashion is by no means the whimsical, wayward, contrary little minx she would have you believe. It is the same as the legend of woman's "mystery," this fable that fashions change like a zephyr between one night-club opening and the next. Canny propagandists keep the fable alive by creating daily fireworks about a significant collar, about a "new" color. (Turkey red becomes a new color if it's rechristened "vermilion *au jus*"), or about a piece of costume jewelry which is as smart this year as it was vulgar last. It all serves its purpose in keeping the public confused and restless, and manages to conceal the fact that fundamentals change slowly.

Sears, however, is no debating society. It does not care why women wear clothes at all or even a particular kind of clothing. It is completely indifferent to Marxian interpretations of lace-trimmed silk panties; Veblen's theories of clothes and the leisure class leave it cold; Westermarck's concepts of wearing apparel and sexual modesty have never yet gone into the making of a catalog page. When Sears looks at women's clothes in a manufacturer's sample room, it asks two questions with the cash register, and not Benedetto Croce, in mind: Will they sell? At what price?

Every Woman Her Own Chanel

Once upon a time in the United States—from colonial days until some years after the Civil War—nearly every woman was her own Chanel. She bought a length of yard goods, a dress pattern (when they became available), lace, embroidery, trimmings, thread, buttons, and wrought in her own way and according to her own whim by hand or on a sewing machine. It was expected of every woman that she be able to sew; it was indispensable to most women that they should sew. There is no place in a pioneer society for women who cannot ply a needle. And for more than 150 years, American women, save for a tiny minority who bought ready-made imported clothes, fabricated their own clothing or had it made by a dressmaker. During these times, the sale of yard goods and of sewing notions expanded and dress-pattern manufacturers grew rich. But shortly after the Civil War came the changes that were to revolutionize women's wearing apparel. First of all, women both North and South began to go to work in offices and factories. These women had little time to make their own clothes and soon lost their skill with the needle or the machine. Second, large numbers of tailors poured into the country in the 1870's and 1880's and began to produce women's clothes cheaply on a mass-production basis. Third, women found, or thought they found, that these clothes were cheaper than those they could make by hand at home. Fourth, as the automobile, the motion pictures, and the radio broke down isolation, women became increasingly sensitive to fashion and changes of fashion. They demanded what was being worn by Greta Garbo in Hollywood or by Chanel's mannequins at Longchamp. The names of great Paris dressmakers became household words in Calico Rock, Arkansas, and the girls of the town wanted imitations of the dresses wrought on the faraway Rue de la Paix by Monteil or Schiaparelli instead of originals created by Miss Annie Wickham of South Main Extended who used to sew for the best people in the county. The girls got what they wanted; dress-goods sections of stores withered; ready-to-wear departments increased almost without end.

Between 1920 and 1930, apprentices to dressmakers decreased by 2,200; dressmakers (in the home) by 75,000, and women's tailors by 10,000.*

So far has the once almost universal ability to sew declined that, in New York, wealthy women of the conservative set demonstrate abortively once a year that they still have the skill of the needle, anciently taught women of all classes. Mary Van Rennselaer Thayer reports this social phenomenon in *Vogue,* March, 1939:

> Most of The Old Guard cherish the happy illusion that they sew beautifully—and, in Lent, every one polishes up her gold thimble, ready to stitch for the poor. Sewing

* Source: Machinery and Allied Products Institute.

classes are arranged by smart parishioners of the leading churches. . . . A ten-dollar fee covers the cost of materials and, while the members sew or make a polite pretence of sewing, there is some sort of entertainment, usually of a musical nature, to distract them. . . . At the end of the session, each lady takes her sewing home. The garments are returned with a flourish the following week—many of them having been ripped apart and re-sewn by more expert maids.

What Every Woman Knows

The pages that follow record in part some of the struggles of American women to wear the kind of clothes they choose to wear when they want to wear them, despite the outcries of prudish men and women. If clamorous voices were raised against the right of women to wear the clothes of their choice, quiet voices were sometimes raised in behalf of that right. The following quotation from *In Maiden Meditation,* by E.V.A. (a woman), published in Chicago in 1894, is interesting not only because it reveals a rising point of view among American women forty years ago, but because the doctrine she preaches has now become accepted feminine gospel among all classes of women in this country:

> . . . A woman never appears to better advantage than when she is conscious of looking her best. . . . Each woman should know that the very folds of her drapery, each frill of lace, are expressions of the inner self. . . . Is it not, then the part of wisdom in women to stand for hours before the mirror in adorning this 'perishable body,' to twist carefully the silken tresses, to guard tenderly the single cuticle that divides youth and gaiety from wrinkled old age and loneliness, to puzzle their minds lest they should fail to calculate properly the angle at which to wear their bonnets or the symmetrical ratio of a tie-back?
>
> It is exquisitely absurd to tell a girl that beauty is of no value, dress of no use. Her whole prospect and happiness in life may depend upon a new gown or a becoming bonnet; and if she has five grains of common-sense she will find out that love itself will hardly survive a winter hat worn after Easter.

Men may pretend to like intellectual women, but they can pardon anything better than an ill-fitting gown. Better a thousand times be frivolous than badly dressed. . . .

The Rise of Ready-to-Wear

The development of machine-made clothing for the masses of American women had its origin in the miseries of Europe, and particularly Russia, where thousands of Jews—many of them tailors—found life intolerable under persecution and fled to the United States. It was wrought by pale, undersized, poverty-stricken east-European tailors in New York who toiled incredible hours in dark, stinking workshop-apartments, or in fire-dangerous, dirty lofts, working with the fury and persistence of a people intent not only upon earning a living but also upon demonstrating their right to live.

The story of their early efforts is vividly told by Levinsky, the cloak-and-suit manufacturer hero of Abraham Cahan's novel, *The Rise of David Levinsky*. The hero of the book is speaking:

The time I speak of, the late 80's and the early 90's, is connected with an important and interesting chapter in the history of the American cloak business. Hitherto in the control of German Jews, it was now beginning to pass into the hands of their Russian co-religionists, the change being effected under peculiar conditions that were destined to lead to a stupendous development of the industry. If the average American woman is to-day dressed infinitely better than she was a quarter of a century ago, and if she is now easily the best-dressed average woman in the world, the fact is due, in a large measure, to the change I refer to. . . .

The German manufacturers were the pioneers of the industry in America. It was a new industry, in fact, scarcely twenty years old. Formerly, and as late as the 70's, women's cloaks and jackets were little known in the United States. Shawls were worn by the masses. What few cloaks were seen were on women of means and fashion and were imported from Germany. But the demand grew. So, gradually, some German-American merchants and an American shawl firm bethought themselves of manufacturing these garments at home. The industry progressed, the new-born great Russian immigration—a child of the massacres of 1881 and 1882—bringing the needed army of tailors for it.

Levinsky gives us, too, a glimpse of the hard conditions under which cheap clothing for the masses was turned out by the toiling poor:

> . . . Things brightened up at our factory. I ordered an additional sewing-machine of the instalment agent and hired two operators—poor fellows who were willing to work fourteen or fifteen hours a day for twelve dollars a week. (The union had again been revived, but it was weak, and my employees did not belong to it.) As for myself, I toiled at my machine literally day and night, snatching two or three hours' sleep at dawn, with some bundles of cut goods or half-finished cloaks for a bed. Chaikin spent every night, from 7 to 2, with me, cutting the goods and doing the better part of the other work. Mrs. Chaikin, too, lent a hand. Leaving Maxie in care of her mother, she would spend several hours a day in the factory, finishing the cloaks.

How rapidly the manufacture of women's clothing grew is shown vividly by a comparison of two periods separated by twenty years:

Value of output in 1909. . . . .$ 384,000,000
Population (1910 census)   92,000,000

Value of output in 1929. . . . .$1,678,000,000
Population (1930 census)   123,000,000

Parasols

In 1939, when Queen Elizabeth of England visited Washington during its notoriously hot summer, fashion writers made much of the fact that she used a parasol and commented with surprise upon how the parasol accentuated the femininity of its royal wearer. But in 1905, in America, parasols were almost always part of woman's standard equipment, and the catalog lists nearly a page of them. They were frilly and sometimes silly but they were feminine and the women of that day, conscious of the allure of femininity, wore them everywhere in spring and summer.

The choice of parasols offered by the catalog was wide. One might have chosen "Ladies' Plaid Coaching Parasol, made of very pretty China silk, with a puff of the same material on top. Mounted on fancy, assorted sticks to contrast with parasol. Plaids will be very stylish this season. . . . Comes in either red or blue plaids. . . . Price $1.05."

The extreme of elegance and of price was "No. 18C1952 Ladies' Parasol. This is a very stylish affair, made of good quality China silk, trimmed with two generous ruffles of fancy, figured border, sewing silk veiling, closely shirred. A very rich and attractive parasol. Large puff of same material on top. Mounted on fancy designed sticks, large cord and tassel. . . . Can be ordered in black or white. Price $3.25."

Death of the Parasol

The parasol, which had maintained a long vogue in American fashion since the Civil War, came to its end in 1915. Its obituary is written in the catalog for that year which contains only this notice: "Parasols, toy."

An Old American Custom

The shirtwaist seems to be one of America's few original contributions to women's wearing apparel. It began in 1890 and by 1905 the wearing of shirtwaists was already an old American custom. Throughout its entire regime, haughty Paris dressmakers sniffed at it and pronounced the death sentence upon it three times before 1909, whereupon American women sniffed back and bought more shirtwaists, until by 1910 New York's production alone was valued at $60,-000,000.

Responsive to the enormous demand for shirtwaists, the 1905 catalog lists and illustrates no less than 150 models,

ranging from one made of lawn and selling for 39¢ to the taffeta-silk waist at $6.95. Almost every fabric known to domestic and foreign textile mills was used in the making of this garment, including some that survive now only in museums: lawn, organdy, sateen, sicilian, albatross, nun's veiling, linen, flannel, velvet, and silk, while great quantities of laces and embroidery for their manufacture were imported from France, Belgium, Switzerland, and Germany.

The shirtwaist was sometimes almost as elaborate as a baroque church. For example:

"This pretty waist is made entirely of fine Jap silk. The entire front is heavily tucked and trimmed with lace insertions and embroidered medallions. Yoke effect. Very large sleeves richly trimmed with lace insertion and embroidered medallions. Fancy cuffs tucked all around. Buttons in back only. Very stylish and up to date. Price $3.75."

The height of fashion as late as 1912—nearly twenty-five years after its first appearance—the shirtwaist began to decline in popularity shortly before the World War, and had completely disappeared by the end of 1919.

Rainy Daisies

The short or shorter skirt, like the shirtwaist with which it was worn, is also an American innovation in women's wearing apparel, and here again American women were guilty of *lèse-majesté* against the Paris dressmakers. The so-called walking skirt, short enough so as not to drag along the ground, came into fashion in the 1890's over the usual protest of conservatives. In New York, women organized The Rainy Day Club to promote the use of short skirts—that is, skirts two or three inches above the ground—and for their troubles were denounced for immorality and called "Rainy Daisies." By 1905, the catalog is featuring "Ladies' Walking Skirts" of which it says:

". . . These garments are made expressly for convenience, and are also known as the Health Skirt. Very appropriate garment for rainy day, street wear or shopping and always looks neat. *To get the benefit of the walking skirt, be sure to order one that will clear the ground by about two inches."*

A few years later, women's skirts were to be the subject of sermons in churches, of resolutions in clubs, of suits in courts, and of editorials in newspapers and magazines.

Wrappers and Silk Jackets

Wrappers—one of the most grotesquely ugly and unflattering garments ever worn by women—were part of the wardrobe of nearly every woman in 1905. Really a kind of house dress, wrappers were unshapely, ungainly, elaborate, and drab. The cheapest model made of calico—a once widely used fabric that has now almost disappeared—sold for 49¢. This is a description of the de luxe model at $1.49:

"Ladies' Wrapper. Made of fast colored percale. This is the well known and well advertised 'corset fitting' easily adjusted, well made wrapper. Is neatly tailored, front trimmed with same material and neatly stitched. New sleeves with belt, wide flounce around the bottom. Cuffs are made with button and buttonholes and can be easily opened. Fancy yoke in front and back. Inside vest made of cambric, is made with draw strings and can be easily adjusted. Colors, black, blue, gray or red with fancy figures."

Fashionable ladies in 1905 wore short silk jackets or long silk coats which sold (in the catalog) for prices ranging from $3.75 to $12.75, and at that time it was the ambition of thousands of women to own one of these garments. Generally they were made of taffeta silk which shone and rustled, thus somewhat relieving the somberness of their funereal black. Close-buttoned around the throat, ground length, elaborate, and almost stifling in warm weather, nothing could have been more uncomfortable or less well adapted for the use to which long silk coats were put: traveling and street wear. Yet indomitable women wore and liked such a garment as this:

"Ladies' Coat. Made of very fine taffeta silk. Very dressy and appropriate for traveling or the street. Made with collarless effect, leg-of-mutton sleeves, fancy turnover cuffs.

Double breasted front, half tight fitted back, finished with pockets in front. Box plaits. Similar trimming around the neck and on back of jacket. . . . Very high grade in every respect."

Plush coats and jackets had been fashionable since 1895, and they still linger on ten years later in the catalog of 1905. This material which matched much of the furniture of the times was made up into plain plush jackets or highly embroidered garments trimmed with imitation bear, thus making a woman who wore one with an ostrich-plume hat a dead ringer for Lady Hildegarden.

The Struggle of the Skirts

The struggle of the skirts began in the 1890's and continued for nearly a quarter century almost without armistice.

Shirtwaist Suit with Carpet-Sweeping Skirt

The popularity of bicycle riding at this period made it imperative to devise a costume to take the place of the then universally worn trains which were bound to become entangled in the wheels, and so the shorter skirt was made for bicycle riders. This first tentative step in shortening the skirt aroused no indignation among conservators of public morals anywhere except in Boston, but here the attack was centered upon the bicycle itself. Boston, which seems to have been enveloped in a strange darkness ever since Paul Revere's lantern went out, expressed itself through the Boston Woman's Rescue League. It said:

> Thirty percent of the unfortunates who come within the field of this organization's work, have at one time or another of their existence been bicycle riders, and therefore wheeling has a demoralizing influence on women.

Despite this warning against the bicycle as a vehicle that would take the rider to Venusberg even if she set out for Concord, Boston women continued to use bicycles and shortened skirts. This led to a remarkable discovery. If short skirts were comfortable for riding, why not for walking? Hence they were shortened again in the form of the walking skirts we have discussed, and by 1908 they no longer touched the ground.

Then, from 1909 to 1912, came the vogue for tight skirts accurately described as the "hobble" because they made walking and movement so difficult that a woman who wore one moved with the ease of a hobbled horse. Having got themselves into this dilemma, the ladies struggled to regain their new-found, but suddenly lost, freedom, and after toying with the wide-bottomed skirt and the divided skirt or harem trousers, they released their constricted legs by adopting the slit skirt and again shortening its length. Sometimes these skirts were made of thin, transparent materials which, when the wearer stood against the sun, gave the male eye a stimulating optical cocktail. These radical departures brought on the storm, and it is a mark of the poverty of imagination of reformers and of their own lewdness of thinking that, whenever women change their clothes or their customs, all that reformers can do is to compare women with prostitutes. Thus,

Mr. Edward Bok feverishly raved in a *Collier's Weekly* article of August 30, 1913, entitled "The Remedy for the Present Wave of Indecent Dressing":

> Whatever may be the opinion of the present indecent styles in women's dress . . . we know where they come from, and in view of that fact the remedy lies in the hands of every decent American woman.

Here Mr. Bok departs to blame it all on the French—an old Anglo-Saxon and American custom. To the English and the Americans, the French are irremediably a people addicted to immorality and light wines. In the 1890's, a well-known American ladies' magazine would not print a short story involving love outside the holy bonds of wedlock unless its locale was France. Mr. Bok continues:

> During the past five years . . . Paris dressmakers have . . . shown the steady degeneration of their waning art in the so-called "Paris styles" which they have sent over here. . . . No Frenchwoman of the slightest refinement wears these "styles." They are the hallmark of the French underworld that frequent the Paris boulevards. . . . As Mme. Sarah Bernhardt said after her last visit to America, it was a perfect amazement to her to see perfectly decent American women dressed like the *demi-monde* of Paris. . . . They are the creations of disordered minds of French dressmakers who have lost all sense of art and decency, have become pure commercialists, and who, laughing in their sleeves at the American woman, are . . . making damn fools of the American women.
>
> This is known to every woman of the underworld in America. As one of these recently said. "Here are a lot of girls and women who draw their skirts aside when they meet us, and yet are dressed exactly like us." A walk along Fifth Avenue verifies this statement that two classes of girls are today dressing exactly alike. A social service worker only a few days ago said that more decent girls had been approached during the last year by men in the streets of New York, under a misapprehension as to their standing, than ever before in her recollection.

What Mr. Bok did not seem to know or realize is that chic demimondaines play an important role in the world of fashion, and that their respectable sisters simply pant to ape them. If he had taken the trouble to step out into *Collier's* office and ask the typists whether they would rather resemble Cleopatra or Florence Nightingale, he might have saved much wear and tear on his spleen.

While Mr. Bok was groaning over the decline of woman, Richmond, Virginia, the capital of the Confederacy and allegedly a citadel of gallantry toward all women, including those who were human, all too human, was going into action. There in July, 1913, Mayor Ainslie and Police Chief Werner arrested a young lady named Blossom Browning for wearing a slit skirt, and took her to jail from which she was bailed by friends. Miss Browning said that her gown was the fashion, that she bought it in a local department store, and that it suited her taste. The next day she was fined $25 and ordered to leave the city.

The East and the South have now had their say about what women should wear, and the Middle West makes its contribution to the subject. *The New York Times* of August 2, 1913, carried the following dispatch from St. Paul, Minnesota:

> Asserting that the present styles in women's dresses are not fit for modest gentlewomen, and that women who refuse to wear tight skirts are obliged to do without new garments, a district board of the Federation of Women's Clubs has started a dress reform which it is proposed to make nation-wide.
>
> Next week the board will write to every manufacturer . . . of ready-made clothing for women and every manufacturer of dress patterns, making an appeal for modifications of the present styles. . . .

Two days later, Mrs. Edwin Gould "returning to New York in the private car *Dixie,* in which the Gould party has been making a tour of the West, took occasion to make some caustic comments upon the prevailing fashions in women's apparel, asserting with some asperity that women who displayed themselves in slit skirts and skirtless bathing suits were not 'ladies.' "

Soon business and the church took a hand in the controversy. At New Britain, Connecticut, reported *The New York Times* in August, 1913, "The slit skirt and hobble and diaphanous garb are things of the past among young women employed . . . by Landers, Fray & Clark, a large manufacturing concern.

"The management has issued an edict to the young women that they will be expected to garb themselves with decorum.

"The polite hint that they must change their style was conveyed by means of a note each girl found in her pay envelope yesterday, stating that all must appear for work in businesslike and modest clothes.

"Many of the young women took umbrage at the order, while others to whom the ultra modern garments did not appeal, said it was 'good enough for them.' Several hundred stenographers and clerks are affected."

A favorite theme of preachers is the denunciation of women's clothes and morals, because they afford preachers the opportunity to preach juicy sermons that titillate their congregations, while at the same time the preachers appear to be soldiers in the fight against sin. Bishop Luther Wilson, addressing the annual camp meeting at Ocean Grove, New Jersey, in September, 1913, took for his text the old stand-by of the pulpit and the stump—"Pure American Womanhood."

"The women of today," said the Bishop, "are responsible for the future of these little ones. Can any true American Woman indorse the fashions of today? Women who wear the new styles are not representative of true American womanhood. They tend to degrade the small girls who are soon to become women.

"Women in this congregation who leave here will go to the big cities and towns all over the United States. It is their moral duty to do all they can against these fashions."

One lone male voice was raised in defense of women's

clothes during this heated controversy. It was the voice of
Judge Latshaw of the Criminal Court of Kansas City, Missouri, who said:

"There is nothing immoral in the slit skirt, diaphanous
gown, or any other present form of woman's attire. Narrow
skirts and trim figures do not mean immorality, as some insist. One of the most vicious epochs of society was when hoop
skirts were worn."

This was treason enough, but not content, the Judge asked
a devastating question:

"The women of today," he continued, "have only one idea
in view—to dress in a manner that appeals to men. Well,
hasn't it always been so?"

After the War, skirts went up again and they continued
to go up until, by 1926, they were above the knees. And the
catalog's skirts followed the procession, carefully and cautiously, never leading, but never entirely out of step with the
leaders. Once more women had demonstrated that they wear
what they want when they want to wear it. And the time was
to come when the catalog would boldly say that women wear
clothes to please men.

Wear the Clothes Men Like

In 1939, the catalog says of a group of clothes illustrated
in its pages:

PICKED BY THE MEN THEY'RE WORN FOR.

"Men like women in simple, casual clothes. They vote for
dresses that don't need fussing with . . . dresses like these
that will take you from dawn to dusk superbly groomed,
beautifully at ease, and fashionably perfect."

Again: "Men don't like gaping plackets. They know there's
no excuse for them in this modern age. . . ."

This is a complete reversal of the feminine tradition of the
nineteenth and the early twentieth century in the United
States. Feminine allure was then based on the principle that
women must never admit they wished to attract the attention
of men, and must carefully conceal the fact that they did de-

sire to attract them. Their success lay in the "Oh! this is such a surprise" method when the man whom a woman had furtively been stalking for months at last proposed marriage. Under these circumstances, it could not have been advertised that women wore or desired to wear clothes that would please and attract men, for that would have let the cat out of the bag. But now that we are in an era when women may openly hunt down their men, such advertisements as the foregoing from the catalog merely confirm a practice that is universally accepted.

Romance

Once upon a time Sears was content to sell clothes and clothes alone in the catalog's pages devoted to the subject. As late as 1925, evening gowns were not to be found in the catalog, but, in 1939, they are offered and described as more than mere clothes—they are the stuff of rayon of which dreams and romance are made. In a manner reminiscent of the old days of copywriting, when a bit of flamboyance was not out of place, and in the language of the smart fashion magazines, the catalog lets go in a paean to clothes:

THIS ISN'T JUST ANOTHER SPRING . . . IN THIS ROMANTIC ERA

The curtain rises on a new era of Fashion. A romantic young figure takes the center of the stage . . . an elegant Lady who enchants us with the age-old appeal of femininity. . . .

What does the young and elegant Lady wear? She wears:

THIS YEAR'S MOST ROMANTIC GOWN

An enchanting evening gown, symbolic of all the old-world charm of this romantic era! A gown that might have graced a glamorous beauty of the court of Marie Antoinette—thrillingly dramatic with its off-the-shoulder neckline, its boned bodice accentuating a tiny waist, its full seven yards of billowing ruffles on a flaring skirt. It has been made in ethereal clouds of lustrous Rayon Net, a filmy, fragile-looking fabric, perfect choice for this ro-

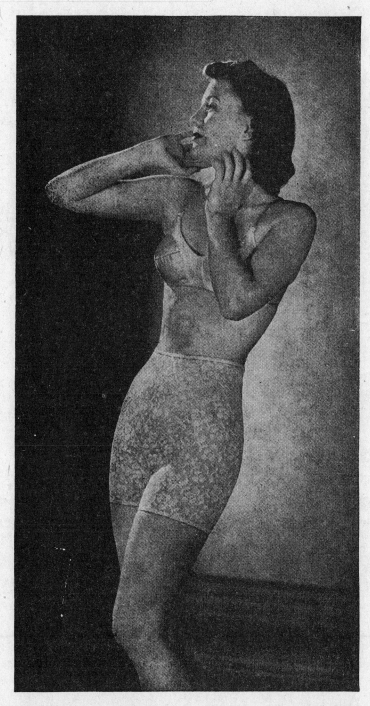

The Ideal Of Millions of Women. Also The Reason Why The Wheat Grower's Loss Is The Lettuce Farmer's Gain.

The Just A Song At Twilight Touch. Every Woman Knows That An Ounce of Wistfulness Is Worth a Ton of Wisecracks In Catching Her Man.

mantic fashion. . . . A modern picture gown, destined for the most brilliant events of the year.

This is perhaps the most purple and delirious passage ever printed in the catalog, and it was not published to please the whim of some unsung Baudelaire in Sears' advertising department. The girls out in the country and all over the country are reading fashion and motion-picture magazines in whose pages such dotty chat is commonly employed, and the catalog, therefore, to convey the impression that its clothes are just as smart as those seen in *Vogue* or *Harper's Bazaar*, gurgles and coos, even if it does make some of the old-timers around the organization sick to their honest stomachs.

It is fashionable for smart dressmakers and shops in New York to give names to their dresses as names are given to race horses and Pullmans, and, nothing daunted, the catalog does the same. Here is:

"Moonlight Sonata. You—winsome and desirable in clouds of Rayon Net, your tiny waist sashed with whispering Rayon Taffeta! . . ."

Or, if you don't care to be caught up in clouds of rayon net while rayon taffeta whispers to you, you may choose:

"Whispers in the Dark. You—pretty as a picture in a formal of Celanese Rayon Ninon agleam with rayon satin stripes. Proud puffed sleeves, softly shirred bodice slashed in a V, a gay flower. . . ."

These dresses undoubtedly have their points but the dress that is not only romance but the dream of romance is:

"Waltz Song. You—a dream of romance in a gown of rustling Moire Rayon Taffeta. A frilly little Rayon Taffeta evening hat included! Gay Nineties puffed sleeves and a sweeping skirt to float you through any dance. . . ."

One would expect that such dresses as these would cost what was called a king's ransom in the days when anybody bothered about ransoming a king, but here we have romance on a mass-production basis. "Moonlight Sonata" and "Whispers in the Dark" go for $3.98; "Waltz Song," for some reason not disclosed, may be had for only $2.98, including a "frilly little Rayon Taffeta evening hat."

Everything in the dress section of the 1939 catalog and in all America seems to have been romantic, except for a disconcerting lack of ready cash on the part of some people. Hence the catalog, abruptly interrupting its hymn to romance, drops for a moment into the language of the workaday world to say:

REMEMBER!
You Can Buy Anything at Sears on
Easy Payments.

Grandma Goes to Town

The dresses we have been describing were designed for the young, but we are now in an era when all women and most men try to look young. Grandma is young, mother is juvenile, daughter has to hold her own. Everywhere the accent is on youth, and in its golden name, women suffer tortures in beauty parlors and at the hands of plastic surgeons, diet as religiously as Moslems during Ramadan, and puff like The Old 97 as they bend their creaking backs in severe exercises. Youth worship is as potent now in America as ancestor worship in China, and the catalog of 1939, casting its eyes on dancing mothers and golfing grandmothers, says to the woman who would defy her arteries:

"Make A More Beautiful Woman Of Yourself In These Romantic Fashions Designed With A Young Point of View. . . ."

In the pioneer days, boys of twenty-one commanded Salem vessels on long and dangerous trading voyages around the world to China; girls of seventeen shouldered the heavy responsibilities of wifehood and motherhood in the wilderness. Even in 1900, a boy of eighteen was a man, and a girl of fifteen or sixteen was a woman. Now a boy often is not a man when he finishes college at twenty-four, while many girls never get over being girls. The box-office heroines of the movies are young—Shirley Temple and Deanna Durbin. There is no place in our culture for elderly actresses, unless they are content to take small character parts. The Duchess of Windsor, middle-aged ladies said gleefully in the intervals when they were not racked with envy, has proved that forty is the age at which woman is most alluring. In the drawing rooms of the land, wit, conversation, and music have given way to games that would have been played in the nursery thirty years ago. Across the fields of fox-hunting Virginia gallop fortyish women, drawing three breaths to every one taken by the horse as they try to keep pace with authentic youngsters.

Grandmas now golf, swim, play tennis, and even have bathing-beauty contests. In Worcester, Massachusetts, eleven grandmothers, improving on Walter Pitkin's formula that *Life Begins at Forty,* have organized a lifeguard swimming club with the slogan, "Life Begins at Fifty." And recently, just ahead of the great European war, a group of Battle Creek, Michigan, grandmothers returned together from Europe. Their ages ranged from sixty to seventy-three, and among them they had thirty-eight grandchildren, but this did not prevent them from "doing" Europe in six weeks, during which they went everywhere without pause from England to Finland. This throws some light, however, upon the fact that while America is filled with widows there are few widowers. It is the rare American who survives his wife.

In a country, then, where the accent is on youth and grandma is on the go, the catalog, in designing clothes "with a young point of view," is merely recognizing the phenomenon that this is the land of youth, natural or synthetic.

The Passion for Uniformity

If evidence is needed that the passion for uniformity in America is at work everywhere and affects all classes except the bottom stratum, it is to be found in the page of women's riding clothes in the 1939 catalog. The horse is vanishing from the farm but it is coming around to the front door and entering the parlor. The United States Department of Agriculture estimates that the number of horses on farms has dropped from (round numbers) 18,000,000 in 1900, to 11,000,000 in 1939. But if the catalog is to be believed, the horse that once plowed the farm is now taking the farmer's daughter out on gallops across the countryside, and she goes attired in "Kerrybrookes. Because they are smart looking and beautifully tailored by experts. . . . Because the sturdy fabrics stand hard riding and wear much longer than you would expect. . . ."

The decline of the horse on the farm and its renascence in the parlor are of recent origin. The horse went out as farm machinery came in, but it came back as the country's prosperity rose. Some genius among the *nouveaux riches* discovered that it is easier to enter the best drawing rooms of the country on a horse than to sail into them on a yacht, and, following this discovery, social climbers climbed on the best horses that money could buy and were soon leaping the social hurdles that had barred them from the social sets in which they desired to move. The cult of the horse, hitherto confined to a small group of people, rapidly became as popular and claimed as many devotees as Elk's Clubs during prohibition; horse shows were held in towns that had not had a good look at a horse since Buffalo Bill came through with his wild West show, and, finally, the girls took Horace Greeley's advice and began to go West where they put up at dude ranches and bestrode steeds whose poison fangs had been extracted. The catalog, taking this equestrian revolution in its stride, rushed into rotogravure a page of riding clothes for women. Here are to be found such horsy items as "Colorful plaid sports shirts. . . . Brand new Dude Ranch shirt in bold cowboy plaids"; jodhpurs; whipcord riding breeches; suede-leather jackets, and riding boots. What we thought were the last days of that decrepit gelding, democracy, turns out to be a fiery stallion with the farmer's daughter atop.

We have gone a long way from the time in 1837 when Donald Walker, in his *Exercises for Ladies,* said that horseback riding produces "unnatural consolidation of the bones of the lower part of the body, ensuring a frightful impediment to future functions which need not here be dwelt upon."

Death of a Woman

For many years, the catalog and dress shops advertised clothes for fat women under the euphemistic term of "stylish stouts." Nowadays if a woman is stout she cannot be stylish. Hence the stylish stout has been killed and resurrected in the

Killed by Fashion

form of "the larger woman"; a none too subtle evasion which pleases fat ladies without reducing their tonnage. These victims of glands or gluttony are offered "slenderizing styles" designed to make sweet Afton gently flow, or, in the catalog's words, "they are skilful at hiding pounds. . . . Designed to make you look slimmer than you ever thought you could!"

Where now are the pounds of the Baskervilles? Hidden beneath a slenderizing coat. "The coat hangs in slim flowing lines that turn you into a slim column of a woman." Mass production has brought to the twentieth century the sweet confusion of Anthony Munday's seventeenth-century dream:

> *Into a slumber then I fell,*
> *And fond imagination*
> *Seemed to see, but could not tell*
> *Her feature or her fashion. . . .*

What's Her Income?

A survey of the dress sections of the catalogs for thirty-five years reveals three principal tendencies aside from endless variations of detail and changes of styles:

(*a*) The accent on youth—a comparatively recent development.

(*b*) The constant tendency toward the dropping of frills and the movement toward simplicity.

(*c*) The approximation of the clothes of the middle classes in appearance, and often in materials, to those worn by the rich.

Class distinctions in dress, which were so common throughout the Western World in the sixteenth to the nineteenth centuries, were achieved not only by the use of costly materials but also through excessive ornamentation. When, however, in the nineteenth century, French esthetes discovered Japanese culture, a movement toward simplicity in both dress and household furnishings began which is now reaching its apex. Yosoburo Takekoshi, in his *Economic Aspects of the Civilization of Japan,* tells a pretty story out of Japanese lore of which the catalog's makers may not have been conscious but which has nonetheless influenced them.

In the seventeenth century, when the Tokugawa Shoguns closed Japan's doors to foreign trade because they feared that contact with vulgar, grasping Europeans would endanger the hierarchical and agrarian society of the country, merchant's wives (members of an inferior caste) were forbidden to wear the cloth of gold that could thereafter be employed only by women of the upper castes. Whereupon the lovely Nakamura Karanosuke, wife of a rich Kyoto merchant, set out to make her clothes more beautiful than ever and yet stay within the law. She called in for advice, not a dressmaker, but an artist. He suggested that she wear only black and white, and when she appeared in garments employing only these colors she looked so dignifiedly elegant that soon the great ladies of the court threw away their cloth of gold and their clothes of many colors to appear in the moving simplicity of the merchant's wife. And when Europe, particularly France, discovered cultural Japan in the nineteenth century (America was content to find a new market), it discovered also new subtleties of tone and, above all, how beauty may be achieved in dress or in house furnishings through emphasizing surface and line rather than ornamentation. Thus slowly, and through many devious turns and windings, we have arrived at a point where materials employed in clothes are simple and are simply cut, while the whole tendency of dressmaking is toward following and setting off the natural lines of the human figure instead of denying their existence or grotesquely caricaturing them.

At the same time, the machine has been a great leveler. Mr. Bok pointed out with indignation some years ago that it was becoming more difficult on the streets of New York to distinguish the prostitute from the lady, apparently on the assumption either that ladies then dressed like prostitutes or prostitutes like ladies. The point is of no importance. This is not, as Czarist Russia was, a "yellow-ticket country," and women do not wear their virtue or lack of it on their sleeves. What is important is that it is now difficult to distinguish one woman of an economic class from another as both walk down Fifth Avenue. The manicurist is as smartly dressed as the woman whose hands she manicures, and, while the customer's clothes may cost more than those of the employee, distinctions of material, tailoring, and cut are certainly not discernible at a glance to the untutored eye. The machine makes excellent imitations of the finery of the rich; silk is so cheap that millions wear it; rayon is used by all classes; with the result that within recent years there has been an extraordinary approximation toward uniformity in dress among all women, and the American woman has become the best-dressed woman in the world.

Progress toward democracy has made amazing strides in this matter of personal decoration. Formerly it was the ladies of the court who used it most; today it is the serious concern and dearest pastime of all three estates. It was the spread of the use of furs, to take but one example, to all classes (and also to all seasons) which inspired the just description of woman as America's greatest fur-bearing animal. And nowadays no one can tell, either by the quantitative or the qualitative test, whether a given person lives on Riverside Drive or East Fourth Street.*

This is a matter of great importance, even if well-fed ministers deplore our insistence on what they call "the development of the material at the expense of the spiritual"; even if lady tourists and romantic writers "oh" and "ah" over the spiritual beauty of poverty-stricken, disease-ridden Mexican and Guatemalan peasants. It has to do with the vexed question of the separation of body and spirit upon which the West has always insisted. The case for the machine and for the oneness of soul and body is stated by Dr. Charles A. Beard in *Whither Mankind*. Dr. Beard is commenting upon the article contributed to this symposium by Dr. Hu Shih, the noted scholar and present Chinese Ambassador to Washington:

> As he goes about the Far East, seeing sickness that elementary medicine could cure or prevent, starvation due to defective transportation, and appalling poverty near undeveloped resources, Dr. Hu Shih cannot look with amused indifference on well-fed persons gathered in comfortable drawing-rooms to deplore the materialism and black despair of science and the machine. Far from it. Instead of conceding that they may have some right reason on their side, he boldly denies the correctness of their terms, demonstrates the shallowness of the old antithesis between matter and spirit, turns the customary conceptions of the East and West upside down, and comes out with the firm conclusion that inventors, scientists, and producers of goods deserve the blessings of mankind as spiritual leaders, while the mumblers of mystic formulas are to be set down as slaves of circumstance, themselves fundamentally materialist in their surrender to starvation,

* Devere Allen, "Personal Decoration," *The World Tomorrow*, VIII (1925), 77.

misery, and darkness, called fate. Naturally this will be shocking, particularly to those Westerners who, pained by the hardness of the machine and baffled by the inconclusiveness of science, seek refuge in one or more of the two or three hundred varieties of religious exercises given to the world by the fruitful Orient.*

Style Show at Central High School

It is a platitude of American life that this is a fashion-mad country. All over the land, style shows are constantly being held in big towns and little with such variations in elegance, in chic, in mannequins, and in the quality of clothes displayed as derive from the greater wealth of the cities. In the cities, the shows are professional and smart; in the small towns, they are amateur and folksy; but wherever they are held, they denote the same passionate interest of women in clothing.

Hotels have found that style shows held in their dining rooms during or after luncheons bring crowds of customers; small-town churches use them for money-raising purposes in place of the old-fashioned supper or social, and local women, single or married, are glad to parade before their fellow townsmen in dresses bought or lent for the occasion by local merchants. Even the high schools now have style shows of their own. The Lynds, in *Middletown in Transition,** report one held there a few years ago:

"The following from the daily press in February, 1933, strikes a high-style note not present in 1925, and exhibits at once the momentum of clothing pressure under commercial sponsoring even at the worst of the depression, and the efforts of the high school to channel it so far as the girls were concerned into the domestic-science classes:

A style show, from which the mode of dress for Central High School's 1933 graduation exercises will be selected, will be staged Thursday . . . in the high-school auditorium. All seniors and their parents are invited to

*Charles A. Beard, *Whither Mankind,* p. 405.

attend. Sixty seniors will serve as models during the show. Displays will be made of boys' suits . . . and of girls' dresses in white and pastel colors in sports, semi-sports, and afternoon styles. Decision as to the vogue for next June's graduating class is being made early so that dresses may be made in the senior sewing classes.

The circulation of smart fashion magazines is relatively limited, but newspapers with millions of readers print thousands of fashion-chat columns annually. Sunday society sections of newspapers in cities as large as New Orleans and Memphis publish rhapsodic descriptions of clothes worn during the week by various leaders of society. Here we learn what Miss Waterrene Ethrington Sanderson wore when she played tennis at the Country Club; the details of Mrs. Williamson Williamson's gown in which she danced at the annual Fata Morgana ball of the exclusive Club de Dix Heures, and the costume favored by Miss Andrea Magdalena Jones when she "poured" at the tea given in fashionable Puyallup Place for the benefit of the starving Bulgarians. Such notices are read with avidity not only by the women concerned but also by all the working girls in town, and local merchants testify to their approval of the practice by placing more clothes advertisements in the society sections of the newspapers.

Small-town newspapers report every social gathering of women not only in terms of the names of those present but also in terms of what they wore. The following descriptions are taken from a single issue (June, 1939) of the Greenville, Mississippi (population 20,000), *Democrat-Times*:

A wedding and what was worn by the ladies present. First, the bride:

> The white marquisette bridal dress over a sheath of shining satin was designed with bodice of row on row of white silk lace. The long, full train was bordered with bands of the same lace. . . .

*R. S. & H. M. Lynd, *Middletown in Transition*, p. 171n.

*Mannish Clothes for Feminine Women. Woman Finally Comes Into
Her Own and Man's But Both Seem to Like It.*

Young Business Woman Looking For a Job from a Balcony Of The Empire State Building. Even Glue Factories Demand Well Dressed Typists.

Second, the matron of honor:

> Mrs. Howard Knowles . . . matron of honor, wore a tea-rose marquisette and lace designed along the same lines as the dress worn by the bride.

Third, the bridesmaids:

> . . . The bridesmaids wore similar dresses of starlight blue marquisette and lace.

Fourth, the flower girls:

> . . . Rosemary Arnold and Ann Uzelle . . . flower girls, wore miniature replicas of the bridesmaids' dresses.

Fifth, the mother of the bride:

> Mrs. Sharkey, mother of the bride, wore orchid chiffon with corsage of flowers in pastel shades.

Sixth, the mother of the bridegroom:

> Mrs. Burke, mother of the bridegroom, wore blue lace with corsage of pink carnations.

Description of a luncheon from the same newspaper:

> Mrs. A. D. Simmons, feted Miss Mayers with a lovely luncheon.
> The hostess was attired in a gown of turquoise sharkskin. Miss Mayers was attractively dressed in a trousseau model of linen, with which she wore a corsage of yellow gladioli and water lilies, and accessories of white.

Miss Mayers, a popular bride-to-be, appears at two other luncheons reported on the same day as the foregoing. We have seen what she wore at the Simmons luncheon.

Then "Mrs. Alfred Stone honored the bride-to-be with a lovely luncheon, entertaining at the Stone home on North State Street.

"Miss Mayers was lovely, attired in a gown of aqua and

dusty rose imported linen, with which she wore a hat topped with a bouquet of real flowers in shades of aqua and dusty rose, and other accessories of matching shades."

Finally, she appears at a "charming informal party given by Mrs. T. E. Wilson. The hostess received her guests wearing a sports frock of white sheer. The honoree selected a beautiful gown of aqua and yellow spun linen, with which she wore a pretty matching corsage."

Negro newspapers of the area, following the trend, also report the clothes worn by ladies at their parties, and colored ladies, it seems, outdo the white folks by wearing not one but two costumes during the evening. Last year, a Negro newspaper in the Mississippi Delta contained the following note of local society:

"Mrs. William Henderson entertained at her home on Edison Street last night for Mrs. Cynthia Hays of Vicksburg. During card playing the honoree wore a beige sports dress, and for dancing afterwards changed into a wine transparent velvet evening gown. Delicious refreshments of mints, cocktails, and hot tamales were served."

The inevitable result of this endless outpouring of news about women's clothes is the building up of an acute clothes-consciousness on the part of all women at every economic level. The newsreels, too, carry on the good work, and every week millions of women see new clothes on the screen; Hollywood pours its great volume into the swollen flood of fashion publicity; while photographs of what's what in Paris flash continually above the ocean wastes.

Fashions move through the country, moreover, with the speed of lightning, and woe to that manufacturer or distributor who thinks that small-town women are hicks who do not know this year's styles from those of last year. Main Street, Fifth Avenue, Hollywood, and even Paris are now next-door neighbors. Once merchants could trace the peregrinations of clothing styles as they slowly moved from Fifth Avenue in New York downtown to Fourteenth Street, and to Main Street six or twelve months later. Now Main Street, Fourteenth Street, and Fifth Avenue wear the same styles almost simultaneously, with, of course, variations brought about by cost and local divergencies of taste. Copyists in the garment trade move fast,.style information moves fast, and the express moves fast, so that the merchant or manufacturer who lags behind the procession is soon out of the procession and business. The very speed of this process works a hardship upon catalog dress merchants such as Sears who are necessarily faced by a lag of four to six months between the time when their buyers select women's clothing and the time when the customers receive the catalog.

The consequences of the operation of all these processes of publicity, of speed-up of manufacture and distribution were somewhat drily noted in *Recent Social Trends,* which said that "Men's clothing is apparently more responsive to business declines than women's." Depression or no depression, women buy clothes to the utmost extent of their purchasing power, while men, in hard times, reduce their expenditures for clothing.

The catalog offers a dramatic demonstration of the enormous importance of women's clothes in the country generally and in Sears own business. In 1905, its opening pages were devoted to buggies, and in 1915, to small items of hardware selling at two, four, and six cents each, but the 1925 edition opened with women's clothing, and it has ever since occupied the premier place with constantly increasing numbers of pages allotted to it. The 1939 edition is filled with photographs of models who might have stepped out of the pages of *Vogue* or *Harper's Bazaar*. Its language is the language of Paris: "inspired by Schiaparelli," a French woman whose name is known to millions of American small-town women who do not know the name of the President of France; "the pet dress of Paris inspired this two-piece charmer. . . ."

In a statement made by Sears at the time it issued its fall and winter catalog of 1939–40, it was said that "the traditional lapse between the acceptance of new fashions in women's ready to wear, millinery, accessories, as well as home furnishings, in metropolitan centers and in the small towns and on farms apparently no longer exists."

The catalog, "which reflects changing tastes, requirements and living conditions of our customers, projects in the current edition a picture of a standard of living which would have been unthinkable as recently as two decades ago," and recognizes "a sharpened style consciousness on the part of farm women."

IN 1893, *The Chicago Tribune* published an extremely ungallant editorial. The man who wrote it must have suffered much at the hands of primping women, because the studiedly courteous tone of his editorial betrays the repressed impatience of one who had cooled his heels for long minutes in the parlors of Chicago, while the ladies of his acquaintance arranged their "rats" and distributed their "transformations" amid the hair they had not bought in stores.

"Women," said the *Tribune,* "should not occupy the dressing room indefinitely; from one-half to three-quarters of an hour. It is true that it is difficult for a woman to arrange her hair in her berth . . . but it behooves the courteous traveler of the fair sex to shorten as much as possible the time devoted to her morning toilet, postponing some of the details until later in the day or until arriving at her destination."

This was mere whistling in the wind, and it is not likely that the ladies paid much attention to the editorial even if it did appear in "the world's greatest newspaper." It is to be hoped, however, that the grumpy writer of this suggestion to women lived until that happy day when the bobbing of woman's hair shortened the time devoted to arranging it. In 1893, however, and for many years later, millions of women yearned for floor-length tresses such as those shown to an admiring and envious country by the Seven Sutherland Sisters as they toured the land exhibiting their clouds of hair and selling the preparations which they said had caused their scalps to flower with such riotous abundance.

Switches, Waves, and Bangs

When the catalog—as we have often said before—devotes a whole page to an article of commerce, it is certain that that article is in great demand. In 1905, it bestowed this accolade on:

Our 60-Cent Princess Tonic Hair Restorer

The bottle containing the tonic carries a label depicting a woman literally embowered in hair that swirls and foams from the top of her head to her hair-hidden waist. The Princess, it seems, was capable of doing anything, and the advertising copy which celebrates it begins by asking a perhaps useful but brutal question: Are You Bald? We are not told whether any of the catalog's customers admitted they had been overtaken by this direst of female afflictions, but the copywriter goes on grimly with his probing:

"Does your hair come out easily and gather on the comb and brush when you brush it?

"Does your head itch?

"Do you have dandruff or scurf and do white, dustlike particles settle on your coat collar?

"Is your hair stiff and coarse and hard to brush?

"Is your hair fading and has it turned prematurely gray?"

If the answer to any or all these questions was "yes," then the need for Princess Hair Restorer was clearly indicated. And urgently needed "if you want a head of fine, silk, glossy hair, the pride of every woman."

The Princess, we are told, at one and the same time, and for only sixty cents a bottle (money back if you are not satisfied), made two hairs grow where only one languished before, while it destroyed dandruff, removed crusts and scales, restored gray hair to its natural and youthful color, and soothed itching surfaces. In view of these accomplishments —these miracles created in Sears' own laboratory—we can sympathize with the catalog's indignant warning against amateur and shoddy dermatologists:

"Don't Send Away to a Cheap Specialist and pay

OUR 60-CENT PRINCESS TONIC HAIR RESTORER.

A WONDERFUL NEW HAIR TONIC AND PRODUCER.

No.
8C1101

Per
Bottle,
60c.

Restores the Natural Color, Preserves and Strengthens the Hair for Years, Promotes the Growth, Arrests Falling Hair, Feeds and Nourishes the Roots, Cures Dandruff and Scurf, and Allays all Scalp Irritations.

THE ONLY ABSOLUTELY EFFECTIVE, UNFAILINGLY SUCCESSFUL, PERFECTLY HARMLESS, POSITIVELY NO-DYE PREPARATION ON THE MARKET that restores gray hair to its natural and youthful color, removes crusts, scales and dandruff, soothes irritating, itching surfaces, stimulates the hair follicles, supplies the roots with energy and nourishment, renders the hair beautifully soft, and makes the hair grow.

EVERY SINGLE BOTTLE OF PRINCESS TONIC HAIR RESTORER is compounded especially in our own laboratory by our own skilled chemists, and according to the prescription of one who has made the hair and scalp, its diseases and cure, a life study.

PRINCESS TONIC HAIR RESTORER IS NOT AN EXPERIMENT, not an untried, unknown remedy, depending on enormous, glittering advertisements for sales, but it is a preparation of the very finest and most expensive ingredients, that will positively cure any case of falling hair, stimulate the growth of new hair on bald heads, cure dandruff and other diseases of the scalp.

Regular Retail Price, per bottle, **$1.00**
Our Price, per bottle, ... **.60**
Our Price, per dozen bottles, . . **6.00**
Unmailable on account of weight.

ARE YOU BALD?
Is your hair thin or falling out?
Does your hair come out easily and gather on the comb and brush when you brush it?
Does your head itch?
Do you have dandruff or scurf and do white, dust-like particles settle on your coat collar?
Is your hair stiff and coarse and hard to brush?
Is your hair fading or has it turned prematurely gray?

IF YOUR HAIR SUFFERS in any one or more of these particulars, we would urge you by all means to order a bottle of Princess Tonic Hair Restorer as a trial, for speedy relief. Use it according to directions and you will be surprised and delighted at the wonderful results. It acts direct on the tiny roots of the hair, giving them required fresh nourishment, starts quick, energetic circulation in every hair cell, tones up the scalp, freshens the pores, stops falling and sickly hair, changes thin hair to a fine heavy growth, puts new life in dormant, sluggish hair cells on bald heads, producing in a short time an absolutely new growth of hair. If your hair is fading or turning gray, one bottle of Princess Tonic Hair Restorer will give it healthy life, renew its original color and restore it to youthful profusion and beauty.

USE IT ALWAYS IF YOU WANT A HEAD OF FINE, SILKY, GLOSSY HAIR, THE PRIDE OF EVERY WOMAN.

PRINCESS TONIC HAIR RESTORER IS GOOD FOR BOTH MEN AND WOMEN.

IS EQUALLY EFFECTIVE ON MEN'S, WOMEN'S AND CHILDREN'S HAIR.

AS A CURE FOR DANDRUFF, as a tonic for thin and scanty hair, Princess Tonic Hair Restorer acts with quick and wonderful success. It removes crusts and scales, keeps the scalp clean and healthy, the roots at once respond to its vigorous action, dandruff is banished and a thick and healthy growth of hair is assured.

Princess Tonic Hair Restorer Grows Hair Like This.

FOR A TOILET ARTICLE, as a fine hair dressing, no one who takes any pride in a nice head of hair can afford to be without a bottle always on the dresser. Princess Tonic Hair Restorer is delicately perfumed, and one light application imparts a delightful, refined fragrance. Neither oils, pomades, vaseline or other greases are required with our preparation.

DON'T SEND AWAY TO A CHEAP SPECIALIST and pay $1.00, $1.50 or $2.00 a bottle for a worthless and perhaps injurious preparation. Don't be misled by catchy advertisements with baits of free trial sample bottle and fake examination offers—such people will draw you in, make you believe something awful is the matter and scare you into paying enormous prices for alleged remedies, when you can get the genuine, tried, tested Princess Tonic Hair Restorer at 60 cents a bottle, the actual cost of the ingredients and labor of bottling, with our one small profit added.

PRINCESS TONIC HAIR RESTORER IS ABSOLUTELY HARMLESS. **IT IS NOT A DYE.** It will not injure the most delicate hair, it will not stain the daintiest head dress. Princess Tonic Hair Restorer works wonders with the hair. We get letters daily from people telling how much good it has done for them. It will do the same for you. You can sell a dozen bottles at a profit to yourself in your immediate neighborhood to people who see the good it has done and the wonderful results on your hair.

ORDER A BOTTLE AT 60 CENTS which you can easily sell at $1.00, and if you do not find it all and more than we claim for it, if you do not find it is just the hair tonic you want, stimulating the growth, cleansing the scalp, stopping hair from falling out, restoring natural color, curing dandruff or promoting a new growth of hair on a bald head, return it to us at once **AND WE WILL CHEERFULLY REFUND YOUR MONEY.**

EVERY BOTTLE OF OUR GENUINE PRINCESS TONIC HAIR RESTORER IS STAMPED WITH THIS LABEL AS SHOWN IN THE ILLUSTRATION,

OUR GUARANTEE OF HIGHEST QUALITY.

This Label is your Protection. It shows that only the purest and finest ingredients are used.

YOU WILL FIND VARIOUS SO CALLED HAIR TONICS and hair restorers widely advertised in the newspapers and magazines. Some of them possess merit and others do not. Those that possess merit are sold for two and three times the price we ask for the genuine Princess Tonic Hair Restorer, and are not equal to the preparation we put out under our binding guarantee for quality. If you have any doubt as to the merit of the Princess Tonic Hair Restorer as against the preparations advertised and offered by others, we would be willing for you to order our preparation, and then send for any other preparation in the market, give both preparations a fair and honest trial, and if you do not find the Princess Tonic Hair Restorer better by far than any other hair tonic, you need only write us to this effect and we will return your money. We reproduce herewith a few of the many letters we have received from pleased customers, telling us of the good they have received from the Princess Tonic Hair Restorer.

No. 8C1101 Price, per dozen bottles, $6.00; per bottle **60c**

CURES ITCHING SCALP, FALLING AND GRAY HAIR.

Maynard, N. Y.

Sears, Roebuck & Co., Chicago, Ill.

Dear Sirs:—In regard to the Princess Tonic Hair [Restorer] I will say that it was used for itching scalp [and] hair, and also gray hair, and it cured [the]es. I think your remedy is all right.

Yours truly,

One bottle is u...
No. 8C10...

A. L. VAN HATTERS.

ONE BOTTLE OF PRINCESS TONIC HAIR RESTORER GIVES WONDERFUL RESULTS.

Sweetwater, Neb.

Sears, Roebuck & Co., Chicago, Ill.

Dear Sirs:—My wife used your Princess Tonic Hair Restorer for hair falling out, and it gave wonderful results, the hair stopped falling out and grew thicker after using one bottle of your famous Hair Restorer. We keep a bottle on hand all the time. I would recommend this Restorer to everybody who has trouble with their hair. Respectfully yours,

REV. E. HERZBERG.

THE BEST HAIR TONIC EVER USED.

Royal, Iowa.

Sears, Roebuck & Co., Chicago, Ill.

Dear Sirs:—Should you wish to know if the Princess Tonic Hair Restorer did any good towards the purpose for which it was bought, I would say that I bought it for falling hair and it stopped the trouble at once. Princess Tonic Hair Restorer is the best hair tonic I ever used.

Respectfully yours,

O. TOELLE.

WAVES, BANGS AND WIGS.

ALL WIGS, TOUPEES, WAVES, ETC., BEING MADE TO ORDER, WE ASK THREE TO TEN DAYS' TIME IN FILLING YOUR ORDER, AND

WE REQUIRE CASH IN FULL WITH ORDER ON ALL HAIR GOODS, GUARANTEEING SATISFACTION OR REFUND OF MONEY.

— BE SURE AND SEND A GOOD SIZED SAMPLE OF HAIR —

The Melba Bang.

No. 18C4378 Melba Bang. Made of the best quality naturally curly hair, with vegetable lace parting, most suitable for youthful faces and a very popular style of hair dressing.

Price....................$1.50
Gray and blonde hair..........2.50

If by mail, postage extra, 5 cents.

Parisian Bang.

No. 18C4382 Parisian Bang. Ladies who do not require large, heavy front, will find this a little gem; light and fluffy, ventilated foundation. Price...............$1.35
Gray and blonde hair.........2.00
If by mail, postage extra, 5 cents.

Alice Wave.

No. 18C4386 Alice Wave, invisible hair lace foundation; natural curly hair; 3-inch part, 12 inches from side to side. Price.......$3.25
Gray and blonde hair...........4.50

If by mail, postage extra, 6 cents.

The Pompadour.

No. 18C4390 The Pompadour. This style, unlike the old style pompadour, is very light in weight. The soft wavy hair is combed over one's own hair in which small rolls of crape hair are placed to produce a puffy effect on sides and top. Price....................$3.50
Gray and blonde hair..........5.00
If by mail, postage extra, 6 cents.

The Patent Pompadour.

No. 18C4394 The Patent Pompadour for simplicity, elegance and style is far superior to anything ever shown. It slips right on, is as dainty as a feminine heart could desire; it produces the fluffy fullness now so much in vogue and possesses none of the disagreeable qualities of the ordinary roll or pad. It is made on twisted wire, of the best long, curly hair and weighs only half an ounce. Can be worn with just the ends concealed under the lady's own hair, or may be used in place of the rolls and the wavy ends coiled in with the natural hair. Send sample of hair.
Price....................$1.50
Blonde and gray hair..........2.25
If by mail, postage extra, 6 cents.

The New Patent Dip. Pompadour.

No.18C4395 This is the latest style Pompadour, made from the best quality of human hair, to match any color hair, designed to give the new dip and rolling front effect which is the prevailing style of hair dressing. Light and wavy, at the same time giving the appearance of great fullness. Effect produced is same as shown in illustration. Send sample of hair. Price..$3.50
Gray and blonde hair..........5.00
If by mail, postage extra, 8 cents.

Ladies' Wigs—Short Hair.

Send measurement of head.

These wigs are all made of fine selected hair on ventilated open mesh foundation. Absolutely perfect in fit, having that graceful and natural appearance.

Short Curly Wig.

No. 18C4402 Ladies' Curly Dress Wig, made of natural short hair, with or without part, mounted on fine open mesh cotton foundation. Price.$10.00
Gray or blonde hair..........15.00
If by mail, postage extra, 14 cents.
No. 18C4406 Ladies' Wig. Same as above but mounted on silk foundation.
Price....................$12.00
Gray or blonde hair...........18.00
If by mail, postage extra, 8 cents.

Ladies' Wigs—Long Hair.

Can be arranged in many different ways.

No. 18C4410 Made of the best selected hair on silk foundation, 18-inch hair.
Price, $15.00
By mail, postage extra, 10 cents.
No. 18C4414 Made same as above on silk foundation, 24-inch hair.
Price, $18.00
By mail, postage extra, 10 cents.

The above prices are for ordinary shades of hair. Red, Blonde and Gray Hair cost 50 per cent more, which please add when you send order. Be sure and send sample of hair. Send measurement of head.

The Eugenia Wave.

No. 18C4398 The Eugenia Wave. This is a new and very becoming wave for middle aged and elderly ladies, made of the best quality natural curly French hair; easily dressed and cared for; 3¼-inch parting.
Price....................$4.00
Gray and blonde hair...............6.00
If by mail, postage extra, 8 cents.

'3 to 10 days' time required to fill orders on Toupees and Wigs made to order.

To measure for a Toupee or top piece, cut a piece of paper the exact size and shape of the bald spot, mark the crown and parting, enclose a lock of hair, and state if hair is to be straight or curly.

No. 18C4418 Men's Toupee, weft foundation. The weft foundation is a cotton net and weft parting suitable for ordinary wear. Price........$5.50
Postage extra, 8 cents.
No. 18C4422 Men's Toupee, ventilated foundation. The ventilated toupees are made on a fine gauze foundation with natural parting, showing scalp through. Price....................$10.00
If by mail, postage extra, 8 cents.
No. 18C4423 Toupee Paste, which is used to keep toupee in place; heat and apply. Price, per stick...............42c
If by mail, postage extra, 5 cents.
Red, Blonde and Gray Hair cost extra. Allow one-half more than above prices.

Remember, we guarantee a perfect fit and match if you follow instructions, or your money back.

Men's Toupees.

How to Measure a Wig.

State style of wig, kind of parting, whether for right or left side; price and description as per list; to insure a good fit mention number of inches. Send sample of hair. Inches. No. 1 Circumference of head. No. 2 Forehead to nape of neck. No. 3 Ear to ear, across forehead. No. 4 Ear to ear, over top. No. 5 Temple to temple, around back.

Gentlemen's Wigs.

Gentlemen's Wigs are made of the finest selected hair. We guarantee our work the highest grade, and they cannot be distinguished from the natural growth.

No. 18C4426 Men's Full Wigs. Weft with crown, cotton foundation. Price............$8.00
No. 18C4430 Men's Full Wigs. Gauze or silk parting. Price.....$12.00
No. 18C4434 Men's Wigs. Ventilated with hair net parting. Price.............$21.00
If by mail, postage extra, 8 cents.

Red, Blonde and Gray Hair cost extra; allow one-half more than above prices

Street Wigs for Colored People.

No. 18C4438 Street Dress Wig for colored women, made of human hair, bang with parting in front, the hair in back is 18 inches long, and done up high in back with a knot. Send measurements as shown in illustration in rules for measurement on this page. Price..(Postage extra, 8 cents.)..$5.50
No. 18C4442 Street Dress Wigs for colored men, made of human hair with parting on side. Send measurement as per instructions. Price, $4.50
If by mail, postage extra, 8 cents.

Theatrical Wigs and Beards of Every Description.

No. 18C4446 Mustache on wire spring, common.
Price.... 8c
Postage extra 1 cent.
No.18C4450 Mustache, ventilated.
Price...(Postage extra, 1 cent)...12c
No.18C4454 Goatees. Price....8c
If by mail, postage extra, 1 cent.

No. 18C4458 Whiskers, side.
Price...........60c
Beards come in black, brown, gray, red and blonde colors.
If by mail, postage extra, 3 cents.
No. 18C4462 Full Beard, on wire. Price....68c
No. 18C4466 Full Beard, on ventilated net. Price......$1.75
If by mail, postage extra, 3 cents.

Full Beard.

Minstrel and Character Wigs.

No. 18C4470 Minstrel or Plain Black Negro Wigs. Price........49c
Postage extra, 8 cents.

Theatrical and Character Wigs for Stage and Masquerade Purposes.

No. 18C4472 Bald Head Wigs, all colors, including white, for Irish and Dutch comedians.
Price............$2.25
Postage extra, 6 cents.
No. 18C4475 Crop or School Boy's Wig. Colors, brown, red or black.
Price............$2.00
Postage extra, 6 cents.
No. 18C4476 Chinese Wig. Price...........$1.50
No. 18C4477 Mikado Wig. Gents'. Price, $2.25
If by mail, postage extra, 8 cents.
No. 18C4479 Mikado Wig. Ladies'. Price.......$2.50
No. 18C4480 Shoulder or Lord Fauntleroy Wigs, black, brown or blonde. Price............$2.50
If by mail, postage extra, 10 cents.
No. 18C4481 Dress Wig for Gents, all colors. Price............$2.50
No. 18C4483 Lady or George Washington, white only. Price......$3.00
If by mail, postage extra, 12 cents.
No. 18C4485 Fright Wigs, all colors. Price............$3.50
No.18C4486 Court Wigs, white only. Price..(Postage extra, 12c)..$3.25
No. 18C4494 Pencils for Eyebrows, brown or black. Price..(Postage extra, 3 cents.)..20c
No. 18C4498 Blue Pencil for the veins. Price...(Postage extra, 1 cent.)......20c

Court Wig

$1.00, $1.50 or $2.00 a bottle for a worthless and perhaps injurious preparation. Don't be misled by catchy advertising with baits of free trial sample bottle and fake examination offers—such people will draw you in, make you believe something awful is the matter and scare you into paying enormous prices for alleged remedies, when you can get the genuine, tried, tested, Princess Tonic Hair Restorer at 60 cents a bottle, the actual cost of the ingredients and labor of bottling, with our one small profit added."

This warning, incidentally, is interesting for two reasons: one, that whatever the merits of Sears' hair remedy, it is a blast against "fear" copy that in later years was to become so popular and to enrich so many fakers in the fields of cosmetics and medicines; two, that Sears frankly makes it clear that it is not in business for reasons of "service" or for the good of humanity but to make a profit.

Human hair is all things to all people. To biologists, it is a secondary sexual character; to men and women, it is essential to their beauty or attractiveness; to poets, the theme of song; to Marquesans and Democrats, it is part of the apparatus of revenge; to manufacturers, it is the source of a profitable industry. In *The Golden Bough,* Frazer reports of the Marquesans that "occasionally they have their head entirely shaved, except one lock on the crown, which is worn loose or put up in a knot. But the latter mode of wearing the hair is only adopted by them when they have a solemn vow, as to revenge the death of some near relation, etc. In such case the lock is never cut off until they have fulfilled their promise." And in the United States, good Democrats, emulating the Marquesans, let their hair and beards grow pending the time when William Jennings Bryan should be elected President.

The ladies of 1905 demanded voluminous quantities of hair on their heads and, when niggardly nature did not respond to the demand, they resorted to the stores. Sears imported bales of hair from Europe and worked it up into switches and wigs for women, thereby strangely paraphrasing Canning's famous remark: "The Old World will redress the baldness of the New." The demand was so great that the catalog devotes a whole page to switches, and tells us that "We Sell More Hair Goods Than Any Five Houses In The Country."

The prospective switch customer was instructed to "send us a good sized sample of hair cut as close to the roots as possible. . . . We will then send you the switch you select by mail."

The cheapest switch available was one weighing two ounces and measuring twenty inches in length for fifty cents; the most expensive weighed four ounces, was twenty-eight inches long, and sold for $3.75.

Sears' switches were guaranteed against fading, but if one of them seemed to fade on the head or in the drawer, the customer was told "to wash same in cold tea, which is very beneficial and darkens the color."

Many ladies of 1905 must have had the convictions of their coloring, because the catalog lists "white or nearly all white hair switches," and they were considerably more expensive than ordinary shades, ranging in price from $2.10 to $8.75.

The bald woman, or the woman not content with the niggardliness of switches, could buy a long or short wig, any color she desired, at prices ranging from $10 to $18, or the very popular Patent Pompadour:

". . . For simplicity, elegance and style it is far superior to anything ever shown. It slips right on, is as dainty as the feminine heart could desire; it produces the fluffy fullness now in vogue. . . . Can be worn with just the ends concealed under the lady's own hair, or may be used in place of the rolls and the wavy ends coiled in with the natural hair."

Years after the appearance of the 1905 catalog, the English historian, Arnold Toynbee, stated a doctrine that is the foundation of an American business with sales mounting into the millions: *

* Arnold Toynbee, *A Study of History,* vol. 1, p. 228.

This craving for the normal in physical appearance (whatever the normal may be in the particular circumstances) is not of course confined to the single feature of colour. For example, in the United States, where the physical appearance of the White People is the norm for the Coloured people, the Coloured women try to lessen their unlikeness from the White women by straightening their hair. On the other hand, the White women, who have no fear of looking like Negroes, take pleasure . . . in having their hair curled or waved. Thus, in the same town at the same moment, some barbers may be busy straightening women's hair in the Negro quarter while others are busy curling women's hair in the White quarter—in both cases alike, for the satisfaction of the universal human craving to be in the fashion.

In other words, parallel lines meet in the beauty parlor. And the catalog, recognizing the "craving for the normal in physical appearance . . . and to be in fashion," lists:

"Street Dress Wig for colored women, made of human hair, bang with parting in front, the hair in back is 18 inches long, and done up high in back with knot."

Toupees for Gentlemen

Forty years ago, Gertrude Atherton visited the United States Senate and recorded her impression many years later in her *Adventures of a Novelist*:

". . . So, in December of that year of 1899, I found myself seated in the members' gallery of the United States Senate on the first day of its annual assembling. It was a brilliant scene; the galleries were crowded; diplomats were in full uniform; women of importance superbly gowned; every seat on the floor occupied by more or less dignified senators—a spittoon beside each desk!

". . . I had never seen so many bald heads in my life. I became fascinated noting the varying tints on those polished domes. Some were as marble-white as the Father Christmas beards that depended below. Others were as pink as new-born babies. Some were of delicate ecru, Jersey cream, old ivory; two were freckled, and three jaundice yellow. One was bright scarlet, doubtless from temper, for its owner was quarreling violently with his neighbor. . . ."

It is perhaps fitting that Senators should be bald, because baldness in them is at once a badge of high office, a symptom (in the popular mind) of profound thinking, and an outward reassurance of inward magisterial wisdom. But bald gentlemen who were not Senators rebelled against baldness as a cruel trick played on them by nature which made them look old and foolish in the eyes of their fellow men, and, still more important, old and futile in the eyes of the ladies. Here the catalog stood ready with the easy mail-order method to repair the ravages of nature with wigs and toupees made to order. All that the bald man had to do was:

". . . Cut a piece of paper the exact size and shape of the bald spot, mark the crown and parting, enclose a lock of hair, and state if hair is to be straight or curly. Gentlemen's Wigs are made of the finest selected hair . . . and they cannot be distinguished from the natural growth." Prices ranged from $10 to $21, unless one wanted red, blonde, or gray hair, which cost fifty per cent more.

Making of a Mail-Order Samson

After the expense of the first cost, the upkeep was slight. One then needed only "Toupee paste, which is used to keep toupee in place, heat and apply. Price, per stick 42¢."

Hair Ornaments

Women's heads in 1905 were garnished as liberally with hair nets, hairpins, side combs, back combs, rat combs, puff combs, neck combs, hair binders, and barrettes as a hamburger with onions. It was a man-sized job for a woman to arise in the morning and, beginning with the small material given her by nature, work it up with the aid of rats, transformations, switches, wigs, pompadours, and combs into an imposing mass of beautiful hair second only to that possessed by the Seven Sutherland Sisters. At night, when the process had to be reversed, it was again the work of a titan to dismantle the hairy superstructure, comb and brush the rats and transformations, arrange the combs and hairpins in neat array against the morning, and rub in a bit of Princess Hair Restorer before jumping into bed.

So extensive indeed was the hair paraphernalia needed by the women of 1905 that the catalog lists nearly three pages of hairpins and combs, including such exotic and long-vanished items as:

"Ladies' Jewelled Pompadour Comb. Imitation tortoise shell, set with forty-two brilliant rhinestones. . . . Very high grade. Price 25¢."

Pompadour Comb to Keep the Rats in Their Place

"The New Rat Comb . . . does away with the hair roll . . . creates a fine, fluffy pompadour for young and old. Price 8¢."

"Jeweled Hair Barrette . . . with highly polished teeth . . . inlaid with nineteen brilliant rhinestones. . . . Price 40¢."

"Dr. Scott's Electric Hair Brushes are recommended by leading physicians. A wonderful help for headache and neuralgia; splendid to prevent falling hair, dandruff, etc. The curative powers of these brushes have been known and tested for a number of years. . . ."

Hair in the Second Year of the World War

For ten long years since 1905, women had been buying more and more hair at Sears, until the 1915 catalog devotes two pages to hair goods, and warns its customers that "For sanitary reasons we do not buy combings or take old switches as part payment on orders for new." The hair switch enjoys, therefore, the unique distinction of being one of the very few things in American life which has no trade-in value.

The featured hair on Sears' shelves in 1915 was:

(*a*) "The Basket Twist. This is a real hit. Made of lovely wavy hair mounted on neat foundation and braided into a fashionable modest effect." It was obviously the ornament of the ingénue.

(*b*) "The Handy Single Puff. Just what every woman needs for the new style of hair dressing."

(*c*) "Becoming Coronet Braids."

(*d*) "Transformation Band Switches . . . of the greatest benefit to women with thin hair. . . . Gives the desired fullness entirely around the head, instead of in only one place as . . . when an ordinary switch is worn."

Gentlemen are still buying toupees by mail, and the business has grown to such proportions that Sears issued a booklet: "Toupees and Wigs," containing instructions for measuring for a toupee. One enthusiastic customer wrote:

"The wig fits as if it grew on my head. It is a splendid piece of artistic work."

Acres of Rhinestones

Women's heads in 1915 blazed with rhinestones set amid hair purchased in Chicago. The catalog lists and illustrates nearly one hundred combs—all of which are set with rhinestones, sometimes to the number of one hundred and thirty-five, while imitation tortoise-shell hairpins were set with as many as sixty-seven. And inasmuch as a woman might wear

You Can Dress a Three Separate Strand Switch
in as Many Ways as Your Own Hair Divided Into Three Parts.

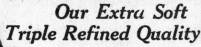

Our Extra Soft Triple Refined Quality

One of the Arrangements Made With Our Three-Strand Switch.

No. 18V4458 We take pride in this quality. It is carefully selected genuine human hair refined by our Secret Process to an exquisitely soft pliable texture. It will blend perfectly with your own hair. The ideal quality for graceful stylish hair dressings. Has the loveliest natural wave that is positively permanent. Made in our sunlight hair factory by the most skillful workmen. Mounted with high grade silk on three separate stems, the handiest arrangement ever invented. In this quality we can match almost every shade except gray.

Weight	Length	Price
2 ounces	20 inches	$2.48
2¼ ounces	22 inches	3.25
2½ ounces	24 inches	3.98
2¾ oz. A Real Bargain 26 in. A Popular Size		4.95
3 ounces	28 inches	6.35
3¼ ounces	30 inches	7.25
3½ ounces	32 inches	8.35

WE GUARANTEE
A Perfect Match.
A Permanent Wave.
Faultless Workmanship.
Full Length and Weight.

NOTE.—For sanitary reasons we do not buy combings or cut hair, or take old switches as part payment on orders for new. Cleanliness is a big feature in our hair goods.

BE SURE
to send a good large sample with your order and to read **HOW TO ORDER HAIR** on opposite page.

Our Well Known Fine Medium Quality

No. 18V4457 Here we offer a superior medium quality carefully selected genuine human hair, which has become popular. While our Triple Refined Quality must receive our highest unqualified recommendation, this standard quality will be found an excellent value at the extremely low prices we quote. It has a beautiful lasting wave and, being made up in this favorite three separate strand style, can be dressed in a great number of pretty braid and coil effects. Seven sizes fitted with silk mounts. Black and ordinary brown shades only. For drab, blond or auburn shades refer to the Triple Refined Quality; for grays see No. 18V4378 on opposite page.

Weight	Length	Price
1¾ ounces	20 inches	$1.69
2 ounces	22 inches	1.98
2½ ounces	24 inches	2.95
3 oz. A Favorite Size 26 in. Special Bargain		3.75
3¼ ounces	28 inches	4.65
3½ ounces	30 inches	5.25
4 ounces	32 inches	5.95

The Clever Basket Twist.

Choice of Two Fine Grades.

This is a real hit. It is one of the most becoming pieces ever designed. Made of lovely wavy hair mounted on neat foundation and braided into a fashionable modest effect. Width, 5 in. Length, 6½ inches. Shipping weight, 7 oz.

No. 18V4475 Our Well Known Fine Medium Quality. Black and ordinary brown shades only. Price....**$1.95**

No. 18V4476 Our Extra Soft Triple Refined Quality. All shades in this dainty grade, including slightly gray. Price..................**$2.95**

Charming Biscuit Coils.

One of the most popular styles of low hair dressing ever known. Becoming to so many faces. Handily arranged. Easily redressed. Natural wavy hair woven on light wire foundation. Shipping weight, 7 ounces.

No. 18V4340 Our Well Known Fine Medium Quality. Black and ordinary brown shades only. Price..........**$1.49**

No. 18V4341 Our Extra Soft Refined Quality. All shades in this grade, including slightly sprinkled gray. Price..................**$2.59**

Transformation Band Switches.

This arrangement is of the greatest benefit to women with thin hair. It gives the desired fullness entirely around the head instead of in only one place, as is the case when an ordinary hair is worn. The hair, which finishes 18 inches in length, is woven on a fine weft and mounted on a narrow ribbon, 22 inches long, to encircle the head. It is worn under the natural hair and is light and comfortable. Builds either front or back pompadours. We send illustrated directions. Shipping weight, 6 ounces.

Our Extra Soft Refined Quality.
No. 18V4424 The lovely grade of genuine human hair which blends so naturally for becoming headdresses. Beautiful lasting wave. All shades in this quality, including the slightly sprinkled gray. Price..................**$2.89**

Our Well Known Fine Medium Grade.
No. 18V4432 A carefully selected quality of genuine human hair that is fine and fluffy with a permanent wave. Black and ordinary brown shades only. Price..................**$1.95**

We Make Perfect Fitting Toupees and Wigs
For Men and Women

One customer writes:
"The wig fits as if it grew on my head. It is a splendid piece of artistic work. Another wigmaker quoted me a price of $50.00 for the same wig. Your firm saved me almost $22.00 on this one purchase."

Men's toupees at $14.95 and $21.65. Full wigs from $14.35 up. Women's wigs and transformations from $11.95 to $37.50.

WE SAVE YOU ONE HALF.
Write today for our booklet, "Wigs and Toupees," containing full descriptions and instructions for measuring.

Regal Coronet Braids.

No. 18V4445 Excellent quality genuine human hair, with natural wave, made up in our widely known "Handy Braid" style. Joined in center with neatly woven weft which is cleverly covered. We offer remarkable values in this popular headdress. Prices are for usual ordinary shades. Shipping weight of braids, each, 6 ounces.

Weight	Length	Price
2 ounces	30 inches	$1.79
2½ ounces	32 inches	2.59
3 oz. A Favorite 35 in. Bargain at		2.98
3½ ounces	38 inches	3.35

Outside Front Pompadour.

WITH NATURAL PARTING.

A really effective front covering. Made of the very finest first quality French convent hair with beautiful lasting wave. Mounted on a lace net foundation 3½ inches wide. Formed to fit across forehead from ear to ear. Skillful handiwork throughout. Hair can be drawn back about the ears. Has natural ventilated parting in center or either side. State choice. Send a good sample of your hair. Shipping weight, 6 ounces.

No. 18V4479 For usual shades. Price..................**$6.75**

Lovely Hair Goods To Match Your Own

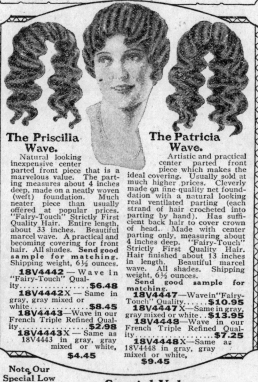

a dozen combs, barrettes, and the popular rhinestone-studded "question mark" pins, in addition to a rhinestone bandeau around her forehead, the effect must have been that of a department-store jewelry counter out for an evening stroll.

Rhinestone Bandeau

Man's Last Stand

In the 1920's, with the shortening of skirts women began to shorten their hair; the boyish figure became the fashion, and the "boyish bob" the hair fashion. We have moved far from the ample days of the past characterized by double beds, double chins, large-busted women with wasp waists, and heavy meals for men and women. A few pioneers had bobbed their hair in 1918. By 1924, women were moving by hordes into the last stronghold of man's privacy—the barbershop. The presence of the ladies made it impossible for the men to cuss, tell dirty stories, and lie about their exploits in catching fish or shooting game; impossible to enjoy a few minutes of unalloyed masculinity. They endured these deprivations silently, however, as is the wont of American men. But hairdressers complained that vulgar barbers were pre-empting their expert field, while barbers, in the good old American way, said, "There ought to be a law"—a law that would forbid hairdressers to cut hair unless they were licensed barbers.

Whereupon *The Hairdresser* retorted that *The Police Gazette*-polluted atmosphere of the barbershop was no place for ladies, and eloquently defended the purity of our womanhood:

"The effort to bring women to barber shops for hair-cutting is against the best interests of the public, the free and easy atmosphere often prevailing in barber shops being unsuitable to the high standard of American womanhood."

American womanhood, however, was more interested in its appearance than in its morals, and continued to haunt barbershops, hairdressers, "beauticians," or the establishment of anyone else who could and would cut, shingle, clip, snip, or otherwise shorten the hair. At the same time, women adopted small hats which fitted tightly over the head, and this meant throwing overboard tons of hairpins, hair nets, combs, switches, and other impedimenta, to the sorrow of manufacturers of these things who saw fashion taking bread out of the mouths of their babes and to the distress of foreigners who had given their hair for a few pennies to the greater glory of American womanhood.

But while the clicking of shears and the clacking of tongues announced that woman's hair was being bobbed all over the United States, Sears and its customers went serenely on their old ways, and there are few indications in the 1925 catalog that woman's head and woman's hair are not what they were twenty years before.

Replace Bobbed Hair with Bought Hair

Hair bobbing, strangely enough, opened a new market for hair-goods manufacturers, and the alert catalog is on the ground to garner the profits offered by unchanging but ever changeable woman. It was the fashion, apparently, to bob the hair and then replace it with store-bought hair to produce a new effect, rich and strange. Ladies who had had their hair bobbed were told to:

"Dress Up Your Bobbed Hair With the Mignon Bandeau. Style tendencies in all fashion centers indicate that the well dressed woman is now wearing her hair up. This wonderful headdress, designed especially to wear over bobbed hair, is a quick, practical and stylish accessory for this purpose. Our finest Fairy-Touch quality, $3.95."

Ladies with bobbed hair also bought Minerva Ringlet Clusters, and the "New Coronet Swirl . . . a very effective and practical covering for bobbed hair or short ends."

Switches, transformations, and pompadours are still as popular in 1925—despite the bobbed-hair fashion—as they were in 1905, and the catalog continues to give two pages to hair goods. The rhinestone splendor of the previous decade is somewhat dimmed, but it gleams fitfully in barrettes and in the new bobbie combs and pins.

Gentlemen are still hiding the nudity of their skulls beneath Sears' wigs, despite the fact that prices have risen sharply in the past twenty years, making the cost of the best quality wig $63. The hair-raising revolution of the outer world has not yet penetrated the ranks of catalog conservatives, and, as we shall see, it never became completely effective in rural and small-town America.

Beauty on Easy Payments

In his *Treatise on the Hair,* published in London in 1770, David Ritchie lays down this doctrine:

". . . For such is the matter of the brain, such is the vapor of hair arising from it in color, quantity and quality and the ancients were in their observations thereon very particular. For Aristotle, Galen, Hippocrates, etc., having laid down rules for discovering the temper, talents, wit, judgment and imagination, etc., of men and women, esteemed the hair a principal sign from which they drew their observations. . . ."

One hundred and sixty-five years later, the catalog tells its readers:

LOVELY HAIR . . . YOUR AID TO NATURAL,
ALLURING BEAUTY

"Meet the test of searching eyes confidently—don't let thinning or straggly locks spoil your appearance. Sears approved smart hair styles add charm to feminine loveliness. . . ."

Men and women in search of beauty were offered an invaluable aid in the form of Sears' "New Illustrated Hair

Fashion Booklet." "Shows actual photographs of hair pieces on live models, including wigs and toupees." And for the first time, elusive beauty may be captured and held by almost anybody because "pieces costing $25 or more may now be purchased on Easy Payments."

There are few things in the catalog—especially those subject to changes of fashion—that persist through three decades, but the switch and the wig belong to this elect company. Decade after decade, the catalog has listed them, and in 1935 they are again listed in the same form that they had taken thirty years ago. The transformation is also present and it has suffered no transformation whatever, although nearly everything else in America had changed in the long interval between Roosevelt, Theodore, and Roosevelt, Franklin D. By 1935, there were thousands of beauty parlors in the United States, and no hamlet was so small that it did not have at least one shop where beauty dwelt in bottles on shelves or in the nimble fingers of the beautician; millions of women had bobbed their hair; others were letting their bobs vanish in growing hair; still others were concerned with "setting waves," making ringlets or curls. But the wig, the transformation, and the switch still claimed the allegiance of large numbers of women, and gentlemen continued to avoid the horrors of baldness by buying toupees and paste from Sears. And out of it all emerges a beauty industry employing thousands of men and women, producing sales greater than those made by a giant corporation such as United States Steel.

15 · THE BIRD ON NELLIE'S HAT

"THERE ought to be a law," many an outraged American husband has growled in impotent wrath as he looked at his wife's hat. For some reason unexplored by poets and unplumbed by psychiatrists, males who do not know whether their women are wearing a Mother Hubbard or a Fortuny tea gown are sensitive to women's hats.

The usual American method of dealing with almost any problem is to appoint a committee or pass a law, and, although we have had laws governing everything from the filing of mule's teeth to the length of hotel bed sheets, we have never had one to control what woman wears on her head. The politician with nerve enough to introduce such a measure is yet to be born, and even if it should be passed, the direst despotism would be broken in an effort to control the uncontrollable. In the United States, consequently, where women have had to fight for higher education and shorter bathing suits, for wearing pants and retaining their maiden names after marriage, for the dubious privilege of having their votes counted out in elections and of serving on juries, their apparently inalienable right to wear the hats of their own sweet choice has never been threatened. Men may mutter for the iron hand of the law, but their domination of women stops at the hairline.

In 1905, living was simpler than it is now, but hats were more complicated. The typical hat of that period was no mere snip of felt decorated with a simple buckle, but an intricate high-piled confusion of feathers, wings, flowers, fruits, straw, and lace. This, for example, is what the catalog calls "a very plain but exceptionally stylish hat that will go well with any tailored suit":

"THIS CHARMING TURBAN IS NEAT AND DRESSY, $2.30. This is a very large turban developed in brown with a touch of light blue. The facing . . . overlaid with closely tucked brown silk chiffon, same trimmed around the brim with a

The Bird Walk

fold of brown, satin braid, caught with hub ornaments, made of brown and light blue combination satin braid. The large bell crown is made of folds of light blue and brown satin braid. Directly in the front is a novelty gilt ornament from which two quills are drawn and extending to the left over the brim. An all around bandeau completes the trimming of this hat. Very pretty as described in brown and light blue, but also can be ordered in all brown or white and pink, which also looks good."

After a glimpse of a "plain" hat of 1905, we may now look at some of the more "dressy" hats. We shall never know by what inversion of values or through what excesses of repression, the head of Sears' millinery department—a fierce libertarian perhaps condemned to selling hats—was induced to name several of his most distinguished models THE CHARLOTTE CORDAY. That brave young woman of the French Revolution who dyed Marat's bath water with his own blood achieves—for whatever reason—a New World, mail-order immortality in THE NEW CHARLOTTE CORDAY, A $4.00 HAT; OUR PRICE, ONLY $2.05.

But the catalog loses no time in vain speculations why a girl revolutionist of the eighteenth century was turned into a hat of the twentieth. It gets right down to business and tells us that:

"The very latest hat is known as the Charlotte Corday. At present it is the rage of Paris and New York. It is a small dress shape with edge drooping in mushroom effects. . . . The very large bell crown is developed in gathered and shirred brown silk. On the left side is a wheel silk rosette; six brown silk and velvet flowers elegantly arranged in front on the large bell crown complete the trimming of this hat. This is a hat that no swell dresser should overlook, as it is without doubt the very latest offered by the very highest class milliners. There may be more becoming hats than this one, but we can assure you that no more stylish hat has ever been offered."

The Descats, the Agneses, the Lewises of the 1905 catalog were the distinguished Mesdames Frances, Rentau, and Lemar. These Gallic ladies working wonders in New York and Chicago by remote control from their Montparnasse ateliers—and in the carefree Parisian manner humming snatches from *La Bohème* as they sewed—contributed several creations to the catalog and America. Indispensable creations, for just as we once played the sedulous ape to the painters and writers of France and the Continent, we still ape the fashions of Paris. On the eve of St. Catherine's day, 1905, Madame Frances sent us No. 39C9072. DESIGNED BY MADAME FRANCES COMBINING STYLE AND QUALITY, $2.80. This was a fine example of subtly beautiful effects achieved through the simple device of placing "shaded silk and velvet flowers between serpentine rosettes."

Madame Rentau, on the other hand, was made of sterner stuff. She seems indeed to have been afflicted with that secret sorrow not uncommon to Parisiennes, and which even the most casual tourist must have observed in the eyes of the mustached, bombazined sisterhood who usher you to your seat (*pourboire* one franc) in Paris theaters. Madame Rentau begins gaily enough, but soon she tosses in a somber note. Thus, DESIGN BY MADAME RENTAU, $3.30, was "very tastily trimmed all around the crown with mercerized pink satin flowers and imported foliage," but before things get out of hand, she adds "a fold of black satin [which] surrounds the flowers on the left and extends to the back over the brim where it is made into milliner's loops and bows. The facing trimmed with pink silk and mercerized satin flowers completes the trimming of this hat."

As befits a race of passionate individualists, Madame Lemar was quite unlike her sisters Frances and Rentau. It is evident, however, that she possessed the French genius for clothes because, says the catalog, No. 39C9063 DESIGNED BY MADAME LEMAR, BEAUTIFULLY TRIMMED, $2.68, "is another one of those hats we can recommend."

This is high praise indeed, for the catalog, knowing that objectivity is a quality of the gods and that in any event it was doing business with farmers, made no pretense in that direction. And while it attempted to persuade the customer by skillful and legitimate use of the arts of description and illustration, it rarely, as in the case of Madame Rentau, suggested that the customer should pluck a particular flower from the midst of all those that bloomed in its garden. It is comforting, therefore, to find that the Madame's work was worthy of the distinction. The recommended hat was:

"Strictly hand made on a wire frame. . . . The large bell crown is trimmed with folds of black fancy braid. The facing is trimmed with black allover lace, same overlaid with folds of silk chiffon ruching. The upper trimming consists of a long wreath of black satin and black silk flowers. Trimmed on the right side with large loops of black satin taffeta ribbon, same ribbon extending around the crown and falling over the back of the brim, where it is made into milliner's bows." Madame Lemar knew, however, that all American women were not cast in dark Goyaesque mold, and for more pastel ladies she provided the same model "also in black and pink or white and pink."

While Sears' millinery department gave French designers a chance to show what they could do, it was by no means their slave and manifested none of that scabrous snobbism and obsequiousness to Paris that still marks many New York shops and their clientele. Nor was it pugnaciously parochial, glorifying the American designer above all others simply because he was American. It took the best where it could be found, and, searching for the best, sometimes grafted American buds upon a French stem. For example:

A PARISIAN DESIGN. VERY SWELL, $3.55. This was a "very large and beautiful dress hat," for summer. It was a cool confection of "white silk chiffon edged with white satin braid and white silk hair braid . . . and inlaid with maize color satin taffeta ribbon. The large bell crown . . . is very tastily trimmed with two large American Beauty rosebuds, imported foliage and long stems."

Our native millinery designers, once they are turned loose, display their skill by concocting hats made of materials alien to our soil—lace and ostrich feathers. The first of these was a VERY STUNNING CREATION IN LACE AND OSTRICH, $5.50. Its charm derived from allover lace combined with white satin-taffeta ribbon and "twelve ostrich small white half plumes surrounding the upper half brim."

The second was A BECOMING AND BEAUTIFUL GAINSBOROUGH EFFECT, $4.50. Here the much-desired Gainsborough effect, which made the wearer look like a mistress of Charles I, was achieved by the use of "two white French curl half plumes beautifully arranged, one on the left side of the crown and the other under the facing extending over the brim."

Mourning Bonnets

Executive Mansion

MY DEAR MADAME:

Your bonnets were received on yesterday. The black with colors, I liked very much. Also the black crape. I wished a much finer black straw bonnet for mourning—without the gloss. Could you get me such a one? I want you to send me a bow of black crape, for the top of the black straw bonnet, *exactly* like the one on top of the black crape bonnet—of the *same crape* two bows on each side of the loup, like the other. I wrote you about the veils—did you receive the letter. I want you to select me the *very finest,* and blackest and lightest crape veil. . . . Please get the finest that can be obtained. Want a *very very* fine black crape veil, round corners and folds around . . . for summer. . . . The *long veil* I should like to have by Friday . . . black and light—please send *this* immediately. . . . I have your money ready for you.

Very truly yours,

MRS. LINCOLN *

Hitherto we have been considering hats for the gayer moods of living. But, when death came, Sears made appropriate provision for the conventional clothes to be worn in an era when it was little short of scandalous for women not to observe the prescribed ritual of mourning. In this respect at least, 1905 was like 1862. For mourners, the catalog offered A MOURNING BONNET TRIMMED IN BEST MANNER WITH FINE MATERIALS, $2.50. This hat, while conforming in color and trimmings to the somber spirit demanded of the occasion, in no way indicated that the widow who wore it was so brokenhearted over the death of her husband that she had to be violently restrained from killing herself. On the contrary, it was flattering and attractive, with "the edge of the brim surrounded with black gathered nun's veiling while a long grenadine silk veil appears in the back. Two long black silk ties complete the trimming of the mourning bonnet."

Grandma, in 1905, was content to be grandma and did not try to look like one of the girls of the Florodora Sextette. She generally wore a hat as characteristic as that worn later by Queen Mary of England. It was a "PRETTY BONNET, TASTILY DESIGNED, $1.65. The crown is made of black hair braid edged with jet black spangles. Trimmed in front with a jet spangled aigrette, held to the frame with a black orna-

* From an undated letter written by Mrs. Abraham Lincoln to an unknown correspondent, after the death of her son, Willie Lincoln, in 1862. Quoted in Sandburg and Angle, *Mary Lincoln, Wife and Widow.*

ment. In back of the brim are bows of black silk taffeta ribbon through which are drawn streamers of the same material. This is a very pretty bonnet and can be ordered as described in black only."

The Old Gray Bonnet

The catalog of 1905 is filled with hats which are described as "dressy and nobby." But even in the faraway—and to our tired eyes—Indian summer of that year, living and hats were not always nobby and dressy but sometimes plain and workaday. The catalog now ditches its French modistes; drops ostrich feathers and jet; throws away its silk and satin ribbons, and turns to a hat as American as the covered wagon. It is a hat indeed that crossed the continent in the covered wagon, and long before that time had sheltered the pioneer head as it bent over the wild-raspberry bushes of colonial New England. It is:

"No. 39C9482. Ladies' Percale Sunbonnets in plain colors with ruffle edge around front. The body is fancy stitched,

American Madonna

has a long full cape with a bow at back and strings. An exceptionally well made bonnet. This is a better quality than is usually retailed at 25 cents. Colors, royal blue, cardinal, light blue or pink. Price 15¢."

This was the bonnet in its most Spartan form, but, however plain, it blazed with color and attractively framed the face madonna fashion. It was useful as well as ornamental; it was washable, and supremely cheap. At the slightly higher price of twenty-three cents, women were offered "Ladies'

Figured Percale Sunbonnets, made of good quality cloth, with large full cape. Trimmed with a plaited ruffle on edge of bonnet, also one around edge of cape. Ruffles, neatly stitched and trimmed with valenciennes lace edge. Comes in light blue, pink, cardinal or royal blue."

Plumes of Africa

Thirty to fifteen years ago the life of the ostrich was made miserable by the demands of women for his plumes. He was pursued and plucked by Bedouins of the Arabian desert, by the Indians of South America, by the Negroes of Africa. His feathers, cured, dyed, and curled, eventually turned up on hats and fans everywhere. Sears, the ever careful, waiting until the ostrich-feather vogue had passed the fad stage and had become firmly established, then announced:

WE ARE DIRECT IMPORTERS OF
OSTRICH FEATHERS
WE WISH TO CALL PARTICULAR ATTENTION TO
OUR OSTRICH PLUMES AND TIPS

After assuring the reader that Sears has the goods and is selling them at prices lower than "you could buy them from any wholesale house in the country," the catalog devotes nearly a whole page to seventy-five kinds of ostrich plumes and tips.

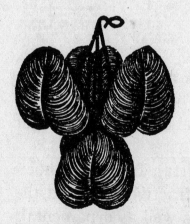

When an Ostrich Buried Its Head in the Sands of 1905, It Emerged Naked

The quintessence of quality in plumes was "No. 39C3631. FRENCH CURL OSTRICH PLUMES. Very finest and highest

Cross Aigrettes.

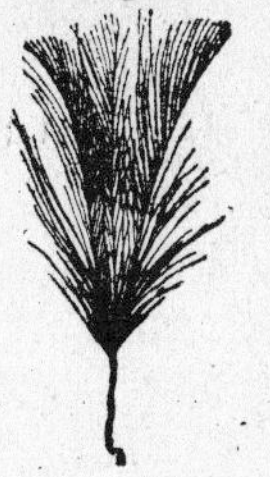

No. 39C3522 Three-piece Cross Aigrette. This is a full and rich trimming which is extremely popular this season. Colors, black or white.
Price........................20c
Postage extra, 4 cents.

No. 39C3525 Four-piece Cross Aigrette. Same as above, only branched by four. Colors, black or white.
Price........................25c
Postage extra, 4 cents.

High Aigrettes, Brush Effect. Very Stylish.

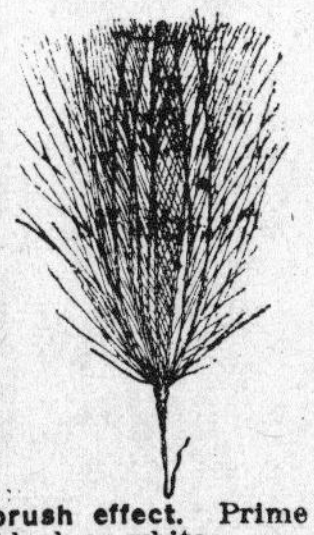

No. 39C3528 Three-piece, Fine Quality Aigrette, brush effect. Eight inches high. Colors, black or white, branched by three bunches. Makes a very full show.
Price, per bunch...19c
Per three bunches, as per illustration......55c
If by mail, postage extra, 4 cents.

No. 39C3531 Nine-piece Aigrette, brush effect. Length, 6 inches, fine quality. Colors, black or white only. Price..40c
Postage extra, 4 cents.

No. 39C3534 Nine-piece, 8-inch Aigrette, brush effect. Prime quality of stock. Colors, black or white.
Price.....(Postage extra, 4 cents)........55c

No. 39C3537 Eighteen-piece Aigrette, brush effect. Length, 8 inches. This makes a very full and showy trimming. Equal to what you would pay $1.50 for elsewhere. Colors, black or white. Price....................$1.00
If by mail, postage extra, 4 cents.

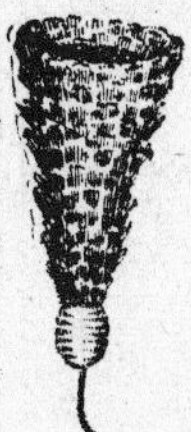

No. 39C3540 Feather Pompon set in chenille ball. This pompon will be very much used this season. Stands 6 inches in height. Colors, black, brown, green, navy or red.
Price, each...... ....$0.21
Per dozen............. 2.25
If by mail, postage extra, each, 4 cents.

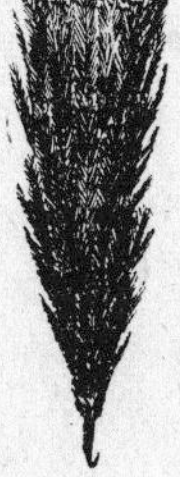

No. 39C3543 Feather Pompon. This is a soft, feather pompon, 7½ inches long. Makes a very pretty trimming for either ready to wear or dress hats. Colors, black or white.
Price, each.............$0.10
Per dozen............... 1.00
Postage extra, each, 4 cents.

Ostrich Feather Boas.

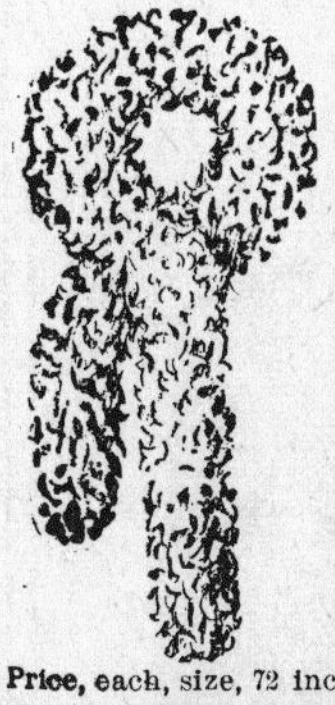

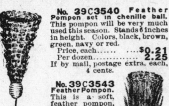

No. 39C3570 Finest Real Ostrich Feather Boas. Rich, glossy black; only the fullest, finest stock. Very dressy and stylish. Black only. We quote them in two different lengths, as follows:
Price, 36-inch.$ 7.50
Price, 54-inch, 11.25
If by mail, postage extra, 8 to 15 cents.

No. 39C3572 Fine Ostrich Feather Boas, heavier and fuller than above. We guarantee them equal to much higher priced boas sold elsewhere. Black only.
Price, each, size, 36 inches.......$9.25
Price, each, size, 54 inches.......13.75
Price, each, size, 72 inches..............18.50

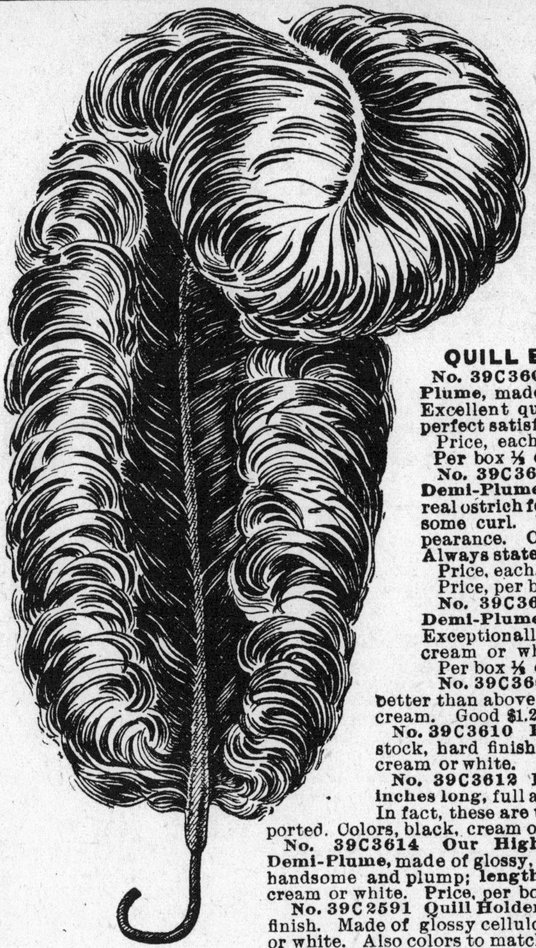

WE ARE DIRECT IMPORTERS OF

OSTRICH FEATHERS.

We Wish to Call Particular Attention to Our Ostrich Plumes and Tips.

ALL OF OUR OSTRICH FEATHERS are made of the best grade hard flue, selected stock, are the best black and look rich and glossy. We do not handle the poor fluffy, woolly stock. **WE GUARANTEE YOU BETTER VALUES THAN YOU COULD BUY THEM FOR FROM ANY WHOLESALE HOUSE IN THE COUNTRY.** If after receiving ostrich plumes or tips ordered from us, you are not perfectly satisfied that you are getting value such as we claim, you are at liberty to return them, and we will refund your money with postage added. **If sent by mail, allow 10 to 15 cents extra for postage.**

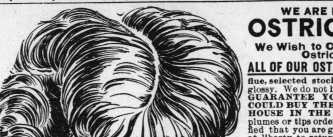

HALF PLUMES WITH LARGE FULL HEADS

QUILL ENDS IMPROVE THE OSTRICH PLUMES.

As soon as you receive your ostrich feathers open them out and comb them in the dry air. It will greatly improve their appearance.

No. 39C3602 Our Special 9-inch Demi-Plume, made from real ostrich feathers. Excellent quality and warranted to give perfect satisfaction. Black only.
Price, each.........................$0.29
Per box ½ dozen......................... 1.50

No. 39C3604 A Very Full 10-inch Demi-Plume, made from extra quality real ostrich feathers. Fine fibre and handsome curl. Very rich and glossy in appearance. Colors, black, cream or white. Always state color desired.
Price, each.........................$0.49
Price, per box ½ dozen.............. 2.75

No. 39C3606 Real Ostrich Feather Demi-Plume, 11 inches long, very heavy and plump, with fine soft curl. Exceptionally handsome. Fine fibre and glossy finish. Colors, black, cream or white. Always state color desired. **Price, each**..........$0.75
Per box ½ dozen.......................... 4.25

No. 39C3608 Real Ostrich Demi-Plume. These are the next grade better than above. Fine selected stock. **Length, 12 inches.** Black, white or cream. Good $1.25 value. Price, per box ½ dozen, $5.00; each..........90c

No. 39C3610 Fine Ostrich Demi-Plume, 13-inch. Made of fine selected stock, hard finish, long and glossy fibres. Exceptional value. Colors, black, cream or white. Price, per box ½ dozen, $6.00; each..........$1.10

No. 39C3612 Finest Quality Real Ostrich Feather Demi-Plume, 14 inches long, full and heavy, with exceptionally fine curl, glossy and beautiful. In fact, these are the richest and finest appearing plumes we have ever imported. Colors, black, cream or white. Price, per box ½ dozen, $8.00; each..........$1.38

No. 39C3614 Our Highest Grade and Best Quality Genuine Ostrich Feather Demi-Plume, made of glossy, hard fibre, ostrich stock, a rich, glossy black, fine curl, very handsome and plump; **length, full 15 inches.** Exceptionally handsome. Colors, black, cream or white. Price, per box ½ dozen, $9.75; each..........$1.69

No. 39C2591 Quill Holders, to put on end of ostrich plumes. Gives the plume a pretty finish. Made of glossy celluloid to imitate a large quill end; very stylish. Colors, black or white. Also colors to match colored French plumes. Length, 5½ inches.
Price, per dozen, 8c; each..........................1c

LONG FRENCH CURL PLUMES.

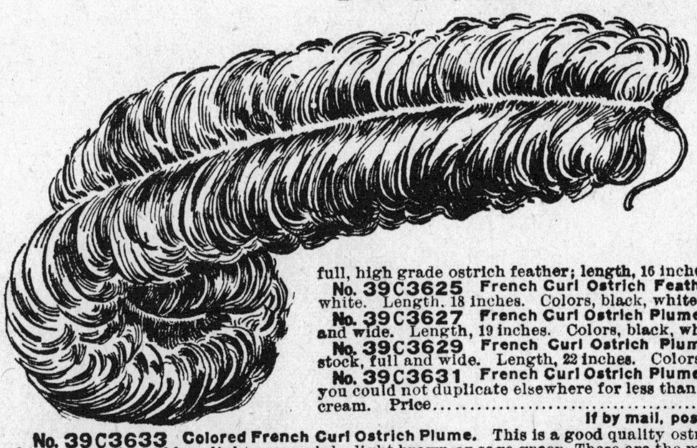

French Curl Plumes have the large, full drooping head. These French plumes are made of the best selected hard flue stock from the male ostrich bird, which retain their luster and are always best. The **black is rich** and glossy and we guarantee it absolutely fast. The finest black in the whole world. **The white feathers are the natural pure white and are very beautiful.** Every feather is one piece, full and wide fiber. We are satisfied that we give you at least 100 per cent more value for your money than any other concern. **You run no risk whatever in sending your orders to us.** If you are not entirely satisfied, after receiving our ostrich plumes, that they are almost one-half the price you have to pay elsewhere, you can return same and we will immediately refund your money and postage.

No. 39C3621 French Curl Ostrich Feather, a splendid full feather; length 15 inches. Colors, black, white or cream. Price..........$1.69

No. 39C3623 French Curl Ostrich Feather, a nice, full, high grade ostrich feather; length, 16 inches. Colors, black, white or cream. Price..........$2.75

No. 39C3625 French Curl Ostrich Feather, fuller and larger than above, glossy black and pure white. Length, 18 inches. Colors, black, white or cream. Price..........$3.95

No. 39C3627 French Curl Ostrich Plumes, an exceptionally handsome and beautiful feather, full and wide. Length, 19 inches. Colors, black, white or cream. Price..........$5.00

No. 39C3629 French Curl Ostrich Plumes, a large and very beautiful feather, very best quality stock, full and wide. Length, 22 inches. Colors, black, white or cream. Price..........$7.00

No. 39C3631 French Curl Ostrich Plumes, very finest and highest quality stock, such a feather that you could not duplicate elsewhere for less than $12.00 to $15.00. Length, 24 inches. Colors, black, white or cream. Price..........$8.50

If by mail, postage extra, 6 to 20 cents.

No. 39C3633 Colored French Curl Ostrich Plume. This is a good quality ostrich feather. French curled. Regular $1.50 value. Colors, white, cream, light blue, light navy, pink, light brown or sage green. These are the most popular colors for the coming season. Length, 13 inches.
Price, per box ½ dozen, $6.25; each..........(If by mail, postage extra, each, 10 cents.)..........$1.15

No. 39C3635 French Curl Ostrich Plume. This is a very elegant, good quality ostrich plume. The colors are the best shades and the quality exceptional value. Colors, white, cream, light blue, pink, light navy, light brown or sage green. Length, 15 inches.
Price, per dozen, $22.50; each..........(If by mail, postage extra, each, 10 cents.)..........$2.00

No. 39C3637 French Curl Ostrich Plume. This is the best number that we run in colors. Is a large, beautiful feather in very pretty shades, the prevailing colors for this season. Values cannot be equaled anywhere. Colors, white, cream, light blue, pink, light navy, light brown or sage green. Length, 17 inches. Price, per dozen, $33.00; each..........(If by mail, postage extra, each, 12 cents.)..........$3.00

AMAZON OSTRICH PLUMES.

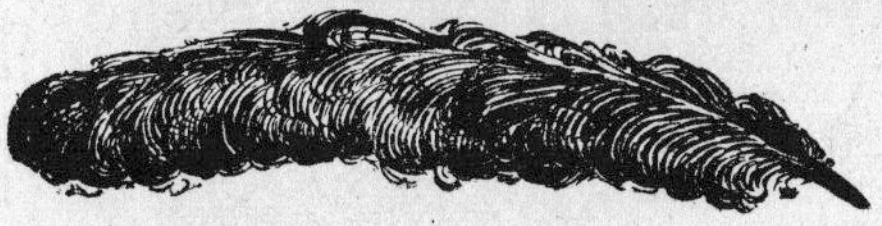

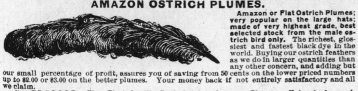

Amazon or Flat Ostrich Plumes; very popular on the large hats; made of very highest grade, best selected stock from the male ostrich bird only. The richest, glossiest and fastest black dye in the world. Buying our ostrich feathers as we do in larger quantities than any other concern, and adding but our small percentage of profit, assures you of saving from 50 cents on the lower priced numbers up to $2.00 or $3.00 on the better plumes. Your money back if not entirely satisfactory and all we claim.

No. 39C3638 Fine First Quality Real Ostrich Amazon Plumes. Extensively used, especially for the Gainsborough effects. Length, 14 inches. Colors, black, white or cream.
Price, for ½ dozen, $8.25; each..........$1.50

No. 39C3640 Amazon Real Ostrich Plumes. Finer and larger than above. Length, 15 inches. Colors, black, white or cream.
Price, for ¼ dozen, $5.50; each..........$1.95

No. 39C3644 Amazon Real Ostrich Plumes. Rich, glossy stock, long fibers. Length, 16 inches. Colors, black, white or cream.
Price, for ¼ dozen, $6.50; each..........$2.29

No. 39C3648 Amazon or Flat Plumes. An extra quality, hard fiber, glossy, black ostrich. Length, 17 inches. Colors, black, cream or white.
Price, for ¼ dozen, $8.50; each..........$3.00

No. 39C3650 Amazon Plumes. Very full, very extra fine stock. Length, 19 inches. $6.00 value. Colors, black, cream or white.
Price, for ¼ dozen, $12.25; each..........$4.25

No. 39C3652 Amazon Plumes. The very highest grade, beautiful full stock. Equal to any plume at $10.00 and $12.00. Length, 22 inches. Colors, black, white or cream.
Price, for 1-6 dozen, $13.50; each..........$6.95

If by mail, postage extra, 5 to 10 cents.

See the New Quill Stem Holder, as used for the ends of ostrich plumes, described under our No. 39C2591, at 1 cent each.

OSTRICH TIPS.

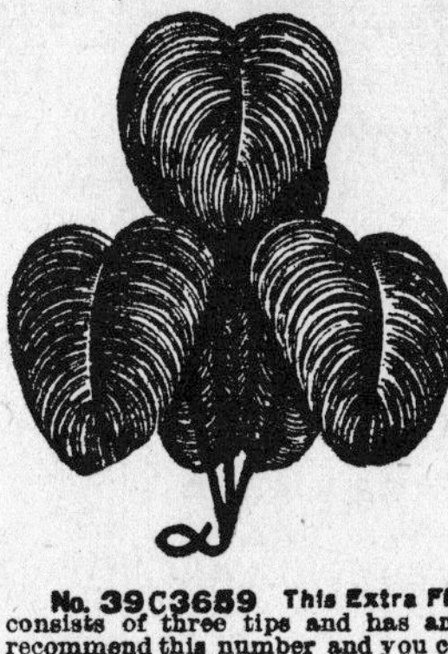

Ostrich Tips come three in a bunch, made from the best selected stock. We do not use the woolly or cheap ostrich, but only sell the best grade. Ostrich tips will be very stylish as a trimming this season, and nowhere can you get such good things for so little money as what we offer.

No. 39C3653 Handsome Bunch of Real Ostrich Feather Tips, made of good quality ostrich, very handsome bunch at the price. We can furnish these tips in black only.
Price, per bunch of three..........$0.30
Per box of ½ dozen.......... 1.65

No. 39C3655 This Exceptionally Fine Quality Bunch Real Ostrich Feather Tips consists of three tips, heavy stock, select ostrich. We offer these tips at a special price, a price that you could not possibly duplicate for nearly twice what we ask. Colors, black, white or cream.
Price, per bunch of three..........$0.55
Per box ½ dozen.......... 3.00

No. 39C3657 This Elegant Bunch of Real Ostrich Tips, three in the bunch, is made of good, hard, glossy ostrich stock. These tips are made for our special use and are unexcelled for beauty and richness. Colors, black, cream or white. Price, per bunch of three..........$0.90
Per box ½ dozen.......... 5.00

No. 39C3659 This Extra Fine Bunch of Rich, Full and Glossy Ostrich Feather Tips consists of three tips and has an exceptionally fine curl and full appearance. We specially recommend this number and you could not duplicate same elsewhere for less than $2.50. Colors, black, cream or white. Price, per bunch of three..........$1.50
Per box ½ dozen.......... 8.25

If by mail, postage extra, 5 to 10 cents.

See the new Quill Holders, used on end of ostrich plumes, our No. 39C2591, at 1 cent each.

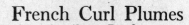

Fine Broad-Head Plumes

Large Full Heads. *Beautifully Curled.*

This style is designed with the idea of producing a very broad effect in the head of the plume. This curling shows the width of the feather to the best advantage. The quality will please you. Come in both black and white (except No. 18V3602, which comes in black only). *State color.* Average shpg. wt., 12 oz.

Catalog No.	Length, In.	Price, Each
18V3602	9	$0.33
18V3604	10	.55
18V3608	12	.98
18V3612	14	1.59
18V3615	16	2.98
18V3616	17	3.75
18V3617	18	5.45

So You Will Know

how we have prepared to take care of your plume order, we will tell you that years ago we laid down the following rules for conducting this department:

1st. To sell only good plumes; plumes which would give a full measure of satisfactory wear.

2d. To establish a high standard of quality and maintain it.

3d. To sell at a small margin above cost and depend on a big volume of sales for a profit.

4th. To establish a fixed selling price and give the greatest possible value for this price.

Upon this good foundation we built a tremendous ostrich plume business. It is still growing. This is evidence that we have secured our customers' confidence. And without confidence in the seller, no woman can be entirely satisfied with her plume. Our increasing reputation as value givers proves that we have convinced the buyers of our ability to give them *better* plumes at *lower* prices. Order now and satisfy yourself as to the value of our plumes. Examine them carefully: see if they are not all and more than we claim.

Our guarantee makes you the judge.

French Curl Plumes

Are Always Popular.

These beautiful Ostrich Feathers are second only to our Supreme Royal Curl quality, and carry our highest recommendation to those who wish a good plume at a very moderate price. Made of fine selected stock, the width of each feather being in good proportion to the length. Colors, black or white. *State color.* Average shipping weight, 1¼ lbs.

Catalog No.	Length, In.	Width, In.	Price, Each
18V3621	15	8	$1.95
18V3623	16	8½	2.98
18V3624	17	9	3.75
18V3625	18	9½	4.88
18V3627	19	10	5.89
18V3629	22	10	7.95
18V3631	24	10	9.45

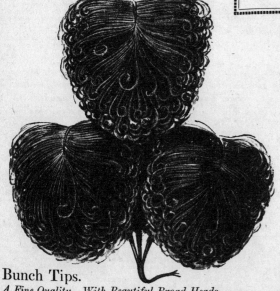

Bunch Tips.

A Fine Quality   With Beautiful Broad Heads.

Can easily be separated and used singly. The fine quality will surely please you. We do not quote sizes in these tips as their value lies in the weight and fullness of the head and not in the length or width. Black or white (except No. 18V3653, which comes in black only). *State color.* Average shipping weight, 13 ounces.

Prices are for bunch of three tips.

No. 18V3653	Price...$0.35	No. 18V3661	Price...$1.95
No. 18V3655	Price... .63	No. 18V3662	Price... 2.48
No. 18V3657	Price... .98	No. 18V3663	Price... 3.48
No. 18V3659	Price... 1.59		

Willow Plumes

of Genuine Ostrich.

No other trimming can replace the beautiful rich looking and graceful willow plume for all styles and sizes of hats. Is a complete trimming for the largest hat. These plumes are made of three full layers of hand-tied ostrich feathers. Colors, black or white. *State color.* Average shipping weight, 1½ pounds.

Catalog No.	Length, Inches	Width, Inches	Price, Each
18V3660	19	17	$3.25
18V3664	22	22	4.75
18V3665	24	21	6.25
18V3666	27	24	7.98

quality stock, such a feather that you could not duplicate elsewhere for less than $12.00 to $15.00. Length, 24 inches. Colors, black, white or cream. Price $8.50."

For those who could not afford the regal magnificence of full-length plumes, tips were available. They came "three in a bunch, made from best selected stock. Ostrich tips will be very stylish as a trimming this season." Tips, in bunches of three, sold at prices ranging from 30¢ to $1.50.

Aigrettes Without Regrets

In the early years of the twentieth century, millions of birds were killed and mummified for the trimming of women's hats. Fashion demanded that they die, and fashion can be a savage arbiter deaf to reason and mercy. A parlor gathering of ladies in the period 1900–15, when looked down upon from above, resembled nothing so much as the bird section of a museum of natural history, made up of thrushes, orioles, red-wing blackbirds, the gray mourning dove, the purplish-black grackle, the man-loving wren, and the common pigeon. Even the Shelleyan skylark was taken for a last ride by many a lady of the land, and, thereafter watching from the vantage point of her hat with the all-seeing eyes of the dead, saw her raise funds for missionaries to convert the savages of Africa to the amenities of civilization.

All God's chillun literally had wings in 1905. They were stylish, abundant, and cheap. For twenty-five cents, one could buy "Fine quality soft pliable wings. Nice full size." Fifty cents bought "Extra Large Size, fine quality, soft, pliable wings. Can be used for any style trimming."

The long-continued and never-ending battle for bird protection in the United States has been directed as much against women as against predators and hunters. A report of the New York State Audubon Society, in 1899, stated:

"About 150 persons were present, most of them women, and fully three-fourths wore birds or parts of birds in their hats, a practice on which the Society frowns."

But whether the Audubon Society frowned or smiled, and

however many ladies joined it, swearing to stop the extermination of birds while wearing their bodies on their hats, the "world traffic in feather millinery reached its height in the period between 1870 and 1908, and the quantities of plumage used during these years was beyond calculation. . . . As a single example, in an auction room in London, where great sales took place monthly, there was displayed in June, 1900, in one lot, white egret plumes that had cost the lives of more than 24,000 birds." *

The most prized of all the feathers of birds were the plumes of the egret. This graceful and beautiful white heron was a few years ago on its way to extinction along with the vanished passenger pigeon and the heath hen. The demand for its plumes, which could not be plucked harmlessly from the live bird like those of the ostrich but could be obtained only by killing the bird, was so great that thousands were annually killed wherever they existed in the world. It is during the mating and nesting season that the plumes of the egret are at their best, and this fact was sufficient to threaten the existence of the species. At other seasons, this bird is wild and difficult to approach, but, when the young have been hatched, the parental instinct among egrets is so strong that they return time after time to succor their young, despite the blazing guns of hunters and the sight of other birds dropping around them. As the old birds were killed, the young were left to starve or to become the prey of snakes and owls, while few remained to reproduce their kind. But despite the savage cruelty involved in the taking of egrets' plumes, and despite the strange fact that the feathers of this bird and of the beautiful bird of paradise became so popular among pleasure ladies that they were almost the hallmark of their profession, years were to pass and the egret was to face extinction before a Federal law made traffic in their plumage illegal.

On April 16, 1913, a letter addressed to the editor ap-

* Gilbert Pearson, *Adventures in Bird Protection.*

peared in *The New York Times*. It was signed by Minnie Maddern Fiske and George Arliss. They wrote:

> Members of the Audubon Society are deeply interested in legislation relating to the protection of birds. Col. Roosevelt says, "It is a disgrace to America that we should permit the sale of aigrettes." When some aigrette company tried to establish itself in New Jersey, President Wilson, who was then governor of that State, killed the bill that would have allowed this indecent traffic and expressed himself in these words. "I think New Jersey can get along without blood money."
>
> The aigrette is torn from the live mother bird in the nesting season and the little ones are left to starve. One of the plume hunters in a Southern coutry writes:
>
> "The natives of the country do virtually all the hunting for feathers. I have seen them pull the plumes from the wounded birds leaving the crippled birds to die of starvation unable to respond to the cries of their young which were calling for food. I have known these people to tie and prop up wounded egrets on the marsh where they would attract the attention of other birds flying by. These decoys are kept in this position until they die of their wounds or from the attacks of insects. . . . I could write you many pages of the horrors practiced in gathering aigrettes in Venezuela for the millinery trade of Paris and New York."
>
> Congress has convened in special session for the purpose of passing the revised tariff act. The Audubon Societies support the provision prohibiting the importation of aigrettes. . . .
>
> There will undoubtedly be strong opposition to the proposed law . . . on the part of merchants and milliners who encourage the aigrette atrocities as a source of revenue.
>
> The matter is in the hands of the American women.

Egret atrocities were committed as ruthlessly in the United States as in Venezuela. When a bill seeking to outlaw sales of egrets was before Congress in 1913, a film was shown which revealed the methods of egret hunters. It was made by Mr. Edward McIlhenny, the famous bird conservationist of Louisiana.

"Into a large colony of snowy egrets which he has long nurtured near his home on Avery Island, plume hunters entered and from a boat shot egrets about their nests. The film showed the hunters pushing through the bushes in their quest, showed the birds falling dead or wounded before the gunfire, and revealed the helpless young left in their nests. Then there was the camp scene on shore, where the bodies of dead birds were skinned for their feathers, and soon a line of dried scalps were waving gently in the breeze." *

The bill to protect egrets had smooth sailing in the House, but in the Senate there was much difficulty and some Senators campaigned against it. Among them was Senator James A. Reed of Missouri, who said:

"I really honestly want to know why there should be any sympathy or sentiment about a long-legged, long-beaked, long-necked bird that lives in swamps, and eats tadpoles and fish and crawfish and things of that kind; why we should worry ourselves into a frenzy because some lady adorns her hat with one of its feathers, which appear to be the only use it has. . . . If the young are left to starve, it would seem to me the proper idea would be to establish a foundling asylum for the young, but still let humanity utilize this bird for the only purpose that evidently the Lord made it for, namely, so that we could get aigrettes for the bonnets of our beautiful ladies."

("Eighteen-Piece Aigrette, brush effect. Length, 8 inches. This makes a very full and showy trimming. Colors, black or white. Price $1.00.")

Senator Reed, who was apparently privy to the mind of the Lord, was a powerful figure in his time, but nonetheless a bill prohibiting the importation of aigrettes and many other kinds of bird feathers became law—after twenty-seven years of agitation—on October 3, 1913.

* Pearson, *ibid.*

T. S. Eliot evidently did not know the history of American birds or fashion-mad American women when he wrote of "white birds and tall women," for when a white bird met a tall woman before 1913, it was soon glued to her hat. And not even the Federal law deterred the ladies in the beginning.

On October 27, 1913, *The New York Times* reported that "A feathered headdress valued at $600.00 was seized from the baggage of Miss Edna McLaughlin of 60 East 183 Street on her arrival yesterday from Liverpool. . . ." A few days later, the same newspaper described another seizure:

"When Mrs. Robert S. Winsmore walked down the gangway from the Cunarder *Mauretania* yesterday with her husband . . . an inspector noticed she wore one of the forbidden plumes in her hat.

"Gently but firmly, the representative of the Federal Government approached Mrs. Winsmore and informed her . . . that she would have to remove the aigrette and hand it to the Inspector.

"Mrs. Winsmore was very indignant and said that it was all nonsense because the plume was an artificial one, and in addition had been purchased in New York.

" 'That must be settled afterward,' said the Inspector. . . .

"Mrs. Winsmore went on board the *Mauretania* again to her cabin where she removed the aigrette as quickly as her indignation would permit, while her husband stood on the deck and aired his opinions of the customs generally and those of New York in particular."

From the passage of the law of 1913 until 1922, the story of egrets closely parallels the story of prohibition. The ladies were bound to have their aigrettes and were willing to pay high prices for them—with two results. One was that a brisk business in smuggling soon developed, for no law forbade the wearing of aigrettes once they were in the country. The other was that imitation aigrettes—like imitation Scotch whisky in 1929—were sold for the genuine article. Finally, in 1922, a Federal law was passed, providing that if anyone offered for sale the plumage of wild birds, he must produce proof satisfactory to the Customs officials that they were legally imported prior to October 3, 1913.

At last the traffic in birds came to an end with the passage of protective legislation in the United States, Great Britain, and Canada. The bird gradually disappeared from Nellie's hat and emerged white and beautiful against the dark beauty of the swamps and marshes of Louisiana and Florida.

Hatpins

In 1905, when ladies wore small mattresses of natural or store-bought hair, hats were clamped to them by means of hatpins. The catalog lists these useful but potentially dangerous instruments in only their most primitive form: "Round Jet Hat Pins, made of best quality blued steel, good size head. Price per dozen . . . 3¢." A few years later, the hatpin assumed the proportions of a full-fledged ornament and became a menace to the public safety.

The World Hatpin War

Less than one year before that summer's day of 1914 in the Serbian town of Sarajevo when a young student, Gavrilo Princip, touched off the World War with pistol shots that killed the Austrian Archduke Ferdinand and his wife, women's hatpins touched off a world-wide hatpin war. And that war, like the great conflict that was soon to come, began in Europe and eventually engulfed the United States. On April 20, 1913, the following dispatch from Berlin appeared in *The New York Times:*

> Police President Von Jagow's embargo against murderous hatpins came officially into force in Berlin this week. Women who are fond of decorating their millinery with prongs which endanger life and limb, henceforth will be subject to a fine of $15 for the first offense and imprisonment for the second offense. Police "spotters" are at work . . . trying to catch offenders. . . . The shops report a landoffice business in the sale of hat pin protectors, which have been named "jagow-nibs."

A few days later in New York, an enraged man wrote to the *Times,* complaining that:

> A friend of mine, while riding on the Brooklyn elevated received a deep and painful cut from a hat pin which protruded over two inches from the hat. . . . It began to swell, and at the end of a week his chin had swollen to twice its normal size. He was compelled to go to a physician who told him that blood poisoning had set in, and an operation on his chin would be necessary.
>
> . . . He has now fully recovered, but will always bear the reminder of the incident in the shape of an ugly scar on his chin. He not only had to pay a heavy doctor's bill, but lost two weeks work, and for a young fellow with a mother dependent on him this is no small matter.

Soon it was Austria's turn to fight the hatpin. In May, 1913, the Ministry of Railways issued an order that women wearing unprotected pins should not be permitted to ride on the State Railways, and Vienna conductors were ordered to put off the trams women whose pins were likely to put out a fellow passenger's eye. Austria, however, as Metternich said long ago, was "an absolutism tempered by *Schlamperei.*" So the news dispatch concludes with this sage observation. "The fair Viennese will probably continue to ride on the municipal tramways, whether their hat pins be long or short, and protected or not."

In the spring of 1913, New Jersey, unable to make the ladies listen to reason, in desperation passed a law prohibiting the wearing of hatpins protruding more than one half inch without protection of the points. And even New Orleans —a deep South stronghold of gallantry—legislated against the ladies. One's melancholy at this defection from traditional Southern politesse is relieved only by the fact that the city's policemen were ordered to be courteous in making arrests. It was an order, however, which may have proceeded as much from discretion as from chivalry.

"Six women have appeared as defendants in two courts of this city [New Orleans]," says *The New York Times* of May

11, 1913, "for wearing hat pins that were too long, violating a new ordinance. The police made the arrests in a very polite manner. Large crowds followed them. The policemen endeavored in every way not to give the impression that the matter was a joke, at the same time being careful not to offend any of the women they approached.

" 'I beg your pardon,' the policemen would say, 'but I must call your attention to the fact that you are violating the law. . . . Kindly give me your name and address.'

"Invariably the woman so approached would smile, take the matter good-naturedly, and respond by telling where she lived. Some of the women arrested were well known. One of the policemen, who is six feet three inches in height, and weighs 253 pounds, said:

" 'I'd like to have you understand that it's no joke to watch for those shining points and then approach the owner and warn them.' "

The Portable Veranda

$2.63
No. 18T6879 Brevort

The time was now approaching—February, 1914—when the World War would soon begin, but in that month France joined the Austro-German alliance against hatpins. The Paris Prefect of Police, M. Hennion, "issued stern edicts against unprotected hat pins, yet Parisiennes still cheerfully disobey them."

American, German, and Austrian women might be kicked off trams and trains, be arrested and pay fines, but not the ladies of Paris. It was not long before this doleful fact was to become apparent to the Paris police, for as the *Times* reported a week after the order against hatpins had been issued:

The police are beginning to believe that la belle Parisienne is invincible. Twice has the Prefecture issued a stern edict against unprotected hat pins, but the Parisienne merely smiles, shrugs her shoulders, and goes her way, often bristling like a hedgehog.

To Prefect Hennion was first given the task of rebuking careless hat pin wearers, but, although he had become the terror of the Apaches, he failed ignominiously to bring about the slightest change in the Parisienne's dangerous habit.

. . . This week M. Hennion made a new rule. Since the majority of gouged and lacerated cheeks occurred in the Underground or in omnibuses, he ordered the guards to refuse admittance to all women with unprotected hat pins, but the subway guards, who are reputed to be the most heartless of men living, proved too gallant.

Inquiry at headquarters shows that not a single report of such exclusion has been made, although in every train the deadly hat pins are plainly visible.

Thus French women, by a combination of passionate individualism and charm, that glorious indifference to discipline which is a mark of the French people, and the gallantry of subway guards, evaded the rulings of the Paris prefect. What is a gouged cheek or a lacerated eye by comparison with the necessities of fashion in Paris, the capital of fashion?

The Parisiennes, however, who were not struggling for the vote or "women's rights" in 1914, and apparently cared not a snap of their chic fingers for either, must have been surprised to note how their addiction to the hatpin was interpreted by a leader of the woman's movement in the United States. Miss Harriet Stanton Blatch's letter to *The New York Times* is highly revelatory of the state of thinking among so-called "advanced" women in 1914. Miss Blatch wrote:

In your telegraphic news from Paris recently we are informed that Prefect Hennion . . . has twice issued edicts against unprotected hat pins, but that the Parisi enne merely smiles and goes her way. . . . This is but another argument for Votes for Women and another painful illustration of the fact that men cannot discipline women. . . .

Women have never had the advantage of being disciplined by those who could discipline them. Men have made laws unjust to women, and they have made laws sometimes that favor women, but they have never been able to discipline them. One of the leading railroad corporations declared recently that if a woman met with an accident on its railway, and wore a hobble skirt, she could not recover damages, but mere man, when he gets on the bench and in the jury box, does not seem to fall in line with the corporations and discipline the women. The Mayor and City Council of a Southern town declaimed very brave things about disciplining women who wore slit skirts, but the fair dames of the South laughed the plan to scorn. . . .

Women need discipline; they need to be forced, if not led, out of their barbarisms, but women never have and never will submit to the discipline of men. If they are to be civilized, their rulers will have to be the wise and good of their own sex. Give women political power and the best among them will gradually train the uncivilized, just as the best among men have trained their sex. . . .

In April, 1914—when spring was there with the last April of regattas, flowers, and peace that England was to know for four years—the hatpin war reached that country and the English ran extraordinarily true to form in the presence of this menace.

Two members of the London County Council suggested that the Local Government Records and Museums Committee should report on the desirability of introducing a new by-law to cope with hatpins. One of the members, Mr. Shearman, said that a friend of his, a doctor at St. Thomas's Hospital, had told him that there were frequent cases of hatpin injuries treated in the out-patient department. At a large establishment in the West End, it was stated that, although hatpin protectors were stocked, women refused to buy them.

A Charming Style, Very Pretty Trimming.

$1.25

No. 39C9000 This is a large dress hat, made of Canton and lace straw. The shape raised on the left side and drooping in the back. Trimmed very effectively with gathered folds of white silk mull. Rosettes of white chantilly lace appear on both sides of crown. Bows and folds of white silk taffeta ribbon are handsomely arranged in the back and also on the side of the left brim, same extending to the bandeau, which is trimmed with violets. Two clusters of violets and foliage complete the trimming of this hat. Can be ordered as described, in natural color shape trimmed in white, or black shape trimmed in black. Price.........$1.25

Very Effective and Becoming Dress Turban.

$1.65

No. 39C9003 This is a dress turban, made of firm black, fancy straw braid, shape rolling on the left side. The upper trimming consists of a loose drape of black silk, same overlaid with rows of black satin straw braid. On the left side appears a long wreath of light blue velvet forget-me-nots, same wreath extending to the back of the crown, which is caught with a long novelty ornament. A black bandeau on the left side, trimmed with light blue velvet forget-me-nots, completes the trimming of this turban. As described in black trimmed with light blue is very pretty, but can also be ordered in black trimmed in pink, or white trimmed in pink or light blue. Price....................$1.65

Large Pretty Dress Hat, $3.00 Value, only $1.75.

$1.75

No. 39C9006 This is a large dress hat, hand made on a wire frame, shape slightly raised on the left side. The facing and upper brim are covered with light blue silk mull, same overlaid with a pretty pattern of light blue lace straw braid. The large bell crown is covered with a firm straw braid. The front as well as both sides of the upper brim, is trimmed with an extra large cluster of blue wild flowers. The crown is surrounded with folds and loops of white China silk, same falling over the brim and extending to the bandeau, where they are made into bows. The facing trimmed with a fold of white China silk and white wild flowers completes the trimming of this hat. Very pretty as described in light blue and white, but can also be ordered in black and pink or white and pink. Price..$1.75

A Stylish and Becoming Dress Hat, $1.80.

$1.80

No. 39C9009 A large black dress hat. Made of firm black straw. The shape is raised on the left side and drooping in the back. Very effectively trimmed around the crown and the entire upper brim with serpentine rosettes made of black taffeta silk edged with a row of pink satin straw braid. A large wreath of pink velvet forget-me-nots ornaments the upper trimming. The facing is overlaid with a row of satin braid and a large cluster of pink velvet forget-me-nots in the back over the upper brim, complete the trimming of this hat. Very pretty, as described in black and pink, but can also be ordered in white, pink or light blue, with trimmings to match. Price.................$1.80

This is a Very Beautiful Turban, $1.85.

No. 39C9012 This is a very beautiful turban, hand made on a wire frame. The shape, upturned high in the back, is closely fitted to the head. The facing is developed in stitched and shirred brown silk chiffon, edged with folds of brown novelty imported German braid. The upper brim is developed in brown shirred and stitched silk chiffon. The low crown is made of German folded hair braid, trimmed very beautifully on the left side with six brown silk and velvet flowers and folds of brown silk, same falling over the left side. An all around bandeau completes the trimming of this hat. This is an unusually becoming turban in brown, as described, but can also be ordered in all black, white or light blue, with trimmings to match. Price...................$1.85

A New and Pretty Idea, $3.00 Value for $1.88.

$1.88

No. 39C9015 No prettier hat has been shown this season. The workmanship, style and material must be seen to be appreciated, it is hand made on a wire frame. Facing as well as upper trimming is made of navy blue silk chiffon, while the wide brim is made of shirred chiffon, with a fold of maize color satin braid. The bell crown, made of maize color satin braid and edged with navy blue silk chiffon, is handsomely trimmed in the back with two wheel rosettes of navy blue satin ribbon caught with two imported novelty ornaments from which folds of ribbon extend and fall over the brim. An all around bandeau completes the trimming of this hat. As described in navy blue and maize color is very pretty, but can also be ordered in black, brown, white or light blue. Price.....................$1.88

A Very Becoming and Stylish Turban, $1.90.

No. 39C9018 This is a large dress turban, hand made on a silk wire frame. The facing and upper rim as well as crown are overlaid and trimmed with black tucked silk chiffon. The entire rolling brim is trimmed with red mousseline flowers and foliage, and the flowers are overlaid with black chantilly lace. Directly in the center over the crown is a large cluster of red mousseline flowers and imported foliage, surrounded with a fold of black silk, which extends to the left side of the brim where it is made into wired bows. A bandeau on the left side completes the trimming of this elegant dress turban. This turban is exceedingly becoming and stylish and would recommend same in the color as described in black and red, but can also be ordered in black and pink, white and pink or light blue with trimmings to match. Price....................$1.90

Very Latest Three Cornered Design, $2.00.

No. 39C9021 This is an exceedingly pretty hat of the very latest design and shape, hand made on a wire frame. The shape is three cornered and uprolling in the back. The facing is made of gathered and shirred black silk chiffon while the upper brim is overlaid with folds of soft black peroxiline braid and tucked black silk chiffon. Pink silk and velvet flowers and imported foliage with long stems are arranged on the left side between the crown and the brim, while the left facing is trimmed generously with the same material. A bandeau on the left side, trimmed with a loop of black ribbon and loops of the same material in the back, falling over the brim, complete the trimming of this hat. As described, in black and pink, it is very pretty, but can also be ordered in white and pink, or light blue and white, which makes a very good combination in this hat. Price..................$2.00

The New Charlotte Corday, a $4.00 Hat; Our Price, Only $2.05.

$2.05

No. 39C9024 The very latest hat, known as the Charlotte Corday. At present it is the rage in New York and Paris. It is a small dress shape with edge drooping in mushroom effect. The facing is made of folds of brown silk chiffon, while the rolling drooping brim is trimmed with gathered and shirred brown silk. The very large bell crown of the newest shape is also developed in gathered and shirred brown silk. On the left side is a wheel silk rosette; six brown silk and velvet flowers elegantly arranged in front on the large bell crown complete the trimming of this hat. This is a hat that no swell dresser should overlook, as it is without doubt the very latest offered by the very highest class milliners. There may be more becoming hats than this one, but we can assure you that no more stylish hat has ever been offered. As described in brown it is very pretty, but can also be ordered in all black, white or light blue. Trimmings to match. Price.....................$2.05

It's Here~~
in time for the party

MOTHER knew, when she mailed us the order, that the new dress would arrive in time.

She was confident that Sears, Roebuck and Co. would ship it promptly. In all the years she had been dealing with us she had never been disappointed. Now Marjorie could wear the dress to the party—her cup of happiness was full.

This was proof again that a customer's faith was justified. It is an everyday occurrence in thousands of homes, because our customers have come to expect the best of service from the World's Largest Store. And that's just the kind we give them — *the best service.*

One customer writes: "My shipment arrived so quickly I think the goods and my order must have passed each other on the way!"

Another, living in the third zone from our store says: "It was only 48 hours from the time I mailed my order until I was carrying the goods into the house."

We ship more than 130,000 packages a day from our four great stores at Chicago, Philadelphia, Dallas and Seattle.

We know that 99 out of every 100 of these shipments leave our store *within 24 hours after the orders are received.* Orders received before noon are *shipped the very same day!*

Here is a great organization, built to serve our customers better than they can be served anywhere else. Not only must our values be bigger, but our service must be better. That combination has brought us the continued patronage of over nine million families.

Let the World's Largest Store supply all YOUR needs—we give you our assurance that

"In less than a day your order is on its way"

Hatpins and Nations

It is both amusing and illuminating to see how the movement against exposed hatpins was treated in different countries.

In Berlin, law-abiding German women, in dread of the law, rushed out and bought hatpin protectors when the police ordinance ordaining their use was passed. In Paris, the ladies charmed the guardians of the law who were too gallant to arrest them, while the subway guards were too chivalrous to kick them off the trains. In London, a committee was appointed to consider and report on the desirability of hatpin legislation—a forerunner of the policy that J. M. Keynes was later to call the "wise policy of cunctation" and cause Britain the gravest difficulties—while the women, in the interim, ignored hatpin protectors. In New Orleans, the police, with the respectful politeness that women in those days commanded, arrested offenders somewhat nervously, not only because the offenders were women but also because police officers frequently lose their jobs for applying the law to important persons in the community. At the same time, the spectacle of a six-foot policeman with large crowds following him as he begged a woman's pardon for arresting her appealed to the American sense of humor and made of an incident that would seem serious in Europe merely a little comedy played out on the streets.

The whole hatpin controversy came to an end in Europe in 1914. Eyes then began to be gouged out by bayonets and high explosives. And to America, shortly, came bobbed hair and the end of hatpins.

Wartime Plumes

The War in Europe brought a boon to millions of ostrich-plume lovers in the United States. The catalog for 1915 announces ALL PLUME PRICES SMASHED and then tells us why.

"Disturbed market conditions," it says, "had caused a sudden drop in plume prices, and, for a few weeks, the prices stood at the lowest levels in twenty-five years. We took immediate advantage of this sudden flurry and bought an immense stock of our regular high-grade quality plumes. We now give you all the benefit of this big saving. . . ."

Fortunate America! High prices for wheat and low prices for ostrich plumes. Both the demand and Sears' stock of plumes must have been immense, for the catalog devotes two pages to them. So firmly established was the vogue for plumes at the time that a promise of their popularity in perpetuity is given. "A fine plume," we are told, "never goes out of style. It is the only trimming in the millinery world which is considered staple and always in good taste." Plumes, then, were like money in the bank. But in the catastrophic years that were to come, neither money in the bank nor the plume was to be safe.

The craft of dyeing had evidently made great strides since 1905 when plumes were produced in only a few simple colors. Now one can wear a feathered rainbow by buying BEAUTIFUL COLORED PLUMES. ALL OF FASHION'S FAVORITE SHAPES.

"No other trimming," says the catalog, "lends as much charm and beauty to a hat as a richly colored plume. These have the Medallion Spot style of shading, which is a big favorite. The lighter shade in the center of the head blends in a charming effect with the darker part on the outside. Furnished in the following colors:

"American beauty red with Nell rose spot; mahogany color with pink spot; emerald green with nile green spot; or tango color with deep cream spot."

The hats of 1915 are smaller than those in 1905, made of velvet or silk plush, and those "for dressy wear," almost invariably topped off with a plume or two. TRIMMED HATS WITH STYLE were in the manner of No. 78D9002:

"Charming hat made entirely of silk velvet. . . . Beautifully curled band of fine quality ostrich laid around crown and over upper brim. Trimming ornament has ostrich rosette with six curved striped quills, called whips. Price, $3.98."

One passes with a shock of surprise—so great is the contrast—from the elaborate ostrich and plush confections to a severe, new kind of hat evidently designed for a new kind of woman who is wearing "Good Felt Hats." These depend for ornamentation only upon a simple buckle or a piece of ribbon around the crown, and sell for prices ranging from 98 cents to $2.48.

In the same manner of simplicity are HIGH GRADE GENUINE BEAVERS. RICH LOOKING LOW PRICED HATS. They seemed to be so firmly established in fashion's favor that the catalog ventured upon a prediction which time was to prove rash: "We consider beavers a staple millinery article, just as we consider an ostrich plume a staple article. They are always in good taste."

Plumes Pass

The catalog, which so confidently predicted in 1915 that "a fine plume never goes out of style," lists one mere wisp of an ostrich tip in 1925. Since that time, ostrich growers, aided by Paris milliners and a corps of press agents with large sums of money at their disposal, have tried in vain to make women wear plumes again. But the ostrich goes about today shedding its feathers on the desert air in its native habitats, or kicking up its heels for the benefit of visitors to zoos. Milliners long ago handed it back to naturalists.

In 1925, Sears employed a millinery fashion arbiter, known to posterity only as Pauline, who ventured to tell the ladies what was what in hats for the season. She says:

"Most heartily do I urge every woman who desires to keep in style to include in her wardrobe a hat of satin. Fashion has been most generous to satin; it is not confined to a short season in spring, summer, fall or winter. Satin hats are seen during all months in the smart style centers. They are very popular for wear with a suit or a coat; and there is no material more pleasing and altogether correct for evening wear with a dress than satin. . . ."

Pauline was not a lady to be caught off base. When mere men ran Sears' millinery department, they were likely to make rash prophecies about the enduring style qualities of plumes or beaver hats, but Pauline, with feminine conservatism, played safe. "There is," she says, "no one material that is 'it' for this fall. Style leaders are wearing felts, both fancifully trimmed and tailored, the lovely ribbon hats, hats of velvet and combinations of silk and satin and velvet, and of satin which is good all year around. Trimmings this fall are of flowers, ribbons and fancy feathers, in all the new stylish colors."

Silk Roses amid Crushed Velvet—A Neat Little Number in 1915

It is common experience among merchants that if an article will not sell for $1 it may sell for $1.50, because buying is frequently done not on value but on price. Thus if two shirts are put in a shopwindow, one with a red label priced at $1 and one with a blue label at $1.50, a large percentage of buyers will walk into the shop and buy the blue-label shirt without even asking to look at the red label. Why should they? A shirt at $1.50 simply must be better quality than one at a dollar.

Pauline, knowing this propensity of buyers, therefore addresses a few words on the subject to the ladies.

"Many Women Write Me," she says, "and ask if we have some 'more expensive hats'. They say they always pay from $10 to $15 for hats, and they wonder how it is possible to offer hats that are good style and quality at our low prices. Now I am sure all of you know that a high price does not make a stylish hat. Is it not true that among our friends there is always a 'Mrs. Brown' who can take a $2 shape and $1 worth of ribbon and make a hat which looks more stylish than one which was made for 'Mrs. Jones' for $25? The price does not decide. Sears-Roebuck . . . sell on value—not making a charge for style. . . . Order and convince yourself."

Following this blunt dissertation addressed to the large group who do not know how to differentiate between value and price, the catalog turns to the rescue of another large group: the fat women of the land. It is a striking paradox of American life that a depression-ridden country should have so many fat men and women, for in those lands—China, Japan, Arabia, and others—where food is not abundant, only the rich are fat. Not only do we have great numbers of fat people but they spend millions of dollars annually trying to become thin.

Typical of the EXTRA LARGE SIZES FOR STOUTS offered by the 1925 catalog is No. 78D8165:

"This unusual style keeps the same youthful appearance that a small size represents, and looks equally as smart. Made of alternating sections of silk faced velvet and good grade Rayon [artificial silk] taffeta. Inside brim is velvet. Handsome flower appliqué of shaded novelty ribbon outlined with effective embroidery stitches. . . ."

Go West, Young Woman

In the fashion world of 1905, Paris was the first word and the last in the buying and selling of women's clothes. Thirty years later (1935), fashion—certainly popular mail-order fashion—looks to Hollywood. Europe, in fact, has long been grumbling that it is being Americanized with cocktails, ice water, chewing gum, Coca-Cola, bathtubs, quick lunches, and above all, the motion pictures of the United States. The screen and the shadows that flit across it have captivated America and now exercise a prodigious influence on American life, including fashions. In this changing world, poor Madame Rentau, the great French modiste of the 1905 catalog, has been forced into retirement at her villa near Cannes; Pauline, the fashion arbiter of 1925, is running a beauty parlor at South Bend, and Adrienne Ames—AUTOGRAPHED HOLLYWOOD FASHIONS—becomes the girl's guide. The catalog tells us that:

"Adrienne Ames is clever! She puts her autograph on one of the most important, best liked felt hats for Fall! And she wears it in a very fine quality felt. . . . She knows there's nothing smarter than the casual easy lines of the brim, that turns down in front, up in back, the jaunty, soft crease in the crown. And she's right! Sears customers get the benefit of her fashion judgment!"

This paragraph, as peppered with exclamation points as rye bread with caraway seed, strikes the mood for the 1935 presentation of hats. It reveals America as a country where people may, perhaps, die but in which there are no middle-aged or elderly persons. The people of the country and their hats are "young." Youth must be served, agrees the catalog, and at the lowest price that will bring the greatest volume of profitable business.

Thus No. 78K6245 is "A young hat that fits large head-sizes, too! Just a single natural crease in the crown, jabbed with a gay quill."

And No. 78K6230 is certainly the last word in chic because it was "Copied from a style worn by Kay Francis!" Now you have the opportunity to dress and look like her for only $1.69.

One looks in vain for dear old Grandma and her poke bonnet that endured for nigh on to thirty year. Both have vanished from the catalog, and Grandma, if she is living at all, would not be found dead in that old hat.

It was smart to be horsy in 1935. All over the land, fat-bellied men and big-bottomed women were jogging heavily along the bridle paths of city parks on hired nags as ancient as those slaughtered in Spanish bull rings. Northern Virginia was undergoing a second Yankee invasion and rich New York Gauchos were falling off horses where Virginian gentlemen once rode. None of this was lost on the catalog, which grouped a large number of hats under the general heading: GRAND NATIONAL FAVORITES. THOSE JAUNTY FELTS WITH CREASED CROWNS AND BRIGHT FEATHERS! RIGHT FOR EVERYONE!

1935 was the year, too, of the beret. The national headgear of the mysterious Basques became the fashionable hat of the American woman. The catalog pictures dozens of berets and describes them in language that is already obsolete:

"What luck! To think you can enjoy this young, new *peppy* fashion, etc." And then in a distinctly uncatalogish gurgling burst: "Look lovely and angelic in this brand new off-the-face beret."

Ostrich Redivivus

It appears that, after all, woman's face and woman's figure which have gone through so many transformations in thirty years are about to go through another metamorphosis and emerge in the feminine likeness of 1915. In June, 1939, a fashionable New York store—Saks Fifth Avenue—published this advertisement:

SAKS FIFTH AVENUE
says
WATCH OSTRICH

it's due for a revival

"Back to curves and hips and bustles! Back to the frankly feminine figure! Back to the elegance of pre-war days. That's the current trend in fashion. And we forecast a big revival for ostrich—surely the prettiest, most flattering, most alluring feminine fashion that Art and Nature ever devised."

If ostrich does come back, Sears' task will be simple. It will merely have to buy some plumes and dig up its catalog copy of 1915 so similar to that employed by Saks Fifth Avenue in 1939.

FOREIGNERS traveling in the United States have recently had a new marvel to write about along with the New York skyline, our gulp-and-gallop lunch counters, the wonders of Hollywood, the mysteries of our politics, and the American missionary attitude toward Europe. It is the silk-stockinged legs of American women. Elsewhere there are wonders of architecture matching or exceeding those of our skyscrapers; the mysteries of European politics are as strange to us as our politics are to Europeans, and Europe even assumes the missionary pose when it serves its purposes. It may even be conceded that elsewhere one may find women's legs matching or exceeding in beauty the legs of American women, but nowhere else do so many women's legs move to work and to play in silk. And if ever the barricades should be erected in the streets of our cities, a diligent press, passionate for the reporting of records, will say that this is the first revolution marked by the presence of great quantities of silk hosiery; let the runs come when they may and go where they list.

Soviet Russia showed a newsreel to its citizens in 1933. It was made in America and pictured long lines of people standing before soup kitchens. The obvious purpose, of course, was to demonstrate to the comrades the distress of the people of a rich democracy. After a few showings, the reel was abruptly withdrawn. The comrades were mumbling in their beards. "If the unemployed in America are so well dressed," they said, "what must be the condition of those who have jobs."

In the United States, more than in any other country of the world, women's apparel tends to approach that of a classless society; here the luxuries of other nations are common necessaries. Nowhere is this fact more sharply demonstrated than in the case of silk stockings, whose phenomenal increase in use during the past twenty years is clearly marked in the catalog's pages.

When Silk Stockings Were a Luxury

One looks in vain for mention of silk hosiery in the 1905 catalog. At that time, it was the luxury of a few women who brought silk stockings home from Europe, or bought them at high prices in America.

The overwhelming majority of women who shopped for stockings, in the catalog or elsewhere, contented themselves with black cotton or lace stockings selling at prices ranging (at Sears) from ten cents for a pair of plain stockings to forty cents for a pair of silk embroidered on cotton. These stockings were coarse, thick, ill-fitting, clumsy around the toes, sleazy, and became a bilious green black after a few

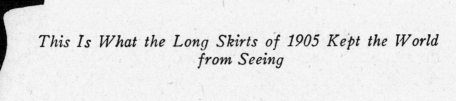

This Is What the Long Skirts of 1905 Kept the World from Seeing

trips to the washtub. They were as devoid of allure and sex appeal as a damp fish, but this was of no importance because the skirts of the times were long and the shoes were high, and if amateur Casanovas watched skirts fly in the wind that whistled around the Flatiron Building in New York, or caught a glimpse of an ankle as a lady ascended the steps of a streetcar in a small town, this was thrill enough without the beauty of silk.

In any event, women contented themselves with cotton stockings until the beginning of the World War, when skirts and

wages went up together, and the greatest cotton-growing country in the world became the largest silk-consuming country on earth. War, that grim phenomenon whose mysteries no man fully understands, works strange wonders in the field of fashion and wearing apparel as it does in so many other fields more important to the life of man, but it is enough to note here that Government buying of hosiery during the Civil War forced the development of our hosiery industry, and the World War precipitated the rise in the use of silk stockings. The cold figures are that from 1914 to 1923 American production of cotton hose decreased 6.17 per cent, while during the same period there was an increase of 26.77 per cent in silk hosiery and of about 417 per cent in hosiery made of rayon and mixed fibers.

Legs Come Out of Hiding

Shortly after the beginning of the World War, the legs of American women began to come out of their seclusion, and made their first public appearance in stockings of silk or artificial silk—as rayon was then called. The beginnings of the emerging of legs from hiding and of the stockings in which they were encased were modest enough. The catalog lists only two styles of full-fashioned silk stockings. They were heavy in weight and therefore lacking in sheerness; their prices were $1 and $1.37 a pair, and the only color available was black. These were luxury models. Women shopping for cheaper stockings bought, at eighty-eight cents a pair, ho-

Advertising—and Women—Grow Bolder in 1910

siery with cotton tops and a silk body, or artificial-silk stockings at prices ranging from twenty-four cents to forty-six cents a pair.

In 1915, millions of American women in the cities as well as in the small towns and on the farms tried to dress warmly in winter; the time had not yet come when they would go about in freezing temperatures attired in a few ounces of silk or rayon, while their husbands, bundled up to the ears, impotently grumbled, "You're crazy to dress like that." At this period, women wore black, ribbed mixed-wool-and-cotton stockings, warm, shapeless, heavy, ugly, and cheap, at twenty-five cents a pair; black pure-wool stockings, bulky and unattractive, at forty cents a pair; and even bulkier and uglier fleece-lined cotton stockings, at fifteen or twenty cents a pair. Neither silk hosiery nor rayon hosiery had yet achieved general acceptance among the masses.

Gertie's Garter—a Factor in Production

During the prosperous years 1919–28, the demand for silk hosiery became so great that production rose by 250 per cent, and this despite the fact that silk stockings, measured by to-day's prices, were high. The 1925 catalog features one number at $1.89 a pair, and it was by no means made entirely of silk, because its soles and heels were cotton as were those of all the other silk stockings in the catalog for that year. White, black, and brown are popular colors, and indeed these are all the colors except champagne, peach, and gray.

At this period, hosiery manufacturers began to cope with the problem of preventing Gertie's garter from destroying Gertie's expensive silk stockings by making "runs" in them. At home, Gertie would dress to go out for a party, put on a pair of round garters or attach her stockings to the garters on her girdle, and, while bending over to kiss Grandma good-by, would often at the same time say an unwitting farewell to her stockings as they gave way under the strain. And this was a serious matter to Gertie, because stockings cost from one to two dollars, yet runs or no runs, expense or no expense, she would not be found dead in cotton or wool hosiery. Whereupon manufacturers began to tinker with devices that would stop runs—ravel stops, garter stripes, reinforcements of fabric—but the runs have not been stopped and Gertie wears silk stockings just the same. Years ago, the wife of a workingman with an income of $1,600 a year told the Lynds a fact of American life which they reported in their *Middletown:*

"No girl can wear cotton stockings to high school. Even in winter my children wear silk stockings with lisle or imitations underneath."

If silk is a luxury, then we are obviously the most luxury-loving people on earth, enjoying an unprecedented mass distribution of at least this one item among the people. By 1929, we had achieved the astonishing feat of taking eighty-five per cent of total world deliveries of silk to mills—about half of which went into hosiery—and by 1930, American manufacturers were producing 300,000,000 pairs of silk stockings in a single year. American women literally lived, played, and slept in silk.

Technology Rescues Gertie

In all probability, Gertie had never heard the word technology; the Mitsui and Mitsubishi families of Japan would have struck her as just so much chop suey; the development of rayon from cellulose was a story that would have bored her; labor troubles in the North resulting in the migration of silk-hosiery mills to the cheaper nonunion labor areas of the South was a tale she had never heard, and Joan Crawford's make-up naturally interested her more than technical improvements in hosiery-knitting machines. Yet all these things played a part in enabling Gertie to buy her silk stockings for less money. The price drop may be graphically shown:

The average retail price for silk stockings during the period 1923–28 was $1.51 a pair.

The average retail price for silk stockings during the period 1933–38 was $0.91 a pair.

These are catalog prices, but, wherever Gertie bought her stockings in the latter period, she bought them for about sixty cents a pair less than in the earlier period. Whether she saved money in the long run (no pun intended) is doubtful, because, as time passed, Gertie wanted her stockings sheerer and sheerer, transparent and yet more transparent, until they finally became wisps of silk gossamer so finely spun that Gertie's legs seemed bare. And it was obviously impossible that such a fragile fabric should be able to withstand the stresses and strains of walking, dancing, or bending in the normal course of living. But this was of no importance. Gertie wanted her legs to look as beautiful as possible, and the sheerer the stockings the greater the beauty.

The 1935 catalog seems to think that Gertie desired the stockings worn by Hollywood stars—a thought well founded in reality—and consequently it offers her "Royal Purple

Chiffons Autographed and Worn in Hollywood by Loretta Young." What was good enough for Loretta Young was the height of perfection to Gertie Smith. The copy lays stress not on the wearing qualities of these stockings, for by now nobody expects stockings to wear, but on their sheerness—the indispensable quality that no one would do without.

"Lovely full fashioned chiffons, luxuriously fine in texture and finish. That's why Loretta Young chose them! Now finer-gauge; sheerer; flawless, ringfree. . . ."

Note too that these stockings differ sharply from those of 1915 and 1925, not only in the fact that they are gossamer thin as opposed to the heavier fabrics of the earlier stockings, but they contain no cotton at all. "All silk even to the picoted double tops, shadow welts, the reinforced French heels and sandal soles. . . ."

Yet Gertie paid only ninety-four cents for a pair of these stockings, or about half the price she had paid ten years before. All unknowing to Gertie, the complicated machinery of the modern world had been at work behind the scenes to lower the price of silk hosiery for her especial benefit.

First of all, raw silk dropped in price. As a nation, we went from silk in 1929 to sackcloth and ashes by 1932. There had been a time when we had worn silk regardless of price; now the time had come when we could afford it only at a low price. If we could not afford to buy silk, the Japanese could not afford to keep their silk crops at home, although they once tried silk control as we are now trying agricultural crop control. Raw silk is Japan's most important export and doubly important because it requires no imported raw materials to finish it for foreign markets; also it brings her a hundred per cent return of badly needed foreign exchange. Japan was therefore driven to sell her silk to us, who are the world's largest buyers, and to sell it at lowered prices. Even if this had not been sufficient compulsion, another powerful force was at work that inevitably drove down silk prices. That force was rayon. Cheaper than silk and, as technology improved it, highly competitive with silk, rayon decreed that silk must come down in price or dwindle to unimportance in the world market. Silk came down; invention and depression worked to make Gertie's stockings cheaper and to enable her

Putting Their Best
Legs Foremost

to buy more pairs of gossamer hosiery to match or contrast with each of her costumes.

Technology again gave Gertie a helping hand in producing superior knitting machines which now enable one operator to turn out ninety-six pairs as against seventy-two pairs during the period 1923–31. And wages came down. The silk-hosiery knitter who got $60 a week in 1923–28 got $50 a week after the depression, while producing more pairs of stockings per day than ever before. And because millions of women wear silk hosiery which is one of the most important items in their clothing budgets, there is intense competition among retailers for Gertie's stocking business. They reduce their profit margins on stockings because they hope also to sell Gertie a more profitable girdle or dress, and whether they succeed or not, she buys her hosiery at prices lower than are available to any other woman in the world.

In the short space of thirty years, we have moved from the point where silk hosiery was a luxury of the rich to the point where it is a necessary of the masses. No other nation has ever worn silk so universally. Down the avenues of the cities, down the streets of small towns, down the quiet paths of farms, bending over typewriters, and manipulating machines move the silk-stockinged legions of American women, presenting a fashion phenomenon unique to the United States and without parallel in history. The reputation of American silk hosiery, moreover, has spread abroad, with the result that, although we were long known as makers of excellent machinery, we are also now famous as the leaders in this field of fashion. Wherever silk hosiery is worn American silk stockings, produced at home or in our factories abroad, are in great demand.

The economic foundations of the country may be shaken by depression, but the hosiery industry, secure upon the rock of woman's legs, feels no tremors save that of the pulsing machinery turning out stockings in ever-greater numbers.

Gertie Attacks the Japanese

In 1938–39 Gertie and thousands of her sisters attacked the Japanese in order to rescue the Chinese. ("I admit," wrote De Tocqueville, "that America has no poets; but Americans have no lack of poetic ideas.") It was all so simple. Gertie was told that she could defeat Japan in her China war by throwing away her silk stockings and wearing cotton or lisle hosiery made in America. Japan, so the argument ran, simply could not live if her vital exports of silk to the United States were stopped or sharply reduced. It looked reasonable to Gertie and it appeared that women eight thousand miles away from an Asiatic war could win it by changing their stockings. Where the League of Nations, Great Britain, France, and the United States government had failed, Gertie would succeed. And in a short time, the pages of magazines and newspapers all over America bloomed with photographs of Gertie, of Vassar and Bryn Mawr girls, and of small-town women burning their silk stockings and flaunting their legs in lisle hosiery.

Japan seems, however, to have been little disturbed by this crusade. She knew that while Gertie didn't like Japan, Gertie's boy friend liked cotton stockings even less, and it was too much to ask of any girl that she sacrifice Bill's dates for China's future. It may be, in the language of Gertrude Stein, that a leg is a leg is a leg, but it is also true, in the language of Gertie Smith, that a leg encased in lisle has no more sex appeal than a wet towel. The great stocking crusade came, therefore, to an abrupt end. Gertie shamefacedly put her lisle hosiery away and bought new pairs of silk stockings. If China was to be rescued, the job was not to be Gertie's.

THE figures of corseted ladies in the 1905 catalog remind one of the lines of Gelett Burgess:

A wonderful bird is the pelican
His beak holds more than his bellican.

For these ladies wore viscera-crushing corsets in order to achieve small waists. They cherished large breasts if they had them, or did their damndest to get them if they did not have them. And they threw their crumpled stomachs into dismay by eating the large meals of the times. All this in obedience to a fashion. It is part of the history of fashion that it can be uncomfortable, torturing, ugly, and ridiculous, and yet be obeyed in a civilized society with an obedience that has no parallel save in the taboos of savages.

The unhappy-looking ladies sketched in the corset pages of the 1905 catalog have pulled-in, wasp waists, and what was then called a "big bust," while their well-tempered clavichords, propelled into space by the constriction of their middles, project at an angle that would be dangerous in this period of crowded streets, and practically impossible in modern small apartments. The instrument of these achievements was a strait jacket of steel and cloth whose severities were concealed but not tempered by froufrous of ribbon or lace, and whose stern function is indicated by heavy brass eyelets which were drawn together by strong hands pulling upon the laces. Illustrative of these bonebreakers gladly worn in the sweet name of fashion was:

"Straight Front Fine Batiste Corset, Bias Gored, at 50¢.

"Straight front, military erect figure, has 2 side steels and 4 bone strips with extra heavy front, 10-inch steel boned underneath, making a perfectly smooth surface. This is a medium weight with low bust, adapted for a wide range of figures. Handsomely trimmed with pretty lace on top."

An Undistributed Surplus

It appears from the description of this model that the ladies of 1905 wanted a straight and militarily erect figure with a wasp waist, and they had the equally strong desire for a large bust. The catalog assures us that large busts were the fashion, and in a half page of space it extols the merits of: THE PRINCESS BUST DEVELOPER AND BUST CREAM OR FOOD.

The developer itself was an instrument made of nickel and aluminum, and was merely a large, bell-shaped cup attached to a rod, enabling the user to massage her bust. "Comes in two sizes, 4 and 5 inches diameter. . . . The developer gives the right exercise to the muscles of the bust, compels a free and normal circulation of the blood . . . through the flabby, undeveloped parts, these parts are soon restored to a healthy condition, they expand and fill out, become round, firm and beautiful. Will enlarge any lady's bust from 3 to 5 inches.

"IF NATURE HAS NOT FAVORED YOU with that greatest charm, a symmetrically rounded bosom full and perfect, send for the Princess Bust Developer.

"The Princess Bust Developer and Food is the only treatment that will actually develop and enlarge the bust, cause it to fill out to nature's full proportions, give that swelling, rounded, firm bosom, that queenly bearing, so attractive to the opposite sex. It brings a thin, awkward, unattractive girl or woman nearer to an exquisitely formed, graceful fascinating lady, and absolutely without harm."

Dr. Fuller's Bust Developer—the Fairy Wand of the Bigger Bust

Here then, if anywhere, is a clue to the mystery. Do women's figures change in response to the demand on the part of men for figures of a certain kind? Are the favored women of Tunisia fat because the fat woman is attractive to Tunisian men, and is the modern woman in America and the Western World generally thin because thinness in women is attractive to modern men? The catalog makes no bones about it but states flatly that the "swelling, rounded, firm bosom" is attractive to "the opposite sex." And this in 1905 when the demands of modesty made breasts a bust, while at the same time the bust could be extolled frankly as an important secondary sexual character.

So strong indeed was the pull of fashion that nursing mothers wore the same kind of corsets as those worn by unmar-

THE PRINCESS BUST DEVELOPER AND BUST CREAM OR FOOD

glish Lavend'

Regular retail price, each............$5.00	
OUR PRICE, EACH 1.50	
With one bottle Bust Expander, and	
one jar Bust Food FREE.	
OUR PRICE, PER DOZEN........ $16.00	

WILL ENLARGE ANY LADY'S BUST FROM 3 TO 5 INCHES. PRICE FOR DEVELOPER, BUST EXPANDER AND BUST FOOD, COMPLETE - - - - - - - $1.50

With every order for Princess Bust Developer and Bust Food, we furnish FREE one bottle of the GENUINE FLEUR DE LIS BUST EXPANDER and TISSUE BUILDER (retail price, 75 cents) without extra charge.

THE PRINCESS BUST DEVELOPER

IS A NEW SCIENTIFIC HELP TO NATURE.

COMBINED WITH THE USE OF THE BUST CREAM OR FOOD, FORMS A FULL FIRM WELL DEVELOPED BUST.

It will build up and fill out shrunken and undeveloped tissues, form a rounded, plump, perfectly developed bust, producing a beautiful figure.

THE PRINCESS BUST DEVELOPER AND CREAM FOOD is absolutely harmless, easy to use, perfectly safe and the only successful bust developer on the market.

IF NATURE HAS NOT FAVORED YOU with that greatest charm, a symmetrically rounded bosom full and perfect, send for the Princess Bust Developer and you will be surprised, delighted and happy over the result of one week's use. No matter what you have tried before, no matter if you have used other so called bust developers (paying $4.00, $5.00 or $6.00) the Princess Developer will produce the desired result in nearly every case. If you are not entirely satisfied with the result after giving it a fair trial, please return it to us and we will gladly refund your money.

Unmailable on account of weight.

PRINCESS BUST DEVELOPER.

Comes in two sizes, 4 and 5 inches in diameter. State size desired. The 4-inch Developer is the most popular as well as the most desirable size.

THE DEVELOPER is carefully made of nickel and aluminum, very finest finish throughout. Comes in two sizes, 4 and 5 inches in diameter. In ordering please state size desired. The developer gives the right exercise to the muscles of the bust, compels a free and normal circulation of the blood through the capillaries, glands and tissues of the flabby, undeveloped parts, these parts are soon restored to a healthy condition, they expand and fill out, become round, firm and beautiful.

THE BUST CREAM OR FOOD

IS APPLIED AS A MASSAGE.

It is a delightful cream preparation, put up by an eminent French chemist, and forms just the right food required for the starved skin and wasted tissues. The ingredients of the Bust Food are mainly pure vegetable oils, perfectly harmless, combined in a way to form the finest nourishment for the bust glands. It is delicately perfumed and is

UNRIVALED FOR DEVELOPING THE BUST, ARMS AND NECK,

making a plump, full, rounded bosom, perfect neck and arms, a smooth skin, which before was scrawny, flat and flabby.

FULL DIRECTIONS ARE FURNISHED, SUCCESS IS ASSURED.

You need no longer regret that your form is not what you would like it to be. Ladies everywhere welcome the Princess Bust Developer and Cream Food as the greatest toilet requisite ever offered. We have letters from many of our lady customers, telling us the good results of the Princess Developer, how their busts enlarged from two to six inches, and expressing their gratitude for the big benefit derived.

BUST CREAM OR FOOD UNRIVALLED FOR ENLARGEMENT OF THE BUST SEARS, ROEBUCK & Co. CHICAGO, ILL. SOLE AGENTS.

THE PRINCESS BUST DEVELOPER AND FOOD is the only treatment that will actually develop and enlarge the bust, cause it to fill out to nature's full proportions, give that swelling, rounded, firm bosom, that queenly bearing, so attractive to the opposite sex. It brings a thin, awkward, unattractive girl or woman nearer to an exquisitely formed, graceful, fascinating lady, and absolutely without harm.

$1.50 is our Special Introductory Price for the PRINCESS DEVELOPER and BUST FOOD, Complete, the Lowest Price Ever Made on this Article.

DON'T PAY an extravagant price for a so called bust developer. Be careful of the medicines and treatments offered by various irresponsible companies. Send for the Princess Developer, complete with the Bust Food, at our special introductory price of $1.50, state whether you wish the 4 or 5-inch developer, and if you are not entirely satisfied with the results, if it does not meet your expectations, without the slightest harm or inconvenience, return it, after giving it a trial, and we will refund your money. Don't put off ordering. Nowhere else can you buy a Princess Bust Developer for only $1.50.

No. 8C1098 Our Princess Bust Developer, with one bottle Bust Expander, and one jar Bust Food, FREE. Price, complete..................$1.50

FLORAL MASSAGE CREAM.

COMPLETE COURSE OF INSTRUCTIONS FOR FACIAL MASSAGE SENT WITH EACH ORDER.

Floral Massage Cream (antiseptic). Regular 50-cent size jars, - - - - - 39c

Extra large size jar (½-lb.), enough for 60 treatments, only - - - - 67c

A new, purifying, antiseptic, cleansing and beautifying massage cream, a most excellent preparation. Makes the old young, makes the plain beautiful, removes the telltale marks of time.

FULL DIRECTIONS for taking a complete course of massage treatment sent with each jar, the same course of treatment and the same preparation that society ladies receive in the fashionable city massage parlors at $1.00 per treatment. This is our latest and most improved toilet preparation, a high grade and perfectly satisfactory facial massage cream, to be used by anyone according to the plain and simple instructions for the course of massage treatment sent with every package.

FOR REMOVING HORIZONTAL LINES ON THE BROW, laughing wrinkles and crows' feet, wrinkles under the eyes, to make the cheeks plump and round, and to make your complexion just what you want it to be, healthy, clear and rosy. Floral Massage Cream is a toilet luxury which no woman, young, middle aged or old should deny herself. Our Floral Massage Cream contains no grease of any kind. It is composed of the purest ingredients, perfectly harmless to the most delicate skin. Its emollient effects are greater, its cleansing and beautifying results more marked than could be obtained from any other combination prepared for massaging purposes.

OUR FLORAL MASSAGE CREAM is the genuine massage preparation used so successfully by all massageurs of prominence in the massage parlors of every large city in this country and Europe, and is supplied by us exclusively to our customers for home massaging.

HAVE YOU EVER TRIED FACE MASSAGE? Have you ever experienced the peculiarly delightful, stimulating and exhilarating effects upon the facial nerves and muscles produced by a scientifically prepared and properly applied massage cream? Do you know that massaging the face is now considered a function which no progressive lady omits in order to produce and preserve that healthy glow, that pink of complexion which makes the beautiful features more beautiful, and adds to irregular ones attractions, the effect of which is really remarkable. We all know that exercise means increased circulation of the blood, but generally exercise is not entirely sufficient to produce the right results in the fullest measure for the facial perfection. Local exercise, in other words massage of the face, becomes necessary to induce increased circulation through the facial blood vessels, but even this is incomplete unless you use in connection with it the famous Floral Massage Cream which cleanses and clears the skin, arouses to activity every facial nerve and muscle, stimulates and feeds them, removes wrinkles under the eyes, on the brow, fills out the cheeks, making them plump and round, and insures a beautiful complexion in all cases. It is not surprising that the foremost professional massageurs will use nothing else in their work but Floral Massage Cream, which can be found in every fashionable massage parlor, where it is used almost exclusively.

IT IS NOT GREASY, it does not contain any animal fats, and therefore is not subject to decomposition. It is absolutely pure, therefore harmless and cleanly. It is prepared in the most scientific manner, therefore reliable and certain in results. It is, however, not necessary that you should employ the services of a professional massageur, for with our Floral Massage Cream you can massage your face in the privacy of your home, and at an expense of only a few cents. We supply the regular large $1.00 size jar of the genuine Floral Cream to our customers for 67 cents, sufficient for many months of facial massage treatment. Complete instructions are sent with each jar.

FLORAL MASSAGE CREAM HEALS THE SKIN, removes from the pores the impurities that make the skin rough and unwholesome. Its use renders the skin soft, white and beautiful. It is antiseptic and eradicates the germs of disease, yet it is perfectly harmless to the most delicate skin. Floral Massage Cream is non-irritating, purifies and invigorates the pores of the skin, giving at the same time activity to the glands, which is always very desirable.

FLORAL MASSAGE CREAM IS A DELIGHTFUL PREPARATION and speedily renders facial muscles firm and healthy, clarifying the complexion quickly and permanently. Soothes and rests the nerves of the face, and produces a healthy glow and a sensation of ease and comfort.

No. 8C1099 Floral Massage Cream. Price, regular 50-cent jars, dozen, $3.90; each.............

If by mail, postage extra, 14 cents.

No. 8C1100 Large size (holding three times the quantity of 50-c). Price, per dozen, $6.00; each........(Not mailable)...

FLORAL PURIFIED MASSAGE CREAM AND ANTISEPTIC SKIN BEAUTIFIER SEROCO CHEMICAL LABORATORY CHICAGO ILL

A BOOK ON "SELF MASSAGE," WITH ILLUSTRATED LESSONS AND COMPLETE INSTRUCTIONS, WILL BE SENT ON APPLICATI

Comfort Corsets With Woven Boning

"WOVEN BONING Bends With The Body"

Favorite of Thousands

For Average Figures. **$2 48**
18V220—Pink.
Medium Bust, 3 in. Skirt, 14 in. Clasp, 7½ in. Sizes, 21 to 30.
Order your corset size 2 inches smaller than waist measure taken over corset. Shipping weight, 1⅛ lbs.
Splendid value, beautiful back lacing corset in a free hip, full skirt model. Made of fancy mercerized pink brocade material, combining fine appearance and splendid wearing qualities.

$1 98
Fashionable Clasp Around.
18V219 Pink only.
Just Hook Up—No Lacers. Length, top to bottom, 14 inches. Bust, height, 2 inches. Front clasp, 8½ inches. Sizes, 22 to 30; also 32.
Order your actual waist measure taken over corset and dress. Shipping weight, 1 lb.
Firm surgical elastic, alternating with fancy cotton brocade. This combination prevents bulging and gives a straight flat figure. No lacing; you just put it around the body and hook it. Moderately stayed with our famous woven boning. Four hose supporters.

Very Popular Back Lacer. **$2 95**
For Average to Full Figures.
18V205—White Coutil.
Medium bust, 4 inches. Skirt length, 14 inches. Clasp, 10½ in. Sizes, 20 to 30; also 32.
Order your corset size 2 inches smaller than waist measure taken over corset. Shipping weight, 1 lb. 9 oz.
This favorite woven bone model is worn by thousands of pleased customers. Made of fine white coutil. Roomy skirt and bust. Well boned. Strong broad end front clasp. Stitched belt across abdomen adds strength. Four hose supporters.

Woven Bone Comfort Model With Abdo Belt
$2 98

Fine quality elastic, 3 in. wide, extends across top at front and sides. Four good hose supporters.

COMFORT TOP

DO NOT GUESS YOUR WAIST SIZE USE A TAPE MEASURE

For Average and Stout Figures.
18V299—White Coutil.
Bust, 3¾ in.; skirt, 14 in.; broad end clasp, 9½ in. Sizes, 24 to 30. **$2 98**
Order corset size 2 inches smaller than waist measure taken over corset. Shipping wt., 1¾ lbs.
Women who have refrained from corseting, and those with a large abdomen who wish to reduce, will find this garment ideally suited to them. Elastic inner belt gently lifts and reduces the abdomen and holds it in its natural place. The inner belt is attached to each side of the corset and is made of strong elastic with coutil reinforcing at center. It fastens with strong hooks and eyes, giving real support and smooth, stylish lines. Back lacing model of strong white coutil, well stayed with woven boning. Four supporters.
18V301—Same as above. Extra sizes, 32, 34 and 36. State size..................$3.25

☞ **$1 79** Average and Slender.
18V239—Pink.
Low Bust, 2 in. Skirt, 12¼ in. Short 7-in. front clasp. Sizes, 20 to 28.
Order your corset size 2 inches smaller than waist measure taken over your corset. Shipping weight, 1⅛ pounds.
Back lacing corset of fine quality pink coutil. Fancy elastic sections under bust. Short clasp ends at waistline with a soft, comfort top preventing digging in at top. Very comfortable. Elastic fastens above clasp with hook and eye. Lightly boned with our famous woven boning. Four supporters.

Average and Stout Figures. **$3 69**
18V244—Pink.
Low bust, 2 inches. Long skirt, 14¼ in. Clasp, 9 in. Sizes, 22 to 30; also 32, 34 and 36.
Order your corset size 2 inches smaller than waist measure taken over your corset. Shipping weight, 1¾ pounds.
Laced front corset of strong pink coutil with woven wire stays. Elastic sections in bust and at bottom of back. Special sewed down section of double thickness coutil tends to comfortably suppress fleshy thighs and abdomen. Six strong supporters

SEARS. ROEBUCK AND CO.

ried girls, with merely such variations as were necessary to the functional purpose of nursing. The catalog offers:

"A Most Satisfying, Comfortable and Durable Nursing Corset, 75c. S., R. & Co's Nursing Corset, five-hook, reinforced clasp. Made of good corset jean . . . easily adjusted, with patent snap button, and will permit use of nipple without the slightest inconvenience. Very pliable over sensitive parts; a boon to mothers."

A woman of 1905 in fashionable heavy marching order wore not only the formidable corset of the times but other articles which more or less clustered about the corset. Among them were:

"The Popular Habit Hip Pad and Bustle, made of light tampico. . . . The only style of hip pad to wear with the new, modish, form fitting skirts which are the prevailing fashion at the present time."

"Fairy Bust Forms," the modern brassière by another name, which "conform with every movement of the body and give the figure a graceful form," were also worn, as well as The Parisienne Wire Bustle. Over the corset, the well-dressed

The Parisienne Wire Bustle, or, How to Have That Overstuffed Look

woman wore an embroidery- and lace-trimmed corset cover. Thus accoutered in several pounds of confining steel, iron, sateen, lace, embroidery, and wire, she was equally ready for a tennis match, a matching of wits in the parlor, or a matching of attractiveness with other women in the presence of men.

The Battle of the Corsets

The corset has been the object of a battle that has lasted ever since the French Revolution. Like other long-continued wars, it has had its ups and downs, its victories or defeats for one side or the other, and temporary periods of peace and armistice arising from the exhaustion of the combatants.

In the first instance, it took no less than the shock of the French Revolution and the Napoleonic period to free women of the torturing steel and leather corsets which constricted the waists of ladies of fashion to the incredible circumference of thirteen inches. Under the impetus of the Revolution, corsets were discarded and waists relaxed for a little while in simple Directoire gowns that fell straight from bust to ankle. But not for long. By 1810, the wasp waist returned, and the growing knowledge of medicine and anatomy, combined with the growth of new ideas about woman, filled English and American journals with indignant protests against tight lacing. At the same time, however, equally vitriolic defenses came from those who considered the wasp waist both fashionable and enchanting to the roving eye of the male.

The fight against corsets in America began early in the century, and typical of the fighters was Hugh Smith, M.D., who published in 1827 a volume of *Letters to Married Ladies* which included a "Letter on Corsets, and copious notes by an American Physician." Here he deplores the practice of the preceding century when mothers commonly laid their daughters upon their faces, on the floor, and, with one foot on their backs, tightened the cords of their stays. He then goes on to lament the wearing of corsets:

"I would condemn corsets with or without busks," he writes. "They are a slow and fashionable poison, which has laid many a lovely form, at an untimely hour, prostrate with the listless dead." He blames the wearing of corsets for "that now very fashionable disease—the liver complaint. Hence arise faintings in public assemblies, or crowded, overheated apartments . . . and a long train of fashionable evils *too tedious to mention.*"

The italics are Dr. Smith's, and he expresses a feeling that must have been shared by a great number of husbands, lovers, and weary brothers throughout a long period of the nineteenth century. During the first part of that century and throughout the 1860's and 1870's, sickness was fashionable and the lady of fashion was much given to paleness, aches, vapors, pains, dizziness, sick headaches, migraines, and fainting spells.

Dr. Smith continues: "This constant and unnatural pressure upon . . . all the contents of the abdomen, becomes a great source of uneasiness. This often sometimes becomes almost insupportable after a hearty meal, for the stomach cannot carry on its important function of digestion without bitter and sometimes loud complaints. . . . Often, indeed, I have blushed for ladies . . . and often too, has the blush crimsoned their own cheeks, when, by a hem or a cough, they have been compelled to drown the dull music of the screaking cord, or the hollow rumbling mutter of the suffering tenant within."

Then follows an awful warning: "It is a fact well known to physicians, that there is scarcely any power equal to continued pressure, where it can be conveniently applied, for the removal of glandular swellings. This principle operates powerfully upon those two, not only highly ornamental, but essentially useful glands, situated upon the superior and anterior position of your chest. The constant and unyielding pressure of your corsets very gradually, cause an almost total disappearance of these glands, and not unfrequently an entire absorption of them takes place; so that many of our females, before they are five and thirty, are actually obliged to use some deceit, in order to produce the appearance of breasts . . . with many ladies it is often a matter of very serious lamentation, when they pass the rubicund (as some waggish pensmen have seen fit to denominate the line between the girl and the old maid) and yet no plan could be better adapted to hasten that period, than to level down these two attractive prominences."

The ladies paid no attention whatever to the warnings of Dr. Smith and continued to wear corsets at the risk of the loss of their "two attractive prominences." In 1849, a great reformer arose in the person of O. S. Fowler, editor of the *American Phrenological Journal*, who was determined to abolish the corset. Mr. Fowler, in the sound American tradition, got up a motto for his campaign and hurled it into the teeth of the country. It was: "Total Abstinence or No Husbands—Natural Waists or No Wives."

The enraged phrenologist contributed an article to his journal entitled "Tight Lacing, or the evils of Compressing the Organs of Animal Life," and, after announcing with much satisfaction that a previous work of his, called *Matrimony,* had led to the formation of Anti-Lacing Societies throughout the country, he launched into an impassioned protest against the practice of tight lacing. His words must have brought blushes to the cheeks of the young females who read them:

"Who does not know that the compression of any part produces *inflammation?* Who does not know that, therefore, tight-lacing around the waist keeps the blood from returning freely to the heart, and *retains* it in the bowels and neighboring organs, and thereby *inflames all the organs of the abdomen,* which thereby EXCITES AMATIVE DESIRES?

"It is high time that virtuous woman *should blush for very shame* to be seen laced tight, just as she *should* blush to be caught indulging impure desires. I know indeed, that I have now appealed to the most powerful motive possible—to that of woman's modesty, and I make this appeal *because* it is thus powerful. . . . No woman who reads this will dare to be seen laced tight, because she *knows* it to be true, both from experience and from physiology."

The conclusion drawn from all this by the practical phrenologist Fowler was, however, one which did not seem likely to cause ladies to abandon tight lacing.

"I will add," he concludes, "that tight lacing explains the fact that tight-lacers so easily get *in love*. It is true . . . that tight-lacing kindles impure feelings, at the same time that it renders their possessors weak-minded, so as to be the more easily led away by temptation. And *this,* aye, this, is the reason why certain men keep up this immodest fashion."

The conflicting opinions of Dr. Smith and Mr. Fowler on the vices of tight lacing must have thrown the ladies of the times into a fever of indecision. The one told them that the

CORSET DEPARTMENT.

SHAPES FOR ALL FIGURES.

PRICES TO SUIT ALL PURSES. We present for this season the latest models and styles. We have given considerable attention to selecting the very best wearing styles as well as the most comfortable and stylish figures. The prices we quote are less than the average retail stores can buy them for. We sell only such corsets as we can guarantee and recommend. If you have never bought a corset from us, please let us try and fit you. If you are not entirely satisfied after receiving same, both as to price and quality, you may return same and we will cheerfully refund the price you have paid for it, in addition to the postage or express.

BE SURE AND GIVE YOUR ACTUAL WAIST MEASURE

and the size corset you now wear, and observe the following rules in taking your measure: If you measure with corset on, deduct 2 to 2½ inches from waist sizes as shown on tape; this allows for spread of lacing in back. For example, if waist measure is 23 inches over corset, order size 21. If you take actual body measure, without corset or underclothing, you should deduct 3 to 4 inches, depending on how tight you lace. For example, if your waist measure is 25 inches without corset or underclothing, your size will be 21 or 22. Again we remind you to give your waist measure or size of corset, as this is frequently forgotten by customers when ordering a corset. For complete line of corset covers refer to index.

Our Special Four-Hook Corset. . . . 50c

No. 18C8000 Four-Hook Short Corset for medium form. This is a finely made corset of fine jeans, well boned and side steels, boned bust. A perfect fitting corset and meeting with popular favor. We predict an immense sale on this number, and especially at the price we quote. Colors, white, drab or black. Sizes, 18 to 30. Be sure and give actual waist measure. Price................50c
If by mail, postage extra, 15 cents.

The Kabo Five-Hook Corset for the Average Figure 90c

No. 18C8004 Long waist, medium form, five-hook. This is a corset made of fine French coutil, strips of French sateen with silk edging. Moulded on perfect French model; stayed with double girdles at the waist lines. The bones and steels are made with a protecting covering for the ends, which prevents cutting through. A perfect fitting garment that will give entire satisfaction. Equal to the $1.50 kind elsewhere. Made in white, drab and black. Be sure to give waist measure. Sizes, 18 to 30. Price...$0.90
Sizes, 31 to 36. Price........ 1.15
If by mail, postage extra, 15 cents.

The New Kabo Hipless Corset with Elastic Sides, 95c

No. 18C8026 Kabo Hipless Corset, medium waist, full form, made of French sateen, single strip, full boned, cut out over hip, with elastic sides. Matchless for athletic purposes and comfort. No brass eyelets. Colors, white, drab or black. Sizes, 18 to 30. Always give waist measure. Price.......95c
Extra sizes, 31 to 36, 25 cents extra.
Price..........................$1.20
If by mail, postage extra, 15 cents.

Kabo High Bust Corset, for Tall, Slender Figures, 98c

No. 18C8030 Kabo, high bust, extreme long waist, dress form; 6-hook, shaped shoulder straps, sateen covered strips, embroidered edge. Suitable for tall, slender figures. No brass eyelets. Colors, white, drab or black. Sizes, 18 to 30. Give waist measure. Price......98c
If by mail, postage extra, 15 cents.

Kabo Abdominal Corsets, Highly Recommended by Everybody $1.50

No. 18C8038 Kabo Abdominal Corset, medium waist, extension front, very heavy boning, made long below the waist, giving ample abdominal support. Elastic self conforming gores on side, sateen covered strips and improved side lacings. No brass eyelets. Colors, drab or black. Sizes, 19 to 30. Do not fail to give waist measure.
Price.......................$1.50
Extra sizes, 31 to 36, 25 cents extra.
Price.......................$1.75
If by mail, postage extra, 15 cents.

The Sahlin Perfect Form and Corset Combined, for Grace and Comfort . . 90c

No. 18C8052 Sahlin Perfect Form and Corset Combined. Retains all the good and avoids the evil of ordinary corsets. Nothing lost in the style or shape. The bust will not cave in, and therefore padding and interlining are avoided. The effect as here shown is an exact reproduction of a perfect form, obtained only by wearing the Sahlin. No corset is necessary, as it is a corset and form combined. Approved and endorsed by physicians and health reformers. Made of good quality corset coutil, white or drab. Give bust and waist measure. Sizes, 18 to 30. Price.................90c
No. 18C8058 Sahlin Perfect Form and Corset Combined. Same as above, made of fancy summer netting, white only. Give bust and waist measure. Sizes, 18 to 30. Price....90c

How to Send Correct Measure When Ordering Sahlin Perfect Form and Corset Combined.

MEASURES: The measure from B to C is the most important measure and should be taken with the greatest care. To secure a perfect and comfortable fit take measure as for a dress. The necessary allowance of 1½-inch for armhole will be allowed by us. For example, if you measure 8½ inches give us this measure and we will send you a form which measures 7 inches to waist line. To prevent mistakes, please give actual measurement from B to C, and state in order actual measure. We will then allow 1½ inch as above stated. The Sahlin Perfect Form and Corset Combined is made in the following sizes:

Bust	Waist			Under Arm		
30 in.	18, 20, 22		in.	7,	8,	9 in.
32 in.	20, 22, 24		in.	7,	8,	9 in.
34 in.	20, 22, 24, 26		in.	7½,	8½,	9½ in.
36 in.	22, 24, 26, 28		in.	7,	8,	9 in.
38 in.	24, 26, 28, 30		in.	7,	8,	9 in.
40 in.	30, 32		in.	6½,	7½,	8½ in.

These under arm measures as shown in this table are the actual measure before the allowance for armhole is deducted.

In measuring for size of waist, D to C, remove corset, draw measure as close as desired and give this measure. The bust measure from A to B is a matter of taste and is left to the judgment of the wearer, therefore give actual measure from A to B and also state bust measure desired.
Sizes different from front must be made to order and will cost 50 cents extra.

The Jackson Favorite Waist Is the Best Corset Waist In Every Way 85c

No. 18C8044 The Jackson Waist combines in the highest degree the embodiment of an elegant waist and corset combination. Its stays are ample, outlining a most graceful poise of figure, at the same time easy and comfortable; it is also adaptable as a negligee by the removal of side steels, which can be replaced at will. Made of good sateen, in black or drab. Sizes, 18 to 30. Always give waist measure. Price.......$0.85
Extra sizes, 31 to 36. Price..... 1.15
If by mail, postage extra, 15 cents.

A Most Satisfying, Comfortable and Durable Nursing Corset. . . . 75c

No. 18C8064 S. R. & Co.'s Nursing Corset, five-hook, reinforced clasp. Made of good corset jean, entirely new principle, as it is easily adjusted, with patent snap button, and will permit use of nipple without the slightest inconvenience. Very pliable over sensitive parts; a boon to mothers. Boned bust, strong jean girdle, two side steels. Color, drab only. Sizes, 18 to 30. Always give waist measure. Price....75c
If by mail, postage extra, 15 cents.

Straight Front Nursing Corset, 95c

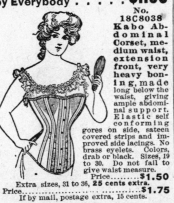

No. 18C8080 Straight Front, Bias Gored Nursing Corset. A particularly useful garment at this time and a very clever one. Made of finest Imperial drill, with glove snap fastenings. Front clasp 10 inches long. Made with garter extension tabs. This model has a medium waist and skirt, low bust and back. Colors, white, drab or black. Sizes, 18 to 30. Do not fail to give waist measure....Price, 95c
If by mail, postage extra, 15 cents.

Kabo Nursing Corset, Made of Batiste . . 96c

Light and Easy for Summer Wear.
No. 18C8088 Exact same model as No. 18C8080, but made of good strong quality batiste in white only, and is boned with non-rustable material. Sizes, 18 to 30. Do not fail to give waist measure. Price......96c
If by mail, postage extra, 15 cents.

Bias Cored, Straight Front, Perfect Fitting, Erect Form 50c

No. 18C8100 A New, Popular, Bias Gored, Straight Front Corset, with set-in gored busts. The latest low bust effect. Made of good imported coutil, with extra heavy 10-inch front steel. This is equal to many of the regular $1.00 straight front corsets sold elsewhere. Colors, white or drab. Sizes, 18 to 30. Always give waist measure.
Price...........................50c
If by mail, postage extra, 15 cents.

Straight Front Fine Batiste Corset, Bias Cored, at 50c

No. 18C8104 Full Bias Gored Batiste Corset. Straight front, military erect figure, has 2 side steels and 4 bone strips with extra heavy front, 10-inch steel boned underneath, making a perfectly smooth surface. This is a medium waist with low bust, adapted for a wide range of figures. Handsomely trimmed with pretty lace at top. White only. Sizes, 18 to 30. Always give waist measure.
Price...........................50c
If by mail, postage extra, 15 cents.

Kabo Straight Front Corset, 90c

No. 18C8120 Kabo Straight Front Bias Gored Corset, with 10-inch front clasp. Made of good quality Imperial drill with satin ribbon trimming and bow finish; long waist, medium skirt and low bust. Has hose supporter attachments. This corset will give the wearer a straight, military like figure; is equal in value to those sold elsewhere at $1.50. No brass eyelets. Colors, white, drab or black. Sizes, 18 to 30. Do not fail to give waist measure.
Price..............................90c
If by mail, postage extra, 15 cents.

No. 18C8124 Kabo Straight Front Bias Gored Corset. 10-inch front clasp. A beautifully made, very pretty garment; the exact same model as No. 18C8120, same colors and sizes; made of fine French coutil, finished with hand buttonhole, 5 gores. Regular $2.00 corset. Colors, white or drab.
Price..............................$1.50
If by mail, postage extra, 15 cents.

No. 18C8130 Identical same model as Nos. 18C8120 and 18C8124, made of strong, light weight, fine batiste. Boned with non-rustable material and trimmed with Swiss embroidery. An exceptionally desirable and comfortable corset. White only. Sizes, 18 to 30.
Price..............................90c
If by mail, postage extra, 15 cents.

No. 17C2990 THIS BEAUTIFUL SHIRT WAIST SUIT OR DRESS, is made of fine figured lawn. Consists of handsome shirt waist, richly trimmed with cream colored medallions. Yoke effect front. Narrow velvet ribbon in front on waistband, around yoke and belt. Pretty sleeves. Detachable collar. Side plaits in back from neck to waist. Skirt nicely tailored, with flounce effect, trimmed with velvet ribbon and embroidered medallions. Colors, pink or blue, with fancy figures. **State color when ordering.** Price.............**$2.98**
If by mail, postage extra, 30 cents.

No. 17C2991 THIS ELEGANT LADIES' SHIRT WAIST SUIT, made of good quality white linen, strictly tailored, consists of nice shirt waist, of which the yoke front is richly tucked and trimmed with openwork embroidery insertion. Detachable collar. Side plaits on the sleeves and side plaits in back from neck to waist. The skirt is trimmed to match, with tucks and embroidered insertion. Nicely tailored and made very full. Color, white only.
Price.....................**$3.25**
If by mail, postage extra, 35 cents.

No. 17C2993 ONE OF THE PRETTIEST SHIRT WAIST SUITS SHOWN. Made of very fine madras cloth. Consists of a stylish shirt waist with plaits, white piping, and circular embroidery trimmings. Very full sleeves, side plaits in back from neck to waist. The skirt is nicely tailored, made with side plaits all around. Very full. Special value, strictly up to date. Colors, blue or ecru (light shade of tan), with trimmings to match.
Price....................**$3.98**
If by mail, postage extra, 40 cents.

No. 17C2994 THIS BEAUTIFUL SHIRT WAIST SUIT OR DRESS. Made of very fine dimity in beautiful Dolly Varden pattern. Consists of handsome shirt waist with circular yoke in front, large shoulder cape neatly trimmed with lace insertion. Large sleeves made with fancy cuffs also trimmed with lace. Round yoke in back. This waist buttons in back only. The skirt is made very full on double flounce style. Lace insertion over each flounce. Very pretty; good value. Color, white with rose or violet figures. **State color when ordering.** Price.......**$3.75**
If by mail, postage extra, 35 cents.

No. 17C2995 THIS HANDSOME SHIRT WAIST SUIT OR DRESS is made of very fine Luzon Ponge. It consists of a beautiful shirt waist, made with fancy circular yoke. Shoulder cape trimmed with lace insertions, and side plaits in front from yoke to waist. Full sleeves, fancy cuffs. Stylish collar. Yoke in back. This waist buttons in back only. The skirt is extremely stylish, has a double flounce, nicely trimmed with lace insertion and shirring over each flounce. Very handsome Color, tan (champagne color) only. **State color when ordering.** Price **$4.95**
If by mail, postage extra, 40 cents.

SAILOR SUITS
ARE VERY POPULAR AND WE SHOW A BEAUTIFUL LINE OF THEM. They are especially adapted for young ladies. Sizes from 32 to 38 inches around the bust, 36 to 44 inches length of skirt, and 22 to 30 inches around the waist.

——— STATE COLOR AND SIZE WHEN ORDERING. NO EXTRA SIZES. ———

No. 17C2997 MISSES' WASH SUIT. Made of tan grass cloth. Consists of skirt and sailor blouse made with a large sailor collar. White dickey in front embroidered with an anchor. Anchor embroidery on right sleeve. The collar and bow in front are bound in red. Belt of same material with a postillion back. Skirt is trimmed with red piping on side plaits on each seam. For 14, 16 and 18-year old young ladies, measuring 32, 34 and 36 inches around the bust, respectively. Skirt lengths, 36 to 40 inches, only. Color, tan only, with red trimmings.
Price.................**$1.95**
If by mail, postage extra, 35 cents.

No. 17C2998 THIS PRETTY SAILOR SUIT is made of good quality madras cloth, consists of nice sailor waist with large collar with inlaid front or dickey. Stylish sleeves. Plaits on cuffs and on waist in front. Embroidered anchor on the dickey and on the sleeves. Skirt is nicely tailored, and very full. French seams all around. Wide hem around the bottom. Bow of the same material in front. Colors, blue or oxblood.
Price....................**$2.35**
If by mail, postage extra, 35 cents.

No. 17C3000 THIS HANDSOME SAILOR SUIT is made of good quality linen finished percale. Consists of stylish sailor waist with inlaid front, otherwise called dickey. Trimmings of white cording on the front and around the collar, as well as on the cuffs. Large sleeves. Embroidered anchor in front and silk embroidered eagle on the sleeves. Silk stars on the collar in back. Skirt is nicely tailored, made with side plaits and trimmed with three rows of cording around the bottom. Color, blue with white trimming.
Price....................**$2.98**
If by mail, postage extra, 35 cents.

No. 17C3003 THIS HANDSOME SAILOR SUIT is made of fine grass cloth. Consists of blouse sailor waist with large sailor collar, richly trimmed with three rows of cording. Tie in front of same material. Pointed yoke effect. Cord trimming on the sleeves, on the tie and around the collar. Large sleeves. Silk embroidered anchor in front and eagle embroidered on the sleeves. The skirt is nicely tailored and is made with side plaits all around, trimmed around bottom with three rows of cording. Color, tan only, with red trimmings.
Price.................**$2.25**
If by mail, postage extra, 35 cents.

No. 17C3004 HANDSOME SUIT. Made of good quality white linen. Consists of beautiful sailor waist. Stylish collar trimmed with straps of same material, side plaits in front, neat cuffs, large sleeves. Silk embroidered anchor on inlaid front and American eagle embroidered in silk on sleeves. Very rich. Skirt is nicely tailored and has side plaits all around with wide hem around the bottom. Beautiful garment, strictly up to date, and we can highly recommend it. Color, white, with light blue or red silk embroideries.
Price.................**$3.50**
If by mail, postage extra, 40 cents.

practice would cause them to lose all sex appeal; the other that it would cause so much sex appeal that tighter lacers would "get in love" all the time, excite "amative desires," and yet be rendered so weak-minded as "the more easily to be led away by temptation." We do not know what the ladies thought of the opinions of these gentlemen, but we do know that they went right on pulling their waists in as far as they could.

When Tight Makes Right

In 1874, the influential novelist, Louisa May Alcott, enters the lists determined to free her suffering sisters of the stays that bind them. In her stories, she had advocated higher education, sports, and exercise for women, and the cultivation of domestic arts for girls. Now, in *Eight Cousins,* she strives to write the *Uncle Tom's Cabin* that will free women from the slavery of corsets. Uncle Alec is telling Rose, the heroine, to run. He says:

> "Very well done, child. I see you have not lost the use of your limbs even though you *are* in your teens. That belt is too tight; unfasten it, then you can take a long breath without panting so."
>
> "It isn't tight, sir; I can breathe perfectly well," began Rose, trying to compose herself.
>
> Her Uncle's only answer was to lift her up and un-hook the new belt of which she was so proud. The moment the clasp was open the belt flew apart several inches, for it was impossible to restrain the involuntary sigh of relief that flatly contradicted her words.
>
> "Why, I didn't know it was tight! I didn't feel so a bit. Of course it would open if I puff like this, but I

never do, because I hardly ever run," explained Rose; rather discomfited by this discovery.

"I see you don't half fill your lungs, and so you can wear this absurd thing without feeling it. The idea of cramping a tender little waist in a stiff band of leather and steel just when it ought to be growing," said Dr. Alec, surveying the belt with great disfavor as he put the clasp forward several holes, to Rose's secret dismay, for she was proud of her slender figure, and daily rejoiced that she wasn't as stout as Lucy Miller, a former schoolmate, who vainly tried to repress her plumpness.

"It will fall off if it's so loose," she said anxiously as she stood watching him pull her precious belt about.

"Not if you keep taking long breaths to hold it on. That is what I want you to do, and when you have filled this out we will go on enlarging it till your waist is more like that of Hebe, goddess of health, and less like that of a fashion-plate—the ugliest thing imaginable."

The Corset Becomes Important Business

In the meantime, American manufacturers, paying no attention to the controversies that raged about the corset, had not been idle. Just as the World War gave them the long-sought opportunity to produce toys, gloves, and other articles usually imported from Europe and Asia, the Franco-Prussian War enabled them to get a start in the corset business, because it sharply reduced importations from the principal source—France. Even before this period, there were corset makers in this country, and the Convex Weaving Company, publishing its first annual report in 1866, proudly announced that it had built a loom which produced thirty-six corsets a day, and then went into calculations which sound much like those of rabbit salesmen who point out the prodigious rate of increase of rabbits which is followed, of course, by an equally prodigious increase of profits. The report stated that it cost $7.80 to weave one dozen corsets on its looms and these, if sold for $14 a dozen, would produce (less certain deductions for taxes) a net profit of $5 a dozen or $1,500 a day on the production of 100 looms turning out 36 corsets each, while the "demand for corsets in the United States is equal to 50,000 per day."

The Corset War Goes On

Throughout the last half of the nineteenth century, the corset war was carried on without abatement, and the manufacturers, using a method widely employed later by press agents of the twentieth century, induced obliging doctors to announce that "a well-fitting corset does no more harm than a well-fitting glove," or, "As a medical man (and not one of the old school) I feel justified in saying that the ladies who are content with a moderate application of the corset may secure that most elegant female charm, a slender waist, without fear of injury to the health."

Bird in a Gilded Cage

Mothers wrote that by early adjustment of the corset, on daughters of the age of seven or eight, the waist could be gradually tapered and become accustomed to its small size. Elegant women said that "to me the sensation of being tightly laced in a pair of elegant, well-made, lightly fitting corsets is superb." Old women murmured that "No young ladies could go into good society with a coarse clumsy waist like a rustic." And young men—the all-important young men—spoke their minds in the letter columns of magazines and newspapers, saying they "were slaves to the little waist," and that "girls with slender waists were the queens of the ballroom," while young gentlemen of leisure in fashionable assemblies declaimed on the clumsy figures of uncorseted girls.

— 373 —

The result of all this was that the slender waist became essential to elegance and fashion; girls of fifteen and sixteen actually slept in their corsets, and fashionable English boarding schools advertised (with repercussions here) that they could achieve the reduction of the waist at the rate of one inch per month to a final circumference of thirteen. Two strong maids would come in every morning to strap up the girls who gladly suffered it, in spite of the fact that after a year or two of such treatment their muscles were unable to hold them erect unsupported.

By 1899, waists were slimmer than ever before, and the possession of an "illusion waist," as it was called in the United States, was to be desired even at the risk of "whooping cough, obliquity of vision, polypus, apoplexy, stoppage of the nose, pains in the eyes and earache, palpitations, flushing and red noses"; all of which corset critics said came from tight lacing. But by 1900, the domestic corset production was valued at $14,000,000.

The Tide of Battle Changes

As we have seen, there had been since the early years of the century a constant barrage of protest against the slender waist and tight lacing; a protest that had proved totally ineffective. But in 1889, newer and more terrifying arguments against the corset were made, and these seem to have made some dent on women's minds and eventually on their bodies. In 1889, Dr. Robert L. Dickinson, a lecturer on obstetrics at the Long Island College Hospital, published a paper in *The New York Medical Journal* called "The Corset; Questions of Pressure and Displacement." In a calmer and more logical manner than preceding corset critics had used, he gave the results of his experiments and observations of corset pressure, concluding that:

(1) The maximum pressure of the corset is 1.625 pounds to the square inch during inspiration, making the total estimated pressure 30 to 80 pounds.

(2) The capacity of expansion of the chest is restricted one-fifth when the corset is on the body.

(3) The thoracic character of women's breathing is largely caused by wearing corsets.

(4) The abdominal wall is thinned and weakened by the pressure of stays; the liver suffers great direct pressure and is more frequently displaced than any other organ.

(5) The pelvic floor is bulged downwards, by tight-lacing, one third of an inch.

Up to this time, corset manufacturers had had little to worry about, because theatrical warnings and dramatic appeals to modesty had constituted the bulk of the opposition to corset wearing—an opposition that lent corsets the attractiveness of forbidden fruit. But now a new and more formidable enemy appeared on the scene, and he came equipped not with moral posturings but with apparently precise medical facts, specific details, and frightening, horrendous photographs of twisted livers, telescoped lungs, and bladders and stomachs crumpled like wet blotting paper. A waggled finger was one thing, but charts, figures, and discoveries announced in reputable medical journals were quite something else again. And the doctor found powerful allies in the husbands of the times.

These long-suffering and helpless creatures had grown sick and tired of listening to descriptions of their wives' vapors, and they were equally tired of paying their medical bills. It now seemed that salvation was at hand for husbands and they eagerly seized it. After the publication of Dr. Dickinson's paper, Papa no longer looked sympathetic and applied cold compresses to Mama's brow when she complained of migraines, but produced a copy of the medical journal, showed her pictures of her compressed liver and lungs, and sneeringly asked: "Well, what the hell can you expect when you strap yourself up like a bale of hay?" The embattled husband was soon to receive additional aid from England where it was proved that corsets would kill monkeys.

Corsets Fatal to Monkeys

In 1904, Dr. Arabella Kenealy published in London an article entitled "The Curse of Corsets." She records the results of an appalling experiment made by putting miniature corsets—replicas of those worn by the women of the times—on monkeys, and recording the results of the experiment.

Dr. Kenealy says at the outset—by implication—that monkeys evidently have more sense than women of fashion. "Their distress at the constriction and discomfort—their unceasing efforts to release themselves—did credit to their intellectual perception and sagacity. The physical results were as disastrous as they are instructive. For it was found that those which were corseted and laced at once to the regulation V-shape of fashionable woman died in the space of a few days, as though stricken by some mortal malady. Those in whose case a more gradual process was adopted lived some weeks in sickliness and suffering; whilst others the 'improvement' of whose figures extended over a still more lengthy period, did not succumb at all, showing that tolerance became established.

"But that tolerance was established obviously at the expense of health and happiness. These rudimental martyrs to a civilized vice fell off grievously in appetite and spirits. They were attacked by gastric and other internal disorders. They moped and lost flesh, alternating between extreme languor and marked nerve-irritability. Their tempers rendered them unapproachable, and although they did not die actually of stays, they died in a few months of some disorder of which stays with the health deterioration consequent on their use, were the undoubted cause."

The Waistland Blooms Again

Manufacturers, frightened by increasing medical attacks on corsets—attacks which seemed to be supported by sound evidence—got busy trying to find ways in which the corset might be anchored other than at the waist and so avoid pull and pressure on the abdomen. And in 1903, an ingenious corset maker added hose supporters to corsets, the waistline expanded in some cases to twice the previous size, and the days of the wasp waist were numbered.

A few years later came the World War, and wars and revolutions strongly influence fashion. We have seen how the French Revolution shook women of the period out of their steel and leather corsets and gave them a brief period of comfort in Directoire gowns, but how, by 1810, they showed they could not stand freedom and again took up their corsets. Now, one hundred years later, war was once more to liberate the feminine figure from stays.

In France—the center of fashion—the birth rate had long been falling; men were dying at the front by tens of thousands, and it became the patriotic duty of women to bear children. To be *enceinte,* therefore, was to be patriotic and hence fashionable. French women embraced pregnancy and abandoned corsets as an expression of love of country; the waistline went down to the hips; skirts rose to the knees, and in no time at all American women, aping the French as usual, were walking around without waistlines or corsets.

The days of wasp waists were over—the days when a seventeen- or eighteen-inch waist was merely ordinary, and when the waist of a woman of fashion could easily be spanned by her husband's hands. It is a measure of the almost incredible smallness of the waists of American women during the nineteenth century and part of the twentieth that the twenty-inch waist of Miss Ginger Rogers is today regarded as phenomenally slender. In the 1890's, such a waist would have been considered almost gross among ladies of fashion.

The Corset in the Catalog

The corseted women sketched in the 1915 catalog differ so radically from those of the 1905 catalog as to seem an entirely different species. The waist is no longer compressed; the breasts no longer bulge outward, and the *derrière* seems an integral part of the figure rather than a hastily added superstructure. Every corset is fitted with hose supporters, and the catalog reminds women but lately emerged from the waist-anchored corset that "the hose supporters are an important part of the garment."

TALL STOUT

Portrait of a Lady Wearing Newfangled Garters

It is apparent, however, that a great many ladies still desired large busts and, where nature had not provided them, Sears came to the rescue of the flat-chested. The catalog lists a Featherbone Bust Extender, "well made in a graceful rounded effect and Ventilated Forms. Strikingly life-like, light, cool, comfortable . . . a necessity for most well dressed women. So perfect that they can scarcely be detected from natural bust by either sight or touch. Expanded by resilient filling which can be removed and washed and returned in a few minutes."

Embittered men—sometimes too late—complained of these deceptions, and hastily backed away from matrimony when they suspected that the opulence they saw in a woman was not of nature but of the store or the mail-order catalog. Charles Macomb Flandrau in his *Loquacities* (1931) says:

> The bustle and the "form improver," moulded not only anatomies, but entire lives; they determined female fates —changed destinies. In my hearing at an early age a young man passionately declared that he had decided never to propose to a certain girl because, as he delicately expressed it, "I think, by God, that there's deception in that bust."

On the other hand, nature was sometimes too prodigal in its gifts, and, for ladies afflicted with a superabundance of bust, the catalog offered the Treo Bust Support and Bust Reducer and Cambric Bust Confiners.

The Fight Against Fat

The corset section of the 1925 catalog expanded to enormous proportions and Sears proudly told its customers that "You have helped us build the largest corset department in the world; there is no place else where such an enormous and varied selection can be made."

And now a new kind of corset comes into being—the rubber corset—as a weapon in modern woman's fight against fat. This fight is to introduce absurd and often harmful food fads and is to make diet prescribers rich and famous; it is to enrich manufacturers of dangerous drugs that have the alleged power to "dissolve fat while you eat all you want"; it is to send women by the millions to masseurs, beauty parlors, gymnasiums, and health farms—and in some cases to their graves. As in the case of wasp waists, it is to make women oblivious to all warnings on the part of reputable medical men. Anything and everything is to be used in the fight against fat, and, in 1925, the rubber corset was one of the principal devices. The catalog tells us that:

"Excess fat is not stylish; it is injurious; it overtaxes the heart. Realizing these facts women everywhere are very much interested in the new discovery, the rubber reducing girdle. Remove your excess fat! Increase your vitality! Improve your health! Be stylish!"

These boons were to be conferred on suffering woman without any effort whatever on her part. She simply put on a rubber corset in the morning and took it off at night, while her figure meanwhile progressed from a mass of bulges and lumpiness to a breath-taking loveliness of line.

"Figure improvement is immediate from the moment the garment is put on, and the gentle continuous massage caused by every movement of the body induces healthful perspiration, thereby massaging away the fat."

The limits of the credulity of allegedly hardheaded woman seeking youth and a fashionable figure have not yet been found.

American women of 1935, in search of youthful bodies and slim, willowy figures, continued to be of great comfort to the rubber planters of the world. The catalog lists a large number of corsets made wholly or in part of rubber, while "Madame La Mont Demonstrates How to Reduce Above and Below the Waistline with Comfort."

It has now become possible, we are told, to "reduce in comfort with our Slim-a-Hip Reducer. Fresh springy perforated rubber, covered with glove silk on the outside, soft felted cotton inside! It massages gently while you walk or sit!" Or a woman could reduce "the air-cooled way with Sears ventilated rubber girdles."

At the same time hips go down, breasts must come out, because "bosoms and curves are in fashion!" and the catalog lists "Removable Pads—to correct that flat chest! Shaped Kapok pads are indetectable and fit inside the Rayon jersey bust."

Would You Like to Look Like Ginger Rogers?

The Ideal Girl of the 1935 catalog is Ginger Rogers, and the catalog offers a number of corsets "autographed and worn" by the distinguished star. A new magic called "Co-Ed Corsetry" has been found, and Sears' lady Ponce de Leon, Madame La Mont, says: "Co-Ed Corsetry Smoothes this curve! Ask the College Crowd! They know! They like Co-Ed Figure Control!"

These corsets promise things more to be desired than pearls or a Phi Beta Kappa key: "a flat tummy," "a slim young waist," and "looking firm and lovely to the eye." The colleges, the corset makers, and Ginger Rogers were transforming the American woman's body, while biologists and evolutionists looked on in amazement as a fat and fortyish woman was

2^{98}

poured into one end of a "slenderizing" girdle and emerged at the other the spitting image of a page boy in the train of Lorenzo de' Medici.

Big Figures

Youth and beauty and slender waists may be the eternal desiderata of womankind, and they may also become big business. A large section of American business is engaged in keeping the public young or attempting to make it look young, and the girdle is used to stay the hands of time for millions of women. The ultimate results of its use are reflected in Department of Commerce statistics. These reveal that in 1935 more than 31,000 workers turned out nearly $67,000,000 worth of corsets and allied garments in the United States.

The Wasp Waist Again?

On August 1, 1939, the Associated Press sent the following dispatch from Chicago: "The business of putting women back into corsets, the kind with laces and stays, came to light at the Merchandise Mart style clinic today.

"There was an emphasis on bustle effects and smaller waists, posing the immediate question of how to get that smaller waist line.

" 'By corsets, and in some instances, of course, corsets that lace,' said Mrs. Katherine Ratto, stylist in charge of the clinic, a feature of the fall-winter wholesale apparel market."

Traditionally, the official opening of the American clothing season is the week after Labor Day. This also happened to be the week in which the European war began. But showings of French imported clothes and American-made designs were staged as usual in smart women's apparel stores. Among the French exhibits which created the widest interest and the greatest discussion among women was Mainbocher's back-laced, wasp-waist corset which had been brought over from Paris on the *Normandie* shortly before the new war started. "One New York department store," reported *Newsweek* in September, 1939, "by last week had sold 500 wasp-waist corsets, while another's stock was exhausted a few days after the ballyhoo started.

"Despite the sudden rush of publicity, the revival of laced, slim-waisted corsets is nothing new. A number of American manufacturers introduced such models as long ago as last spring, but sales lagged until the Paris openings confirmed them as an important style trend."

France marching into the trenches and American women marched into department stores to buy French-inspired, wasp-waist corsets reminiscent of the liberal, easygoing nineteenth century—that is one bit of brittle colored glass in the confused mosaic of 1939.

18 · FROM COTTON DRAWERS TO SILK PANTIES

WRITING forty years ago in England, Samuel Butler said:

> On Hindhead, last Easter, we saw a family wash hung out to dry. There were papa's two great night-shirts and mamma's two lesser nightgowns and the children's articles of clothing and mamma's drawers and the girl's drawers, all full swollen with a strong north-east wind. But mamma's nightgown was not so well pinned on and, instead of being full of steady wind like the others, kept blowing up and down as though she were preaching wildly. We stood and laughed for ten minutes. The housewife came to the window and wondered at us, but we could not resist the pleasure of watching the absurdly life-like gestures which the night-gowns made. I should like a *Santa Famiglia* with clothes drying in the background.*

This sight might also have been, and may still be, seen in the back yards of homes everywhere in the United States, and in the rear of city tenements, where the family wash floating in air is often the only touch of color in otherwise drab surroundings. The age-old aerial ballet of clothes drying in the wind and sun is still enacted all over the country. The choreography remains unaltered but the actors, as compared with those who danced in the innocent American air of thirty years ago, have changed almost beyond recognition. For America has gone from cotton drawers to silk and rayon panties in one generation.

* Henry Festing Jones (ed.), *The Note-Books of Samuel Butler.*

— 383 —

Ladies' drawers in 1905 seem to have been much more the private concern of the person wearing them than they later became in the 1920's. No department-store dummies, despite their papier-mâché rigidity, flaunted drawers in the public's

Reunion in Vienna, Georgia

face; no drawers-clad figures, almost naked and completely unashamed, wore scanty garments in the pages of family magazines. And in keeping with this tradition of privacy, the 1905 catalog, with a fine feeling for the times and the modesty of ladies, illustrates its drawers with simple sketches instead of picturing them on models.

All the drawers in the 1905 catalog were made of cotton. The change to silk or rayon was still some years in the future, but, at the beginning of the century, women contented themselves with underwear made of cotton—a fabric that is washable, durable, cool in summer, warm in winter, absorbent, easily dyed, highly flexible in manufacture, cheap—but lacking in sex appeal. For nineteen cents, the catalog offered "Ladies' Drawers, made of muslin . . . 4-inch cambric flounce with one row of hemstitching and a neat hem around bottom, made extra full, open or closed style." Drawers made in the fashionable umbrella style and the ultimate in catalog luxury cost $1.35:

"Very Pretty Umbrella Style Ladies' Drawers, made of soft nainsook. Has a 5-inch flounce made of point de Paris lace alternating with narrow torchon lace. Triangular pieces of

Bloomers for Schoolgirls

Ages, 8 to 16 Years

Price, 29c Each

No. 38V6729 Black.

SCHOOLGIRL'S GOOD QUALITY SATEEN BLOOMERS. Well made. Elastic band at knees. Saves washing. For ages 8 to 16 years. State age. Average shipping wt., 5 ounces.

Price, 39c Each

No. 38V6736 SCHOOLGIRLS' BLOOMERS. Made from extra fine quality black sateen. Well made throughout and finished with elastic at knees. Ages, 8 to 16 years. State age. Shipping weight, 4 ounces.

Price, 29c Each

No. 38V6734 SCHOOLGIRLS' BLOOMERS. Made from good quality blue chambray gingham. Cut in full sizes; finished with elastic at knees. Ages, 8 to 16 years. State age. Shipping weight, 4 ounces.

Price, 35c Each

No. 38V6730 Black. SCHOOLGIRLS' FINE QUALITY SATEEN BLOOMERS. Good full cut and well made. Ages, 8 to 16 years. State age. Average shpg. wt., 5 ounces.

Price, 89c Each

38V4552 Black. 38V4553 Gray. SCHOOLGIRLS' JERSEY KNIT BLOOMERS. Made from pure wool worsted yarn. Closed at side with patent snap fasteners. Fitted elastic waistband. 8 to 16 yrs. State age. Shpg., wt., 7 oz.

Price, 29c Each

No. 38V6735

Blue and white stripe. SCHOOL-GIRLS' BLOOMERS. Made from good quality striped seersucker gingham. Finished with elastic band at knees. This fabric washes beautifully and does not require ironing. Ages, 8 to 16 years. State age. Shipping wt., 4 ounces.

Bloomers and Trouserettes for Women

Price, 19c Each

No. 38V6726 White.
No. 38V6727 Black.

WOMEN'S KNEE LENGTH BLOOMERS. Knit from fine quality lisle yarn. Has elastic at waist and knees. Small, medium and large. Shipping weight, 9 ounces.

Price, $1.79 Each

No. 38V6700 Tango or mahogany.
No. 38V6701 Black.
No. 38V6702 Navy blue.
No. 38V6703 Cerise or Nell rose.
No. 38V6704 Emerald green.

TUSSAH SILK ANKLE LENGTH TANGO BLOOMERS. Made from a soft lustrous fabric of half silk and half cotton that will wear extremely well. Beautifully made and finished with couleette cuffs at the ankles. Self adjusting elastic waistband, closed at side with patent snap clasps. Lengths, 38 to 44 in. State length. Shpg. wt., 15 oz.

Price, 55c Each

No. 38V6140 Gray stripe.

WOMEN'S BLOOMER DRAWERS of Amoskeag flannelette in neat gray stripe. Closed style, opening at side. Elastic band at knees. Small, medium and large sizes. State size. Shipping wt., 9 ounces.

Price, 99c Each

No. 38V4556 Black.
No. 38V4557 Gray.
No. 38V4558 Navy blue.

WOMEN'S FINE QUALITY MEDIUM WEIGHT BLOOMERS. Knit from 100 per cent pure wool worsted yarn in the jersey stitch. Fitted elastic waistband. Closes at side with patent snap fasteners. Elastic at knees. This is a very practical garment and is priced very low. Medium and large sizes. State size. Shipping weight, 9 ounces.

Price, 49c Each

No. 38V4546 Gray.
No. 38V4547 Navy blue.
No. 38V4551 Black.

WOMEN'S FINE COTTON ELASTIC RIBBED BLOOMERS. Winter weight. Has draw string at waist and elastic band at knees. This takes the place of a knitted petticoat and drawers. Medium and large sizes. State size. Shipping weight, 10 ounces.

Price, $1.29 Each

No. 38V6720 Cerise.
No. 38V6721 Black.
No. 38V6722 White.

WOMEN'S FITTED TOP SIDE CLOSING KNEE LENGTH TUSSAH SILK BLOOMERS. Elastic in waistband and at knees. Finished with narrow plaiting. Length, 27 inches. Shipping weight, 10 ounces.

Price, 69c Each

No. 38V6144 Black.
No. 38V6145 White.

WOMEN'S BLOOMER DRAWERS. Good quality sateen. Closed style. Has elastic band at knees and waist. Small, medium and large sizes. State size. Shipping weight, 7 oz.

Price, $2.48 Each

No. 38V6713 Royal blue.
No. 38V6714 Tango or light mahogany.
No. 38V6715 Cerise or Nell rose.
No. 38V6731 Emerald green.

BROCADED ANKLE LENGTH TROUSERETTES OR TANGO BLOOMERS. This is a very practical undergarment, having the appearance of a petticoat with the deep plaited flounce, at the same time giving the perfect lines so essential to the styles of the day. The material is a soft clinging silk and cotton fabric, which is very pretty and durable. Self adjusting waistband. Lengths, 38 to 44 inches. State length. Shipping weight, 1 pound.

So Chic—So Smart—So Very Becoming

Descriptions of Dresses Shown on Opposite Page.

This pretty, dressy frock of fine, lustrous all silk crepe back satin can be appropriately worn for most any occasion.

The sufficiently full apron front, over a slim-line tubular frock, has a border of contrasting color all silk crepe de chine, which matches the simulated collar, tabs suggesting pockets at either side and is used as a background for the tiny metallic buttons appearing on loose hanging streamer directly at the center. These tiny buttons also set off the pocket tabs.

Lastly, but by far the most important style feature of this beautiful frock, is the artistic embroidery design of vari-colored and tinsel thread, which most effectively embellishes the apron style tunic.

WOMEN'S AND MISSES' REGULAR SIZES—32 to 44 inches bust measure. State size and give length from back of neck to bottom of skirt. Shipping weight, 1½ pounds.
31V5650—Black with green.
31V5651—Navy blue with king blue. **$17.95**

This little summertime costume, with its crisp, cool looking organdie collar and cuffs, and scalloped frilled band centered from neck to hemline, adapts itself admirably to the ever reliable, durable, striped cotton ratine, of which it is made.

A pretty colorful touch is added by fancy stitching on the organdie decoration, which matches in color the cotton charmeuse finishing on the slashed pockets, and narrow kid belt.

You could not make a more profitable selection than this frock, so perfectly adapted to all around summer service. An incomparable bargain at the low price of $6.98!

WOMEN'S AND MISSES' REGULAR SIZES—32 to 40 inches bust measure only. State size and give length from back of neck to bottom of skirt. Shipping weight, 1½ pounds.
31V5655—Honeydew heather.
31V5656—Green heather.
31V5657—Geranium heather. **$6.98**

Individuality and perfection of the slim-line silhouette is revealed in this fascinating frock of fine quality all silk satin Canton crepe.

A soft, dainty style touch is achieved by the front of closely knife pleated all silk crepe de chine, showing beneath the open tunic and inside of the narrow V shaped collar. In addition to this, a most striking effect is given by artistic chain stitch embroidery, which matches front of frock and embellishes the entire skirt. Narrow sleeve band and edging on collar, which falls in graceful narrow streamers, are in a shade to match the pleating beneath the tunic.

A strictly high class frock, and one of the many unusual values you will find on the fashion pages of this book.

WOMEN'S AND MISSES' REGULAR SIZES—32 to 44 inches bust measure. State size and give length from back of neck to bottom of skirt. Shipping weight, 1½ pounds.
31V5660—Rust.
31V5661—Navy blue.
31V5662—Cranberry red. **$15.95**

Nothing could be more effectively simple yet extremely modish, than this delightful summer frock of striped washable all silk broadcloth.

It is almost impossible to ignore fashion's preference for stripes; for they're here, there and everywhere, and they are particularly striking on this cleverly designed model.

Not only is the style one which will give you much pleasure during warm summer days, but in addition it will render unlimited service, as this rich all silk fabric launders so easily. All silk moire grosgrain ribbon tie at neck is drawn through piped buttonholes.

WOMEN'S AND MISSES' REGULAR SIZES—32 to 40 inches bust measure only. State size and give length from back of neck to bottom of skirt. Shpg. wt. 1½ lbs.
31V5665
Fancy stripe. **$9.98**

SIZES Dresses on this and the opposite page (except 31V5655) come in Women's and Misses' Regular Sizes, 32 to 44 inches bust measure, proportionate waist measure, and length from back of neck to bottom of skirt, 47 to 54 inches. Give bust and waist measure; also length from back of neck to bottom of skirt.

Our Finest Silk Dress

31V5640 All Silk Satin Faced Canton Crepe $23.95

Our Finest Silk Dress.

Fashion features the apron style tunic in this charming gown of heavy quality all silk satin faced Canton crepe, trimmed with wide lavishly silk embroidered openwork banding.

Border and bands of reversed self material have been applied in a most unique manner to further accent its beautifully graceful lines and dressy appearance. Note the rich artificial silk braid frogs which are placed at either side of waistline and add a finishing touch to the snug fitting lace adorned sleeves.

Material used for both dress and tunic is of our very best quality, heavy in weight and extremely beautiful.

WOMEN'S AND MISSES' REGULAR SIZES—32 to 44 inches bust measure. State size and give length from back of neck to bottom of skirt. Shipping weight, 1½ pounds.
31V5640—Cocoa brown.
31V5641—Navy blue.
31V5642—Black. **$23.95**

31V5645 Novelty Crepe with Silk Check $7.89

This frock, of strikingly feminine charm, shows the possibility of combining silk checked cotton crepe with allover embroidered net.

A style which adopts a surplice line from the right shoulder, extending to the hipline at left, and gracefully suggests a continuation of the tapering lace front.

A dainty and very effective form of adornment is contributed by narrow Valenciennes lace edging, appearing on the lacy cuffs as well as on the unique triangular lace panel. Tiny colored glass buttons add a decidedly modish touch. Wide sash ties in flying bow at left side where lace panel and fashionable Directoire rever meet.

WOMEN'S AND MISSES' REGULAR SIZES—32 to 44 inches bust measure. State size and give length from back of neck to bottom of skirt. Shipping weight, 1½ pounds.
31V5645—Cocoa brown.
31V5646—Empire blue.
31V5647—Henna rust. **$7.89**

14V2

India lawn set between each insertion, giving flounce a nice flare, 2-inch lace edge to match flounce, including lace edge, 7 inches deep. Open style only."

Here Comes the Bride

Since public policy favors marriage, it must regard with a kindly eye any act, or acts, that tends to aid or increase marriages. From this point of view, the catalog of 1905 is seen in retrospect to have been both a public benefactor and a dancing girl strewing flowers in the path of Eros. No lady of the period need have hesitated to marry because of the high cost of a trousseau when the catalog presented her with a choice of Great Bargains in Trousseau Outfits, ranging in price from $4.35 to $8.65—sums which were not likely to keep any woman away from the sweet delights of holy matrimony. The golden mean between these extremes was:

"Our $5.98 Trousseau Outfit . . . fit for an American queen, made of fine cambric, in four pieces, gown, underskirt, drawers and corset cover."

The End of a Perfect Day—Song by Carrie Jacobs Bond, Clothes by Sears, Roebuck & Company

Queen or no queen, there is something heartening in the spectacle of a young girl of that time going out of her parents' home to face both the world and a husband with nothing between her and the unknown except a nightgown, an underskirt, a pair of drawers, and a corset cover.

Underskirts

The nineteenth-century American landscape was thickly cluttered with underskirts as women reduced the number they wore from six or seven to the single petticoat of the 1890's. Wearing but one petticoat at a time enabled a woman to concentrate her attention on it. She could choose one or a whole collection with great care, and the result in the catalog of 1905 is a bewildering variety of petticoats. There are cotton petticoats, plain and lace-trimmed petticoats, petticoats of washable gingham, sateen, spun glass, and taffeta silk.

$148

35T5735

"Sister Annie, Can You See Them Coming?"

For many years, silk petticoats were expected to emit a silken rustle or "froufrou"—a music not only fashionable but, it was supposed, enchanting to the male ear. At first, only the more expensive petticoats made music as they moved, but later manufacturers found how to put a rustle into bargain-counter petticoats. This caused the genteel to demand that the music be muted. An advertisement in *Vogue* for 1905 shows which way the music was blowing:

"Heather Bloom Taffeta (for petticoats) Looks, Feels, Sounds Like Silk. Possessing all the strength, sheen, swish of . . . the purest silk (but) is without that harsh rustle abhorrent to women of taste."

The catalog makes no musical claims for even its most expensive underskirt "of very fine taffeta silk" at $7.25, but is content to describe merely its ruffles and laces and its blue and green changeable colors once so fashionable.

Thirty Years After

In 1928, the Department of Agriculture issued a report, written by Edna Clark, called *The Changing Uses of Textile Fibers in Clothing and Household Articles*. It is strange enough to find information about women's panties within the austere portals of the Department that concerns itself with wild hay, setting hens, alfalfa, and the woes of agriculture, but Miss Clark's document poses an even greater wonder. The fact that women began to shift from cotton to silk and rayon underwear in the 1920's is a readily demonstrable fact. But, suggests Miss Clark, single women discarded cotton underwear and adopted silk and rayon far more extensively than married women. Why? Is the mystery to be solved in terms of Marx or Freud or Hollywood? The Department is silent; Miss Clark betrays no secrets of her sex; consequently, the fascinating question of why married women still clung to their cotton drawers while their unmarried sisters took to silk and rayon panties is one that some investigator of the future must probe.

The shift to new fabrics for women's underwear marked a great change in fashion; even greater was the change to underwear fashions in 1935 that would have been considered wildly impossible for respectable women in 1905.

The old-fashioned word "drawers" has been dropped from the catalog, and, by whatever name this garment is called, its essential virtue is that it must be scanty. Women now wear little underwear and the little they do wear must be almost imperceptible.

"Sears Briefs! Sleeker! Smoother! Skin-Light! Skin-Tight!

In Union There Is Length

"Knit Rayon Panty and Bandeau Set. Cuddles, clings and flatters, and is young and gay looking." In 1905, the catalog would not have dreamed of using such terms to describe drawers, but in 1935 it emphasizes again and again the scantiness and skintightness of the underwear demanded by women whether on the farm or in the city.

"Little Britches. They Fit Without a Wrinkle! Brief Panties—light as a feather. Beautifully tailored to fit your body like a silk glove. . . ."

Or, "The Briefest little Brief you ever did see! It hugs you tight—stretches and 'breathes' when you do! Very comfy! . . ."

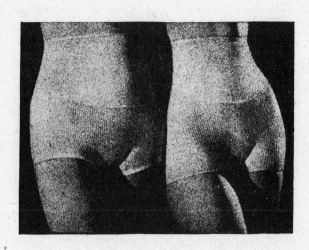

Brevity Is the Soul of It

Ginger Rogers, kindly letting other women in on one of the secrets of her success, wears the same panties that are in the catalog, and, since they cost only forty-five cents, millions of girls may dress like their heroine.

"Ginger Rogers Lace Panties. No wonder Ginger Rogers chose this clever little panty for herself! Three rows of the sweetest lace trim at bottom."

Miss Rogers' colleague, Miss Loretta Young, not to be outdone in generosity, lends the prestige of her name to a "combination that takes the place of 4 garments: panty, brassiere, girdle, and vest. Loretta Young is keen about this 4-in-1 combination—says it is all she needs to wear under most dresses."

While the ladies were changing their underwear, they were also changing their nightgowns. The old-fashioned nightgown, shapeless, long-sleeved, lace-trimmed, high-throated, gave way to form-fitting silk nightgowns made in Puerto Rico or simple, hand-embroidered nainsook gowns from the Philippines—one of our few tangible gains from imperialism, our grandiose "manifest destiny" of the 1890's. In historical retrospect, all this seems to have been a long detour to enable American women to arrive at more attractive dress for bed.

"Let us not forget," wrote Paul Poiret, "that man is the only one of all the animals who has discovered clothing. And is it not his punishment that he is obliged to be continually changing it, and never able to find a fixed formula? He is the Wandering Jew of compulsive fantasy."

IN 1886, a young Southern woman spending the summer at the fashionable watering place, Narragansett Pier, Rhode Island, wrote a letter to one of her friends at home. It was a friendly, catty, feminine letter, written with the dash and accuracy of description that seem to come spontaneously to the woman who is engaged in the delicate surgical art of taking the hide off another woman, and, since it bears on bathing suits which will be considered in this chapter, it is here quoted:

> DEAR COUSIN,
>
> I am snatching a few moments from the daily rush to again urge you to join Me. . . . With the idea of enticing you, I will attempt to give a fleeting glimpse of the passing show.
>
> During the bathing hours at high tide . . . the beach and hotel verandas are crowded with onlookers. An hundred or more bathers—men and women—afford us no end of entertainment. Charlie Dudley is here and, as you know, one permits him to say outrageous things. The combination of his charm and daring humor are disarming. He sat beside me today while all eyes were riveted on one Mrs. Gissing from Chicago. She is supposed to be beautiful. I make a guess that her auburn tresses have been assisted and her figure is described by Charlie as being roBUST and HYPnotic. Some say, "divorcee," others "grass-widow." Well, no matter. In any case it would take a horse race to keep up with her. I, of course, know her only by sight, and *sight* she is! The men buzz around her like bees and gather about the bath rooms to see her pass, en route to the waves. She always lolls on the sand a bit before making a kittenish dash—she's

surely in the thirties if a minute. Her costume and antics this morning were paramount to anything yet. ("Yet" is significant as there is no telling what she may do.)

Black silk bathing suit—*very* short skirt—*very* low neck NO sleeves—transparent silk stockings. On her arm a gold bracelet, if you please! After she had done building sand hills (childish aspect) with several male bathers, she referred to the billows. Catching hands with a favored gentleman, they made a grand rush and sprawled. From then on, where her corset began and left off was very apparent.

Mrs. G., with one exception, is the only good female swimmer, yet, with an arm around the man's shoulder, his arm around her's, swimming with one hand apiece, they made good headway to the deep water raft. Not satisfied with this, she mounted his back and pitched off head foremost. Some women seated next me got up and left. I didn't feel that way about Mrs. Gissing. For all I care she may be as brazen as she likes.

Charlie Dudley watched the whole performance through his field glasses—such remarks!! He leaves next week for White Sulphur. . . . All said and done, what a charming and entertaining man he is—wicked thing. . . .

Both Charlie Dudley and the writer of the letter were in the line of an old tradition. Throughout the Regency, young blades of Bath gazed through binoculars at ladies bathing in ankle-long suits; throughout the nineteenth century and until well into the twentieth, so-called immodest bathing clothes for women were deplored by other women. The letter quoted here indicates that a bathing suit was immodest in 1886 if it had a short skirt, a low neck, and no sleeves; immodest even if the bather wore silk stockings and a corset in the water.

These attitudes were manifested in so-called liberal circles of fashionable society, and it may be expected, therefore, that we shall find them even more pointed among those who were not in "society."

Bathing Suits of 1905

Beach bathing or swimming was plainly not a popular form of amusement for Sears' customers in 1905. Salt water was inaccessible then to the greater portion of the population who lived inland; cheap automobiles, vacations, and good roads were yet to come. Private swimming pools were rare and public pools even rarer; boys might swim in the creeks and men in the lakes or rivers but women seldom swam. And the catalog, because of lack of demand for bathing suits for women, lists only two models in 1905. They conformed to prevailing canons of modesty; they were frightfully ugly, ungainly, and, because of their weight and long skirts, dangerous to the wearer in the water. Black cotton stockings and a collar tightly buttoned up around the throat were the inevitable features of every bathing suit of the times. The catalog describes one chic number as follows:

"Ladies' Bathing Suit, with attached bloomers, made of brilliantine. Has large sailor collar trimmed with two rows white cord and one row of braid. Sleeves trimmed to correspond. Detachable skirt, waistband trimmed with rows of cord and a row of braid, trimmed around the bottom to correspond. Colors, black or navy blue with white trimmings. Price . . . $2.98."

Water, Water, Everywhere and Not a Man in Sight

The caps worn with the suits might also be used as dust caps. "Bathing or Dust Caps, made of pure gum rubber. . . . These caps are also useful as dust caps when house cleaning, etc."

While suits such as the one described conformed with prevailing canons of modesty and taste, and fierce opposition was aroused by attempts to change them, voices were occasionally raised on the other side. *Eve's Glossary,* for example, in 1897, contained this criticism of bathing suits:

> In the United States, where there are to be found exceptionally pretty feet and ankles, women are forced to conceal them and were any of them to venture on the beach at any one of the popular seaside resorts with limbs bare from the knee downwards, an outcry would be raised on the score of injured morality. People with whom I have recently been discussing the subject claim that the strict ideas which prevail in America with regard to bare ankles and feet are a remnant of the old . . . laws and notions of our puritanical forefathers. That is all very well, but what, if you please, would those passengers of the *Mayflower* have said to the present state of *décolletage?* Surely there is less impropriety in displaying the feet and the legs as far as the knee, than in furnishing such a general and liberal exhibition as is to be seen in the boxes on any good night of the New York opera season.

This, too, was all very well, but deep-rooted notions of modesty in woman's dress continued to prevail unchanged in rural and even urban America. *Harper's Weekly* for August, 1913, contained an article called "Modesty in Women's Clothes," in which the author, Francis R. McCabe, reports the following incident:

". . . Recently . . . a farmer advertised for a wife, and after correspondence with the young woman agreed to marry her, but when he met her at the railroad station declined to carry out his agreement because he wanted a modest woman for a wife.

" 'Am I not modest?' asked the girl.

" 'What! Modest with those bare arms?' exclaimed the farmer.

"The girl was wearing a dress with short sleeves."

The attitude of this farmer was broad-minded and generous compared with that of a mob who assaulted a woman at the Atlantic City beach in 1913 because she appeared in a short bathing suit. The incident moved *The New York Times* to remark editorially:

> . . . In Atlantic City . . . a woman has just been fiercely assaulted by the local populace (because her bathing suit was too short). . . . Outright killing doesn't seem to have been the purpose of the offended throng but they frightened the too close imitator of the naiads something more than half to death, by pelting her with epithets and sand, and what they would have done had it not been for the rescuing police is unknown.
>
> The episode can be viewed in various ways. Some will take it as illustrating the noble virtuousness of the general American public; others will wonder why the women who go in swimming must wear any skirt at all, that garment being, in the water, quite unnecessary for decency, and a danger to life as well as a wearying burden that no man will tolerate for an instant on himself. We will not attempt to decide which view is the right one.

If shapely ladies occasionally attempted to burst out of their unshapely bathing suits, gentlemen, more conservative, continued to display their unshapely figures in suits that had been good enough for their grandfathers. The 1905 catalog lists:

Suit Worn by Man Who Opposed Votes for Women

"Our One-Piece Best Cotton Bathing Suit . . . made like a union suit (buttons over shoulder). It is like an ordinary shirt and knee pants, but all in one piece, made in solid colors and fancy stripes. . . . Price 65¢."

Ten Years Pass

It is astonishing to find that in the ten years from 1905 to 1915 the tiny demand on the part of Sears' customers for bathing suits did not increase, and the suits themselves remained relatively unchanged. The time is yet to come when all America, like the lemmings of Norway, will rush head-long toward and into the sea.

Bathing-Beauty Contests

Three overrated institutions—sex, the California climate, and the jury system—we have always had with us, but the first two seem to have been discovered only after the War to end War. It was when we had made the world safe for democracy, and grown rich in the bargain, that the Holly-wood producer and student, if not creator, of American folk-ways, Mr. Cecil B. DeMille, concluded that Americans were interested in only two things: money and sex. Sex in a sim-ple flat is sin; in a palace it is row-mance, and Mr. DeMille, putting two together in a palace, made a smashing box-office success which proved the soundness of his theory. Strangely enough, the guinea pig selected for his experiment was *The Admirable Crichton* by the well-known whimseymonger, James M. Barrie; the play in which an amazingly resource-ful butler shipwrecked on a desert isle with his aristocratic but useless employers rose to every emergency with the ease and aplomb that had distinguished him when at home in Belgravia. This simple play, which Mr. DeMille renamed *Male and Female,* emerged from the Hollywood studios filled with row-mance, excitement, and sex appeal, furnished by a former Mack Sennett bathing beauty—Miss Gloria Swanson —who in one sequence, fading from the present time to the guileless past, was revealed in a Garden of Eden background costumed as the great mother of the race, with Thomas Meighan hovering around her in the role of Adam. This was sex, but it was not money, and consequently, after some more fading out and fading in, Miss Swanson and Mr. Meighan appeared in a splendid Oriental palace, he as the king and she as the maid his majesty loves.

Male and Female was an instantaneous success at the box office, other producers imitated the master, and in no time at all sex and the California climate came to be established as the other parts of the great American trinity.

On the East Coast is Atlantic City where the Gulf Stream obligingly sweeps inward in order to give this town a year-around warm climate for the benefit of the tired millions of near-by New York and Philadelphia. And the town, out of gratitude, has made the Gulf Stream famous with the hotels and boarding houses that it has built near its current, with its Million Dollar Pier, and its famous bathing-beauty contests.

These contests, sprung from the minds of Atlantic City's elder statesmen (assisted by the troubadours of pageantry and publicity, called press agents by the vulgar), were for years as much a part of the life of the town as was the annual ceremony of marrying the sea in Atlantic City's nearest rival for fame—Venice. The doges of the Eastern seaboard, looking westward to Mack Sennett's bathing girls and Mr. De-Mille's profitable incursions into American folkways, decided that the next business cycle in Atlantic City would be based on sex, just as others elsewhere had been based on cotton, oil, or automobiles. All that was necessary was a number of shapely girls in bathing suits, prizes for the winner, and publicity. The doges were right.

The bathing-beauty contests were an enormous success. All over the United States, in towns remote from the sea or even a lake, girls paraded in skimpy bathing suits and high-heeled shoes before local judges. The winner went to the state contest, and the girl adjudged Miss South Dakota was sent to the national contest in Atlantic City to the accompaniment of pages of newspaper chat about her, the prayers of the homefolk, and the plaudits of the mayor and governor of her state.

As usual, voices of protest were raised, and, as usual, no attention was paid to them. A convention of the Southern Baptist church, held in Houston, Texas, denounced bathing-beauty contests as evil things tending to "lower true and genuine respect for womanhood"; the National Council of Catholic Women for once saw eye to eye with the Baptists and condemned the beauty shows as "an exploitation of feminine pulchritude" and "a backward step in the civilization of the world," while the Philadelphia Federation of Women's Clubs adopted a resolution stating that "the demoralizing effect of the Atlantic City Beauty Beach parade is an established fact."

At the same time, the United States navy, recognizing the spiritual kinship of all who go down to the sea, whether in ships or bathing suits, sent its dirigible *Los Angeles* to soar over the city where the fairest of America's fair was being chosen; newspapers printed millions of photographs of the beauties; the winner went on to fame and fortune; rival bathing-beauty contests sprang up over all the country, and advertisers found that a photograph of a bathing-beauty girl was helpful in selling everything from automobiles to mucilage.

It is not surprising, therefore, to find the bathing beauties of the catalog of 1925 attired in "California style bathing suits," with bare arms, knee-length trunks, and rolled silk stockings, while in the city, where the catalog is published, a new Venus was soon to arise from the prairies, build a bubble into a business, achieve international fame, overshadow a great international exhibition, and pave the way for bigger and better nudity.

The creator of these miracles was Miss Sally Rand, a onetime leader in the Christian Endeavor Society at the Jackson Avenue Christian Church in Kansas City, Missouri, whose bubble dance at the World's Fair in Chicago in 1933 was so sensationally successful that within a short time her earnings jumped from $125 a week to $6,000 a week. This led Miss Rand to the sage observance that "I never made any money until I took off my pants"; to the confession that she was "fanning her brother through college," and to the final accolade of receiving many invitations to address luncheon clubs. These groups listened earnestly while the well-to-do and successful Miss Rand spoke on the subject "Bubbles Become Big Business." Finally, the fame of this Middle West ballerina

BATHING SUPPLIES.

Women's One-Piece Mohair Bathing Suit. Latest style and very neatly trimmed throughout. Has fancy sateen collar and trimmed set-in sleeves. Good quality undersuit with each. Cap and slippers are extra. If wanted see below. Sizes, 32 to 42 inches bust measure. State size. Shipping wt., 1 lb. 3 oz.
No. 6V7260 Black. Price, each..**$3.48**
No. 6V7261 Navy. Price, each..**$3.49**

Girls' Bathing Suit. Fast color, good weight, closely woven cotton fabric. Very attractively trimmed. Bloomers with each suit. Comes in ages 6 to 16 years. State age. Shipping wt., 1 pound 3 ounces.
No. 6V7263 Navy blue. Price, each..**$1.47**

One-Piece Wool Juvenile Suit. Heavy sweater stitch, fancy "V" neck trim. A very warm, comfortable suit for a youngster. Sizes, 22, 24 and 26 inches breast measure. State size. Shpg. wt., 1 lb.
No. 6V7242 Oxford with white trim. Price, each..**97c**
No. 6V7243 Navy blue with red trim. Price, each..**98c**

Medium Weight Cotton Juvenile Suit with plain round neck. Trimmed around armholes and trunks. Sizes, 22, 24 and 26 inches breast measure. State size. Shipping weight, 6 ounces.
No. 6V7244 Price, each..**38c**

Women's One-Piece Bathing Suit with set-in sleeves and sailor collar effect. Made of closely woven cotton fabric and neatly trimmed with braid and buttons. Undersuit with each. Cap and slippers are extra. If wanted note selections shown below. Sizes, 32 to 42 inches bust measure. State color.
No. 6V7262 Navy blue. Price, ea..**$1.87**

Men's Two-Piece Suit. Made of a selected combed cotton yarn. A very well made, well shaped cotton garment. Made in round neck style as illustrated and guaranteed not to fade. Color, navy blue with white or red stripe trim. Sizes, 34 to 44 inches breast measure. State size and color trim. Shipping weight, 12 oz.
No. 6V7229 Price........**95c**
Extra sizes, 46, 48 and 50 inches breast measure, in the above garment, extra..........**40c**

Men's Two-Piece Elastic Rib Medium Quality Cotton Bathing Suit. Navy blue, attractively trimmed. This suit possesses excellent wearing qualities. Has "V" shaped neck. Sizes, 34 to 44 inches breast measure. State size. Shipping weight, 12 ounces.
No. 6V7231 Price, each..**65c**

One-Piece Solid Comfort Bathing Suit. Has the appearance of a two-piece suit. This is a style suit that is very popular, especially serviceable, and at the same time highly recommended for propriety. Made of selected combed cotton yarn. Navy blue with white or red trim. Sizes, 34 to 44 inches breast measure. State size and color trim.
No. 6V7228 Price, each....**$1.09**
Extra sizes, 46, 48 and 50 inches breast measure, in the above garment, extra..........**40c**

Medium Weight Cotton Suit; style as above. Navy blue with contrast trim. Sizes, 34 to 44 in. breast measure. State size. Shpg. wt., 12 oz.
No. 6V7239 Price, each......**47c**

Men's Wool Combination Suit in this popular style. Very neatly trimmed, well shaped and carefully finished throughout. Sizes, 34 to 44 inches breast measure. State size.
No. 6V7240 Navy blue with white trim. Price, each..**$1.93**
No. 6V7241 Oxford with white trim. Price, each..**$1.94**

Men's Two-Piece All Wool Worsted Bathing Suit with quarter sleeves. Trimmed around armholes, and at bottom of shirt and trunks. Made of finest French all wool worsted yarn, very closely spun, and possesses exceptionally warm, comfortable qualities. Will dry quickly and not lose its shape. A suit for the man who wants the best. Navy blue with red or white trim. Sizes, 34 to 44 inches breast measure. State size and color trim. Shipping weight, 1½ lbs.
No. 6V7225 Price, each......**$3.00**

Boys' Two-Piece Cotton Bathing Suit, made of a good weight cotton yarn. Navy blue. Well finished and attractively trimmed throughout. Sizes, 26 to 32 inches breast measure. State size. Shipping weight, 10 ounces.
No. 6V7230 Price, each......**47c**

Men's Two-Piece Wool Bathing Suit, sleeveless style, with "V" shaped neck. A strong, firmly knitted, especially well appearing garment. Sizes, 32 to 44 inches breast measure. State size and color trim. Shipping weight, 12 ounces.
No. 6V7226 Navy blue with white or red trim. Price, each..**$1.95**
No. 6V7227 Dark Oxford with white or red trim. Price, each..**$1.96**

Boys' Skirt Style Combination Bathing Suit. Made of good weight cotton yarn. One of the most practicable, serviceable styles for boys. Also can be worn by girls. Navy blue. Buttons on shoulder. Neatly trimmed throughout. Sizes, 28 to 32 inches breast measure. State size. Shipping weight, 8 ounces.
No. 6V7232 Price, each......**47c**

Women's Juliet Style Bathing Cap. Made of rubber lined polka dot sateen. Black or navy blue. State color. Shipping weight, 4 oz.
No. 6V7267 Price, each....**23c**

Women's Pure Gum Rubber Bathing Cap in Juliet style. Blue or red. State color. Shipping weight, 4 oz.
No. 6V7268 Price, each....**48c**

Rubber Lined Bathing Suit Bag, black in color, fitted with drawstrings. Strongly made and finely finished throughout. This is an exceptionally big value and a very useful adjunct to a bathing outfit. Shipping weight, 6 oz.
No. 6V7278 Price, each....**23c**

Men's Worsted Bathing Cap in sweater stitch. Trimmed as illustrated. Oxford gray with white trim; navy blue with red or white trim. State color. Shipping weight, 6 ounces.
No. 6V7223 Price, each....**36c**

Men's Black Elastic Rubber Bathing Cap. Fits tightly over head. Keeps hair dry and water from ears. Shipping weight, 3 oz.
No. 6V7222 Price, each....**40c**

Women's Good Quality Bathing Slippers. Fancy black and white pattern. Buckle fastening. Composition soles. Sizes, 3 to 8. State size. Shipping weight, 6 ounces.
No. 6V7272 Price, per pair..**39c**

Canvas Bathing Slippers; medium quality. Women's sizes, 3 to 8; children's sizes, 11 to 2. State size. Colors, black or white. State color. Shipping wt., 6 oz.
No. 6V7273 Price, per pair..**18c**

Ayvad's Water Wings, 19 Cents.
When inflated will support an adult of 250 pounds as easily as a child at the proper level for comfortable swimming. When deflated can be rolled into a package small enough to be carried in pocket. An excellent support to use when learning to swim. Shipping weight, 4 ounces.
No. 6V7221 Price.................**19c**

Boys' Swimming Trunks. Assorted stripe designs. Sizes 24 to 30 inches waist measure. Shipping weight, 4 oz.
No. 6V7219 Price, per pair..**10c**
Larger sizes, for men, see No. 6V7204 Tights, shown on page 819.

Cork Surf Ball. A great fun producer for bathers. Size, 9 inches in circumference. Shipping wt., 4 ounces.
No. 6V7215 Price, each......**17c**

Men's Canvas Bathing Slippers. Good quality black canvas, composition soles. Sizes, 6 to 11. State size. Color, black. Shipping weight, 8 ounces.
No. 6V7248 Price, per pair..**21c**

For Parcel Post Shipments Include Amount of Charges Extra.

SEARS, ROEBUCK AND CO., CHICAGO, ILL.

Attractive, High Quality Bathing Suits

Complete Suit $3.88

NOTICE—All our bathing suits are California style, with the exception of our Men's Two-Piece Suits. They are all exceptionally well made of fine quality yarns, extra full sizes and are unusual value for the prices we ask. Not to be confused with cheaper suits that are skimped in size and lighter weight.

Men's Medium Weight All Wool Worsted Bathing Suit. Brown heather with orange and royal blue chest stripes. Sizes, 36 to 46 inches chest measure. State size. Shipping weight 1¼ pounds.
6V2125 ....$3.20

Men's Heavy Ribbed All Wool Worsted Bathing Suit. A very high grade snug fitting suit. Navy blue with white skirt stripes. No chest stripes. Sizes, 34 to 42 inches chest measure. State size. Shipping weight, 2 pounds.
6V2148 ....$4.15

Women's Butterfly Style Rubber Diving Cap. Shipping weight, 4 oz.
6V2107 — Red, blue trimmed..38c
6V2110 — Green, white trimmed..38c
6V211 — Blue, white trimmed..38c

Aviator's Style Bathing Cap in Colors. The very latest aviator's style cap in colors to match your bathing suit. Made of heavy Para rubber. Suitable for both men and women. Shpg. wt., 4 oz.
6V2112—Navy Blue.....54c
6V2113—Red 54c
6V2114—Green 54c

Aviator's Style Rubber Cap. Natural color. Pure Para rubber. Suitable for women as well as for men. Shpg. wt., 3 oz.
6V2109..42c

Women's Bow Style Rubber Diving Cap. Very attractive. Shpg. wt., 3 oz.
6V2126—Blue, with green and orange striped bow..36c
6V2128—Red, with blue and green striped bow..36c
6V2129 — Green, with blue and orange striped bow..36c

Boys' All Wool Worsted Bathing Suit. The very latest style for boys. Can also be worn by girls. California style suit, white upper and navy blue skirt and trunk with white web belt. Sizes, 28 to 34 inches chest measure. State size. Shipping weight, 1 pound.
6V2130 $2.58

Women's All Wool Worsted Bathing Suit. Medium weight, California style, with belt to match. Gold braid trim, lustrous finish. Sizes, 36 to 46 inches bust measure. State size. Shipping weight, 1½ pounds.
6V2167—Peacock blue with gold braid...$4.45 | 6V2166—Kelly green with gold braid...$4.45

Women's All Wool Worsted Bathing Suit. Regular and extra sizes. Medium weight, California style, trunk sewed to skirt, round neck, winged sleeve (no belt). Sizes, 40 to 50 inches bust measure. State size. Shipping weight, 1½ pounds.
6V2163—Navy blue with white trimming....$3.98

Divers' Style Rubber Cap. For both women and men. Plain colors. Shipping weight, 3 oz.
6V2101—Blue 19c
6V2102—Green 19c
6V2104—Red 19c

Divers' Plain Style Rubber Cap. Natural color. Heavy Para rubber. Shipping weight, 4 ounces.
6V2105 ....37c

Women's Canvas Bathing Slippers, Black only. Cork soles. McKay sewed. Sizes, 3 to 8. No half sizes. State size. Shpg. wt., 6 ounces.
6V2156 46c

Women's Rubber Bathing Slipper. The very latest style. Made entirely of rubber. Sizes, 3, 4, 5, 6 and 7. State size. Shipping weight, 1 pound.
6V2188 Black 74c
6V2189 Red 74c

Women's Sateen Bathing Slippers with strap and buckle. Cork soles. McKay sewed. Sizes 3 to 8. No half sizes. State size. Shpg. wt., 6 oz.
6V2176 Black 67c
6V2177 Green 67c
6V2178 Red 67c

Misses' All Wool Worsted Bathing Suit. Medium weight, California style. Very attractive. Sizes, 28 to 34 inches bust measure. State size. Shipping weight, 1¼ lbs.
6V2193 Peacock blue, with black and white skirt stripes..$2.65
6V2192 Jockey red with black and white skirt stripes..$2.65

Misses' All Cotton Bathing Suit. Navy blue with trimming of contrasting colors. Sizes, 28 to 34 bust. State size.
6V2187 86c

Flapper Style All Wool Worsted Bathing Suit. Medium weight, popular plain style, trunks sewed to skirt. Sizes, 34 to 42 inches bust measure. State size. Shipping wt., 1¼ lbs.
6V2154 — Jockey red, with black and white skirt stripes...$3.14
6V2150—Navy blue with white skirt stripe...$3.14
6V2151—Plain black $2.98

Women's Heavy Ribbed All Wool Worsted Bathing Suit. California style, trunk sewed to skirt. Sizes, 34 to 42 in. bust measure. State size. Shpg. wt., 2 lbs.
6V2152—Jockey color (bright red) $3.95
6V2153—Peacock blue $3.95

Women's Cotton Bathing Suit. Medium weight, navy blue with trimmings of contrasting colors. Sizes, 36 to 46 in. bust measure. State size. Shpg. wt., 1½ lbs.
6V2160 ....98c

Men's Medium Weight All Wool Worsted Bathing Suit. Navy blue with white skirt stripes. Excellent value for the money. Sizes, 36 to 46 inches chest measure. State size. Shipping weight, 1¼ lbs.
6V2140 $2.93

Men's All Cotton Bathing Suit. Medium weight. Style as above. Navy blue with trimming of contrasting color. Sizes, 36 to 46 chest measure. State size. Shpg. wt., 1¼ lbs.
6V2139 85c

Men's Athletic Two-Piece Bathing Suits. Very latest style for boys and men. Exceptional value. When ordering complete suit give catalog number, size of shirt and size and kind of trunk wanted. Shipping weight, each garment, 12 ounces.
6V2144—White, Medium Heavy Weight All Worsted Supporter Shirt Only. Sizes, 34 to 46 chest measure. State size $1.75
6V2145—Navy Blue, Knitted All Wool Worsted Trunks, fly front, with white web belt. Sizes, 30 to 44 waist measure. State size.....$2.13
6V2147—Navy Blue, All Wool Flannel Trunks, fly front, fast color, with white web belt. Sizes, 30 to 44 waist measure. State size..$2.13

Boys' All Wool Worsted Bathing Suit. Medium weight, California style. Sizes, 28 to 34 inches chest measure. State size. Shipping weight, 1 pound.
6V2123—Maroon with orange and blue chest stripes.....$2.40
6V2120—Navy blue with white and old gold chest stripes.....$2.40

Boys' All Cotton Suit. Navy blue with trimming of contrasting colors. Sizes, 28 to 34 chest. State size.
6V2131......72c

Bathers' White Web Belt. Nickel plated, non-tarnishable buckle. Adds style to bathing suits. Sizes, 26 to 42 inches waist measure. State size. Shipping weight, 5 ounces.
6V2195 ....15c

Juvenile One-Piece All Wool Worsted Suit. Upper part is white color and lower part navy blue color, making a very good looking suit for the little tot. White web belt included. Sizes, 22 to 28 chest measure. State size. Shipping weight, 1 pound.
6V2122.....$1.48

Juvenile All Wool Bathing Suit. Scarlet red, no trimming, no belt. Sizes, 22 to 28 inches chest measure. State size. Shipping weight, 1 lb.
6V2124.....$1.25

Ayvad's Water Wings. When inflated will support an adult of 200 pounds at the proper level for comfortable swimming. An excellent support to use when learning to swim. Shipping weight, 4 ounces.
6V2121—Pair 35c

It's Easy to Order. See Order Blanks in Back of Catalog.

SEARS, ROEBUCK AND CO.

became so great that children bounced their rubber balls to the tune of:

Sally Rand has lost her fan,
Give it back, you nas-ty man.

The movies, the spread of sports, the cult of the sun, and bathing-beauty contests, all played a part in stripping down

The Nudest Thing in Bathing Suits for 1915

the bathing suits of 1935 to a minimum of fabric. The catalog for that year lists "Ginger Rogers smart two-piece effect suits backless and skirtless," which are as near to no clothes at all as the now somnolent law allows. Yet only twenty years had passed since an Atlantic City mob had hurled insults at a woman who appeared on its beach wearing a short bathing suit.

Peace Hath Its Victories

In September, 1939, Atlantic City held its annual bathing-beauty contest. *Life* made the following comment on it:

The tidal wave of war, which engulfed men's plans and thoughts in New York and Washington throughout September, lapped gently on the sands of Atlantic City, N.J. There fighting echoed only faintly from a far-off unreal world, for the minds of businessmen, concessionaires and vacationists were on girls not guns, busts not bombs, legs not Lwów.

Forty-two "pulchritudinous goddesses of American girlhood," had come from all parts of the land for the annual Miss America contest, staged for the greater glory of Atlantic City and the feminine form. . . . At its end the crown of "Miss America 1939" was bestowed on the ruddy-brown head of Miss Michigan—a 19-year-old Detroit model named Patricia Mary Donnelly. She was promptly launched on a flood tide of commercial and theatrical offers.

Michigan's Governor Dickinson, she declared, had sent her off to the contest without any warnings about the evil East. "He was awfully nice to me," chirped she, "but very old. He gave me a crab apple."

Conservative Men

While women had gradually been dropping their old-fashioned, cumbersome bathing suits until they were near to nudity, slow-plodding, conservative men continued to cling to their old models as late as 1925. It is not until 1935 that the catalog pictures men wearing short, close-fitting trunks, and these are still worn with an athletic shirt. Catalog men, with a decent respect for the proprieties, loll about the beach with their shirts on, and it is only until they take to the water that the catalog indicates their new-found freedom: "Take off shirt for free swimming."

Mrs. Maria D. Brown celebrated her hundredth birthday at Fort Madison, Iowa, in 1927. Here she recalls memories of her home in Ohio:*

After periods at the Brice House or in Logan or Somerset, we were always glad to get back to our own father's dear old home. Nowhere else did we have the same conveniences. We did most of our work there in the summer kitchen. That was where we had the big brick oven. We used to fire it twice a week and do a sight o' baking all at once. We'd make a hot fire in the oven, and then, when the bricks were thoroughly heated, we'd scrape out all the coals with a big iron scraper, dump the coals into the fireplace, and shove in the roasts and fowls, the pies and bread. . . . When we went to keeping house in 1845, Dan'l and I, he bought me a little iron stove, a new thing in those days. It was no good, and would only bake things on one side. I soon went back to cooking at an open fireplace.

You know the look of andirons, crane, spit, reflectors. Our heavy iron vessels were swung from chains. When we wanted to lift the lids off, we'd have to reach in with a hook and swing them off. . . . We used to bake Indian pone—that is, bread made of rye and corn meal—that way. We would set it off in a corner of the hearth covered with coals and ashes, and there it would bake slowly all night long. In the morning the crust would be thick but soft—oh, *so* good. . . .

Ma put us girls to work early. It was taken as a matter of course that we should learn all kinds of housework. I know that before I was seven years old I used to wash

* Harriet Connor Brown, *Grandmother Brown's Hundred Years.*

the dishes. . . . There was need of many hands to get all the work done. It required more knowledge to do the things for everyday living than is the case nowadays. If one wants light now, all one has to do is pull a string or push a button. Then, we had to pick up a coal with tongs, hold it against a candle, and blow. And one had to make the candles, perhaps. . . .

Even without candle making, there was certainly a plenty to do to keep life going in those days. Baking, washing, ironing, sewing, kept us busy. Not to mention the spinning and weaving that had to be done before cloth was available for the seamstress. . . .

We had all the things that were really necessary for our comfort in those days, and we had quite as much leisure as people have now. Always, too, we had time to attend church and Sunday school.

In Washington in 1936, Mr. J. P. Morgan told reporters: "If you destroy the leisure class, you destroy civilization. . . . By the leisure class I mean the families who employ one servant, 25,000,000 or 30,000,000 families."

Hardly were the words out of the financier's mouth before the Housewives' League of America had pounced on him to prove that he must have got his ideas of American domesticity from Hollywood. It was shown that according to the 1930 census there were less than 30,000,000 families in this country, and fewer than 2,000,000 servants to attend them all. The League, and editors critical of Mr. Morgan, failed to say, however, that while there were relatively few human servants in American homes, there were millions of mechanical servants, and that labor-saving devices in the home have done at least as much as women's rights champions to liberate American women.

Whole categories of labor once done at home have been largely transferred to machines or to outside agencies. These include canning, baking, dressmaking, lighting, water heating, and laundering. Where these operations are still performed wholly or partly within the home, the labor involved has been sharply decreased by mechanical devices. Electrical

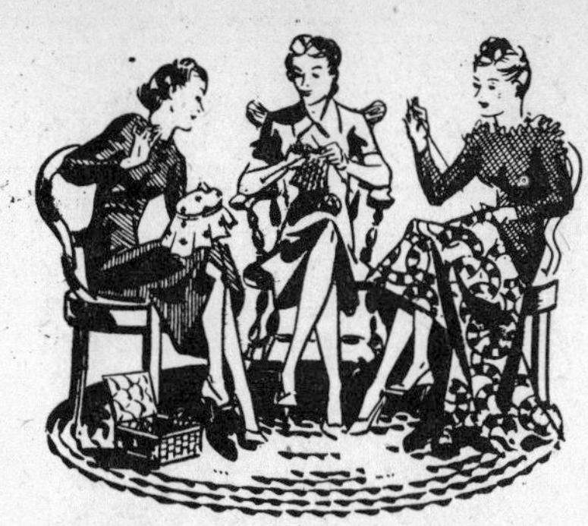

Why Not

MAKE YOUR OWN RUG FOR AS LITTLE AS $2.69

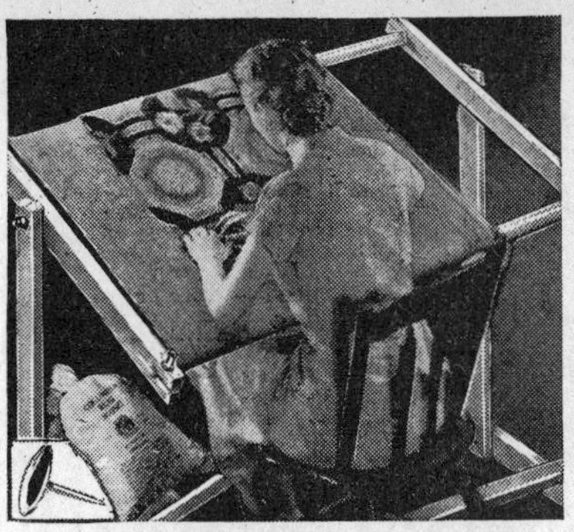

Hearthside Rug Frame

Tilts to any angle for comfortable working position. Strong stand of finished pine and basswood; 30 in. high. Adjustable roller bars at top and bottom hold rug firmly in place. Can be adjusted up to 20x38 in. Easy assembly instructions included.
25 L 4776—Shpg. wt., 7 lbs.5 oz. **Each $1.79**

Rug Sizing—Prevents edges curling.
25 L 4114—Shpg. wt., 10 oz. **½-lb. Bag. 23c**

1½-Inch Rug Pins. Holds material on frame.
25 L 4780—Shpg. wt., box, 3 oz.; 2 boxes, 6 oz.
Box of 50.....9c 2 Boxes (100 Pins)...**17c**

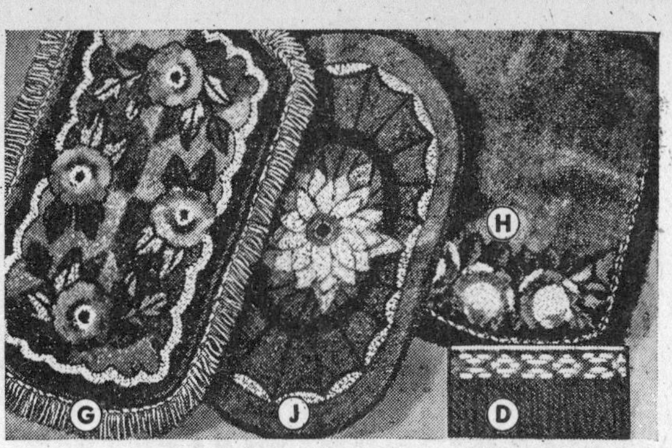

Stamped Hooked Rug Patterns

New Hearthside designs stamped on art burlap—will make up into rich-looking rugs. Choice of (G) Southern Rose; (H) American Beauty Rose or (J) Star of Hope. **State pattern letter.** Instructions.

24x36 Inches	31x48 Inches	36x54 Inches	36x72 Inches
25 L 4236	25 L 4237	25 L 4238	25 L 4239
17c Each	25c Each	33c Each	45c Each
Shpg. wt., 6 oz.	Shpg. wt., 7 oz.	Shpg. wt., 12 oz.	Shpg. wt., 15 oz.

(D) 25 L 4097—**Rug Fringe.** Part wool, part rayon. 3 in. wide. Contrasting multi-colored border with fringe in colors: Black, Blue, Brown, Dark Red, Light Red, Old Rose. **State color.** Shipping weight, 3 ounces. Yard.......**24c**

Hooked Rug Needles

Parisian hooked rug shuttle needle—easiest, fastest metal rug needle made. Make a rug in a day. Does beautiful work. Sturdy construction. Automatically regulates length and spacing of pile. Wood handles. Has extra point and looper. Complete and simple directions. Shpg.wt.,6 oz.
25 L 4693—Each............95c

Shown at far right. For beginners or average workers. Similar to 25L4693 but without interchangeable point or looper. No wooden handles.
25 L 4694—Shpg. wt., 6 oz.
Each..........19c

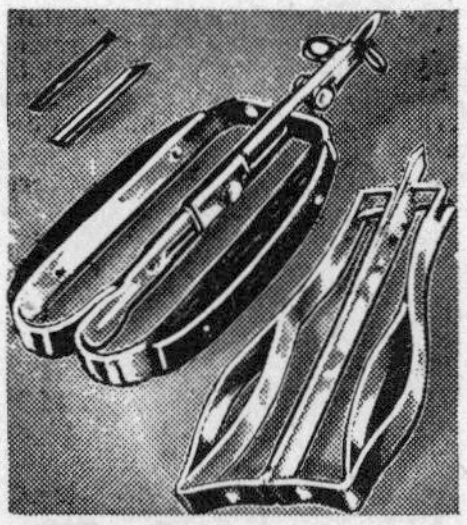

Rug Burlap

Make your own rug designs with this better grade burlap woven from heavy jute yarns—actually weighs 11½ oz. to the yard. Smooth finish, easy to tint or stencil. 40 in. wide. Natural Brown only. Imported from India. Shpg. wt., 12 oz.
25 L 4129
Yard.......15c

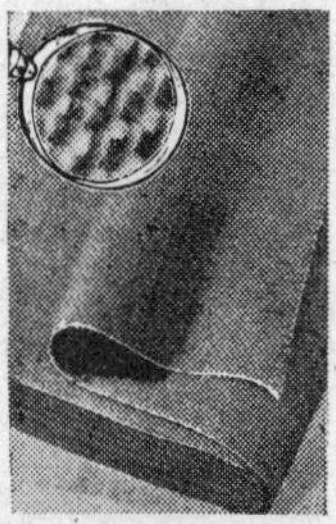

Cotton Chenille Yarn

No clipping! About 27 yards to ball. Velvety soft, about ⅛-inch thick. **Washable** in lukewarm water.

American Beauty 513, Old Gold 709, Lt. Reseda Green 306, Old Rose 527, Dk. Reseda Green 307, Lavender 405, Olive Beige, Mulberry 515, Rose 507, Pink 504, Yellow 704, Royal Blue 208, Brown 608, White, Cardinal 511, Taupe, Lt. Blue 206, Lt. Taupe 637, Purple 414, Black, Nile 302, Orange 509, Jade 314, Bronze 720

Shpg. wt., each, 2 oz.; twelve, 14 oz.
25 L 4872—**State color.**
1-oz. Ball 12c 12 Balls $1.39

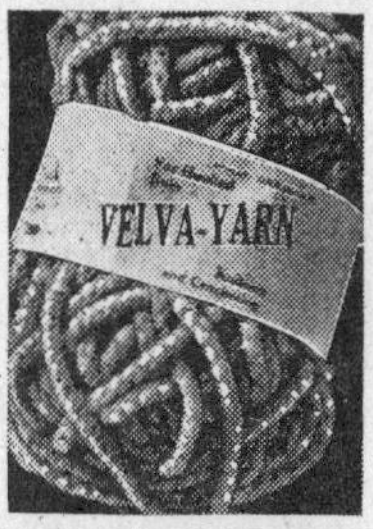

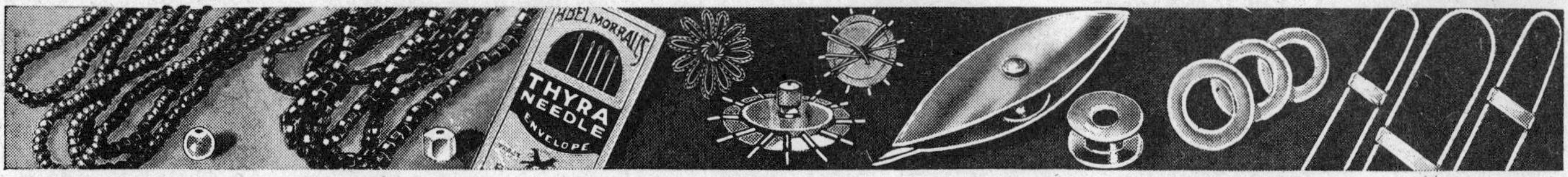

Indian Seed Beads

Diameter, abt. ¹⁄₁₆-in. Small bead shows size. Opaque. For embroidery. Czech. import. 1000 beads to hank.
Colors: Canary Yellow, Chalk White, Medium Green, Cherry Red, Orchid Pink, Royal Blue, Pearlized (imitation pearl), Gold, Turquoise or Black.
State color. Shipping wt., 3 hanks, 2 oz.
25 L 4678...**3 Hanks. 14c**

Colored Glass Beads

Diam., abt. ¹⁄₁₆-in. Actual size illustrated above. Czech. import. 1000 beads to hank. Colors: Amethyst, Crystal, Amber, Cherry Red, Emerald, Black, Med. Pink, Nile, Sand, Turquoise, Canary, White Satin, Wine Red, Steel; or Iridescent Blue, Brown, Purple; Gold or Silver. **State color.** Shpg. wt.; 2 oz.
25 L 4677—**3 Hanks 13c**

For Beads

Best quality imported English steel needles. For all beading. Extra fine ones for threading tiniest beads. Shipping wt., 2 oz.
25 L 5232
5 to a paper **9c**

Daisy Knitter

Use it for fashioning daisies which can be made into bed jackets, pillow tops. Italian import. Small, 1⅞-in. diameter, or large, 2⅛ in. diam. **State size.** Instructions and needle included. Shpg. wt., 3 oz.
25 L 4700
Each.........49c

Tatting Shuttle

Nickeled spring steel with pick. Removable bobbin permits winding on sewing-machine and the easy changing of colors. **About 3 in. long.** Shpg. wt., 2 oz.
25L4685—Each. 12c

Extra Bobbins
Shipping weight, 2 oz.
25 L 4686—2 for **9c**

Ass't'd Rings

Bone Rings. White or Black. Sizes about ⅝-inch; ¾-inch or 1-inch in diameter. **State color and size.** Shpg. wt., 2 oz.
25 L 4741—Dozen.... 9c

White Pearl Rings. Dainty in appearance. For your nicest fancy work. **State size.** Shpg. wt., 2 oz.
25 L 4150
⁹⁄₁₆-in. Diam. 12 for...**9c**
1⅛-in. Diam. 6 for...**12c**

Lace Makers

For making maltese lace—for pillows, collars, blouses, scarfs! Metal needles in three sizes: two 9-inch, one 12-inch length for narrow, medium or wide lace. Shpg. wt., three, 6 oz.
25 L 4119
3 for 22c

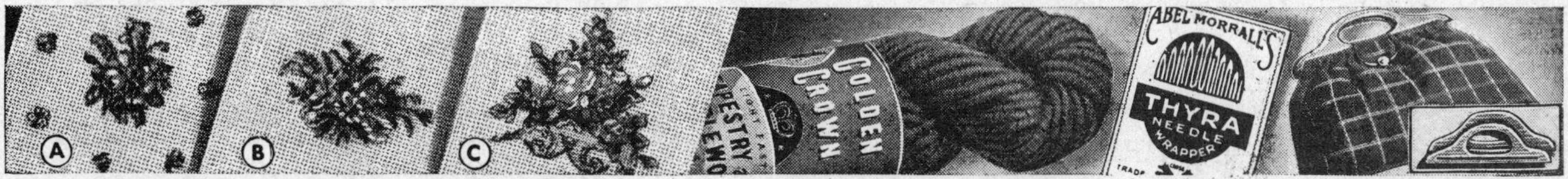

Unusual Values in "Commenced" Needlepoint

Beautiful "started" patterns—all you do is fill in the background. Handworked on firm quality needlepoint canvas. The colorings are exquisite. Usually handworked pieces like these cost a lot more, but we made a quantity purchase and thus secured more savings for you! Suitable for chair seats, radio benches, cushions, foot-stools and hand bags. Assorted patterns. Imported from China.

(A) 25 L 4400	(B) 25 L 4401	(C) 25 L 4402
15x18 Inches	18x18 Inches	23x23 Inches
67c Each	83c Each	$1.35 Each
Shpg. wt., 5 oz.	Shpg. wt., 9 oz.	Shpg. wt., 11 oz.

Tapestry Yarn for Needlepoint

Permanently mothproofed virgin wool—a hard twist yarn for fine needlepoint embroidery. Lightfast.

Colors: Black, White, Tan 604, Copen 215, Brown 614, Peacock 217, Antique Gold 711, Aqua Green 338, Beach Sand 624, French Beige 637, Marine Blue 212, Seal Brown 613, Wild Rose 507, Garnet 609, Maroon 514, Burgundy, Chamois 718, Mulberry 417, Parchment, Reseda Green 305, Lt. Navy 212, Mahogany 611, Moss Green 314, Tile Green 307, Spruce Green 313, Champagne 701, Pottery Rust 605

State color. Shpg. wt., skein, 3 oz.; 4 skeins, 9 oz.
25 L 5669—30-Yd. Skein...17c 4 Skeins..65c

For Tapestry

Best quality steel. Used by experienced workers for fine needlepoint. English import. Sizes 19 to 23 (asstd.) to paper. Shpg. wt., 2 oz.
25 L 5124
Paper of 10..9c

Knitting Bag

Made from assorted upholstery fabrics at a fraction of usual cost! Multicolor designs. Buttoned flap. Large handles with roomy hand opening. **Size: 11x15 in.** Shpg. wt., each, 13 oz.
25 L 4028—Each......59c
Polished wood handles. Abt. 12 in. long. Shpg. wt., 10 oz.
25 L 4055
Set of Two..........21c

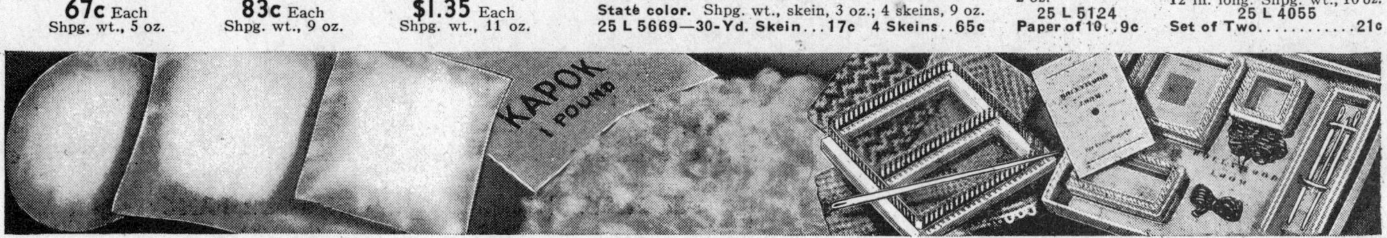

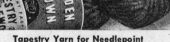

Kapok Filled Pillow Forms

White cambric covered. Dress them up in brocade or velvet—or use for bed pillows. Kapok, you know, doesn't easily pack or crush, and is moisture-proof. Pillows will retain their fluffiness. **State catalog number and size.**

25 L 4121—Oblong			25 L 4120—Square			25 L 4122—Round		
Size In.	Shpg. Wt.	Each	Size In.	Shpg. Wt.	Each	Size In.	Shpg. Wt.	Each
14x16	13 oz.	29c	12x12	8 oz.	18c	12	7 oz.	18c
16x20	1 lb. 2 oz.	35c	14x14	10 oz.	23c	14	14 oz.	23c
16x22	1 lb. 3 oz.	43c	16x16	1 lb.	27c	16	1 lb. 7 oz.	27c
18x24	1 lb. 9 oz.	52c	18x18	1 lb. 2 oz.	35c	18	1 lb. 9 oz.	35c
20x26	2 lbs.	98c	20x20	1 lb. 8 oz.	49c	20	2 lbs.	49c

Remember! You Can Buy Everything at Sears on Easy Terms. ***See Page 5.***

Kapok for Pillows

Prime Japara Kapok. Moisture-resistant, vermin-proof; retains its springiness. Chosen by experienced campers for pillow and mattress filling . . . just as practical for home use. 1-pound package makes an 18x18-in. pillow. Imported from Java. Shpg. wt., 1 lb. 2 oz.
25 L 4756
One-Lb. Bag....27c

Jiffy Hand Weaving Loom Outfits

Weave gay little squares for scarfs, afghans, sweaters. Use about one-fourth as much yarn as for knitted articles. 4-inch frame with adjustable bar for different sizes. Needle and instruction book. Shpg. wt., 4 oz.
25 L 4240—Set........23c

4x8-inch Jiffy Loom for larger pieces. Two adjustable bars. Shipping weight, 7 oz.
25 L 4782—Set.......47c

Complete set for weaving various sizes of squares, oblongs, etc.—think of the dresses, sweaters, dainty baby things you can fashion! Includes one 4x4-in.; one 2x2-in.; one 4x2-in. and one 2x8-in. loom; 3 loom needles; 3 pieces of yarn (enough for 1 square); instruction leaflet.
25 L 4255—Shpg. wt., 14 oz.
Set.......95c

Book for Jiffy Looms (Describes Novelty Weaving.) Tells how to make fancy woven squares and combine colors. Shipping weight, 2 ounces.
25 L 4784—Each........9c

AWNINGS and CURTAINS

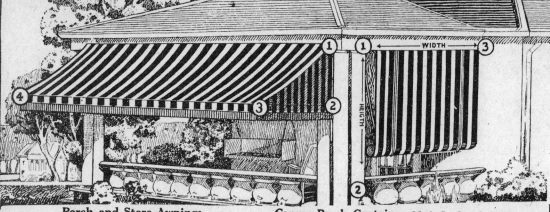

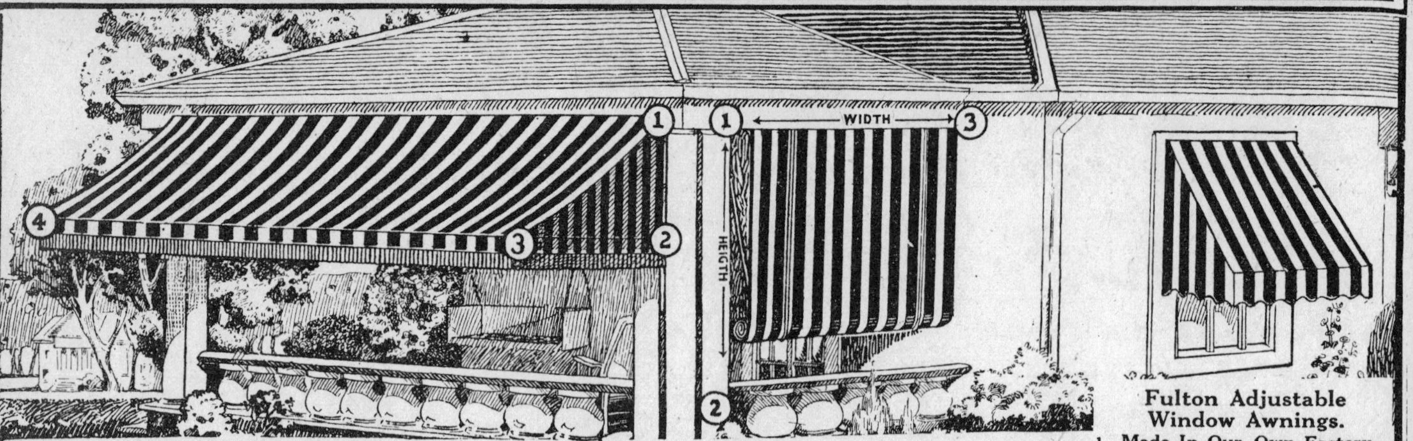

Porch and Store Awnings.
Made In Our Own Factory.

Of plain white, green and white or tan and white **painted striped duck** with long white fringe around the curtain. Full weight duck of first quality. When ordering give height from number 1 to 2, projection from number 2 to 3 and width of front from 3 to 4. Allow four to seven days to make; in June or July allow seven to ten days. Not shipped C. O. D. For lettering awnings allow four days extra.

All exposed metal parts are japanned or galvanized. Awnings 7 feet or less in width are made with a one-piece iron frame across front; over 7 feet, wood front. We will be pleased to quote on any sizes not in the following list. The prices quoted herewith are for awnings complete, ready to be set up. Shipping weight given below is for the 10-foot size. 12-foot size weighs one-fifth more; 14-foot, two-fifths more; 16-foot, three-fifths more; 18-foot, four-fifths more; and 20-foot, twice the 10-foot size weight.

State size; also if to be fastened to wood or brick building.
6V7656½—Green and white painted striped duck.
6V7657½—Tan and white painted striped duck.
6V7655½—Plain white 10-ounce duck.

Height, From 1 to 2	Projection From 2 to 3	Width of Front—From 3 to 4						Shpg. Wt. for 10-Foot Size
		10 Feet	12 Feet	14 Feet	16 Feet	18 Feet	20 Feet	
4 ft.	4 ft.	$12.06	$13.81	$15.56	$17.31	$19.06	$20.82	22 lbs.
4 ft. 6 in.	4 ft. 6 in.	13.03	14.90	16.77	18.64	20.51	22.36	27 lbs.
5 ft.	5 ft.	14.22	16.17	18.12	20.07	22.02	23.97	29 lbs.
5 ft. 6 in.	5 ft. 6 in.	15.33	17.51	19.69	21.87	24.06	26.24	32 lbs.
6 ft.	6 ft.	16.38	18.58	20.80	23.02	24.91	27.12	34 lbs.

If cover only is wanted, deduct 20 per cent, or one-fifth, from the above prices, and state whether for wood or iron front bar. Lettering on roof of white awnings, 15 cents per letter; on white curtains, 12 cents per letter extra.

Canvas Porch Curtains. Made In Our Own Factory.

Plain white or painted striped duck. Furnished complete with pulleys, ropes, roller, etc., ready to attach. By pulling the rope you revolve roller, the curtain being raised or lowered as desired. When ordering, give height, and width as illustrated. We sell the curtains by the square foot, the price per square foot including all accessories. A curtain 7 feet high and 10 feet wide contains 70 square feet, and at 7 cents per square foot would cost $4.90 when made to order. Allow four to six days to make and **be sure to state height from 1 to 2 and width from 2 to 3. See illustration. Also state color.**

Made to Order.
6V7677½—8-ounce white duck. Per square foot..............6½c
6V7668½—Green and white painted striped duck. Per square ft..7c
6V7669½—Tan and white painted striped duck. Per square ft..7c

Sizes Carried in Stock.
Following sizes carried in stock for immediate shipment. State size.
6V7673¼—Plain white only. 8-ounce duck.
Height, 6 ft., width, 6 ft., **$2.34.** Height, 6 ft., width, 8 ft., **$3.12**
Height, 7 ft., width 7 ft., **3.18**

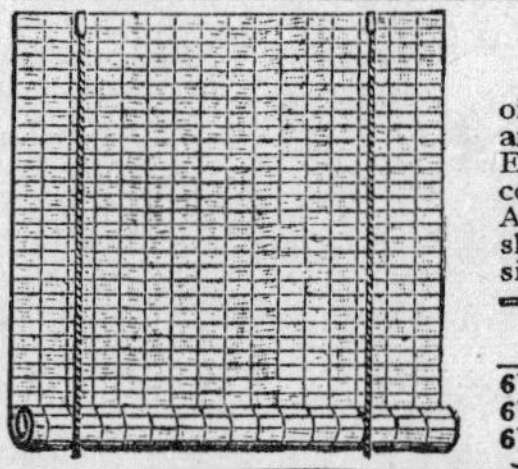

Wood Porch Shades.

Made of smooth sawed basswood strips, oil stained dark green color only. Strong and durable, woven with strong cord. Equipped with easy hanging device and cords and are easily raised or lowered. Allows free circulation of air. Ideal for the sleeping porch. Can only be furnished in sizes listed below. **Unmailable.**

Catalog No.	Hght.	Width	Each	Shpg. Wt.
6V5972¼	7 ft.	6 ft.	$4.90	13 lbs.
6V5973¼	7 ft.	8 ft.	6.60	18 lbs.
6V5974¼	7 ft.	10 ft.	8.10	22 lbs.

Fulton Adjustable Window Awnings.
Made In Our Own Factory.

Of regulation woven blue and white awning stripe, with scalloped curtain bound with braid. Complete, ready to set up and can be shipped immediately. These awnings give much better shade than those usually retailed because they extend down the window 3 feet 6 inches and out from the window 3 feet. The steel frames are very rigid and the awnings are very strong. Not to be confused with the narrow, short awnings usually retailed. Five sizes, to fit windows 2 feet 4 inches to 4 feet 6 inches wide. Height, 3½ feet; projection, 3 feet. Give width of your windows from center to center of casing on each side, and specify catalog number of awnings wanted. Be sure to order awning wide enough.

6V5981¼—Will fit window from 2 feet 4 inches to 2 feet 7 inches. Weight, 6¼ pounds............**$2.75**
6V5982¼—Will fit window from 2 ft. 8 in. to 3 ft. Wt., 6¾ lbs. **$2.85**
6V5983¼—Will fit window from 3 ft. 1 in. to 3 ft. 6 in. Wt., 7 lbs. **$2.98**
6V5984¼—Will fit window from 3 feet 7 inches to 4 feet. Weight, 7½ pounds.........**$3.18**
6V5985¼—Will fit window from 4 feet 1 inch to 4 feet 6 inches. Weight, 8 pounds........**$3.30**

We can furnish at the same price these awnings made of green and white painted stripe or tan and white painted stripe to match our porch awnings and porch curtains. State color.

Canvas Covers

HAYCOCK COVERS

Made of standard full weight duck with brass eyelet and rope loop in each corner. Shipping weight of 8-oz., 2, 3 and 4 pounds each. In lots of twenty covers and over allow three to five days for making.

6V7642¼—State size wanted.

Size, Feet	8-Oz. Duck	10-Oz. Duck	12-Oz. Duck
4¾ x 4¾	$1.15	$1.40	$1.64
6 x 6	1.75	2.14	2.52
7 x 7	2.41	2.94	3.49

EMIGRANT WAGON COVERS

Full weight plain white duck. Our covers are strongly made and carefully finished throughout. Carried in stock for immediate shipment. Weight given below is on 8-ounce covers; 10-ounce weighs one-fourth more than 8-ounce; 12-ounce weighs one-half more than 8-ounce.

6V7640¼—State size wanted.

Size, Feet	8-Oz. S. F. Duck	10-Oz. S. F. Duck	12-Oz. S. F. Duck	Wt. Lbs.	Size, Feet	8-Oz. S. F. Duck	10-Oz. S. F. Duck	12-Oz. S. F. Duck	Wt. Lbs.
10x10	$4.80	$5.95	$7.08	8	11x13	$6.85	$8.47	$10.08	11
10x12	5.70	7.04	8.40	9	11x15	7.84	9.60	11.55	13
10x14	6.76	8.37	9.97	11	12x16	9.42	11.63	13.86	15

Brown Waterproof Covers for Wagons.

Made of heavy brown waterproof duck weighing about 11 ounces per yard after waterproofing. Shipping weights: 6x8 size, 5 lbs.; 6x9 size, 6 lbs.; 6x10 size, 6 lbs.; 6x12 size, 7 lbs.; 6x14 size, 8 lbs.; 7x9 size, 6 lbs.; 7x10 size, 7 lbs.; 7x12 size, 8 lbs.; 7x14 size, 9 lbs.; 8x10 size, 8 lbs.; 8x12 size, 9 lbs.; 8x14 size, 10 lbs.; 8x16 size, 12 lbs.; 9x14 size, 12 lbs.

6V7636¼—State size wanted.

Size, Ft.	Each	Size, Ft.	Each	Size, Ft.	Each
6x 8	$2.91	7x 9	$3.82	8x10	$4.85
6x 9	3.28	7x10	4.25	8x12	5.82
6x10	3.64	7x12	5.10	8x14	6.79
6x12	4.36	7x14	5.95	8x16	7.76
6x14	5.10			9x14	7.64

Stack and Machine Covers.

Made of standard 29-inch wide white duck, finished around edges with brass eyelets and ropes, thoroughly reinforced. Our covers are all cut a little oversize to allow for what is taken up in the seams, hems and reinforcements, so that when you buy a cover from us you get one which is FULL IN SIZE and the only duck we use is STANDARD duck, full to weight and properly woven. We make our own covers and as there is only one small margin of profit between our cost and selling price, you can be sure of receiving the best possible value by buying from us. Write for samples of canvas and compare them with others. Weights given are for 8-ounce covers. 10-ounce weigh one-fourth more and 12-ounce one-half more than 8-ounce. Shipped promptly from stock.

6V7630¼—State size wanted.

Size, Feet	8-Oz. Duck	10-Oz. Duck	12-Oz. Duck	Wt. of 8-Oz.
9½x16	$ 6.75	$ 8.34	$ 9.93	12 lbs.
9½x18	7.69	9.48	11.25	14 lbs.
12x14	7.60	9.36	11.11	13½ lbs.
12x16	8.51	10.51	12.50	13 lbs.
12x18	9.69	11.93	14.17	16 lbs.
12x20	10.71	13.20	15.69	17 lbs.
14x16	9.47	12.39	15.09	16 lbs.
14x18	11.59	14.28	16.97	18 lbs.
14x20	12.65	15.64	18.62	20 lbs.
14x24	15.25	18.83	22.40	25 lbs.
16x16	11.45	14.16	16.83	18 lbs.
16x18	12.85	15.84	18.83	19 lbs.
16x20	14.25	17.47	20.91	23 lbs.
16x24	17.00	20.99	24.96	29 lbs.
18x20	16.41	20.24	24.07	26 lbs.
18x24	19.08	23.55	28.01	32 lbs.
18x28	22.13	27.33	32.52	37 lbs.
18x30	24.69	30.51	36.32	40 lbs.
20x24	21.45	25.95	34.95	34 lbs.
20x36	31.88	39.45	47.01	51 lbs.

Brown Waterproof Paulins or Machine Covers.

Made of fine grade double filling brown duck, weighing about 12 ounces per yard after waterproofing. This duck is strongly constructed. The covers are suitable for automobile trucks, machinery or anything that needs protection from the weather. Finished with eyelets and ropes and the seams are double stitched.

6V7645¼ State size wanted.

Sizes, Ft.	Each	Shpg. Wt.
10x12	$ 9.27	12 lbs.
12x14	13.04	15 lbs.
14x16	17.38	18 lbs.
16x20	24.85	26 lbs.
18x24	33.52	38 lbs.

engineers, as much perhaps as Elizabeth Arden and Harriet Hubbard Ayer, have been the saviors of the housewife.

Fifty years ago, *Scribner's Magazine* felt safe in saying: "There can be little doubt that electricity will be adopted in all households . . . and adapted for purposes of adornment. In the parlor an illuminated painted vase, lighted from within may vie in attractiveness with the pictures on the wall." Five years later, so rapidly had electrification progressed, *Everyday Housekeeping* said:

"Nothing remains practically, but what my lady herself, with some assistance from a little maid, or a friend perhaps, will find it her pleasure to attend to. . . . There will be no domestic problem to solve. . . . If one wishes to go off for a spin on the bicycle before the bread has finished baking it is only necessary to set the clock . . . and the fire goes out when the work is done."

This alluded, of course, to city women. But the time was soon to come when the blessings of electricity would be extended also to the farm and the small-town household. With the catalog as our guide, we may trace the relative liberation of the servantless housewife during the past thirty years.

Blue Monday

If white American women had the Negro's gift for song, they would certainly have made and sung one called, "I Got the Wash-Day Blues," but since they have no such gift they were content to call the weekly day of clothes washing Blue Monday. And it was blue. Throughout the world, this task falls to women and it is a back-breaking one wherever it is done, because it entails long hours of heating and carrying water to the tub, bending over a washboard, wringing out clothes to dry, hanging them on lines in the sun, and ironing them when they have dried. Some women escaped the task by hiring a laundry to do it; others employed washwomen; but millions of women in the United States laundered, and still launder, the clothes of their families.

In 1905, home laundresses bought from Sears a tin or copper wash boiler (90c), a washboard (32c), a washtub (56c), 100 feet of clothesline (45c), a hand-operated wringer ($1.98), and a sadiron weighing four to five pounds (83c).

A Muscle Builder of 1905

With these instruments, and the application of long hours of hard labor, they could launder the family's clothes; nothing then remained to do but cleanse the paraphernalia, put it away, and wait for the next Monday to come around. But even in 1905, the shape of things to come in the home laundry was already visible.

The catalog lists a number of the crude, wood washing machines of the times, hand-operated it is true, but less diffi-

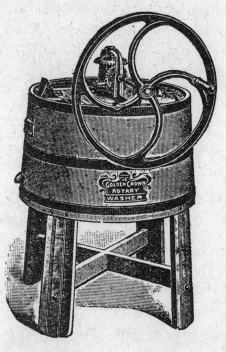

*Man's Gift to Toiling Woman—
a Clothes Churn of 1905*

cult to manipulate than the washtub and scrubbing board. One model moved to the ancient rhythm of the cradle: "Rocks like a cradle and almost as easily. You can do your washing while sitting on a chair." For another model—The Revolving Wheel All Steam Metal Washer—it was promised that

The Curtis Washer.

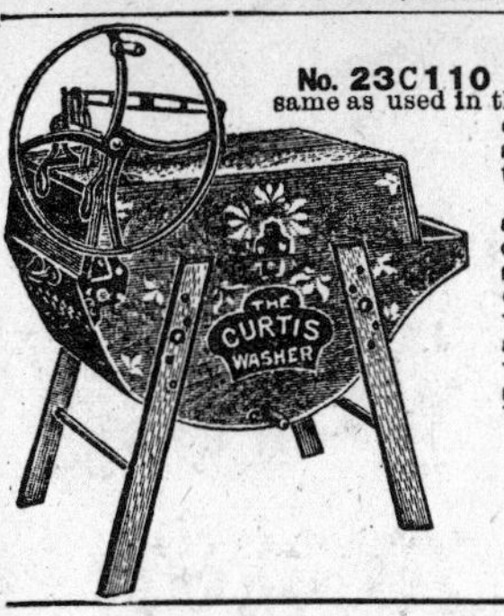

No. 23C110 **This machine is made on the rubber principle,** the same as used in the Quick and Easy, but has two cylinders working in opposite directions at the same motion of the crank shaft, thus cleaning the clothes quicker and more thoroughly than the former machine.

It will not tear the clothes, and on account of the balance wheel the machine will work so easily that a child can work it without being fatigued. Made of selected Louisiana cypress, finished with two coats of paint and one coat each of graining color and coach varnish. Has heavy non-rusting galvanized bottom and all the iron parts coming in contact with the water are heavily tinned or galvanized to prevent spotting the clothes. Inside dimensions, 18x34x13 inches. Weight, 103 pounds.

Price, wringer not included **$5.10**

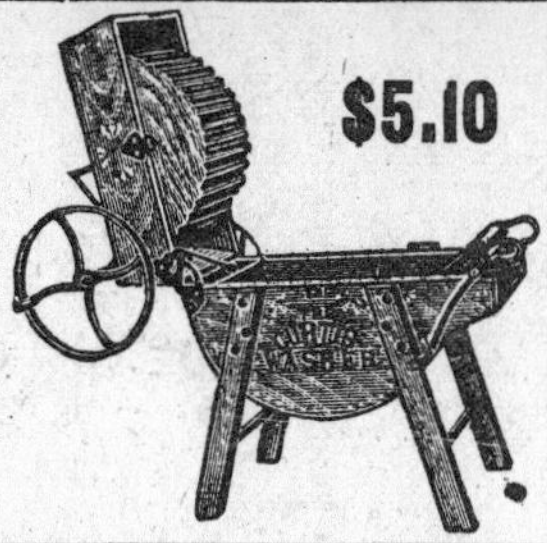

$5.10

Columbia Rotary Washer.

$4.98

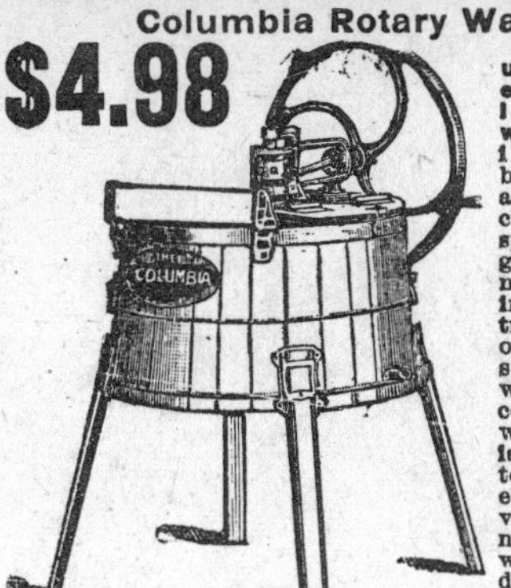

No. 23C144 Columbia Rotary Washer. Easiest and lightest running washer made. Has improved roller bearings, metal parts aluminum coated; no clutches, cams or springs to wear or get out of order. The mechanism is never in the way. Has extra large tub made of perfectly seasoned selected Virginia white cedar, fully corrugated like a washboard. Top hoop is flat, middle and bottom hoops are of electric welded galvanized wire, can never come off. It washes the most delicate laces or the heaviest bedding easily, quickly, perfectly. Balance wheel turns in either direction and washes equally well when turned slowly or rapidly. The tub is steamtight as well as watertight giving out no odor of foul steam, and making no sloppy floors. No other machine combines so many labor saving devices with good workmanship and perfect material. Fully guaranteed, and if not the easiest running machine made, can be returned at our expense and money will be refunded. Weight, 65 pounds.

Price....................................**$4.98**

Our Cascade Rocker Washer.

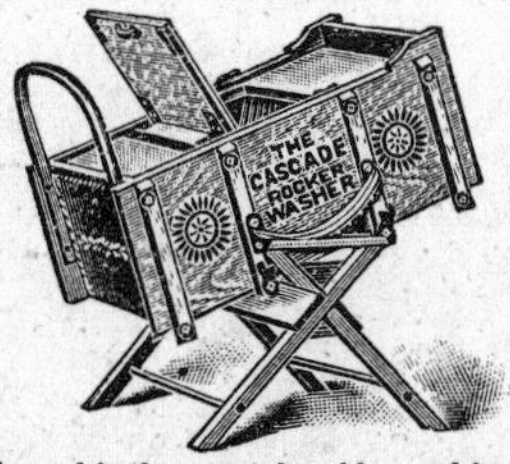

No. 23C121 **Rocks like a cradle and almost as easily. You can do your washing while sitting on a chair.** Cannot possibly tear the clothes, has large capacity and washes quickly and easily. The galvanized cover is water and steam tight. No sloppy floors or foul steam to endanger your health if you use our Cascade Rocker. Has space for attaching a wringer, and can be instantly locked in a level position. It is extra well made and strongly braced, has no parts to wear or break and is the most durable machine manufactured. Inside dimensions, 16x25 inches. Weight, 60 pounds. Price....................................**$3.98**

The Golden Crown Rotary Washer.

A $10.00 WASHER AT ONLY $5.45

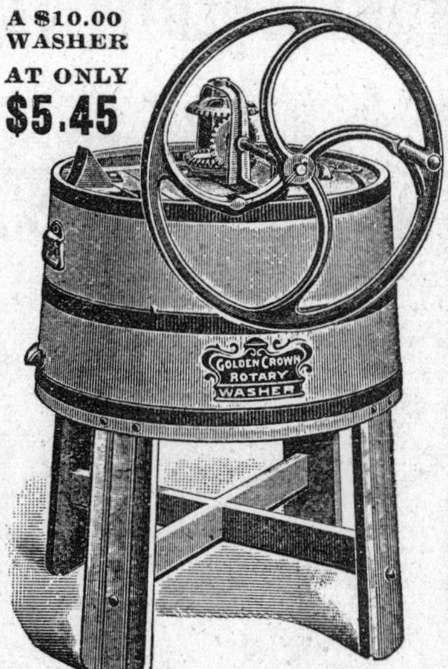

No. 23C137 **This is the genuine Golden Crown Washer, a machine that has always sold for $10.00. Exactly the same as the $10.00 machine in every way—has every improvement, including the high speed heavy draft gearing,** by which you can wash a heavy load in one-half the time required to wash a light load in any other machine. We fully guarantee the Golden Crown Washer to wash more clothes at a time and to do it in one-half to two-thirds the time of any other washer. This illustration, which is reproduced from a photograph, gives a little idea of the strength and durability of this machine. It is built of selected red Louisiana cypress, which will resist the action of water and acid better than any other known wood, the extra heavy stave legs are strongly bolted to the chime of the tub, cross braced and reinforced with steel rods. We guarantee the gearing for five years and should any part give out within that time we will replace it entirely free of charge. The inside is fully corrugated. The heavy well balanced fly wheel can be run either way with little effort and the machine washes anything from a lace curtain to a horse blanket perfectly. Finished with three coats of cream colored pure lead paint, with red hoops and gold bronzed gearing and fly wheel. Remember, we guarantee the Golden Crown washer to wash one-third easier and quicker than any other. Every one is shipped out on 30 days' trial and if after using it 30 days you are not more than satisfied with your purchase, return it to us at our expense and we will refund your money and all transportation charges you have paid. Shipped set up and ready for use by attaching fly wheel which can be done in a few moments. Shipping weight, 80 pounds. Price....................**$5.45**

The Genuine Improved Scott's Western Washer.

The standard family machine. The make up and finish of our **Scott's Western** will be the same as heretofore, and will not be excelled by any other make. All of the bolts, washers, nuts, nails, in fact all iron parts that come in contact with the clothing are heavily tinned, absolutely no danger of rust spots on the clothes. Fitted up with our patent post and pinwheel, the greatest invention of the age in washing machines. Made in two sizes, No. 2 and No 3. The former is the family size.

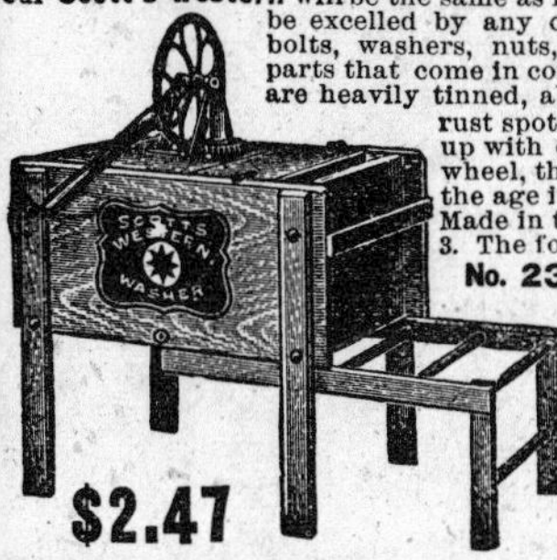

No. 23C124 **Scott's Western Washing Machine, Size No. 2.** Inside dimensions, 17¾x23½x10½ inches. Weight, 62 pounds. Price.......**$2.47**

No. 23C126 **Scott's Western Washing Machine, Size No. 3.** Inside dimensions, 19½x25½x11½ inches. Weight, 68 pounds. Price....................................**$2.67**

$2.47

The Revolving Wheel All Metal Steam Washer.

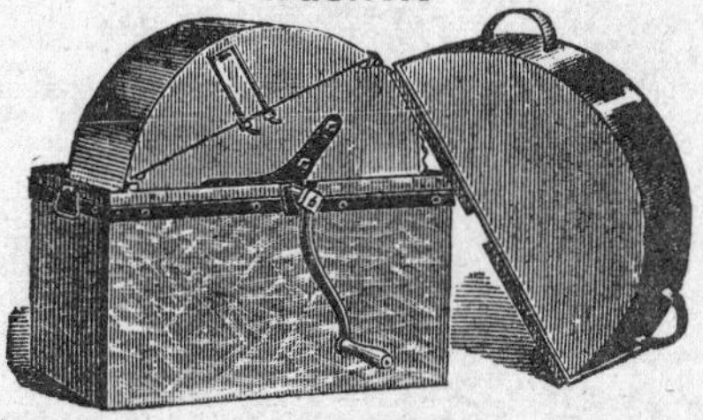

No. 23C149 **Having all the latest improvements. Boiler is made of heavy galvanized iron, 21¾x12x10½ in., inside measurement.** The cylinder is made from heavy tin plate, is 18¼ inches in diameter and 9¾ inches wide. The clothes are placed in this cylinder and washed by the action of the steam. Prints and ginghams can be washed in from five to eight minutes, white flannel in five minutes; red flannel in about one minute; lace curtains in from ten to fifteen minutes. No washboard rubbing is necessary, and clothes will last twice as long. In washing it is not necessary to turn all the while. You turn the cylinder one or two minutes, then go about your other work for a while, then turn the cylinder a minute or two again. You can wash much cleaner in this washer than you can by hand, and the clothes will always keep white and never turn yellow. Does not wear the clothes or pull off the buttons. This machine is made of the best material and should last from five to ten years. Remember, the clothes are not boiled, but cleansed by steam. This is a process which is used by the celebrated French steam cleaning establishments. A heavy tin cover fits closely on the top of this machine, and closely confines the steam. Shipping weight, 30 pounds. Price....................**$3.75**

Quick and Easy Washer.

No. 23C135 **This machine is called the Quick and Easy Washer** and we are satisfied that by buying it every householder will find that it is true to its name and will relieve his wife of a great burden. Sides are each made of one piece of selected lumber, has heavy, rustless galvanized iron bottom, removable corrugated double rubbers, nicely finished in red with iron parts japanned. Inside dimensions, 19x28x13 inches. Weight, 43 lbs. Price....................................**$1.98**

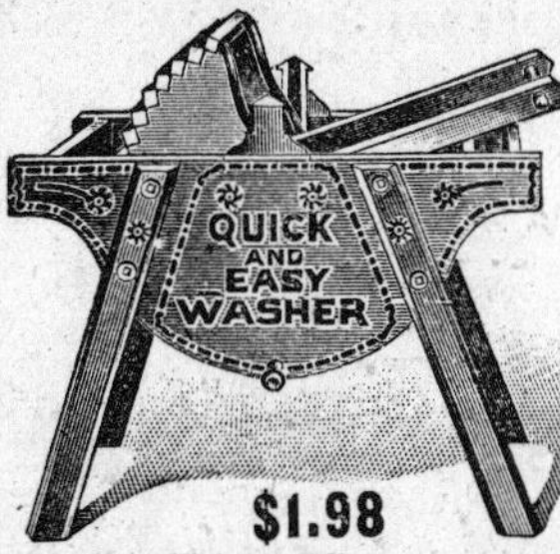

$1.98

Electric Washer.

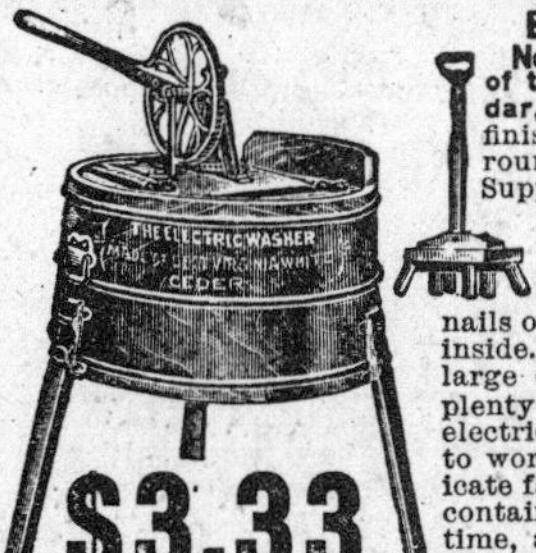

$3.33

No. 23C140 **Constructed of the best Virginia white cedar,** and is stronger, more nicely finished, and larger than any round machine on the market. Supplied with our improved gearing fully galvanized. Inside of machine is fully corrugated, similar to a washboard, there being no nails or blocks of any kind on the inside. The machine is made with large end of tub down, allowing plenty of room for water and clothes. The hoops are made of extra heavy galvanized wire, are electric welded, and are warranted not to break or fall off. Instead of using a square wooden post to work the dolly, we use a square galvanized iron rod, making it impossible to tear the most delicate fabric, as the dolly and standard are automatically adjusted to the quantity of clothes contained in the machine. **The Electric** closes tight and retains the heat in the water for a long time, and prevents the odor of foul steam from clothes. The washer can be used on a carpet without soiling same. Large, convenient place for holding the wringer, which need not be moved while using the machine. Shipping weight, 50 pounds. Price....................**$3.33**

Our Ideal Washer.

No. 23C154 **Our Ideal Washer. It does washing equal to any large washing machine,** but with greater ease and more rapidity. It washes a tub, pail or boiler full of clothes all at one time, without the usual wear and tear

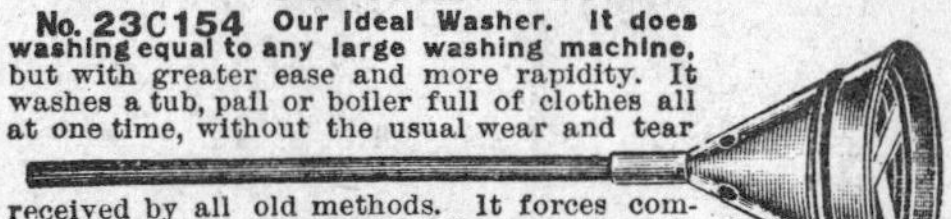

received by all old methods. It forces compressed air, steam and water through the fabric, quickly removing all dirt. It has no equal for dainty fabrics, lace curtains, blankets, woolens, disagreeable cloths, etc. If it does not do all we claim for it, it may be returned and money will be refunded. Made of best tin. Weight, 1½ pounds. Price....................**42c**

WRINGERS.

Rolls in our warranted wringers are made of solid white rubber, and vulcanized immovably to shaft. When we state that a wringer is guaranteed for a certain period, we mean, that should the rolls turn on the shaft, become loose, bulge, or give out because of defects within the time specified, we will replace them free of charge. When we guarantee a wringer for one year, it does not mean that we do not think, and that you cannot expect that the wringer will last longer than that time. If a wringer is defective it will certainly show within one year, and if it does not show within that time, we take it for granted that the wringer is perfect in material and workmanship, and will last according to the care and usage it receives, from five to twenty years. **When ordered with a washing machine a wringer adds little or nothing to the freight charges.**

The Curtis Star Wringer.

With large 11-inch rolls.

No. 23C206 **The Genuine Curtis Star 5-Year Guaranteed Wringer** with relief screws is similar to the Acme Star in design but has the highest grade solid white rubber rolls made, size, 11x1¾ inches. Sets down close to tub and is easy to operate. The best wringer made for galvanized tubs. Weight, boxed, 22 pounds. Price....................**$2.87**

The Keene Wringer.

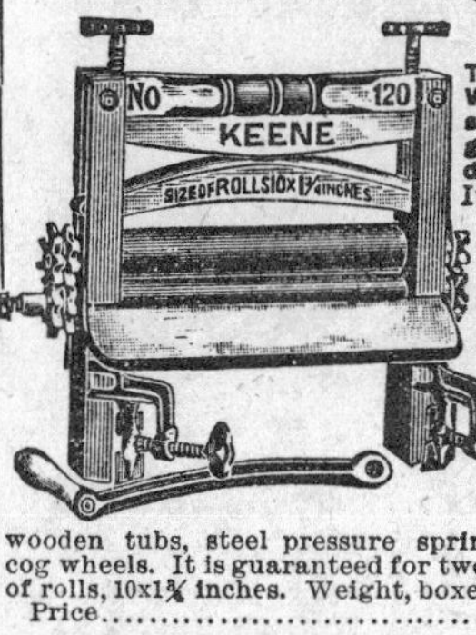

No. 23C210 **The Keene Wringer is a strictly high grade, up to date wringer.** It has all the improvements known to wringer manufacturers. It has wheel top screws, tub screws that will fasten to galvanized iron, fibre or wooden tubs, steel pressure springs, double cog wheels. It is guaranteed for two years. Size of rolls, 10x1¾ inches. Weight, boxed, 21 pounds. Price....................**$1.98**

The Wonder Wringer.

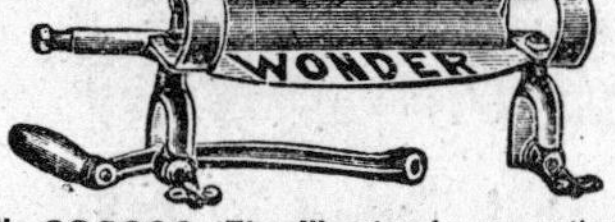

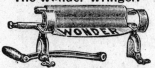

No. 23C200 **The Wonder is an ordinary grade wringer,** not guaranteed. It has iron frame, and apron, iron tub clamps, steel springs; rolls are 10x1¾ inches. This wringer is not warranted, and we do not advise its purchase. Weight, boxed, 14½ lbs. Price. **$1.25**

The Acme Star Wringer.

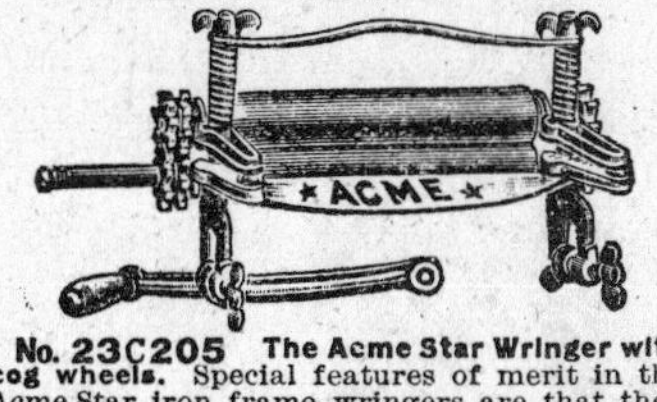

No. 23C205 **The Acme Star Wringer with cog wheels.** Special features of merit in the Acme Star iron frame wringers are that they have steel spiral pressure springs and thumb nuts, by which the pressure can be adjusted the same as any wood frame wringer. They are furnished with high grade rolls, size, 10x1¾ inches, guaranteed for three years. Weight, boxed, 21 pounds. Price....................**$2.08**

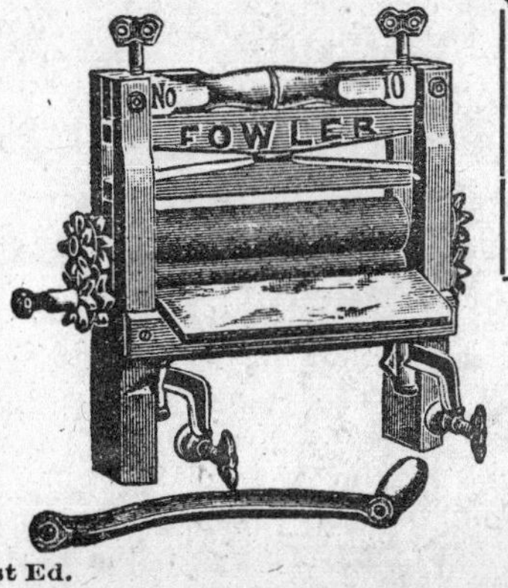

The Dandy Wringer.

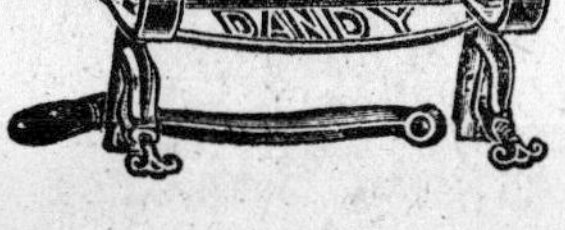

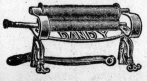

No. 23C202 **The Dandy Wringer has a frame and apron** of the same general appearance as the Wonder wringer, but the rolls are high grade and are warranted for one year. It is furnished with tub clamps that will fasten to galvanized iron, fibre or wooden tubs. Size of rolls, 10x1¾ inches. Weight, boxed, 15 pounds. Price....................................**$1.65**

The Fowler Wringer.

No. 23C208 **The Fowler Wringer has wood frame with two adjusting screws, iron tub clamps,** as shown in illustration. The rolls are ordinary grade, not warranted, and while we recommend our 5-year guaranteed Curtis wringer, we offer this as a wringer for less money. Rolls, 10x1¾ inches. Weight, boxed, 20 pounds. Price....................**$1.45**

BURBANK

BRADSHAW

SHROPSHIRE DAMSON

ABUNDANCE

HARDY PLUM TREES

30c Ea.

In Lots of 25
2 to 3 Ft.
POSTPAID

Sears offer varieties of plums best suited to this area. Our trees are hardy and grow vigorously in almost any soil. Succeed best in one that is medium fertile. Can be planted in odd corners and other waste areas, where they will grow readily with little care and produce valuable crops of fruit. Plant 16 to 18 ft. apart.

Abundance: (Early) Large Japanese Plum. Pinkish red color. Flesh yellow, tender, juicy. Popular. Trees grow large and bear heavily.

Bradshaw: (Midseason) Very large. Reddish purple, sweet and juicy. Strong growing variety. Excellent for canning.

Burbank: (Midseason) Fruit large excellent quality. Cherry red with lilac bloom. Flesh amber yellow. Well flavored.

Shropshire Damson: (Late) Purplish black, flesh golden yellow, juicy and firm. Tree is vigorous and heavy producer.

Fellenburg: (Italian Prune) Delicious sweet prune. Hardy and very productive. Large, purple, oval-shaped fruit.

State variety. Shipped Postpaid from Nursery near you.

Size	Caliper	Cat. No.	Each	5 Trees	10 Trees	25 Trees
2 to 3 ft.	5⁄16 to 7⁄16-in.	91 L 142	38c	$1.79	$3.29	$7.50
3 to 4 ft.	7⁄16 to 9⁄16-in.	91 L 143	46c	2.15	3.89	8.95
4 to 5 ft.	9⁄16 to 11⁄16-in.	91 L 144	59c	2.79	4.75	10.95
5ft. and up	11⁄16 in. and up.	91 L 145	79c	3.79	7.25	17.15

See Nursery Stock Guarantee on Page 886.

BLACK TARTARIAN   **MONTMORENCY**   **YELLOW SPANISH**   **NAPOLEON**

SEARS CHERRY TREES—EASY TO GROW

Fragrant Blossoms - then Delicious Fruit

SOUR OR PIE CHERRY

39c Ea.

In lots of 10
2 to 3 Ft.
POSTPAID

Cherries are a dependable market fruit, always in large demand. A cherry orchard will increase in value from year to year and bring handsome returns on your investment. Sears trees have 2-year old tops on 3-year old roots. Strong, healthy and well-branched. Sour varieties should be planted 15 to 18 ft. apart, and sweet varieties 18 to 20 ft. apart.

Montmorency: The best late sour cherry. Extra large fruit, bright red; firm and fine for shipping. Early bearers, hardy and fruitful. Good pie cherry. Leading commercial variety.

Early Richmond: The earliest of pie cherries. Fruit medium large, bright red and juicy. Trees strong, hardy heavy bearers. Valuable variety.

State variety wanted.
Shipped Postpaid from Nursery near you.

Size	Caliper	Cat. No.	Each	5 Trees	10 Trees
2 to 3 ft.	5⁄16 to 7⁄16-in.	91L162	45c	$2.15	$3.90
3 to 4 ft.	7⁄16 to 9⁄16-in.	91L163	55c	2.65	4.75
4 to 5 ft.	9⁄16 to 11⁄16-in.	91L164	67c	3.15	5.98

SWEET CHERRIES

47c Ea.

In lots of 10
2 to 3 Ft.
POSTPAID

Governor Wood: Fruit large; pale yellow with pink blush. Excellent early quality. Delightful flavor.

Black Tartarian: Perhaps the most popular of the sweet varieties. Fruit large, purplish black and heart shaped. Flesh is mild, sweet and firm. Trees are vigorous and adaptable to many soils and climates. Ripens middle of June. One of the best varieties.

Yellow Spanish: Fruit large, pale yellow with light red cheek. Best yellow variety.

Napoleon: Very large fruit. Yellow and amber, with bright red blush. Very firm, juicy and sweet; vigorous grower and very productive. Fruit keeps well, making it an excellent shipper.

State variety wanted.
Shipped Postpaid from Nursery near you.

Size	Caliper	Cat. No.	Each	5 Trees	10 Trees
2 to 3 ft.	5⁄16 to 7⁄16-in.	91L162B	52c	$2.49	$4.70
3 to 4 ft.	7⁄16 to 9⁄16-in.	91L163B	59c	2.89	4.98
4 to 5 ft.	9⁄16 to 11⁄16-in.	91L164B	72c	3.45	6.15

CONCORD

PLANT GRAPE VINES

Will Grow Well in Any Soil

5½c Ea.

And Up
in Lots of 250
POSTPAID

Grapes are easy to grow. They can be grown in many types of soil, from light blow sand to heavy clay. One of the most profitable fruits—can be grown on hillsides, along boundary lines, or on arbors and trellises. Grapes require very little care and should be planted in every home garden. Sears offer only strong two-year old plants, grown for us in the leading grape growing sections. Varieties offered produce big crops of quality fruit. Plant Sears high quality vines and be assured of success. Plant 8 to 10 feet apart.

Concord Grapes

16 strong Concord vines. Generally considered the finest blue grape for all around purposes. Good as table grape or for jellies, preserves and juice. Large, compact bunches, sweet and delicious. Make delightful arbors. Strong one-year old plants.

91 L 599

Postpaid from Nursery,

16 vines, 85c

Popular Tested Varieties

Concord: The best black grape. A very popular commercial variety. Bunches are large and compact. Flesh juicy, sweet and tender; excellent flavor. Hardy and produces good crop.

Caco: New red grape. Quick growing, young bearing, early ripening; deliciously sweet. Berries large, rich wine red. Bunches are good sized. One of the best for home use.

Catawba: Standard late red grape. Berries when fully ripe are dark copper color, with rich musky flavor; good wine grape.

Delaware: Best red grape. Very delicious for table use; keeps and ships well. Berry and bunch are small and compact. Color, light red, with heavy bloom.

Fredonia: Earliest good black grape. Berries large, round and hang to bunch. Flesh juicy, solid but tender. Good market variety, excellent shipper. One of the best new varieties.

Moore's Early: Early black grape. Berries are large, sweet, and juicy. Excellent shipper. Very hardy.

Niagara: Best white grape. Bunch and berry large. Very productive and disease-free. For home use and shipping.

Portland: A delicious new white variety; earliest of all grapes. Very hardy, vigorous and productive . . . berries sweet, juicy and of fine flavor. Highly recommended for home or market.

Worden: Bunch and berry are large and compact. A seedling of Concord, but of better quality. Ripens ten days earlier. Berries are black, with heavy bloom.

Postpaid from Nursery near you. State variety wanted.

Name	Cat. No.	Each	10	25	50	100	250
Concord	91L552	12c	$0.95	$2.00	$3.59	$6.45	$13.75
Caco	91L567	29c	2.39	5.79	11.25	20.50	49.00
Catawba	91L551	19c	1.75	3.89	6.45	11.25	26.50
Delaware	91L553	17c	1.35	3.25	5.85	10.45	24.50
Fredonia	91L587	25c	2.35	5.69	10.45	17.50	39.50
Moore's	91L555	17c	1.35	3.25	5.85	10.45	24.50
Niagara	91L556	17c	1.35	3.25	5.85	10.45	24.50
Portland	91L588	25c	2.35	5.69	10.45	17.50	39.50
Worden	91L557	17c	1.35	3.25	5.85	10.45	24.50

NIAGARA

CACO

RED DELAWARE

△ **SEARS**

Garden Grape Arbor

A collection of the very best grape varieties, including black, white and red grapes. An ideal combination for a home grape arbor or backyard vineyard. Consists of 6 Concord; 1 Niagara; 1 Fredonia; 1 Moore's Early; 1 Delaware. Shipped Postpaid from Nursery near you.

91 L 592

10 plants as listed......**$1.29**

Planting Guide

Planting and Pruning Guide furnished with every order for nursery stock. Contains valuable information on Planting and Pruning Trees, Roses, Flowering Shrubs, Hedges, and Grape Vines. Contains other interesting data to help you grow better crops.

Planting and Pruning

Roebuck and Co.

WASHINGTON ASPARAGUS

MYATT LINNAEUS RHUBARB

HORSERADISH

Strong 2-Year Asparagus Roots

Asparagus is one of the best vegetables grown by the home gardener. It is a very profitable commercial crop. A small patch will bring in surprising returns. We offer the **Mary Washington Asparagus**, a rust-resistant variety. It produces large straight shoots of a dark green color, tender and flavorful. Buy Sears extra strong roots. Set roots 1 to 2 feet apart in rows 3 feet apart, in rich, well drained soil. Quantities up to 500 shipped from Nursery near you. Postpaid.

91 L 675—Mailable

| 25 roots | 49c | 100 roots | $1.59 |
| 250 roots | $3.50 | 500 roots | $5.35 |

91 LM 675—Not mailable

| 1000 roots | $8.35 | 5000 roots | $39.50 |
| 10,000 roots | $69.50 | | |

1000 or more shipped by express from central Connecticut, southern Delaware, Michigan or Iowa. Not Prepaid. Shipping weight, 60 pounds per 1000 roots.

Rhubarb Roots

For early spring pies and sauces, there is nothing better than rhubarb. Sears offer the **Myatt Linnaeus** variety. Large, early, tender and prolific. Bright pink to red. Set four feet apart, preferably in rich deep loam. Will do well however in any ordinary garden soil with little care. Shipped from Nursery near you. Postpaid.

| 91 L 680—6 roots...... | 42c |
| 12 roots, 66c | 50 roots, $2.19 |

Horseradish Roots

Horseradish will grow any place. Requires no special care. Valuable when properly prepared as a relish and appetizer. Set roots straight up and down, and leave top one inch below surface. Postpaid from Nursery near you.

| 91 L 685—12 roots..... | 35c |
| 36 roots, 98c | 100 roots, $1.95 |

the operator would not have to give it her constant attention but could do other work while the clothes were being washed. At the same time, the catalog's copy reveals what went into the tubs of 1905:

". . . Prints and ginghams can be washed in from five to eight minutes, white flannel in five minutes; red flannel in about one minute; lace curtains in from ten to fifteen minutes. No washboard rubbing is necessary. . . . You turn the cylinder one or two minutes, then go about your other work for a while, then turn the cylinder . . . again."

These washing machines ranged in price from $1.98 to $5.10.

The Home Laundress Looks at Beauty

After the passage of thirty years, washing machines have become one of the most important items in the catalog. They occupy four pages of the 1935 edition and run up sales in millions of dollars. So efficient have these machines now become that the catalog takes efficiency of operation for granted, and addresses its sales argument to their beauty:

"Beautiful, None Bigger. The beautiful lines of the Mottled Green porcelain tub are accentuated by polished aluminum body bands and top edges. Green lacquered base has sturdy legs with splash-proof casters. The tub washes a full 60 pounds of dry clothes per hour, making short work of the biggest family wash."

These machines are now designed by the best American industrial designers who work not only with an eye to their efficiency but also to their beauty, and, measured by modern standards, they are beautiful. Their lines are simple; their surfaces enameled; there are no exposed gadgets to catch the dust; they are easy to clean.

Operated by electricity or by gasoline motors where current is not available, modern washing machines notably lessen the once savage drudgery of laundering. "Cut washday to one hour," suggests the catalog. "Why go on spending hours of hard work each week over a washboard? . . ."

If washing was once drudgery, so was ironing. It was a hard task to manipulate the old-fashioned sadiron weighing four or five pounds; pushing it a mile or two in the course of a day; testing its heat with a bit of spittle on the finger, and keeping it hot over a charcoal stove which had to be constantly watched. Electricity now takes over the task once done by hand.

"The Heatmaster iron . . . handles heavy damp linens with as much ease as sheerest fabrics. You set control at proper heat for fabric and that temperature is automatically maintained. Cannot overheat. . . ."

This does not, however, mark the end of progress in the home laundry. Just as the electric iron is an enormous improvement over the old-fashioned iron, so is the electric ironer an improvement over the electric iron. This machine (price $36.95) requires "Only ⅓ the Time, ½ the Effort and ½ the electricity cost of a hand iron. . . ."

In thirty years, therefore, technological change has taken most of the drudgery out of laundering; given women more leisure, or released them for other tasks, and permitted the servantless housewife to accomplish with a minimum of effort and time a job that once took back-breaking hours of labor. Women have not been slow to respond to the machine that makes this possible. By 1936, it is estimated that there were 10,300,000 washing machines in American homes.

In October, 1939, the United States was in the joyous throes of celebrating National Washer and Ironer Week. For the seventh successive year, sales of washers had passed the one million mark, and the estimate for 1939 was close to two million. But even better days lay ahead. "Despite the widespread distribution already gained for home laundering units," said Mr. J. H. Connors, vice-president of the B. F. Goodrich Co., "the saturation point is no where near being reached. More wired homes are without electrical washers and ironers than sixteen years ago, and nine out of twenty wired homes are without washers."

Easy Monthly Payments
ELECTRIC WASHING MACHINES

The Most Necessary of

The electric washing machine is today recognized as the most helpful home equipment that was ever invented. It is not a luxury, but an actual necessity for every family, no matter whether that family is small or large. As an economizer of labor and time and a conserver of women's health, there is no household utility that is the equal of the electric washer. Once you have installed one in your home, you wouldn't be without it.

$84.95 Cash Price

Customers Praise Our Washing Machines.

Sears, Roebuck and Co.
My wife is very enthusiastic over your electric washer. We tried it on your 30-day free trial money back guarantee, and it has come up to our fullest expectations.

Although we have an unusually big wash, the work is turned out in one-third the time with little effort, and a cleaner, whiter product one could not wish for. The swinging wringer is the last word in par excellence and convenience.

Since operating the washer, we have wondered how we got along without it. And last, but not least, your easy time payments made it possible to own an electric, enjoy its convenience and incidentally turn Blue Monday into a holiday.
Yours very truly,
P. F. EGGESON, Quincy, Ill.

A New, Improved Design.

This is the very latest type of electric washing machine on the market. It was designed by skilled engineers and is built by a great factory long experienced in the manufacture of the highest quality washers made. It has all the features which make for the most efficient operation. Because of its sturdy workmanship, the Liberty will give years of satisfactory service. Read below about the new all metal wringer, the corrugated copper tub and the other details of construction which make the Liberty the greatest of all electric washers on the market, regardless of name, make or price.

We sell electric washing machines just like we do any other household equipment, such as furniture, rugs, stoves and the like. We have no place in our catalog for anything, including washing machines, unless we can offer you a big saving. Moreover, we couldn't afford to offer any but the very highest quality washer it is possible to build—one that is free from breakdowns—one that will do the very best of work—one that will give years of satisfactory service. We offer just that kind of washing machines—machines backed by our Guarantee of Satisfaction or Your Money Back! Built of the highest quality materials the market affords and designed according to the latest accepted clothes cleansing principles, these electric washers are unbeatable bargains.

Save $50.00 to $75.00!

From every standpoint either of these washers is the washer you want. In finish and handsome appearance they reflect quality throughout. Quality insures long life. For many years they will render willing service. Their economy in price, freedom from breakdown, easy and efficient operation, all combine to make them the best electric washing machines you can buy anywhere.

There's everything in these Electric Washers that you get in the higher priced machines for which you are asked to pay $150.00 to $175.00. Save the difference! The extra high price of other washers is not extra quality but extra profits and commissions paid to salesmen, dealers, distributors. Our method of distributing electric washing machines direct from our factory to the homes of our customers, enables us to eliminate these excessive expenses which add not a particle to the quality.

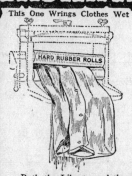

The Liberty Oscillator.

Features

The Liberty is the type of electric washer that will stand up week after week, month after month and year after year. It will give you the kind of trouble free service every woman demands. Every single part of this machine has been most carefully designed and constructed with this purpose in mind. You'll find the Liberty ready for its task every time washday comes around.

Here are the Reasons Why:

FRAME. Sturdy and substantial iron construction, painted in battleship gray. Fitted with large strong casters, enabling anyone to move the machine with the least possible effort.

WRINGER. Motor driven, full size, all metal, ball bearing, swinging wringer. The soft Para-elastic rubber rolls protect all buttons and are the most efficient rolls ever made for wringing the most water from the clothes. Detailed description is given at the right.

TUB. Solid copper, corrugated, heavily tin planished on the inside. Large eight-sheet capacity. Oscillates rapidly, forcing the water and suds through the clothes at every backward and forward motion. Water rushes from front to back, washing every particle of dirt from the clothes. In ten to fifteen minutes a big tubful of clothes is clean—much cleaner than you can get them with the ordinary washer. There is nothing in the tub to rub, drag or injure the clothes. When through washing, simply drain the water through the drain cock and wipe the inside, and the machine is ready for the next week's washing.

OPERATION. There is nothing complicated about the operation of the Liberty. It is so simple any child could run it. No mechanical knowledge whatsoever is required. After you have removed the lid of the tub, poured in the water, added the soap and inserted the clothes, fasten the lid back in place and turn the switch. The motor does all the work, rocking the tub rapidly back and forth. No better or easier way of washing clothes than this tried and proved way has ever been discovered. There is nothing to get out of order, no fancy, expensive, troublesome parts to require attention. You will be delighted with the simplicity, the sturdiness and the efficiency of the Liberty.

MOTOR. Before ordering be sure to read motor description on opposite page.

Catalog No.	Liberty Copper Tub Electric Washer	Shpg. Wt. Lbs.	Cash Price	Easy Payment Price	Payment With Order	Monthly Payments
26V624⅓	With motor for alternating current 105 to 115 volts, 60 cycles.	300	$84.95	$98.50	$8.50	$9.00

Shipped from factory in SOUTHERN MICHIGAN.

Practically a Whole Year to Pay!

So easy are the terms of payment on our electric washing machines that anyone can own one. Send only a small payment with your order and the balance in monthly payments so small you will hardly notice them. We offer you practically a whole year's time in which to complete payment because we know the service the Liberty and the Allen will give. For years and years, long after you have made final payment, either will be on the job, doing its weekly task.

Fill out the Time Payment Order Blank on page 951 now!

The All Metal Wringer

This One Wrings Clothes Wet · This One Wrings Clothes Dry

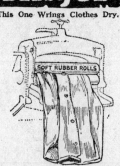

HARD RUBBER ROLLS · SOFT RUBBER ROLLS

Soft Rubber Rolls Are the Best.

Both the Liberty and the Allen Washers are equipped with the very latest and most efficient wringer ever devised. This is the all metal wringer on which every part except the rolls is made of wear resisting steel. All the metal is galvanized before it is enameled. This is a special precaution we take to prevent rust. It is sure to last as long as the life of the machine itself, for there is no wood to become waterlogged and to rot. The same motor that drives the machine operates the wringer and will do this while you are washing a tub full of clothes, thus saving considerable time. Ball bearings make it work smoothly and silently. It swings to any position necessary.

If you order on our easy Time Payment Plan use the order blank on page 951.

SEARS, ROEBUCK AND CO.

From the Old Spring to the New Refrigerator

American literature contains many allusions to the old, cool, sweetly flowing spring. There watermelons were cooled and fetched to be eaten in the heat of the day; around it grew beds of mint from which were plucked leaves to become (in the South) part of the poesy of a mint julep; there water flowed grateful to the parched throat. There are good American scenes, too, of New Englanders cutting the ice of their ponds in winter to store it away for use in the summer. But one finds few allusions to the household hardships suffered by people in those sections of the country—notably the South and the West—where there were few or no springs; where ice did not form in the winter, and where the population consequently endured the discomforts of heat without ice or nature's refrigeration.

Nor were the difficulties of the people living in these regions much relieved by the coming of artificial ice. The ice factories were in large towns and their ice was not available to millions living in villages and on farms. Consider the plight of a farm family in the hot cotton-growing area of Arkansas when a child burned with malaria fever. No cold compresses were available; if ice was to be had at all, it meant sending a buggy ten or twenty miles over hot, dusty roads while the precious frozen water dripped away on the slow journey. Consider also, the fortunate family that had a cool spring on the premises. Sometimes the spring was a quarter or a half mile away from the house. This made it necessary first to put vegetables or other provisions in the spring, and then retrieve them for use in the home—another task of endless going to and fro for the heavily burdened housewife.

Or—to come now within the purview of the catalog—consider the old-fashioned icebox used by those to whom either natural or artificial ice was available. Its use involved summoning the iceman, mopping up the kitchen where the cake of ice he dragged in had melted, and forever emptying the pan or bucket into which ice had dripped. Yet in 1905, the householder had either to do without ice, or else use the spring, or the icebox.

In keeping with the passion of the times for ornamentation, iceboxes were frequently carved and decorated as in the "Michigan Large Double Door Family Refrigerator ... beau-

A Sprig of the Anheuser-Busch

tifully carved solid ash case, dark antique finish, solid bronze trimmings, most perfect insulation. . . . Very economical for natural or artificial ice. . . . Price $13.80."

Every Home Its Own Ice Factory

The icebox of 1935 bears no resemblance to the icebox of 1905, while the electric refrigerator was not dreamed of thirty years ago. The boxes of the 1935 catalog are made not of wood but of steel. Interiors and exteriors are enameled, there is no decoration on them and consequently no dust traps, and they are easy to clean. But the demand for them has become so small that iceboxes occupy less than half a page in the 1935 edition of the catalog. The electric refrigerator is now in the ascendant, and millions are being sold everywhere.

Letters from purchasers of Sears' electric refrigerators testify not only to their quality but to the once hard conditions of living which they have ameliorated.

REFRIGERATORS

OUR MICHIGAN REFRIGERATORS are built to last and to be economical in the consumption of ice, as a refrigerator that wastes ice is dear at any price. The inside case is made of thoroughly seasoned lumber, upon which is placed our special insulation, mineral felt, which is securely held in place by hardwood cleats, to which is fastened the outside case or cabinet, leaving a space for dead air between the outer wall and filling, the whole forming the most perfect insulation known to science. Outside cases are made of thoroughly seasoned selected ash lumber, finished in antique and handsomely carved and ornamented.

ALL OUR REFRIGERATORS have full metal lining, highest grade solid brass or bronze trimmings, galvanized iron provision shelves, swinging baseboard, which permits the use of a large pan to catch the drippings from waste pipe. Lids are constructed of 1¼-inch lumber, making them very heavy, which prevents warping. Backs are hardwood, paneled. Waste pipe is removable for cleaning. Have perfect dry air circulation. All are thoroughly well built, and have every modern improvement. We give extreme outside measurements, including casters.

THE ICE CAPACITY IS OBTAINED FROM THE NUMBER OF CUBIC INCHES IN THE ICE CHAMBER.
REFRIGERATORS THAT HAVE ICE CHAMBER DOOR IN FRONT ARE NOT MADE WITH WATER COOLER.

CATALOGUE OF REFRIGERATORS FREE.

WE ESPECIALLY RECOMMEND that you select a refrigerator from the ones illustrated and described in this big catalogue,

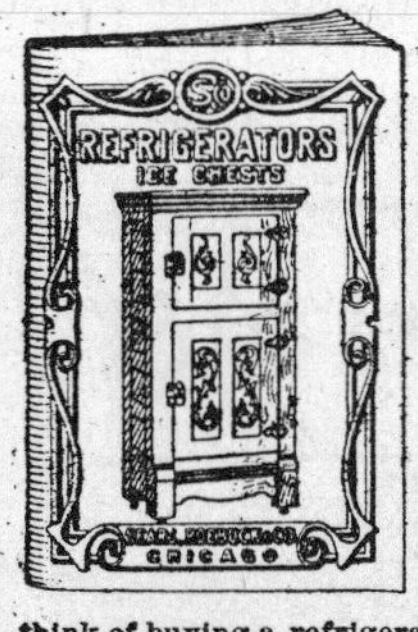

rather than to delay to first write for our free Special Refrigerator Catalogue, since we guarantee that any refrigerator you may order as selected from these pages will reach you in perfect condition, will prove in every way satisfactory to you and that you will find it a very much better refrigerator than you could buy elsewhere at anything like the price we offer, guarantee you will make a big saving in cost; otherwise you can return the refrigerator to us at any time within 10 days at our expense and we will immediately refund your money, together with any freight charges paid by you. **If, however, you are unable to make a selection from the illustrations and descriptions shown in this catalogue,** and you feel that you would like to have a larger variety to select from, larger illustrations and more complete descriptions, then don't think of buying a refrigerator of any kind from anyone until you first get our free Special Refrigerator Catalogue.

OUR FREE SPECIAL REFRIGERATOR CATALOGUE shows by very large, handsome illustrations, bringing out every little detail, our complete line of refrigerators, all that are shown in this catalogue and many more. Tells how it is possible for us to sell the highest grade refrigerators made at about one-half the prices charged by others. This free catalogue tells all we know about refrigerators, and unless you order at once from these pages, don't think of buying a refrigerator elsewhere until you first write for our free Special Refrigerator Catalogue. In a letter or on a postal card simply say "Send me your free Refrigerator Catalogue" and it will go to you by return mail, postpaid, free with our compliments.

OUR BINDING GUARANTEE. **We guarantee every Michigan Refrigerator to be made of the very best materials throughout,** to be constructed on the latest improved and most scientific principles, to be found exactly as represented in every respect, **and to give universal satisfaction,** and if found otherwise than stated we will refund any money sent us and pay freight charges both ways.

REFRIGERATORS are shipped from our factory in Southern Michigan. Refrigerators are accepted as second class freight rate by all railroad companies, which is usually from 40 to 60 cents per 100 pounds for 500 miles. By referring to pages 7 to 11 in front of the book you will get the second class freight rate per 100 pounds to a point nearest you, which is almost exactly the same as to your town, and you will see the freight will amount to next to nothing as compared to what you will save in price.

MICHIGAN SINGLE DOOR REFRIGERATORS

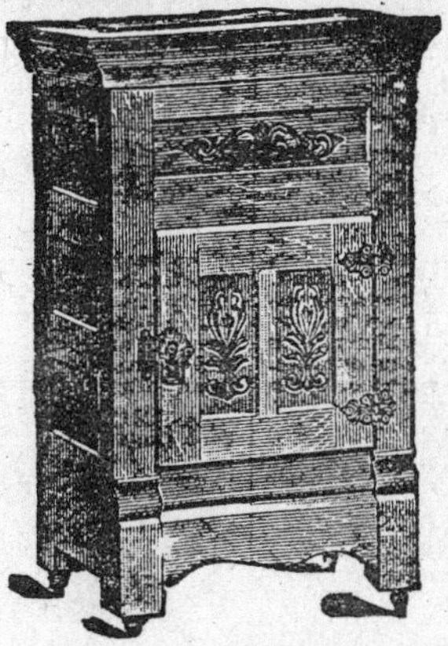

have handsomely finished solid ash cases, solid bronze trimmings, full metal linings, galvanized provision shelves.

A HIGH GRADE LINE AT A LOW PRICE

No.	Width	Depth	Height	Ice Capacity	Shipping Weight	Price
23C970	23 in.	15 in.	37 in.	25 lbs.	90 lbs.	$ 5.18
23C971	25 in.	16 in.	39½ in.	30 lbs.	100 lbs.	6.35
23C972	26 in.	17 in.	40½ in.	40 lbs.	110 lbs.	7.68
23C973	28 in.	19 in.	43 in.	50 lbs.	125 lbs.	8.85
23C1007	30 in.	19 in.	44 in.	60 lbs.	135 lbs.	9.45
23C1009	32 in.	21 in.	46 in.	75 lbs.	150 lbs.	10.75

The following refrigerators are exactly the same as Nos. 23C970 to 23C1009, except that they are furnished with a porcelain lined water cooler, and faucet to match trimmings, which reduces the capacity of the ice chamber.

No.	Width	Depth	Height	Ice Capacity	Shipping Weight	Price
23C976	25 in.	16 in.	39½ in.	25 lbs.	110 lbs.	$ 8.38
23C977	26 in.	17 in.	40½ in.	35 lbs.	120 lbs.	9.55
23C978	28 in.	19 in.	43 in.	40 lbs.	135 lbs.	10.75
23C1015	30 in.	19 in.	44 in.	45 lbs.	145 lbs.	11.50
23C1016	32 in.	21 in.	46 in.	65 lbs.	165 lbs.	13.20

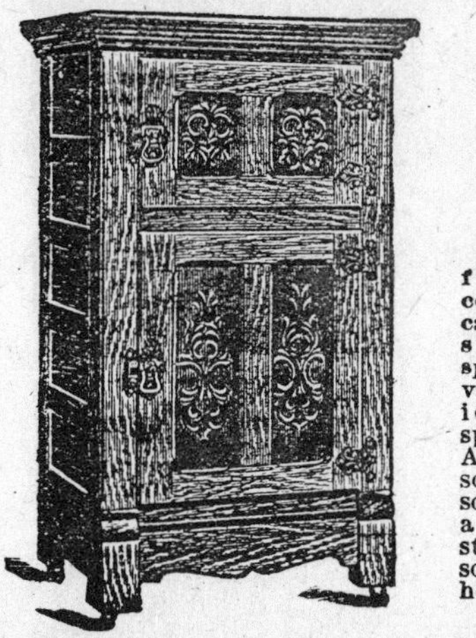

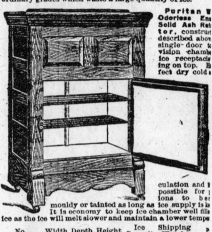

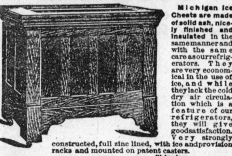

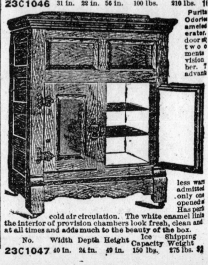

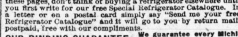

Michigan Refrigerators. These refrigerators combine large capacity with small floor space and are very convenient where space is limited. All have handsomely carved solid ash cases and are constructed as described in the heading.

No.	Width	Depth	Height	Ice Capacity	Shipping Weight	Price
23C1017	24 in.	18 in.	50 in.	50 lbs.	120 lbs.	$ 9.80
23C1018	28 in.	19 in.	55 in.	75 lbs.	160 lbs.	12.05
23C1020	31 in.	22 in.	57 in.	100 lbs.	195 lbs.	14.30

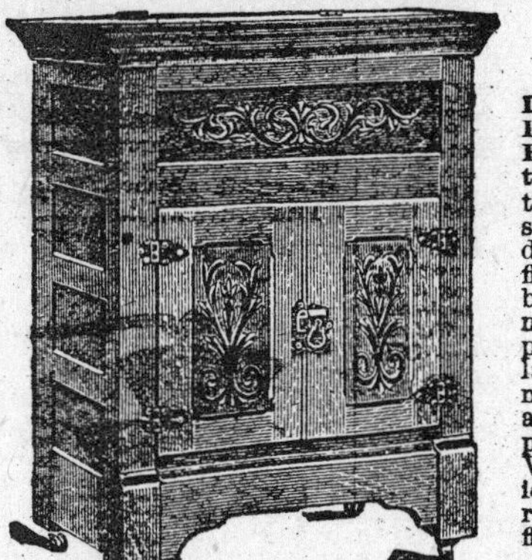

Michigan Large Double Door Family Refrigerator, has beautifully carved solid ash case, dark antique finish, solid bronze trimmings, most perfect insulation, full metal lining, and all improvements. Very economical for natural or artificial ice.

No.	Width	Depth	Height	Ice Capacity	Shipping Weight	Price
23C1022	36 in.	21 in.	46 in.	100 lbs.	165 lbs.	$13.80

No. 23C1024 Same as No. 23C1022, but with porcelain lined water cooler and faucet, which reduces ice capacity to 80 pounds. Shipping weight, 185 pounds. Price..........................**$16.25**

This elegant line of large double door refrigerators for hotels, boarding houses and private families, are stylish in appearance, of the most durable construction and very economical; have hand carved cases, beautifully finished, and solid brass trimmings. See heading for description of construction and insulation. Fully guaranteed in every way. All have provision chamber divided into two compartments, except smallest size.

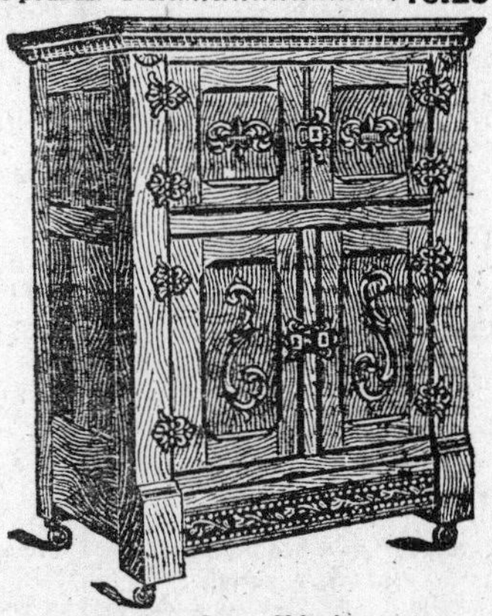

No.	Width	Depth	Height	Ice Capacity	Shipping Weight	Price
23C1026	37 in.	20 in.	51 in.	125 lbs.	195 lbs.	$17.15
23C1027	40 in.	24 in.	52 in.	170 lbs.	290 lbs.	21.60
23C1028	42 in.	27 in.	54 in.	190 lbs.	340 lbs.	24.45
23C1029	45 in.	28 in.	56 in.	220 lbs.	370 lbs.	26.95

MICHIGAN ICE CHESTS.

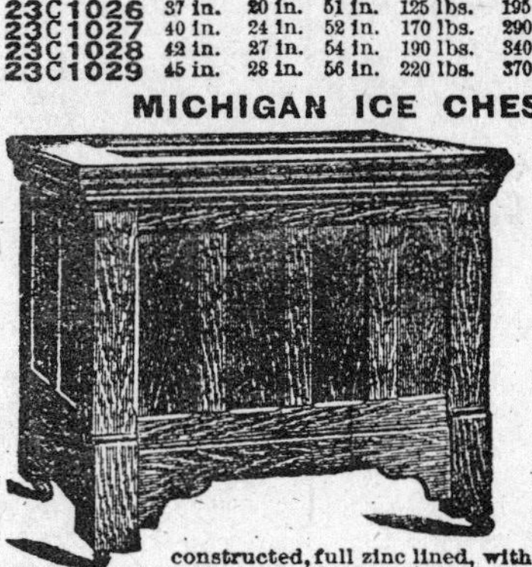

Michigan Ice Chests are made of solid ash, nicely finished and insulated in the same manner and with the same care as our refrigerators. They are very economical in the use of ice, and while they lack the cold dry air circulation which is a feature of our refrigerators, they will give good satisfaction. Very strongly constructed, full zinc lined, with ice and provision racks and mounted on patent casters.

No.	Length	Depth	Height	Shipping Weight	Price
23C1031	25 in.	17 in.	25 in.	70 lbs.	$ 4.45
23C1032	29 in.	20 in.	25 in.	85 lbs.	5.50
23C1034	32 in.	21 in.	26 in.	105 lbs.	6.20
23C1035	35 in.	23 in.	29 in.	125 lbs.	7.50
23C1036	37 in.	25 in.	31 in.	145 lbs.	8.65
23C1037	41 in.	27 in.	33 in.	185 lbs.	10.10

Puritan White Odorless Ename Refrigerators.

In this line is embodied the latest and best ideas of sc and sanitary refrigerator construction of the best grade. there are many higher priced refrigerators on the marke is no other line in which all the essentials, **namely:** dur economy in the use of ice, and ease of cleaning are comb such an extent as in our Puritan line.

Construction—Made of selected thoroughly seasoned a ber. Paneled on side, top and back to prevent warping ornamented with raised beveled panels, finished in a handsomely polished. Hinges and automatic air tight loc are solid brass, Roman gold finish. Lids are extra heavy a not warp. Ice racks and ice chambers are heavy galv steel, fitted with self closing drip cup, removable wast swinging baseboard and patent casters. The metal lining vision chamber, shelves and drain pipe are enameled with white sanitary odorless enamel, which is a mineral sub containing no white lead, oil or turpentine. It is app three coats and baked on in ovens under a high tempe after cooling, a coating of white shellac is applied, which a high glossy finish, easily cleaned with warm water and cloth. Others use an enamel the same as used on iro which is poisonous, bad smelling and not sanitary.

Our system of insulation is acknowledged to be th known, and consists of six distinct walls as follows: Outs casing, sheet of mineral felt, dead air space, sheet of mine inner casing and metal lining. The doors are insulated same manner, with mineral felt and dead air space. The you will save in the smaller consumption of ice through th fect insulation will in a single season more than p difference in cost between a Puritan refrigerator a ordinary grades which waste a large quantity of ice.

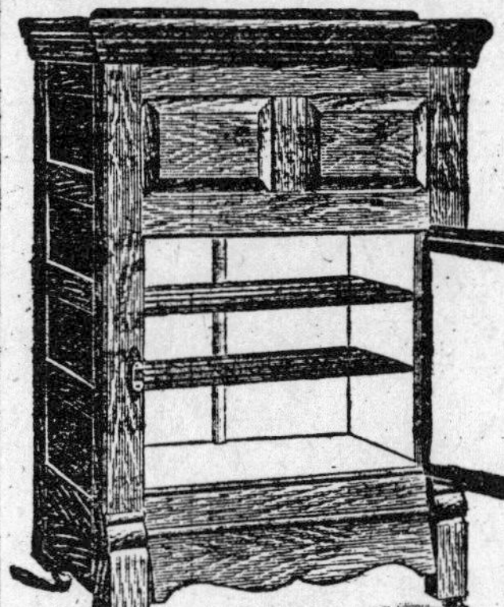

Puritan W Odorless En Solid Ash Ref tor, construc described abov single-door t vision chamb ice receptacle ing on top. H fect dry cold culation and possible for ions to be moldy or tainted as long as ice supply is k It is economy to keep ice chamber well fill ice as the ice will melt slower and maintain a lower temp

No.	Width	Depth	Height	Ice Capacity	Shipping Weight	P
23C1038	30 in.	20 in.	46 in.	75 lbs.	150 lbs.	$12
23C1039	33 in.	22 in.	48 in.	90 lbs.	180 lbs.	15

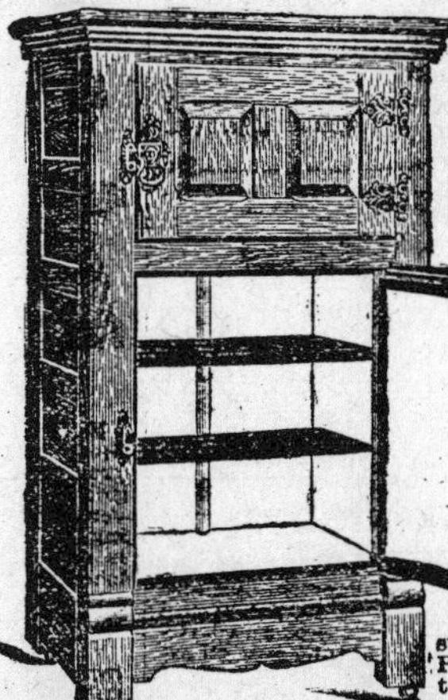

Puritan Odorless En Refrigerator. style is very c ient where sp limited, as the bine large c with small space. Ice c door is in making it eas cess. If p supplied with Puritan line wil tain the lowest ature and use than any other

No.	Width	Depth	Height	Ice Capacity	Shipping Weight	P
23C1045	29 in.	20 in.	54 in.	65 lbs.	175 lbs.	$1
23C1046	31 in.	22 in.	56 in.	100 lbs.	216 lbs.	1

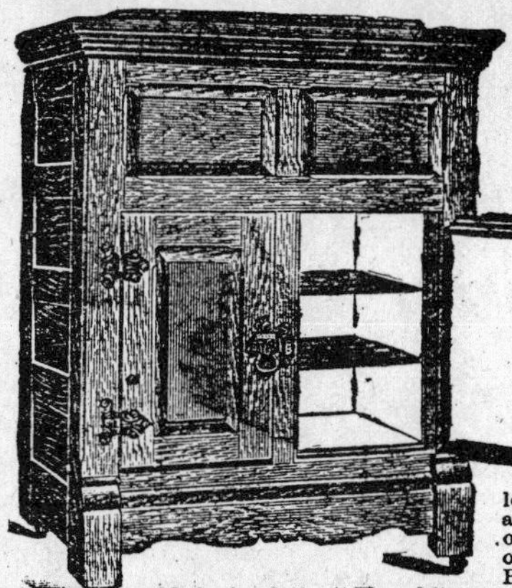

Purita Odorle ameled erator. door s two ments vision ber. T advan less war admitted only on opened Has perf cold air circulation. The white enamel linin the interior of provision chambers look fresh, clean and at all times and adds much to the beauty of the box.

No.	Width	Depth	Height	Ice Capacity	Shipping Weight	
23C1047	40 in.	24 in.	49 in.	150 lbs.	275 lbs.	$2

REFRIGERATORS

THE CASE.
The outside case of our refrigerators is made of selected oak, Northern ash or elm, as mentioned in the description of each refrigerator, the three best woods for outer case refrigerator construction, specially selected and thoroughly air seasoned and kiln dried and absolutely guaranteed not to warp, crack, check or shrink. The inner wood section of the case is made of seasoned hardwood selected for its perfect adaptation to a cold temperature.

HOW THEY ARE BUILT.
Each section of the wall is a perfect non-conductor of heat or cold, making it absolutely impossible for heat to penetrate or cold to escape. Each wall is made with an outside wood section, a thick sheet of mineral felt, a dry air space, another sheet of mineral felt, a section of wood and the metal lining. Note especially that two sections of mineral felt are used in the walls of our refrigerators and read what we say about mineral felt at top of page 1013. Each wood section is framed and fitted in a most careful manner. The tongue and groove joining is used, instead of miter joints, making it practically impossible for the joint to break loose. The galvanized steel lining and porcelain lining are fastened securely to the inner wood casing, covering it entirely and rendering it impossible for the water to come in contact with the wood in any part of the chambers. There are no cracks or crevices for the

accumulation of dirt or impurities. The mineral felt is held in place against the wood section by strong cleats. Solidity, cleanliness and durability are combined with perfect sanitary and germproof inner chambers. A perfect dry cold air circulation and every degree of this coldness is utilized in the preservation of the food.

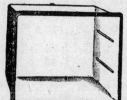

THE PORCELAIN LINING.
The porcelain lining used in the provision chamber of the four refrigerators shown on this page is made of 16-gauge steel. It is cast in one piece, as shown in the small illustration to the left. There are no cracks or crevices to catch and hold any food that may be spilled. The inner surface of the chamber has a pure white porcelain finish. Many other makers use plates of porcelain steel and fasten them with screws, with open joints at all the corners, which makes an uneven rough surface which catches food particles and makes it hard to keep the food chamber clean and sweet. Our porcelain lined food chamber is one of the strongest, most durable and most easily cleaned of all food chamber linings.

ADDITIONAL DESCRIPTION OF OUR REFRIGERATORS IS GIVEN AT TOP OF PAGE 1013.

Four Splendid *Porcelain Lined Refrigerators*

Single Door. Lift Lid.

Only $15 25

Porcelain Lined Food Chamber.

OUTSIDE CASE.
Northern ash, high gloss golden oak finish. Front corner posts and top have rounded edges. Lift lid top. Airtight joints. Swinging baseboard.

ICE CHAMBER.
Made of galvanized steel. All metal ice rack. No. 1V62878⅓, width, 20 inches; depth, 13 inches, height, 10 inches. No. 1V62880⅓, width, 22 inches; depth, 14 inches; height, 11 inches.

FOOD CHAMBER.
Single door with two panels. Porcelain finished, steel lining. All steel wire shelves, tinned finish. Removable drain pipe. Floor on level with bottom of door. No. 1V62878⅓, width, 22 inches; depth, 13 inches; height, 17 inches; No. 1V62880⅓, width, 24 inches; depth, 14 inches; height, 17 inches.

TRIMMINGS.
All door hinges made of solid metal, nickel plated. Heavy patent nickel plated lever locks, holding door into an airtight joint. Self retaining spring socket casters. Automatic self closing air trap fitted to bottom of drain pipe.

Catalog No.	Outside Width, Inches	Outside Depth, Inches	Outside Height, Inches	Ice Capacity, Pounds	Shipping Weight, Pounds	Price
1V62878⅓	26	17	44	85	160	$15.25
1V62880⅓	28	18	46	100	175	18.35

Shipped from factory near GRAND RAPIDS, MICH.

Two Doors. Open Front.

Only $21 65

Porcelain Lined Food Chamber.

OUTSIDE CASE.
Made of Northern ash, high gloss golden finish. Panel ends. Front posts and top have rounded edges. Airtight joints. Swinging baseboard.

ICE CHAMBER.
Single door opening in front, three panels. Galvanized steel lining. Removable flues. Solid metal ice rack. Width, 20 inches; depth, 15 inches; height, 17 inches.

FOOD CHAMBER.
Large single door, full paneled. Porcelain lining. All woven steel wire shelves, tinned finish. Removable drain pipe. Top, bottom and sides pure snowy white. Width, 23 inches; depth, 15 inches; height, 23 inches.

TRIMMINGS.
All door hinges made of solid metal, nickel plated. Heavy patent nickel plated lever locks, holding door into an airtight joint. Self retaining spring socket casters. Automatic self closing air trap fitted to bottom of drain pipe.

Catalog No.	Outside Width, Inches	Outside Depth, Inches	Outside Height, Inches	Ice Capacity, Pounds	Shipping Weight, Pounds	Price
1V62884⅓	27	20	55	100	230	$21.65

Shipped from factory near GRAND RAPIDS, MICH.

Four Doors. Two Food Chambers.

Only $24 95

Porcelain Lined Food Chambers.

OUTSIDE CASE.
Northern ash, high gloss golden oak finish. Paneled ends. Swinging baseboard. Airtight joints. Front posts and top have rounded edges.

ICE CHAMBER.
Conveniently placed on left hand side. Single door with center panel. Galvanized steel linings. All metal ice rack. Width, 15 inches; depth, 17 inches; height, 23 inches.

FOOD CHAMBERS.
Extra large chamber and small chamber below ice chamber. Porcelain finished, steel lined. Metal steel wire shelves. Removable drain pipe. Large chamber, width, 15 inches; depth, 17 inches; height, 33 inches. Small chamber, width, 15 inches; depth, 17 inches; height, 7 inches.

TRIMMINGS.
All door hinges made of solid metal, nickel plated. Heavy patent nickel plated lever locks, holding door into an airtight joint. Self retaining spring socket casters. Automatic self closing air trap fitted to bottom of drain pipe.

Catalog No.	Outside Width, Inches	Outside Depth, Inches	Outside Height, Inches	Ice Capacity, Pounds	Shipping Weight, Pounds	Price
1V62889⅓	34	20	46	125	225	$24.95

Shipped from factory near GRAND RAPIDS, MICH.

Three Doors. Two Food Chambers.

Only $29 95

Porcelain Lined Food Chambers.

OUTSIDE CASE.
Solid oak, high gloss golden finish. Heavy front posts and top rails have rounded corners. Full paneled ends. All doors have thick raised bevel edge panels. Swinging baseboard.

ICE CHAMBER.
Door in front. Galvanized steel lined. All metal ice rack. Width, 15 inches; depth, 15 inches; height, 23 inches.

FOOD CHAMBERS.
Two compartments. Steel linings, porcelain finished, pure snowy white. All steel woven wire shelves, tinned finish. Removable drain pipe. Large compartment, width, 15 inches; depth, 15 inches; height, 33 inches; small compartment below ice chamber, width, 15 inches; depth, 15 inches; height, 7 inches.

TRIMMINGS.
All door hinges made of solid metal, nickel plated. Heavy patent nickel plated lever locks, holding door into an airtight joint. Self retaining spring socket casters. Automatic self closing air trap fitted to bottom of drain pipe.

Catalog No.	Outside Width, Inches	Outside Depth, Inches	Outside Height, Inches	Ice Capacity, Pounds	Shipping Weight, Pounds	Price
1V62893⅓	35	20	47	130	260	$29.95

Shipped from factory near GRAND RAPIDS, MICH.

Mr. Charles A. Bly, Jr., Needles, California, writes: "We live in the heart of the Mojave desert where the temperature is often as high as 120° in the shade. Have kept milk fresh 14 days during summer."

Here again Sears, intent not only upon providing a refrigerator of high mechanical efficiency but also a beautiful one, hired a famous industrial designer to create the cabinets.

The features of the electrical refrigerator are so well known that they need no elaboration here. It is sufficient to say that, although the 1925 catalog does not mention electric refrigerators, they occupy three pages in the 1935 edition, and by 1936, 9,200,000 were in operation in the United States.

Spring Cleaning

In the early years of this century, the dweller in an American small town or on the farm knew that spring had come by one infallible sign: the housewife or her servant was beating rugs and carpets with a stick or a carpet beater. Spring came to America not only in flowers blooming along the wayside but also in clouds of dust arising from the cleaning of carpets. This sight is still to be seen but far less frequently than in the past, for in a land which once possessed no vacuum cleaners there were, in 1936, nearly eleven millions of these instruments at work.

The housewife of 1905 had only two important implements for chasing dust: the broom and the carpet sweeper. The use of the broom entailed severe manual labor; the carpet sweeper was inefficient. The housewife of 1935, however, wherever electricity was available, could use vacuum cleaners that almost effortlessly performed in a few minutes the work formerly done by hours of broom pushing.

In *This Week* (September, 1939), a New York housewife —Mrs. Annette Burkelman—tells how she successfully managed without a servant to take in a number of paying guests who were attending the World's Fair. The key to her success was in labor-saving devices for the home.

"While I'm getting breakfast," said Mrs. Burkelman, "I turn on the automatic washer that I've loaded the night before and let it do a load of clothes. . . . Hanging the clean clothes that are waiting for me in the washer is my next job. Then I start a second load of clothes and go back upstairs to clean the bathrooms, dust and dry-mop the bedrooms.

"That is where my vacuum cleaner and attachments come in. I can dust moldings, woodwork, odd corners and floors in a twinkling. . . . I make no schedule for the ironing. With the ironer, I find that I can work it just any time. I can sit down and do a few pieces while dinner's cooking. . . . I try to be finished by one o'clock. Then I have time for a bath and rest. . . ."

Wood for the Stoves of America

Inseparably mingled in the memories of the small boy of the South of twenty or thirty years ago are scenes associated with gathering of wood for stoves and grates. In July or August, after the cotton crop had been laid by and picking had not yet begun, many plantation Negroes earned some much-needed cash by cutting cordwood in the forests and selling it to white folks in the towns. Long before dawn, while the stars still shone in the Southern sky, heavily loaded mule-drawn wagons accompanied by one or two sleepy Negroes began to move toward the nearest town, perhaps ten or fifteen miles away. Shortly after breakfast, they would arrive at their destination. The wagon would drive into the white-folks' back yard, and the loads of oak, ash, hackberry, and cottonwood would be removed and neatly stacked in cord lengths, while barefooted white boys stood by with wondering eyes watching the muscles of the Negroes' arms dart beneath the skin, watching for snakes that sometimes came with the wood, sniffing the sweet odors of newly felled trees, and climbing on top of the piles to survey the earth beneath. Then the black men would be given breakfast at the kitchen, paid in shining silver dollars, and would finally drive slowly out of the yard standing upright on the frame of the wagons like Ben-Hur driving in the chariot race.

₤6.70 BUYS OUR ACME TRIUMPH.

$26.70 to $30.45

THE HIGHEST GRADE
BLUE POLISHED NICKEL TRIM-MED STEEL RANGE MADE.

Complete with high warming closet and deep porcelain lined reservoir, exactly as illustrated. (Burns coal or wood.)

BLUE POLISHED STEEL PLATE by reason of its high cost, is only used in ranges by a very few makers and then always sold at very high prices, usually ranging from $40.00 to $60.00. Blue polished steel is the natural color of the steel as it comes in its finished state from the rolling mills, a handsome high natural polish in a soft bluish tint, and makes the handsomest steel range yet produced; blue polished steel is very hard, there is no wear out to it; it will practically wear forever.

THIS IS A SIX-HOLE RANGE exactly as illustrated, we use a thicker plate of steel than is used by any other maker. Main top, covers and centers are cast plate from Birmingham iron, and are guaranteed against fire cracks. One of the covers has two rings and a small cover in the center, being a graduated lid. The range has heavier inner lining, bracing and staying than in any other range made.

OUR FREE TRIAL OFFER. We will send you this range with the understanding that after using it 30 days, if you are not satisfied you have saved $20.00 to $30.00 in cost and have received the best range in your neighborhood, you can return it to us at our expense and we will return your money, together with the freight charges you paid. See page 14 for our liberal $1.00 to $5.00 C. O. D. subject to examination offer.

ACME TRIUMPH

NEWARK STOVE WORKS CHICAGO

$26.70 TO $30.45

WE ADVISE you to buy one of our best ranges, either our Acme Regal at $23.67 to $27.44 or this, our Acme Triumph at $26.70 to $30.45, for either range will outwear **THREE** of the cheaper ranges, besides saving you the whole cost in economy of fuel used.

NICKEL TRIMMING. With the heavy nickel bands all along the front edge of

OUR SPECIAL PRICE $26.70 TO $30.45

BLUE POLISHED STEEL RANGES

We can always furnish repairs for Acmes. See page 19 about how to order repairs.

SAVED AT LEAST $20.00.
Anderson, Ind.

Sears, Roebuck & Co., Chicago, Ill.

Dear Sirs:—We are very much pleased with our blue polished steel range purchased of you. It has given satisfaction and feel that we have saved at least twenty dollars by buying of you.
H. E. WARD, M. D.

main top and front of the warming closet, with the large nickel closet brackets, tea shelves and trimmings, large nickel doors, heavy nickel trimmed oven door and reservoir, heavy nickel polished corners, nickel plates and panels, with the extra high finish of this range throughout, you must see, examine and compare it with other ranges to appreciate the value we are offering, for really no such a steel range goes out of any other foundry in America.

Price List of the Acme Triumph 6-Hole Polished Steel Plate Range with High Closet and Porcelain Lined Reservoir. Prices do not include pipe or cooking utensils. For Cooking Vessels see index on pink pages.

Catalogue Number	Range Number	Size of Lids	Size of Oven, Inches	Main Top Including Reservoir	Height to Main Top, Inches	Length of Fire Box for Wood, Inches	Size of Pipe to Fit Collar, Inches	Shipping Weight, Lbs.	PRICE
22C20	8-17	No. 8	16x21x14	46x29	30½	26½	7	505	$26.70
22C21	8-19	No. 8	18x21x14	48x29	30½	26½	7	520	28.29
22C22	8-21	No. 8	20x21x14	50x29	30½	26½	7	535	30.40
22C23	9-19	No. 9	18x21x14	48x29	30½	26½	7	520	28.34
22C24	9-21	No. 9	20x21x14	50x29	30½	26½	7	535	30.45

Cook Books for easy, economical meals

American Woman's Cook Book

$1.98 Postpaid

- Prepare appealing, energy-giving meals in less time . . . for less money. Over 5000 recipes.
- How to prepare leftovers to taste as delicious as original dish. How to arrange food.
- 300 photographs . . . 32 in appetizing, beautiful color.

If your time's on a budget, and your family needs double-energy, double-delicious meals these work filled days, here's your cook book. Every page contains many valuable cookery helps. Recipes for every occasion and every taste. Separate sections on feeding your family on a budget, substitute foods (especially helpful to a wartime meal schedule), and others. How to set a table for any occasion, how to carve meat and fowl. Complete table of vitamins and calories. New and original ideas on serving leftovers. Book is covered in washable cloth binding, and back is reinforced for hard wear. Thumb indexed for easy reference. Size, 8¼x5¾ inches.

3 K 2332—Postpaid............................$1.98

Good Housekeeping Cook Book

Helps you overcome the food problems that face every homemaker. The hundreds of kitchen-tested recipes have been check for accuracy and clearness so that even the beginner can be a good cook. Shopping information, food budgets, etc., Over 900 pages Indexed.
3 K 2325—Clothbound. Postpaid.$2.75

Modern Family Cook Book

Booklet, Canning, Drying and Freezing for Victory included with cookbook at no extra charge. By one of America's best-known home economists. Cookbook contains 1,000 pages of information on planning meals, marketing, budgeting, cooking; tested recipes of hundreds of dishes. 107 illustrations . . . many are in color.
3 K 2326—Clothbound. Postpaid.$2.83

Bradley Menu-Cook Book

Day by day menus, recipes, and marketing lists covering 56 whole weeks are designed to bring variety to your daily diet. No menu repeated and very few foods served in the same way. Other helpful suggestions. Indexed. 944 pages.
3 K 2327—Clothbound. Postpaid. $2.42

Joy of Cooking

Make cooking a joy for yourself . . . and the results a pleasure for your family. Easy-to-follow recipes by one of America's foremost cooks, Irma Rombauer. A cook book that is a "best seller." Contains 884 pages.
3 K 2331—Clothbound. Postpaid. $2.42

World Famous Chefs' Cook Book

Secret recipes of world-famous chefs can now be yours. With these recipes you can prepare delicacies to match those served in the costliest eating places for a very small sum. Many illustrations. Contains 637 pages.
3 K 2334—Clothbound. Postpaid.$3.39

Southern Cooking

A daughter of the South tells how to prepare the tempting and excellent dishes of that section. This book is for the bride as well as the matron or chef who delights in serving fine food. There are many illustrations . . . 12 pages in full color. Indexed. Contains 384 pages.
3 K 2342—Clothbound. Postpaid.$2.39

You Are What You Eat

Do you know that health, pep and vitality are largely dependent on what you eat? Even some physical disturbances such as heart burn, rheumatism, have been traced to incorrect diet. Thrilling new discoveries about the nutritional values of food have proven that you are what you eat. 87 interesting food charts and tables. Contains 128 pages.
3 K 2350—Paperbound. Postpaid...47c

Mystery Chef Cook Book

Radio's famous "Mystery Chef" presents co-ordinated recipes—entire dinners with directions for every move in its preparation complete to time schedule. With this book in hand, you can prepare an appetizing and perfectly cooked meal with a minimum of effort.
3 K 2330—Clothbound. Postpaid...95c

Soy Cook Book

This book is all about the much discussed soy bean. It tells how to bake with soy flour, how to sprout soy beans, how to cook soy beans, how to use soy cooking oil, soy sauce. Hundreds of tested recipes by expert cooks.
3 K 2341—Clothbound. Postpaid.$1.46

1000-page Vitamin Cook Book

This book tells what vitamins are and how they function. A detailed guide to vitamin cooking for better health. Over 1000 pages of new recipes and household economies. Illustrated—16 pages in color. Imitation leather bound.
3 K 2328—Postpaid.............$2.18

23 Booklets of tested recipes
13c each . . . any four for 46c

A collection of cook booklets that covers practically every phase of cookery from soup to dessert. Each book contains 250 to 500 tasty, tempting and nourishing recipes . . . each one thoroughly tested. Photographs appear on almost every one of the 48 pages . . . so luscious-looking they'll make your mouth water. You can rely on these booklets to give you lots of new ideas for delicious meals, appetizing lunch boxes and unusual party snacks. 48 pages each. Strong paper binding.

3 K 2335—Postpaid ....Each 13c   4 for 46c

Be sure to state titles wanted

Dishes from Leftovers	Meat	Eggs
Potatoes	Dairy Dishes	Ways to Prepare Poultry
Refrigerator Desserts	ABC of Canning	Soups
Cakes	Breakfast and Brunch	Candy
Every-day Menus	Tasty Sandwiches	Cookies
Vegetables	Delectable Desserts	Fish and Sea Food
Superb Pies	Facts about Food	500 Food Extenders
Salads	Snacks	

A few days later, there came to the yard a Negro with an ax, saw, and wooden "horse," to cut the wood into lengths for the stove or the grate. Again the white boys gathered to watch him, to see the saw eat through wood while sawdust fell quietly like snow. The flashing ax rang as it bit through the stout heart of oak; the saw's blade was anointed with grease every little while to make it move more easily through the timber. Afterwards, the boys helped the black man stack the wood in the woodshed, and envied him the happy life he led—he who would not have to go to school in September.

Stoves Lead All the Rest

So overwhelmingly important in Sears' business were stoves and ranges that the catalog of 1905 opens with them. The first thirty pages describe the many kinds carried in stock, all of which were manufactured in the Company's

How Mother Made the Pies that Mother Used to Make

"largest stove foundry in the world located at Newark, Ohio."

All the stoves of the times were alike in being inordinately ugly and hard to keep clean. Women demanded that their stoves be ornamented; they got what they wanted, and paid for it in the form of labor—polishing not only the black surfaces but also the nickel-plated ornaments that splotched the surfaces. This is a description, in part, of a typical kitchen stove of the period: "It has the same highly finished nickel plating throughout, made of the same beautifully polished steel with the same ornamental cast base, highly ornamented, trimmed and finished in the same manner."

Six fuels were employed in the stoves of 1905: wood, coal, coke, gas, kerosene, and gasoline. Wood, coal, and coke were heavy to handle and left residues of ashes which had to be removed; kerosene stoves often smoked and gave off an unholy odor, while both kerosene and gasoline were dangerous. Only gas stoves offered cleanliness and ease in action, but they were few in number because the production of artificial gas was limited, and gas pipe lines had not yet spread about the country. The result was, in general, that the housewife of 1905 not only spent a great deal of time preparing meals and keeping the heating stoves going, but also had to carry fuel to the stoves and cart the ashes away. Finally, in the intervals when the stoves were permitted to cool, they had to be cleaned and polished.

A Prophecy Realized

In 1905, the catalog ventured a prophecy: "Kerosene oil for fuel has proven so far superior to all other fuels during the recent coal famine, that its future for cooking purposes is established and rooted as firmly as the Rock of Gibraltar."

Thirty years later, the catalog shows full-fledged kerosene ranges capable of doing anything done by other ranges, and they are so popular that four pages are employed to describe four models.

Gasoline does more these days than run the family car; it

also runs the family stove in thousands of homes. The catalog tells us of gasoline ranges "with everything that a city gas-range can give you," simple, easy to clean, and enameled in "artistic two-tone colors."

One of Sears' customers—Mrs. John Fraher of Elmwood Park, Illinois, writes (in 1939) to say what her catalog gas range has done for her: "I Bake 60 Loaves of Bread Daily, besides half a dozen pies, several pans of muffins—and on Saturdays an additional dozen pans of pecan rolls. I find your oversize oven, with its perfect insulation, a big help in my baking—it bakes so evenly—and the temperature of my kitchen doesn't become uncomfortable. Your gas range is certainly a beauty."

But what if natural or artificial gas is not available in a given community? It makes no difference. Gas may be used just the same. It is available as bottled gas. The catalog says: "Bottled Gas. . . . We factory-equip our gas ranges to burn almost any make of Bottled Gas furnished in steel tanks. When ordering be sure to tell us the B.T.U. content and which make of Bottled Gas you are going to use."

Sears points out the time- and work-saving advantages of its De Luxe Electric Range—Price $134.95. "Gives you a new lease on home-life. Gives You Time Off From Kitchen Duty. Oven Heat Control and Automatic Timer do oven watching for you. Cooking Timer watches top cooking for you. Set it for any time from a minute to an hour."

Women are no longer tied to the kitchen or to the kitchen stove.

Every Man His Own Barber

The 1905 catalog offers many models of hair clippers for home use, and the traveler in rural regions of the country is familiar with the spectacle of parents clipping their children's hair, or (among Southern Negroes) of families seated on the front porch in summer looking carefully through one another's hair with a fine-tooth instrument locally known as a "can't-you-don't-you" comb. But by 1935, even the simple manual-labor job of hair clipping has been taken over by electricity, and the catalog offers "the ideal electric hair clipper for home use." Here, too, are listed many labor-saving devices and comfort-giving gadgets unknown in most cases thirty years ago.

Sewing-machine motors: "Here's a real labor saver for your home! Why not let it take over the drudgery of running your sewing machine?"

Electric waffle irons: "Every waffle baked just right without watching!"

Bread toasters: "Toast turns automatically when door is lowered."

Electric ice-cream freezers: "Turn over the tough job of cranking the freezer to this powerful motor-driven machine."

Electric coffee percolators; electric mixers for foods; juice extractors; nursery-bottle warmers; heating pads for the body, and for an America that has recently discovered the sun, electric sun lamps. The list of these gadgets is endless but, of the more important electrical devices, the following numbers were in use in 1936:*

Ranges	1,450,000
Flatirons	21,750,000
Toasters	10,250,000
Percolators	6,000,000

Home Heating

The American home is the best heated—or, according to foreign visitors, the most overheated—home in the world. It is only within the past thirty years, however, that central heating has come to be widely used in the American home, and the catalog of 1905 has little to say on the subject.

But in 1915, Sears introduces the subject with a little lecture on the Eskimo: "CONSIDER THE ESKIMO. What a hard winter he has of it! Six months of continuous darkness and extreme cold.

"His home is a snow igloo. . . . He never builds anything larger than a small one-room house with low ceiling and no

* Source: Edison Electric Institute.

windows. If he built anything larger he would be unable to keep it warm enough to live in, for he depends upon a small open oil flame burning from a hollowed out stone lamp. . . . The result is the entire family is compelled to eat, sleep, work and live in a single small, close apartment. A bare existence is all the Eskimo gets out of life."

It isn't enough merely to pity the poor Eskimo. The point is that some Americans, according to the catalog, are living almost like Eskimos:

". . . There are still many people throughout our land who spend their winters in a manner approaching somewhat the life of the Eskimo. With the coming on of cold days in the fall they abandon the summer kitchen and do the cooking in the dining room. The parlor or front room is closed off with folding doors and the upstairs bedrooms are practically uninhabitable. The family life is contracted into the two or three rooms which can be kept comfortably warm."

This is an unquestionably veracious picture of life as it was lived in thousands of American homes. Because it was true, a wide field lay open for the sale of central-heating appliances. The catalog then gets down to business: "Our Warm Air Heating Plants are installed in old houses practically as easily as in new houses. With the heating plant installed, the whole house . . . is pleasantly and comfortably warmed all winter long. Any handy person who can use the common tools found in every home can do the work in first class manner with the assistance of our simple and complete directions. . . . Our average price for a complete Warm Air Heating Plant . . . for the average six or seven-room house, is about $70.00. . . ."

As time passed, more and more heating plants were installed in American homes; the catalog found it no longer necessary to draw pictures of shivering Eskimos wrapped in arctic gloom, and in 1939 it merely described and illustrated a large variety of furnaces spread over eleven pages. Central heating has long been accepted as necessary. Now comes an innovation. "Fresh Warm Air in Every Nook and Corner with Hercules Modified Air Conditioner." Once the home in cold climates was almost hermetically sealed in order to retain the heat of the stove and keep out cold air, but now the order of the day is warmth plus *fresh* air. The Hercules Air Conditioner "rapidly circulates clean, filtered air throughout the house. Filters remove 95% of dust, germs and pollen. Stale air is replaced with this clean air from four to seven times an hour. . . ."

And in the summer, the Hercules "Delivers cool basement air to living rooms in hot weather—a great comfort."

In the old days, even when a family had installed a coal-burning furnace, somebody had to keep the fire going and frequently regulate it in order to control the temperature. These days, says the catalog, are gone forever, because many of its coal furnaces are fitted with thermostatic controls which automatically control the heat and automatic stokers that pitch the coal: "Save steps, save fuel, save doctor bills, with Sears Temperature Controls. . . . With the Hercules Electric Clock Thermostat you can plan your 24-hour program of heating. . . . You can sleep in fresh cool rooms and arise in a warm cozy house. . . ."

If you have a Hercules Coal Stoker, "You'll cut down exposure to colds if your living room is not roasting one hour and chilly the next—as is frequently the case with old fashioned hand-firing. You'll save endless trips to the basement trying to nurse along a fire on a cold day. . . ."

Through the use of devices such as these, the glowing stove and the crackling hearth fire of the American home are gradually being extinguished. They were, it is true, cheerful and colorful and intimate as the family life centered about them, but they were also relatively inefficient, they required constant watching and work, and so their doom is upon them in a country that yearly becomes more and more mechanized.

The Saturday-Night Bath

The Saturday-night bath was a reality in American life long before it became a joke in the standard vaudeville repertoire. Personal cleanliness itself is largely a product of modern times; for long centuries, the generality of men rarely bathed or washed more than their exposed features such as the face and the hands. Thus, according to Lancelot Hogben, in his *Genetic Principles in Medicine and Social Science*:

> Adequate toilet facilities . . . were only slowly introduced into the homes of the middle class (England) late in the nineteenth century. Earlier the bathtub was regarded as a superfluity in the palace of Versailles, and the bathtub was removed and put in the garden for a fountain. There is ample evidence that the inhabitants of the palace acted in the spirit of Philip of Spain, who had authorized the destruction of all public baths left by the Moors on the grounds that washing the body was a heathen custom dangerous to believers.

The world may once have been filled with chevaliers pure and above reproach, but the drab fact is that they did not wash behind the ears.

The Great American Desire to Wash is now such a marked feature of this country that we are likely to believe it is of ancient origin on our soil. But it is a relatively new desire. In the 1840's, the bathtub was widely denounced as an epicurean English innovation whose widespread use would surely corrupt the democratic simplicity of the republic. The medical profession warned against its use on medical grounds. The bathtub, it said, produced rheumatic fevers, inflamed lungs, and zymotic diseases. It was not enough, however, merely to warn the people against this dangerous agent; some persons would be foolhardy enough to use the bathtub despite all warnings. This situation obviously called for a law, and in 1843 an ordinance was introduced into the Philadelphia Common Council prohibiting bathing between November first and March fifteenth of each year. The ordinance failed of passage by only two votes. In Virginia, heavy water rates were levied against those who had bathtubs, and a tax of thirty dollars was assessed against their owners in certain towns. When President Fillmore installed a bathtub in the

White House in 1851, he was widely denounced for importing a "monarchial luxury into the official residence of the Chief Executive of the Republic," and was pointedly told that he could dispense with it since other Presidents had struggled along without bathtubs.

The present American frenzy for bathing and washing is the result, in part, of the advance of scientific knowledge which brought about the Germ Era. The horrible consequences of germ ravages were soon made known to every man, woman, and child in the country. But it is also the result, in part, of the release from pioneer days. Americans were then crowded together in little cabins lacking everything except the bare necessaries of living, so that the bath was a luxury to be yearned for, and was later to become a symbol of plenty. "Cleanliness is next to godliness" is an attitude which sprang more from a starved dream of a heaven filled with oceans of warm, clean, sudsy water, than a stern ambition merely to have everyone wash his neck. The spread of this attitude is vividly shown in the increasingly large numbers of pages devoted by the catalog to bathtubs and bathrooms.

The tubs of 1905, by comparison with those of today, are primitive-looking, ugly, and employ materials which have long gone out of plumbing fashion. For example: "Nickeloid Bath Tubs . . . constructed with an inner lining of heavy sheet zinc, both sides deposited with copper, and outside heavily nickel plated and polished to a mirror finish. Finished on the outside in a beautifully tinted nile green. . . . Legs bronzed in pure gold." This basin of beauty, for all its colors and metals, sold for only $10.50.

Here, too, we find Plunge Bath Tubs made of tin with a wood bottom; the kind that are associated with the legend of the Saturday-night bath. It was tubs such as these that kept millions of Americans reasonably washed throughout long years of the growing republic. These tubs were placed in the warm kitchen close to the supply of hot water boiling on the stove, and one by one the family bathed.

Everything for the Bathroom

SICK ROOM COMMODE.

No. 1V4815
Price **$3.68**
Solid oak, golden gloss finish. Top, 16x16 inches. Removable granite vessel. A very convenient and necessary article for every home. **Shipped from CHICAGO.** Shpg. wt., about 25 lbs.

No. 1V4805
Price **$1.95**
This Washstand is made of thoroughly seasoned Northern hardwood, golden oak finish, and has one drawer and lower shelf. Top, 15¼x22¾ inches. **Shipped from CHICAGO.** Shipping wt., about 40 pounds.

No. 1V4808
Price **$3.45**
Oak, golden gloss finish. Height, 27 inches. Top, 17x17 inches. Linen drawer and vessel cupboard. Claw feet. **Shipped from CHICAGO or factory in INDIANA.** Shipping weight, about 50 pounds.

No. 1V4831
Price **$4.55**
Oak, golden gloss finish. Entire height 36 inches. Top, 18x26 inches. Serpentine front. French legs. Linen drawer and vessel cupboard. **Shipped from CHICAGO or factory in INDIANA.** Shipping weight, about 60 lbs.

No. 1V4811⅓ Imt. Plain Oak Quar. Oak
Price..........**$3.55** **$3.65**
Oak or hardwood in imitation quarter sawed oak, golden gloss finish. Top, 17x30 inches. Brass trimmings. Matches Dresser No. 1V4410⅓, and Chiffonier No. 1V4716⅓. **Shipped from factory in INDIANA.** Shpg. wt., abt. 70 lbs.

No. 1V4823⅓
Imitation Plain Oak. Quar. Oak
Price....**$4.15** **$4.25**
Oak or hardwood in imitation quarter sawed oak, golden gloss finish. Top, 18x32 in. Brass trimmings. **Shipped from factory in EAST or WEST.** Shipping wt., about 70 lbs.

No. 1V4827⅓
Price ...**$4.45**
Hardwood in imitation quarter sawed oak, golden gloss finish. Top, 18x30 inches. Wood knobs. Matches Dresser No. 1V4414⅓. **Shipped from factory in INDIANA.** Shipping wt., about 70 lbs.

No. 1V4841⅓ Price.**$5.25**
Made of oak, golden gloss finish. Top, 18x34 inches. Fitted with wood knobs. Quarter sawed oak serpentine top drawer. Carved claw feet. Matches Dresser No. 1V4457⅓. **Shipped from factory in INDIANA.** Shipping weight, about 80 pounds.

No. 1V4845⅓ Price.**$5.65**
Made of hardwood in imitation quarter sawed oak, golden gloss finish. Top, 18x32 inches. Wood knobs. Large top drawer and two small drawers and cupboard below. Matches Dresser No. 1V4467⅓ and Chiffonier No. 1V4741⅓. **Shipped from factory in INDIANA.** Shipping weight, about 70 pounds.

A Big Value AT $8.45

This splendid Washstand is made of thoroughly seasoned oak in high gloss golden finish. Base, 20x34 inches. The rounded mirror frame and standards are tastefully carved. French bevel plate mirror, 16x24 inches. Serpentine front veneered with rotary oak. French legs. This handsome washstand is very convenient for small bedrooms as it occupies but small space and supplies the need of a dresser. A special feature of construction is the three-ply built-up stock used in the end panels, back panels and drawer bottoms; won't warp, split, swell nor break. **Shipped from factory in INDIANA.** Shipping wt., about 100 pounds.

No. 1V4877⅓
Price, **$8.45**

No. 1V4854⅓ Price.**$6.25**
Made of seasoned oak, high gloss golden finish. Base, 20x32 inches. Three drawers and cupboard. Full serpentine quarter sawed oak front. Carved claw feet. Wood knobs. Matches Princess Dresser No. 1V4523⅓, shown on page 1050. **Shipped from factory in INDIANA.** Shipping weight, about 80 pounds.

No. 1V4858⅓
Imitation Walnut Oak
Price.....**$5.85** **$5.95**
Made of curly grained gumwood, finished in imitation walnut, or of oak with quarter sawed oak front, high gloss golden finish. Top, 18x32 inches. Large top drawer. Two small drawers and door have swell front. Matches Dresser No. 1V4472⅓. **Shipped from factory in INDIANA.** Shpg. wt., about 100 lbs.

No. 1V4836⅓ Price....**$4.95**
Made of Northern hardwood. Finished in imitation of quarter sawed oak, high gloss finish. Base, 16x23 inches. French plate mirror, 12x18 inches. Two drawers and cupboard. Towel hangers each side. **Shipped from factory in WISCONSIN.** Shipping weight, about 80 pounds.

No. 1V4849⅓ Price....**$5.75**
Especially adapted for small bedrooms. Made of seasoned oak, golden finish; large, roomy drawer and spacious compartment below the drawer. Top is 18x32 inches. Mirror, French plate glass, 12x18 in. in size. Lacquered brass handles, knobs and casters. **Shipped from factory in INDIANA.** Shpg. wt., abt. 90 lbs.

No. 1V4862⅓ Price....**$6.45**
Especially constructed for hotel use; also very attractive for the home. Made of oak, golden finish. Has 18x32-inch double top and 12x18-inch French plate mirror. Serpentine shaped top drawer, roomy cupboard below. Good quality casters. **Shipped from factory in INDIANA.** Shipping wt., about 85 lbs.

No. 1V4867⅓ Price....**$6.95**
Made of seasoned Northern hardwood, in imitation quarter sawed oak, high gloss golden finish. Top, 18x32 inches. Full swell top drawer. Double door cupboard. French bevel plate mirror, 14x24 inches. Brass finished handles. Good quality casters. **Shipped from factory in INDIANA.** Shpg. wt., about 100 lbs.

No. 1V4872⅓ Price....**$7.65**
Made of oak, high gloss golden finish. Serpentine swell front top drawer with two drawers and a cupboard below. Has 18x34-inch double top. Mirror, French bevel plate, 14x24 inches. Knob and handles are lacquered brass. Complete with casters. **Shipped from factory in INDIANA.** Shpg. wt., about 100 lbs.

18x40-Inch Base.

$8.95

Oak, high gloss golden finish.
Base, 18x40 inches.
Four drawers and cupboard.
Top drawers swell front.
French bevel plate mirror, 16x24 in.
Shipped from factory in INDIANA.
Shipping wt., about 120 pounds.
No. 1V4881⅓
Price..**$8.95**

20x40-Inch Base.

$9.85

Oak, high gloss golden finish.
Extra large base, 20x40 inches.
Swell front top drawer.
Three drawers and cupboard.
French bevel plate mirror, 16x24 in.
Shipped from factory in INDIANA.
Shipping wt., about 125 pounds.
No. 1V4886⅓
Price .**$9.85**

20x42-Inch Base.

$10.75

Oak, high gloss golden finish.
Base, 20x42 inches.
Full swell front.
Three drawers and cupboard.
French bevel plate mirror, 16x28 in.
Quality guaranteed.
Shipped from factory in INDIANA.
Shipping wt., about 130 pounds.
No. 1V4891⅓
Price, **$10.75**

Long before 1939, the bathroom had become one of the most important rooms in the American home, while bathrooms and bathing had acquired an eminence scarcely achieved since the great days of Rome. For a number of years, fashion magazines have been publishing photographs and rhapsodic descriptions of the luxurious and often bizarre bathrooms of society leaders in Europe and America. Two seasons ago, one scene of a successful play on the New York stage—*The Women*—was laid in a bathroom. Here the audience saw one of the heroines splashing about in the tub, greeting friends, and chatting gaily over the telephone within arm's reach.

In small towns, too, the bathroom is the pride of thousands of homes, and the traveler in America is no longer astonished when his hostess insists upon showing him the beauty of her bathroom with its recessed tub, its mother-of-pearl-decorated johnny, its electric heaters, and innumerable other gadgets. It is not surprising, therefore, to find in 1939 that Sears has a Bath Shop and that the catalog advises its readers to "Splash Your Bath With Color," by using, among other things, colorful shower curtains: "A new bathroom for an old one with Sears stunning new shower curtains! . . . Five lovely colors . . . so your bathroom can be joyously bright or delicately subdued."

If the daily bath is now an essential part of the living routine of millions of Americans, so is the daily weighing of the body in a country where fat is feared as a supreme enemy. The catalog tells us: "You . . . are not as young as you look . . . But as young as you weigh! . . . So make it a habit to weigh yourself daily on an accurate Sears scale." And the scales are in the bathroom where one may weigh without clothes.

In 1939, Sears sells bathtubs and other fixtures separately if you want them. But in order to achieve proper bathroom beauty and harmony of design, it recommends "This Charming Ensemble," consisting of bathtub, lavatory, and johnny (elegantly called "closet" by the catalog). Efficiency is now taken for granted, and Sears addresses itself to beauty: "Simple, straightline beauty in the modern manner. . . . Fittings are brass, finished in jewelry type chrome that gives a rich gleaming surface. . . . A unique design to impart even more beauty to your bathroom. . . . They're the finishing touch to a perfect bathroom ensemble."

The humble johnny is no longer permitted to be merely utilitarian. It, too, must be beautiful, and the catalog, speaking of those it offers, says they "Gleam And Glisten For Years. . . . Made Like The Finest China. . . ." Sears' Aristocrat johnny seats are guaranteed for five years against cracking, peeling, or discoloring, and the prospective customer is offered a wide choice of materials and colors, including Mother-of-Pearl finish in heavy sheet celluloid applied by a special process that welds the sheets together. Beautiful flake design. . . . Comes in choice of five attractive colors: White, Orchid, Ivory or Black. Price $3.95."

Luxuries such as The Corinth, The Downsurge, and The Elite johnnies, with their mother-of-pearl seats, are only for homes that having running water. Vast numbers of American rural homes are, however, without running water and their inhabitants must resort to the old-fashioned outdoor privy. These privies are a characteristic feature of the American rural landscape, and their importance in our scheme of living is attested to by the fact that one of the great jobs of rural rejuvenation undertaken by the Federal government was to build thousands of new privies designed in Washington by competent toilet architects. Characteristically, this innovation sometimes aroused resentment as well as approbation. A North Carolina mountaineer, residing near Hung Yearling Gap, said bitterly that the government had done him wrong, because his WPA privy had been built with an in-swinging instead of an out-swinging door and this kept him from talking to his friends as they walked along the near-by road. But in 1939, even this last landmark of rural America seems about to be flushed away by the torrent of modern invention.

"If Your Home Is Without Running Water," says the catalog, "Your Family Deserves the Comfort And Health Protection Of The New DeLuxe Handee Indoor Toilet." We are then told that:

> Public health officials . . . agree that failure to provide convenient, sanitary toilet facilities in many American homes is a serious health menace. They know that much of the stomach disorders and intestinal ill-health suffered by our adult rural population can often be traced to lack of convenient toilet facilities and the resultant development of the "deferring habit."
>
> You owe it to yourself and to your children to break the "deferring habit." Your children especially are entitled to a life of good health, which must be started when they are young.
>
> The Indoor Sanitary Toilet is a real aid to good health. Unsanitary outdoor toilets are a menace to the community as well as to the individual, since they spread the germs of typhoid, dysentery and hookworm diseases. . . .

Fortunately for rural Americans, the price of the DeLuxe Handee Indoor Toilet is low. It costs only $7.79. And it marks perhaps the passing of one of the few remaining pioneer institutions—the outdoor privy.

The Highest Level of Comfort

The consequence of invention and technological progress in machines for the home is that the American home has become the most comfortable home in the world. It is easier to run than homes elsewhere, and the American housewife enjoys more leisure than any other. The problem, however, of extending the use of these machines to the homes occupied by millions of persons who cannot now afford them has so far defied solution.

IT IS springtime in Charleston, South Carolina, and the old town is filled with tourists come to see her famous gardens. Among them is Mrs. Oscar B. Tutwiler, the vitamin-irradiated gardener of Julian Meade's *Adam's Profession and its Conquest by Eve*. Mrs. Tutwiler ignores her Negro guide while she takes charge and discourses to her friends:

". . . This," she exclaims, stopping by an English holly . . . "is that darling of the Ilex family, *Ilex aquifolium*. Isn't it superb? And it's another superb treasure the Yankees can't have. Doesn't like New England winters and I can't blame it. Now, Boy, you must be sure to tell the visitors that it's *aquifolium*. Don't you mix it with *yunnanensis*.

"Why, only the other day I was telling Oscar B. that I had never given the Ilex family the attention they deserve. I've never grown any except *aquifolium* and that plain, vulgar American one, *Ilex opaca*. But Oscar B. seems to think I should keep to the same old varieties. Sometimes I feel that Oscar B. has so little *zest* when it comes to horticulture. He'll buy me anything in the world but he leaves me too much by myself. . . ."

There have always been Mrs. Oscar B. Tutwilers in America; now they are merely more numerous than ever before in a richer and more leisurely country. They were once missionary-society ladies, crusaders for this or that Cause, or implacable hunters of Culture; recently they have gone in for gardening. All over the country, garden-club ladies now dig, weed, and reap; visit one another's gardens singly and in droves; go off on long trips, called pilgrimages, to the famous gardens of Charleston, Mobile, and Natchez. They pore over seed catalogs; exchange bulbs and information; torture the peacefully dead Latin language; study Japanese flower arrangement; hire lecturers; construct Oriental rock gardens in Louisiana and formal English gardens in Kansas; lobby against billboards that deface the highways; insist that roadsides be planted with trees and shrubs to beautify them; encourage the preservation of birds, and spend millions of dollars annually for seeds, plants, fertilizers, gardeners' labor, and garden accessories. Amateur gardening is now big business in the United States, and a constant source of amazement to foreign visitors. Mrs. Constance Spry, an English authority on flowers, reports her observations in *Harper's Bazaar* for July, 1939:

> To a stranger from a country where flowers are used lightheartedly and where women seem to be preoccupied with digging to the exclusion of getting together, the Garden Club movement in America is a bewilderment and its first impact staggering. With every trip I make I learn more and more of its activities and ramifications—the restoration of ancient houses and gardens, the road beautification, the preservation of wild life, and the spread of knowledge about gardens and gardening. My first, last, and all-the-time feelings about this garden movement are of admiration and amazement. . . .

Gardening in America is not a mere matter of millions of individual women casually playing with spades and watering pots among their shrubs. It is a Movement, and since there cannot be a Movement without an organization, and since America is addicted to both movements and organizations, garden-club ladies are highly organized into local clubs which are affiliated with state clubs and these in turn with national organizations. No country in the world exhibits such a passion for individuality and for communal effort as America, and here the ladies are running true to American form. Their gardening activities, moreover, are marked by an appalling and almost demonic energy.

Consider the Garden Club of America. This organization,

writes Mary Van Rennselaer Thayer in *Vogue* for March, 1939, ". . . is a rich and distinguished organization, whose leading light in New York is probably Mrs. Harold Pratt. More cosmopolitan than it sounds, members of this paragon of Garden Clubs make an annual junket to some spot of unusual interest. This year, they'll be off, en masse, to Texas, for a short jaunt for those more ardent ones who once trekked all the way to Japan to look at a few gardens. . . ."

If gardening is a fashionable and vigorous activity among wealthy women in wealthy communities, it is equally fashionable and is conducted with equal vigor in poorer communities by women of modest incomes. The state of Mississippi is the poorest state in the Union, but nonetheless it is an active gardening state. Some glimpse of its activities may be had from an article by Mrs. J. D. Duncan, President of the Garden Clubs of Mississippi, that appeared in *Holland's Magazine* (June, 1939):

> . . . Our membership . . . has studied conscientiously to make our gardens conform more carefully to certain established rules which make for a more beautiful garden picture. . . . Interest in developing perfect specimens has created specialists in roses, dahlias, peonies, camellias, and azaleas. The Mississippi Rose Society was formed as a result of interest in rose culture. . . .
>
> . . . Our Junior Chairman is very active in forming new clubs, that they may develop a sweet appreciation of nature, and a realization of the need for the preservation of our wild flowers and bird life. Many clubs have demonstrated, in rural communities, the proper planting of native trees and shrubs, showing that home beautification can be accomplished with little expenditure of money. . . .

Moreover, in a country where the sexual virility of the male gardener was once suspect, there are now men's garden clubs and unashamed male gardeners. The observer of million-faceted American life cannot but be struck by the recent widespread interest in gardens. And all this, like so many other developments, is fully recorded in the catalog.

The Verbena of Yesteryear

It was not until 1905 that Sears opened its seed department "which we have been compelled to establish at the urgent demand of our customers who were daily sending us inquiries for seeds and plants from all parts of the country. . . ." The new venture began with a special seed catalog and two pages in the general catalog, shared equally between flower and vegetable seeds. The star offering was:

"Yellowstone Flower Seed Collection. Eighteen Varieties of the Most Beautiful Flowers of the Best and Most Popular Varieties, only 29 cents."

For 29 cents, the customer received:

1 package Alyssum	1 package Poppy
1 package Astor	1 package Sweet Peas
1 package Batchelor's Button	1 package Verbena
1 package Calliopsis	1 package Marigold
1 package Foxglove	1 package Mignonette
1 package Butterfly Flower	1 package Mourning Bride
1 package Phlox	1 package Nasturtium
1 package Pink	1 package Pansy
	1 package Petunia

Canned Gardens

The 1905 catalog was content merely to list seeds and leave it to the gardener to plant them as she saw fit, on the theory that a woman who bought flower seeds knew what to do with them. In 1935, however, there were apparently thousands of women who wanted gardens and yet who knew nothing about gardening; who wanted flowers but did not want to take the trouble of cultivating and weeding flower beds. For these tired novitiates, Sears prepared, as nearly it could, a canned garden. Open the package, stir according to directions, and flowers in planned arrangements rise before your eyes with the magic of a Hollywood film and the opulence of nature on the loose.

"The NEW Way To Grow A Garden.

"A gorgeous garden . . . professionally planned . . . perfectly balanced . . . a garden that thrives with little or no weeding or watering.

"Here is flower gardening at its best. Hundreds of varied blooms . . . daring colors and delicate pastels . . . yet each one fits into the carefully planned patterns so as to contrast its loveliness to the utmost. . . ."

It is now as easy to have a canned garden as to have canned soup. It is all done through "The New Come-Pakt Planned Garden [a patent and product of International Paper Company]. The seeds are in numbered packets to correspond with numbered sections on the pattern. You simply plant the seeds through the holes in the pattern. Come-Pakt brings you a symphony of loveliness."

Old-fashioned dirt gardeners who know their way about with a hoe, who do not mind looking a weed full in the face, and who have minds and floral prejudices of their own, are not compelled to buy canned gardens. They are given a large choice of bulbs, vines, roots, shrubs, shade trees, and hedges, among which they may root and grub and water from dawn until that evening sun goes down. So numerous now have these gardeners become that ten pages of the catalog are required to exhibit the wares collected for them under Sears' roof: cash-register eloquence testifying to the great growth of gardening in America.

Our Beloved Enemy—Leisure

The gardens and garden clubs of America are thickly sprinkled with Mrs. Oscar B. Tutwilers: fugitive ladies whose interests are one day in Babylon and the next day in China relief. They are as much a part of American life as Coca-Cola and chewing gum. But the nation-wide spread of gardening cannot be accounted for merely because of their present passion for it, or because many former culture-club ladies have dropped Napoleon to take up tuberous begonias. The reasons lie farther afield.

Gardening, in part, is the result of greater leisure avail-

OUR SEED DEPARTMENT

WE present to our customers our newly organized Seed Department, a department which we have been compelled to establish at the urgent demand of our customers who were daily sending us inquiries for seeds and plants from all parts of the country. We have therefore inaugurated this new department of seeds, in which we sell all kinds of farm seeds and field grasses, all kinds of trees and shrubs and all kinds of flower and vegetable seeds. We have made close and very favorable arrangements with the largest and most reliable seed farms in America, and in accordance with our established policy of asking only a small, narrow margin of profit above our cost, we are able to furnish to our customers the very best in this line at the lowest possible prices, lower prices than can be had from any other seed house.

We are able to fill any order, no matter how large, for FARM SEEDS, GARDEN and FLOWER SEEDS of any description.

WE ARE DETERMINED TO HANDLE ONLY THE BEST AND MOST RELIABLE SEEDS.

We have the unlimited confidence of our millions of customers throughout the entire country, and we could not afford to risk losing the confidence of any single one of our customers by sending out poor and unreliable seeds. Not only that, but the majority of our customers depend on reliable seeds for their living, and we would not solicit orders for this department unless we would be absolutely sure that the seeds we send out and the trees and shrubs we furnish from this department would prove a good advertisement for us and would be a means of strengthening the hold we have on our trade. We can assure you that the seeds we offer are the same kinds and varieties that have been used for years by farmers and market gardeners in all parts of the country, people who depend on reliable seeds for their means of livelihood, and who use nothing but the best seeds that grow.

OUR FREE SEED CATALOGUE.

Our Free Seed Catalogue is a complete book showing everything in the line of vegetable and flower seeds, field grasses, trees and shrubs as well as garden material, and we ask everyone who is interested in this line, as a special favor, to please write and get our free Seed Catalogue. Before you make up your spring order for seeds, or even if you intend to buy only one dollar's worth of flower seeds or vegetable seeds, send us a postal, ask for the free Seed Catalogue, and we will send it to you immediately by return mail, postpaid.

Our Free Seed Catalogue shows lower prices, more liberal offers than any other seed catalogue published. It is interesting from cover to cover. We can sell you the very best to be had in every variety at a lower price than you can find offered by any other concern, and we can save you a great deal of money in this line. Please write for our Special Free Seed Catalogue.

FLOWERS.

In our Free, Special, Descriptive Seed Catalogue, you will find a selection of the most popular and easily grown Flower Seeds.

Our selected varieties of flower seeds come from strictly first class stock of highest vitality and we know that in ordering from us you will get the most satisfactory results with your seeds for annual and perennial plants.

SEND FOR OUR SPECIAL SEED CATALOGUE. IT'S FREE.

VEGETABLE SEEDS.

Seroco Reliable Vegetable Seeds Cheap.

NONE BETTER. NONE CHEAPER. ALL TESTED.

Our stock of vegetable seeds, we are sure, cannot be excelled either in quality or selection by any firm in the country. Every variety listed is desirable and has our recommendation. Our packets are, we believe, as well filled as any reliable dealer's in the United States, and in fact, a comparison has shown that they contain more seeds on the average than those of any other firm whose packets we have secured.

Write for our Special Free Seed Catalogue and get our low prices on the best garden seeds in the best selected varieties ever grown.

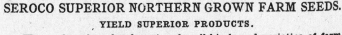

SEROCO SUPERIOR NORTHERN GROWN FARM SEEDS.

YIELD SUPERIOR PRODUCTS.

We are American headquarters for all kinds and varieties of farm seeds. Our contracts with some of the most reliable northern seed farms in America enables us to sell the best strains of all standard varieties, thoroughly dried and tested seeds. Send for our new Special Descriptive Seed Catalogue, and you can, from this special catalogue, make up your order for the best and most reliable seeds at the lowest prices.

The price on some farm and field seeds is subject to the fluctuation of the market and while the prices in our Special Seed Catalogue are correct according to market conditions at the date of the catalogue, we reserve the right to change these prices without notice, charging you the difference, which advance represents only the difference in cost to us. If the prices decline so that we can fill your order at a lower price than those printed in our Special Seed Catalogue, you will always get the benefit of such prices and the difference will be returned to you in cash.

TREES, SHRUBS AND PLANTS.

For the convenience of those of our customers who send to us for nearly all they buy, we have made arrangements with some of the largest and most reliable nurseries for our supply of trees, shrubs and perennial plants. From our Special Seed Catalogue, you can make your selections of trees, shrubs, etc., and send your order to us and we will have the stock sent you direct from the nursery.

REMEMBER.

We ship all orders for trees and shrubs direct from the nursery, fresh dug and carefully packed.

WRITE FOR OUR SPECIAL SEED CATALOGUE.

THESE TWO PAGES ARE MERELY TO INTRODUCE OUR NEW SEED DEPARTMENT to everyone who receives this catalogue. Our space to them all in this catalogue. We have prepared a very attractive and complete Special Seed Catalogue, and this catalogue will be sent to anyone by mail, postpaid, on application. **Write for our Free Seed Catalogue.** If you are interested in this line, if you use any seeds of any kind, don't fail to first write and get our Free Seed Catalogue before you place your order. We are sure that we can save you just as much money on your seed purchases as we can save you on any other line of merchandise, such as stoves, sewing machines, clothing, etc., depending on the amount of the purchase. You will find our prices throughout our Special Seed Catalogue just as much lower than the prices asked by seed houses generally or by retail dealers, as our prices on other lines of merchandise are lower than the prices asked by all other dealers.

YELLOWSTONE FLOWER SEED COLLECTION, 29 CENTS.

THE GREATEST BARGAIN IN FLOWER SEEDS EVER OFFERED.

Eighteen Varieties of the Most Beautiful Flowers of the Best and Most Popular Varieties, only 29 Cents.

1 package **Alyssum.**	1 package **Marigold.**	1 package **Phlox.**
1 package **Astor.**	1 package **Mignonette.**	1 package **Pink.**
1 package **Bachelor's Button.**	1 package **Mourning Bride.**	1 package **Poppy.**
1 package **Butterfly Flower.**	1 package **Nasturtium.**	1 package **Snap Dragon.**
1 package **Calliopsis.**	1 package **Pansy.**	1 package **Sweet Peas.**
1 package **Foxglove.**	1 package **Petunia.**	1 package **Verbena.**

REMEMBER—For only 29 cents, we will send you these eighteen separate packets of flower seeds as named above. This collection of pretty and easily grown annuals is made up of fresh, high grade seeds, packed in a neat lithographed carton. This collection cannot be broken under any condition.

No. 56C100 Yellowstone Flower Seed Collection. Price...............**29c**

If by mail, postage extra, 3 cents.

OUR ASTONISHING VEGETABLE SEED OFFER, YOUR GARDEN PLANTED FOR 33 CENTS.

REMEMBER, WE DO NOT ACCEPT ORDERS FOR LESS THAN 50 CENTS.

(SEE PAGE 2.)

If you want to take advantage of these three great bargains in seeds be sure to make your order 50 cents or more. Look over our other departments and include other needed goods with your order if you can use only one of these three seed offers.

SEROCO EXCELSIOR 33-CENT COLLECTION OF VEGETABLE SEEDS. Eighteen Varieties of Vegetable Seeds, 33 Cents. This Astonishing offer of the following:

1 package **Beet,** Crimson Globe	1 package **Lettuce,** Hanson	1 package **Radish,** Non Plus Ultra.
1 package **Cabbage,** Early Jersey Wakefield.	1 package **Melon,** Osage or Water Ice Cream.	1 package **Spinach,** Victoria.
1 package **Cabbage,** Holland Favorite.	1 package **Melon,** Musk, Rocky Ford.	1 package **Squash,** Hubbard.
1 package **Celery,** Golden Self Blanching.	1 package **Onion,** Yellow Globe Danvers.	1 package **Tomato,** Sparks' Earliana.
1 package **Carrot,** Guerand or Oxheart.	1 package **Onion,** Prize Taker.	1 package **Tomato,** Ponderosa.
1 package **Cucumber,** Evergreen, White Spine.	1 package **Parsnip,** Long White Dutch or Sugar.	1 package **Turnip,** Early White Milan.

THIS COLLECTION is made up of our highest grade seeds and costs more than double this amount if bought elsewhere. We cannot make any changes in this collection

No 56C110 Seroco Excelsior Vegetable Seed Collection. Price..**33c**

If by mail, postage extra, 5 cents.

COMBINATION FLOWER AND VEGETABLE SEED COLLECTION, 43 CENTS.

TWENTY-FIVE VARIETIES Valuable Vegetable and Beautiful Flower Seeds, for only 43 cents. Our special vegetable and flower collection. Never were reliable seeds offered at such a low price. It would cost you three times as much to buy these seeds elsewhere. Take advantage of this unusual offer by ordering now, twenty-five varieties of the best vegetable and flower seeds, at our low price, 43 cents. Seeds that grow.

VEGETABLES.

1 package **Beet,** Early Egyptian.	1 package **Onion,** Large Red Wethersfield.
1 package **Cabbage,** Early New Jersey Wakefield.	1 package **Parsnip,** Hollow Crown.
1 package **Celery,** White Plume.	1 package **Radish,** Early Scarlet, Wide Tipped.
1 package **Carrot,** Improved Long Orange.	1 package **Spinach,** Long Standing.
1 package **Cucumber,** Early Cluster.	1 package **Squash,** Mammoth Bush.
1 package **Lettuce,** Prize Head.	1 package **Turnip,** Early Snowball.
1 package **Melon,** Champion Market.	1 package **Tomato,** Dwarf Champion.

FLOWERS.

1 package **Aster.**	1 package **Pansy.**
1 package **Marigold.**	1 package **Pink.**
1 package **Petunia.**	1 package **Poppy.**
1 package **Phlox.**	1 package **Sweet Peas.**
1 package **Snap Dragon.**	1 package **Verbena.**
1 package **Calliopsis.**	

All of these twenty-five Vegetable and Flower Seeds only 43c.

REMEMBER—We cannot make a single change in this collection and no other varieties can be sold so cheap.

No. 56C120 Our Combination Flower and Vegetable Seed Collection. Price..**43c**

If by mail, postage extra, 6 cents.

able to middle-class women who now have smaller families and greater numbers of labor-saving devices in the home than they had earlier in the century. Leisure itself has come suddenly and as something of a shock to a hitherto pressed and hurrying country, and we do not yet know what to do with it or how to employ it. It is also the expression of an esthetic awakening on the part of many women and, if it is an awakening still clouded with drowsiness and obscured by remembrance of things past, it is nonetheless the mark of a healthful awareness that once did not exist. Women have become sensitive to the bleakness and ugliness of the towns and the homes in which they dwell, and of the dreariness of the streets that crisscross their town. They have found that extraordinary transformations may be wrought around unpainted, shabby houses by planting heavenly-blue morning glories to twine up their porches; that nasturtiums blooming in the window boxes of tenements relieve the grayness of their surroundings; that lonely cabins high in the Appalachians are gayer for dahlias blooming in the front yard.

It is indubitable, too, that the rose, like the horse, has played its part in social climbing. Many a small-town woman has used her garden to get into parlors she had never before entered. But the evidence is convincing that, apart from a few Mrs. Oscar B. Tutwilers and social climbers, interest in gardening, among the majority of women who practice it, is a healthy interest flowering out of a realization of the amenities it affords.

Part Three

GENTLEMEN

This section is devoted to the merchandise satisfactions of men. These satisfactions, by contrast with those of women, are pale and puny; they reflect creatures who, when compared with women, seem like primitives, still in a primitive state of development.

Here we begin with pistols—one of the male's imperative needs in 1905—and end with a study of the changing tools and the changing farm of the man on the land. But even the American male has his moments, and we consider him at play in a chapter on sports and sporting goods. Finally, because men must cover their nakedness and because the slowly changing wearing apparel of men affords some clues to the changing manners of this group of archconservatives, we have included two chapters on men's clothes.

This section is concerned with: pistols and sports and sporting goods; men's clothing and men's furnishings; tools, agricultural machinery, and the farm.

Andrew Jackson, seventh President of the United
States, had been living with his wife Rachel for two years
when they learned that her divorce from her first husband
was not valid. A proper decree was obtained, and they re-
married at once. Then he got out a pair of pistols, cleaned
and oiled them, and put them in condition to use upon the
first man who made a slighting remark about his wife.

These pistols were kept ready for use for 37 years. At
least twice they were used. The first time no one was hurt
except a bystander, presumably innocent, and he not badly.
But the second offender died. Therafter, people eschewed
reference to adultery when Andrew Jackson was within
earshot.*

PISTOL toting is an old American custom. There was a time
not so long ago in many parts of the country when men
carried pistols with the same nonchalance with which Eng-
lishmen carry umbrellas. And just as in the uncertain climate of England an umbrella may become necessary at any
moment, so, too, in the uncertain moral climate of America a
man could never know when he might need his pistol. Consequently, the citizen, particularly in the South and West,
would no more leave home without his pistol than without
his pants.

If the catalog is a criterion, the number of pistols in the
hands of the people in 1905 must have been enormous. It
devotes six pages to revolvers and revolver cartridges, and
that means sales running into thousands of pieces. By this
time, the frontier had already been practically closed for fif-

* Gerald W. Johnson, *Andrew Jackson, An Epic in Homespun.*

teen years (since 1890), but in many sections of the South and West, the law did not reach far from the county seats; the roads were poor; communications were uncertain; the lands were sparsely settled; pioneer habits of self-protection persisted, and men continued to be a law unto themselves. In many cases, the law itself, with its delays, circumlocutions, miscarriages of justice because of technicalities, and the high cost of litigation, frequently led to homicide. Typical of the point of view of the frontier—and its attitudes still persist in the South and West—was the action recently taken in the large city of El Paso, Texas, by an old rancher.

This man, well along in years, had lived for a long time on a small ranch near El Paso earning a meager living for himself and his wife. Then oil was discovered in his neighborhood, and a young lawyer of El Paso—we shall call him Suggs—hailed old man Edwards into his office and induced him to sign a document that swindled him out of his ranch. Edwards might have gone to the law, but he went instead to his pistol, put it in his pocket, and visited Suggs' office.

"Mr. Suggs," he said, "I've come to kill you. I hate to do it because I haven't killed a man since 1889, and I hate to kill you, but there just ain't anything else I can do. I'm an old man and you're about to put me and my wife in the poorhouse. I ain't got the money to go to law, and even if I did have it, it would be so long before the court decided that I'd be dead by then, so I'll just have to kill you and be done with it. Maybe it'll learn you a lesson."

The lawyer, who knew that the old man meant business, said he didn't have any intention of cheating Edwards out of his land, and that if he thought so he'd immediately give him back his deed to the ranch.

"No, sir," replied Edwards, "that ain't no good at all. I know you'll give me a deed and just as soon as I'm out of this office, you'll call Sheriff Jimmy Brown and tell Jimmy that you give me a deed under duress and not to record it. Then I'll just have to come back here and kill you anyhow, and I reckon I might as well do it now."

MERIDEN FIRE ARMS CO. LATEST MODEL REVOLVER

NOTICE TO PURCHASERS OF REVOLVERS AND PISTOLS.

We keep a record of the name, caliber and serial number of every revolver and pistol we sell, together with the name and address of the purchaser and the date of purchase. This record is open at all times to any accredited peace officer. We solicit only the trade of responsible and reputable persons who have a legitimate right to purchase and own a revolver or pistol. We particularly solicit the trade of policemen, sheriffs, deputies, constables, game wardens, forest rangers, express and bank messengers and sportsmen o' unquestionable charac

To enable us to properly discriminate in the filling of orders for revolvers or pistols, we m insist that purchasers comply with the following requests: Give age. (We do not sell to mino Give occupation. Give names of two citizens of your town as character references.

Automatic Shell Ejecting Double Action Revolver

Reliable, accurate, and sure fire. Made of the best material. Double action. Pulling the trigger automatically raises and trips the hammer and discharges the cartridge. Fitted with open rear sight and improved front sight. Accurately machined and handsomely finished. All parts are interchangeable and are guaranteed against defect in material or construction. This revolver fitted with pearl stocks looks very handsome. For cartridges see foot of page.

Catalog No.	Caliber	Length Barrel	No. of Shots	Wt., Oz.	PRICE, RUBBER STOCKS	
					Nickel Plated	Blued Finish
6V1111¼	32 C. F.	3 inches	5	12	$2.95	$3.20
6V1112¼	38 C. F.	3¼ inches	5	15	2.95	3.20
6V1115¼	32 C. F.	5 inches	5	15	$3.40	$3.65
6V1116¼	38 C. F.	5 inches	5	18	3.40	3.65

Shipping wts., 32-caliber, 1 to 1½ lbs.; 38-caliber 1⅜ to 1⅝ lbs.

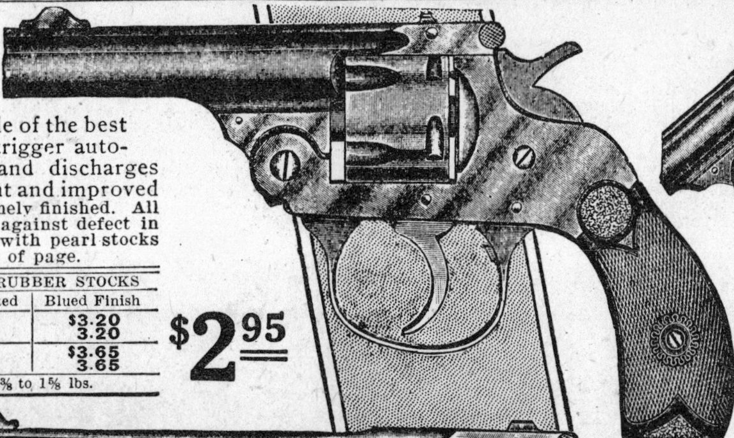

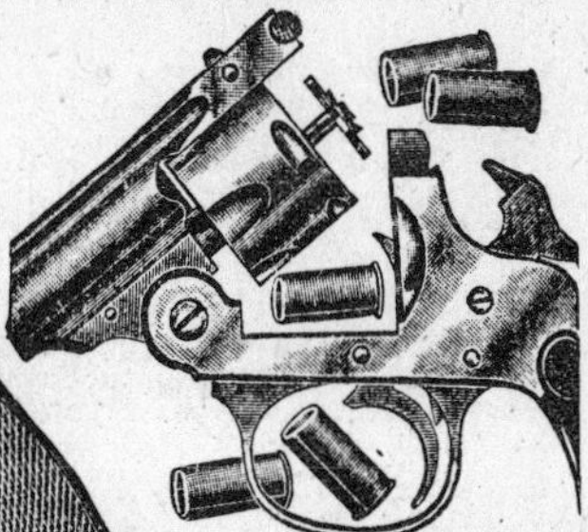

$2.95

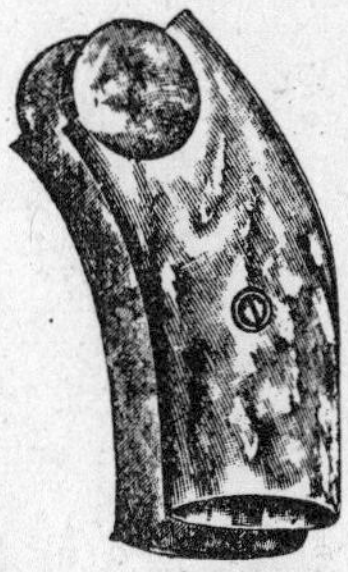

Pearl Stock
$1.25 Extr

Meriden Target Model Revolver

In answer to the demand for a special revolver for target shooting, we offer this Meriden improved model, fitted with automatic shell ejector and improved cylinder stop. Can be used as either a double or single action revolver. Furnished in blued or nickel plated finish. Fitted with special black rubber target stocks, extra long grip and large full butt 1¾ inches wide, having solid end extending ¾ inch over the frame; scored sides. Special attention is paid to alignment, balance and the securing of an ideal hang. The barrel is well rifled to insure the greatest possible accuracy and uniformity in shooting. This revolver is fitted with a new design front sight and an improved model rear sight. These features make this an ideal arm for target practice as well as one of the most practicable general purpose revolvers. For cartridges see foot of page.

Catalog No.	Caliber	Length of Barrel	No. of Shots	Wt., Oz.	PRICE	
					Nickel Plated	Blued Finish
6V1150¼	32	5 in.	5	15	$3.90	$4.15
6V1151¼	38	5 in.	5	18	3.90	4.15
6V1152¼	32	3 in.	5	12	$3.50	$3.75
6V1153¼	38	3¼ in.	5	15	3.50	3.75

Shipping weights, 32-caliber, 1⅜ to 1⅝ pounds; 38-caliber, 1⅝ to 1⅞ pounds.

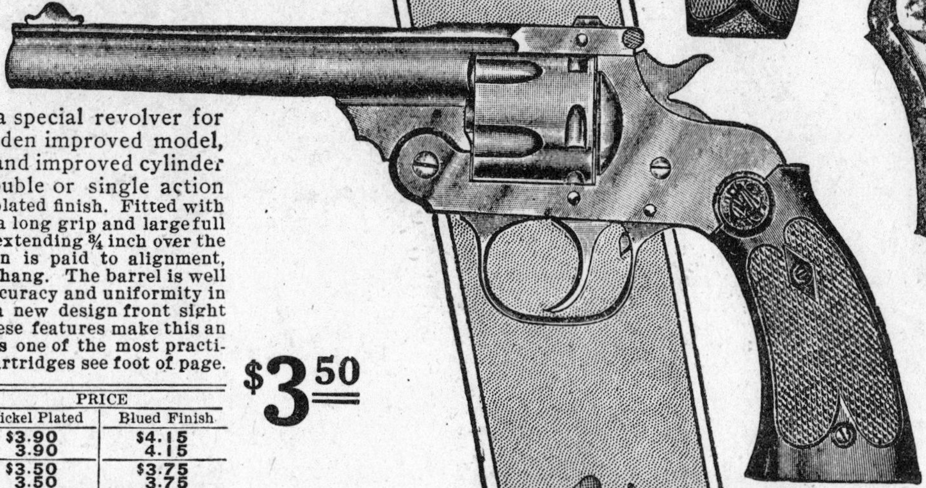

$3.50

Meriden Latest Model Hammerless Revolver

The Meriden Improved Model Hammerless Revolver is of practically the same construction as that above described. Guaranteed for accuracy, sure fire and penetration. Fitted with polished and scored black rubber stocks. Guaranteed equal in every way to any of the revolvers on the market selling at considerably more. The Meriden Fire Arms Co. revolvers are manufactured exclusively by us. We own the factory and control its entire output and our price is based on the actual cost of material and labor, making our price to you, quality considered, very low. For cartridges see foot of page.

Catalog No.	Caliber	Length of Barrel, Inches	Finish	Wt., Oz.	Price, Rubber Stocks
6V1141¼	32 C. F.	3	Nickel Plated	12	$3.50
6V1142¼	38 C. F.	3¼	Nickel Plated	15	3.50
6V1143¼	32 C. F.	3	Blued Steel	12	$3.75
6V1144¼	38 C. F.	3¼	Blued Steel	15	3.75

Shipping wts., 32-caliber, 1 lb. to 1 lb. 3 oz.; 38-caliber, 1 lb. 5 oz. to 1½ lbs.

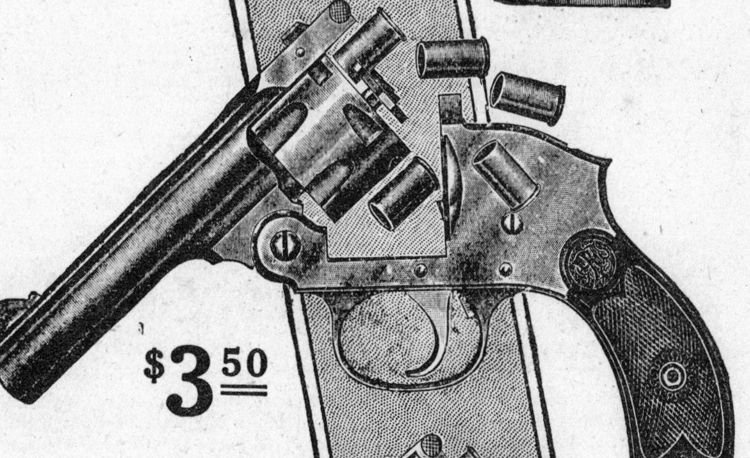

$3.50

Engraved Model Meriden Revolver

This is the same as our model No. 6V1111¼ above described, with the exception of the handsome hand engraving, as illustrated. This engraving is all done by hand by skilled artists. The illustration does not do it justice, as we cannot bring out the fine detail, but, nevertheless, it gives you a fair idea of the beautiful finish of this revolver. We can furnish it either blued or nickel plated and when fitted with pearl stocks (at an extra charge of $1.25) it presents a handsome appearance. For cartridges see foot of page.

Catalog No.	Caliber	Length of Barrel	Finished, All Hand Engraved	Number of Shots	Wt., Oz.	Price, Rubber Stocks
6V1121¼	32 C. F.	3 in.	Nickel Plated	5	12	$3.75
6V1122¼	38 C. F.	3¼ in.	Nickel Plated	5	15	3.75
6V1123¼	32 C. F.	3 in.	Blued Steel	5	12	$4.00
6V1124¼	38 C. F.	3¼ in.	Blued Steel	5	15	4.00

hipping wts., 32-caliber, 1⅛ lbs.; 38-caliber, 1⅜ lbs.

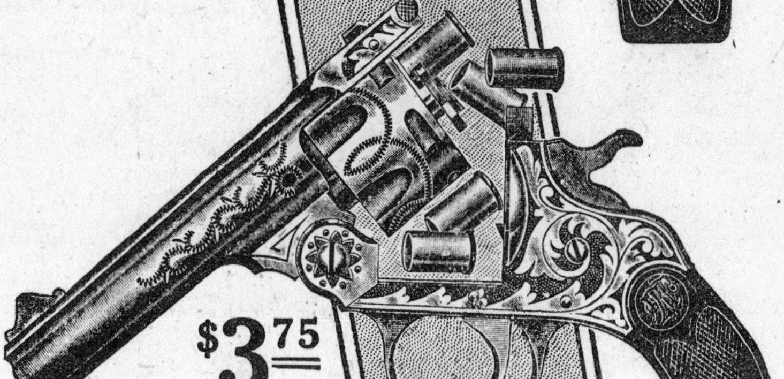

$3.75

Cartridges.

Catalog No.	Caliber	Price for 50	Price for 100
6V2377	32 S. & W.	36c	70c
6V2388	38 S. & W.	47c	92c

$2.75 BUYS OUR AUTOMATIC --SELF-- COCKING REVOLVER.

MANUFACTURED FOR US BY ANDREW FYRBERG & CO., HOPKINTON, MASS.

AT $2.75 we offer you from our own revolver factory, in Hopkinton, Mass., an automatic shell ejecting, double action, 32 or 38-caliber revolver, under our guarantee that it is superior in every way to automatic revolvers of other makes that sell at much higher prices. We established our own revolver factory at Hopkinton, Mass., for the sole purpose of turning out a uniformly higher grade revolver than those usually furnished by other makers, and yet at a cost to us that would enable us to supply our customers at a lower price than we could possibly supply other makes

MAKERS HAVE, in our judgment, for several years been asking too much money for revolvers. There has been too much profit to the manufacturer and too much profit to the retail dealer, and it was with a view of changing this condition, getting a lower cost and a lower price to our customers, and a better made revolver, that we have established our own revolver factory.

THE CUSTOMER who reads this description can have little idea of the effort and outlay of money necessary to produce such a revolver for $2.75. From the time the manager of this department conceived the idea of building a factory and making our own revolvers, nearly two years, we have been busy with a large force of men making special machines, getting out designs, making dies, jigs, gauges, tools, etc., before the first revolver could be produced.

IT HAS REQUIRED nearly two years time, a large force of mechanics and a big outlay of money to first build the equipment necessary to produce the finished revolver at the price. We are now fully equipped. Our revolver factory, like one of our gun factories, is also located in Hopkinton, Massachusetts, is in charge of one of the best revolver makers in the country. We have one of the most, if not the most modern, up to date revolver making plants in America. We have every facility for turning out the neatest, handsomest, most up to date design, best finished and best shooting revolver on the market and at the very lowest possible cost, and our special $2.75 price to you represents the net cost to us with but our one small percentage of profit added.

IF YOU WANT A REVOLVER you will find far greater value in one of our own make, one of the revolvers illustrated on this page, than in any other revolver made. This we positively guarantee. We will accept your order with the understanding that if the revolver is not perfectly satisfactory when received, if you are not convinced that it is the greatest revolver value offered by any house and in every way equal, and in many ways superior, to revolvers that sell at double the price, you can return it to us at our expense of express charges both ways, and we will immediately return your money.

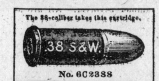

$2.75

FROM THE ILLUSTRATION, engraved by our artist from a photograph, you can get some idea of the general appearance of the revolver. This illustration shows the exact size of the 32-caliber revolver just as it appears in the photograph, but you must see, examine and compare the revolver with others to appreciate what we are turning out and how much money you save by sending your order to us.

WE HAVE ENDEAVORED to make this revolver superior to the regular line of automatic revolvers, not only in what we consider a handsomer design, a neater and better shape, and a more beautiful outline, but we believe we have the best shell extracting device, the best cylinder catch and barrel latch, the simplest, strongest and best self-cocking action that is produced on any revolver made, regardless of price, and you order one of these revolvers we leave it to you to be the judge. All are six shot and take center fire cartridges. Same size as Smith & Wesson revolvers. In our nickeling and bluing department we believe we get a finer finish

than is furnished on other revolvers. We have endeavored in this respect to turn out a revolver unexcelled, if equaled by any revolver made.

THESE REVOLVERS are made from the very finest decarbonized steel procurable. The cylinders are neatly fluted, the barrels are bored true to gauge and full rifled. They have the latest style high rib, as illustrated, are accurately sighted, made with handsome monogram rubber handle, neatly shaped trigger guard, trigger and hammer, a compact, well made and well finished automatic revolver, built with a view of combining the good qualities of all automatic revolvers with the defects of none, and yet offered at a price lower than offered by any other concern, a price that barely covers the cost of material and labor, with but our one small percentage of profit added, only $2.75.

OUR BINDING GUARANTEE. Each and every one of these revolvers is covered by our binding guarantee, by the terms and conditions of which we will replace or repair any part which may break within one year by reason of defective material or workmanship.

38-CALIBER CARTRIDGES		
91 CENTS Per 100		
☞ SEE PAGE 317. ☜		

The 38-caliber takes this cartridge.
.38 S&W
No. 6C2388

The 32-caliber takes this cartridge.
32 S&W
No. 6C2377

32-CALIBER CARTRIDGES		
70 CENTS Per 100		
☞ SEE PAGE 317. ☜		

No. 6C1161 32-caliber, 3-inch barrel, full nickel plated finish, rubber handles, 5-shot, weight, 12 ounces, shoots cartridge No. 6C2377. Price........$2.75
No. 6C1162 38-caliber, 3¼-inch barrel, full nickel plated finish, rubber handles, 5-shot, weight, 15 ounces, shoots cartridge No. 6C2388. Price....... 2.75
No. 6C1163 32-caliber, 3-inch barrel, blued steel finish, rubber handles, 5-shot, weight, 12 ounces, shoots cartridge No. 6C2377. Price............ 3.15
No. 6C1164 38-caliber, 3¼-inch barrel, blued steel finish, rubber handles, 5-shot, weight, 15 ounces, shoots cartridge No. 6C2388. Price............ 3.15

If by mail, postage extra, 32-caliber, 18 cents; 38-caliber, 22 cents.

OUR 5-INCH BARREL AUTOMATIC REVOLVER.

THE 5-INCH BARREL REVOLVER is made the same as our regular 3 and 3¼-inch revolver, except the length of barrel. A 5-inch barrel revolver is preferable for target shooting while the 3 or 3¼-inch barrel is used mostly for defense.

When ordering, write catalogue number in full and mention caliber, length of barrel and finish wanted. All these revolvers are 5-shot.

$3.25

Catalogue Number	Caliber	Length of Barrel	Finish	Handles	No. of Shots	Weight, ounces	Shoots Cartridge	Price
6C1165	32 C.F.	5 inches	Nickel Plated	Rubber	5-shot	15	6C2377	$3.25
6C1166	38 C.F.	5 inches	Nickel Plated	Rubber	5-shot	18	6C2388	3.25
6C1167	32 C.F.	5 inches	Blued Steel	Rubber	5-shot	15	6C2377	3.65
6C1168	38 C.F.	5 inches	Blued Steel	Rubber	5-shot	18	6C2388	3.65

If by mail, postage extra, 32-caliber, 22 cents; 38-caliber, 26 cents.

ON RECEIPT OF $1.00 we will send any revolver by express, C. O. D., subject to examination, balance to be paid after the revolver is received and found perfectly satisfactory. We recommend, however, that you send cash in full with your order and save the small extra charge which the express companies ask on a C. O. D. shipment. Nearly all our customers send cash in full with their orders.

OUR PEARL HANDLE AUTOMATIC REVOLVER.

THIS IS OUR REGULAR AUTOMATIC REVOLVER, as illustrated and described on this page, but fitted with first quality pearl handles instead of rubber handles.

When ordering, write catalogue number in full and mention caliber, length of barrel and finish wanted.

If by mail, postage extra, 22 to 25 cents.

$3.75

Catalogue Number	Caliber	Length of Barrel	Finish	Handles	No. of Shots	Weight, ounces	Shoots Cartridge	Price
6C1161P	32 C.F.	3 inches	Nickel Plated	Pearl	5-shot	12	6C2377	$3.75
6C1162P	38 C.F.	3¼ inches	Nickel Plated	Pearl	5-shot	15	6C2388	3.75
6C1163P	32 C.F.	3 inches	Blued Steel	Pearl	5-shot	12	6C2377	4.15
6C1164P	38 C.F.	3¼ inches	Blued Steel	Pearl	5-shot	15	6C2388	4.15
6C1165P	32 C.F.	5 inches	Nickel Plated	Pearl	5-shot	15	6C2377	4.25
6C1166P	38 C.F.	5 inches	Nickel Plated	Pearl	5-shot	18	6C2388	4.25
6C1167P	32 C.F.	5 inches	Blued Steel	Pearl	5-shot	15	6C2377	4.65
6C1168P	38 C.F.	5 inches	Blued Steel	Pearl	5-shot	18	6C2388	4.65

All this very quietly, without rancor on the part of the old man, but with apparently unshakable determination to go ahead with his murdering. The lawyer, however, pleaded and begged for his life. Edwards finally took his word that he would give him a deed and say nothing to the sheriff. In a few minutes, he marched out of the office with the document in his pocket and went to the courthouse to record it. On arriving there, he found the sheriff waiting for him on the steps.

"Ned," said the sheriff, "Joe Suggs just told me on the phone that you said if he didn't give you a deed to your property and let him record it, you'd kill him."

"And what did you tell him?" asked the old man.

"I told him I thought you would," replied the sheriff.

Whereupon the rancher went into the courthouse, recorded his deed, and returned to his wife and his lands.

If homicides sometimes arise from the inadequacies or the delays of the law—and not all cases end as happily as this Texas case—they arise also from unwritten codes of honor—particularly in the South and West. In these sections, it was almost obligatory upon a man to kill his wife's lover. If, instead of resorting to his pistol, he had resorted to the courts and sued the lover for the alienation of his wife's affections, he would have been laughed out of the community. So, too, he was called upon to fight or to kill if another man called him a son of a bitch or impugned his honor in general. And on the other side, women, instead of going to Reno when they found that their husbands were having a love affair with another woman, were likely to go to the hardware store, buy a pistol, and shoot the other woman full of holes. In these cases, the approval of the community was manifested by the fact that the killer rarely, if ever, went to jail, and frequently was not even arrested or subjected to any annoyance greater than a perfunctory hearing before a sympathetic justice of the peace.

The absence of effective libel laws in this country has also resulted in many killings, especially of local politicians in the

South and the West. It is, of course, a monstrous thing that these gentry are permitted to go about the country assassinating the characters of honest men, libeling and lying about them, without any curb whatsoever upon their clattering tongues. But often the curb has been applied in the form of a Colt's .45, and it is still occasionally applied, although, in the South, some concession to the softness of modern times is made. Warnings now often precede shootings—warnings in the form of newspaper notices to a politician that if he persists in lying about Joe Jones on the public platform Joe will kill him at sight. These notices are usually sufficient to reduce the flow of slander to a reasonable volume.

This, however, must be remembered. Whatever the state of the law, whatever the degree of civilization or settlement in a community, we are the most lawless and violent people in the world, with our violence expressing itself so frequently in homicide that we lead all other nations in this category of crime. And the common instrument of homicide is the pistol.

Nowadays we associate killings with the brawls and battles of frontier mining camps and cattle towns, and they certainly contributed their share to our bloody legend. But the farther we recede in time from frontier days, the higher goes our homicide rate. According to Hoffman, an authority on American homicide statistics, the rate for thirty-one cities, with a total population of 25,000,000 in 1930, rose from 5.1 per 100,000 in 1900 to 10.9 in 1930. The Wickersham Commission estimated 8,720 homicides for the whole country in 1930.

The homicide industry is at its lowest ebb in the industrial New England states; at its highest point in the agricultural Southern states. This is in keeping with what seems almost a universal law of crime throughout the world: the homicidal tendency is greatest in warm countries. In our own South, the high rate of killing is given a sharp boost by the large percentage of Negroes in the population, whose unhappy distinction it is that they excel their white competitors in murder and manslaughter by a ratio of seven to one. It must be noted, however, that the homicidal tendencies of Negroes are not confined to Southern Negroes but apply to Northern Negroes as well, both in rural and urban areas. Whether the high homicide rate of Negroes arises, as some investigators maintain, from repressions suffered at the hands of whites which cause them to become violent and express their violence in murder (usually against their own brethren), or whether it arises from a complex of other causes, is a moot point. In the state of Mississippi, we see the homicide rate responding to the law of warm countries, and we note the effect upon it of its Negro group which makes up more than one half of the total population. L. J. Folse, executive director of the Mississippi State Planning Commission, has issued a report in which he describes Mississippi as the world's leading center of crime:

> There is no place in the world where homicides are more prevalent than in Mississippi. In 1935 the homicide rate in Mississippi was higher than the homicide rate of any other country in the world. . . . Such a record is an indictment of the state. In 1935 there were 535 homicides in Mississippi, with the homicide rate of 26.2 for 100,000 population. Florida, with a homicide rate of 25.1 was second to Mississippi, and New Hampshire with a homicide rate of 1.0 was the lowest among the states. It is interesting to note that the homicide rate in Mississippi was 26 times greater than that of Maine.

The whites of the South, while committing their share of shootings and killings, often encourage Negroes to follow in their footsteps. "Negroes are frequently released from jail when an important white man telephones to protest that 'you got a nigger of mine in jail there, and I wish you'd let him come on back home and finish picking his crop.' That frequently marks the end of the case. It often happens, too, that when a Negro sharecropper shoots or stabs another on the plantation premises, he is never arrested or molested by officers of the law. The planter is not willing to lose the services of a good worker, and in any event, he feels that violence among Negroes is naturally to be expected, is of no moral or social consequence whatsoever, and the whole affair is soon forgotten. Obviously, this encourages crime among Negroes." *

Many Southern Negroes attach themselves, in the feudal manner, to a white man for protection. They are certain that their "white folks" are all-powerful men whose voices could make kings and potentates, as well as sheriffs, tremble. Without question, they believe, the white protector can get "his niggers" out of jail at any time anywhere in the world. The result, of course, is that these Negroes, believing themselves immune from the law, are much more likely to commit a homicide than a Negro who has no white folks. An incident occurred in Vicksburg a few years ago which, although it ended peacefully enough, illustrates at once the attitude of Southern Negroes toward their white folks and their profound reverence for "de Law" in the person of a policeman.

A Memphis banker by the name of Saunders drove from his home to Vicksburg, a distance of about 250 miles, with his Negro chauffeur, Son James. On the return trip, Mr. Saunders asked Son what he had done in Vicksburg. Son said: "Well, suh, w'en I lef' you de other night, I went to git me some vittles. I went at de café an' w'en I come in I heard a rattlin' an' went out in de back. It was a big nigger on de flo' huntin' for a nine. Naw, suh, I didn't git in de game. Dem niggers had too many diffunces [razors].

"I come on out front an' wuz drinkin' me a soda-pop an' talkin' to a cullud lady w'en a white po-liceman come in. He say, 'Nigger, what you doin' here?' I say, 'I come to Vicksburg drivin' my boss-man.' 'Who is yo' boss-man?' I say it was you, Mr. Saunders, what's at de bank. I say he had shorely heard tell of you. He didn't say no mo', an' I didn't say no mo'. Jes' kep' a-talkin' to de cullud lady.

"One of my foots was kinder 'vanced out in front of de other an' de po-liceman he was spittin' 'baccer juice on it. I kep' on drinking my pop an' de po-liceman he kep' a-spittin'

* David L. Cohn, *God Shakes Creation*, p. 158.

an' a-spittin' on my foot." Mr. Saunders asked him why he did not pull his foot out of the tobacco-juice stream. "Naw, suh," Son replied, "I wasn't goin' to pull in *my* foot whilst de Law was spittin' on it."

Another reason, perhaps, for the frequency of homicide in the South is the leniency of punishment. Men are rarely hanged for murder. Prison sentences are seldom entirely served. In Mississippi, for example, the average time actually served on a life sentence is seven years.

Thus the homicide capital of the United States in 1930 was not New York or Chicago, despite their widely publicized gang killings. It was Memphis. While New York had a homicide rate of 7.1 per 100,000 of population and Chicago 14.4, Memphis left them far in the rear with its prodigious rate of 58.8. One's chances, therefore, of coming to a violent end were almost eight times greater in Memphis than New York and about four times greater than in Chicago. Consequently, Memphis was equally desirable for the man who wanted to enter the cotton business or the Nietzschean disciple anxious to "live dangerously."

Rural Crime

"Rural residence," says Dr. Earnest A. Hooton, "puts a premium upon physical hardihood and restricts the choice of crime. Countrymen are prone to violence against persons, partly because of their physical equipment and partly because rustic life affords few opportunities for acquisitive offense. In general, one must rape, murder, or behave."

In the light of this theory, it is illuminating to look at the ledgers of the Mississippi State Penitentiary in 1935, containing the records of 787 prisoners committed from the rich Delta agricultural section of the state. They were serving sentences for the following crimes:

Murder	304
Manslaughter	92
Burglary	149
Burglary and larceny	70

Grand larceny 69
Assault and battery with intent to kill 46
Robbery 19
Forgery 8
Arson 3
Attempt to rape 4
Rape 1
Violating age of consent 1
Obtaining property under false pretense 3
Attempt to commit robbery 2
Aiding jail breaks 3
Robbery with firearms 2
Highway robbery 5
Possessing stolen goods 1
Distilling 1
Counterfeiting 2
Uttering forgery 2

Thus, more than one half of this group, or 396 persons, were in prison for homicides; 447 had committed crimes against the person, and even the crimes against property usually took the violent forms of robbery and burglary.

"The Right of the People to Bear Arms"

The second article of the Bill of Rights says: "A well-regulated Militia, being necessary to the security of a free State, the right of the people to keep and bear Arms, shall not be infringed."

In 1905, this seems to have been interpreted in many sections of the country to mean the right to keep weapons open or concealed. In any event, it is certain that Sears at that period sold pistols with no strings attached. No questions were asked. No permits from law officers were necessary. Pistols were sold as freely and with as little formality as rice and sugar.

As cheap as they were, however, other lethal weapons offered by the catalog were still cheaper. Pistols had certain disadvantages which might have shocked some delicate and sensitive maimers and killers. Guns made loud, vulgar noises when fired; they made messes of their victims. For men who desired to knock out their enemies without noise and with a minimum of messiness, the catalog offered three kinds of shot-filled billies. The golden mean seems to have been "Leather Billy, sewed down the side, loaded with shot, made

Every Man a King

of the best material, and cannot be equaled at the price. Length, 9 inches. Weight, about 9 ounces. Price, 35¢."

Straight and Fancy Shooting

For the benefit, presumably, of the younger generation toting pistols for the first time on their unaccustomed hips, the catalog lays down a few instructions in nontechnical language:

"When testing a revolver always take a muzzle rest, and shoot 5 or 6 consecutive shots at a bull's eye without stopping, then examine your target and see how the shots group and how near the group is to your bull's eye. This will give you an idea whether you should hold high, low, to the right or to the left of your mark. . . . In order to become an expert shot it is quite necessary for you to become acquainted with the revolver you intend to shoot. . . ."

Yes, Sir, She's My Baby

The affection in which good men once held their pistols is shown by the name of one of the catalog's models: OUR

The Voice of Experience

BABY HAMMERLESS REVOLVER. Our Baby was a cozy little trick with a long stock and a short barrel that a man could keep snug and warm in his vest pocket. But this mere child, only four inches long and selling for $1.80, could spit fire and lead just as effectively as its bigger brothers.

It was, however, but one of a number of vest-pocket revolvers that were so common that it must have been difficult in 1905 to know whether a man was reaching for a fountain pen to sign a contract or for a pistol with which to sign a death warrant. Gallantry dictated, of course, that the ladies be protected, but, when gentlemen were not present to protect them, they could rely confidently on Harrington & Richardson's Young America, Ladies' Revolver. Ladies, in the American legend, are notoriously accurate pistol shots, but, since neither the demands of protecting honor nor of accuracy could interfere with the stern necessities of chic, Young America was made with admirable compactness that prevented an unsightly bulge when worn to picnics or dinners. "It can be carried in the vest pocket as conveniently as a watch."

"But You Can't Pass My Thirty-eight"

In that deathless mountain ballad, "Love, O Love, O Faithless Love," the lady who was wronged sings of vengeance and the lover who abandoned her in these lines:

> *You pass my door, you pass my gate,*
> *But you can't pass my thirty-eight.*

Our Baby and revolvers of the same ilk were merely, so to speak, household instruments for easy shooting in and around the home. But when serious business was ahead, when the game was big and tough, men (and women) wanted pistols that, in the apt phrase, "spoke with authority." And the catalog provided them.

Our $3.65 Frontier Revolver, a portable cannon, belonged in the category of stern weapons. It was a .44-caliber six-shooter, for "large and strong shooting," and ingeniously constructed so that, if the battle became hot and you ran out of pistol cartridges, you could reload with rifle ammunition and keep going.

This gun, however, was just a mere killing weapon, good enough for ordinary bank robbers or crude deputy sheriffs. Men who loved the beauty of firearms would not have them, and the fact is that throughout the ages craftsmen have lavished extraordinary skill and care on instruments of death. The swords of Toledo and Damascus; the kris of the Malay; the intricately chased steel barrels and silver-inlaid stocks of flintlock rifles, and the beautiful Belgian and English shotguns of our times testify to man's love of beauty in his weapons. For connoisseurs of the pistol in the United States, the catalog provided one that was both decorative and useful. It was Colt's Special Pearl Handle Revolver. "Cowboy's

Cowboy Jewelry

Six Shooter with pearl handles. The right handle has an Ox Head carved in raised design and makes a handsome revolver. Weight 41 ounces. Price $20.00."

The Times Change

As we have seen, no permit to buy a pistol from Sears was necessary in 1905. Ten years afterward, in 1915, it was still possible to buy a gun without a permit, but the catalog contains this:

NOTICE TO PURCHASERS

We keep a record of the name, caliber and serial number of every revolver and pistol we sell, together with the name and address of the purchaser and the date of purchase. This record is open at all times to any accredited peace officer. We solicit only the trade of responsible and reputable persons who have a legitimate right to purchase and own a revolver or pistol. We particularly solicit the trade of policemen, sheriffs, constables, game wardens, forest rangers, express and bank messengers and sportsmen of unquestionable character.

To enable us to properly discriminate in the filling of orders for pistols, we must insist that purchasers comply with the following requests: Give age. (We do not sell to minors.) Give occupation. Give name of two citizens of your town as character witnesses.

These provisions were not sufficiently stringent to prevent anybody from acquiring a pistol through the mails, but it is significant that the pistol business had sharply dwindled since 1905. The six pistol pages of the catalog have now shrunk to only three pages, and 1915 was moving fast toward 1917, when millions of American boys would have the best pistols that money could buy put in their hands free of charge by the United States itself.

Sears continued, however, to sell pistols until the spring of 1924. The catalog of that year gives no explanation why this action was taken, but it seems there were three reasons: One, the Company desired to co-operate with the law-enforcement agencies of the country; two, Sears was receiving a certain amount of unfavorable publicity due to the fact that when a shooting occurred the newspapers frequently stated that the weapon used was a "cheap mail-order pistol"; three, the difficulty of adhering to the many local pistol regulations that had come into force throughout the nation.

The year 1924, therefore, saw the extinction of what had been considered an inalienable right of the freeborn American: the right to order his pistol along with his shoes and plow points. Along with the abolition of this right, there seems to have gone the quenching of the last fitful fires of the pioneer spirit. Hereafter, if a man should be called a son of a bitch, he would assert that this was a biological impossibility; if slandered by a lying politician, he would sue for slander; if another man ran off with his wife, he would bring an action for alienation of affections.

THE oldest and most widespread forms of American sports are fishing and hunting. From the time the first settlers landed to this day, Americans, more than any other civilized people in the world, have been a race of hunters and fishermen. The pioneers, it is true, hunted and fished more for food than for fun, but the urge to kill game and catch fish is still strong in Americans when the necessity to do so for a livelihood has long passed. Nowadays, about seven million men annually procure hunting and fishing licenses, while untold thousands avoid this formality but take to the fields and the streams just the same. So strong indeed is the hunting instinct in Americans that, throughout the small towns and in rural areas, the standard present for parents to give a young boy is a shotgun or a .22-caliber rifle. The curious but unintended consequence is that nonmilitary America possesses vast numbers of men who acquired a familiarity with firearms in their youth, and who may be of much importance to the country in time of war.

It is one of the miracles of America that, despite its enormous industrialization, it still contains a large variety of game in abundance, while, strangely enough, some of the most heavily industrialized states afford excellent shooting and fishing. Thus, both New York and Pennsylvania are famous for deer shooting, and almost within sight of the busy cities of New Jersey one may find good pheasant hunting. At the other end of the country, wild duck are shot within forty-five minutes' ride of the main street of New Orleans.

It is also a uniquely American phenomenon that this is the

only heavily populated country in the world where the poor man may shoot or fish without let or hindrance. In Europe, these have been the sports of the rich who maintained private game preserves over which none but the owner and his guests could shoot or fish, and stringent poaching laws kept out the poor intruder. But in the United States, the humblest Southern Negro, the Iowa farm boy, the Pittsburgh clerk, may pick up his rod or rifle and find a place to pursue his pleasures unmolested. Some of the states, moreover, have set aside public game preserves open to all citizens; have erected lodges where guests may stay at reasonable rates, and they supply boats and guides. Louisiana, for example, maintains such a preserve near the mouth of the Mississippi where one may get some of the best wild-fowl shooting and fishing in America.

Hunting and fishing may therefore be said to be the classical sports of Americans, and the catalog's pages teem in consequence with the guns, rods, and other paraphernalia used by hunters and fishermen.

The Guns and Rods of 1905

The catalog of 1905 devotes the enormous space of fourteen pages to shotguns, and so intense was the interest of prospective purchasers that thousands of words in tiny type were devoted to describing a single shotgun in infinite detail. The barrels, the frame, the action, the stock, the shooting qualities were gone into at great length. Americans, whatever their impulsiveness in other fields, took their shotguns seriously. And it was not enough to stock merely the multitudinous varieties of guns made in America. The catalog offers also "Our Line of Imported Double Barrel Shotguns. . . . It embraces the products of some of the best European makers. . . . All our imported guns are tested by the government of Belgium. . . ."

The purchaser could choose from a wide variety of hammer and hammerless shotguns, single, double-barrel, or repeating, at prices ranging from $2.98 for The Long Range Winner to $33.50 for a Winchester trap gun.

The Long Range Winner was "one of the highest grade automatic shell ejecting, single barrel breech loading shotguns made for white or black powder."

From Europe came "The Belgian Muzzle Loading Double Barrel Shotgun, $6.98. Our Bar Lock Gun has genuine patent breech, genuine twist barrels, case hardened bar lock plates, checkered pistol grip stock, wood ramrod, German silver escutcheons, iron butt plate, case hardened and blued mountings. Made in 12 and 14-gauge, 34 inch barrels; weight 7½ to 8 pounds. . . ."

The catalog offers another gun which is no longer manufactured in this country, although old ones are still to be found in remote rural districts. This was "Giant 8-Gauge Goose Gun, 36-Inch Barrels. Weight 12 to 14 pounds." Such a gun was in reality a small cannon which could be fired only by a powerful man because of its tremendous recoil. It was a favorite gun of wild-fowl-market hunters who could kill or cripple as many as fifty wild ducks with it at one time when they fired into the great flocks that were so common in the United States forty to thirty years ago.

Among the better-quality guns listed in 1905 was "Model 1897. Latest Repeating Shotgun Made. This Gun Is Known As The Winchester Pump Gun. Best gun made for ducks, chickens or partridges. . . . Number of shots, 6. Price $17.82."

Rifles

It is seldom that the catalog lists an article and then goes out of its way to urge the customer *not* to buy it. Yet this is what it did in the case of the $2.20 Remington System Flobert Rifle. In a boxed notice, the customer is told that "We Do Not Recommend Nor Guarantee Flobert Rifles. Buy a good rifle. It will pay you in the end. . . ."

Recommended and guaranteed rifles were sold at prices ranging from $2.50 for "The Genuine New Pieper, just the rifle for squirrels, rabbits and small game," to "Winchester Model 1894 Repeating Rifles at $14.75."

The Pioneer Tradition in 1905

Rifle cartridges and shotgun shells—measured by today's prices—were cheap in 1905. For example, Sears sold a box of twenty-five smokeless shells (12 gauge) for forty-seven cents as against the 1939 price of $1.05. But in 1905, the pioneer tradition of a man loading his own cartridges and shells was still alive, and the catalog devotes two pages to tools and materials necessary for this purpose. Here everything for shell making is sold except gunpowder, which Sears was forbidden by law to sell.

Listed, however, were: apothecaries' scales for weighing smokeless powder; shot and bar lead; empty shells and cartridges; reloading tools; dippers for running bullets; melting pots; bullet molds; shell crimpers; gun wads; primers and gun caps, and shell-loading blocks.

American boys have read many stirring stories of the pioneer hastily reloading his long rifle from his powder horn as the Indians swarmed to the attack, or how the powder horns of the Americans ran out on Bunker Hill. By 1905, the pioneer and the Indians and the powder horns were gone, but the catalog is still offering the modern version of the horn in the form of "Powder Flasks. Holding 8 ounces of black powder, with cord, common top. Price 24¢." And accompanying the flasks, "Leather Shot Pouches, for holding 2½ to 3 pounds shot. Price, 45¢."

Hunting Accessories

Perhaps the sole indigenous form of sculpture that has ever existed in America was the making of wood decoys. By 1905, this seems, however, to have become a lost art. The job was then being done by factories, and the catalog offers "Cedar Wood Decoy Ducks. . . . Great care has been used to select only sound white cedar for their construction and to secure a perfect balance. They are light, substantial and naturally painted." Many a duck hunter, in the excitement of the sport, has shot his own decoys but, says the catalog, "They will not sink if you shoot them. $2.50 and $3.70 per dozen. Each dozen contains 8 drakes and four females."

Some wild birds may be lured by calls, and so the catalog lists duck, turkey, wild-geese and -duck, and snipe callers. The farmer troubled by hawks is offered "Our Hawk Call, 45 Cents. . . . It is designed and manufactured by a man who has had much trouble by hawks killing his chickens, and the hawk caller pays for itself many times over every time a hawk is killed. . . ."

Skiing in 1905

Skiing has recently become fashionable in America and highly publicized. It is generally assumed, too, that the use of skis is almost new in this country. But in 1905, the catalog lists "Ski or Norwegian Snow Shoes. Our Expert Ski, made especially for us in accordance with suggestions made by expert ski men. The Expert Ski are broad in the front and curved a little at the side in the center of the ski, to facilitate turning without lifting the ski. The bottom is grooved. They are hand shaved and oiled . . . are made of the best white ash. . . ." Then the catalog adds a sentence which indicates that a number of manufacturers were making skis in 1905. "We consider ash better adapted for work of this kind than any of the cheaper woods used by various manufacturers in making these goods. Our 9½-foot Expert Ski, Price, per pair, $4.95."

Indian snowshoes, too, were in common use in 1905. The catalog describes: "Snow Shoes. Genuine Indian Made. . . . Strung with the best cariboo gut and furnished with tough moosehide thongs, we are offering this top notch snow shoe, the best made anywhere, for $3.00."

Fishing in 1905

The catalog presents its fishing-tackle department in 1905 with these words: "We carry an assortment of the highest grade fishing tackle to supply the wants of anglers of all kinds. We do not handle the cheap grade of tackle which has no practical value, but have selected our line with considerable care and handle only the very best of the hundreds of rods, reels, hooks, lines and baits on the market. There are hundreds of baits and specialties in fishing tackle on the market, but very few which have practical merit, and you can rest assured that any article you select from this catalogue is exactly as represented, is full value for the money, and fully answers the purpose for which it is intended."

Then follow five pages of fishing tackle, listing hundreds of items which do not materially differ from those sold today.

Golf

An English visitor to the United States in the 1890's wrote: *

> There is perhaps no game that requires more patience to acquire satisfactorily than golf, and the preliminary steps cannot be gobbled. It is therefore doubtful whether the game will ever become extensively popular in a country with so much nervous electricity in the air. . . . The skill already attained by the best American players is simply marvelous; and it seems by no means beyond the bounds of possibility that the open champion of (say) 1902 . . . may be trained on American soil. The natural impatience of the active-minded American makes him at present very apt to neglect the etiquette of the game. The chance of being "driven into" is much larger on the Western side of the Atlantic . . . and it seems almost impossible to make Brother Jonathan replace that divot!

Twenty-five years later, when the 1905 catalog appeared, golf had already become a popular game in the United States, but it was still played largely by the urban and the wealthy. The game is not mentioned in the catalog of 1905. "The history of American recreation for the half century after 1870," says Faulkner, "is largely a story of urban amusement. The rural population had little time or energy left over for recre-

* Muirhead, *Land of Contrasts.*

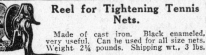

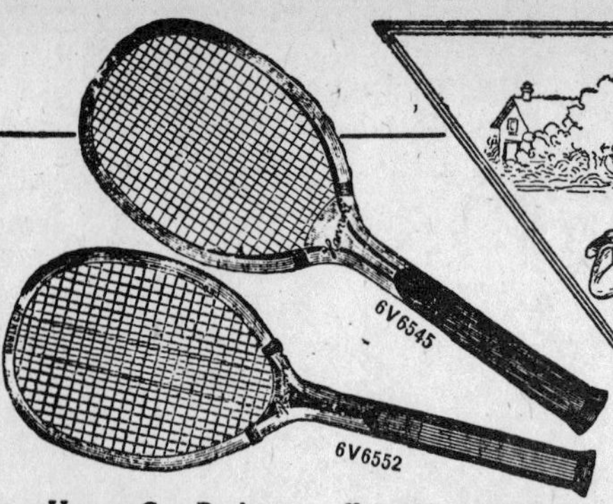

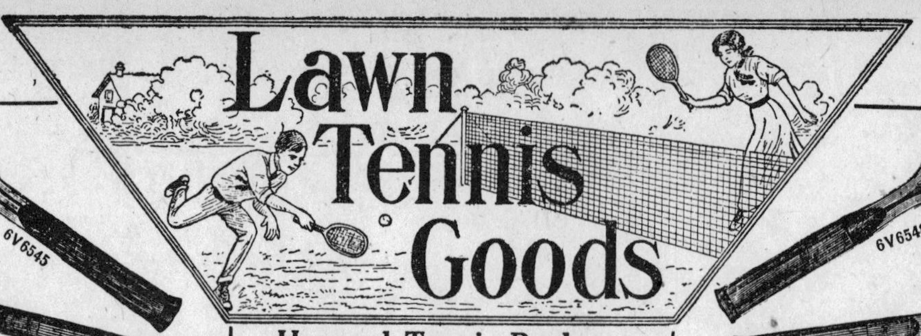

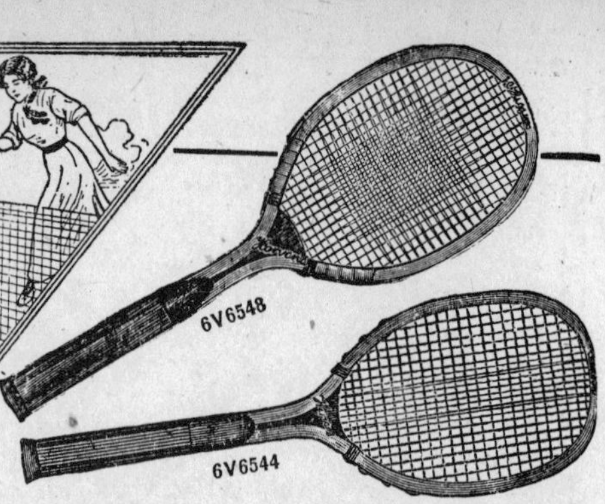

Harvard Tennis Rackets.

Sold Exclusively by Us.

The Harvard Tennis Rackets are of the latest popular shapes and models. Well balanced. Selected second growth ash frames. Laminated throats, combed cedar handles, and strings of best quality gut. We guarantee the Harvard Rackets to be unexcelled in finish, fitting, swing and balance, and that our prices are one-third lower than you would have to pay for corresponding quality and grade elsewhere.

Homan Cup Racket.

This racket is a new departure in many features of construction. The concave throat is lined with a curved reinforced strip, which extends upward, strengthening the shoulders of the frame. The racket is also wound at shoulders with light weight gut to reinforce frame and throat, and to overcome excess vibration. Extra large grip handle. Perfectly strung with best quality medium weight English gut. A rubber moisture proof envelope furnished with each racket. Furnished in 13, 13½, 14 and 14½-ounce weights. **State weight desired.** Shipping weight, 1¾ pounds.

No. 6V6552 Price.**$5.85**

Improved Volley Racket.

Full size highly polished head; is made from selected second growth ash, shoulders wrapped with tape at throat, five-piece walnut and maple throat, polished and scored cedar handle, closely strung with a fine quality imported gut, leather capped and well balanced. A racket suitable for amateur or expert work. Furnished in 13 to 14½-ounce weights. **Give weight wanted.** Shipping weight, 1¾ pounds.

No. 6V6543 Price.**$2.40**

Harvard Improved Expert Racket.

Made of selected straight grain air dried ash, with extra reinforced walnut strips on the inside running from bottom of throat to center of racket, with a five-piece white holly throat. Wound at shoulders next to throat with light weight gut to insure great strength. Full size head, finely beveled, hand polished, white ivory finish. Neatly scored genuine cedar handle, leather butt. These rackets are made by experts and every attention is paid to balance, swing and hang. Very closely strung in center, giving great driving power. Furnished in 13, 13½, 14 and 14½-ounce weights. **State weight desired.** Shipping weight, 1¾ pounds.

No. 6V6545 Price.**$4.20**

Glencoe Tennis Racket.

Regulation size, made of selected second growth ash, five-piece hardwood and maple throat; cedar handle, leather capped; closely strung with best clear gut; nicely finished and polished, and well balanced. A good, serviceable racket at a low price. Furnished in 12½ to 14½-ounce weights. **State weight desired.** Shipping weight, 1 pound 9 ounces.

No. 6V6536 Price.**$1.30**

Lawn Tennis Nets.

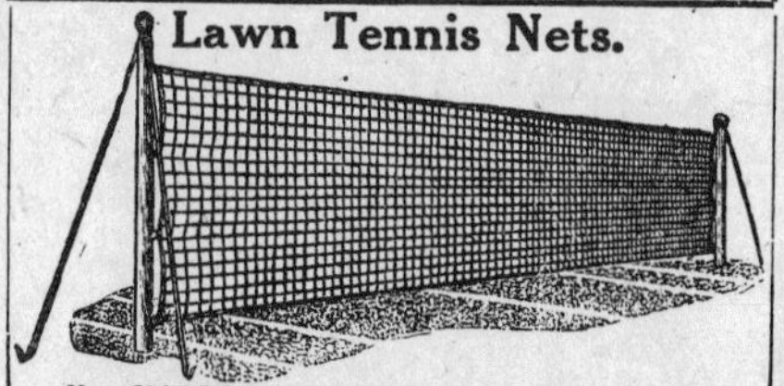

No. 6V6601 Tennis Net, 27x3 feet, 12-thread. Shipping wt., 1 pound 15 ounces. Price......**72c**

No. 6V6602 Tennis Net, 36x3 feet, 15-thread. Shipping weight, 2½ pounds. Price........**$1.12**

No. 6V6603 Tennis Net, 36x3 feet, 15-thread, canvas bound. Shipping wt., 3½ lbs. Price.**$1.38**

No. 6V6604 Tennis Net, 42x3 feet, 15-thread, canvas bound. Shipping wt., 3½ lbs. Price.**$1.56**

No. 6V6605 Double Center Net, 42x3 feet, 21-thread, hand made, canvas bound. Weight, packed, about 6¼ pounds. Price..............**$3.25**

No. 6V6606 Back Stop Net, to prevent balls from rolling out of grounds, 50x8 feet, 12-thread. Weight, packed, about 6¼ pounds. Price...**$2.13**

J. C. Higgins Professional Racket.

Intended especially for professional tournament use. The frame is made of the finest straight grain, two-year air dried white ash; heavy shoulders, reinforced with silk tape wrappings. Full size oval shaped head, five-piece walnut and maple throat, finely scored cedar handle with leather butt. A feature of this racket is the double mesh stringing in the center. The mesh in the center is ⅛-inch, instead of the ordinary ⅜ or ½-inch mesh, giving double the resiliency and driving power. The racket is hand polished. Every racket guaranteed perfect balance. Furnished in 13, 13½, 14 and 14½-oz. weights. **Give weights desired.** Shipping wt., 1¾ lbs.

No. 6V6548 Price.**$5.50**

Service Racket.

Full size head, made from selected second growth ash, with five-piece walnut throat, cedar handle, strung with good quality selected imported gut, leather capped. Designed for rapid, effective work; well strung and well balanced. Furnished in 12½ to 14½-ounce weights. **Give weight wanted.** Shipping weight, 1¾ pounds.

No. 6V6542 Price.**$1.70**

Improved Champion Racket.

Now furnished with concave throat, beveled frame and reinforced gut wound shoulders, full size large head, full size grip. Made of selected air dried second growth ash, with five-piece concave walnut throat, finely scored cedar handle with leather cap. Closely strung with selected Oriental gut and trimmed at throat and top of racket. Guaranteed to be equal in finish, balance, strength and quality to rackets sold elsewhere at a great deal more than our price. Furnished in 13, 13½, 14 and 14½-ounce weights. **State weight wanted.** Shipping wt., 1¾ pounds.

No. 6V6544 Price.**$3.00**

Aztec Racket.

Medium size head, made from second growth ash, with five-piece walnut throat, cedar handle, closely strung with best American gut, leather capped, well balanced. An excellent low priced racket for youths and misses. Furnished in 12½ to 14½-ounce weights. **State weight desired.** Shipping weight, 1 pound 9 ounces.

No. 6V6534 Price...**90c**

Lawn Tennis Balls.

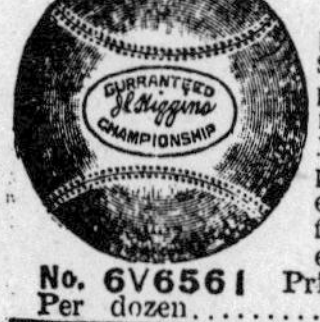

J. C. Higgins Championship Tennis Balls. Specially designed for professional and tournament use. Imported from Manchester, England. Best pure rubber center, covered with finest felt cover, firmly cemented and sewed. Shpg. wt., each, 3 oz.

No. 6V6561 Price, each.........**$0.30**
Per dozen.........**3.50**

Our Country Club. Imported English ball, felt cover, full size, guaranteed to give satisfaction. Shipping wt., each, 3 oz.

No. 6V6558 Price, each........**$0.20**
Per dozen.........**2.30**

No. 6V6559 Goodrich Championship Tennis Balls. Regular retail price, 40 cents.
Price, each..........................**$0.32**
Per dozen..........................**3.80**

Ayres Championship Ball, used in all English tournaments. None better made. Endorsed by the N. L. T. A. Ship. wt., each, 3 oz.

No. 6V6563 Price, each........**$0.35**
Price, per dozen..................**4.00**

Wright & Ditson Championship Tennis Balls. Shipping weight, each, 3 ounces.

No. 6V6560 Price, each........**$0.35**
Per dozen..........................**4.00**

Paramount One Seam Tennis Ball. No plug inside. Air cannot escape. Standard size and weight. Approved by U. S. L. T. A. Shipping weight, 3 ounces.

No. 6V6562 Price, each........**$0.32**
Per dozen..........................**3.75**

Canvas Center Strap.

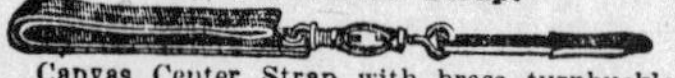

Canvas Center Strap with brass turnbuckle and galvanized stake, for holding center of net at regulation height. Will not chafe the net. Shipping weight, 1½ pounds.

No. 6V6610 Price, each...........**80c**

Tennis Net Poles.

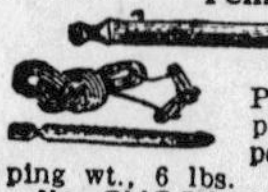

Solid (one-piece) Tennis Poles, nicely finished, complete with guy ropes and pegs. Weight, 4 pounds. Shipping wt., 6 lbs.

No. 6V6617¼ Price, per pair......**70c**

Mackintosh Racket Covers.

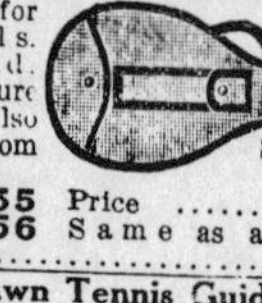

With pocket for three balls. Fabric bound. Keeps moisture from racket, also protects it from injury. Shipping wt., 12 ounces.

No. 6V6555 Price **50c**

No. 6V6556 Same as above, without pocket...............................**40c**

Lawn Tennis Guide.

Annual Tennis Guide, giving rules and instructions. Shipping weight, 11 ounces.

No. 6V7029 Price...................**10c**

Restringing Tennis Rackets.

Rackets restrung with medium grade gut, $1.50; best grade gut, $1.90.

For rackets drilled for narrow mesh stringing, similar to our No. 6V6545, add 35 cents extra to the above prices. Allow postage for return of racket. Time required for restringing, about seven days.

Double Court Marking Tapes.

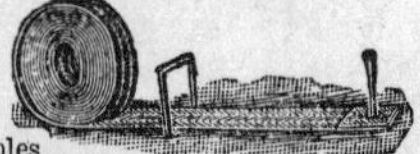

Double Court Lawn Tennis Marking Tapes, complete with pins and staples. Put up in cardboard box with complete instructions. Shipping weight, 7½ pounds.

No. 6V6629 Price, per set....**$2.87**

Reels for Tightening Tennis Nets.

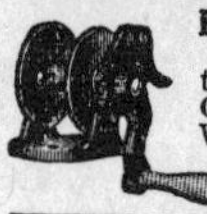

Made of malleable iron, extra strong. Black enameled. Can be used for all size nets. Weight, 2¼ pounds. Shipping weight, 3 pounds.

No. 6V6620 Price**$1.10**

Tennis Scorer.

No. 6V6630 Four movable discs to record points in games of opposing players or teams. Made of solid celluloid. Indispensable to scorer or referee. Size, 5x1¼ in. Shpg. wt., 2 oz. Price...............**6c**

Automatic Fly Back Racket Press.

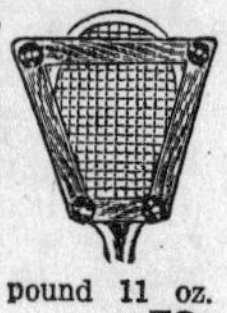

Keep your racket in a press when not in use, to prevent warping and twisting. This press is made of selected straight grained ash wood with thumbscrews, as illustrated. There are four springs between press to hold press in right position at all times. Shipping weight, 1 pound 11 oz.

No. 6V6549 Price...............**72c**

Elastic Tennis Sweatbands.

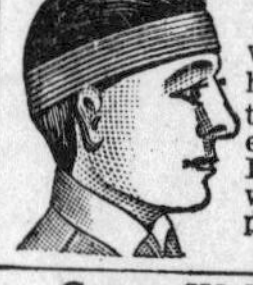

Ideal for those who do not wear a regular hat. Keeps hair and perspiration from the eyes. Made of cotton elastic web, 3 inches wide. Furnished in one size, which will fit any size head. Shipping weight, 3 ounces.

No. 6V6632 Price..**15c**

Cotton Web Belt.

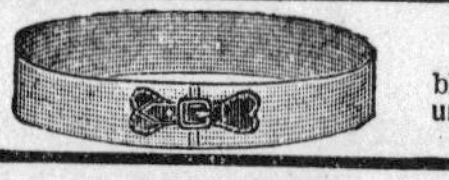

To fit Pants No. 45V1240. Furnished in white, black or navy blue. Sizes, 28 to 46 inches waist measure. **State waist measure and color wanted.** Shipping weight, 2 ounces.

No. 6V6638 Price...........................**18c**

Dry Tennis Court Marker.

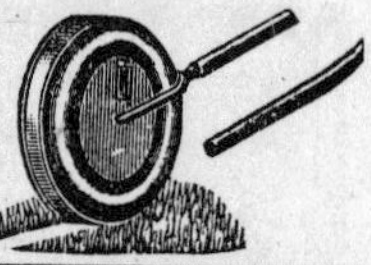

Fill with marble dust or air slaked lime; no mixing material required. Comes fitted with handle. Wt., 2¼ lbs. Shipping wt., 2¾ pounds.

No. 6V6628
Price **70c**

White Canvas Tennis and Golfing Hat

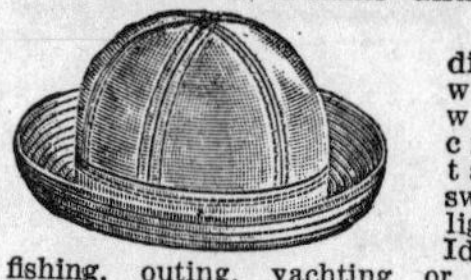

Made of medium weight white canvas, with round crown, inside taped seams, sweatband. Very light and cool. Ideal hat for fishing, outing, yachting or general wear. Sizes, 6⅜ to 7¾. **When ordering state size wanted.** Shipping weight, 4 ounces.

No. 33V4832 Price, each.........**39c**

White Duck Tennis, Golf and Outing Pants.

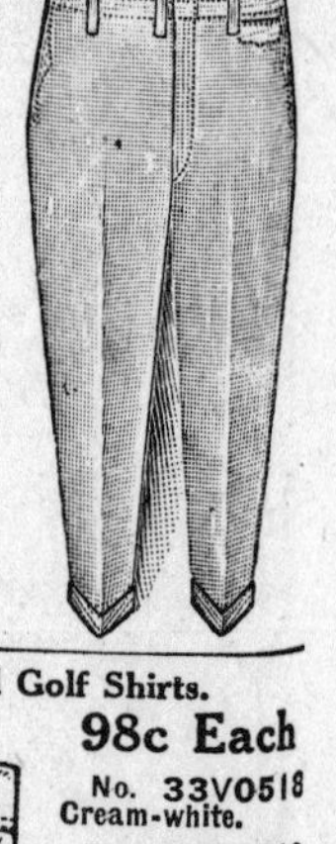

Made on the latest outing pattern, closed welt seams, cuff bottoms, belt loops, two side and one hip pocket, and small watch pocket. Very comfortable. Can be washed. Ideal for fishing, yachting, picnic or street wear. Sizes, 28 to 46 inches waist measure. **When ordering give waist and inseam measures.** Shipping wt., 1⅝ to 2 pounds.

No. 45V1240
Price, pair...**$1.35**

Dumbbells and Indian Clubs.

Sold in pairs only. First quality rock maple, finely polished. Weight given is the weight of each club or dumbbell. For shipping weight add about 1 pound to actual weight of dumbbells or clubs. **State weight wanted.**

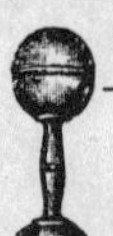

Dumbbells No. 6V6857 Per Pair	Weight	Indian Clubs No. 6V6856 Per Pair
18c	½ lb.	18c
20c	¾ lb.	20c
23c	1 lb.	23c
Not made	1½ lbs.	26c
28c	2 lbs	28c
44c	3 lbs.	44c
51c	4 lbs.	51c
60c	5 lbs.	60c

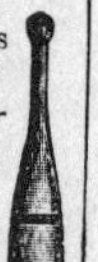

Dumbbell and Indian Club Hangers.

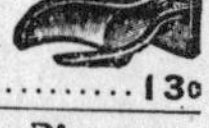

Made of iron, black enamel finish. For all weights. Shpg. wt., per pair, 12 oz.

No. 6V6855 Price, per pair...........................**13c**

Exercising or Swinging Rings.

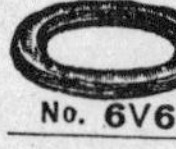

Three pieces, walnut and maple, glued together. Six inches in diameter. Shipping weight, 1⅛ pounds.

No. 6V6879 Price, per pair......**45c**

Vaulting Poles.

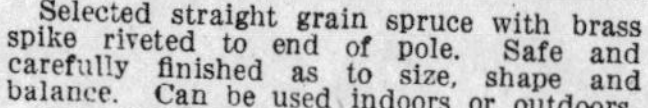

Selected straight grain spruce with brass spike riveted to end of pole. Safe and carefully finished as to size, shape and balance. Can be used indoors or outdoors.

No. 6V6775 14 feet. Shipping weight, 8 pounds. Price, each...............**$4.96**

No. 6V6776 16 feet. Shipping weight, 10 pounds. Price, each...............**$5.95**

Horizontal Bars.

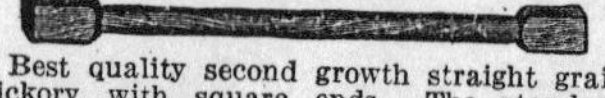

Best quality second growth straight grain hickory with square ends. The standard bar, used in all gymnasiums. Made in three lengths.

No. 6V6880A 5 feet long. Price, each (Shipping wt., 4 lbs.)...........**$1.00**

No. 6V6880B 5½ feet long. Price, each (Shipping wt., 5 lbs.)...........**$1.15**

No. 6V6880C 6 feet long. Price, each (Shipping wt., 5 lbs.)...........**$1.25**

Gymnasium Mats.

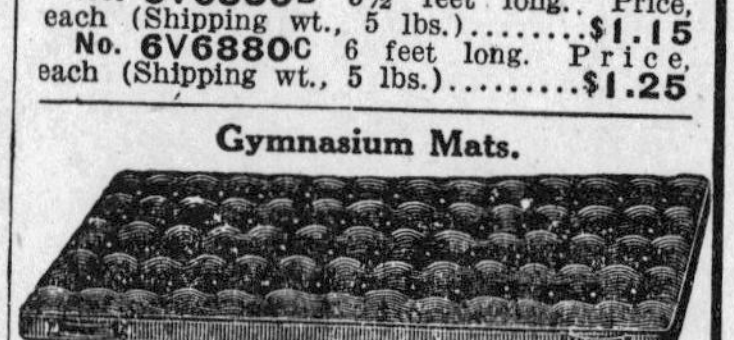

Made of 8-ounce white canvas, filled with two layers of best quality hair felt with burlap between the layers and around the felt, then tufted to hold same in place. The mats are also tufted on the outside, through the canvas. **When ordering give catalog number and size wanted.** Shipped from CHICAGO factory. On special sizes, not listed below, allow 58 cents per square foot.

Catalog No.	Size	Shpg. Wt.	Price
6V6700⅓	3x 5 ft.	30 lbs.	$ 8.00
6V6702⅓	4x 6 ft.	48 lbs.	12.00
6V6704⅓	5x 6 ft.	70 lbs.	15.50
6V6706⅓	5x10 ft.	100 lbs.	25.75
6V6708⅓	5x20 ft.	200 lbs.	52.00

For indoor and outdoor shots, throwing hammers and iron quoits, see page 819.

Tennis and Golf Shirts.

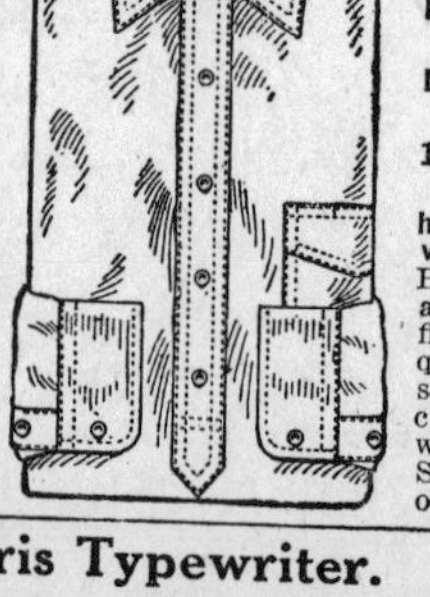

98c Each

No. 33V0518 Cream-white.

No. 33V0519 Light blue.

No. 33V0520 Light tan.

Sizes, 14½ to 17. **State size.**

Made from handsome closely woven pongee cloth. Highly mercerized and has a lustrous finish. A shirt of quality. Attached soft collar and cuffs. Trimmed with pearl buttons. Shipping weight, ounces.

ation . . . in the towns and cities . . . increasing wealth gave . . . opportunity for amusement."

Croquet

As long ago as the 1880's, the National Croquet Association held its first tournament, with the then new short-handled mallets, hard-rubber balls, sanded courts, and narrow wickets. Croquet was widely played because of its simplicity, the cheapness of the equipment required, and because it provided an unchaperoned diversion. In 1880, the *Journal of Social Science* said: "If, as some detractors have intimated, it [croquet] has given opportunity for flirtation, it has more than made amends by teaching the fair sex that a long afternoon can be pleasantly and profitably spent out of doors."

In 1905, croquet was still popular, and the catalog offers a number of sets. These ranged from "Our Junior Four-Ball Croquet Set, Price 55¢," to "Our Professional Eight-Ball Croquet Set. Consists of eight finely finished and striped mallets . . . eight hard maple striped and varnished balls, two striped fancy stakes, heavy pointed wire arches . . . put up in strong wood box with hinged cover. Weight, about 27 pounds. Price, per set . . . $1.50."

Tennis

Tennis was introduced into the Untied States from England in 1875 and grew so rapidly in popularity that by 1879 *Leslie's Illustrated Newspaper* contained drawings of gentlemen of the Union Club of Chicago wearing their high silk hats as they played. Two years later, the first women's tournaments were played. But despite the rise of tennis in the cities, it was by no means a popular sport of rural America in 1905. The catalog devotes to tennis equipment about the same space that it gives to croquet.

The cheapest racket sold for eighty-five cents; the highest priced for $3.50. "Regulation Newport Finals Lawn Tennis Balls" sold for twenty-five cents each.

"Our Boxing-Glove Department"

The catalog of 1905 devotes as much space to boxing gloves as to tennis and croquet combined. "Our Department of Boxing Gloves is strictly up to date. You will find gloves to suit all tastes for either amateur or professional. These gloves are selected by an expert who is posted on this class of goods. . . . We send free a copy of the Marquis of Queensbury Rules with every set. A set consists of four gloves, two pairs, packed in a box."

In 1905, John L. Sullivan was still alive and still a potent legend in American sporting life. Nearly twenty years had then passed since his epic battle of seventy-five rounds with Jake Kilrain at Richbourg, Mississippi. The men fought with bare knuckles under a blazing sun and, while it was the last of the bare-knuckle fights, it was also the last of the genuine tooth-and-claw battles of the ring. From that time almost until his death, Sullivan was the revered hero of thousands of American youths who wistfully dreamed of following in his mighty footsteps.

It was in 1905, too, that the great John J. Jeffries retired, with a fortune and nation-wide fame gained in the ring after knocking out such heroes as James J. Corbett and Bob Fitzsimmons. Popular interest in amateur boxing must have been great, judging from the space allotted boxing gloves in the catalog. Amateurs were offered a wide choice of gloves. "Youth's size, made of wine colored kid leather . . ." sold for $1.10 a set; "George Stoll's Corbett Pattern" for $3.25. Professionals bought "Our Geo. Peacock Pattern Professional Fighting Glove, price, per set, $2.10."

"Hold 'Em, Yale!"

Football is a relatively old sport in the United States, but for years interest in it was largely confined to the colleges, their students and alumni. It is only comparatively recently that interest in football, both inside and outside the colleges, has risen to almost hysterical proportions.

In 1880, the rules of the game were changed by the initiative of Walter Camp, so that it little resembled English Rugby, and emerged as American football. It was, as *The New York Evening Post* described a game in the '80's, as much of a battle as an athletic contest:

> The spectators (at a Yale-Princeton game) could see the elevens hurl themselves together and build themselves in kicking, writhing heaps. They had a general vision of threatening attitudes, fists shaken before noses, dartings hither and thither, throttling, wrestling and the pitching of individuals to earth. . . . Those inside the lines, the judges, reporters . . . were nearer and saw something more. They saw real fighting, savage blows that drew blood, and falls that seemed as if they must crack all the bones and drive the life from those who sustained them.

Since there were few regular coaches of football in the early days of the game, teachers often assumed the role of coaches. In 1889, Connecticut Wesleyan College turned out a successful team under a teacher coach which defeated Pennsylvania, Amherst, Rutgers, and Trinity. The coach was Professor Woodrow Wilson.

But football, whatever its popularity in the colleges in 1905, occupied a small space in the scheme of rural living, and the catalog allots it a correspondingly small space in its pages. It offers merely a few footballs at prices ranging from seventy-five cents to $3.25; football shoes and sweaters, and football pants. The lowest-priced pants sold for fifty-eight cents and were made of "white twilled drilling"; the highest priced at $1.25 were made of "colored army khaki cloth, which is popular this year by reason of its strength, durability and color . . . cane reeds at thighs, the latest thing in football pants. . . ."

Jingle Bells

All that now remains in America of the great days of sleighing, save in a few districts where occasional sleighs still survive, is a nostalgic memory palely perpetuated on

Christmas post cards. But once the lonely and silent woods of America were filled with the music of sleigh bells and the merry shouts of men and women as horses bore them swiftly over hard snow. The vehicles themselves were gay with gilt, paint, and decoration; the harness was of elegant design; the bells harmonized, and the horses ran the faster for the music.

Sleighing was extremely popular with women, and, since it was a sport that could not be carefully chaperoned, it was sure to arouse the criticisms of prudes. In 1816, such a critic wrote a letter to the *Daily National Intelligencer,* and was soon answered in verse by a defender of the ladies who wrote:

> *All that is stuff—I know it well,*
> *A girl of virtue and true worth*
> *Need never dread the sleighman's bell*
> *She's armed against all the power of earth.*
>
> *And virtue that's safe by day,*
> *Which melts before an evening's chilling*
> *And cannot keep, tho in a sleigh,*
> *I would not give for it a shilling.*

More than a half century later, sleighing was still a popular sport in America, as noted by an English visitor, George M. Towles, in his *American Society:*

> On one of the wide roads of the outskirts of the town (New York), any clear winter afternoon, you will see hundreds of sleighs dashing hither and thither, the daintiest and jauntiest of equipages, luxuriously warm and cozy by the aid of blankets, drawn by spirited horses of finest temper and occupied by the male and female fashionable world. There is racing and in spite of all that legislators can do; the very air tempts it and intoxicates and makes hilarious.

In rural districts, sleighs were at once a source of transportation and recreation where dirt roads lay deep-buried in snow in winter. They bulked so large in Sears' sales that in 1905 a special sleigh catalog was issued. "Our Special Free

Duck Hunting Pants.

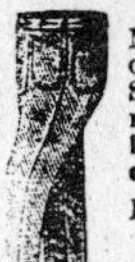

No. 6C5158 Hunting Pants. Made of 8-ounce duck; dead grass color, with four patch pockets. Sizes, from 28 to 40 inches waist measure. **Give waist measure and leg measure of inseam when ordering.** Price, per pair.......**73c**

If by mail, postage extra, 25 to 30 cents.

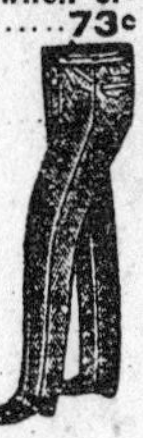

No. 6C5159 Duck Hunting Pants. Made of 10-ounce army duck, dead grass ..r, business style. Cut in front back pockets. Sizes, from 30 inches waist measure. **Give ..st measure and leg measure of ..am when ordering.**

..ce, per pair............**$1.20**

..y mail, postage extra, 30 to 35c.

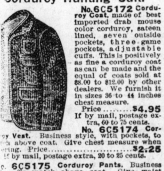

Corduroy Hunting Suit.

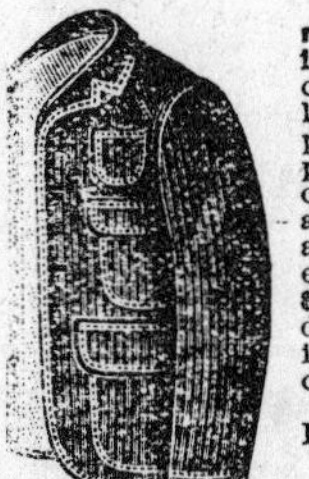

No. 6C5172 Corduroy Coat, made of best imported drab mouse color corduroy, sateen lined, seven outside pockets, three game pockets, adjustable cuffs. This is positively as fine a corduroy coat as can be made and the equal of coats sold at $8.00 to $12.00 by other dealers. We furnish it in sizes 36 to 44 inches chest measure.

Price.........**$4.95**

If by mail, postage extra, 60 to 75 cents.

No. 6C5174 Cor..oy Vest. Business style, with pockets, to ..h above coat. Give chest measure when ..ering. Price..............**$2.25**

If by mail, postage extra, 20 to 25 cents.

No. 6C5175 Corduroy Pants. Business .. To match above coat. Give waist ..ure and inseam of leg measure when ..ring. Price, per pair..............**$3.25**

If by mail, postage extra, 30 to 38 cents.

..IL TANNED HORSEHIDE AND CORDUROY REVERSIBLE COATS.

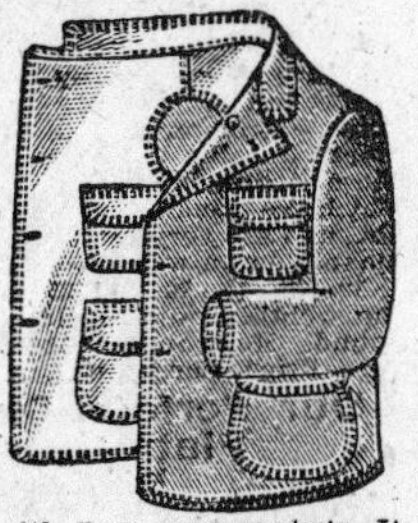

..o. **6C5179 ..Tanned Horsehide Coat,** russet ..r, waterproof, .. and pliable, ..will always re..in so. A splen.. garment for .., cold and ..my weather, ..'s made so that ..y be reversed, .. corduroy on ..de and horse.. on the other, ..t has three ..kets on the ..r side and .. pockets on ..orduroy side, with flaps over pockets. It ..y be worn either as a horsehide or corduroy .. Sizes, 36 to 46 inches chest measure. ..tively the best reversible coat on the ..ket, regardless of price. Give chest measure ..ordering. Weight, 4¼ to 4½ pounds.

..rice..............**$11.35**

..ur Reversible Leather and Corduroy Hunting Coat, $7.50.

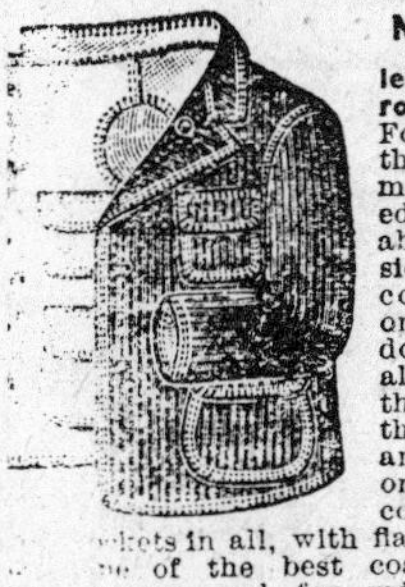

No. 6C5180 Our Reversible Leather and Corduroy Hunting Coat. For $7.50 we furnish this hunting coat, made of tan colored, soft tanned, pliable leather on one side and mouse colored corduroy on the reverse side, double stitched at all essential places, three pockets on the leather side and three pockets on the reverse or corduroy side, mak.. ..ockets in all, with flaps over pockets. ..ne of the best coats ever offered ..ouse, and for rainy or stormy ..is by far the best, warmest and ..eful coat ever made; it can be ..stormy weather with the leather ..and in clear weather it may be worn ..orduroy side out, making a nice, neat, ..at, a coat which will please you. ..out 4½ pounds. These coats come .. 42 and 44 inches chest measure. ..urement of chest when ordering.

..........**$7.50**

..ING HATS AND CAPS.

..s Cape ..8 Cents.

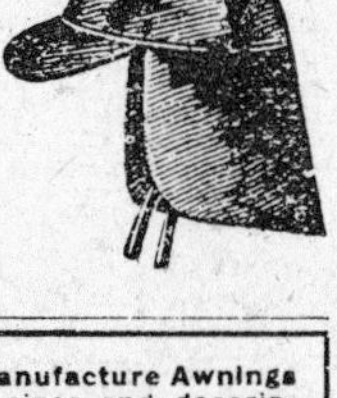

..189 Can..as, made of .., dead grass .. stiff visor, ..annel lined, .. rough or ..r cap. State

..........**38c**

.. postage ..cents.

..GS We manufacture Awnings of all sizes and descriptions. It is surprising .. money buys a good Awning.

Our $1.32 Klondike Cap.

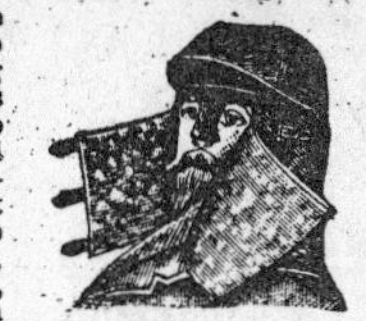

No. 6C5197 The greatest winter cap made. Just the thing for farmers, teamsters and the Klondike. Made of heavy duck, lined with soft tanned sheepskin with the wool left on, with flap over face and strap and buckles, large visor, green lined, to protect the eyes, with nose protector. The best cap on the market to protect you from extreme cold weather. State size wanted. Price..........................**$1.32**

If by mail, postage extra, 20 cents.

DOG MUZZLES.

NOTICE—When ordering Dog Muzzles, please give measurement around the dog's neck and around snout, 1 inch from the tip of the nose, and the length from tip of the nose to the top of head where the strap goes around his neck, and you will assist us in fitting the muzzle, for muzzles vary considerably in size.

Leather Strap Dog Muzzle.

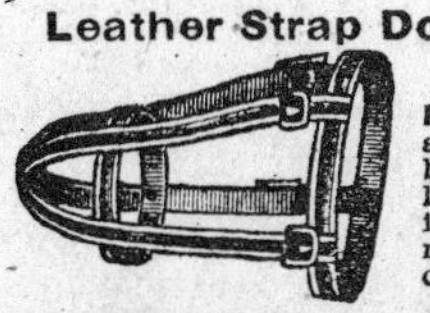

Leather Strap Dog Muzzle, to buckle around neck and buckles to take up length around head if too large. Give measure when ordering.

No. 6C5347 Small size. Price........**30c**
No. 6C5348 Large size. Price........**40c**

If by mail, postage extra, 4 cents.

OUR LINE OF DOG COLLARS.

Big Bargains.

We engrave names on collars for 3 cents per letter. Cash with order. If you wish a name engraved on the name plate, write the name PLAINLY, so we will not get it wrong.

NOTE—In taking measurements for dog collars the measures below are the length of collar from staple and middle hole, but for convenience of our customers we suggest that you give us the actual measurement around dog's neck by inches, specifying in the order actual measurement, and we will fit him every time. **Prices on dog collars do not include padlocks.**

Our Chain Dog Collars.

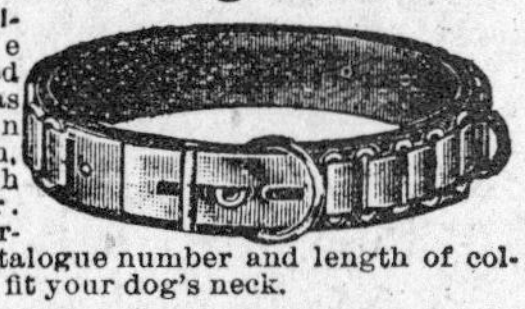

These collars have nickel plated flat links, as shown in illustration, lined with leather. When ordering, give catalogue number and length of collar that will fit your dog's neck.

Catalogue Number	Neck Measure	Width of Collar	Price of Collar	Postage Extra
6C6260	11 inches	½ inch	20c	5c
6C6262	13 inches	¾ inch	25c	7c
6C6264	15 inches	1 inch	30c	12c
6C6266	17 inches	1 inch	35c	16c

Engraving extra, 3 cents per letter. Write name plainly and send cash with order.

Our Studded Dog Collars.

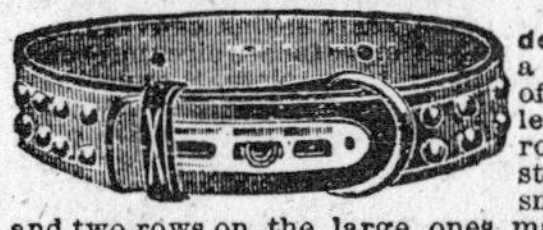

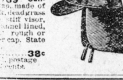

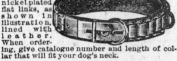

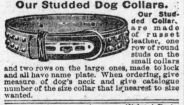

Our Studded Collars are made of russet leather, one row of round studs on the small collars and two rows on the large ones, made to lock and all have name plate. When ordering, give measure of dog's neck and give catalogue number of the size collar that is nearest to size wanted.

Catalogue Number	Neck Measure	Width of Collar	Price of Collar	Postage Extra
6C6290	7 inches	½ inch	20c	6c
6C6292	9 inches	½ inch	22c	8c
6C6294	11 inches	¾ inch	25c	10c
6C6296	13 inches	¾ inch	30c	12c
6C6298	15 inches	1 inch	35c	14c
6C6300	17 inches	1 inch	40c	16c
6C6302	19 inches	1 inch	45c	18c
6C6304	21 inches	1¼ inch	50c	20c

Engraving extra, 3 cents per letter. Write name plainly and send cash with order.

Our Heavy Collars for Mastiffs and Large Dogs.

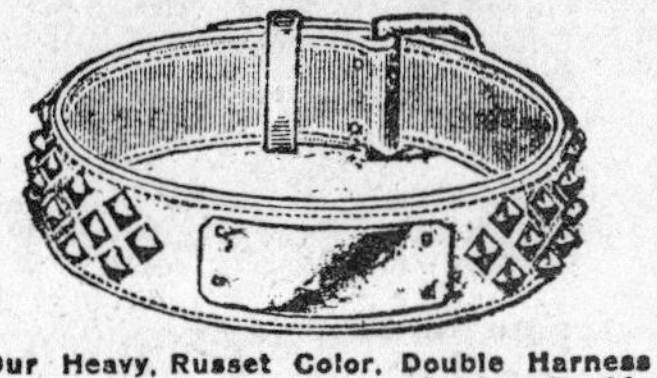

Our Heavy, Russet Color, Double Harness Leather Collar, fine russet finish. Double stitched. Heavily studded, with nickeled studs, solid D ring, nickel plated. Nickeled name plate, staple and trimmings, made to lock; for large dogs. Give catalogue number and length of collar that will fit your dog's neck.

Catalogue Number	Neck Measure	Width of Collar, Inches	Price of Collar	Postage Extra
6C6306	15 inches	1¼	$0.53	18c
6C6308	17 inches	1¼	.60	20c
6C6310	19 inches	1¼	.65	22c
6C6312	21 inches	1½	.85	25c
6C6314	23 inches	1½	.90	27c
6C6316	24 inches	2	1.15	30c

Engraving extra, 3 cents per letter. Write the name plainly so we will not get it wrong, and send cash with order.

Drilled Key Dog Collar Locks.

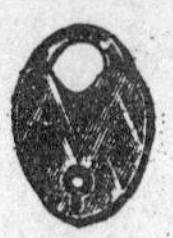

No. 6C6400 Padlock, 1x¾ inch, all nickel plated, with key. Price..........................**17c**

No. 6C6401 Padlock, 1x¾ inch, brass, with key. Price...**15c**

If by mail, postage extra, 1 cent.

No. 6C6402 Our Little Secret Dog Collar Lock. A very neat and substantial lock; as strong as any lock and does not require a key. Keyhole has centerpost and is opened by pressing pin to the right. Price......................**10c**

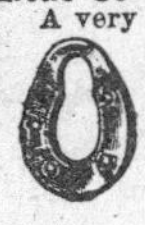

If by mail, postage extra, 2 cents.

Kennel Chains.

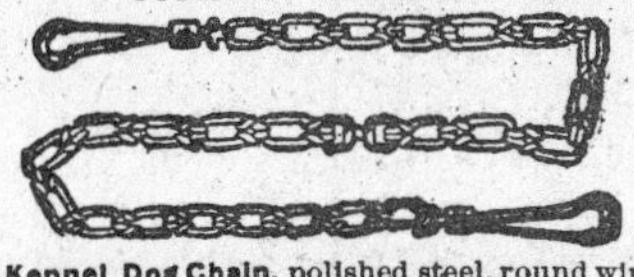

Kennel Dog Chain, polished steel, round wire, new style safety links, three swivels, two snap hooks, so it will not kink; well made and durable; no dog can break it; comes in two lengths and two sizes.

Catalogue No.	Size Links	Length Chain	Price	Postage Extra
6C6420	Medium	4½ feet	22c	10c
6C6421	Medium	6 feet	27c	10c
6C6423	Heavy	4½ feet	30c	12c
6C6425	Heavy	6 feet	35c	16c

Spratt's Dog Cakes.

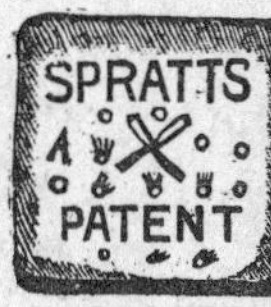

No. 6C6454 Spratt's Patent Fibrine Dog Cakes (with beetroot); these celebrated biscuit are supplied to all the leading kennels and are used at the principal dog shows in America and England, and have been before the public for more than a quarter of a century; 5-pound boxes. Per box....**$0.40**

No. 6C6455 25-pound boxes. Price, per box.................. **1.60**

Each cake weighs 5 to 6 ounces. 2 to 4 cakes per day for pointers and setters, 3 to 5 cakes per day for mastiffs, is considered sufficient food.

LAWN TENNIS GOODS.

Our line of tennis rackets has been selected with great care and we know that we are offering better rackets for far less money than any other house. Even our cheapest racket is a hand polished racket. These rackets are made especially for us; we guarantee them to exceed any rackets on the market in finish, stringing and balance. We recommend our Seroco Racket, in 12-ounce weight, as being an excellent racket for ladies.

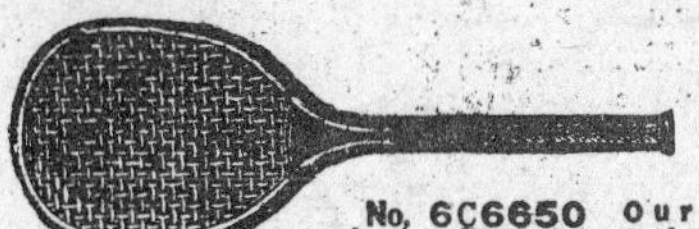

No. 6C6650 Our Junior Racket is made from second growth ash, walnut throat, cedar handle, well strung with American gut, well balanced; for boys and girls.

Price....................................**85c**

No. 6C6651 Our Oak Park Racket, full size head; made from second growth ash, with walnut throat, cedar handle; closely strung with best American gut, leather capped, well balanced. An excellent low priced racket for youths and misses. Price..............**$1.25**

No. 6C6652 Our Seroco Racket, full size head; made from selected second growth ash, with walnut throat, cedar handle; strung with good quality selected imported gut, leather capped. Designed for rapid, effective work, well strung and well balanced.

Price....................................**$1.75**

No. 6C6653 Our Volley Racket, full size, highly polished head; is made from selected second growth ash, five-piece walnut and maple throat, polished and scored cedar handle, closely strung with a fine quality imported gut, leather capped and well balanced. A racket suitable for amateur or professional work.

Price....................................**$2.50**

No. 6C6655 Our Expert Racket. This is a racket which is especially built for us, has full size extra highly polished head; the frame is made of the very best selected second growth ash, and head tapers slightly from the rim toward the gut; five-piece walnut and maple throat; polished and scored cedar handle; strung with the very finest imported gut, leather capped, well balanced; designed especially for professional work, 12-ounce, 13-ounce and 14-ounce weights. This racket is as well made as any racket can be regardless of price, name or brand and usually sells at $5.00 to $6.50.

Our price..............................**$3.50**

If by mail, postage extra, 14 to 16 cents.

RACKETS RESTRUNG WITH BES. CLEAR GUT, $1.50.

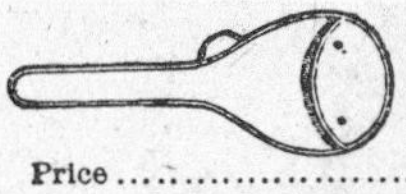

No. 6C6657 Soft Felt Racket Cover. Keeps moisture from racket, saves racket and gut from injury.

Price....................................**35c**

If by mail, postage extra, 6 cents.

Lawn Tennis Balls.

No. 6C6658 Regulation Newport Finals. No. 350A.

Price, each..............**$0.25**
Per dozen.................. **2.70**

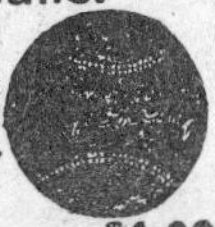

No. 6C6659 Victor Championship Tennis Balls, No. 350. Positively the best ball made.

Price, each, **35c**; per dozen..........**$4.00**

If by mail, postage extra, 3 cents.

Lawn Tennis Nets.

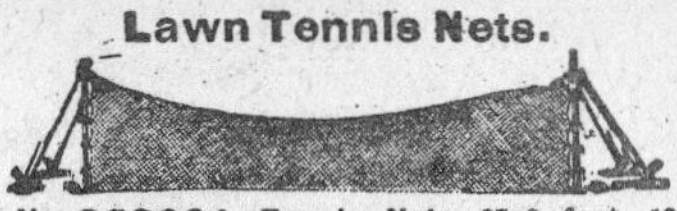

No. 6C6661 Tennis Nets, 27x3 feet, 12-thread. Weight, packed, 31 ozs. Price.....**65c**

No. 6C6662 Tennis Nets, 36x3 feet, 15-thread. Weight, packed, 36 ozs. Price **$1.00**

No. 6C6663 Tennis Nets, 42x3 feet, 15-thread. Weight, packed, 36 ozs. Price **$1.25**

No. 6C6664 Tennis Nets, 42x3 feet, 15-thread, canvas bound. Price..........**$1.65**

No. 6C6665 Tennis Nets, 42x3 feet, 21-thread, canvas bound. Price..........**$2.00**

No. 6C6666 Back Stop Net to prevent balls from rolling out of grounds, 50x8 feet, 12-thread. Price..............................**$2.25**

Seroco Tennis Net Poles.

No. 6C6667 Solid (one piece) Tennis Poles, nicely finished, complete with guy ropes and pegs. Price, per pair............**98c**

Dry Tennis Court Marker.

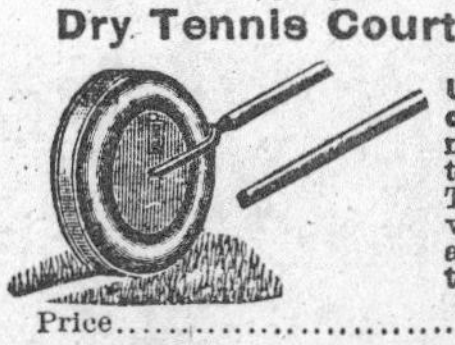

No. 6C6668 Uses marble dust or air slaked lime, no mixing of material required. The wheel revolves on its axle. Comes fitted with handle.

Price....................................**$1.00**

Our Seroco Croquet Sets.

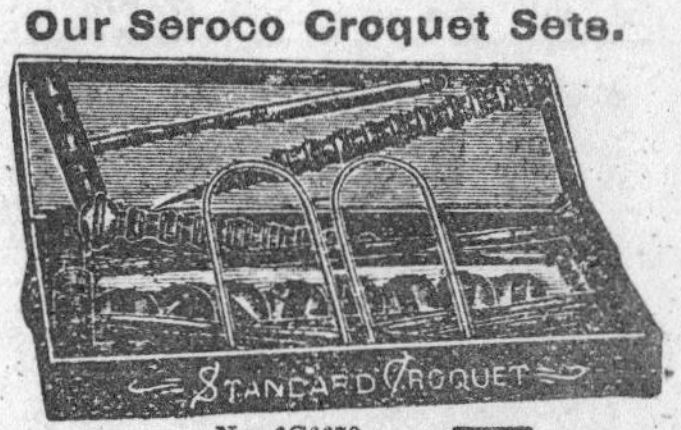

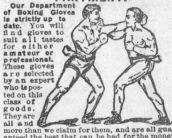

No. 6C6678

No. 6C6670 Our Junior Four-ball Croquet Set, four striped mallets, four hardwood varnished and striped balls and striped and varnished stakes, ten wire arches; put up in neat, strong wood box with hinged cover. Weight, about 13 pounds. Price, per set.**55c**

No. 6C6672 Our Amateur Eight-ball Croquet Set, eight striped mallets, eight hardwood varnished and striped balls, two striped and varnished stakes, ten wire arches; put up in a strong wood box with hinged cover. Weight, about 22 pounds. Price, per set..........**75c**

No. 6C6674 Our Favorite Eight-ball Croquet Set, consists of eight nicely painted and varnished mallets with five-inch heads, eight striped and varnished balls, two large fancy striped stakes, heavy wire arches; an excellent set at a low price; put up in a strong, durable wood box with hinged cover. Weight, about 24 pounds. Price, per set..................**$1.25**

No. 6C6676 Our Champion Eight-ball Croquet Set, consisting of eight finely finished striped mallets, with eight-inch heads, eight hard maple striped and varnished balls, two striped fancy stakes, heavy pointed wire arches; well made and finished set in every respect; put up in strong wood box with hinged cover. Weight, about 27 pounds.

Price, per set..............................**$1.50**

Our Professional Croquet Set.

No. 6C6678 Our Professional Eight-ball Croquet Set, consists of eight finely finished varnished and striped mallets, with eight-inch heads, eight finely finished striped hardwood balls, two handsome beaded striped stakes, heavy wire arches; an excellent set in every respect; put up in a strong wood box, hinged cover. Weight, about 31 pounds.

Price, per set..............................**$2.25**

OUR BOXING GLOVE DEPARTMENT.

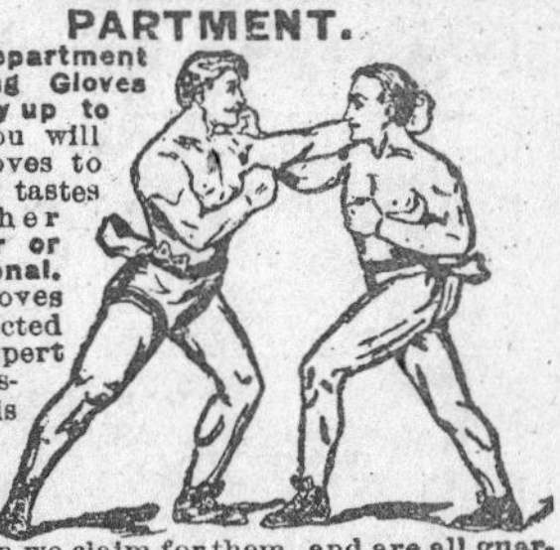

Our Department of Boxing Gloves is strictly up to date. You will find gloves to suit all tastes for either **amateur or professional.** These gloves are selected by an expert who is posted on this class of goods. They are all and more than we claim for them, and are all guaranteed the best that can be had for the money. **We send free a copy of the Marquis of Queensbury Rules with every set. A set consists of four gloves, two pairs, packed in a box.**

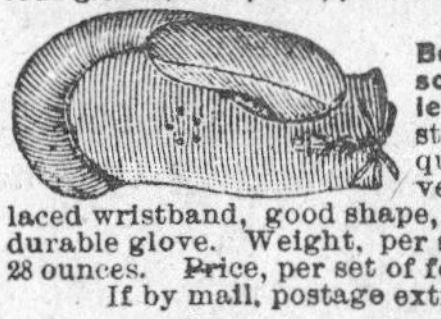

No. 6C6800 Boys' size, made of soft tanned kid leather, ecru color, stuffed with good quality short hair, ventilated palm, laced wristband, good shape, a well made and durable glove. Weight, per set, boxed, about 28 ounces. Price, per set of four gloves.**85c**

If by mail, postage extra, 31 cents.

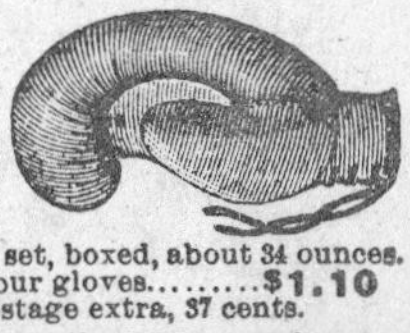

No. 6C6801 Youths' size. Made of wine colored kid leather, soft and pliable, stuffed with good quality curled hair; stitched fingers, laced wristband, ventilated palm. Weight, per set, boxed, about 34 ounces. Price, per set of four gloves..........**$1.10**

If by mail, postage extra, 37 cents.

BOXING GLOVES continued on next page.

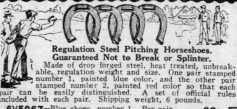

Catalogue of everything in this line will be ready October 1st, and if you expect to buy anything in the way of a cutter, sled, or runner attachments, be sure and write for the Free Cutter Catalogue. . . ."

Ten years later, in 1915, the general catalog carried a full page of cutters. (Vehicles drawn by two or four horses were called sleighs, while those drawn by one horse were called cutters.) New terms are grafted onto old vehicles. "The New Automobile Seat Spring Cutter. Upholstery—Dark green broadcloth. Trimming—Nickel plated dash rail. Painting— Body, black, neatly striped; gear, blood carmine, striped. . . . Price, complete, with leather trimmed shafts, $33.50." Here, too, are "The Old Comfort Spring Cutter, $30.95," and "The New Round Front Portland Cutter, $22.60." The catalog advises customers to "Order Early. . . . Place your order with us early in the season so as to have your cutter or bob sled on hand when the first snow comes. . . . We have put in a big supply of cutters and bobs this season as we expect a heavy winter. . . ."

Sleigh bells were made standard equipment by law because sleighs made no noise to warn pedestrians of their approach. Since it was a point of pride to own musical bells, the catalog of 1915 offers fourteen kinds. Among them were "Swiss Pole Chimes. Six harmonized graduated Swiss open face bells, iron knockers, nickel plated, highly polished. Price, $1.69," and "Our Brewster Sleigh Bells. . . . The tone is clear and distinct and from small to large bells the volume increases. Price, $1.53."

Batter Up

American baseball celebrated its one hundredth anniversary in the summer of 1939, and the catalog accurately calls it "America's National Game." In 1905, baseballs, gloves, masks, uniforms, and other paraphernalia of the game occupied two catalog pages. Baseball equipment has changed but little in the past thirty years; the gloves and bats of 1905 would suffice for the game today.

The catalog lays great stress on its made-to-order baseball uniforms, and, in its instructions to customers, we note how large a part amateur baseball played in the lives of Americans in 1905 when, almost invariably, great contests were held on important holidays. "Our baseball suits are made to order, which involves a delay of four to ten days, except just prior to *Decoration Day and Fourth of July,* when we require orders for suits to be furnished on these days to be placed two weeks in advance . . . on account of the enormous demand for suits at this time of the season."

Bicycling

Bicycles, like sleighs, were used both for utilitarian transportation and for amusement. During the 1880's, they were employed only by intrepid professional riders, because of the dangers of the huge front wheel. Nonetheless, an amateur rider, Thomas Stevens, left the United States in 1883 on one of these cumbersome contrivances, and returned home four years later after having covered fourteen thousand miles. Mr. Stevens left posterity a memoir of this journey in his *Around the World on a Bicycle.*

With the improvement of the bicycle and the lessening of its dangers came more riders and more bicycles, so that by 1886 The League of American Wheelmen had more than ten thousand members. It fought village ordinances and municipal regulations which barred bicycles from roads and streets; agitated for bicycle paths, macadam roads, and instituted a campaign for the building of good roads throughout the country. The safety bicycle, as it was called, with equal-size low wheels and pneumatic tires, gave a great impetus to the sport of bicycling, in which the ladies were soon to join wholeheartedly with the invention in 1888 of the drop-frame bicycle. Before the turn of the century, millions of Americans were cyclists; professional bicycle races called "scorchers" were very popular, and the place of this vehicle in American life seemed assured.

In 1905, Sears issued a special bicycle catalog, and devoted six pages to bicycles and accessories in the general catalog. The star of the stable was "The Celebrated Three-Crown Nickel Joint Napoleon Bicycle, the Highest of High Grade, Brought Right Up To Date for 1905, Price, $13.85." With each Napoleon went a "Special finished leather tool bag, complete with wrench, pump and tube of quick tire repair cement."

Ladies were advised to buy Napoleon's mate—"The Josephine. It is the Ladies' Model of our highest grade wheel, the Napoleon. . . . Equipped with the highest quality 1905 combination rubber pedals, mud and chain guard, handsomely striped, varnished and laced to match color of frame. Price, $14.35."

Girls and boys rode "Elgin Red Head Juvenile Bicycles. . . . Made of the very best material, of same quality and finish as our celebrated Elgin King and Elgin Queen. Price, $11.95."

Little did the millions of cyclists dream that they would soon be roughly shoved off the roads by the automobile which was then beginning to appear, and which they regarded as a vulgar, noisy nuisance.

Thirty-five Years Later

It was inevitable, among the manifold changes that came to America in the period 1905–39, that sports, too, should change. Increased wealth and leisure, growing emphasis on sports for health and slenderness, and the use of the time-saving, far-ranging automobile, all worked to spread American interest in sports. In some cases, old forms of sport have almost vanished; other old forms are more popular than ever before, and new forms have come upon the scene.

The American passion for hunting and fishing has not only not diminished since 1905 but has grown. The automobile now makes it possible for a small-town or city man to fish or shoot in the early morning and be at his desk by nine o'clock; it enables him to spend a Sunday or a holiday on distant streams or in distant fields and return home at nightfall;

while new roads have opened for the sportsman game areas hitherto inaccessible to all save those who had time and money for extended expeditions. And this, in turn, threatened the extinction of certain species of game, especially migratory wild fowl, so that stringent Federal game laws have had to be passed for their protection, with the result that once again, as in pioneer days, the flyways of this continent are black with wild geese and ducks. Man, the destroyer, appalled by his own powers of destruction, has come to nature's aid. He is breeding some species in captivity and releasing animals and birds into the woods and fields; billions of fish are annually put into streams from Federal and state hatcheries. The passion to shoot and fish is still strong in urban as well as rural Americans, and the catalog of 1939, like that of 1905, caters to their wants.

It is significant of change that Sears no longer uses thousands of words (printed in minute type) to describe a shotgun. Perhaps men no longer love guns so well that they are eager to study every detail of their construction as they did in 1905; perhaps the purchase of a cheap gun in richer America is no longer so keenly anticipated and thrilling an event that one thought about it and read about the gun for weeks in advance of the purchase, or, perhaps, men now take efficiency in guns for granted and buy them as casually as they buy handkerchiefs. Whatever the reasons, the 1939 catalog indulges in no extended descriptions of its shotguns and rifles.

Two new kinds of guns now appear. One kind puts a high premium on skill and gives game a greater chance; the other kind puts little premium on skill and is highly destructive. The former is represented by light-caliber weapons—.20 gauge and .41 gauge; the latter by the heavy, fast-shooting automatic.

Firearms cost more in 1939 than they did in 1905. The cheapest single-barrel shotgun is now $6.95, as against the $2.98 gun of 1905; the 12-gauge, full-choke Browning automatic sells for $57.20.

In 1905, thousands of hunters loaded their own shells and cartridges. But in 1939, whether for lack of skill, lack of time, or loss of the sense of thrift, few make their own ammunition but buy it ready-made. The catalog now lists no equipment for shell loading.

Golf in 1939

The word "golf" did not appear in the catalog of 1905. It had not yet become a small-town game, although it was widely played even at that time by urban folk. By 1939, however, hundreds of small towns had golf courses where the local citizenry played, and the catalog talks to them in golf language right from the start. "Here's Real Tournament Quality, Says Vic Ghezzi, North and South Open Champion." Real Tournament Quality, according to Sears, is to be found in "X-Pert Golf Clubs. Beauties—you bet! . . . from Woods to Putter. . . . Irons, $3.79. Woods, $4.79." The golfer may now buy his complete equipment from the catalog, ranging from balls to rain jackets.

"Hit the Winter Trail"

"WHETHER IT's . . . A Stem Turn . . . A Figure Eight . . . Or A Fast Run . . . Let Sears Practical Sports Styles Add Zest To Your Winter Fun! Seen at Lake Placid . . . Seen at Sun Valley . . . Seen at St. Moritz! Yes Sir! Seen everywhere red-blooded sportsmen gather! These are the style winners at top-notch resorts in America and Europe. . . . Look like an expert . . . and you'll be an expert that much sooner. Discard bundlesome outdoor duds . . . zip into the latest in winter-sport togs. . . ."

These are the introductory words to two pages of skiing equipment in the 1939 catalog. Skiing, a European sport, that has recently shot into tremendous popularity in the United States, began here as an urban sport. Each week end in winter, and on holidays, thousands of city men and women, transported by snow trains, embark on skiing expeditions. But already this sport, as the catalog's pages eloquently testify, has become the sport of small-town folk as well. While the rich may go to Lake Placid, Sun Valley, or St. Moritz, and buy their skiing equipment from Norwegian makers and their ski clothes in London or Paris, the middle class are going to more modest resorts or are skiing near home and buying their equipment and clothes from Sears. Nor is that all. Such is the wonder of America that one may now do figure eights on the installment plan; make fast runs on "easy terms."

The catalog devotes one page to ski clothes and another to equipment. "Double Breasted Tyrolean Jackets and Gabardine Downhill Ski Pants" sell for $4.79; ski caps for forty-nine cents; wool-knit gloves for seventy-nine cents. You don't have to be rich to be a catalog skier. "Sears Bargain Special Pine Skis" cost only seventy-nine cents. But if you want the best in skis, you must buy "Finest Ridge Top Hickory; Tempo Tip. Equal to fine imported skis. . . . Hand worked oval ridge for utmost strength, flexibility. Improved bend assures maximum amount of skiing surface. . . . Clear bottom. . . . Sizes 7 ft. and over. Price, $12.69."

In 1905, the farmer used the skis which he had paid for to reach his stock or move about his snow-buried lands. In 1939, the farmer's daughter and the farmer's son are doing installment-plan *slaloms* for fun.

Tennis—A National Game

Tennis, like golf, had become a national game by 1939. All over America, in big towns and small, thousands of men, women, and children, including Negroes as well as white, were playing tennis. The rich field for tennis equipment and clothes is, of course, tapped by the catalog, and its copy makes an appeal both to thrift and the players' assumed expert knowledge:

"Save Up To 50% on Australian Type Racket. Sears Finalist—Worth $10. Patterned after the nationally famous Australian type, etc. . . . Price $4.59."

The catalog now offers everything for tennis players and tennis courts, while Sears will even restring your racket on "easy terms."

The Ups and Downs of Sport

As time passes, some sports decline, others arise, and still others seem to maintain an even keel of quiet popularity. In 1939, Americans were still fighting as much perhaps as ever, but they were not using so many boxing gloves. Amateur boxing, as measured by the catalog's pages, has sadly declined since 1905, and boxing gloves occupy an inconspicuous place in the edition of 1939.

But croquet, on the other hand, is still going strong. "9 or 99—You'll Enjoy Croquet," says the catalog, and follows up this admonition with one half of a page devoted to croquet sets.

Sleighs, however, have disappeared from the catalog and belong now with America's pioneer past. The Department of Commerce census of manufactures reveals that only six hundred and fifty-seven sleighs and sleds were produced in 1931.

Bicycles have staged a strong comeback after long years of desuetude. In 1929, America manufactured more than three hundred thousand bicycles valued at $6,184,000, and the catalog of 1939 devotes as much space to them as did the edition of 1905.

The new bicycles are sold in automobile terminology: their great feature is speed. "Amazing New 2-Speed Twin-Bar Elgin Bicycle. Shifts into low or high like modern motor cars! Levels out the hills . . . makes for quick getaway! . . . The powerful electric horn in that good looking paneled tank clears the way for action; mere toe-pressure on the pedals and the famous Elgin air-cooled coaster brake hauls you to a quick stop. Price, $28.95."

And for girls: "Girls' New 2-Speed Elgin. . . . Designed to breeze along with the greatest of ease . . . to dates, to picnics, to school or movie! . . ."

Sports as Pleasure and Business

Sports, player-participant as well as spectator, have become a characteristic part of our national life. Millions of Americans of all social and economic classes, and Negroes as well as whites, now hunt, fish, shoot, golf, ski, play tennis or other games. And back of their playing lies a giant industry employing thousands of men to manufacture equipment for sportsmen, and to transport, feed, and guide them.

SLAVERY or freedom; secession or union; Mr. Lincoln and Mr. Jefferson Davis; First Bull Run and Appomattox. These great issues, men, and battles seem unrelated to the grime of clothing sweatshops in New York and Chicago; to well-regulated clothing factories in New York and Chicago; to the whir of clothing machinery and flashing shears wielded by men but lately come from Europe. Yet they are related. For the technique of mass production of men's clothing by machinery is the result, in the United States, of the Civil War. The need for soldiers' uniforms for the Federal armies led to the establishment in New York of factories which superseded the handicraft or semihandicraft methods in use up to that time, and to the necessity for importing uniforms and materials from Vienna and Prague. In the South, uniform factories were organized at Richmond, Savannah, New Orleans, and other places. After the war, the mass-production techniques learned in clothing factories were employed in the making of men's suits at low prices, and so successful were they, that from 1889 to 1899, the growth of the garment industry in the United States, measured by number of workers employed and the value of the products made, was two or three times as great as the average for all industries. This was the period in which factory-made clothing—the once inferior "hand-me-down"—gained dominance over the homemade or tailor-made suit, and as time passed, the improvement in quality of tailoring and materials employed was such that it came to be accepted by people of all incomes and all positions in society.

Jodie Eubanks Shops for Suits

It is a hot night in June, 1905, and Jodie Eubanks, a young cotton farmer of Desha County, Arkansas, draws the lamp nearer him so that its rays will fall directly on the catalog outspread on his knees. Jodie will need some new clothes next fall, and he thumbs the pages with joyful anticipation because his crop looks good and today he heard that old man Haley, the best cotton planter in the county, told Mr. Nelms, the banker, the happy news that "the old lady's nightgown is up over her head and it's gonna stay there, I reckon, the balance of this month." This was the message for which the county waited annually, because when old lady Haley's nightgown was reported to be above her head everybody knew that the nights were ideally hot for growing cotton, and now old man Haley promised a whole month of them. Jodie's fingers linger long over the many pages of men's clothing in the catalog containing bewildering selections of Sunday suits, suits for everyday wear, loud and sober suits, and tailor-mades as well as hand-me-downs. The suits are in Chicago and he is in his home in Arkansas, but the vividness of the catalog's descriptions enable him to see them almost as well as though he were shopping at The Leader Store in Lake Village, the county seat. Here, for example, is a beautiful Sunday suit that any young man would be glad to wear, even if its glorious coloring suggests Turner's *The Fighting Téméraire* rather than so utilitarian a thing as clothing to cover one's nakedness:

"Fancy Tweed Round Cornered Sack Suit. This is a very pretty combination of white, gold, green, and red threads on a dark background, the white threads being sprinkled very thickly and the other colors somewhat subdued, the general effect is somewhat of a brownish shade sprinkled with white —a very rich pattern and one that will have numerous admirers." Fortunately its price is as modest as its colors are riotous: $6.50 for coat, vest, and pants.

The woolen-goods manufacturers of the early 1900's had none of the morbid fear of color that marks the efforts of their brethren of today, but worked a full palette overtime, secure in the belief that one good color deserves another. The consumers of the time, whether they pitched hay for a living or ran a livery stable, exhibited a passion for color not experienced in the Western World since the death of the gallants of the Italian Renaissance. Consider this beauty in the light of today's clothing of undertaker drabness:

"Fancy Colored Mummy Effect Worsted Round Cut Sack Suit. This is a mixture of black, pale green and pale blue worked into a sort of faint small check effect with the pale green forming squares of one-half an inch diameter and the pale blue squares of the same size, the two being combined and forming borders for the small checks, the middle of which is composed of black. . . . Price for suit, $8.50."

Even in those days, however, there were men whose souls were the souls of undertakers, of note shavers, of mortgage holders waiting to get their clutches on the farm lands of widows and orphans, and they wore funereal black sack suits, or, if they were lawyers running for Congress, they took to the "four-button frock style to be worn with but one button closed. Especially suitable for dress or Sunday wear. Price $12.00."

Northern Civil War veterans were introduced to a neat trick of clothing economics in the catalog; a trick strangely reminiscent of the methods of present-day Chinese soldiers who wear uniforms until the Japanese come along, then bury them until the enemy has passed, when they emerge again as soldiers in regulation dress. One of the catalog's suits enabled a man to be a civilian during weekdays and a veteran on Sundays or during encampments, without the expense of buying two suits:

"Standard Navy Blue Flannel Round Cut Sack Suit. . . . These garments are made with eyelets and detachable civilian buttons. Owing to the fact that these garments can be worn as the regular Grand Army men's suits we will furnish an extra set of G.A.R. buttons free if you mention them in your order. . . . Price for suit, $10.00."

No such economic boon was offered, however, to the boys

Man About Town in a Hand-Me-Down

who had once worn the Confederate gray; sad evidence that the soul of Thaddeus Stevens had marched as far west as Chicago.

Men who did not care what their suits cost were offered a limited selection at the catalog's top price for hand-me-downs —fifteen dollars. For this price, one could buy the ultimate in luxury, such as:

"Tillotson's Extra High Class Silk Mixed Worsted Round Cornered Sack Suit. A very beautiful pattern, a brownish cast in a spring and summer weight, the background is composed of a dark and dull brown shade, and sprinkled over this very thickly are gold threads, with an almost invisible over-

A Natty, Nobby, Nifty Number at a Low Price

plaid of a single red thread; there are also fine, but faint stripes. . . . An immensely popular and dressy pattern in a high grade quality, very richly tailored; serge linings, and in every respect a high grade suit, guaranteed to please the most stylish dressers. . . ."

Custom Tailoring

In 1905, as now, many men dissatisfied with ready-made clothing resorted to tailors, and Sears, nothing daunted by distance or the vagaries of the human figure, established a large custom-tailoring department for the benefit of the multitudes of exquisites. This department did not cater to the sloppy and vulgar in dress but, according to the catalog:

"OUR LINE APPEALS TO GOOD DRESSERS. We have as permanent customers many of the most careful dressers in every town and city of the United States, business and professional men (lawyers, doctors, ministers, and prominent persons in

Home-Made Measurements Make a Tailor-Made Man

every locality), such people as require neat, dressy, up to date wearing apparel. Our custom tailoring department also appeals to young men in every part of the country, whether in the city or on the farm, such as enjoy wearing the latest novelties made into the snappiest and most up to date styles. . . ."

Prices, however, along this mail-order Savile Row were agreeably modest, ranging from $12 to $25 for suits.

Fashion in Men's Suits

Fashions in men's clothes change more slowly than in women's, and the effect sought in men's suits in 1905 differs widely from the effect sought today. An anthropologist of the future, peering into the catalog's illustrations for clues to the physical size of American men in the early 1900's, would be totally deceived if he accepted the conclusion that the men

—466—

No Tailor Gets $6.00 for Taking My Measure
—Said Sam

"When did your ship come in?" said Tom.

"Why?" asked Sam. "Do I look so prosperous?"

"You sure do," said Tom. "You're all spruced up."

"You don't call paying $12.00 for a new suit of clothes prosperous?" queried Sam.

"I'd call that thrift," said Tom, "if you can get all that style for $12.00. It looks like an $18.00 suit to me, every inch of it. You must have got it at a sale."

"Not on your life," said Sam. "That came from Sears, Roebuck and Co., Chicago, Illinois, and is one of their regular values."

"You're certainly taking long chances on getting a fit," replied Tom. "I should call it an expert tailor's job to take measurements."

"NO TAILOR GETS $6.00 FOR TAKING MY MEASUREMENT," replied Sam, emphatically. "I take 'em myself. It's as easy as rolling off a log. Besides, Sears, Roebuck and Co. guarantee to fit me or give me my money back, so why should I worry?"

And that was the shot that knocked Tom over. "Just to think," said he, "that I have been spending money like a millionaire all these years, just to get my measure taken."

Now he is a customer of Sears, Roebuck and Co.'s Clothing Department and often tells his friends of the measurement joke that fooled him for so many years.

See our Men's Clothing pages, 422 to 449 in this catalog, or write for our Sample Book No. 89V, which will be mailed free and postpaid on request. It includes an order blank that makes the taking of your measurement as simple as A B C.

Take Your Own Measure—We Guarantee to Fit or Return Money—No Worry. SEARS, ROEBUCK AND CO., CHICAGO, ILL.

were as large as they looked in their clothing. Men of that time wanted to appear big and strong and modeled along the herculean lines of Paul Bunyan or the entire Yale eleven, and tailors, giving them what they wanted, built them up to look big and strong through the cut of their coats and bales of padding stuffed into the shoulders.

Clothing Miscellany

The 1905 catalog devotes nearly two pages to articles of men's clothing popular then but almost museum pieces or curiosities now. For example: fancy-silk and wash vests much affected by men about town, village *boulevardiers,* and gallants of the old school. Gentlemen took the air of a summer evening, afoot or in a carriage, wearing perhaps No. 45C9916:

"Men's Fancy White and Red Dot Wash Vest. The background in white is a sort of basket weave effect, over this there are rows of red dots three-quarters of an inch apart, each red dot having four small black dots around it. A very pretty light colored wash garment."

The serious work of life, however, called for more somber clothes and the bookkeeper of 1905, for instance, on coming to work, took off his coat and put on a black-cotton coat (price 50 cents) or a black-alpaca coat (price $1) before settling down to his ledgers.

The alpaca coat was also the badge of the preacher—white and black in 1905—and the catalog lists coats made especially for men of the cloth.

"We have two special ministerial coats. . . . These coats are made extra long, ministerial style, from a good quality of black alpaca. . . . Price $2.50."

Men's Clothing in a New World

In fast-moving America, great changes occur sometimes from year to year; in the twenty years that passed between 1905 and 1925 the changes were fantastic. Men and men's clothing changed too.

The well-dressed man of the catalog now looks far smaller than his prototype of 1905. He no longer yearns to loom over the landscape like a chunk of the Rocky Mountains, but instead aspires to slender lines, which he achieves by omitting the bales of padding that formerly went into the shoulders of his coat and by using the military cut. Here war again takes a hand. Just as the Civil War brought mass production of men's clothing into existence, the influence of World War uniforms brought a new development of the waistline, and collars that came closer to the throat.

Much has happened to men's fashions in twenty years but much has happened also to prices. The catalog tells us that Sears is "America's Largest clothing store—where over 1,000,000 men yearly buy their suits, topcoats, trousers and the like," but they are paying far higher prices than they paid twenty years before. The de luxe suit of 1905 sold for $15— the catalog offered none more expensive—but by 1925, the featured suit sells for almost double this price, or $25.

The passion for uniformity has also been at work, one suit looks much like another, and all betray the Brooks Brothers-Harvard-Princeton note of conservatism, while over and over again, the catalog stresses "quiet dignity in every line." The country is going to college, and the college is going to the country. Clothing scouts lurking in the cloisters of Eastern universities note what Yale '24 is wearing, and the catalog of 1925 reflects their reports in the clothes that go to all America. Individualism is passing, and with its departure comes a new snobbery.

Young men buy their suits at Sears, but many of them will not admit it, and Sears, more interested in putting clothes on the backs of customers than in taking kinks out of their minds, is content to accept cash for its clothes and let the credit go to the fashionable shops where some of its customers say they buy their clothes. The boys like to brag about the shops in which they buy; it is apparently part of the success tradition to boast that one's clothes are expensive and bear the labels of fashionable clothiers. So, just to make it easier

ALL WOOL BROWN SERGE FANCY NORFOLK SUITS.

A very handsome little garment, made as illustrated, with large shield front and one plait in the center of it, which has a neat silk embroidered emblem on it. The front is also ornamented with four clusters of brown pea buttons. The back of the garment has two box plaits and a belt of the same material is attached.

We also furnish a bow of peau de soie silk with it. The little pants are lined and taped throughout.

No. 40C2145 Price for Eton Norfolk suits, for boys from 4 to 8 years of age only...........**$3.50**

FANCY ROUGH RIDER SUITS.

This is one of the handsomest styles ever produced for the little fellows. The material is a beautiful shade of golden brown corduroy. The illustration will give you an idea as to how the suit is made. It has a small Eton collar trimmed with silk stars on each corner, two outside breast pockets with flaps made to button, the cuffs are turned up and a belt of the same material is attached. Belt, cuffs and shoulder straps are bound with yellow silk soutache. A silk embroidered emblem will be found on the left arm, and the whole suit is trimmed with neat firegilt brass buttons. Pants are lined throughout and have a yellow silk stripe down the side. One of the most popular novelties. We are confident that it cannot be obtained elsewhere at our price.

No. 40C2147 Price for Rough Rider suits, for boys from 3 to 8 years of age only...........**$3.50**

BOYS' BLOUSE SUITS.

Sizes, 3 to 8 years. Order by age only and state if boy is large or small for age.

BLUE CHEVIOT SAILOR BLOUSE SUITS.

Made of a good quality of wool and cotton mixed cheviot. The blouse is made with large sailor collar which is trimmed with black tape and two rows of red silk soutache. A detachable shield is attached and cord and whistle are furnished with the suit. The material is wool and cotton mixed cheviot in a navy blue and we consider the suit the best which possibly can be produced for the price.

No. 40C2151 Price for blouse suits, for boys from 3 to 8 years of age only.....**$1.35**

FANCY CASSIMERE ETON BLOUSE SUITS.

A beautiful little garment made in double breasted style, as illustrated, is neatly trimmed with metal buttons. It has a small Eton collar, neatly plaited, cuffs made to button and a black silk tie is attached. The material is a very handsome mixture of green, brown and olive.

No. 40C2153 Price for blouse suits, for boys from 3 to 8 years of age only.**$1.75**

MEDIUM GRAY STRIPED CHEVIOT SAILOR BLOUSE SUITS.

The material we use for this is all wool, in medium gray shade in a striped effect. The large sailor collar on this number is trimmed with five rows white silk soutache. The suit has a neatly embroidered shield of the same material attached, and a black silk bow tie is furnished with it. It is the best all wool suit which can possibly be produced for the price.

No. 40C2155 Price for blouse suits, for boys from 3 to 8 years of age only...........**$2.00**

FANCY GRAY MIXED CHEVIOT ETON BLOUSE SUITS.

The material for this suit is a handsome mixture of dark gray and green in a striped effect, relieved by green and brown silk spots. The blouse is made in double breasted style, as illustrated, has neatly plaited cuffs, elastic bottom, and a black silk bow tie is furnished with it. Pants are taped and made closed front.

No. 40C2157 Price for Eton blouse suits, for boys from 3 to 8 years of age only........**$2.50**

ALL WOOL RED SERGE SAILOR BLOUSE SUITS.

A very handsome garment, which is very popular. The material is all wool serge in a handsome red shade. The garment is made with a large sailor collar trimmed with seven rows of silk soutache. It has a neatly embroidered shield, a silk embroidered emblem on the left arm and a silk tie is attached. Pants are taped and lined throughout.

No. 40C2159 Price for blouse suits, for boys from 3 to 8 years of age only...........**$2.75**

ALL WOOL NAVY BLUE SERGE BLOUSE SUITS.

This is another very handsome garment, made of strictly pure wool navy blue serge with a large sailor collar, which is trimmed with four rows of black silk tape; a handsomely embroidered shield is attached and a black silk tie is furnished with it. The cuffs on the garment are neatly plaited and made to button. Pants are fully lined and taped and made with closed front.

No. 40C2161 Price for blouse suits, for boys from 3 to 8 years of age only........**$3.00**

BUSTER BROWNS AND RUSSIAN SUITS.

Sizes, 2½ to 6 Years only. Order by Age only, and State if Boy is Large or Small for Age.

RED FLANNEL BUSTER BROWN SUITS.

Made of a splendid quality of all wool red flannel, with a large shield front, neatly trimmed with fancy metal buttons and provided with a belt of the same material. The collar is trimmed with black tape and a black silk bow tie is furnished with the suit. Pants are taped through seat and made in bloomer style. A remarkable value.

No. 40C2163 Price for Buster Brown suits for boys from 2½ to 6 years of age only........**$2.00**

BLUE SERGE BUSTER BROWN SUITS.

Another handsome suit, made exactly as shown in illustration, with an Eton collar, which is neatly trimmed with black tape and black soutache, and the shield front is trimmed with handsome white pearl buttons and a belt of the same material is attached to the suit. The material is a splendid quality of navy blue serge, which will give satisfactory wear. Pants are fully lined and taped and made in bloomer style.

No. 40C2165 Price for Buster Brown suits, for boys from 2½ to 6 years of age only...........**$2.35**

DARK BROWN ALL WOOL BUSTER BROWN SUITS.

A very handsome garment, made with Eton collar, plaited cuffs, and has a substantial black leather belt attached. The front is trimmed with two rows of fancy brass buttons, and the left sleeve has a silk embroidered emblem on it, and a silk bow to match the material is attached to the suit. Pants are fully taped and made in bloomer style. A beautiful, dressy garment.

No. 40C2167 Price for Buster Brown suits, for boys from 2½ to 6 years of age only....**$2.50**

FANCY MIXED CHEVIOT BUSTER BROWN SUITS.

The material is homespun and its color is a medium shade, a gray and green mixture, relieved by green, yellow and red silk lines which give it a very dressy effect. It is made double breasted, front neatly trimmed with ivory buttons, has open plaited cuffs, a detachable white linen collar and black silk bow tie are furnished, and a black patent leather belt is attached to the garment. For a dressy summer suit there is nothing equal to this number.

No. 40C2169 Price for Buster Brown suits, for boys from 2½ to 6 years of age only...........**$2.75**

ALL WOOL RED SERGE BUSTER BROWN SUITS.

A red serge is a very popular material for this style and is sure to give satisfactory wear. This number is made with three plaits down front, trimmed with neat brass buttons and is ornamented with three black and white silk stars in front. A black silk bow tie is attached to the suit and a black leather belt is furnished with it. Pants are lined throughout and made in bloomer style.

No. 40C2171 Price for Buster Brown suits, for boys from 2½ to 6 years of age only...........**$2.75**

FANCY MIXED CASSIMERE SUITS.

This is one of the handsomest materials we have been able to obtain. Its color is a medium shade of gray in a small check formed by dark gray and olive lines. The front is neatly trimmed, as shown in illustration, and the edges of the collar and front are bound with black and red cord and a red silk bow tie is attached. A handsome leather belt to match the material is furnished with it. Pants are double sewed and taped and made in bloomer style.

No. 40C2173 Price for Buster Brown suits, for boys from 2½ to 6 years of age only...........**$3.00**

ALL WOOL NAVY BLUE RUSSIAN SUITS.

A very handsome style, made fly front, has a large, neatly trimmed sailor collar and a handsome silk embroidered shield attached. A black leather belt is furnished with the garment, cuffs are neatly plaited (made to button) and on the left arm is a handsomely embroidered emblem. Nothing has ever been produced to equal this suit for the price.

No. 40C2175 Price for Russian suits, for boys from 2½ to 6 years of age only........**$3.50**

FANCY SHEPHERD PLAID BUSTER BROWN SUITS.

If you desire something especially dressy for your little boy, there is nothing better than this number. The material is all wool black and white checked shepherd plaid cheviot. The front of the garment is ornamented with a red silk embroidered emblem and has two rows of small black buttons. The edges are bound with red cord. Cuffs are made to button and are neatly plaited, and suit is furnished with a black patent leather belt. A black silk bow tie is attached. Pants are made in bloomer style and are fully lined and taped throughout.

No. 40C2177 Price for Buster Brown suits, for boys from 2½ years of age only

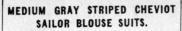

CHILDREN'S CLOAKS.

CHILDREN'S DRESSES. AGES, 1 TO 5 YEARS.

$1.98

21c   25c   75c   98c

No. 38C4164 Child's Military Cloak, made of fine all wool flannel. Has wide military collar trimmed with flannel in contrasting color, followed with gilt braid and three small gilt buttons; collar trimmed with braid to match; full fashioned sleeves; cloak trimmed with large gilt buttons and interlined with wadding and lined with sateen. Colors, royal blue or cardinal.
Price................$1.98
If by mail, postage extra, 34 cents.

No. 38C4700 Child's Dress. Made of good quality washable gingham. Hubbard style, revers on each side trimmed with fancy braid and trimmed in center with novelty braid to match, sleeves trimmed with novelty braid to match, hem at bottom. Colors, blue or pink checks. Price, each......$0.21
Per dozen.............. 2.40
If by mail postage extra, each, 8c.

No. 38C4704 Child's Dress, made of gingham. Solid color yoke trimmed with three rows of fancy braid, ruffle edged with wash lace, hem at bottom. Colors, pink or blue, in checks or stripes.
Price, each........$0.25
Per dozen............. 2.85
If by mail, postage extra, each, 10c.

No. 38C4712 Child's Dress made of fancy check suiting. Cashmere yoke trimmed with two rows of soutache and small pearl buttons, ruffle all around yoke. Dress lined throughout with cambric. Deep hem at bottom. Colors, fancy checks, blue or red predominating.
Price..............75c
If by mail, postage extra, 20 cents.

No. 38C4716 Child's Dress made of cashmere. Hubbard style. Fancy circular yoke. Trimmed with tucks and baby ribbon. Plaited ruffle all around yoke and edged with two rows of baby ribbon. Collar and cuffs have two rows of stitching. Lined throughout with cambric. Deep hem at bottom. Ages, 1 to 5 years. Colors, royal blue or wine.
Price.................98c
If by mail postage extra, 19 cent

CHILDREN'S FRENCH DRESSES. AGES, 2 TO 6 YEARS.

$2.48

39c   45c

48c

89c

No. 38C4167 Child's Cloak, made of good quality velvette. Has wide shoulder cape, neatly trimmed with five medallions, followed with fancy braid, also squares of sateen trimmed with soutache. Collar and cuffs trimmed with fancy braid. Fancy gilt buttons. Interlined with wadding and lined with sateen. Color, black with fancy trimmings.
Price..............$2.48
If by mail, postage extra, 33 cents.

No. 38C4730 The New Suspender Dress, made of chambray. Suspenders made of same material as in dress, and edged with wash lace. Collar and cuffs edged with wash lace, full blouse, hem at bottom. Ages, 2 to 6 years. Colors, royal blue or red (oxblood).
Price, each............$0.39
Per dozen.............. 4.50
If by mail, postage extra, each, 10c.

No. 38C4732 Child's Lawn Dress, very neat yoke made of white striped lawn, the fancy bertha neatly trimmed with valenciennes lace and edged with neat wash lace, sleeves trimmed to match, collar edged with lace, hem at bottom. Ages, 2 to 6 years. Colors, pale blue, tan or white.
Price................45c
If by mail, postage extra, 9 cents.

No. 38C4734 Child's Dress, made of good quality wash gingham; trimmed with three box plaits back and front, made to button on side and trimmed with white pique. Newest style plaited sleeves, belt of same material as in dress, white pique collar. Ages, 2 to 6 years. Colors, blue or pink.
Price............48c
If by mail, postage extra, 12 cents.

No. 38C4738 Newest Style Suspender Dress. Body made of white lawn, neatly trimmed with six plaits. Skirt made of good quality percale, with belt to match. Suspenders trimmed with row of white pique and edged with neat embroidery; collar and cuffs edged with embroidery to match; deep hem at bottom. Ages, 2 to 6 years. Colors, pink or blue stripes. 89c
If by mail, postage extra, 10 cents.

98c

$1.15

98c

$1.48

75c

$1.10

No. 38C4742 Child's Sailor Dress, made of chambray. Very neat sailor collar trimmed with two rows of white tape, white pique dickey. Full blouse trimmed in back and front with three box plaits; tie, cuffs and belt trimmed with white braid. Box plaited skirt with deep hem at bottom. Ages, 2 to 6 years. Colors, blue or tan.
Price.................98c
If by mail, postage extra, 12 cents.

No. 38C4746 Child's Dress, made of chambray. Very neatly trimmed in back and front with six plaits, dress made to button on side. Neatly trimmed with two rows of white tape. Collar and belt trimmed to match. Newest fashioned sleeves trimmed with ten rows of white tape. Ages, 2 to 6 years. Colors, blue or tan.
Price.........$1.15
If by mail, postage extra, 12 cents.

No. 48C4750 Child's Dress, made of chambray. Has wide sailor collar, neatly trimmed back and front with box plaits, back and front with two pearl buttons, newest fashioned sleeves with plaits. Full plaited skirt, with deep hem at bottom. Ages, 2 to 6 years. Colors, blue or tan. Price.....98c
If by mail, postage extra, 12 cents.

No. 38C4754 Very Pretty Dress, made of fine dimity, in very neat floral effects. Round yoke, trimmed with clusters of tucks alternating with three insertions of neat embroidery; the very neatly designed bertha is edged with embroidery, neck and sleeves trimmed to match. Full blouse and also trimmed with embroidery. Ages, 2 to 6 years. Colors, neat stripes in blue or pink with floral design.
Price..............$1.48
If by mail, postage extra, 11c.

No. 38C4758 Child's Dress, made of fancy checked suiting. Trimmed with two cashmere straps, each with two rows of soutache and small pearl buttons. Collar and cuffs trimmed with two rows of soutache. Very full blouse. Dress lined throughout with cambric. Deep hem at bottom. Ages, 2 to 6 years. Colors, fancy checks, with blue or red predominating. Price....75c
If by mail, postage extra, 20c.

No. 38C4762 Child's Dress, made of cashmere, plaited front. Fancy stitched strap at left side, trimmed with embroidered silk emblem. Collar, cuffs and belt with two rows of stitching plaited back. Dress lined throughout with cambric. Deep hem at bottom. Ages, 2 to 6 years. Colors, navy blue or wine. Price.$1.10
If by mail, postage extra, 18 cents.

for the braggarts as well as to boost sales, Sears omits its name from all its suits.

Dress for Success

During the period 1870–1900, when men were busy with the giant task of building America, dress and dressing were of little importance to them. Probably at no period in the country's history were empire builders and ditch diggers more shabbily and sloppily dressed than during this great era of national growth. From 1900 to 1929, men dressed far better than they did in the latter half of the nineteenth century, while their clothes were evidence not only of prosperity but also of the healthy vanity of the preening male. But ten years after the beginning of the depression of 1929, when prosperity had vanished and the male's peacock feathers sadly drooped, men no longer dressed to please themselves or women but to please the boss or attract the attention of a putative boss. In 1939, they wear clothes to succeed, and the catalog, whose business it is to know the workings of the American mind, tells its customers to "Prepare for Leadership, Wear The Right Clothes." What are the right clothes? The right clothes, messieurs, are those worn by college men. The college is now as potent in the field of men's fashions as Hollywood is in women's fashions. And so the catalog says: "Up The Ladder To Success With College Shop Clothes."

What is the costume that leads infallibly to success? It is the suit of clothes called Staunton, because here skillful tailors have wrought into wool those esoteric principles discovered by the eminent academician of success, Mr. Dale Carnegie, and generously released by him to a country in travail. The Staunton, we learn, "Wins More Friends, Influences More People," and so smooth has the way to success been made by Sears and Mr. Carnegie, that the wearer of this suit (while winning friends and influencing people) may pay for it at the rate of $2 a month.

25 · GENTS' FURNISHINGS

In THE early 1900's, all items of men's wearing apparel
except suits of clothing were grouped and sold under the
general heading of "Gents' Furnishings," and the stores that
sold them were gents' furnishings stores. It was not until the
1920's that this term came to be superseded by the haughty
"haberdashery" sold in shops, campus stores, or clothing
cathedrals. But under whatever term men's wearing apparel
was distributed, it became increasingly important to retail
stores. Men's fashions change more slowly than women's
fashions and exhibit less variability but they do change, and
since the turn of the century have been affected by the automobile, sports, and an increasing clothes consciousness,
whether aroused by advertising or a rising ego clamoring
for expression. These changes relate not only to what men
wear but even more explicitly to what they no longer wear.

And So to Bed

Readers of George Moore's *Memoirs of My Dead Life*
will recall the author's anguish when, upon arriving at
Orelay with the long-sought but elusive Doris, he found that
he had failed to put his pajamas in his luggage, and how,
after going from shop to shop of the little French provincial
town, the shopkeepers who sympathized with his desperate
plight were unable to produce anything but an old-fashioned
nightshirt. The pajamas of elegant Paris had not yet penetrated to the provinces, and George Moore, to whom the
nightshirt was the death of love, was compelled to take one.

In 1905, a few exquisites of metropolis wore pajamas,
but the great mass of American men were content to sleep in

their skins (weather permitting), their underwear, or their nightshirts; they were disturbed by no fears such as existed in the mind of George Moore, and there is no evidence to prove either that the nightgown was the death of love in America or that the later pajamas were its renaissance. In any event, the catalog pictures quite serene-looking gentlemen wearing:

"Men's superfine nightshirts. Made of finest muslin. . . . Collars and cuffs handsomely trimmed and richly embroidered in silk of contrasting shades, cardinal, baby blue, pink, opal, or lavender."

Yet Women Loved Them

Nowadays most men wear the same weight night clothes throughout the year, because of better home heating, but in the early 1900's they put away their summer nightshirts at the approach of cold weather and changed to those of flannelette. These were "soft and fluffy like swansdown, assorted colors and stripes," which cost as much as ninety-five cents for the luxury models and as little as forty cents for the simpler kinds. The time had not yet come when men would wear pajamas, thus making two garments do the work of one and bind them around the stomach in the bargain. The 1905 catalog does not list pajamas at all.

Celluloid Shirt Fronts and Rubber Collars

Men's shirts of forty to thirty years ago differ markedly from those worn today. The so-called collar-attached soft shirt, now almost universally worn, was then used only by workmen, whose clothes have always been distinguished by a grace, comfort, and utility lacking in those worn by the white-collar classes. Shirts did not button down the front but were pulled over the head, and many a man who got stuck in one as he tried to take it off yelled and cussed until his wife came to the rescue, and with a strong yank liberated the suffering man into the fresh air. The detachable, starched, stiff collars of the times were made either of materials that matched the shirts, or, more commonly, of white linen, rubber, or celluloid.

Shirt, circa 1905

In the heat of summer, linen collars tightly buttoned around the throat were a torture to the flesh; their saw edges rasped the neck, and the victim's sweat soon reduced the once starched collar to a damp band of fabric. Nonetheless, men stuck to collars and collars stuck to men for long years; they were made in hundreds of styles, and were the basis of large firms such as Cluett, Peabody, who at one time made nothing but collars, and whose business was seriously threatened when detached collars finally went out and the collar-attached shirt came in. This firm avoided dissolution by becoming a manufacturer of shirts.

Linen collars were cheap, costing from ten to twenty cents, but it was true of them, as it was later of the automobile, that "it ain't the initial cost that counts; it's the upkeep." They soiled easily, acquired saw edges after a few trips to the laundry, and they could not be washed at home or tossed into the family pile of clothes hauled away once a week by the washwoman. Therefore, they were avoided by the less elegant but thriftier gentlemen who bought celluloid or rubber collars. These could be cleansed by the application of soap and water, or, in a desperate moment, by a lick of spittle applied with a handkerchief; they did not breed laundry bills, and were low in wilting capacity. A man who wore a celluloid collar, however, ran the risk of literally becoming hot under the collar, because it was highly inflammable, and the wearer had to beware of fire.

Modern revolutions, whatever their underlying philosophies or lack of them, lean heavily on shirts. Benito Mussolini, the best press agent the shirt industry has ever had, almost invariably begins his speeches from a fixed or portable balcony with the ringing cry, "Blackshirts of the revolution!" We had black shirts long ago, and now all we have to do is resurrect them and build a revolution around them. In the early 1900's, many American workmen wore, instead of the blue shirt of today, shirts of plain or figured black sateen.

Money Belts

Sneak thieves and robbers have always abounded in America, and the honest farmer going to the city or the gold miner moving in a rough environment, sought to outwit them by the use of money belts secured to their bodies. The prospective customer is offered a choice of three models, of which No. 6C4498 seems to have been the most useful:

"Money and Gold Dust Belts. Four inches wide; made of the very finest oil tanned calfskin; will never get stiff and is just the thing to carry money or gold dust in; made with three compartments; the outside cover folds over very closely and is fastened by snap buttons. This is the finest belt on the market for the purpose. Price, 98¢."

Neckties

In the summer of 1905, half the men in the country, to judge by the space allotted in the catalog, wore with their stiff, plaited bosom shirts the string tie of the legendary Southern colonel. These ties were made of white lawn or black silk—the orthodox tradition—or of colored silk or madras. And they were so cheap they were sold not by the piece but by the dozen. Twelve lawn ties cost ten to twenty-five cents; colored madras ties forty to sixty-five cents; while the more expensive silk string ties ranged from ten to twenty-five cents each.

It can scarcely be assumed that men of 1905 had no time to knot their ties before rushing off in the morning to catch the 6:57 train, yet factory-tied, ready-to-wear cravats were highly popular and outsold all other kinds in the catalog. One can only assume that the hand that ran the plow or milked the cow was not fluent to the niceties of turning a wisp of silk or lawn into a fashionable knot worn at the throat. Sears spared men this job by doing the work itself.

29c
EACH
No. 33T8373

Pampered Men Once Bought Their Ties Ready-Knotted

The highest-priced silk tie in the catalog of this year is "men's finest quality silk imperial," for seventy-five cents; simple silk ties sold for twenty cents, and the extremely popular shield bows went for a dime.

Stretchy Seam Drawers

So radically does men's underwear of today differ from that of 1905, that the terms "stretchy seam drawers" and "balbriggan shirts" are gibberish to this generation. Then, however, both were popular. Stretchy seam drawers were made with inserts of cotton webbing down each side of the leg, "giving easy motion and greater comfort." They were ankle length, highly anaphrodisiac, and some had laces at the bottoms to tie them around the ankles. Balbriggan undershirts were lightweight undershirts usually made of Egyptian cotton and usually having long sleeves. They were ecru or tan in color and buttoned up the front. It is unfortunate that no painter of the times stayed home and preserved for posterity a typical American of the period in a *Portrait of A Man Wearing Stretchy Seam Drawers and Balbriggan Undershirt,* instead of going to Paris and painting conventional nudes after the outworn formalisms of the French academic schools.

In the early years of this century, underwear had to cover a multitude of skin both summer and winter. Drawers were

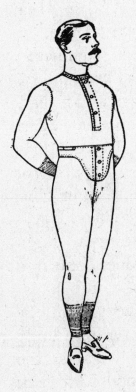

The Long and Simple Flannels of the Poor

almost invariably ankle length; undershirts had long sleeves; union suits were, of course, all enveloping; while many men, even in the hottest weather, wore a hair-shirt device next the skin called "lightweight, summer wool underwear," on the theory that "sweating keeps you cool." When winter came, men took to heavy cotton or wool underwear, the latter being almost as scratchy as sandpaper and frequently scarlet red, because this shade was supposed to have therapeutic qualities good for curing or alleviating the pains of rheumatism. The time was to come, however, when plodding men, following the example of swifter-moving women, would shed their heavy clothes for lighter apparel.

Pajamas—Fresh Air—And Other Novelties

The seesaw of fashion change in men's apparel is clearly shown in the catalog of 1915; clearly shown, too, is the fact that fashion change, like evolution in the physical world, does not advance dizzily upward but in a sidewise manner, and at any given time some species is farther ahead in the march of evolution than others.

Soft shirts with collars attached are now listed in great numbers, but so are rubber collars; pajamas are offered, but so are nightshirts. One of the pajama numbers prominently displayed offers proof that the World War has brought unwonted prosperity to the small town and the farm and is leading the farmer into strange ways. The man who a few years ago went to bed in his skin, his stretchy seam drawers, or a flannelette nightgown (price ninety cents), now prepares for sleep in "Extra Fine Tub Silk Pajamas. Colors light blue, champagne, creamwhite." And the price! Five dollars! It was innovation enough for the thrifty farmer to wear night clothes at all instead of going to bed as he had once come into it; it is nothing short of revolution to find him in silk pajamas; but since radicalism grows by what it feeds upon, the end is not yet in sight. By 1915, the farmer and his family have so far conquered their ancient prejudice against the night air in which dangerous diseases were supposed to lurk that they are voluntarily sleeping out of doors. The catalog lists a number of heavyweight garments:

SPECIAL VALUES IN GOLD PLATED JEWELRY.

A GROWING DEMAND from clothing stores, furnishing goods stores, dry goods stores, traders and others for a grade of gold plated jewelry such as is commonly sold by retail clothiers and dry goods merchants, has induced us to add the following special lines of gold plated jewelry, to our already big line of the highest grade gold plated, gold filled and solid gold jewelry.

THERE IS A GREAT DEMAND among our millions of customers, those who buy for their own use, as well as those who buy to sell again, for a dependable quality of gold plated jewelry that can be sold at a fraction of the price we are compelled to ask for the highest grades of gold plated and gold filled and solid gold jewelry, such as is shown in the other pages of this catalogue.

TO SUPPLY THIS DEMAND, on the following pages we show a variety of jewelry in the very latest styles and patterns which we offer at the lowest price at which any dependable grade of gold plated jewelry can possibly be offered, and at prices very much lower than the same grade of jewelry is or has ever been offered by any other house in any quantity.

THE SPECIAL GOLD PLATED JEWELRY which we offer on the following pages is not to be compared with any of the cheap electro plated jewelry that is so widely advertised and sold by cheap jewelry houses, peddlers, etc. Every piece of jewelry illustrated is well made and beautifully finished, all nicely gold plated, highly polished and finished, and has all the appearance of the higher grade of gold plated and gold filled jewelry which sells at several times the price we ask.

THIS IS THE EXACT SAME GRADE of gold plated jewelry as you will find in the best dry goods stores as well as in many of the most representative retail jewelry stores. For example, the cuff buttons and cuff links which we offer at from 10 to 20 cents each (special prices in dozen lots), are the exact same links and buttons that retail generally at from 25 to 50 cents per pair. The handsome, new style brooches which we offer at 10 to 25 cents are the exact same style and grade of gold plated goods that retail generally at 25 cents to $1.00. The stick pins, scarf pins and other pieces of gold plated jewelry shown in this line, which we offer at 10 to 20 cents (special prices per dozen quantities), are the exact same goods that retail everywhere at from 25 to 50 cents each. The chains which we show in a big variety, at prices ranging from 10 to 50 cents each (special prices in dozen quantities), are the exact same new, late style goods that are retailed generally at from 50 cents to $1.50.

WHILE WE DO NOT GUARANTEE THE WEARING QUALITIES of this grade of jewelry, as before stated, it is the exact same grade of gold plated jewelry that is sold largely by dealers under one, two and three year guarantees at from two to ten times the price we ask. The length of time any piece of this jewelry will wear without the gold wearing off and without tarnishing or discoloring depends on the kind of wear the piece of jewelry gets. For example, a scarf pin, brooch, charm or cuff button will wear much longer than a ring. Every piece we offer will give the best of satisfaction and we guarantee it the equal of any gold plated jewelry retailed generally at from two to five times the price we ask.

SPECIAL OPPORTUNITY FOR DEALERS, JEWELERS, CLOTHIERS, GENERAL STORES, TRADERS AND OTHERS TO BUY IN QUANTITIES AT HERETOFORE UNHEARD OF LOW PRICES.

WE ARE SELLING THIS JEWELRY AT PRICES MUCH LOWER than the same grade of jewelry was ever sold by any manufacturer or wholesale dealer. At our special prices you can supply your wants at a much lower cost than you have ever before been able to buy. If you have a general store or are engaged in the clothing, dry goods or furnishing goods business and do not carry a stock of jewelry, we especially urge that you order a small assortment selected from the following pages. We will guarantee you will find the goods the very latest style, gold plated goods that will give satisfaction, an assortment of gold plated jewelry that will find ready sale with your trade and at prices from three to five times the price you pay us. If you don't carry jewelry, put in a little stock, if only an assortment of $5.00 or $10.00, and you will be surprised how rapidly these goods will sell. A $10.00 assortment at our prices, as selected from these pages, would, at average retail prices, bring $50.00 to $75.00, and we are sure if you make the start you will in time carry a liberal stock and add greatly to your profit by the small investment made.

DEALERS AND TRADERS are especially urged to make up a small order of this popular priced gold plated jewelry as selected from these pages. Make up a $5.00 assortment, if you please, and the shrewd peddler or trader will be able to sell the lot for at least $25.00.

WHILE THE VERY LOW PRICES at which we sell this popular grade of gold plated jewelry will attract thousands of our customers, who may wish to buy one item for their own use, the prices we offer enable you to buy for 10 or 15 cents, one article for which you would have to pay at retail from 25 cents to $1.00. This grade of gold plated jewelry is offered especially to supply the retail jeweler, the peddler and the trader who wishes to buy in dozen lots and take advantage of our very low prices, prices much lower than were ever before quoted on this grade of goods.

YOU WILL NOTE UNDER EACH ARTICLE OF JEWELRY we quote the single price, also the price per one-half dozen and the price per dozen, making a special price where orders are placed for dozen lots, and in ordering a dozen you are at liberty to assort the dozen. For example, if you are selecting cuff buttons and wish to take advantage of our dozen price you can make up the dozen by selecting one or two of each number at the same price. For instance, there may be one-half dozen numbers that sell at $1.50 a dozen, in which case you are at liberty to select two of each number and get the benefit of the dozen price. In this way it gives the dealer, the peddler or the trader an opportunity to get together a very attractive assortment of the showiest cheap gold plated jewelry made for a very small investment. Just a few dollars, $5.00 to $10.00, would make up an assortment of jewelry that would prove very attractive in any clothing store, dry goods store, general store or in the stock of any peddler or trader.

REMEMBER, THESE ARE BEAUTIFUL GOODS, handsomely finished and highly polished, all gold plated, the same grade of latest style goods as is handled usually by the retail clothing trade and dry goods trade, but none of this jewelry is guaranteed by us, nor will it be replaced or repaired by us after being worn except when otherwise specified. We will fill any order for this jewelry, sending it to anyone with the understanding and agreement that if it isn't perfectly satisfactory when received, it can be returned to us at our expense, and the money sent us will be immediately refunded, together with any express charges paid by the customer, but after the jewelry has been worn, used or carried in stock, or offered for sale, it is not returnable to us and no repairs will be made on it by us. If you wish to buy jewelry which is guaranteed to wear for years you should select the higher grade gold plated, gold filled and solid gold jewelry shown in this catalogue.

REMEMBER, WE ACCEPT NO ORDER FOR LESS THAN 50 CENTS. If you wish to buy an item of jewelry for your own use, the price of which is less than 50 cents, select enough more needed jewelry or other merchandise to make your order amount to 50 cents or more.

Collar Button Price List, No. 4C15000 to No. 4C15100.
To order correctly, give catalogue number for shape wanted and letter as shown for quality and style desired.

	Price for 1 Dozen only	Price for ½ Gross only	Price per Gross, for 1 Gross or more
A Gold plated top, post and bottom	$0.18	$1.05	$2.00
B Gold plated, with pearl bottom	.28	1.58	3.00
C Gold plated, with celluloid bottom	.18	1.05	2.00
D Second quality, rolled gold plated top, post and bottom	.36	2.10	4.00
E Second quality, rolled gold plated, with pearl bottom	.39	2.23	4.25
F Second quality, rolled gold plated, with celluloid bottom	.36	2.10	4.00
G First quality, rolled gold plated top, post and bottom	.69	3.94	7.50
H First quality, rolled gold plated, with pearl bottom	.73	4.20	8.00
I First quality, rolled gold plated, with celluloid bottom	.69	3.94	7.50

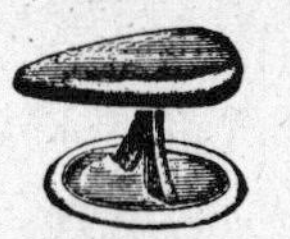
No. 4C15000 Large size pointer.

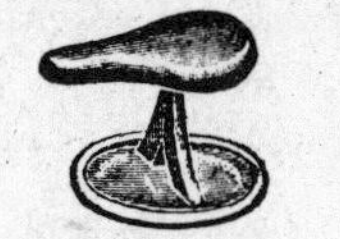
No. 4C15010 Narrow shape pointer.

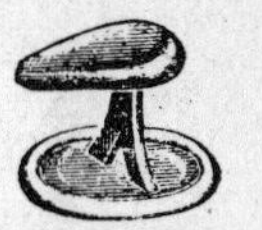
No. 4C15020 Small size pointer.

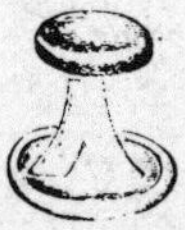
No. 4C15030 Large size lever.

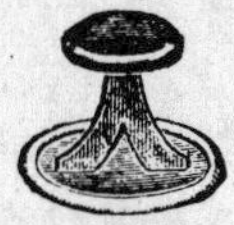
No. 4C15040 Medium size lever.

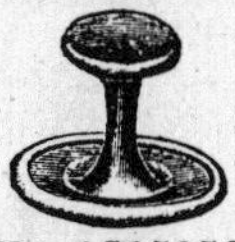
No. 4C15050 Tall flat top post.

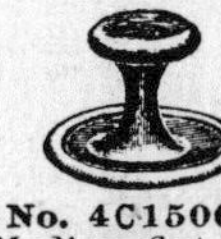
No. 4C15060 Medium flat top post.

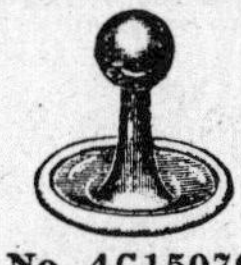
No. 4C15070 Medium size ball top.

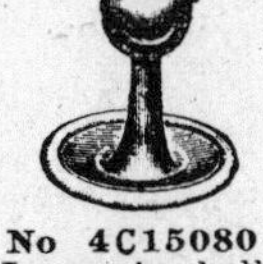
No 4C15080 Large size ball top.

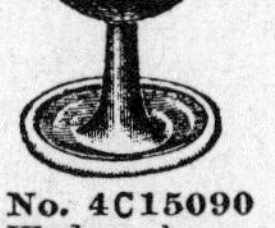
No. 4C15090 Wedge shape, large size, solid post.

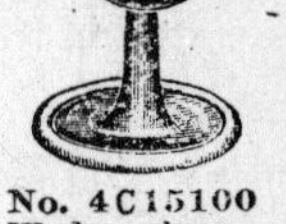
No. 4C15100 Wedge shape, small size, solid post.

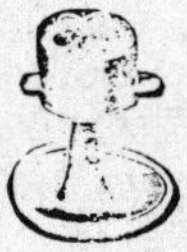
No. 4C15120 Separable, engraved top, solid silver bottom. One dozen.. $0.69 Half gross.. 3.94 One gross.. 7.50

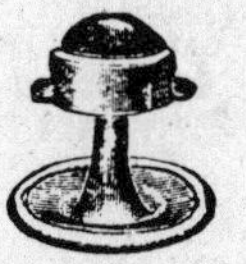
No. 4C15130 Separable, celluloid bottom, fancy stone set. One dozen.. $0.48 Half gross.. 2.76 One gross.. 5.25

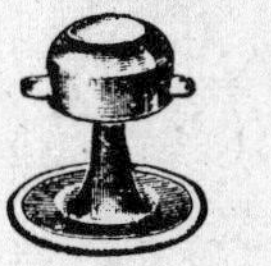
No. 4C15140 Separable, pearl setting, celluloid bottom. One dozen, $0.58 Half gross, 3.35 One gross.. 6.38

Collar Button Sets, Consisting of Two Lever, One Ball Top and One Pointer.

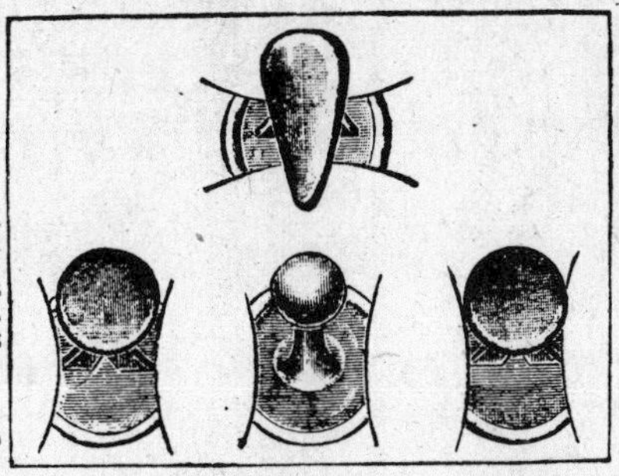
No. 4C15110 COLLAR AND CUFF SETS.

No. 4C15110 Collar Button Set Price List.
To order correctly, give catalogue number of set and letter for quality desired.

	Price for 1 Dozen Sets only	Price for ½ Gross Sets only	Price for 1 Gross Sets or more
A Gold plated top post and bottom	$0.72	$4.20	$8.00
B Gold plated top post, pearl bottom	1.12	6.32	12.00
C Gold plated top post, celluloid bottom	.72	4.20	8.00
D Second quality rolled gold plated top post and bottom	1.44	8.40	16.00
E Second quality rolled gold plated top post with pearl bottom	1.56	8.92	17.00
F Second quality rolled gold plated top post with celluloid bottom	1.44	8.40	16.00
G First quality rolled gold plated top post and bottom	2.76	15.76	30.00
H First quality rolled gold plated top post with pearl bottom	2.93	16.80	32.00
I First quality rolled gold plated top post with celluloid bottom	2.76	15.76	30.00

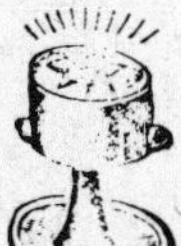
No. 4C15150 Separable, rhinestone, pearl set top, celluloid bottom. One dozen.. $0.58 Half gross.. 3.35 One gross.. 6.38

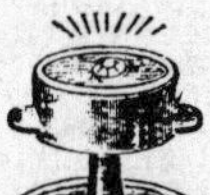
No. 4C15160 Separable, rhinestone, pearl set top, celluloid bottom. One dozen.. $0.48 Half gross.. 2.76 One gross.. 5.25

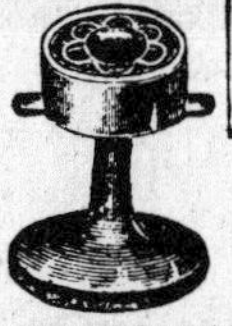
No. 4C15170 Separable, fancy stone set, pearl bottom. One dozen.. $0.58 Half gross.. 3.35 One gross.. 6.38

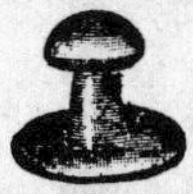
No. 4C15180 Bone collar button, one piece. One dozen...... 5c One gross...... 50c

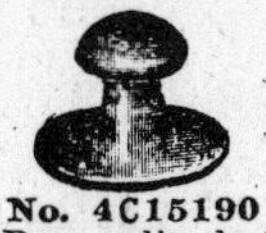
No. 4C15190 Bone collar button, one piece. One dozen...... 6c One gross...... 65c

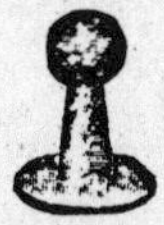
No. 4C15200 Pearl collar button, one piece. One dozen.... 46c

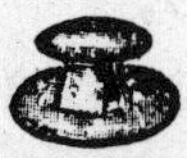
No. 4C15210 Pearl collar but ton, one piece. One dozen.... 42c

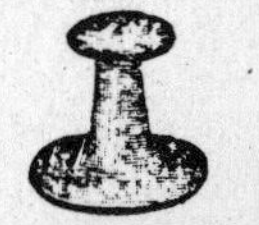
No. 4C15220 Pearl collar button, one piece. One dozen.. 52c

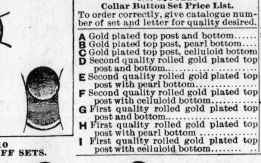

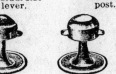

SEE INDEX, PINK PAGES 492 TO 499, TO FIND WHAT YOU WANT.

MEN'S SUMMER UNDERWEAR.

FOR MEN'S WINTER UNDERWEAR, SEND FOR SPECIAL CATALOGUE OF UNDERWEAR.

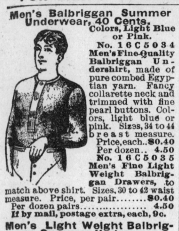

Men's Balbriggan Summer Underwear, 40 Cents.

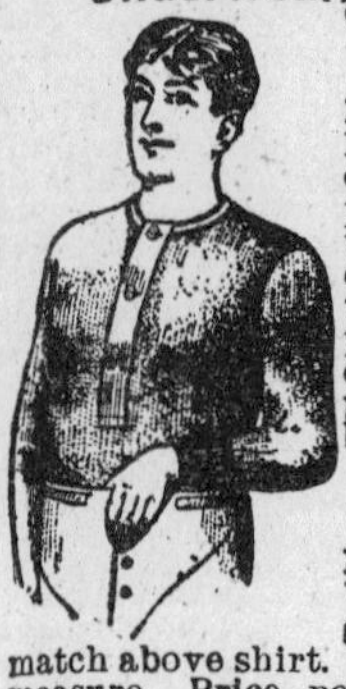

Colors, Light Blue or Pink. No. 16C5034 **Men's Fine Quality Balbriggan Undershirt**, made of pure combed Egyptian yarn. Fancy collarette neck and trimmed with fine pearl buttons. Colors, light blue or pink. Sizes, 34 to 44 breast measure. Price, each..$0.40 Per dozen.. 4.50

No. 16C5035 **Men's Fine Light Weight Balbriggan Drawers,** to match above shirt. Sizes, 30 to 42 waist measure. Price, per pair........$0.40 Per dozen pairs........ 4.50
If by mail, postage extra, each, 9c.

Men's Light Weight Balbriggan Summer Underwear, 40 Cents.

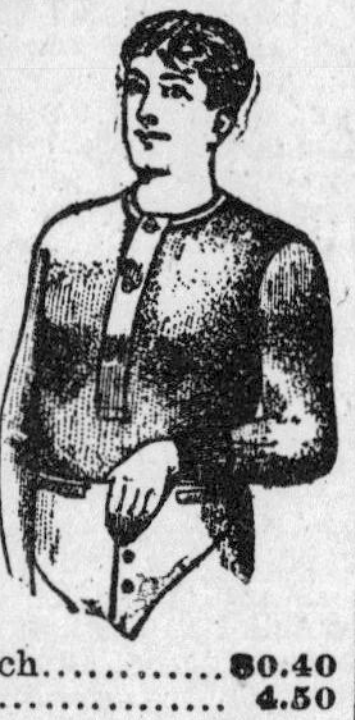

Color, White. No. 16C5036 **Men's Fine Quality Balbriggan Undershirt, very fine light weight garment,** made of pure combed Egyptian yarn, and for a light weight summer garment we consider it one of the best garments; in fact, it is more like a gauze weight. Fancy collarette neck and trimmed with fine pearl buttons. Color, white. Sizes, 34 to 44 breast measure. Price, each............$0.40 Per dozen........ 4.50

No. 16C5037 **Men's Fine Light Weight Balbriggan Drawers,** to match above shirt. Sizes, 30 to 42 waist measure. Price, per pair........$0.40 Per dozen pairs........ 4.50
If by mail, postage extra, each, 9c.

French Balbriggan, 65 Cents.

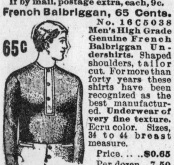

65c

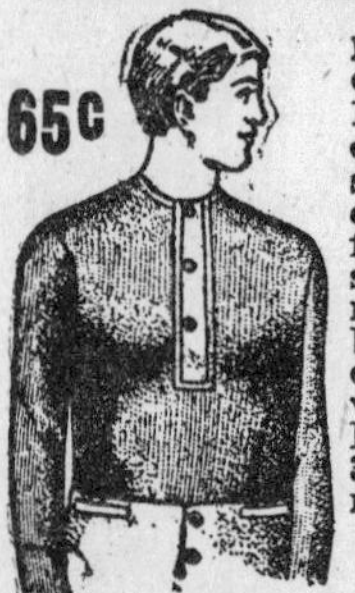

No. 16C5038 **Men's High Grade Genuine French Balbriggan Undershirts.** Shaped shoulders, tailor cut. For more than forty years these shirts have been recognized as the best manufactured. **Underwear of very fine texture.** Ecru color. Sizes, 34 to 44 breast measure. Price.....$0.65 Per dozen. 7.50

No. 16C5039 **Men's Drawers,** to match above shirts. Sizes, 30 to 42 waist measure. Price, per pair..$0.65 Per dozen pairs........ 7.50
If by mail, postage extra, each, 10c.

Our Special Leader in Fine Mercerized Underwear, 85c.

85c

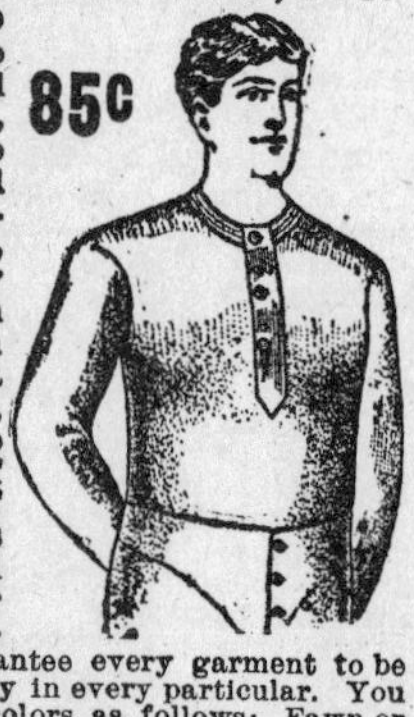

No. 16C5040 **Men's Fine Plain Knitted Undershirts,** made of the new yarn called **American mercerized silk,** which is a very fine Egyptian cotton yarn treated by a special process, which gives the appearance of and many of the properties of silk. It will wear better than a silk garment, and we guarantee every garment to be entirely satisfactory in every particular. You have a choice of colors as follows: Fawn or light blue. Be sure to state the color in your order. Sizes, breast measure, 34 to 44. Price........85c

No. 16C5041 **Men's Drawers,** to match above undershirts. Sizes, waist measure, 30 to 42 inches. Price, per pair........85c
If by mail, postage extra, each 9 cents.

FOR MEN'S WINTER UNDERWEAR send for free Special Catalogue of Underwear

Black Balbriggan Underwear.

40c

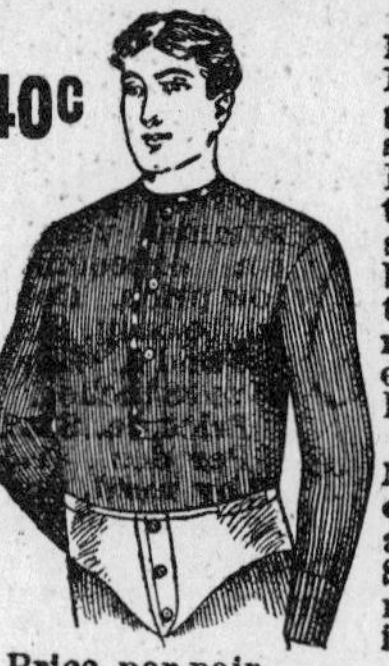

No. 16C5042 **Men's Fine Black Balbriggan Undershirts,** made of Egyptian cotton. Color, absolutely fast black. Sizes, 34 to 44 breast measure. Price, each......$0.40 Per doz.. 4.50

No. 16C5043 **Men's Drawers,** to match above shirts. Sizes, waist measure, 30 to 42 inches. Price, per pair..................$0.40 Per dozen pairs........ 4.50
If by mail, postage extra, each, 9c.

MEN'S FANCY UNDERWEAR.

Men's Cadet Blue and White Striped Balbriggan Underwear, 40 Cents.

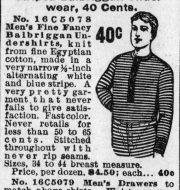

40c

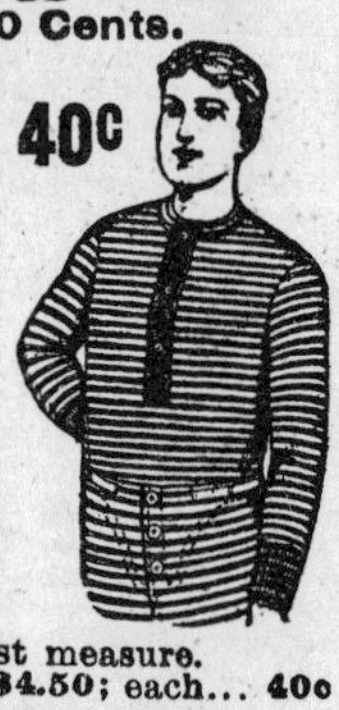

No. 16C5078 **Men's Fine Fancy Balbriggan Undershirts,** knit from fine Egyptian cotton, made in a very narrow ⅛-inch alternating white and blue stripe. A very pretty garment that never fails to give satisfaction. Fast color. Never retails for less than 50 to 65 cents. Stitched throughout with never rip seams. Sizes, 34 to 44 breast measure. Price, per dozen, $4.50; each... 40c

No. 16C5079 **Men's Drawers** to match above shirts. Waist measure, 30 to 42 inches. Price, per doz., $4.50; per pair, ..40c
If by mail, postage extra, each, 9c.

Men's Fancy Tan Mixed Underwear, 40 Cents.

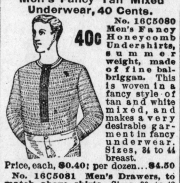

40c

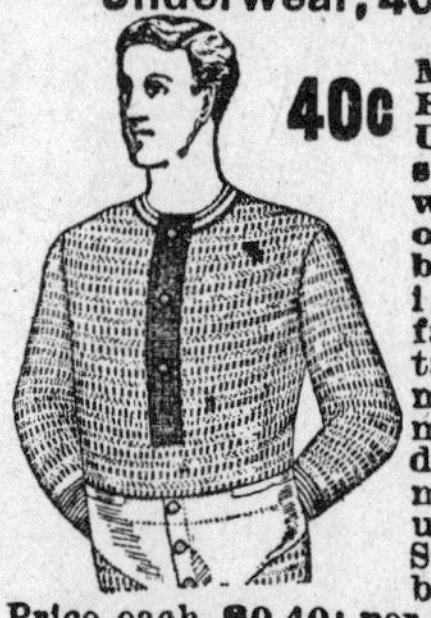

No. 16C5080 **Men's Fancy Honeycomb Undershirts, summer weight, made of fine balbriggan.** This is woven in a fancy style of tan and white mixed, and makes a very desirable garment in fancy underwear. Sizes, 34 to 44 breast. Price, each, $0.40; per dozen...$4.50

No. 16C5081 **Men's Drawers, to match above shirts.** Sizes, 30 to 42 inches waist measure. Price, per doz., $4.50; per pair, ..40c
If by mail, postage extra, each, 9c.

Men's Ecru Jersey Ribbed Underwear, 40 Cents.

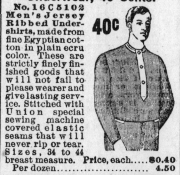

40c

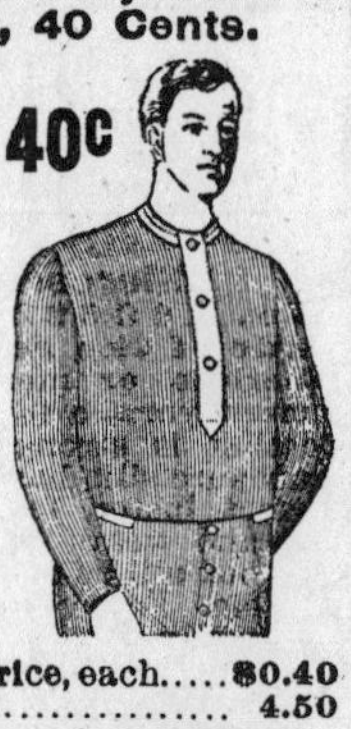

No. 16C5102 **Men's Jersey Ribbed Undershirts,** made from fine Egyptian cotton in plain ecru color. These are strictly finely finished goods that will not fail to please wearer and give lasting service. Stitched with Union special sewing machine covered elastic seams that will never rip or tear. Sizes, 34 to 44 breast measure. Price, each.....$0.40 Per dozen........ 4.50

No. 16C5103 **Men's Drawers,** to match above shirts. Sizes, waist measure, 30 to 42 inches. Price, per dozen, $4.50; per pair, 40c
If by mail, postage extra, each, 9c.

ALWAYS STATE SIZE WANTED.

Fish Net Shirts, 35 Cents.

35c

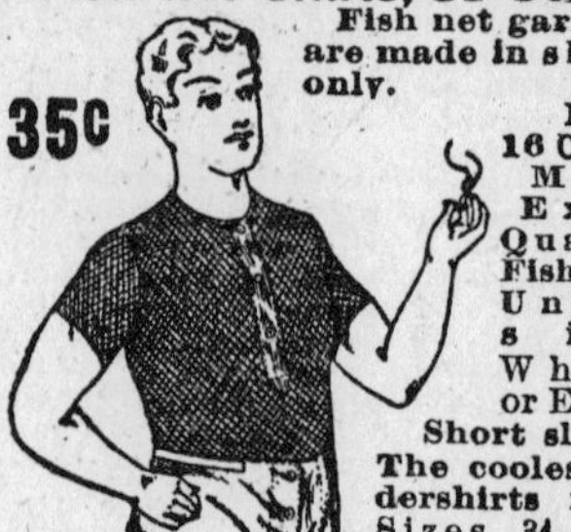

Fish net garments are made in shirts only. No. 16C5112 **Men's Extra Quality Fish Net Undershirts.** White or Ecru. **Short sleeves. The coolest undershirts made.** Sizes, 34 to 44 breast measure. Price, per dozen, $4.00; each.... 35c
If by mail, postage extra, each, 6c.

Men's Jean Drawers, Stretchy Seam, 40c.

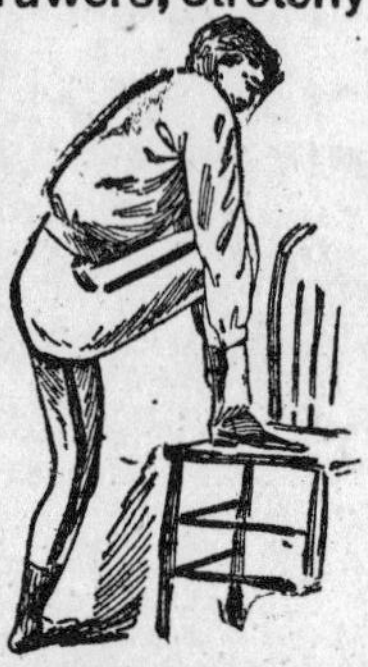

No. 16C5116 **Men's Fine Jean Drawers, made with stretchy seams down each side of the leg, giving easy motion and greater comfort.** The seams are of wide elastic ribbed balbriggan on the sides of the legs and in back, are self adjusting, easy and comfortable. Ribbed anklets. Sizes, 30 to 44 waist measure and 30 to 34 inseam. Color, white. Price, per pair.........$0.40 Per dozen pairs........ 4.50
If by mail, postage extra, per pair, 11c.

Men's Extra Size Underwear, 50 Cents.

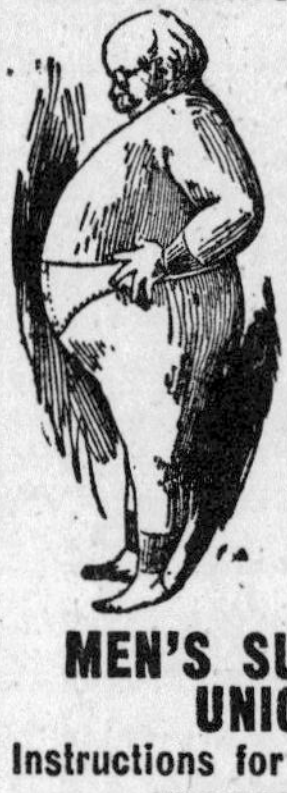

No. 16C5118 **Men's Extra Size Balbriggan Undershirts, very fine summer undergarment.** Strictly high grade, first class undergarment. Made from fine combed Egyptian yarn, stitched with the Union Special. Covered elastic seams. Will not rip or irritate; ecru color. Sizes, 46 to 52 inches chest measure. Price, each........$0.50 Per dozen........ 5.75

No. 16C5119 **Men's Drawers,** to match above shirt. Sizes, 46 to 50 waist measure. Price, per pair....$0.50 Per dozen pairs.... 5.75
If by mail, postage extra, each, 12 cents.

MEN'S SUMMER WEIGHT UNION SUITS.

Instructions for Taking Measurements, FOR BREAST AND WAIST.

A close, firm (but not too tight) measure should be taken over vest with coat off, observing that you do not expand the chest. Take close breast measure and see that the tape is close under the arms and over the shoulder blades.

80-Cent Union Suits.

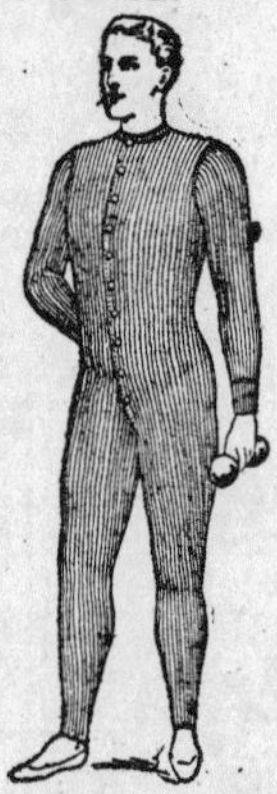

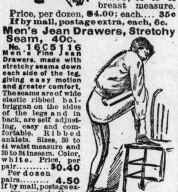

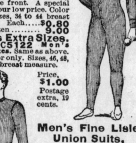

No. 16C5120 **Men's Summer Weight Ribbed Egyptian Cotton Union Suits.** This garment is carefully proportioned on scientific principles and will be found perfect fitting in every particular. They are made with fine pearl buttons, silk tipped cuffs and silk finished all the way down the front. A special value at our low price. Color ecru. Sizes, 34 to 44 breast measure. Each.....$0.80 Per dozen........ 9.00

Men's Extra Sizes. No. 16C5122 **Men's Extra Sizes.** Same as above. Ecru color only. Sizes, 46, 48, 50 and 52 breast measure. Price, $1.00 Postage extra, 19 cents.

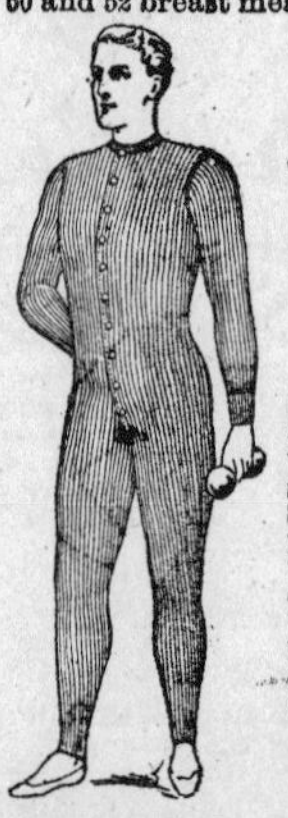

Men's Fine Lisle Union Suits, $1.15.

No. 16C5124 **Men's Fine Lisle Thread Union Suits,** ecru color, summer weight. Fine quality, high grade in every particular. Silk trimmed around neck; pearl buttons; perfect buttonholes; silk tipped cuffs and stitched throughout with Union special sewing machine; never rip elastic covered seams. Sizes, 34 to 44 only. Price, each. $ 1.15 Per dozen........ 13.00
If by mail, postage extra, 12 cents.

Men's Mercerized Union Suits, $1.75.

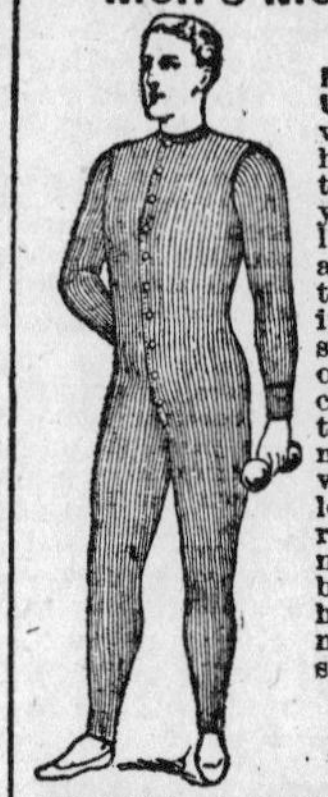

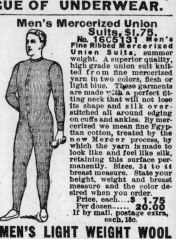

No. 16C5131 **Men's Fine Ribbed Mercerized Union Suits;** summer weight. A superior quality, high grade union suit knitted from fine mercerized yarn in two colors, flesh or light blue. These garments are made with a perfect fitting neck that will not lose its shape and silk overstitched all around edging on cuffs and ankles. By mercerized we mean fine Egyptian cotton, treated by the new Mercer process, by which the yarn is made to look like and feel like silk, retaining this surface permanently. Sizes, 34 to 44 breast measure. State your height, weight and breast measure and the color desired when you order. Price, each....$ 1.75 Per dozen........ 20.00
If by mail, postage extra, each, 18c.

MEN'S LIGHT WEIGHT WOOL UNDERWEAR.

Summer Weight Merino Underwear, 40 Cents.

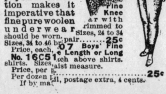

40c

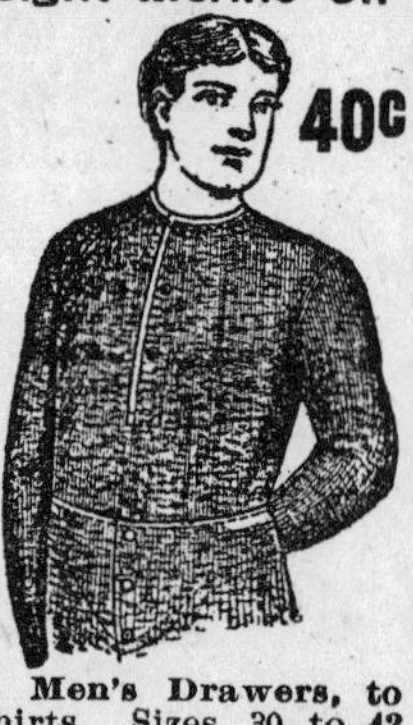

No. 16C5150 **Men's Light Weight Natural Gray Mixed Summer Merino Undershirts.** Soft wool finish, a good spring or fall underwear but preferred by many for summer wear. Retail value, 50 cents. **Fine pearl buttons.** Sizes, 34 to 44. Price, ea. $0.40 Per doz.. 4.50

No. 16C5151 **Men's Drawers,** to match above shirts. Sizes, 30 to 42 waist measure. Price, per pair, $0.40 Per dozen pairs........ 4.50
If by mail, postage extra, per pair, 11c.

Men's Light Summer Weight Wool Underwear, 80 Cents.

80c

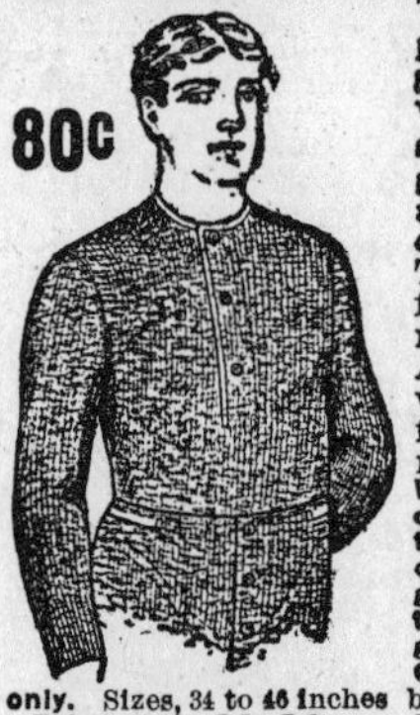

No. 16C5160 **Men's Fine Superior Light Weight Undershirts,** natural gray in color, about 90 per cent pure wool. This is a soft, fine garment, made partly of Australian wool, suitable for all the year round wear. **We strongly recommend goods of this character because of their great merit, and they never fail to give satisfaction. Color, natural gray only.** Sizes, 34 to 46 inches breast measure. Price, each, $0.80; per dozen......$9.00

No. 16C5161 **Men's Drawers,** to match above undershirts. Sizes, 30 to 44 inches waist measure. Price, per pair............$0.80 Per dozen pairs........ 9.00
If by mail, postage extra, each garment, 11c.

Our Special S., R. & Co. Light Summer Weight Wool Underwear.

$1.40

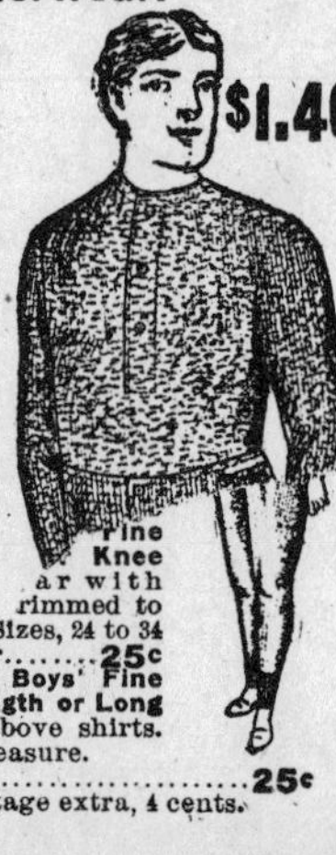

No. 16C5170 **S., R. & Co.'s Finest Grade Medium Weight Health Undershirts,** flat knit, fine soft surface. Made from pure Australian lamb's wool. These are the kind your physician would recommend particularly to those whose physical condition makes it imperative that fine pure woolen underwear should be worn. Sizes, 34 to 46 br... Price, each, ...
No. 16C51... shirts. Sizes, ... Price, per ... Per dozen ... If by ma...

... Fine ... Knee ... ar with ... rimmed to ... Sizes, 24 to 34 ... pair........25c
...07 **Boys' Fine ... e Length or Long** ... ch above shirts. ... aist measure. ... r........25c
... il, postage extra, 4 cents.

For Outdoor Sleepers
With Hood and Stockings to Match

Sleeping outdoors, it seems, is not only not dangerous but actually healthful. "The custom of sleeping in the open air is based on health principles. Buy an outfit and sleep outdoors a few nights and you will soon be convinced that it is the proper way to sleep."

This is an extraordinary change in the American way of sleeping, because the prejudice against night air and fear of its dangers had long been rooted in the people. This prejudice had once found expression in an important source—the Butterick Publishing Company whose dress patterns were used and whose publications were read by hundreds of thousands of women. In a volume called *Home-Making and Housekeeping,* published in 1889, it was said:

> At night, when the perceptions which enable us to detect offensive odors are dulled by sleep, the danger from breathing bad air is much greater than during the day. As the sunlight vanishes, the vapors, from standing water about a house or running water that is tainted . . . ascend unchecked, and while their weight confines their pernicious effects to lower levels than pure dry air seeks, this very fact makes them formidable to the occupants of sleeping rooms on the lower floors of dwelling houses. . . . On general principles . . . it is wiser to close all windows below the second story of a house during the night, as the air which enters from above this distance is apt to be dryer and freer from soil exhalations than that below.

Once the country had conquered its fear of night air, it was ready to take the next step—taking the sun. But this did not come until a few years later.

American men in the second year of the World War had not only adopted pajamas but, as an expression of their new-found sybaritic ways, were wearing bathrobes and smoking jackets—sometimes called house coats. Wheat is high, and cotton and corn; the only way is up, and men are wearing clothes that they would have scorned only a few years before as the apparel of sissies.

Machines are now doing much of the work formerly done by man and beast; hands are less gnarled and calloused by heavy labor; nails less often blackened and broken, and the fingers of 1915, more supple than those of 1905, are skillful for knotting ties. The ready-made tie is consequently going out of fashion; the long-honored string tie has gone or is precariously preserved only by a few Southern colonels; the shield bow is disappearing, and the four-in-hand is the thing to wear.

Women are already kicking over the traces of underwear that clung to their bodies, after a few experimental sheddings, but men, ever conservative about their clothes, continue to change from summer- to winter-weight underwear almost as automatically as nature thickens the coats of her fur-bearing animals when the snows begin to fly. They clung to their heavy shirts and drawers or their woolen union suits, and the catalog, describing the virtues of its "Double-Body Union Suits for Men"—some of them weighing two pounds —warns its customers to beware of the cold.

All Quiet on the Western Front

"Every man who works in the open knows the dangers of sudden changes of temperature if the body is not properly protected. Double-Body Union Suits offer the proper protection. Bad colds bring on la grippe, lumbago and pneumonia. Try this underwear as a preventive."

Friedrich Nietzsche and Huey Long

Once upon a time, Friedrich Wilhelm Nietzsche wrote: "In order to sleep well one must have all the virtues." But Herr Nietzsche did not work as a copywriter for Sears. The catalog's point of view on this subject is altogether different from that held by the German philosopher, and it argues that to sleep well one need only wear "an extra full, extra long, woven cotton broadcloth nightshirt." There is much to be said for the catalog way as opposed to the Nietzschean, for, while it might be difficult to acquire all the virtues as a sedative, it took only eighty-nine cents to acquire a Sears nightshirt with "sound sleep woven into every inch."

The catalog of 1935 is filled with pajamas, but there is also a saving remnant of men with democratic hearts of oak— good, sound, conservative, hog-and-hominy individualists— who will have no truck with newfangled notions in politics or sleeping apparel. This remnant stands for the old-fashioned, long-tailed nightgown, and standing with them on a memorable occasion in the 1930's was that democrat extraordinary, the late Senator Huey P. Long of Louisiana, whose pajamas once caused a coolness in relations to develop between the late German Republic and the United States.

Up the Mississippi River one warm summer's day slowly steamed the German cruiser *Emden,* bound for a courtesy visit to the port of New Orleans, in command of Captain Arnold von Lothar de la Perriere, former U-boat commander, able sailor, and gallant gentleman. In his suite at the Hotel Roosevelt in New Orleans, taking his repose in green silk pajamas, was the Governor of Louisiana, Huey P. Long.

Slowly the war vessel moved up the river, passing, one after another, cotton and sugar-cane plantations that line the river's bank on both sides, until suddenly, around a great bend in the stream were New Orleans, the ship's dock, and standing on the dock, Herr Jaeger, the German Consul. Slowly the hours had passed over the city and over the Governor's suite, as he lay abed in silken ease thinking those thoughts that governors of Louisiana are wont to think on warm summer afternoons.

Suddenly there came a rapping on the Governor's door. "Come in," shouted His Excellency. The door opened and in walked Captain Arnold von Lothar de la Perriere, commander of the German Republic's warship *Emden,* clad in ceremonial dress uniform, and the Republic's consular agent in New Orleans, Herr Jaeger. In accordance with the principles of usage laid down in such cases, these representatives of a friendly nation had come to pay a courtesy call upon the Governor of the state, wearing the clothes and going through the ceremonial prescribed by the rules of diplomatic procedure. The gentlemen clicked their heels, saluted, and immediately presented two stiffened backs to the Governor as they went out the door. Soon a message came to his suite from Washington. Herr Jaeger had complained that the Governor of Louisiana had insulted the German Republic because he had received the commander of the *Emden* while dressed in silk pajamas. Would not the Governor, the State Department asked, put on his clothes and pay a proper visit to the warship?

The Governor had clothes in abundance, but not the kind prescribed by protocol: a cutaway coat, gray striped trousers (locally known as "senator britches"), and a top hat. These Mr. Long borrowed and, hastily going down to the *Emden,* repaired the growing breach between two great powers.

In the meantime, the wires were humming with the story. It was going out to the piny woods, to the creeks and the crossroads, that Huey P. Long, the po' man's friend and champion, the pot-likker democrat, the hater of the rich and all their ways, had been caught wearing green silk pajamas. Wearing pajamas or living in a painted house were crimes, either of which would have ruined the career of an ordinary politician among the plain people, and, even for an extraordinary politician such as Mr. Long, they were dangerous. The Governor, however, who had met and conquered more dangerous enemies in his time than pajamas, did not mean to be politically strangled by them. He settled the question of his democratic integrity simply and decisively. One of his retainers went out and bought a cotton nightshirt which he donned; press photographers were invited in to find the Governor sitting on the edge of the bed conducting the state's business in a nightgown; newspapers all over the state printed these photographs in the morning, and by night, Huey's admirers back in the swamps and up on the hills were saying they knowed it was a lie, that talk about Huey wearing them silk pajamas. Nightshirts had routed pajamas, democratic integrity had been saved, and Governor Long was soon to become United States Senator Long.

Joining the nightshirt brigade in opposing heretic change are the gentlemen who hate laundries and collar-attached shirts. For them, no collar is a collar that is not made of rubber, and the catalog which treats its old customers with tender care, and sometimes humors their whimsies with the sentimentality of a doting grandmother, lists in 1935 "rubber composition collars with a dull linen-like finish. . . . Easily cleaned with a damp cloth. . . ."

Men Lay Down Their Heavy Burden

During the thirty-year period we have been considering, men laid down the burden of heavy clothing and adopted

37c EACH GARMENT NAINSOOK

COAT SHIRT AND PANTS, LOOSE FITTING

These are widely advertised garments and sold the country over at 50 cents each in the largest retail stores. They are in special favor with young men, and men who are out of doors a great deal in the heat of the summer months. They are made from a fine gauge twilled nainsook cloth. The coat shirt is sleeveless and buttons down the entire front; the drawers are fitted at the waist with loose fitting legs to the knee. Splendidly made and handsomely finished. Pure white in color.

No. 16T5118 Coat Shirts. Sizes, 34, 36, 38, 40, 42 and 44 inches breast measure.
Price, each garment..........................37c
No. 16T5119 Pants to match above shirts. Sizes, 30, 32, 34, 36, 38, 40 and 42 inches waist measure.
Price, each garment..........................37c
State size wanted when ordering.
Shipping weight, each garment, 9 ounces.

lighter-weight wearing apparel. They wore less clothing in 1935 than in 1905; less heavy cotton or wool underwear, and more lightweight cotton underwear which they used the year round; high shoes gave way to low shoes; woolen socks to silk, rayon, or thin cotton socks; flannel shirts to broadcloth shirts, and men gave up changing clothes because of the seasons. In general, they have moved toward simplicity and comfort in dress, especially in summer, and it is only in those purlieus of the archconservative—rural backwaters and city banking rooms—that today one may find men dressing in the manner, if not the fashion, of thirty years ago.

26 · THE MAN WITH THE WOE

A GREAT merchandise-distributing organization catering to practically all the wants of farmers must naturally offer for sale those articles by which the farmer makes his living; that is, agricultural implements. Successive catalogs, therefore, devote multiple pages to these implements, and as they change in character and kind through years, as old ones drop out and new ones take their places, and as motor-driven vehicles largely supplant the horse, we may trace some of the transformations which have profoundly affected millions of farmers (and all of America in consequence) during the period 1905–39. In the pages that follow, some attempt will be made to relate the farm problem as it emerges in our times to the changes of technology indicated in the catalog. But inasmuch as a complete discussion of the questions involved would require volumes, little more is attempted here than to point out some of the more dramatic mechanical and economic changes that have occurred within the short space of thirty-five years.

After the Civil War

It is April 9, 1865. General Robert E. Lee has come to Appomattox Court House, Virginia, to arrange terms for the surrender of the army of northern Virginia. Magnanimously, General Grant permits Confederate officers to retain their horses and side arms. "Then," he wrote, "General Lee . . . remarked to me that in their army the cavalrymen and artillerists owned their own horses; and he asked . . . if the men . . . were to be permitted to retain them. I told him that as the terms were written they would not. . . ."

"I then said to him that . . . I took it most of the men in the ranks were small farmers. The whole country had been so raided by the two armies that it was doubtful whether they would be able to put in a crop to carry themselves and their families through the next winter without the aid of the horses they were then riding. . . . I would, therefore, instruct the officers . . . to let every man of the Confederate army who claimed to own a horse or mule take the animal home with him. Lee remarked again that this would have a happy effect."

Thus, the defeated soldier-agrarians of the South rode sadly back to their run-down, slave-deserted farms. (For lack of labor, seventy-year-old Thomas Dabney, once a great land-owner, was to wash his family's clothes for years.) The planter class was ruined and with it the planter civilization which H. L. Mencken, an expert heaver of rotten eggs at the South, has called one of "manifold excellencies—perhaps the best the Western Hemisphere has ever seen—undoubtedly the best that These States have seen." On its wreckage—out of sheer necessity—the share-cropper system was erected, and, in years to come, this question and the low standard of living in the South were to present the nation with a monumental problem.

The old plantation regime was gone but the land remained, and a cotton crop was raised in 1865. This achievement was praised by Henry Grady in a moving oration: "As ruin was never before so overwhelming, never was restoration swifter. The soldiers stepped from the trenches into the furrow; horses that had charged Federal guns marched before the plow, and fields that ran red with human blood in April, were green with the harvest in June."

But before long, farmers were complaining that they were no better off than their slaves had been in 1860. They had become the slaves of an extortionate banking and factoring system. Capital was scarce in the South; interest rates were usurious. *The Nation,* startled by fiery Southerners, advanced one reason why, in its opinion, capital did flow to the South.

If the South, it said, would "suppress the practice of shooting at sight, it would be worth hundreds of millions of dollars to it in the next fifteen years. . . ."

Southern farmers, however, evidently devoted some of their time to farming as well as to shooting. The cotton crop of 1870 was greater than that of 1860; by 1910, it was almost trebled, and, by 1930, nearly one third of all the farms in the United States grew cotton.

A prodigious agricultural expansion also occurred in other sections of this country after the Civil War. Under the Homestead Act of 1862, any able-bodied man or woman was enabled to take up a farm. Between 1860 and 1910, more than 120,000,000 acres were taken up by homesteaders, while other millions of acres, granted to railroads, were sold by them to settlers. The consequence was that, in the short period 1860–90, more land was brought under cultivation than in all the previous history of America. Most of this expansion occurred in the West.

While more land was going under the plow, the rise of machinery, the development of superior techniques, the spreading of knowledge through agricultural schools were enabling farmers to get more produce out of an acre than ever before. Fewer men were needed to grow greater crops; the farm became mechanized; it was no longer the self-contained economic unit that was part of the Jeffersonian dream. Great staple crops such as corn hogs, wheat, tobacco, and cotton depended for price stability on exports. In a country rapidly becoming industrialized under finance capitalism, agriculture ceased to be either the predominant occupation of Americans or the predominant interest of Congress. It became merely a cog in the industrial wheel. Some of the results are that ever since the close of the Civil War the farmer has been The Man With The Woe; the country has witnessed an unending series of agricultural crises, and the farm problem has become a constant x in the equation of American national life.

Machinery

The shape of mechanical things to come on the farm was clearly shadowed forth at the Centennial Exposition held at Philadelphia in 1876. A contemporary book describes the exhibit of agricultural machines as follows:*

> Even a superficial observer could not fail to observe with delight and pride the superior exhibition of agricultural machines. . . . It was immense as to number shown; varied, as to uses intended, and admirable as to workmanship.
>
> Most prominent amid all this array of practical beauty were the reapers and mowers, which, more than anything else, signalize agricultural progress. It is only a few years since the sickle was seen in every grain field, and with its slow and toilsome results each farmer had to be content. When the cradle came it seemed as if the climax had been attained, and the man who could cut three or four acres of wheat in a day, laying it in fair shape for the binder who followed, was doing good work. But the cradle and hand-rake gave way to the reaper and self-raker, and these, year by year, improved and perfected, make of harvesting little more than a holiday. There remains for accomplishment in this direction only the automatic binder, already a partial success, and quite sure to reach perfection in the future.

The mechanization of agriculture had begun in the 1830's, but without making notable progress up to 1860. Then came war, the destroyer, and, at the same time, the colossal accelerator of industrial techniques and invention. The Civil War took men away from the farms and raised the price of grain, with the result that machines were adopted which would enable one boy to do the work of several men. Among these machines was the reaper—two hundred and fifty thousand of which were in use by 1864.

But the machines did not come in without protests. We have before noted the hostility of men to new inventions. Agricultural machinery, too, was faced with hostility:

* Ingram, *The Centennial Exposition,* p. 202.

Electric Light for Farm Homes Has Come to Stay.

It is no longer an experiment. We have shipped plants as far east as Maine, as far west as California and as far south as Texas and Florida. Customers have no difficulty in installing their own plants by following our complete instructions.

Our plants consist of an engine, generator, switchboard, battery and miscellaneous parts. If you have an engine or sufficient power of any kind, we will sell you any of our battery plants without the engine. The storage battery which we furnish makes it unnecessary to run your engine every time you want light.

If desired we will furnish plants without batteries, to be used for power and lighting purposes. Please ask for Electric Lighting Plant Catalog.

Make Your Own Electric Light!

Use a reliable plant, easily understood and operated, guaranteed to give satisfactory results or money returned.

Complete plant with enclosed type of battery. These batteries are charged before being shipped and are very easy to install.

Complete plant with open plante plate battery. Open plante batteries have the plates made from solid sheet lead. These batteries are much larger than the enclosed type of batteries, and will last two or three times as long under the same conditions. We recommend the use of open plante batteries because we feel they are a better value.

TABLE OF SEARS-ROEBUCK ELECTRIC LIGHTING PLANTS USING BATTERIES.

All ratings are based on using 12-candle power lamps, 1¼ watts per candle power.

| Catalog No. | BATTERY | | | GENERATOR | | Price, Less Engine | Engine | Price, Complete | Lamps Furnished |
	Kind	Lights for Eight Hours	Lights for Three Hours	Size	Lights				
57V104½	Enclosed	10	19	6 -Ampere 42-Volt	13	$153.70	1½-Horse Power	$182.20	20
57V105½	Enclosed	10	19	13 -Ampere 42-Volt	28	179.35	1½-Horse Power	207.85	25
57V108½	Enclosed	20	38	13 -Ampere 42-Volt	28	207.30	1½-Horse Power	235.80	30
57V106½	Enclosed	10	19	20 -Ampere 42-Volt	42	203.85	1½-Horse Power	232.35	35
57V107½	Enclosed	10	19	27½-Ampere 42-Volt	59	227.15	2½-Horse Power	267.10	45
57V109½	Enclosed	20	38	20 -Ampere 42-Volt	42	232.70	1½-Horse Power	261.20	35
57V110½	Enclosed	20	38	27½-Ampere 42-Volt	59	256.40	2½-Horse Power	296.35	45
57V112½	Enclosed	30	58	20 -Ampere 42-Volt	42	274.50	1½-Horse Power	303.00	40
57V114½	Enclosed	30	58	27½-Ampere 42-Volt	59	298.80	2½-Horse Power	338.75	55
57V308½	Open Plante	20	42	13 -Ampere 42-Volt	28	247.95	1½-Horse Power	276.45	30
57V309½	Open Plante	20	42	20 -Ampere 42-Volt	42	271.30	1½-Horse Power	299.80	35
57V310½	Open Plante	20	42	27½-Ampere 42-Volt	59	297.15	2½-Horse Power	337.10	45
57V312½	Open Plante	30	64	20 -Ampere 42-Volt	42	329.50	1½-Horse Power	358.00	40
57V314½	Open Plante	30	64	27½-Ampere 42-Volt	59	353.75	2½-Horse Power	393.70	55
57V316½	Open Plante	40	85	27½-Ampere 42-Volt	59	406.20	2½-Horse Power	446.15	60
57V320½	Open Plante	50	107	27½-Ampere 42-Volt	59	459.65	2½-Horse Power	499.60	75

Plants Without Batteries

We have direct connected and belted generating sets to use without batteries. These plants are especially suitable for summer resorts, moving picture work or any place where it is convenient to have the engine running when power or light is being used. These outfits can be furnished in voltages of 42, 60, 110 and 220, and in capacities from 1¼ kilowatts to 5 kilowatts. The equipment is high grade and moderate in price. Please ask for Electric Lighting Plant Catalog.

Tungsten Lamps.
State Voltage Wanted.

Catalog No.	Candle Power	Watts	Volts	Price, Each	Price, Pkg. of Five
57V501½	8	10	25	30c	$1.45
57V502½	12	15	25	30c	1.45
57V503½	16	20	25	30c	1.45
57V504½	20	25	25	30c	1.45
57V509½	8	10	30	30c	1.45
57V513½	12	15	30	30c	1.45
57V517½	16	20	30	30c	1.45
57V521½	20	25	30	30c	1.45
57V533½	32	40	30	30c	1.45
57V508½	8	10	32	30c	1.45
57V512½	12	15	32	30c	1.45
57V516½	16	20	32	30c	1.45
57V520½	20	25	32	30c	1.45
57V532½	32	40	32	30c	1.45
57V540½	40	50	32	40c	1.95
57V510½	8	10	60	30c	1.45
57V514½	12	15	60	30c	1.45
57V518½	16	20	60	30c	1.45
57V522½	20	25	60	30c	1.45
57V534½	32	40	60	30c	1.45
57V542½	40	50	60	40c	1.95

Triple Braid Weatherproof Copper Wire.

To be used when exposed to weather.

Catalog No.	Gauge	Price, per Foot	Price, per 100 Feet
57V805½	No. 4	4½c	$4.25
57V807½	No. 6	3 c	2.90
57V809½	No. 8	2½c	2.00
57V811½	No. 10	1¾c	1.60
57V813½	No. 12	1¼c	1.00

Rubber Covered New Code Insulation. Copper Wire.

Catalog No.	Gauge	Price, per Foot	Price, per 100 Feet
57V804½	No. 4	6½c	$6.20
57V806½	No. 6	4¾c	4.40
57V808½	No. 8	3 c	2.75

Many Advantages

The many advantages of having your own electric plant are found in the use of our low voltage direct current motors, fans, electric irons, vacuum cleaners, and miscellaneous supplies. The electric motor on the washing machine saves much hard work. Electric irons are a great comfort at any time, especially in hot weather.

These items are fully described in our special Electric Lighting Plant Catalog.

Reduce the Fire Risk

Cut Down Repair Expense
by the Use of Concrete Products

Anyone Can Make Them and They Last for Ages

THE durability of concrete is now well known, and the making of concrete products in a machine or mold and then setting the finished product in position is one of the most economical methods of using this material. Our Concrete Machinery Catalog describes and illustrates a very complete line of machines and molds for making blocks, brick, porches, fence posts, door and window sills and caps, steps, chimneys, drain tile, sewer pipe and other concrete products. You can make the products yourself, even though you have no experience in this line, and can use them for practically every purpose that you would use lumber, brick or stone. Our General Information Book, shown at left, tells how.

Send us a postal card today and ask for our free Concrete Machinery Catalog, and learn how little money you need spend for a machine or mold for making concrete products of various kinds. A few examples of our low prices are given on this page. We guarantee to save you money on any kind of equipment and furnish machinery of the very highest grade. Our guarantee means that we must save you money on your purchase, that we must satisfy you perfectly, or the machinery may be send back at our expense, and your money, together with any freight charges you paid, will be returned to you.

Send Us a Postal Card Today and Ask for Our Free Concrete Machinery Catalog.

A Few Examples of What We Offer in This Line.

The Wizard
An Automatic Block Machine With Big Outfit of Plates and Pallets.
$42.50

The Triumph
With Outfit Ready for Use.
$12.50

Concrete Mixers
All Types,
$19.75
and Up.

Fence Post Molds
$2.25
and Up.

Can Be Used for Many Purposes

Building Blocks

Easy to make and can be used for houses, barns, silos, outbuildings, foundations, retaining walls and many other purposes where you would ordinarily use lumber, brick or stone. Our Concrete Machinery Catalog shows machines for making all sizes and styles of building blocks, and the prices of these machines are only $12.50 and upward. We show two models on this page. Our customers say the Wizard is the fastest, easiest working machine ever put on the market. The Triumph is better than machines usually sold at a great deal more than our price.

Fence Posts.

Good wood fence posts are becoming scarcer and higher in price each year. Concrete forms a perfect substitute for wood posts and makes a post that is everlasting, proof against rot, prairie and forest fires, and repair expenses. The concrete post in the first place need not cost more than a wood post and, when the elimination of replacement and repair expense is considered, no one can afford to use anything but concrete fence posts. Our Special Concrete Machinery

Catalog describes in full how concrete fence posts are made, tells what they cost and illustrates molds as low as $2.25 each.

Concrete for Porches.

A concrete porch can be added to any kind of a house, whether built of concrete, brick, stone or lumber, and will add to the appearance and value several times more than the cost of the concrete work. You can make and lay the various porch materials yourself by following the directions in our instruction book. We have an exceptionally fine line of molds for making all kinds of ornamental work for porches and concrete building decoration.

Concrete Pipe.

Easy to make and can be used for drainage, sewerage and irrigation work; in fact, for any purpose where clay tile can be used. Our Concrete Machinery Catalog describes and quotes prices on machines and molds for making both drain and sewer tile, and tells all about the advantages of this new material over the old costly and short lived clay tile. Be sure to get our Special Concrete Machinery Catalog and learn all about how easily and cheaply you can make practically everlasting tile.

Porch Molds
A Full Line of Beautiful Designs
$1.90
and Up.

Molds for Pipe and Tile
$5.65
and Up.

Free Information

The Information Book illustrated above contains full instructions for selecting the various materials and for properly proportioning and mixing them; also contains full instructions for making and curing the various products. The information in this book has been compiled with great care and with a view to giving the information in the most simple manner so it will be easily understood by anyone, even though they have no experience in the making of concrete products.

When requested, this book is sent free of charge with every concrete machine or mold. It is a book you would gladly pay for at any book store. We are also in a position to give you expert advice on the subject of concrete product manufacture, should you need any special information or advice.

"Small-town bankers and businessmen refused for many years to lend money on tractors on the ground that they were a menace to farmers. They argued not only that farmers could not operate the machine profitably, but also that if they were successful, the farmer would have too much leisure time. They had invested in horses and foresaw their eventual decline in price if tractors were utilized. The national horse associations led in circulating propaganda against tractors and were joined by the local bankers. Farmers were easily susceptible to such a campaign for the price of tractors was high, horse-drawn implements became almost a total loss, and the farmers were often sentimentally attached to their horses. Farmers rarely had sufficient evidence one way or the other on the question whether the breakage on the tractor and the amount of fuel required were excessive. The opposition of the farm wage workers, displaced by the tractor, was also great." *

Technological Change on the Farm

Protests were, however, of little avail. As time passed, more farmers bought more machines and new machines came into being. The results are summarized by the Department of Agriculture as follows:

Estimated amounts of man labor used to produce an acre of 100 bushels of wheat, of 100 bushels of corn, and five hundred pound gross weight bales of cotton for designated periods:

	1878–82	1898–1902	1928–32
Wheat-Man labor per 100 bushel-hours	129	86	49
Corn-Man labor per 100 bushel-hours	180	147	104
Cotton-Man labor per bale-hours	304	285	235

* *Technological Trends and National Policy*, National Resources Committee, Washington, 1937.

By 1900, the value of farm implements and machines in this country was $800,000,000. But by 1920—following the fantastic expansion of the World War years—farm machinery had increased in value to $2,300,000,000.

As machines came in, the farm worker's efficiency went up; as production increased, crop prices went down; as capital investment jumped, mortgages multiplied, and tens of thousands of small, one-horse farmers lost their lands and became tenants. In 1880, about one fourth of all farmers were tenant farmers; by 1930, nearly one half were tenant farmers.

At the same time, the human and horse population of the farms dwindled. In the premachine age—1840—agricultural workers comprised more than three fourths of all persons gainfully employed in America; the proportion has steadily dropped, until in 1930 it was about one fifth. Since machines feed on oil instead of fodder, the loss of nine million horses and mules from farms, between 1918 and 1932, released thirty million acres to be devoted to crops for human consumption and so increased the already great surpluses.

These are a few of the spectacular developments in American agriculture since the Civil War. They are developments that have caused the farmer to grumble from 1867 to 1939; to set up powerful organizations for legislative relief, and to create a number of spectacular champions. These included such figures as "Pitchfork Ben" Tillman of South Carolina; Mary Lease, the "Kansas Pythoness," who advised farmers to "raise less corn and more hell"; "Sockless Jerry" Simpson, and the late Senator Huey Long ("Every Man a King") who, during the agricultural crisis of 1933, suggested state legislation throughout the South forbidding the growing of cotton for one year.

The Horse Age

According to evolutionists, it took thirty million years for the evolution of the eohippus into the horse. But it required less than thirty years for the farmer to change largely from the horse to the motor. In 1905, however, America was still

Competent Judge of Harness
to Be Both Judge and Jury

BRIDLES—¾-inch long cheeks; spotted fronts and face pieces; short flat reins.

LINES—1-inch wide, 18 feet long.

HAMES—No. 91 bolt, ball top; four hame straps; two spread straps.

TRACES—No. 1 stock; 6 feet long; 1¾ inches wide; triangular cock-eyes sewed in.

HAME TUGS—1¾-inch, double and stitched.

PADS—Metal bridge, flat harness leather, felt lined, nickel plated spots; folded belly-bands.

BREAST STRAPS—1½-inch, with snaps and slides.

MARTINGALES—1½-inch, with collar straps.

BREECHING—Folded leather body; heavy layer, stitched the full length; 1-inch side straps; 1-inch double back straps; 1-inch double hip straps with trace carriers, nickel plated spots on the outside.

TRIMMINGS—XC white metal; nickel plated spots. Weight of harness, packed for shipment, about 75 pounds.

No. 10V4777¼ Harness without collars. $41.95 Price.

The "Watson" Farm Harness
$41.95

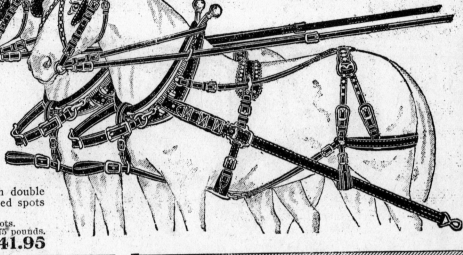

purchase price of a set of harness and pay the shipping charges both ways than have you dissatisfied.

Send your order and be among the hundreds of satisfied harness users who benefit by our special efforts to offer harness that cannot fail to impress you, first by its excellent appearance and later by its unusual wearing qualities, **backed by our reputation.**

SPECIAL NOTICE—We have hundreds of sets of these harness ready for immediate shipment from KANSAS CITY, MO., or CHICAGO, ILL., so can only sell the harness STRICTLY AS DESCRIBED. WE CANNOT MAKE ANY CHANGES.

Harness Bargains

Kansas City, Mo., or Chicago, Ill.

The great popular demand in harness as in other modern necessities is PROGRESS. How we are meeting this demand is strongly and convincingly emphasized here by three important features, which cover the whole harness buying question. First, the special features of the harness, its quality and the way it is made, as explained elsewhere on these pages. Second, the price, and third, our new shipping arrangements. These harness are shipped direct from the city nearer you, thereby making you a saving on the freight charges and in the shipping time.

BRIDLES—⅞-inch box loop cheeks; cupped blinds; ⅞-inch short flat reins.

LINES—1 inch wide, 18 feet long.

HAMES—All steel bolt hames, large ball tops; combination loops; hame straps and spread straps. Concord bolt clip attachment trace to hames.

TRACES—Custom made Concord truck, 6 feet long, 1¾ inches wide; six-link heel chains; 1¾-inch bellybands, folded and stitched.

BREECHING—Extra heavy folded body; 1½-inch layer, stitched the full length; 1⅛-inch hip, back and side straps; padded rump safes; large heavy rings; brass trace carriers.

MARTINGALES—Chicago truck style, 1¾ inches wide, with collar straps.

BREAST STRAPS—1¾ inches wide, 5 feet 2 inches long, with rollers.

TRIMMINGS—Japanned buckles; brass spots. Weight of harness, packed for shipment, about 85 pounds.

No. 10V4778¼ Harness without collars. Price, $49.95

Why Our Harness Prices Are Low

Our low prices create wide interest and are worthy careful consideration. There are many reasons **why** we can make our prices so low, but the reasons are not as interesting to you as the great fact itself and that **we actually do give** our customers the benefit of every possible saving effected from the time the raw hides are purchased until the harness is completed and shipped to you.

Spending good money on a doubtful harness is poor business judgment. A really first class harness at a few dollars more is better practical economy than a lower priced one of questionable quality. The purchase of a good harness is as wise an investment as the buying of good horses. Both are money makers to the farmer or other team owner. Harness should also be a **money saver**, which is something more. Every extra day that a set of these harness lasts will mean an actual saving in cash to you. **Dependable quality** is what we insist upon first, quality is what we get and what we offer you here. Price is merely a secondary consideration. A poor harness will show its defects sooner or later and when it does may mean a dissatisfied customer. These harness are guaranteed to contain all that good harness should contain and to wear splendidly during their entire term of service.

The "Republic" Extra Heavy
Concord Truck Harness
$49.95

Send All Orders to
SEARS, ROEBUCK AND CO., CHICAGO, ILL.

The American Farmer Is a Most
We Therefore Invite *Him*

"National" Single Strap Buggy Harness
AN UNUSUAL BARGAIN
Quality in Every Strap.

$18⁹⁹
NICKEL PLATED.

$19⁹⁹
IMITATION RUBBER.

"National" Single Strap Buggy Harness.

BRIDLE—⅝-inch box loop cheeks; giant patent winker brace with combination front; ring and double billets on the crown; pigskin impression blinds; long throat latch; extra heavy Dexter driving bit, overcheck and overcheck bit.

LINES—13½ feet long, ¾-inch double and stitched, beaded fronts, 1⅛-inch flat hand parts quality equal to that used in higher priced harness.

BREAST COLLAR—2¾-inch, V shape, single strap body, double neck straps; Cooper patent flange layer loops on the lead-ups, that prevent the lead-ups from pulling loose.

TRACES—1¼-inch single strap body, scalloped points stitched to the breast collar. Full length breast collar and traces; 14½ feet.

BREECHING—1⅝-inch single strap body with scalloped layer stitched on each end; ⅝-inch split hip straps, box loop lead-ups with Cooper patent flange layer loops; ⅞-inch side straps, scalloped and stitched turnback with large round crupper sewed on.

GIG SADDLE—Berlin, full padded, flexible tree, hogskin impression skirts; combination shaft tugs and adjustable bearers, double bellybands.

TRIMMINGS—Genuine German silver hook and terrets and nickel plated buckles; or genuine rubber hook and terrets and imitation rubber buckles.

FINISH—Smooth, round edge; no creasing. Weight, packed for shipment, about 25 pounds.

No. 10V4774¼ With genuine German silver hook and terrets, nickel plated buckles. Price, **$18.99**	No. 10V4775¼ With genuine rubber hook and terrets, imitation rubber buckles. Price. **$19.99**

Why Our Harness Quality Is High

Many years ago we began the sale of good harness. As in all great enterprises, our beginning was very small. Our business has grown by leaps and bounds, until today we are acknowledged to be the largest distributers of reliable harness, selling direct to the user, in the United States.

At the outset we established a fixed policy, from which we have **never once** swerved. That policy was to handle and sell only harness of such unquestionable quality and value as to be worthy of an **unlimited guarantee**—the strongest and most durable harness that could possibly be manufactured at a given price. Actual tests proved that harness made from **bark tanned leather** met these requirements better than harness made from leather tanned by other methods and gave the longest and most satisfactory service, therefore we decided that **bark tanned leather** should be used **exclusively** in the manufacture of our harness. Since that time other methods of tanning leather have been discovered and utilized—quicker and therefore cheaper methods—but they were not better methods, they did not produce more serviceable harness, hence we have not adopted them.

Styles have changed and prices have risen and fallen, but the good quality of our harness remains the same, due to the uniform quality of leather which the bark tanning process assures.

Our guarantee is limited only by the American farmer's judgment of quality and its relation to price, length of time and brand of service he, as judge and jury, thinks a harness of that price ought to last and give, considering the use to which he puts it. We want our harness judged by the long service and genuine satisfaction it gives and the buyer to be the sole judge. We do not compare our harness with others, but, having unbounded confidence in its worth, we guarantee it to you in unqualified terms. "Your satisfaction" expresses in the fullest degree what we guarantee to you. We would much rather return to you the

Four of Our Great
Shipped from

Our widely known policy of always giving the greatest possible value has been carried out to the fullest extent in these four harness. Manufactured from genuine bark tanned leather—the leather that insures harness of unexcelled strength and wearing qualities—the particular care taken in cutting and fitting every strap means that no expense is saved in our efforts to give you full value for every dollar you invest in a set of our harness. **Every piece of leather that goes into these four sets of** harness is **genuine bark tanned**.

"Brewster" Double Farm Harness, $30.85.

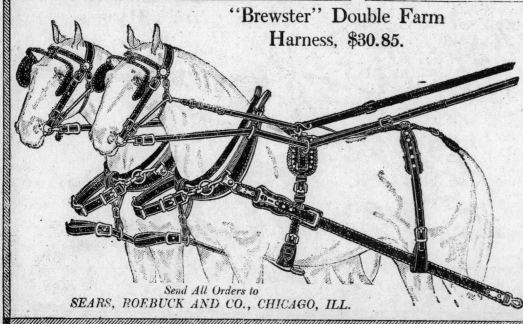

BRIDLES—¾-inch long cheeks; round side reins; patent winker stays.

LINES—1 inch wide, 18 feet long.

HAMES—Square staple, iron over top; jointed Concord clip attachments with Moeller hame tugs; four hame straps; two spread straps.

TRACES—1½ inches wide, 5 feet 8 inches long, Moeller style, with clip cockeyes.

BREAST STRAPS—1½-inch, with snaps and slides.

MARTINGALES—1½-inch, with collar straps.

PADS—Flat; harness leather top; felt lined; nickel plated spots; XC drop hooks and terrets; folded bellybands.

HIP AND BACK STRAPS—1-inch scalloped safe under hip straps nickel plated spots on the outside.

TRIMMINGS—XC buckles, nickel plated spots.

Weight of harness, packed for shipment, about 65 pounds.

No. 10V4776¼
Harness without collars. Price,
$30.85

Send All Orders to
SEARS, ROEBUCK AND CO., CHICAGO, ILL.

in the horse age; millions of horses and mules grazed in green pastures; horse traders and horse trading were still characteristic and picturesque features of rural life, and the catalog made ample provision for horse-drawn vehicles and for some of the needs of the animals that drew them.

Harness

At that time, hundreds of small towns situated in farming districts had a harness and saddle maker, the nature of whose occupation was indicated (following the practice of eighteenth-century England) by a wooden horse standing in front of his store. It was a horse more beautiful to the eyes of schoolboys than the famous Trojan horse across whom they stumbled in their studies. It was full seven feet tall; it had large, noble, agate eyes; a magnificent horsehair mane, and a powerful, sinuous body. At any moment, you expected it to come to life, and dash swiftly down Washington Avenue, fire flying from its hoofs as they struck the brick street, and its head held high in defiance of the frightened townsmen. Now it is one with the Trojan horse in legend. Out of its agate eyes, the harness-shop horse could not see Mr. Henry Ford sneaking up on its rear to deliver a deathblow.

In the days of this horse, the catalog, too—if less picturesquely than the local harness dealer—sold harness in large volume. "We invite attention to our very complete Harness and Saddlery Department. . . . We Handle The Very Best of Harness that is possible to be made. . . ." Then followed page after page of buggy and farm harness. The choice offered was extremely varied. It began with "Our Pan-American Single Web Harness, $3.00," continued with "Our Georgia," "Our Kansas," "Our Iowa," "Our Nebraska," "Our Texas," and concluded magnificently with "Our Very Finest Double Driving Harness, With Solid Nickel German Silver Trimmings, $24.75."

In the latter instance, the sober American farmer, not satisfied with mere utilitarian harness, showed that love of harness finery which is usually associated with the Andalusian hidalgo or the vanished Mexican *haciendado*. "The trimming used on our high grade double buggy harness, is *solid nickel*, commonly known as German silver. All the buckles, rings, the overcheck bit, the snaffle bit and hooks and terrets on the hames are made of this high grade solid nickel German silver metal. . . ."

For Children

Dogs and goats have never been used as draft animals in the United States as they have in some sections of Europe, notably the Low Countries. They have often, however, been the playthings of children, and the farm child of 1905, growing up in the horse age, amused himself and emulated his father by driving harnessed goats and dogs. The all-seeing catalog made provision for children with its "Single Goat or Dog Harness, Price, $2.70."

Homeward the Weary Plowman

Down the million-mile furrows of 1905 America went millions of men and horses, a set of harness to every horse. They wore, among others, "Our Bismarck Concord Farm Harness," "Our Dakota Team Farm Harness," or (before Oklahoma became a state in 1907), "Our Indian Territory Farm Harness." Separately the catalog lists hundreds of horse and harness items, including collars, hobbles, blankets, fly nets, stallion shields, horsetail clasps, horseshoes, cockeyes, sweat pads, bridle rosettes, and breast-collar housings.

The Last Roundup

Nowadays the automobile and even the airplane supplement the horse on Western cattle and sheep ranches, but in 1905, as anciently, cowboys rounded up their herds on horseback. Sears' saddle department is proud of its cowboy saddles: "Our Western and Southwestern trade has been so very large that we have felt justified in making very extensive preparations in the stock saddle line for the coming season. . . ." Cowboys' saddles bear names redolent of the old West: "Our Omaha Saddle, Improved La Platte tree," "Our Spe-

KENWOOD DISC PLOWS.

One-Furrow,	Two-Furrow,	Three-Furrow,
$24.75	$33.50	$42.25

Guaranteed to be as good disc plows as you can buy from anyone at any price and to be better plows than others ask from $32.00 to $60.00. If you want a disc plow don't doubt the quality because our prices are low; the plows are perfect tools, and should you send us your order you have the privilege of returning the plow at our expense if it does not prove perfectly satisfactory. All we ask is that you make an honest comparison, give our plow a fair trial, and we know you would not part with it for double its price, or trade it for any other plow made. These plows are not intended for turf or sod plowing, but they are the best plows made for stubble or old land plowing, no matter how hard the ground may be. They are very strong, of light draft and easy to operate. They will do the most satisfactory work and are convenient to handle for level ground. The discs revolve on chilled bearings. The furrow wheel is flexible, controlled by a lever which permits set of plow in or out of land at will. Depth of furrow is adjusted by a lever within easy reach. When throwing furrow it can be locked for deep or hard plowing or left flexible, but it is under full control of team at all times. All sizes have 24-inch wheels and 24-inch polished discs, and can be adjusted to cut a furrow any depth from 6 to 8 inches. The one-furrow plow will turn a furrow from 10 to 14 inches wide and has a two-horse hitch. The two-furrow plow will turn furrows up to 28 inches wide and has a three-horse hitch. The three-furrow plow will turn furrows up to 36 inches wide and has a four-horse hitch. Will furnish three-horse hitch on the one-furrow plow, or four-horse hitch on the two-furrow plow, without extra charge if so ordered. Shipped knocked down from factory in Eastern Ohio.

They can be made rigid for rolling ground or flexible for level ground. The hitch can be quickly adjusted or changed by a lever. The rear castor wheel permits of a square turn to right or left.

No. 32C157 One-Furrow Disc Plow. Weight, 595 pounds. Price.....................$24.75
No. 32C158 Two-Furrow Disc Plow. Weight, 745 pounds. Price..................... 33.50
No. 32C159 Three-Furrow Disc Plow. Weight, 895 pounds. Price.............. 42.25

Kenwood Steel Frame Sulky Plows.

$29.25 to $29.80

These plows are a perfect combination of strength and simplicity, built to stand hard service. Frame is steel and very rigid. Nearly all cast parts are malleable iron or cast steel. Plow handles with ease and levers are within easy reach of driver. Weight is equally distributed on each wheel. Rear wheel is locked in line and released by foot lever and castors at turn. Loose lever principle makes plow ride and handle easily, and insures even depth of furrow, both on smooth and rough land. They have soft center mouldboard, landside and share, and mouldboards and shares are double shinned. Can furnish either tongueless, as shown in this illustration, or with pole, and either right or left hand. Be careful to state whether you want right or left hand, tongueless or with pole. Weight, from 475 to 525 pounds. Shipped knocked down from factory near Chicago.

Catalogue No.	Price, 12-inch	Price, 14-inch	Price, 16-inch
32C132 Stubble Sulky Plow	$29.25	$29.50	$29.75
32C133 Turf or Sod Sulky Plow	29.30	29.55	29.80

Kenwood Orchard Gang Plows.

$15.65 TO $22.80

STEEL FRAME. RIGHT HAND ONLY.

Adapted to all kinds of shallow plowing. Furnished regularly with outside rear wheel, but can furnish with rear wheel inside the frame so that plow can be used close to vines or trees. Bottoms are each 9 inches wide, entire cut being 27 inches. Steel mouldboards, shares and landsides are all made of soft center plow steel. Will plow sod from 2 to 4 inches deep and stubble from 3 to 6 inches deep. Gangs having chilled shares are furnished with one extra set of shares. Weight, 300 pounds. Shipped knocked down from factory in Western Michigan.

No. 32C150 Orchard Gang Plow, with cast mouldboards, chilled landsides and chilled shares. Price.............................$15.65

No. 32C151 Orchard Gang Plow, with steel mouldboards, chilled landsides and chilled shares. Price................................$17.30

No. 32C153 Orchard Gang Plow, with steel mouldboards, steel landsides and steel shares. Price.............................$22.80

Kenwood Wood Beam Brush Plows.

$8.60 and $9.30

RIGHT HAND ONLY.

A splendid general purpose plow. Beam is made extra heavy directly over and forward of the standard, and has heavy iron strap on under side. Mouldboard is soft center plow steel turf and stubble shape, carefully hardened, ground and polished. Landside and share are wrought steel. Has steel standard and standard cap, and entire plow is strongly braced. Price is for plow complete, with gauge shoe, reversible coulter and adjustable clevis. Shipped knocked down from factory in Western Michigan.

No. 32C165 12-inch Brush Plow. Weight, 95 pounds. Price.............................$8.60
No. 32C166 14-inch Brush Plow. Weight, 100 pounds. Price.............................. 9.30
No. 32C167 Gauge Wheel. Weight, 12 pounds. Price.............................. .68

Kenwood Steel Beam Brush Plow.

$7.80

RIGHT HAND ONLY.

An excellent plow for road work and for breaking up rough and rooty land. Beam is made of two steel bars placed side by side and bolted together. Mouldboard is soft center plow steel, hardened, ground and polished. Share and landside are chilled iron. Handles and entire plow are strongly braced to stand heavy work. Plow measures about 11 inches across the bottom, but will turn a 13-inch furrow. Price includes one extra share, but does not include coulter or gauge wheel. Shipped knocked down from factory in Western Michigan.

		Weight	Price
No. 32C172 Steel Beam Brush Plow		128 lbs.	$7.80
No. 32C173 Gauge Wheel		11 lbs.	.70
No. 32C174 Foot Coulter		11 lbs.	1.40
No. 32C175 Knife Coulter		8 lbs.	.92

Kenwood Sod Breaker Plows.

$6.55 TO $7.05

STEEL BEAM RIGHT HAND ONLY.

This plow is intended for turning heavy sod and for use in prairie plowing, but is not suitable for light or sandy soil. Adjustable steel rods take the place of a mouldboard. Share is wrought steel. Price includes gauge shoe, fin cutter and one extra share. Weight, about 67 pounds. Shipped knocked down from factory near Chicago.

			Price
No. 32C186	12-inch Sod Breaking Plow		$6.55
No. 32C187	14-inch Sod Breaking Plow		6.80
No. 32C188	16-inch Sod Breaking Plow		7.05

Kenwood Vineyard Plows.

$6.50 and $7.80

WOOD BEAM. RIGHT HAND ONLY.

Especially adapted for nurseries, orchards, vineyards and all one-horse work. Beam is adjustable so horse can walk in furrow or on the land. Mouldboard is shaped to make light draft and to clean out the furrow in loose soil. Landslide and share are chilled iron. Will turn furrow from 8 inches to 12 inches wide and from 3 inches to 8 inches deep. Price is for plow complete, with gauge wheel, knife coulter, clevis and one extra share. Shipped knocked down from factory in Western Michigan.

No. 32C190 Vineyard Plow, with cast mouldboard. Weight, 103 pounds. Price.........$6.50
No. 32C191 Vineyard Plow, with steel mouldboard. Weight, 103 pounds. Price.........$7.80

Kenwood Full Chilled Plows.

$1.95 to $5.95

WOOD BEAM. RIGHT HAND.

These are genuine modern, full chilled plows with a general purpose shape. Can be used for any work which a chilled plow will do. Beams are heavy and of good proportions, and entire plow is strongly braced. Mouldboards, landsides and shares are perfectly chilled, ground and polished. One extra share furnished with each plow. Jointers and coulters can only be used on No. 32C207 and larger. Six-inch to 9-inch plows are suitable for one horse; 9-inch to 12-inch plows for two horses. Can furnish Nos. 32C207 and 32C211 in left hand, if so ordered. Shipped knocked down from factory near Chicago.

No. 32C203 6-inch Chilled Plow. Width of furrow, 7 inches. Weight, 43 pounds. Price.....$1.95
No. 32C205 7-inch Chilled Plow. Width of furrow, 8 inches. Weight, 48 pounds. Price.....$2.75
No. 32C206 8-inch Chilled Plow. Width of furrow, 9 inches. Weight, 54 pounds. Price....$3.05
No. 32C207 9-inch Chilled Plow. Width of furrow, 10 inches. Weight, 68 pounds. Price....$4.40
No. 32C209 10-inch Chilled Plow. Width of furrow, 12 inches. Weight, 92 pounds. Price....$5.50
No. 32C210 11-inch Chilled Plow. Width of furrow, 13 inches. Weight, 112 pounds. Price....$5.70
No. 32C211 12-inch Chilled Plow. Width of furrow, 14 inches. Weight, 120 pounds. Price....$5.95
No. 32C212 Cast Jointer. Wt., 12 lbs. Pr...$1.40
No. 32C213 Gauge Wheel. Wt., 13 lbs. Pr. .70

Kenwood Prairie Breaking Plows.

$7.95 TO $8.55

WOOD BEAM. RIGHT HAND ONLY.

These plows are intended for use in breaking either old or new sod in any kind of soil, but can be used for other classes of work. The mouldboard is so shaped that it will turn the sod upside down and lay it perfectly flat. Standard and standard cap are steel. Mouldboard is soft center steel, landside and share are wrought steel, all hardened, ground and polished. Entire plow is strongly braced. One extra share is furnished with each plow. Wheel and coulter are not included in price of plow, and, unless you have them, they should be ordered with the plow. Shipped knocked down from factory near Chicago.

			Price
No. 32C220	12-inch Plow.	Wt., 132 lbs.	$7.95
No. 32C221	14-inch Plow.	Wt., 135 lbs.	8.25
No. 32C222	16-inch Plow.	Wt., 138 lbs.	8.55
No. 32C223	Gauge Wheel.	Wt., 11 lbs.	.65
No. 32C225	Rolling Coulter.	Wt., 21 lbs.	1.85

Kenwood Hillside Swivel Plows.

$3.60 TO $6.50

WOOD BEAM

Especially adapted for hillside plowing, but will also do perfect work on level land.

Swivel is arranged to swing very easy. Mould board, landside and share are chilled iron, ground and polished. One extra share furnished with each plow. The 6 and 8-inch plows are for one horse, the 10-inch for two, and the 12-inch for three horses. Jointer can be used only on 10 and 12-inch plows. Shipped knocked down from factory near Chicago.

		Width of Furrow	Weight	Price
No. 32C226	6-in. Plow.	8 in.	70 lbs.	$3.60
No. 32C227	8-in. Plow.	10 in.	78 lbs.	4.40
No. 32C228	10-in. Plow.	12 in.	105 lbs.	5.70
No. 32C229	12-in. Plow.	14 in.	132 lbs.	6.50
No. 32C230	Gauge Wheel.		Wt., 12 lbs.	.70
No. 32C231	Reversible Jointer.		Wt., 14 lbs.	1.55

IF YOU CANNOT MAKE A SATISFACTORY SELECTION FROM THESE PAGES, DON'T THINK OF BUYING FROM ANYONE UNTIL YOU HAVE SENT FOR AND RECEIVED OUR BIG FREE SPECIAL AGRICULTURAL IMPLEMENT CATALOGUE.

At Your Service

cial Kiowa Stock Saddle," "Our Kit Carson Cowboy Saddle," and "Our Special Montana Stock Saddle."

Agricultural Implements and Machinery

So extensive was Sears' line of agricultural implements in 1905 that it advised customers to "SEND FOR OUR FREE AGRICULTURAL IMPLEMENT CATALOGUE. To Properly Illustrate And Describe one complete line of agricultural implements . . . we have found it necessary to devote the entire space of a very large catalogue to this one line of goods. In This General Catalogue, 'The Great Price Maker,' we show only a few seasonable articles, with small illustrations and short descriptions." Yet these "few seasonable articles" covered eighteen pages of the general catalog.

The most primitive of all agricultural implements—the plow—appears in many variations: Disc Plows, Prairie Breaking Plows, Orchard Gang Plows (for shallow plowing), Sulky Plows, Steel Beam Brush Plows (for breaking rough and rooty land), Swivel Plows (for hillside work), Vineyard Plows (for nurseries and vineyards), and Sod Breaker Plows (for turning heavy sod and prairie plowing).

Here are horse-drawn corn and cotton planters, and combination potato planters and diggers; horse-drawn stalk cutters for cutting corn and cotton stalks to prepare fields for plowing; riding disc cultivators; self-dump hay rakes; hay presses with a capacity of seven to ten tons a day; grist mills, corn shellers, and feed grinders.

The motive power for most of this machinery was the human body or the horse, and the catalog lists several devices to make horsepower available in many fields. Among them was "Fulton One-Horse Sweep Power. A good, strong external geared one-horse sweep power, speeded at 25 revolutions to one round of the horse."

Another source of power offered by the catalog was the windmill. A great many must have been sold by Sears because "Our line of this class of goods is so extensive that we have found it necessary to issue a very large special catalogue, devoted exclusively to windmills and kindred goods."

"Kenwood Back Geared Galvanized Steel Pumping Windmills are the heaviest, strongest, and most handsomely finished mills on the market.. . . . The ends of the sails and the vane are tipped with red and the entire windmill is handsome and strong in every detail."

The final source of motive power—aside from electricity which was but little used on farms in 1905—is the gasoline engine. It is represented in the general catalog by two models: the one-horsepower vertical engine which sold for $71; the eight-horsepower horizontal engine for $265.

Change and More Change

In considering the American farm, certain basic facts must be borne in mind:

(*a*) Whether we like it or not, whether it was a wise policy or foolish, the hard fact is this: the American agricultural plant was built to supply not only the needs of the home market but also a vast foreign market. The collapse of this market must inevitably, therefore, work hardship on the American farmer.

Before the World War we normally exported the following proportions of major crops:

Cotton	66 per cent
Wheat	21 " "
Tobacco	39 " "
Hog products	12 " "

In 1929, the total harvested-crop acreage of the United States was 358,000,000. Wheat, cotton, corn (exported both as grain and as meat products), and tobacco were planted in 210,000,000 acres, or fifty-nine per cent, of the total acreage. Thus, more than one half of our farm lands were devoted to the production of crops largely designed for export.

(*b*) From 1865 to 1915 we were enabled to ship agricultural products abroad in great volume. We were a debtor

"Dry-Sox" and "Profile" Shoes for Men and Boys

Roomy Lasts—Solid as a Rock—Searsmade

SEARS Dry-Sox

No. 15V774   **The Pair, $3.95**
Black Chrome Uppers—Bellows Tongue—
Full Vamp—Goodyear Welt—Two Full Soles
—Special Rubber Welt Around Edge.
Sizes, 5 to 12. Wide widths.
Shipping wt., 3 lbs. 11 oz.

SEARS Dry-Sox

No. 15V772   **The Pair, $3.95**
Black Chrome Uppers—Bellows Tongue—
Full Vamp — Goodyear Welt — Two Full Soles
—Special Rubber Welt Around Edge.
Sizes, 5 to 12. Wide widths.
Shipping wt., 3⅜ lbs.

A Heavy but Dressy Shoe for Postmen, Police-men and Men Who Want Shoe Character as Well as Shoe Service.

SEARS Dry-Sox

No. 15V4000   **The Pair, $4.95**
Genuine Box Calf Uppers—Full Kid Lined
—Goodyear Welt Sewed — Two Full Double
Stitched Soles—Full Vamp Under the Tip—
Special Rubber Welt Between Uppers and
Soles.
Sizes, 5 to 12. Widths, C to EE.
Shipping wt., 3¼ lbs.

SEARS Dry-Sox

No. 15V773   **The Pair, $3.95**
Black Chrome Uppers — Bellows Tongue —
Full Vamp — Goodyear Welt — Soft Toe — Two
Full Soles—Special Rubber Welt Around Edge.
Sizes, 5 to 12. Wide widths.
Shipping wt., 3¾ lbs.

No. 15V786   **The Pair, $3.45**
All Gunmetal Calfskin — Goodyear Welt —
Double Sole — Soft Wide Toe — Sensible Heel
—For Men Who Want a Comfortable Shoe.
Sizes, 5 to 12. Widths, D to EE.
Shipping wt., 2¾ lbs.

Profile

No. 15V742   **The Pair, $3.15**
  Men's sizes, 5 to 12. Wide widths.
No. 15V930   **The Pair, $2.65**
  Boys' sizes, 1 to 5½. Wide widths.
  Shipping wt. 3 lbs. 7 oz.

Profile

No. 15V744   **The Pair, $3.10**
Sizes, 5 to 12. Wide widths.
Shipping wt., 3 lbs. 9 oz.

Profile

No. 15V743   **The Pair, $3.15**
Sizes, 5 to 12. Wide widths.
Shipping wt., 3 lbs. 9 oz.

"Profile" Specifications—Black Chrome Unlined Uppers—Heavy Yet Soft and Pliable—Full Bellows Tongue—Full Vamp
Under the Tip—Waxed Thread Stitched—Standard Screw Fastened—Extra Heavy Sole and Shank—"Heel That Won't Come Off."

PAULINS OR STACK AND MACHINE COVERS.

Weight given below is for 8-ounce duck; 10-ounce will weigh one-fourth more than 8-ounce, and 12-ounce will weigh one-half more than 8-ounce. Protect your crops, implements and machinery from snow, rain and inclement weather.

Made to special order. Allow from two to five days, according to the number of orders we have on hand when we receive yours.

We do not ship Paulins or Covers C.O.D.

Made of white duck. Always state size wanted when ordering. These goods are not tents, but paulins or stack covers. Stack covers have short ropes, BUT NO POLES; machine and merchandise covers have eyelets around side. Paulins are made to order and cannot be returned if sent as ordered. Write for samples of canvas which goes into our covers. Write for prices for special paulins not quoted in this list.

No. 6C10370

Style No.	Size, Feet	Wgt. of 8-oz.	8-oz. Duck	10-oz. Duck	12-oz. Duck
A	10x16	11 lbs.	$ 2.68	$ 3.30	$ 4.63
B	10x18	12 lbs.	3.03	3.72	5.00
C	12x14	12 lbs.	2.93	3.60	4.69
D	12x16	13 lbs.	3.44	4.13	5.57
E	12x18	16 lbs.	3.78	4.64	6.25
F	12x20	17 lbs.	4.23	5.15	6.88
G	14x16	16 lbs.	4.47	5.46	6.73
H	14x18	18 lbs.	5.02	6.15	7.50
J	14x20	20 lbs.	5.60	6.84	8.38
K	14x24	25 lbs.	6.39	7.84	10.13
L	16x16	18 lbs.	4.88	5.97	7.66
M	16x18	19 lbs.	5.48	6.73	8.63
N	16x20	23 lbs.	6.09	7.44	9.63
P	16x24	26 lbs.	7.30	8.95	11.50
Q	18x20	25 lbs.	6.85	8.40	10.78
R	18x24	30 lbs.	8.24	10.06	12.92
S	18x28	36 lbs.	9.62	11.74	15.07
T	18x30	39 lbs.	10.26	12.59	16.18
U	20x24	34 lbs.	9.15	11.18	14.38
V	20x36	51 lbs.	13.72	16.76	21.50
W	24x30	51 lbs.	13.72	16.76	21.57
X	24x40	68 lbs.	18.26	22.38	28.75
Y	24x50	84 lbs.	22.84	27.95	35.94

CANVAS BINDER COVERS.

No. 6C10371 Weight, 6½ to 7¼ pounds. Fitted to cover the binder and not the whole machine. Will fit any binder. Size 7½x15 feet. Made of white 8 and 10-oz. duck. Price, 8-ounce, $2.21; 10-ounce.. $2.47

Allow from two to five days to make.

BLACK OILED OR TARPAULIN WAGON COVERS

These covers, although black and called tarpaulins, have no tar in their composition. Our waterproof dressing is an oil preparation and is entirely free from anything calculated to rot or burn the canvas, but adds to the durability of the cover, being impervious to water and very soft and pliable. It will neither rot nor mildew from damp, or break from being too hard. They are invaluable to persons who are shipping and receiving goods that are liable to be damaged by wet weather. In ordering, give catalogue number, size and price. Weight 9 to 28 lbs.; 6x12, 12 lbs.; 6x9, 9 lbs.; 7x12, 16 lbs.; 7x14, 19 lbs.

Allow from two to five days to make.

No.	Size	Price	Size	Price	Size	Price
6C 10375	6x 8 ft.	$2.32	7x 9 ft.	$3.06	8x10 ft.	$3.87
	6x 9 ft.	2.55	7x10 ft.	3.38	8x12 ft.	4.65
	6x10 ft.	2.94	7x12 ft.	4.02	8x14 ft.	5.42
	6x12 ft.	3.43	7x14 ft.	4.75	8x16 ft.	6.21
	6x14 ft.	4.06	....	....	9x14 ft.	6.12

Prices given on other sizes upon application.

WHITE DUCK EMIGRANT WAGON COVERS.

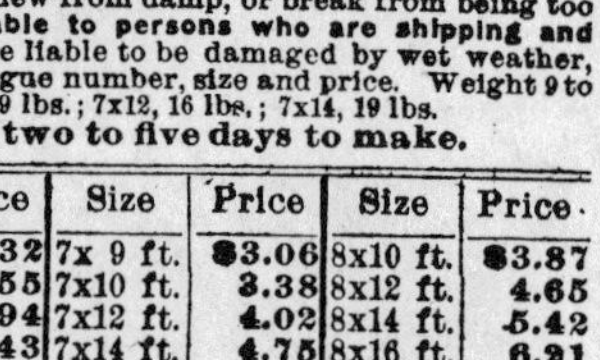

Always give size when ordering. Weight given below is on 8-ounce covers. 10-ounce weighs one-fourth more and 12-ounce about one-half more than 8-ounce. We do not send wagon covers C.O.D. Write for prices on covers not quoted in this list.

No. 6C10380

Size, Feet	Lbs.	8-oz. Duck	10-oz. Duck	12-oz. Duck
10x10	7	$1.78	$2.26	$3.38
10x12	7½	2.15	2.69	4.08
10x14	7¾	2.50	3.14	4.77
10x15	8	2.69	3.36	5.12
10x16	9	2.87	3.62	5.46
11x13	9	2.62	3.38	4.99
11x15	10	3.02	3.80	5.76
12x15	20	3.37	4.22	6.40
12x16	25	3.68	4.50	6.81
12x20	30	4.52	5.73	8.55

Allow from two to five days to make.

Comstock Malleable Iron Tent Pegs.

They last a lifetime. Cannot be broken.

No. 6C10387 Short Peg, 8¾ inches long. Weight about 4½ ounces each.
Price, per dozen..50c

No. 6C10388 Long Peg, 13½ inches long. Weight, about 7¼ ounces each.
Price, per dozen..70c

Our Palmetto Lawn Tents.

These Palmetto Lawn Tents are calculated for temporary use; as playhouses for children and similar purposes. They are made of about 8-ounce awning material and come in stripes of blue and white, are set up with one pole, and a light iron frame sewed into the tent around the eaves; are handsome in appearance upon the lawn and afford great pleasure to children. Order by catalogue number and state size wanted.

No. 6C10393

Size of Base	Size of Top	Height at Center	Height at Side	Wgt., lbs.	Price, each
7x 7 ft.	2 ft. 4 in.	7 ft. 6 in.	6 ft.	17	$4.21
8x 8 ft.	2 ft. 4 in.	8 ft.	6 ft. 6 in.	19	4.87
9x 9 ft.	3 ft. 6 in.	8 ft. 6 in.	7 ft.	23	6.88
10x10 ft.	3 ft. 6 in.	9 ft.	7 ft. 6 in.	26	6.62

Waterproof Ponchos.

No. 6C10394 Our Luster Ponchos, made of finest quality rubber, lined with fine sheeting and have a hole in center, covered with heavy flap. By using this hole and drawing the poncho over the head, it forms a large rubber cape, protecting the entire body. It is absolutely waterproof and may also be used as a rubber blanket. Size, 45x72 inches. Weight, 3½ pounds.
Price $1.25

Our Combination Tent and Cot.

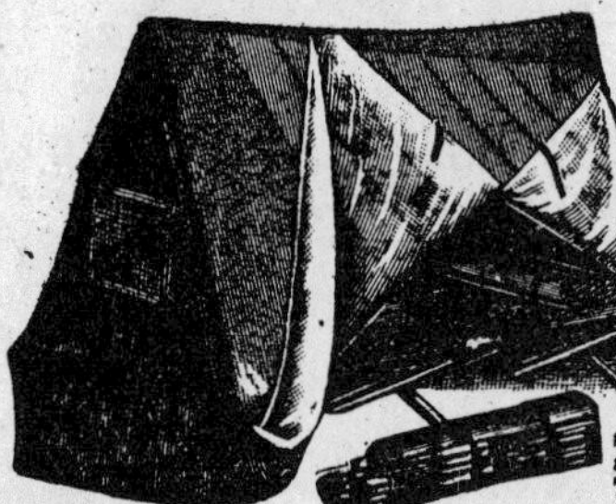

This illustration, engraved from a photograph, will give you some idea of our combination tent and cot, a very desirable article for campers who do not wish to be burdened with a tent. The cot is so constructed that it may be folded into a small package about 3 feet long. The tent frame is constructed on a folding pattern which may be easily attached or detached from the cot and folded in the same manner as the cot, while the canvas tent is made to fit over the cot and tent frame, as shown in the illustration. The cot has a pillow casing attached which may be filled with straw, hay or clothing to act as a pillow, and at each end of the tent there is sewn into it mosquito netting to keep out mosquitoes, as well as to afford ventilation to the occupant. The tent is 6¼ feet long, 2¾ feet wide, 4½ feet high, and is made from 10-ounce duck, which makes it practically a waterproof tent, and the entire weight of the cot and tent complete is about 24 pounds. The entire outfit may be folded up, as shown in the above illustration, and carried from place to place at a moment's notice. Weight, packed for shipment, about 30 pounds.

No. 6C10395 Price of the cot and tent complete, as shown in the above illustration........................$5.50

PORCH CURTAINS.

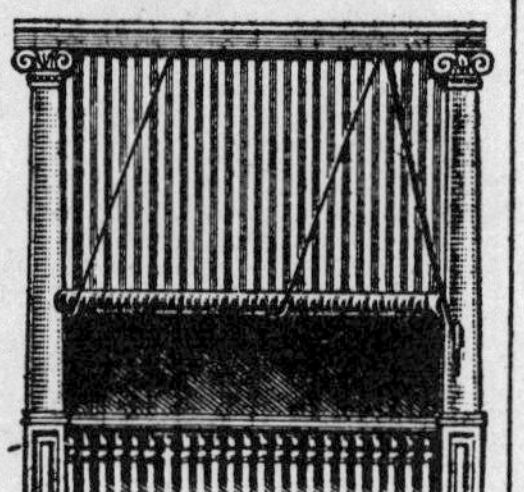

If you have a porch or piazza, a porch curtain will enable you to enjoy the full benefit of same, as it will protect you from the heat of the sun; will also keep out dust and rain, and will help to make your porch very comfortable during the summer months.

Our porch curtains are made of fancy striped duck, furnished complete with pulleys, ropes and roller, and all necessary screws and adjustments ready to attach to your porch. No experience is required to put up one of these curtains. It can be done by almost anyone. This curtain is made with double pulleys—the roller is at the bottom. By pulling the rope you revolve the roller, the curtain being raised or lowered, as desired.

When ordering, give the height and width of your porch; or, if you desire the curtain to cover only a part of your porch, give actual height and width of the opening for which you desire the curtain. These curtains are made to order. Cannot be returned if made as ordered. We sell these curtains by the square foot, the price per square foot includes all accessories. A curtain 10 feet high and 16 feet wide would contain 160 square feet, and at our price of 6 cents per square foot would cost $9.60.

No. 6C10397 Price, per square foot 6c

We are in position to quote prices on special awnings of all kinds. Will be glad to quote prices on store awnings, roller awnings, complete with winding gear, and special awnings for extra wide windows, upon request.

Our Adjustable Window Awning.

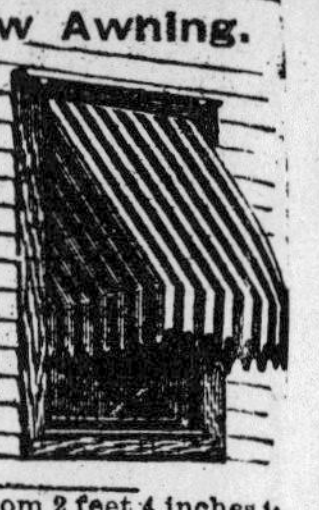

Our Adjustable Window Awning is constructed so that anybody can quickly fit same to a window, and can be as quickly removed if desired. It is not necessary to have an experienced awning hanger to hang these awnings. You can do it yourself just as well. They are made of regular awning material, blue and white striped, with scallops at the bottom, as shown in the illustration, are raised and lowered with ropes over pulleys, same as other awnings. These awnings will help to make your home pleasant, keep the sun from fading your carpets and furniture, and will greatly add to the appearance of the house. They come in three sizes to fit windows from 2 feet 4 inches to feet 5 inches wide. When ordering, give width of your window so that we know which of the three sizes to send you.

No. 6C10399 No. 2 Awning will fit any size window from 2 feet 4 inches to 2 feet 10 inches wide........................$1.75

No. 3 Awning to fit any window from 3 feet to 3 feet 7 inches wide........................1.85

No. 4 Awning to fit any window from 3 feet 10 inches to 4 feet 5 inches wide........................2.00

Weight, packed for shipment, 11 pounds.

Special Awnings for Stores and Residences.

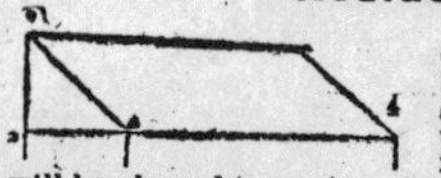

We are able to furnish your home or store with a better awning for less money than you could possibly secure elsewhere. Owing to the great variety of sizes, we do not catalogue special awnings, but will be pleased to quote prices upon receipt of an inquiry, stating size of awning wanted. When writing us regarding special awning, refer to the above diagram, give us height of awning from 1 to 2, projection from 2 to 3 and width from 3 to 4. Distance from 1 to 2 should be governed by height of store ceiling; allow 7 to 8 feet from bottom of frame (2) to sidewalk. Mention if frame is to be fastened to wood, brick, stone or iron columns. Also if columns to which frame is to be fastened are in line. If not in line, state which ones, and how far back they are set. State whether you desire the awning made of plain white or striped duck and if the awning is to be lettered, and whether lettering is to be placed on roof of awning or on curtain. If you desire new cover only, be sure to so state in your inquiry, also state whether the cover is for a wood or an iron frame.

Camp Chairs and Stools.

No. 6C10431 Canvas Top Camp Stool well made. Weight, 2¾ lbs.
Price 22c

No. 6C10432 Canvas Top Camp Chair, same as No. 6C10431, with back. Weight, 3¾ pounds. Price........30c

Our Combination Folding Cot and Litter, $1.50.

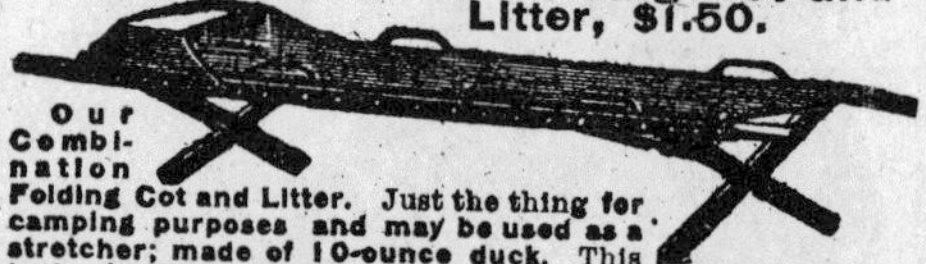

Our Combination Folding Cot and Litter. Just the thing for camping purposes and may be used as a stretcher; made of 10-ounce duck. This is the lightest, strongest and most compact folding cot made. It has the only practical pillow ever put on a cot. It is made so that you can stuff straw or clothing into the pillow casing. Length, 6 feet 3 inches; width, 29 inches. Dimensions, when folded and ready for shipment, 6 feet 3 inches by 5 inches by 5 inches. Weight, 15 pounds.

No. 6C10435 Price, complete with pillow........$1.50

Our Gold Medal Folding Camp Bed.

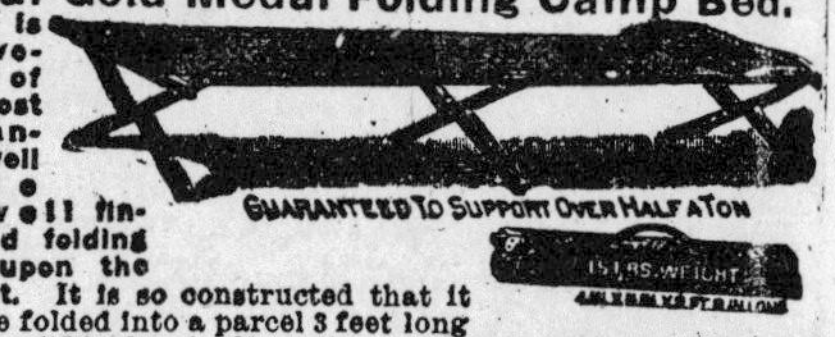

This is positively one of the most substantial, well made and well finished folding cots upon the market. It is so constructed that it may be folded into a parcel 3 feet long and about 5 inches in diameter, and is guaranteed to hold 1,000 pounds. The frame is made strong and substantial, and is covered with heavy brown canvas and has a pillow casing which may be stuffed with straw, hay or clothing to act as a pillow. It is about 6½ feet long and 2⅓ feet wide and weighs about 16 pounds.

No. 6C10438 Gold Medal Folding Camp Bed. Price, $2.15

Camping Outfit Complete at $5.40.

No. 6C10455 Wilson's Kamp Kook's Kit. Just the thing for camping out. 53 pieces. Fire jack, two boilers suitable for using as an oven, fry pan, coffee pot and all utensils and tableware for a party of six. Everything first class. Boilers are made of 26-gauge smooth steel. The entire kit nests in small space, and when packed ready for shipment makes a package 14½x10½x8 inches, all nested together and can be firmly locked up by an ordinary padlock. Weight, complete, 20 pounds.
Price, complete..........$5.40

PAT. MARCH 10, 96.

No. 6C10455 Illustration of kit packed for shipment.

The above outfit together with our No. 6C9170 Rival Camp Stove makes the best and most complete camp outfit ever placed on the market.

country; we were paying the principal and interest on the millions we had borrowed abroad to finance our industrial expansion with farm products, and as a debtor country, despite our own high tariffs, we could sell more than we bought.

(c) From 1914 to 1919, the war demands upon American agriculture were gigantic. We planted the ditch banks; drained the swamps; felled the forests; plowed up the prairie. In the excitement and the prosperity, few noticed, and fewer seemed to understand (the lack of understanding was particularly gross on the part of many so-called international bankers), that we had achieved an amazing transformation within four years from a debtor to a creditor nation. It was time for us to change the rules and play the game the other way by acting like a creditor country; that is, lower the tariff and import more than we exported. We wouldn't change the rules. We would play our way or there would be no game. We desperately needed markets for our war-swollen farms and the world needed our flour and hams. The customers were hungry but they had no money. And we would not take their goods in exchange for our apples and cotton. Our way out was to lend the customers money with which to buy our products; lend them more money to pay interest, and still more money to buy more goods. By 1928, we finally realized what we were doing—even the bankers had begun to get glimmerings of the true situation—and we stopped lending. Then the customers stopped buying. And we went into the tailspin of 1929.

(d) We had made things difficult for our own farm economy by our own actions. Abroad, other stupendous events were in progress. Millions of acres had come into production in Australasia and South America. They had begun to compete actively with us in exports to Europe, and they enjoyed two advantages which had been ours for long decades: they were tilling virgin lands and were debtor economies.

(e) After the World War, the great European countries, impoverished and fearing another war, adopted a policy of self-containment in greater or lesser degree. To the extent that the policy succeeded, they diminished their imports of farm products from the United States.

What were some of the results of these factors on the American farm economy?

In 1919, the gross farm income was (round numbers) $17,000,000,000.

In 1932, the gross farm income was (round numbers) $5,300,000,000.

Farmers did not share in the prosperity of the boom period 1919–29. The share of farm income in the total national income dropped from 18.5 per cent to less than 10 per cent in 1919–29. This was serious enough, but far more serious is the fact that by June, 1932, the prices of farm products had dropped so low, and the prices of the things the farmer bought had risen so high, that he could purchase with his products only forty-seven per cent of what he could have bought in 1914. And he was loaded down with high-priced land and farm machinery; oppressed by heavy taxation, and threatened with dispossession by mortgage holders. But when the sheriffs came around, farmers reached for their shotguns instead of surrendering the old homestead. President John A. Simpson of the National Farmers' Union told farmers:

> Our strike has reached the attention of the Eastern financiers as no other farm movement. It is because a few of our farmers have been shot at. Let them kill a few of us if it will do any good. Governments, courts, laws, and constitutions are inferior to human rights. . . . My authority for this statement is the Declaration of Independence. Under this same authority you have the right to take up shotguns and prevent the big robbers from taking your farms.

America was threatened with a serious revolution and America took it seriously. This country, after all, as Lamar Middleton has shown in his *Revolt. U.S.A.,* is the country where six of the nine major revolutions and rebellions that we have had have been engineered almost entirely by farmers.

One of the first acts, therefore, of President Roosevelt, when he took office in 1933, was to assure farmers that they would not be dispossessed, and shortly thereafter Congress passed the first of a long series of measures designed to relieve agriculture.

The Mechanized Farm of 1939

As we have seen, the Civil War accelerated the invention and use of labor-saving farm machinery; after it, agricultural inventions increased rapidly in numbers and importance. The self-binder for grain came in the seventies; the improved Deering twine binder in the eighties, and at the end of the century the mechanical header was introduced, speeding up harvesting in areas where it was not thought worth while to preserve straw from the wheat stalk. The steam threshing machine revolutionized the separation of grain from the husk, while the cornhusker and corn harvester made their appearance at the end of the century with extraordinary labor-saving consequences in the great American corn crop. The farm revolution may be measured by the fact that the mechanical inventions of the nineteenth century (it is estimated) reduced farm labor by seventy-nine per cent and farming costs by forty-six per cent.

But the most startling advances in farm machinery lay ahead in the rapidly approaching twentieth century. They proceeded from the development of the internal-combustion engine which made it possible for Benjamin Holt to produce an efficient and economical farm tractor in 1903. It was soon followed by the automobile truck. Farmers who used these new vehicles got rid of their mules and horses. The tractor brought the time-saving gang plow and the disk combine, thus completely changing the methods of preparing the soil for planting, while tractor-drawn grain drills hastened the actual planting of seed. When the harvest season came, the work was done by a few men running the harvesting combine which cuts, threshes, cleans, and bags wheat, all in one process.

Other ingenious labor-saving machines have been invented for use in the corn and cotton fields, in orchards and dairies; poultry growing has been revolutionized by the use of incubators, and now the last great stronghold of hand labor— cotton picking—is threatened by the invention of the mechanical cotton picker.

The farm population has been dwindling for decades, yet there are still too many people on the farms for the work that they do and the meager recompense that many of them obtain. O. W. Wilcox, in his *Reshaping Agriculture* and *Nations Can Live At Home,* maintains that we could produce all the food necessary for a high standard of living with one fifth of the persons now on farms working only one fifth of the land now under cultivation, if we employ the best mechanical methods available and the best modes of fertilization.

The catalog of 1939 shows some of the machines and the methods now employed by the American farmer.

The Tractor

The wheat farmer in the horse age could plow only from about two to four acres a day, but with even a small tractor he can plow three or four times as much. Most large farms in the United States, whatever the crops they raise, are partially or completely tractor-equipped. But there are millions of small farmers for whom the large tractor is both uneconomical and a heavy financial burden. Thus, although we tend to think of cotton culture in terms of the Southern colonel surveying his thousands of acres from the back of a spirited horse, the fact is that more than one half the annual cotton crop is produced by men who grow only two to five bales. For the immense group of small farmers, Sears has produced a small, low-priced tractor:

"The Handiman R-T Four Wheel Riding Tractor. Plow ... Harrow ... Seed ... Mow ... Rake ... Cultivate ... Haul. Designed for garden and small farm use. Meets all tillage and cultivating requirements on these places. Built to use standard tools such as disc, drag and spring-tooth harrows, mowers, planters, drills, etc."

These small tractors sell for $355, or roughly one third the price of the standard-size machines.

But if you have an old Ford or Chevrolet (who hasn't?), "you can transform it into a practical tractor. . . . All you need . . . is an old Model T or Model A Ford, or a 1926 to 1931 Chevrolet, and a Sears Thrifty Farmer Tractor Unit. With the auto body removed you can quickly convert the old auto into a tractor that has the pulling power of two to four horses. . . . Price, $99.50."

Modern tractors are equipped with good lighting systems so that the farmer, when pressed for time in planting or sowing, may run them all night. And many tractors carry radios so that the farmer, running his highly efficient machine, may hear the speeches of Congressmen in Washington as they attempt to get greater and greater farm subsidies for him.

Sears manufactures many of its own farm implements and markets them under the trade name of David Bradley Implements. Among them, for use with tractors, are: "David Bradley Hi-Clearance Two-Bottom Tractor Plow. . . . This plow does a marvelously clean and thorough job of turning under all cover crops and refuse for fertilizer, Price $102.00," "Furromaster Tractor Plows, two-bottom, Price, $81.70," and a large number of tractor-drawn harrows.

The Machine and the Cow

Morning and evening, almost every day in the year, the farmer must milk his cow. The cow, however, is a fretful, rebellious creature who often does not tamely submit to milking. She expresses her resentment by kicking, moving, and switching her tail in the milker's face. At least one cow of all the millions that have been milked in the United States during the past sixty years achieved immortality through rebellion. This was Mrs. O'Leary's famous animal which is supposed to have started the great Chicago fire of 1871 by kicking over the lantern Mrs. O'Leary was using for light on a dark morning. But nowadays, the cow may be milked by machinery as well as by hand; the liquid pours into buckets while the farmer looks on.

"Let A Prima Do The Work," says the catalog. "Let the Prima Milker remove the drudgery from the most tedious hours of the day—morning and evening milking. Enjoy new leisure and ease where you once labored and fretted at milking cows by hand. Prima will do all the work for you, and will reduce milking time from one-third to one-half. . . . It never is hurried, never gets tired, and the cows like it. The massaging action of the inflations on the teats is so natural and calf-like that it stimulates the flow of milk . . . the cows actually 'give down' better than when milked by hand. . . . Single Unit Milker, Milks one cow at a time. Price, $44.50."

After the cows have been milked, cream may be separated from the milk by the use of Economy King electric-driven separators, which handle from two to eight hundred pounds of milk an hour. Then the cream may be converted into butter in Elgin Electric Churns.

Even wire and wood fences are giving way to the electric fence. "Fence With Electricity. Save Money. Save Time. Save Labor. You can do all this with a Sears Fence Controller. Only one strand of barbed or smooth wire . . . will turn horses, mules, cattle, or hogs. . . . Fences are quickly built and easily moved. . . . One controller will handle all the inside fences on the average farm, 12 miles or more of wire." Fence Controllers range in price from $7.95 to $15.95.

From Thomas Jefferson to F. D. Roosevelt

American agriculture today is characterized by a high rate of tenancy; a heavy capital investment in machines and high-priced lands; diminishing foreign markets and almost static domestic markets. It is kept from collapse by Federal subsidies. Farming as a way of life is giving way to farming as a business. Mechanized farms are in reality land factories, and the men who run them are industrial workers. Increases in land values and the heavy costs of machines and fertilizer require such large capital that diversified farming and the self-contained farm homestead are rapidly vanishing. It is only in the Southern Appalachians that subsistence farming, eighteenth-century style, is still practiced on a considerable scale. Machines have made farms more efficient; lessened the farmer's hand labor; increased his crops, and driven hundreds of thousands of men off the farms.

Politically, the farmer, despite his agitations, had not been generally successful from 1865 until the present Roosevelt Administration. "With the collapse of the most articulate agricultural group that has ever existed in the United States [the ante bellum Southern planters]," says *The Encyclopaedia of the Social Sciences,* "business interests entered upon a period of almost unchallenged control of the federal government and most of the state governments. Far from being hindered by government regulation, they received at the hands of the central and local governments every favor they desired. . . . What could not be gained by fair means was frequently obtained unfairly. . . ."

Yet from Thomas Jefferson to Franklin D. Roosevelt, it has been held that agriculture is basic, and that therefore the prosperity of the farmer should be the direct concern of government. This point of view has never been better stated than by Theodore Roosevelt: "If there is one lesson taught by history it is that the permanent greatness of any state must ultimately depend more upon the character of its country population than upon anything else. No growth of cities, no growth of wealth can make up for the loss in either the number or the character of the farming population."

Contrast this attitude with the facts of life on the American farm. These are, apart from the dwindling farm population, that the value of farm property in the United States dropped from $78,000,000,000 in 1919 to $44,000,000,000 in 1932. At the same time, farm-mortgage indebtedness increased as follows:

1910	....$3,300,000,000
1920	 7,900,000,000
1931	 9,500,000,000

Yet it was during this period that improved techniques and farm machinery had brought farms to a new high of productivity. Simultaneously, as Southern farm Negroes say, "the interest was eating up the principal." In 1931, eight per cent of gross farm income of this country went to the paying of mortgage interest, as contrasted with three per cent before the World War, while taxes took eleven per cent of gross farm income, as compared with four per cent in 1913.

The burden of these fixed charges was so great that in the period 1927–32 nearly ten per cent of all farms passed out of the hands of their original owners, and nearly four per cent were sold because of failure to pay taxes.

But nonetheless, giant combines and harvesters continued to sweep through Western wheat fields; tractors broke the rich soil of the Arkansas Delta, and airplanes sowed thousands of acres of rice fields in California. Farms and farmers may fail. Machinery marches on.

Part Four

EVERYBODY'S BUSINESS

Throughout this book we have been considering catalog merchandise and have drawn certain conclusions from it. In this fourth section, however, we depart from this pattern to make certain examinations in other fields. Here we consider the vast social and economic force that is advertising, and note how the catalog is affected or unaffected by forces at work in this general field. We consider the hostility that mail-order houses aroused in the breasts of small-town merchants and small-town newspaper proprietors. We treat of a relatively new and dynamic force in American life—installment selling—and suggest briefly that its origins lie not only in economic need but also in changing religious and moral conceptions.

In the last chapter of this book about the Sears catalog, we turn to the catalog itself. Here we tell how the catalog is manufactured and distributed; who gets it and why; the place of the catalog in American life, and finally, how the automobile and the changing circumstances of the past decade have forced the once exclusively mail-order house of Sears to open retail stores all over the United States.

The appendix contains a collection of letters written to Sears by some of its customers.

Thus the book ends with a consideration of the following: advertising; small-town hostility to the catalog; installment selling; the story of the catalog and of Sears' stores; and an appendix containing letters from customers.

THE things that America advertises and displays in its store windows, and the manner in which they are advertised, show us as well as any other indication the direction in which the wind is blowing. It is a wind that blows a stench into the noses of the fastidious but it blows, nonetheless, at gale strength through the pages of our magazines and newspapers and, to a lesser extent, is borne on the radio wings of the air. Almost completely nude figures of men and women in our advertising pages; the loudly extolled virtues of sanitary napkins, of depilatories and deodorants, remedies for offensive mouth and body odors, and brassières that (in the advertising) will give any woman the pear-shaped, moon-pointing breasts of a Balinese virgin are accepted as a matter of course by the American public. These, however, are developments that have come about largely since the World War, and, much as anything else, point to our changing attitudes towards sex and the body generally. Infallibly, the catalog records in text and illustrations the changes as they occurred through the years.

Let us take a single article—sanitary napkins—and contrast their method of presentation in a thirty-year period: 1905–35. In the earlier year, these articles were modestly tucked away toward the end of a page in the latter part of the catalog, and were described as follows:

> Antiseptic Sanitary Towels. These serviettes are made of the finest absorbent cotton, with a layer of absolutely impervious material, which insures cleanliness. . . .These serviettes possess from three to four times the absorbent

qualities of the best toweling. Recommended by the medical profession as indispensable in every lady's wardrobe. . . .

Accompanying the text is a small sketch of the towels; the human figure is absent.

In 1935, sanitary napkins are prominently displayed in large space at the top of a page, with illustrations of the boxes containing them. This is how the catalog describes CELLU-ETTES:

> FORM-FITTING SANITARY NAPKINS. Light as a wisp . . . soft as eiderdown! Form-fitting napkins worn with complete comfort and freedom. . . . Wear with a clinging party frock or for active sports. . . . No tell-tale bulging. . . .

It took years to bring this outspoken kind of advertising into being, and the pioneers moved cautiously for a long time, abandoning their cautious processes only after trial and error had proved that the public had become shockproof and would stomach almost anything. The very name of one of the products—the deodorant Mum—is proof of the caution with which manufacturers at first proceeded. Their eventual success is demonstrated by the 1935 catalog, which advertises a group of deodorants "To Assure Your Personal Cleanliness . . . diverts underarm perspiration to other parts of the body where it can evaporate quickly without becoming offensive and embarrassing." The illustration accompanying the text is a photograph of a nude woman (one hand modestly hides an exposed breast) applying a deodorant under her arm.

The year 1921 saw an avalanche of advertising on the part of makers of such articles as Mum, Kotex, Listerine, and Odorono. Mum, which a few years before had begun with timid, self-conscious little bits of copy, was now having heart-to-heart talks with women readers on the horrors of underarm odors; Odorono was using full-page advertisements. *Printer's Ink,* an important trade publication, wrote in 1921:

"The American public has graduated from prudishness. Self-consciousness about persons and habits and some of the more intimate phases of life have been outgrown."

Motherhood, formerly a taboo subject, by 1921 was being freely discussed by the Young Mother's Institute which headed its advertisements, "Why Risk the Life of Your Coming Baby?"

Rouge, formerly a taboo word in polite society, was made common chat by advertisements in 1921. Other firms, emboldened by the success of the pioneers, began to exploit their products in frank language. A Trenton, New Jersey, firm advertised a silent-flushing toilet; another printed a photograph of a woman sprinkling Sani-Flush into a toilet bowl, a picture that a few years before would have been regarded as indecent and shocking, and soon Lifebuoy and Listerine began to spend millions of dollars advertising their products which allegedly prevented body odors and offensive mouth odors. Under the impetus of this advertising, the profits of the Lambert Company, manufacturers of Listerine, grew from $115,000 in 1920 to $4,000,000 in 1927, and the word "halitosis," which was the basis of its advertisements, was accepted by the younger generation as an everyday part of the English language. Actually, it had been carefully selected from Webster's Unabridged Dictionary, because it was thought that its erudite sound would deodorize the stench of the subject matter itself.

This is not to say that there were no objections on the part of the public to advertising of this kind. There were objections. They came in general from women's clubs and religious groups who protested to the magazines, the manufacturers, and even the Federal government. For obvious reasons, their objections were ignored, the advertising became even bolder, profits mounted, and scores of imitators of the pioneers came on the scene to advertise in more offensive ways more offensive subjects. Finally, the inevitable reaction occurred, and *Printer's Ink* carried the following article by Mary Muldon in 1931:

Women are Getting Tired of Being Told About Odors and Other Terrible Tendencies.

For the last few years women have been deluged with warnings about their terrible tendencies to shock the dear male, and deprive themselves of the pleasures of wifehood, motherhood, girlhood and livelihood in general.

One time it is breath; another time, body odor; another time feet, figure, hair or some other personal matter that need not, methinks, be blazoned in practically every newspaper and magazine that may fall into women's and men's and children's hands. . . . Intelligent women are getting incensed at the constant reiteration of our little personal indiscretions. . . . In many up-to-the-minute clubs women are actually campaigning about the matter. I know two big clubs where the women promised not to purchase goods that are advertised in an impudent manner.

A magazine editor told me that she hated to run the advertisements in her paper. and that many women wrote to her and told her they disliked putting her magazine with these objectionable advertisements on the library table in their homes.

"We can't print filthy literature," she said, "but we certainly print lewd advertisements."

Through the Catalog Looking Glass

As we have seen, the catalog followed the general trend in advertising sanitary napkins, deodorants, and other articles pertaining to the care of the body. In 1935, it lists Essar Health soap, "Large red cakes of pure soap that aid in suppressing body odors"; a group of depilatories for removing hair on arms, legs, and body, and Listerine. "Use it to guard against halitosis (unpleasant breath)."

Copywriters Invent New Diseases

While the catalog went along with national advertisers part of the way, it did not go the whole way. By 1930, all the common ills of the body, such as body odor, bad breath, dandruff, and so forth, had in effect been spoken for by a group of powerful concerns, and for other aspiring manufacturers there remained only the opportunity of inventing new ones. Up to this point, the public had accepted the advertising of hitherto unmentionable products designed to remedy unmentionable ills, and the general point of view of the public was well expressed by Anna Steese Richardson, director of the Good Citizenship Bureau of the *Woman's Home Companion,* who wrote: "Lifebuoy Soap may be as offensive to some of you as the B.O. which it is supposed to remove, but at least it has started a lot of people bathing."

By 1934, however, imaginative copywriters were inventing scores of new ills and advertising products to cure them. These are typical of the plagues with which America saw itself confronted in the pages of newspapers and magazines:

Underarm Offense	Intestinal Toxicity
Pendulosis	Colon Collapse
Hi-Tense-Itis	Ashtray Breath
Barn Odor	Calendar Fear
Undie Odor	Office Hips
Paralyzed Pores	Athlete's Foot

At this point, the catalog bowed itself out of the scene, but it is worthy of note that some magazines which refused to print whisky and cigarette advertising, on the ground that to do so is to promote immorality and offend the morals of their readers, printed without question the advertisements of these imaginary plagues.

Nudity in Advertising

Advertising is not only a potent influence on American habits of mind but also a clue to contemporary morals and manners. Nowhere is this more clearly shown than in the sketches and photographs of the catalog and of advertisers generally, depicting women in corsets, hosiery, or underwear. Here again, the catalog holds a mirror up to American life, and in its pages we see the country in moral transition. Picture following picture gives us almost a motion-picture view of the successive changes in attitudes.

The corseted ladies of the 1905 catalog are extremely modest as they wear the models of the day in rather nondescript and certainly unfleshly sketches. By 1935, the young, slender, and beautiful models wearing girdles are photographed in pose after pose showing not only the girdles and brassières, but also silk-stockinged legs, and often bare expanses of flesh between the brassières and the girdle. These photographs would have been too frank even for *The Police Gazette* in 1905, but in 1935 they aroused no comment in the pages of the catalog.

It was not until 1913 that underwear was shown on full-length women's figures, and this practice, as new as it was, brought no complaints to advertisers, because petticoats came down to the ankles. But the attitude then towards nudity in advertising is shown by the fact that corsets, underwear, and stockings were grouped together as "unmentionables." In 1921, the ladies of the Athenaeum Club, of Kansas City, were shocked by a hosiery advertisement which read: "When you add the windy days of spring to the short skirts prescribed by fashion you have good reason to see that the name 'Gotham' is on your silk stockings!" The ladies threatened to stop buying their hosiery at the shop that ran this advertisement if it did not tone down its language. But ten years later (1931), when other hosiery advertising showed a man lifting a girl's skirts to her thighs with his walking stick, nobody objected. By this time, full-page advertisements containing photographs of girls dressed in nothing but brassières and girdles were being used all over the country, and the permissible limit of freedom of illustration was soon to become the ultimate limit —complete nudity.

In 1939, a country acutely conscious of mammary glands took the following advertisement in its stride. It appeared in at least one magazine which prides itself upon keeping its fiction contents "clean":

A Formfit bra and "glamour" are assuredly synonymous—for this modern and unique creation transforms the breasts into a new, more shapely loveliness—and gives them a poised carriage they have never had before! Lifts them proudly high—separates them oh! so prettily —forms them with a beautifully rising curve on top and moulds them into fashion-right fullness around and below. . . .

The catalog has not yet gone this far. But in general, it has marched with the rest of the country's advertising, and its pages of underwear, brassières, girdles, and hosiery are scarcely to be distinguished from those that appear in *Vogue, Harper's Bazaar,* and other so-called journals of fashion.

Aᴍᴇʀɪᴄᴀ has had its own burnings of the books—the heaped volumes, the kerosene-soaked pages, the kindling match, the leaping flames, the shouting populace, the shooting sparks, the smoldering embers, the crowd going homeward through village darkness.

Here ends the resemblance between these burnings and the literary autos-da-fé of the past in other lands and in present-day Germany. For the books burned in our villages were not the books of literary, religious, political, or economic heretics, and they were not destroyed to obliterate what the Japanese —agile burners themselves—call dangerous thoughts. The books were mail-order catalogs, and they were reduced to ashes at the incitement of local merchants and newspaper editors who believed that to destroy the catalogs was to destroy the competition of the mail-order houses.

Just as the rise of the department store after the Civil War infuriated small merchants and shopkeepers and drove them to futile attempts to ban their big competitors by law, so, too, the rise of the mail-order companies enraged country merchants throughout the United States. Many of these men felt the thrust of the distant Sears, Roebuck in their ribs as directly as though a six-shooter had been thrust into them. Large numbers of country storekeepers were (and are) postmasters, and it must have been bitterly galling to them, first, to deliver catalogs to their own customers (many of whom owed them money); then write out money orders in Sears' name on behalf of their customers, and, finally, hand over parcels containing goods from their remote but potent competitors. It was not easy for the local merchant to forget that when local consumers were short of cash he accommodated them with credit; delivered their messages over his telephone, and otherwise rendered them small services. It was burned in his memory that when flood threatened the village he had shoveled mud all night in the cold rain, along with his fellow villagers and customers, to build a levee against the advancing waters; had voted with them to assess higher taxes on themselves to erect a new school; worshiped together on Sunday; sat fraternally in the same lodge, and as members of the same community had labored to improve it. Yet, when his friends and neighbors had money to spend for merchandise, they chose to spend it over the counters of a distant, anonymous corporation rather than over his friendly well-worn counters. These men consequently would have been saints and not storekeepers if they had not protested against the metropolitan invasion of their rural businesses.

The other merchants in town were also embittered by mail-order competition and they found articulate allies in the editors of local newspapers whose prosperity depended upon the advertising of local merchants. The methods of combating the distant competitor worked out by editors and merchants were both futile and pathetic. Futile because they attempted to stem competition with emotion; pathetic because they represented the confused bewilderment of little men grappling with big business.

Embattled editors and merchants appealed to their fellow townsmen on the ground that to trade at home is to build up the local community; a plea doomed to failure because it is not demonstrably sound and because there is no patriotism of the purse. Men trade wherever they may trade to the best advantage, and if potatoes are cheaper in the bins of the shadowy A & P than they are in the store of Simms Brothers—Fifty Years On This Corner—the A & P will get the business. Flowing from this plea was the implication—carefully fostered by local newspapers—that a man who traded with the mail-order houses instead of at home was a traitor to the community, a sneak thief who would rob a blind man in a cemetery, a bird befouling its own nest. Since few local residents cared to expose either their own selfishness or their own economic concepts, most of them gave at least lip service to the trade-at-home idea while they steadily continued to send their money to Chicago. And the local merchants, fully conscious of this, set out to destroy mail-order competition by destroying the catalogs which were the instrument of the competition.

Sears, too, knew of the hostility against it on the part of local merchants; knew that the townsmen would trade with it if they were protected from public exposure, and consequently there arose the strange situation in which a pair of shoes was sent through the mails with the secrecy and anonymity that might attend the delivery of an opium pipe and pellets. In 1905, the catalog carried this notice on page 2:

HOW WE MAKE EVERY TRANSACTION WITH US STRICTLY CONFIDENTIAL.

"Why our name and address do not appear on any box, package, wrapper, tag, envelope or article of merchandise.

"As many people, especially merchants, townspeople and others, do not care to have others know where or from whom they buy their goods, as many people object to having the name of the shipper spread across every box or package, so that when it is unloaded at the station or express office every one can see what they are getting and where they buy it, to protect all those who care for this protection and make it possible for you to order goods from us with no fear of anyone learning . . . what you bought or where you bought it, our name and address will not appear on any box, package . . . or article of merchandise.

". . . We have learned that thousands of our customers need the protection that omitting the name affords. This applies especially to townspeople."

Mail-Order War in the Northwest

In the period 1916–18, merchants and editors of local newspapers in the Northwest embarked on a vigorous war

This Store is Known

WE ARE an organization of individuals— folks like you and your neighbor—who have the same feelings as other folks.

And as common, everyday people, we like the friendliness that comes with our business relations. We like the frank, kindly letters that our millions of friends write us. We like the feeling that here is one huge family, banded together to buy at the lowest prices. We like the good will that the years have built for us.

That is why we want to take this opportunity of extending our thanks to the folks who have been so generous in their support. We receive each year hundreds of thousands of voluntary requests for our catalogs. The kind words that you passed along to your friends are no doubt responsible for this. And we thank you most sincerely.

We hope that we may long continue to warrant your active support. You may know that never willingly would we allow anything to interfere with the continuance of our pleasant relations.

We want you to think of us as just "plain folks"—men and women who do the best that it is possible to do. As folks—as neighbors— as friends, we thank you for your many kindnesses:

Danville, Ill.

Sears, Roebuck and Co.,
Chicago, Ill.

Gentlemen:

The console phonograph we purchased from your firm three years ago is the finest instrument we have ever heard.

The tone is perfect, the workmanship and finish are equal to or better than machines selling at double the price.

I will also state, that in my 20 years' dealing with your firm, I have found you prompt in your shipments, courteous in your treatment, and above all, I get more for the money and better goods than I have ever received from any firm I ever dealt with.

You can list me as a satisfied customer.

Yours truly,
MRS. GEORGE W. FLORA,
220 East Roselawn Ave.

Above is the beautiful home of Mr. Hy Hoppler who is well known in and around Princeton, Illinois, as a concrete bridge contractor and as a farmer producing excellent seed corn.

Here is what Mr. Hoppler says about us: "We have always found the merchandise bought from Sears, Roebuck and Co. to be as represented. The quick service and 'money returned if not satisfied' guarantee has made your firm popular with our family."

The Guilfoyles are well known and among the most substantial farmers of their neighborhood. They have a fine home with beautiful lawn and shade trees.

Mendota, Ill.

Sears, Roebuck and Co.,
Chicago, Ill.

Dear Sirs:

I have been a Sears-Roebuck customer for around 25 years and your service in prompt shipments together with the lower prices and excellent quality of your goods has always made me feel very friendly to your firm.

Hoping that you may continue to serve us in the same way in the future, I am

Very truly yours,
S. GUILFOYLE.

Springfield, Ohio.

Sears, Roebuck and Co.,
Chicago, Ill.

Gentlemen:

We cannot express to you how well pleased we are with our Hot Water Outfit. We would not have it replaced by any other furnace there is, free of charge.

I also want to mention a few words about other articles we have bought from you. The Merchandise, House Furnishings, Bath Outfit, and in fact everything we have received from you cannot be touched in this town for the same money, as your goods are so much better.

You have always treated us kindly and fairly. We will try to send you trade whenever we can and will always recommend Sears, Roebuck and Co., with whom we have been doing business for the past 17 years.

Hoping our mutual dealings will never cease, I beg to remain

MRS. WM. GLASER,
965 Lagonda Ave.

Although Mr. Holder lives in a big city with many great stores, he bought his furniture from us and saved money.

Toledo, Ohio.

Sears, Roebuck and Co.,
Chicago, Ill.

Gentlemen:

I have dealt with your firm for 25 years and have been well satisfied with everything received. I consider it has been a big saving to me, and hope to remain a customer.

Yours truly,
ALBERT W. HOLDER,
1108 Earl St.

Menlo, Iowa.

Sears, Roebuck and Co.,
Chicago, Ill.

Dear Sirs:

I remember when you sent out your first catalog which was only a small pamphlet. We have been a customer ever since that time and the thing that most impresses me is the prompt and willing manner you have always made adjustments should any goods have to be returned. I have found your guarantee to be just as you say. My family has greatly enjoyed your radio programs. Hope you continue to put on entertaining and helpful programs as you have in the past.

Yours truly,
MRS. WM. MESSINGER,
R. 2, Box 99.

24-HOUR SERVICE

In Less Than a Day, Your Order Is on Its Way

We ship more than 130,000 packages a day from our four great stores at Chicago, Philadelphia, Dallas and Seattle. Actual tests show that 99 out of 100 shipments leave our stores within 24 hours after the orders are received.

"Thrift is Common Sense Applied to Spending"

Theodore Roosevelt

WHEN one-fourth of all the families in the United States buy from one store, you may be fairly certain there is a good reason for their custom. That reason is thrift—getting more value for the money they spend.

And when you know that this army of shoppers is increasing year after year, buying more and more goods from the World's Largest Store, making it possible for us to give them even better values as season follows season, there can be no doubt that they have learned the lesson of thrift.

For years this catalog has been known as "The Thrift Book of a Nation." It is a well deserved title. More than nine million families have found unsurpassed values within its covers. They learned that if they bought a set of furniture from us, their savings would enable them to buy a rug or some new draperies; if they needed a new suit, they could get it, and a dress besides, for the price others would ask for the suit alone. This is common sense spending.

We are the World's Largest Store because we lead in values. We are glad to number more than nine million thrifty folks as our customers. We dedicate to them this issue of "The Thrift Book of a Nation," knowing that it contains the greatest values in our history.

This Catalog is the THRIFT BOOK of the NATION

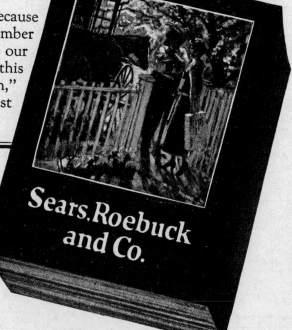

Sears, Roebuck and Co.

against the mail-order houses: a war that not only illuminates attitudes of small towns against big business but was a fore-runner—completely ignored by the chain-store companies—of later attempts to legislate these companies out of business. The following are quotations from newspapers of the North-west.

The Dickinson, North Dakota, *Record-Post* of August 22, 1916, carried this editorial:

LADY WANTED TO BORROW STAMP TO SEND LETTER TO MAIL ORDER HOUSE

One of the local druggists was greatly vexed Monday afternoon, when a lady of this city came into his store with a letter to one of the Chicago mail order houses. She laid the letter on the show case and asked for a stamp, which the clerk gave her. In the meantime she was going through her pocket book but had no money. It was then that everyone in the store were knocked practically on their backs. She asked if she could borrow the stamp until she came downtown again.

Can you become angry at the clerk for turning white and the other members of the sales force for snickering? This merely goes to show how far one will go at times to buy cheap stuff at cheap prices from an out of town firm. This lady had undoubtedly put the last cent she had in a mail order to the Chicago firm, and was then asking a home merchant to lend her a stamp to send her money and her business out of town. . . . The druggist was in tears when he told his tale of woe to a reporter.

The moral is not only that a lady will send her money to Chicago instead of buying at home, but also that in an American village her chances of keeping it secret were those of hiding a ninety-car freight train going over a grade behind two locomotives.

The war goes on, however, and paradoxically we find a vigilant alertness on the part of the embattled merchants of Sleepy Eye, Minnesota, who are not at all asleep. Here the local freight agent plays the part of Nathan Hale for the community and lives to tell his story, and tell it effectively, if we are to believe a news report of August 25, 1916, in the Sleepy Eye *Herald-Dispatch:*

BIG FALLING OFF IN MAIL ORDER BUSINESS

Advertising and Community Co-operation
Causes Decrease of 50%

That the anti-mail order house propaganda and constructive newspaper advertising that has been conducted at Sleepy Eye the past three years has been effectual to a marked degree in re-establishing home trade is attested to by no less a worthy and reliable personage than Josephus Entire Cassidy, local freight censor and juggler. Mr. Cassidy says that when he began his present work at the depot over three years ago, the mail order business reached the pinnacle of its flourishing in Sleepy Eye, every local freight brought in dozens of boxes of Sears Roebuck and Montgomery Ward goods, ranging all the way from toothpicks, hairpins and nut crackers to cook stoves, gasoline engines and windmills. The farmers seemed to be the heaviest purchasers, but there were a number of town people who had formed mail order habits.

At this time, Joe says, only about half as much mail order goods came to the depot at Sleepy Eye as did when he was apprenticing. If this practice of declination is continued at the rate it has been going, it will have been reduced to a minimum three years hence.

From another sector of the battlefield, Mr. Edward Allen, a David employed by local merchants to slay the mail-order Goliath, reported cheering news in the Owatonna, Minnesota, *Junior Chronicle,* on August 4, 1916:

MAIL ORDER HOUSE FUTURE NOT BRIGHT

Conditions Favorable to Growth Cease
to Exist—Already Losing Ground in
Many Communities.

But a week later, disconcerting news came from the neighboring state of Wisconsin, where the Shawano *Advocate* said:

MAIL ORDER CATALOGS RECEIVED HERE

A shipment of mail order catalogs were received here at the local postoffice in this city, Wednesday afternoon. The shipment consisted of fifty-three sacks, each weighing 100 pounds. The total postage on these catalogs amounts to more than some of our merchants spend in a whole year for advertising and then wonder how mail order houses do business in this city. . . .

Counterrevolution

It is the rare revolution that does not breed a counterrevolution whose success depends in part upon secrecy in its initial stages. And in the revolution against mail-order houses, we note the beginnings of a counterrevolution on their behalf. Soon men will go secretly at night accompanied by their wives to pore over the Sears catalog in a shade-drawn room; give their orders and their money to an anonymous correspondent who will dispatch them to Chicago and later deliver a bottle of hair tonic or a pair of stockings with impenetrable secrecy for a small fee.

The Duluth, Minnesota, *News-Tribune* of August 25, 1916, while the mail-order revolution was at its height in the Northwest, carried this advertisement of a local reactionary who had an eye to the main chance:

Orders for Catalog Houses

I take orders for catalogue houses. Any person desiring to buy goods from catalogue houses can leave their orders with me, giving a list of the goods desired and their catalogue numbers. I have catalogues from the leading houses in my place.

Thus, the fortunes of war ebbed and flowed, until one bright merchant, remembering that poets had ever been in the front ranks of the fight for freedom and liberty—even

Shelley, the vegetarian, was a fierce warrior when aroused—enlisted the services of the late Walt Mason, the famous syndicated homespun poet. And just as many wars are forgotten but the poetry they inspired is treasured up for a life beyond life, so it is likely that these verses of the friendly bard will be cherished when Sears and the Sleepy Eye *Herald-Dispatch* no longer exist even in the memory of the oldest citizen. Walt Mason, who threw epics about as lesser men toy with rondelles, and who could point a moral more sharply than any American poet except Edgar Guest, takes his readers on a world tour in order to land them at the country store.

HOMEMADE GOODS

Why send afar, to Cork or Rome
*   For Sunday hats or bales of hay?*
Let's buy the goods we make at home
*   And show we're patriots that way!*
The giant vessels sail the deep,
*   And bring us doodas made abroad.*
We buy such traps and fail to keep
*   Our money on our native sod. . . .*

My wife's new lid was made in France,
*   And 'tis a phoney thing indeed;*
The broadcloth in my Sunday pants
*   Was manufactured by Tweed. . . .*

We sing our patriotic songs
*   And boost the flag and seldom cease;*
But when we want gargoyles or gongs
*   We ship them in from Southern Greece.*

And as I write, a hundred barks
*   Bring curlycues across the foam;*
Oh, profit by these sage remarks
*   And learn to buy your junk at home!*

The War Ends Inconclusively

Despite all the efforts of the poets, the patriots, voluntary one-man intelligence departments such as Josephus Entire Cassidy, and eloquent editors of the rural press, catalogs still continued to pour into rural communities, and, when the frustrated rage of local merchants grew high, catalog burnings were organized. The citizenry were invited to bring books to the burning and the citizenry nobly responded. No one noticed the mail-order-house observer lurking in the shadows; no one took the trouble to note the vintage of the books that were burning. In almost every instance, the local patriots brought to the bonfire not the current catalog but last year's or the year before. And it did not occur to local merchants, when they cranked their Ford Model T's to go home, that the machines in which they rode would within a few years mark off boundaries beyond which the mail-order business could not go, and, more surprisingly, result in the ultimate establishment of retail stores owned by Sears right in their own communities.

By 1935, it had become respectable and not necessarily unpatriotic to order goods from Sears by mail. The catalog for that year makes no promise of anonymity in the shipment of packages. But the war against chain stores is to be carried to the state legislatures and Congress; to what ultimate end, no man may accurately predict.

In every mother's talk to her children, she includes the importance of thrift. We have as much contempt for the spendthrift as for the drunkard. Life is a very serious business; we know saving is as important as industry or politeness or fairness; it is an essential part of life, this saving your money, and avoiding becoming a public or private charge in your old age. . . . Every development in the history of the country is due to thrifty men; men who worked diligently, and save something. We all know these things. Then why do we so generally abuse those who have taken the advice of their mothers? The girls are taught chastity; the boys thrift. Yet we do not say a wanton is better than a virtuous woman. When we say to a boy: "Become a good man," we mean thrift as much as we mean fairness, politeness, industry, temperance. When we say to a girl: "Become a good woman," we include the hope that she will be chaste; chastity is thrift: good conduct for its own sake.*

INSTALLMENT selling is now an American economic institution; the motor force behind billions of dollars of retail sales annually made in this country; the narcotic creating an illusion of prosperity in the breasts of millions of people; an apparently essential instrument in maintaining the flow of goods coming from our assembly lines, and a deeply ingrained form of consumer buying. As goes the country in this respect, so goes Sears. Its installment sales are now huge, and these sales include not only durable or semidurable goods, such as refrigerators or washing machines, but quickly consumed goods, such as shoes and dresses. All this—both in America

* E. W. Howe, *Ventures In Common Sense,* pp. 217-18.

and at Sears—is a comparatively new development in our economic life.

In 1905, the catalog's terms of purchase were short and sweet: cash on the line. If you did not possess what the Italians wistfully call *dolce dollari,* you did not buy until you had acquired the dollars. But by 1915, installment selling had crept into the catalog, and as time passed, the partially opened door was flung wide open by competition and force of the nation's new buying habits. Nowadays men buy everything from false teeth on the "pay as you eat" plan to automobiles on the "pay as you ride" plan; installment selling is accepted by all social classes and is often regarded as a long-established part of our economic scheme. Actually, as we shall see, it is really of recent origin; it once met with great hostility, and its final acceptance by the public illuminates not only important changes in and phases of our economic system but also changing social attitudes.

Installment buying is a way of creating debt, and not long ago in this country debt was looked upon as an evil to be avoided whenever possible. Second only to drink, debt was a cardinal sin whose lurid consequences enlivened even the chapters of etiquette books current in the latter half of the nineteenth century. The definition of a debt was the possession of anything which had not been paid for in full. The debtor became, therefore, *déclassé* under this code as well as afflicted with the stigma of faint immorality.

Installment selling was also in bad odor with many people in the earlier part of the twentieth century, not only because the moral attitude of the nineteenth century continued, but also because of many abuses committed by unscrupulous merchants. Both attitudes are exhibited in a story by Cora Harris, "On the Instalment Plan," that appeared in *Harper's Magazine* in 1913. Two women who live in the mountains of north Georgia are talking:

> "Mary, I'm worried about my stove. The back is burned out already," exclaimed Mrs. Beasley, looking up at her.

"And my sewing machine is out of order. I paid fifty dollars for it. Took me two years," replied the younger woman with a sigh.

"It costs more to get things on the instalment plan from agents," commented Mrs. Beasley.

"But it's the only way for folks like us to get 'em," Mary replied.

The women of Arden had many virtues and one weakness in common. They would purchase anything from a stove to a cabinet organ on the instalment plan. They were always in debt, and they vied with one another in this kind of extravagance. They faced the future as if it were a calamity and provided against it by paying instalments of one kind or another upon their belongings. But up to date they had always paid. . . .

It was consequently an offense to the pride of many people in the early 1900's to buy on the installment plan, because of (*a*) the attitude towards debt; (*b*) the general bad name that installment selling had; (*c*) the fact that goods sold in this way were often of inferior quality; and (*d*) installment buying was an admission of insufficient funds.

"The Ladies' Home Journal" Warns the Ladies

Installment selling is ancient practice in the case of lands and houses, and in certain other categories of goods it has long been common in the United States. The Singer Sewing Machine Company has been doing an installment business since 1856, and numerous piano dealers have been at it for almost as long a time, while farm machinery and sets of books have nearly always been sold through time payments. But in general, and with these exceptions, only the poor in possessions and the poor in character bought goods on installment; the great middle class remained aloof from the practice. That this class was beginning to change its attitude toward installment buying early in the century is proved by an article called "A Trap for the Newly Married," published in *The Ladies' Home Journal* in 1909. The author, Marion Foster Washburne, in the same magazine that is now heavy with adver-

tisements of merchandise sold on installment, warns her readers to beware of this scheme.

If you want a number of things but have no money,
how are you going to get them? The modern answer is:
by means of the installment plan. Houses, furniture,
pianos, sewing-machines, jewelry, clothing, practically
anything you want, can now be obtained in this way.
The partial-payment system, indeed has assumed proportions in recent years that are fairly appalling. Every great
city has clothing houses which offer to clothe you for one
dollar a week; men may buy even their shirts and collars
on· partial payments . . . people in this country may get
steamship tickets for friends in Europe and pay for them
. . . a few dollars at a time. . . .
. . . The price of goods bought in this way is always
high and often exorbitant . . . three or four times the
actual value is by no means an uncommon figure. . . .
The prices of sewing machines sold in this way are
. . . abnormally high, and the price of furniture bought
on the installment plan by ignorant, young married people
eager to set up housekeeping and impatient of the delays
entailed by saving up to pay cash, is often twice what
the articles are worth.

The writer of this article then calls the attention of her
readers to an abuse of the system that is still common in the
United States, and which has just been brought to an end
in Great Britain through the new Hire-Purchase Act:

But there are still greater dangers in this method of
purchasing. . . . It is not simply that they [unwary buy-
ers] do not realize until too late what serious risks they
run when they enter into such agreements. It is not
simply that they are pretty sure to pay for more than the
goods are worth, but that, if they fail to pay their installments when due, they lose both the goods and the money
they have already paid, or, worse still, they lose not only
the goods and the money, but other goods which have
been all paid for. . . .
In Chicago a woman bought furniture costing $221 in

April. The next October 'she bought a parlor stove for $31 from the same firm. She paid for the furniture in full, but was remiss in settling for the stove, after having paid $224 on the whole account. The furniture house thereupon took away both the stove and the furniture and against this injustice she had no redress.

It would seem that these were evils enough to damn any scheme, but our relentless guide goes on to point out greater evils:

> . . . Still another drawback to buying goods on the installment plan is that you cannot safely move without first obtaining the permission of the concern from which you have bought the goods, and these firms sometimes refuse their consent to a change of residence because it makes their collections harder, and every move, of course, means a change of address in their books. Think of the difficulties and inconveniences of such a situation! Imagine having to stay in a house or a neighborhood you do not like because the firm from which you have "bought" your furniture refuses to give you permission to move!
>
> . . . Then too, most dealers . . . charge an exorbitant interest, and the laws of most States permit the imposition. In Illinois ten per cent a month—one hundred and twenty per cent a year!—is often asked.

The author then draws the inevitable conclusion from these facts:

> The installment plan of buying goods . . . is a far-reaching evil; it bears heavily on the poor and the people of only moderate means, the wages of salary earners and the small business people, and it entraps the young at the very beginning of their married life into a mistake which goes far to destroy their faith in the integrity of business methods.
>
> What then, is the remedy for the evils of the installment business? To my mind there is but one safe and sure one; have nothing to do with such a business. Let the sensible part of the buying public refuse to deal in any way with the partial-payment houses.

Sears Warns Its Customers Against Installment Evils

It is clear from these quotations and from other evidence that there was an appreciable amount of installment selling in the United States shortly after the turn of the century. But Sears would have none of it and advises its customers, in 1910, to beware of the dangers of buying without cash.

"THE INSTALLMENT PLAN. If we followed the dealer's method and sold on installments we would be compelled to charge very much more than we do. You can buy practically anything on the installment plan, but what do you pay for the accommodation? Benjamin Franklin, one of the greatest minds that this country has produced, clearly saw the evil of the credit system in the early Colonial days and in his writings will be found the following:

> He who sells on credit expects to lose . . . by bad debts; therefore, he charges on all he sells . . . an advance to make up that deficiency.

"If you buy on the installment plan you sign *notes* for the balance. Who holds the *notes*? *You don't know* until they are presented for payment. *There are concerns who make a business of buying notes at a discount.* Who pays the discount? *You do.* Does everyone pay their notes promptly? *No.* Does the dealer stand this loss? *No.* It is all figured in what he charges for his pianos.

"A dealer takes a risk when he sells on the installment plan and he figures his prices accordingly. That is business. You will save money if you take advantage of our low prices even if you are compelled to make some sacrifice to do it. DON'T BUY ON THE INSTALLMENT PLAN. IT COSTS TOO MUCH IN THE END."

In 1910, Automobiles Were Sold for Cash

The 1910 catalog contains pages describing five models of Sears Motor Cars ranging in price from $370 to $495. But the customer who wanted one had to buy it for cash or go without it. The catalog's language on this subject is clear and strong:

"Our Only Terms Are Cash; We Do Not Sell on Installments or Extend Credit. Send us your order and enclose our price in the form of a postoffice money order . . . or bank check. If you don't want the motor car immediately, send us $25 as a deposit and we will enter your order and then later on you can send us the balance when you want us to make shipment."

In other words: no pay—no ride.

A Radical Change of Face and Plan

The catalog that in 1910 delivered a lecture, on the evils of installment selling, to prospective purchasers of pianos, in 1915 offers pianos on the plan that it had reviled only a few years before. This time the piano copy reads:

High Grade Pianos at $5.00 a Month.

Then follow the details:

"These fine instruments will be shipped to our customers on the monthly payment plan of $5.00 a month, without interest or extras of any kind. We do not ask you to pay anything extra to obtain one of these pianos in this way, and whether purchased on time or cash you get the benefit of the factory price plus one profit. . . ."

What brought about this radical change at Sears within five years? Competition. Other piano dealers were selling their instruments on time-payment plans and Sears was compelled to follow suit; later, as we shall see, competition forced it to place its entire business on an installment basis and to depart completely from the platform laid down in 1910.

Even in 1915, when Sears had begun to offer pianos on the installment plan, it adhered to its doctrine of 1910 that this was a more expensive way of buying, and refused to charge interest on unpaid balances or to charge more for pianos sold on installment than for cash. In so doing, it fell into another dilemma.

If, the customer might ask himself, the price of a piano

is the same under all circumstances and if I have the option of paying the full price at once or paying in installments of $5 a month, would I not be foolish to pay in full? And if enough customers reasoned this way and bought pianos on payments spread over long periods, the following results would flow from their action: one, Sears would in effect be lending large sums without interest; two, customers would be infected with the virus of installment buying who hitherto had been free of it. In a short while, therefore, Sears changed its method, but the virus burrowed into the skins of millions of customers.

The final impetus to the hitherto slow growth of installment selling came in 1915 with the rise of the automobile industry and the beginning of time-payment plans for cars. The tendency continued at a leisurely pace until 1919, when the urge to sell cars became vein-bursting in its pressure. Millions of men then began buying automobiles on installment. Many of them were not eligible for ordinary credit at stores in their own communities but they could buy cars. High-pressure sales methods triumphed. Responsible dealers endorsed promissory notes which, in turn, could be discounted at banks for cash; the car was covered by mortgage, and the man who would not pay his doctor, dentist, or baker would make any sacrifice to pay for his automobile. Other time-payment buyers were conservative men who had always paid cash for the things they bought. But they did not have enough ready cash for a car and, being infected by the general enthusiasm of their neighbors for acquiring things "the easy way," soon succumbed to the prevailing custom. Thus, an immense market was built for automobiles and, more significantly, an even greater market for everything else.

What little conservatism remained on the part of both the public and the merchants was swept away by the 1920–21 depression. Men still wanted goods but lacked cash; merchants wanted business but there were few buyers; the road to the satisfaction of both buyers and sellers was "buy today and pay next year." The public bought and paid. Losses in installment sales have been astonishingly small, amounting in 1929 to only 1.2 per cent.

By 1923, the old prejudices against installment buying had been swept away, people of all classes went in for it, and no stigma was attached to a man who "owned" a car, a piano, a radio, or the clothes on his back, and paid for them in installments.

Prosperity returned in 1923 and was accompanied, as usual, by renewed pressure to make more sales. Sales managers were bound to "beat last year" or bust. Fortunately, there were new instruments at hand in the form of radios and electric refrigerators to make installment selling a potent factor again and keep many factories running.

We have traveled a long way since 1900, but we have farther to go. Installment selling begets installment selling. It must extend farther and farther until, finally, as at present, it reaches all fields of merchandise. The process involves not only our economic scheme but it has marked social consequences.

As we have seen, Sears was driven to sell pianos on time in order to meet competition. The piano is a high-cost instrument, durable, and capable of being recovered by the seller if the payments on it are not made. Why not, then, extend the same system to other categories of goods having the same general characteristics as the piano? That is: refrigerators, stoves, and such. The process was extended by merchants all over America, until, by 1929, it was estimated that installment sales from all sources were $6,000,000,000, or 12 per cent of all retail sales. This would seem to make the United States an ideal country for consumer, merchant, and manufacturer. The wheels turn, goods go out, the merchant clears his shelves, the consumer enjoys the goods while he pays for them. But here we find a whale in the ointment.

If a man pledges his future income for cars, pianos, false teeth, and refrigerators, he will have to reduce his expenditures for things whose use he can limit: food, clothing, education, travel, books, and so on. The only way in which he could meet his time payments and retain his former scale of living would be to increase his income—something beyond the capacity of most men. Many years ago the National Grocers' Association complained that men afflicted with the "easy-way" habit of buying acquired simultaneously the habit of not paying their corner grocer. A lament came, too, from the National Association of Credit Men. In 1926, this group, representing thirty thousand merchants and manufacturers, said that "the events of recent years clearly show that the stimulation of business by the unwise use of credits is merely a temporary measure and has a reaction in the serious disturbance of goods and prices." Statisticians showed conclusively that installment buyers were paying interest rates ranging from eleven to forty per cent per annum. This had no effect, because the American consumer is not one to be deterred by statistics. It meant, however, that he had less money to spend for other things, with the result that makers and sellers of other things—even if they hated installment selling—would be driven to do business on time-payment plans in order to survive. Soon everything would be sold on installment. And with all this would come a new attitude toward debt of potentially dangerous consequences to the entire economy of the country.

The Climate of Installment Selling

A brief flash back to the catalog of 1925 shows that three things are happening in the field of installment sales at Sears: (1) these sales are still limited in general to durable or semidurable merchandise such as radios and pianos; (2) Sears still sells goods for the same price, whether for cash or on time, and charges no interest on unpaid balances; (3) but, significantly, the moral climate in which it makes these sales is changing. Once it was so cold and forbidding that time payments could not flourish; then the climate changed until the first tentative shoots burst forth in the catalog's pages, and now, in 1925, it has become a warm, moist climate in which the once hated installment plan is tenderly nurtured until it achieves a metamorphosis and emerges as the "Easy Payment Plan."

"Low Prices and Liberal Terms," announces the catalog in the introduction to its radio section, and tells its readers to "Use the Easy Payment Order Blank on page 1100."

A Nation Keeps Up with the Joneses

The factors, tangible and intangible, that have caused the phenomenal rise of installment selling in the United States are too complex to be examined in this book with the care that their importance merits. It may be profitable, however, to devote some attention to a few of these factors that seem to underlie our national life.

The first is the continuous and unrelenting pressure for sales directed against that relatively small group in the national community who are able to buy anything beyond the primitive needs of food, shelter, and clothing. If we assume that the year 1929 was the year of our great prosperity in recent times, then we must look at the picture of prosperous America as drawn for us by the Brookings Institution. It is a picture painted with the clarity of outline and economy of stroke that is characteristic of Oriental art at its best, and one glance is enough to fill the observer with an unforgettable vision.

In 1929, one fifth of our families had incomes of less than $1,000 a year.

In 1929, twenty million families, or seventy-one per cent, had incomes of *less* than $2,500.

It is beyond dispute that the families with incomes of less than $1,000 were lucky if they could keep body and soul on speaking terms. They were not lush fruit to be plucked by automobile or radio salesmen; they were thorns in the garden of our discontent.

The twenty million families whose incomes were *less* than $200 a month did have enough money, it is true, to keep going and pay their life-insurance premiums but certainly not enough to enable them to satisfy many of their desires for goods through cash or credit terms. Only two avenues were open to them: their savings and the installment plan. The reduction of their savings would expose them to the perils of the rainy day, and, in any event, billions of dollars of savings among middle-class Americans are tied up in life insurance and usually are not touched save in dire emergencies. But the installment plan was a way out because it merely pledged future income, and many a man was willing to go without steak in the future in order to have a Ford in the present. Consequently, this great group became the target of installment selling, because, in reality, there was no other large group available. Other men had, it is true, more money and greater purchasing capacity, but their consuming capacity was limited by their numbers. This was "that 0.1 per cent of the families at the top (who) received practically as much as forty-two per cent of the families at the bottom," in 1929.

Consequently, hordes of salesmen were turned loose on the large group; they were beseeched to buy this and that on any and all kinds of terms; they were deluged with advertising and radio pleas; one finance company handling automobile "paper"—the Commercial Credit Corporation of Baltimore —by 1930, had paid out over a period of nine years eighty-five per cent in stock dividends in addition to large cash dividends. Those were the days when the slogan of all business executives was "beat last year," and that meant increasing sales by at least ten per cent more than the preceding year, which in turn, by arithmetical progression, meant that business would have to reach astronomical figures in order that the slogan could each year come true. Those were the days when men were supposed to consume themselves into prosperity and when *Punch* took a swift kick at the attitude in a poem by Patrick Barrington (1934). In our process of Americanizing the world and keeping our own plants going, we had stimulated installment selling in Europe by the sale of our automobiles on this plan, so that by 1927–28 the Englishman, the Frenchman, the Swede, and the Finn were meeting payments on their Fords or Chevrolets or radios in the good old American way. *Punch* did not like all this and proceeded to say, "I didn't bring my boy up to be a consumer."

"And what do you mean to be?"
 The kind old Bishop said
As he took the boy on his ample knee
 And patted his curly head.
"We should all of us choose a calling
 To help Society's plan;
Then what do you mean to be, my boy,
 When you grow to be a man?"

"I want to be a Consumer,"
 The bright-haired lad replied
As he gazed into the Bishop's face
 In innocence open-eyed.
"I've never had aims of a selfish sort,
 For that, as I know is wrong,
I want to be a Consumer, Sir,
 And help the world along."

"But what do you want to be?"
 The Bishop said again,
"For we all of us have to work," said he,
 "As must, I think, be plain,
Are you thinking of studying medicine
 Or taking a Bar exam?"
"Why no!" the bright-haired lad replied
 As he helped himself to jam.

"I want to be a Consumer
 And do my duty well;
For that is the thing that's needed most,
 I've heard economists tell.
I've made up my mind," the lad was heard,
 As he lit a cigar, to say:
"I want to be a Consumer, Sir,
 And I want to begin today."

The upshot of all our frenzied consuming and buying for cash, on credit, or on the installment plan, was that the time soon came when we had more automobiles, radios, electric refrigerators, waffle irons, and mined aspirin aboveground than any other country in the world. We did all this, so to speak, in a fit of abstraction, because we had not even begun to strain or even to reach the theoretical limit of our productive capacity; in 1929, according to the Brookings Institution, the productive plant of the United States ran at approximately eighty-one per cent of its capacity. This capacity, moreover, had been largely devoted to satisfying the needs of one great group while the desires of another large group were left for fulfillment in that happy day when all God's chillun should have shoes and crowns. And one may ask whether the installment sales of 1929 did not proceed in part not only from the "prosperity" of that year but also from the general evaporation of old ways and beliefs engendered by the World War.

Keeping up with the Joneses is an ancient American custom, and in the period 1918–29, the Joneses not only kept up with one another but even threatened to trample the competing Joneses in the rush. During that gilded, gaudy, shabby, immensely vulgar, antihumanitarian decade we tended, more than ever before, to judge a man by the number of his servants, the authenticity of his whisky, the cut of his coat, the quality of his mistresses, or the size of his home or apartment. Men desire the esteem of their fellow men; they are conscious of and sensitive to the criteria by which they are measured. Now they were able to live up to the criteria, because, if they did not have enough money with which to buy a Buick or an electric icebox, it was available to them on the installment plan, and they could acquire prestige in the present and pay for it in the future through twelve or more equal installments. And this meant that the last lingering vestiges of nineteenth-century horror of debt had vanished.

The years of the War worked in another way their wonders to perform, although successful sales managers of the period we are considering gave no credit to anything save their own efforts. Long before 1914–19—as far back as the eighteenth century—the process of dechristianization had been sapping the spiritual foundations of the Western World. Millions of men throughout the world, whatever their lip services to religion, grew less and less content to live meagerly in this world as a "vale of tears" in order to reap their reward in heaven. They still wanted heaven if they could get it and at not too great a cost in the present, but they became unwilling to risk the pleasures of earth for the future, priest-promised pleasures of heaven. A Ford on Main Street is worth two chariots on the milky way.

As the belief in the hereafter faded, as the conception of life on earth as a period of trial and preparation for an after-life tended to disappear and be succeeded by a fatalistic conception of a short and material life as the whole of existence, scruples against debt waned, and there arose the passion for possessions that marked the 1920's. It was a passion made fiery and electric through the years of the War, when under war's impulse life and living in terms of the old-established order became impossible, and only the moment, the joys and the possessions and the sensory pleasures of the moment, had value, color, and warmth.

The expansion of installment sales in the United States may, therefore, owe as much—or perhaps as little—to the decay of religion, and the spiritual ravages of the World War, as to the desperate exigencies of our economic system. Growing out of the abandonment of the horror of private debt is another attitude of great importance at this time.

Does it not follow that men who regard their private debts at least with complacency will regard national debts in the same way? Installment sales prove that millions of men live beyond their present incomes and enjoy goods and services in the present by pledging their future incomes. What sense, then, does it make to condemn municipalities, states, and the Federal government for indulging in a practice that we applaud on the part of individuals? If it is sound economics for installment buyers to owe two to three billions of dollars while they use their Fords and Frigidaires, why is it not equally sound for government to make all kinds of expenditures for our benefit in the present and pay them in the future? If, asks the man in the street, installment buyers can owe billions at any given time, why cannot the Federal and state governments, with equal soundness, owe more billions? Haven't we always paid our debts and incurred greater ones? Look at the records of installment sales for the answer.

Debt Marches On

Naturally Sears and its customers were affected by the developments we have been describing. We have seen how Sears in twenty years moved from loathing the vice of debt to extending its first tentative embraces toward the monster. And by 1935, it flung its arms around the monster but still not in complete abandon.

The catalog for 1935 contains three pages lyrically describing the beauties and the virtues of the installment plan. One of the pages contains an illustration of a smartly dressed young woman seated in her living room. She is resting her arm on her catalog-covered knee and has placed her hand under pensive chin while she looks wistfully into space. Underneath the illustration, in big type, is this headline:

How Much Longer Will You Dream About
a Beautiful Home?

The copy then outlines the heaven that is within every man's grasp on easy payments.

"Your credit here can easily bring you the things you want without stinting yourself . . . without waiting until you have the ready cash. At Sears you can buy now and pay little by little each month out of income.

"You, too, can have a modern, comfortable home, just like your neighbors, without waiting. You don't have to deny yourself and your family the enjoyment of pleasant home surroundings . . . the help of modern conveniences . . . for lack of ready cash."

The favorite theme song of installment sellers is that it is easy to acquire possessions at the cost of only a few cents a day. For example, if the selling price of a radio is $36.50, it follows that you can acquire it in a year for ten cents a day, and out of this fact flows advertising of this kind: "Bring the world's music, entertainers, orators, speakers, and statesmen into your own home for as little as ten cents a day." And if this is true of radio, it is equally true of other things. Thus, for two cents a day, you can acquire culture (and keep the radio going at the same time) by reading *Forty Thousand Facts You Never Knew Till Now;* for three cents a day, you can keep your health and acquire a fashionable Florida tan by using the Coral Strand Sunlamp and, at the same time, listen to the radio and read the book; while off in another part of the house (at five cents a day), your wife is glowing under a Venus Vibro-Massage machine, preparatory to putting on her Belvedere evening gown (a dollar a month) and getting out the Extenso-Flex Bridge Table (four cents a day) for a party later in the evening when the children will be sleeping snugly on their Ossiform Mattresses for Growing Young Bodies, at eight cents a day. It's easy, all so easy, because as the catalog tells us:

Payments Never a Hardship

"Do as 75 per cent of the practical home-makers are doing today . . . use credit to get the things you need and want right away, and pay just a few dollars each month. At Sears, even on good-size orders, the payments are never a hardship . . . everything is as simple and easy as A, B, C.

"Turn to page 874 and read the list of things you can buy on credit. . . ."

We do turn to page 874 and find these articles among many others:

Automatic Ranges	Electric Fixtures
Automatic Water Heaters	Electric Motors
Bathroom Outfits	Electric Refrigerators
Building Materials	Farm Implements
Concrete Mixers	Furniture
Cream Separators	Home Furnishings
Dining-Room Suites	Hot-Air Furnaces

Incubators and Brooders	Poultry Supplies
Kitchen Ranges	Radio Sets
Mattresses	Refrigerators
Milking Machines	Roofing
Plumbing Equipment	Windmills and Towers

Note that most of these articles are durable or semidurable; many of them are necessities and not luxuries; some of them are wealth producing. The final step in installment selling—the sale of practically anything under this plan—is yet to be taken.

But already Sears is in tune with the country. It now talks of the ease of buying on easy payments, and it adds a "carrying charge"—that is, interest—to the purchase price of goods bought on installment. The days when banks, schoolteachers, and parents taught children that two cents a day laid away in a bank for twenty years, and held at compound interest, would produce a sizable nest egg are now as remote as the issues of the Pinchot-Ballinger controversy.

Installment Selling Goes to Town

We have traced the various steps by which Sears moved from its cash policy in 1905 to its limited installment-selling policy in 1925 until it adopted the feature of "carrying charges" in 1935. During all this period, however, it had kept installment selling within the bounds of durable or semidurable and wealth-producing goods; luxuries, perishables, and knickknacks were rigidly excluded from its time-payment plan. In 1939, however, under stress of competition from mail-order houses and other competitors, Sears' installment plan really went to town.

The 1939 catalog opens with a drawing of a smartly dressed bride and groom at whose feet is the caption "Two can live. . . ." The copy that follows confirms the concept of American romantic economics that two can live as cheaply as one, and dispels any lingering doubts by telling the young couple that if they cannot live on cash they can certainly live on the installment plan.

"If, at the moment, you don't happen to have the ready cash, don't let that bother you in the least. Take advantage of Sears Easy Payment Plan, and pay out of monthly income.

"The beauty of this comfortable credit arrangement is that the additional cost is painlessly slight. There are no hidden charges. You know exactly what you're paying."

On the page opposite the happy young bride and groom, Sears makes a declaration as radical and as far-reaching in its own history as was the declaration of the Rights of Man in the history of the world when they were enunciated in the American Revolution:

SEARS NOW OFFER

ANYTHING AND EVERYTHING

ON EASY PAYMENTS

(on orders of $10 or more)

"Whatever you need—shoes, clothing, housewares—rugs, furniture, tires—anything and everything from this or any other Sears catalog may be purchased on Sears Easy Payment Plan. Your order need total only $10 or more.

"No need to wait. You don't need the ready cash—you can get and enjoy, right now, the merchandise you want—and pay for it while you use it. Just a small down payment and a little each month will buy anything Sears sell. . . ."

Now all the bars are down and installment selling has become a high, wide, and handsome practice in American economic life. Whether it will prove beneficial or detrimental, only time will tell.

RECENTLY, an obscure, little old man, whose name is known to millions of Americans, turned up at the Chicago offices of Sears and said that he would like to have a job. He had been in retirement for years. He was tired of fishing and puttering around the garden. He wanted something to do once again. Whereupon Sears, Roebuck & Company, The Largest Store in the World, gladly employed Alvah Curtis Roebuck, cofounder, with Richard W. Sears, of Sears, Roebuck & Company in 1886. Shortly after Mr. Roebuck had come again into the bright world of business, he was appointed colonel on the staff of the governor of Kentucky, and it is as Colonel Roebuck that the seventy-six-year-old cofounder attends the opening of new Sears' stores, tells youngsters in the organization of the wondrous days of the beginning, shows himself to amazed customers, and, in general, plays the part of a legend risen from the ashes.

In 1895—after nine years in business with R. W. Sears—Roebuck, then thirty-one years old, walked into his partner's office. He said that his stomach was giving him fits; his nerves had broken down, and he wanted to sell his one-third interest in the business. Mr. Sears bought his partner's share for about $20,000. A one-third interest in Sears today would be worth about $150,000,000. But when the coarse-minded now ask Colonel Roebuck if he does not regret throwing away a vast fortune, he says, no. After all, he replies, Mr. Sears is dead. Mr. Rosenwald is dead. Nearly all the old-timers of the Company are dead. Some worked themselves to death; others just died. But Colonel Alvah C. Roebuck, hale and hearty at seventy-six, is still going strong.

Richard W. Sears—the man who founded Sears, Roebuck —was the breezy, colorful, picturesque type of promoter and supersalesman common in America in the 1890's, although he began his career soberly enough as railroad and express agent in the tiny hamlet of Redwood Falls, Minnesota. Sears' duties took little of his time, so he sought and received permission from his employers to sell coal and lumber to the people in the neighborhood. But one day a package of watches sent by a Chicago wholesaler addressed to a Redwood Falls merchant arrived at the little station. The merchant had refused to accept the watches for the good reason that he had not ordered them.

This was one of the crooked schemes of the times widely employed by wholesalers. They would send a package of merchandise C.O.D. to a village merchant, along with a letter thanking him for his order. The merchant, of course, would refuse the shipment and write the wholesaler to keep his damned goods on his own shelves. Whereupon, the city slicker would write back that it was all a mistake but, inasmuch as the goods had been delivered at the merchant's destination, it would take time and money to retrieve them. The loss would be the wholesaler's. If the merchant would take the goods, he could have them at a discount of fifty per cent. Needless to say, the goods had been marked up in advance, so that even at this discount they would show the wholesaler a profit. Frequently, the merchant would snap at this bait and take the goods, feeling that he had outwitted the city slicker. And here at Redwood Falls, Minnesota, in 1886, when Richard W. Sears was twenty-three years old, lay a package that the local merchant would not take.

Ever watchful to earn a dollar, the young agent wrote the Chicago firm that he would sell the watches for it on commission. By the next mail, he was told to go ahead. Sears then sent a sample watch to other agents of the railroad and, offered a commission to sell them. In a week, all the watches were gone and Sears wrote for another batch. Within six months, he was selling watches for himself by mail in Minne-

A Personal Message

From the President of Sears, Roebuck and Co.

The World's Largest Store is at your service!

Without moving from your own easy chair, you can draw on an almost endless supply of the best of the world's goods. For our buyers go everywhere good merchandise can be bought at prices that insure the biggest savings.

As president of Sears, Roebuck and Co., it is a privilege for me to serve you and the nine million families who buy from us. A privilege, because I feel that we render a genuine service to the country in the form of lower prices; because it was Sears, Roebuck and Co. that first guaranteed merchandise, and that today sells the quality of merchandise that can be honestly guaranteed; because we ship all orders within twenty-four hours.

We have become the World's Largest Store because our customers know that our policy is fair treatment. Through all the years we have been serving this army of thrifty buyers we have taken pride in the fact that we have kept their good will and brought additional members into this great family.

This catalog is the World's Largest Store at its best. It proves the leadership of Sears, Roebuck and Co. It offers 35,000 opportunities to save money. And it is a big factor in the lives of one-fourth of all the families in the United States.

John Kittle
President.

apolis; by 1887, he had moved to Chicago and established the R. W. Sears Watch Company. It is at this point that he struck a partnership deal with Roebuck.

Sears found that his watches seemed to suffer from one slight defect: frequently, they would not run. And some of his customers were ungrateful enough to return them. He found, furthermore, that it was cheaper to repair watches than to buy new ones for disgruntled customers. So he ran a "Help Wanted" advertisement for a watchmaker. This advertisement fell into the hands of young Roebuck, then in Chicago, whose favorite book back in his home town of La Fayette, Indiana, had been *Complete Treatise on Modern Horology*. Roebuck got the job, and later a partnership.

The business, under Sears' dynamic management and the employment of methods common at the time, flourished vigorously. For example, he advertised an expensive-looking suite of furniture for three or four dollars, and the customers got doll's furniture for their money. Once he saw a suit of clothes advertised in a Chicago newspaper, reproduced a drawing of it in his catalog, and received orders for thousands of suits. The harassed partners then had to scurry all over Chicago to find suits to fill the orders, and while scurrying ran into a young clothing manufacturer named Julius Rosenwald. On other occasions, however, when orders from customers exceeded the stock on hand, or when they called for goods which had never been on hand and could not be conveniently located in Chicago, Sears resolved the dilemma by dumping the orders in the stove.

Another favorite Sears scheme was to send out thousands of circulars offering a national prize to the customer who first sent in his order, and smaller prizes to the first order from each of the states. The Prix de Sears was announced in the following letter:

> Kind Friend: We believe if we can induce you to read
> this circular you will favor us with your order at once.
> True, you may not get the $500.00 piano, or even a

$50.00 gold watch, yet, considering the small number of these offers we are sending out, you ought at least be in time for a gold watch if you answer at once. But, in case you do not get the piano, or a watch, you are sure to get some nice present, and the shoes we send you at $2.75 are worth nearly three times the price asked. If you will fill out the enclosed order blank and send to us at once, with $2.75, for a pair of shoes described, we will see that you get a nice present, and, if first, the piano; if not first of all, but first from your State, a $50.00 gold watch. As an *extra inducement,* if your order is received any time within 30 days, we will see that you get an extra nice present. But please answer at once and try to be first. Very truly, Sears Roebuck & Company.

By 1895, Roebuck's health had broken down under the strain of trying to keep up with his restless, dynamic partner. He sold out to Sears, and Julius Rosenwald became the new partner. For some time, the firm of Rosenwald & Weil had been selling more and more suits to Sears, until he had become their biggest customer. Julius Rosenwald asked Sears how he managed to sell so much clothing by mail, and when he had been told, he became a convert to the mail-order method of doing business. He wanted to embark in the business and Sears wanted him to come in because he needed more capital. The two men soon agreed on terms of partnership and in 1895 Rosenwald became a member of the firm of Sears, Roebuck & Company. Thereafter it was to become completely changed in system, outlook, and morality.

The latter part of the nineteenth century—the period 1865–1900—saw the country governed in its economic life by a rule of *caveat emptor* rarely paralleled in savagery and cruelty. In high places and low, the cardinal principle of business conduct was: the customer be damned. Get rich honestly if you can, but get rich. And if a Rockefeller got rich very quickly in oil, or a Gould in railroads, with millions of dollars and empires as the stake, lesser men by the thousands indulged in shameful skulduggery with pennies as their reward. For this is the land where little men with the mechanical fidelity almost of robots play the sedulous ape to their financial superiors, justifying themselves, if justification were needed, by the query: "If they get away with it, why shouldn't I?"

In the golden age of corruption, when adulteration, misbranding, misrepresentation, and false weights and measures were accepted as part of the day's business by nearly everyone, the consumer was robbed by every device except a gun pointed at his head. This, for instance, was common practice in cities having large numbers of newly arrived immigrants. An immigrant woman would try on a hat in a store. Hardly had she got it on her head before the clerk would pull from his pocket a document which he read to the customer who scarcely understood the language and was terrified by the customs of a new country. It stated what purported to be the law of the land, namely, that a woman who kept a hat on her head for two minutes was obligated to purchase it. So-called reputable wholesalers often swindled their customers in this manner. The wholesaler's traveling salesmen would take orders from retailers, but they would not give the customer a copy of the order. When the order, sometimes containing dozens of items, reached the wholesaler, his "write-up man" would go through it and raise prices wherever he thought he could do so without risk of detection. And sometimes, retailers used a scheme which is reminiscent of the title of one of Fielding's plays: *Rape upon Rape, or Justice Caught In His Own Trap*. In this case, whenever the retailer bought men's suits he bought an equal number of cheap watches. Into the trouser pocket of each pair went a watch. Then when the customer was trying them on, he would feel the watch, conclude it had been left by another customer, and would be so intent on stealing it that he would readily pay $25 for a $15 suit.

In thousands of stores throughout the land, prices were on a catch-as-catch-can basis; Oriental haggling was common, and the customer paid all the traffic would bear. Mr. J. C.

Penney, the well-known merchant, writing of his early experiences as a clerk in Denver, notes one method by which consumers were fleeced:

> . . . I found my next job in a store down Larimer Street, but it wasn't long before I walked out on that too. It happened this way. I was keeping stock when I noticed one stock number of men's hose marked at two different prices, the same hose marked one pair for a quarter and two pairs for a quarter. I went to the proprietor.
>
> "There must be a mistake in the price marks on these hose," I said.
>
> "Young man," he replied sharply, "you mind your own business. Sell those socks for a quarter when you can, and when you can't sell them two pairs for a quarter."

Hitherto we have observed the catalog as a recorder of passing events; as a dispassionate chronicle of economic and technological cause and effect; as part of the history of our changing manners and morals. We may now observe it as it steps out on the continental stage of America to bring about salutary and permanent change.

The two-price system was manifestly impossible in catalogs. A mail-order firm could do business only under a one-price system in which prices varied solely with the seasons. Sears, therefore, was compelled to sell to all at one price, and when the influence of its example had penetrated to every hamlet of the countryside, and influential city stores such as Macy's and Wanamaker's inaugurated one-price systems in the cities, one of the knock-down-and-drag-out practices of unscrupulous merchants was dealt a severe blow. In time, the order of the business day everywhere became one price plainly marked and the same price to all.

This change in selling practice, however important, must be considered as secondary to an even more important change brought about in large part by the catalogs. They wrought a revolution in merchandising and tended to make buying safe for the consumer through the principle of the mail-order guarantee:

We guarantee that each and every article in this catalog is exactly as described and illustrated.

We guarantee that any article purchased from us will satisfy you perfectly; that it will give you the service you have a right to expect; that it represents full value for the price you pay.

If for any reason whatsoever you are dissatisfied with any article purchased from us, we expect you to return it to us at our expense.

We will then exchange it for exactly what you want, or will return your money, including any transportation charges you have paid.

Now these are brave words, and similar bravura statements have lured millions of dollars from the pockets of unsuspecting Americans. They were not, however, as Sears employed them, mere brave words at all (although it took courage to use them at first) but a statement of principle upon which its business was founded. Let us see first why Sears was compelled to invoke this principle, and then assess its effect upon American retail business in general.

Sears' problem was this. It listed in the catalog, let us say, a suitcase. Harold Drawwater who grows apples ten miles from Yakima, Washington, gets the catalog. He usually trades at the Banner Store in Yakima, and at the moment is thinking of buying a suitcase and going to Portland after his crop is picked. He sees one that he likes in the catalog. There is a picture of it and a description; it seems to be a bargain and Harold likes to save a dollar. But he can't touch the Sears suitcase or get the heft of it, because it lies on a shelf in Chicago clear across the continent, while a clerk at the Banner would pull one down for him, let him smell the leather, and yank on the straps. There are other drawbacks that make Herald hesitate about buying his luggage from Sears. He has to send those faraway fellows his money in advance without having seen anything but a picture; he has to take their word for it that the suitcase is as represented, and if he is not satisfied he may return it and have his money refunded or get a new suitcase without charge. The guarantee reads convincingly on paper; those Chicago people look honest. Harold takes a chance. He sends Sears a money order, and a week later the suitcase is in his hand.

Then one of three things happens. He likes what he bought and keeps it. He doesn't like what he bought, he returns it, and his money comes back to him. He uses the suitcase for a little while, it does not prove satisfactory, and in response to his complaint, Sears sends him, according to his choice, a new suitcase or the money he had paid for it. But whatever happens, Harold is now convinced that Sears is on the level and he becomes an enthusiastic mail-order customer.

The guarantee thus made buying safe for Harold. But what of Sears? If it did not abide by its promises, if it failed to make a refund for an alleged "all-leather suitcase" that ran down the customer's leg when he was caught with it in a heavy rain, or did not return the purchase price of ten yards of "fast-color cretonne" that became a confused rainbow in the washtub, it would lose the confidence of its customers, and its business was based in the highest degree upon confidence. On the other hand, if too many articles came back and too many refunds were made, it would inevitably go bankrupt.

Sears, therefore, in protecting the consumer had first to protect itself. It had to know, for instance, beyond the shadow of a doubt that a blanket represented by it to be "all wool" was made in fact of the locks of Mary's little lamb instead of a coal-tar and buttermilk concoction shaken up in a chemist's test tubes. How could it know? There was only one infallible way: putting the blankets to test in its own laboratories before they were put into the catalog. This innovation compelled manufacturers to deliver to Sears what they had promised to deliver. It assured Sears it was receiving what it had paid for and—most important—enabled it to stand behind the promises made to customers without fear of serious loss. But the benefits of this practice extended far beyond the circle of Sears' own business. The factories who supplied it also supplied other customers, and as they were held to severe tests and specifications, they were compelled to improve their processes of manufacture. The result was that they delivered better goods to all their customers and these in turn to consumers.

In the course of time, many retailers, faced with the strong competitive pull generated by the money-back guarantee of Sears, had to discard *caveat emptor* and even, as competition increased, transform it into *caveat venditor,* and, finally, embrace the doctrine that "the customer is always right." Retailers were then faced with the same dilemma that had once confronted Sears. Actually their position was more difficult, because while they now had to stand behind their goods, they could not afford to maintain testing laboratories to assure they were receiving what they bought. The obvious solution which they adopted was to turn to wholesalers and manufacturers who had a reputation for fair dealing. These dealers— because their salvation lay in the retailer's survival—were forced to police the quality of the goods they offered. Thus, the consumer came to be protected in some degree, not by measures he had taken for his own protection, but by competitors who had once preyed on him yet who now had to struggle for his custom in a changed merchandise world.

This is not to say that ever was a time when there were not some honest manufacturers and merchants. There was always an honest minority. But competition did not once compel a large number to be honest whether they liked it or not. Nor is this to say that all the representations of Sears have been, or are, mathematically accurate. It, too, like many men and institutions, has sometimes been the creature of its times. Witness Sears' large business in fake medicines when such medicines were commonly sold in this country. It is beyond doubt, however, that the Company has in general offered honest merchandise honestly, and adhered without question to its money-back guarantee, so that if it ever willfully or unwittingly led the customer astray he had immediate and satisfactory recourse. And certainly this is not to say that the influence of Sears, or of any other organization of businessmen, or of consumers, has been sufficient to abolish from this country misbranding, misrepresentation, and other dishonest devices employed to fleece the people. The fact is, as everybody knows, that ingenious and shameless frauds are perpetrated daily upon consumers by some manufacturers and their more or less innocent retail distributors. But this in no wise detracts from the profound influence exerted by the money-back guarantee of Sears in breaking down the once almost universally observed rule of *caveat emptor* in retail selling, and thereby favorably affecting the purses of millions.

In 1896, Sears' sales were $1,273,000. By 1914, they were $101,121,000. In June, 1914, the Committee on Business Ethics of the National Civic Federation asked Mr. Rosenwald his opinion on business practices. He wrote in reply: "Not long ago the general practice in business was to let the buyer look out for his own interests. The man who sold made little or no effort to protect the man who bought. . . . But of late years this has changed. There has come into practice generally a new and wholesome doctrine of business morality. More and more the man who sells has come to realize that he has a very definite responsibility toward the man who buys."

The Farmer's Bible

Twice each year—in the spring and fall—heavy trains roll out of Chicago laden with 7,000,000 catalogs weighing a trifle under three pounds each, making a total weight of 21,000,000 pounds. The cars are bound for ten Sears mail-order branches scattered from Seattle to Atlanta. Here the catalogs are put in the mails and distributed to families who eagerly await them. At other intervals, other cars, heavily laden with special departmental catalogs—agricultural implements, tombstones, and such—and with "flyers" (bargain bulletins), make their way across the continent, so that almost every month in the year the great stream of American mail is swollen by the torrent that pours into it from Sears.

Actually the catalog is not one catalog but a number of catalogs. The editions that are made up for various sections of the country vary in size and content, because the people

...L BE SENT TO ANY ADDRES
FREE
BY MAIL POSTPAID
ON
APPLICATION

SIMPLE RULES FOR ORDERING.

...OUR ORDER BLANK IF YOU HAVE ONE. If you haven't one, use any plain paper.

...L US IN YOUR OWN WAY WHAT YOU WANT, always giving the CATALOGUE NUMBER of each article.

...the letter the amount of money, either a postoffice money order, which you get at the postoffice, an express

...r, which you get at the express office, or a draft, which you get at any bank; or put the money in th...

...it to the postoffice and tell the postmaster you want it registered.

...YOU LIVE ON A RURAL MAIL ROUTE, just give the letter and the money to the mail carrier and he will get the

...r at the postoffice and mail it in the letter for you.

...'T BE AFRAID YOU WILL MAKE A MISTAKE. We receive hundreds of orders every day from young and

...ver before sent away for goods. We are accustomed to handling all kinds of orders.

...L US WHAT YOU WANT IN YOUR OWN WAY, written in any language, no matter whether good or poo...

...nd the goods will be promptly sent to you.

...E HAVE TRANSLATORS TO READ AND WRITE ALL LANGUAGES.

...'T BE AFRAID OF THE FREIGHT OR EXPRESS CHARGES. You must pay them when you get the goods

...ion, but they never amount to much compared with what we save you in cost.

...YOU FIND IT NECESSARY TO HAVE SOME SPECIAL INFORMATION you can undoubtedly obtain it by

...to the matter contained within the first ten pages of this catalogue.

A REGLER ATT IAKTTAGA VID BESTÄLLNING.

...na vår beställningsblankett, om ni har en sådan.
...begagna vanligt rent papper.

...ss på edert eget sätt hvad ni önskar, alltid uppgif-
...talognumret på hvarje sak. Inneslut beloppet i
...ntingen i postoffice money order, hvilken köpes å
...ret; express money order, hvilken köpes å express-
...eller en vexel, hvilken kan köpas å hvilken bank
..., eller också inneslut kontanta penningar i brefvet,
...ll postkontoret och säg postmästaren att ni önskar
...gistrerat.

...ke rädd för att ni gör ett misstag. Vi erhålla hun-
...eställningar dagligen från unga och gamla hvilka
...r sändt efter varor. Vi äro vana vid att expediera
...beställningar.

...ss på edert eget sätt hvad ni önskar. Skrif på hvil-
...t som helst, bra eller dålig stafning, bra eller dålig
...och varorna skola blifva eder prompt tillsända.

...öfversättare som läsa och skrifva alla språk.

...r icke nödvändigt för eder att genomläsa de första
...a i denna katalog, såvida ni icke önskar någon spe-
...lysning. Dessa tio sidor innehålla detaljerad upp-
...så att de som i alla delar önska göra sig förtrogna
...t att beställa och sända varor, fraktkostnader o. s. v.,
...skrifva till oss, utan helt enkelt kunna

...de önska.

Einfache Regeln zum Bestellen.

Gebraucht unsere Bestellungszettel wenn Sie welche haben, me...
nicht nehmen Sie gewöhnliches Papier.

Im Bestellen erwähnen Sie die Catalog Numero an allen
Sachen. Die Bestellung soll das Geld enthalten, entweder eine
„Postoffice Money Order," (welche man gewöhnlich an der Post be-
kommen kann), eine "Expreß Money Order," ein Bank Certificate,
das man an jeder Bank bekommen kann, oder legen Sie das Ge...
in den Brief mit der Bestellung, in welchem Falle Sie den ...
Eingeschrieben schicken sollten. Der Brief wird in der
Eingeschrieben (Registered.)

Wir erhalten jeden Tag eine große Anzahl von Bestellungen von
allen Leuten (Jung und Alt).

Sie brauchen nicht furchtsam zu sein Sachen zu bestellen, wir w...
ben Ihr Bestellung schon verstehen.

Schreiben Sie uns in Ihrer eigener Weise, und in Ihrer eigener Sprache, was Sie wollen, einerlei ob gut oder schlecht geschrie-
ben, und die Waare wird Ihnen sofort zugeschickt.

Wir haben Leute die alle Sprachen schreiben und übersetzen.

Die ersten zehn Seiten in diesem Catalog beziehen sich haupt...
lich an die Frachtbeträge der verschiedenen Waare und hat nur ...
tigteit für Sie im Falle Sie in diesen Einzelheiten interessi... sin...

Paragraph O.

HOW TO RETURN GOODS.

BEFORE RETURNING THE GOODS to us in any manner, we would k that u communicate with us in regard to them, as we are frequently able t adjust .atters in a manner that will avoid the delay occasioned by return of goods.

INVOICE NUMBER. Be sure to mention your invoice number under which goods were shipped to you by us.

NEVER RETURN GOODS BY EXPRESS if the weight is more than wenty-five pounds, as it is cheaper to send heavy packages by freight. When ou return goods by express or freight be sure to enclose in the package your etter of instructions and particulars. **Don't forget** we must always have your .nvoice number. **Never** write us about a shipment and omit the invoice number. **Don't forget** that a letter containing full instructions should be in all express and freight shipments returned. **Don't forget** we must have your full name and address, exactly as given in the original shipment, in order to properly adjust any matter pertaining to an order returned.

WHEN RETURNING A PACKAGE BY MAIL, write your name, address and invoice number plainly in the upper left hand corner, providing you do not have one of the labels which we furnish when we know goods are to be returned. **Send us** by separate mail the particulars and instructions.

DO NOT ENCLOSE WRITTEN MATTER of any kind in mail packages, as by so doing you are liable to a fine of $10.00 and double letter rate postage.

DO NOT UNDER ANY CIRCUMSTANCES ENCLOSE MONEY WITH THE RETURNED GOODS.

THE UNITED STATES POSTAL LAWS AND REGULATIONS require that all packages of merchandise sent in the mails must be wrapped or enveloped in uch a manner that their contents may be readily examined by the postmaster without destroying the wrapper. **Never seal packages returned by mail,** but tie them securely with twine.

DO NOT FAIL TO REGISTER MAIL PACKAGES WORTH $2.00 OR MORE. Merchandise is sometimes lost when sent by open mail. A package can be registered for 8 cents and if necessary can be traced. **Do not enclose money with returned merchandise.** We cannot be responsible for its loss.

Paragraph P.

ABOUT DELAYED SHIPMENTS.

IF YOU HAVE SENT US AN ORDER FOR GOODS and you think it is time they should have arrived, before writing us concerning the delay please consider ? following:

While we are willing and glad to answer all kinds of inquiries, to make very possible kind of research, to quickly look up and trace any shipment aid to have been delayed, we are daily in receipt of hundreds of letters :iming that goods have been delayed, when the orders have been filled by ith all possible promptness, and have been handled by the railroad or exss companies with their usual dispatch. The investigation simply shows e customer is impatient and has not allowed sufficient time for the order to ach us, we to fill the order and the railroad or express company to deliver he goods.

WE FILL ALL ORDERS with the greatest possible dispatch consistent with proper care and safety. It requires from two to six days after your order is received for us to ship goods. Where goods are ordered that have to be made to order or finished after received, such as tailoring, upholstered furniture, vehicles, etc., additional time must be allowed. Goods shipped direct from our factory, such as stoves, sewing machines, furniture and a few other heavy items, require from five to ten days to make shipment, add to this the unecessary time for the express company or railroad company to carry the goods to you and you will seldom, if ever, be disappointed in the arrival of your goods.

BEFORE WRITING us concerning goods ordered or before calling for them at your railroad station, first consider if you have allowed ample time for your rorder to reach Chicago, the required time for us to fill same, as above stated, and for the railroad or express company to carry it to you. If you will always do this, allowing liberal time, bearing in mind that express and railroad companies sometimes delay goods a few days after they receive them, you will seldom, if ever, have occasion to write us concerning a delay. If there is more than one freight or express agent in your town, always make inquiries at each office before writing us concerning non-arrival of goods, as it often happens that a shipment is at one office and the notification card has miscarried, while the customer has been making inquiries at another office.

IN CASE, HOWEVER, an order should be delayed beyond the time above referred to, and you write us, do not fail to mention the date on which you mailed your order, the name and address as given in the original order, the value and nature of the cash you sent, and, if possible, give us your invoice number, for if you received from us a postal card acknowledging the receipt of the order, you will find the invoice number on the card mailed you.

ABOUT MISTAKES. If we make a mistake in filling your order, kindly give us a chance to correct it. We try to fill every order absolutely correct, but errors sometimes creep in. They do in all business houses. You will always find us willing to correct ours. Do not fail to write us in case of an nercror; otherwise we may never know of it.

nt? **CHANGE OF ADDRESS.** We would kindly request our customers to immediately advise us concerning any change of address, as we keep our records according to states and towns, and should you order from one town and then write from another, we would be compelled to send for further information before we could adjust the matter in question.

Paragraph Q.

ABOUT UNNECESSARY CORRESPONDENCE.

WHILE WE EMPLOY OVER ONE HUNDRED STENOGRAPHERS for the commodation of our customers, and are willing and glad to answer all and furnish any special information that may be desired, we daily av hundreds of letters of inquiry about things that are plainly answered it catalogue, hundreds of letters which might be avoided, saving loss of ti and unnecessary expense.

IT IS VERY SELDOM NECESSARY TO WRITE US, asking what the freig or express charge will be on any article to any point, for, from the weig given under each description and from the express and freight rates show on pages 7 to 11, you can calculate very closely what the freight or expre will amount to and save the time and trouble of writing for this informatio

OUR OLD CUSTOMERS rarely ever have occasion to write us, asking wl the freight or express will be on any article, and new customers will ha ever have occasion to if they will refer to pages 7 to 11.

LETTERS CONCERNING SHIPMENTS CAN OFTEN BE AVOIDED. receive hundreds of letters every day from parties who have ordered : have not allowed sufficient time for the order to reach us, the goods to packed and shipped and for the goods to reach them. (See paragra **P.**) Never write about a shipment until ample time has been allowed for goods to reach you. We receive hundreds of letters asking for prices or s cial prices on articles on which the price is plainly printed in this catalog All such letters are unnecessary, for it only means an answer again refer you to the catalogue.

WE RECEIVE HUNDREDS OF LETTERS DAILY from people who ask if we can't make changes in the goods as advertised, that they want the sa thing or things with slight changes. This is all irregular and could not furnished excepting at an advanced price, and we have found it impractical to make any such changes, and to all such inquiries we can save you t time and trouble by saying that no changes can be made from those ma plain in this catalogue. Since we answer as many as ten thousand letter day, you will help us where a reply is necessary by answering on the ba of our letter.

Paragraph R.

INSTALLMENT PLAN OR PARTIAL PAYMENT.

WE RECEIVE HUNDREDS OF LETTERS asking for prices on certain goo especially on organs, pianos and other goods that run into money, fr parties who wish to buy on the installment plan and to make settlement notes. All these inquiries can be avoided for the reason that our only ter are cash, we never extend time, we open no accounts nor allow goods to sold on the installment plan.

Paragraph S.

ABOUT CLAIMS FOR DAMAGE AND OVERCHAR ON TRANSPORTATION.

WE CAREFULLY PACK AND DELIVER ALL OUR GOODS in good co tion on board the cars, either in Chicago or at the factory, as made plain i catalogue. We accept a receipt from the railroad company for the good good order, and it very rarely happens that any goods that we pack ship reach their destination in bad order.

IF IT SHOULD EVER HAPPEN that any article reaches you marred, scratc broken or in any way defective, be sure to have the railroad agent make a tion of such defect on the freight receipt (expense bill) he gives you. You then present your claim for damage to the railroad agent from whom received the goods, it being his duty at that end to take the matter up with officials of that road and collect for you any damage that may have occur

WHILE THE PROPER PLACE FOR TAKING UP ANY CLAIMS FOR DAM OR OVERCHARGE ON TRANSPORTATION on goods in transit, either by freig express, is through the agent who delivers the goods, the trouble, delay an pense of writing us to do this can also be avoided. We, however, guara the goods we ship to reach you in the same perfect condition they leav and to be satisfactory to you in every way, and if you find them dam in transit and you accept them and the agent hesitates to take and co your claim for damage, you can write us enclosing your receipt (exp bill) for the freight charges paid the agent, with the agent's written not on the expense bill, stating what the damage is, and we will take the m up at this end, collect the damage and send the money to you. It will b possible for us to consider claims for damages to shipments unless the ex bill bears a notation to the effect that the shipment was received in bad cond

WHILE WE HAVE a large corps of stenographers and corresponding cle our employ, whose duty it is to promptly and courteously answer all inq and give all desired information, in order to maintain our extremely low [the cost of conducting our business must be cut down to the very minir and to do this our customers are especially requested before writing us cerning freight rates, claims, delays, or before asking us for informatio any kind, to carefully consult this catalogue, and if they will do this will find in nine cases out of ten the information can be had or the ad ment of damage made, without going to the trouble of writing us or pu us to the expense of corresponding on the subject.

ON THE BASIS OF BETTER VALUE THAN YOU CAN POSSIBLY ELSEWHERE, the best possible service, every item you order guarante reach you in perfect condition and to prove perfectly satisfactory or money to be immediately returned to you; under our binding guarant please you in every way in your dealings with us, we respectfully : your orders.

DO NOT FAIL TO GIVE SIZE, COLOR, WEIGHT, ETC., IF REQUIRED, WHEN WRITING YOUR ORD

and their merchandise needs vary sharply from section to section. The ice skates and ski suits that are featured in the New England edition are, of course, omitted from the Southern edition; farm machinery, because of varying crop and soil differences, differs according to the region in which the catalog is distributed. Southern women like bright colors and frilly clothes. The North wants quieter colors and plainer clothes. The Far West prefers modern furniture; the Middle West period designs; the South wants mail-order baroque; the East sticks to the colonial.

At first, the catalog was sold for one dollar. Then the price was reduced to ten cents. Now it is given away but, as we shall see, it is given away with care. The cost of this large book, containing upward of one thousand pages, filled with illustrations and color plates, varies with the years. Its price has fluctuated within recent years between a high of $1.39 and a low of sixty cents; now it costs about eighty cents a copy to produce in quantities of fourteen million.

The catalog is always old and always new; always the same and never the same. Each issue resembles in a general way each preceding issue; but every issue has new merchandise, features, text, and illustrations. And the making of it is never completed, because, at the moment when a Wisconsin farmer is taking the new fall edition out of his mailbox, the new spring edition is getting under way at Chicago.

How the Catalog Is Made

Back of the catalog stands an immense organization. At the top, there is a general advertising manager with numerous assistants. Functioning along with him is a production manager, aided by a large staff, who is in charge of mechanical production. Then there are a number of sales managers, each of whom has his assistants. Typical of this group is the sales manager for automobile accessories. It is his duty to see that this department is adequately represented in the catalog as to space, prices, texts, and illustrations.

These men, so to speak, are the catalog's architects. (Later we shall examine the duties of the draftsmen who work under them.) And the catalog is built to house a display of merchandise. The architect's employer is consequently the man in charge of merchandising—a vice-president of Sears. He must decide, in consultation with departmental supervisors and others, these all-important questions: what is to go into the catalog; the amount of space to be apportioned each department; how much space for the various items, and the one central selling idea, or "theme song," that is to dominate the particular issue. The emphasis varies. Sometimes it is fashion; sometimes thrift; sometimes the soundness of merchandise assured by Sears' laboratories.

The question of what is to go into the catalog and how much space it is to occupy is vital. The pulling power of this huge book, with a circulation of millions of copies reaching out to every post office in the land, is so enormous that, in 1931, pages were sold to outside advertisers (Chevrolet and The Curtis Publishing Company) at $23,000 apiece. (This experiment was immediately thereafter discarded by Sears.) If catalog space is so valuable to outsiders, it is equally valuable to insiders, and the auditing prices set upon pages for Sears' own departments range from $5,000 to $20,000 a page.

Every page is constructed according to a rigid plan. It contains usually a "feature" and a "volume" item besides listings of merchandise at intermediate prices. The feature —usually the highest-priced item on the page—is placed where it is most likely to catch the reader's eye: the upper right-hand corner. Around it are grouped the other and lower-priced items. Experience shows that about sixty per cent of the customers will select the cheapest merchandise from the "volume" items; the remainder will buy the "feature" items at the highest prices, and other goods at intermediate prices.

Sales statistics, a vast experience gained in continental merchandising, and a knowledge of economic conditions all over the country guide Sears in determining how much space shall be allotted any item. Thus the washing machine began its catalog life inconspicuously with small space; as its sales increased, the amount of space devoted to it increased, until now, it is given two or more pages. But if, after a carefully watched trial, its sales had declined; if the public had signified it did not want or was not yet ready for the washing machine, it would have been ruthlessly thrown out of the catalog or shoved into a corner.

Once the merchandise and its space allotments have been decided upon, a page blueprint called a "layout" is made for each page of the catalog. It is the catalog in embryo with marked-out blocks for text, illustrations, and drawings. In New York, Sears maintains elaborate photograph studios and a large staff of photographers, technicians, and artists. Wherever possible, merchandise is photographed on live models and photographs are generally used to illustrate merchandise. But nonetheless, photographs are not used for many categories of goods. Sears must neither overplay nor underplay what is offers for sale. If it overplays its illustrations, customers will be deceived; but (as often happens with photographs) if it underplays its illustrations, merchandise will look flimsier than it actually is. Pictures are vital to the catalog whose customers are the length of a continent away. Consequently, tires, furniture, and other things are pictured by drawings which accurately show their strength and massiveness.

Certain ironclad restrictions are placed upon the men who make the photographs and drawings for the catalog. The farmer is never represented as a rube with straw behind his ears; he never wears the battered straw sun hat and goatee of the vaudeville stage; he is never an Uncle Hiram with tobacco juice staining his white beard. No model, man or woman, is shown smoking a cigarette. And while the pages of women's clothes are thickly sprinkled with photographs of girls who have slender figures, there are numbers of others whose plump, matronly figures are like those of the cow-milking, chore-performing, child-bearing farm women with whom the catalog so largely deals.

While the photographers and artists are at work in New York, the copywriters are busy in Chicago writing the accompanying texts. Finally, all have completed their job, and 1,000 to 1,500 pages are ready to go to the printer. In order to keep up with this large number of pages involving nearly 50,000 items, as they go to and from the printer, Sears has evolved a simple system.

It has a huge chart called a Follow-up Board. Attached to it is a rack containing a thousand or more sections each of which holds a set of cards. There is a section for each page, and the sections are numbered from one to a thousand. At first, each section holds eight colored cards, and when the eight are in the section it is a notice that the printing of that page has not been started.

If you look at the rack and find that the yellow card is gone from page 188, you know that the copy has been written and sent to the editorial department. When the brown card goes out, you know that the copy is at the printer's; the disappearance of other colored cards indicates that various processes of manufacture are in progress. Finally, the blue card goes and this means that proofs have been okayed and sent to the printer. A new catalog is about to be born.

The printing of the catalog is surrounded with secrecy. A stranger cannot get into the printing plant without written permission from Sears. Prices are not inserted in the copy until the moment the catalog goes to press. The obvious reason for secrecy, of course, is to prevent competitors from learning Sears' prices in advance and changing their own accordingly.

The staggering job of printing the Sears catalogs is not done by Sears. Once it had its own printing plant but it soon found that this was uneconomical. During the rush season, it was overworked; at other times, while new catalogs were being prepared, it had little to do. Sears, therefore, has its printing done by two large Chicago firms.

One of the difficult problems of printing the catalog is the paper. The paper required must be light, thin, opaque, tough, and cheap. While the catalog is being printed, the paper is frequently weighed, because even a slight increase in weight would put the catalog into another mail classification and cost Sears thousands of dollars. Even the absorption of moisture from the air may put the weight of the catalog just over the postal border line into another classification.

The job of making the requisite catalog paper was put up to Sears' own chemists who after a number of years of experimentation finally solved it, and so benefited not only Sears but all others who print lightweight books and magazines.

"The Advertising Guide"

Sears annually deals with about ten million mail-order families whose orders result in over two hundred million transactions. These orders come from every social and economic class in the United States. The catalog's text must, therefore, reach and appeal to an audience as wide and as varied as America. It must be vivid but not florid; descriptive but not imaginative; simple but not boring, and, above all, scrupulously honest. *The Advertising Guide,* for use in the catalog division, was first issued in 1908 and, with successive revisions and changes, has continued to be the copywriter's law from which he must not deviate. The following are some of the instructions contained in it:

"Copy reading 'regardless of cost' should be used sparingly, as cost is always regarded.

"Exaggerated claims and unrestrained superlatives undermine customers' confidence. Therefore avoid free use of such expressions as Best, Finest, Biggest, and avoid all statements the truth of which may be questioned.

"Appeals to patriotism as an argument to induce buying are to be avoided."

There are hundreds of trade terms in common use by American consumers. Few know their precise meaning, and this permits unscrupulous advertisers to misrepresent their goods successfully. Sears insists that trade terms be used with precision. Here are some of them:

> Pure Dye—Applied to a silk fabric which contains no more than 10% of any substance (metallic or other type) other than silk. Black pure dye silk may contain as high as 15%. Other things being equal, pure-dye silk will give far better service than weighted silk.
>
> Waterproof—Applied to fabrics which must pass a severe spray test in which 1 qt. (1000 c.c) of water per minute falls from a height of 4 feet on 7 square inches of fabric, supported at a 45 degree angle. No drop of water must penetrate the fabric within 24 hours.
>
> Linen weave may not be used because any weave can be made from linen fibers. There is no weave which is always made of linen. The use of this term cannot be condemned too strongly as being misleading and inaccurate.

On numerous occasions throughout this book, we have seen how the catalog poked out its tongue at the local dealer. Those bawdy days are gone forever. For a long time, *The Advertising Guide* has contained this canon of conduct:

"It has been the practice of mail order selling for many years to present some of our goods on the basis of, for example, *'eliminating the middleman,'* thus speaking in a derogatory manner of the dealer. This practice should be discontinued. . . ." The worm has not only turned but has begun to bite. The lowly middleman is now trying to drive Sears and other chain-store organizations out of business through legislation.

Finally, the catalog is as direct as a hard-boiled top sergeant. When it talks about shoes, for example, it does not start out with a story about the aching feet of Stanley as he searched for Livingston in the African wilds, and end with the conclusion that he would have been a happier man had he been wearing a pair of Sears' Compo Soles. It tells you what the shoes are made of; how they look; what you may expect of them, and the price. In describing its nightgowns, it does not suggest that if you wear one you will wind up in the bed of the Maharajah of Kapurthala; it does not promise that its tooth paste will enable you to flash a smile that will make the Federal Reserve take your promissory note on the spot; it makes no claim that its washing machines will save your hands and give them a fluency unseen since Mary Garden used hers with such effect in Debussy's *Pelléas and Mélisande*. In 1936, *Time* magazine, reviewing an article in *Printer's Ink* about the catalog, said:

Having perused the 928-page "Golden Jubilee" Sears, Roebuck & Co. catalog lately mailed to 6,500,000 customers, *Printer's Ink* last week marked three lessons for the average advertiser:

(1) Though the occasion was its fiftieth anniversary, Sears devoted less than one-tenth of one per cent of the catalog to talking about itself, which might be a good proportion to keep in mind.

(2) Though it is necessary to describe mail-order merchandise in great detail, Sears provides more information than is ordinarily available in a personal transaction.

(3) Nowhere in the volume is merchandise represented as a means to such ends as these:
Getting a husband.
Holding a husband.
Saving the home from wreckage.
Soothing the nerves.
Getting a date for the Junior Prom.
Overcoming social inferiority.
Curing a disease of the "housewife's knuckles" type.
Eliminating sleepless nights.
Preventing the baby from having to have dental plates at age seven.
Stimulating an emotional jag.

Yet somehow Sears seems to struggle along and sell a few items every year.

"Please Send Me a Catalog"

Every year Sears receives 3,000,000 post cards and letters, written in many languages, all of them saying, "Please send me a catalog." It is the business of the circulation department of the ordinary publication to keep circulation up. At Sears, the circulation department is primarily concerned with keeping circulation down. The scale of its efforts may be measured by the fact that it receives an average of 10,000 requests each business day for the catalog. Obviously, the sending of catalogs to persons who do not buy is an expensive luxury that Sears cannot afford. It has, therefore, established these rules: a catalog is sent to anyone who writes for it. If you do not buy, you do not get it again unless you request once more that it be sent you; if you buy a trivial amount, you must also write for the catalog to get it the next time. If, however, you buy enough to become a "preferred customer" (the exact amount necessary to achieve this status is a Company secret), the catalog is automatically sent to you each season.

It might be thought that Sears would lose an irreplaceable asset if its customers' list should be destroyed by fire or other calamity. This is not the case. Apparently Sears' customers are as anxious to be on its list as the Company is to have them on it. It therefore regards the possible loss of its list with equanimity—an attitude confirmed by experiment. Some years ago, in order to obtain light on this potential problem, Sears advertised in the newspapers of certain counties that its list of customers for those counties had been lost. It requested that customers send their names in to Chicago. When the names were checked against the list in Sears' possession, it was found that not only had all the old customers responded but a number of new persons sent in their names. Thereafter, the fire hazard caused Sears executives no more sleepless nights.

What Sears Knows About America

In 1932, *Fortune* magazine said: "To the Company, the

farmer remains a profound and incalculable mystery, a hand that reaches out dollars or keeps them in his pocket, a thin envelope that arrives in the mail. Of the farmer's thoughts and desires and changing tastes practically nothing is indicated, except through what he does not buy."

This is equivalent to saying that if a man had a toothache he might think he was suffering from kidney trouble, because he had not lived long enough with his teeth to spot their exact location in his body. Actually, Sears has a mass of knowledge about the farmer, intimate and statistical, excelled perhaps only by that of the Department of Agriculture. How could it have had billions of transactions with millions of farmers for over fifty years and at the end of that time be in complete ignorance about them?

Sears knows far more about farmers than the average man knows about his own wife. There are men at Sears who can tell you what the farmer thinks about when he gets up in the morning, and why; what the family discuss at the breakfast table; the kind of underwear the farmer's wife wears to church; what the farmer's son says to a girl when he is courting, and who are the farmer's daughter's favorite movie stars. They can tell you the sort of pictures that hang on the walls of the farmer's home; his wife's favorite dishes and how she prepares them; what the farm family does on holidays. Information of this kind is not gathered for academic use. It is vital to Sears' business which, after all, is simply knowing what people want and the prices they can afford to pay to satisfy their wants.

Sears not only goes to the farmer but the farmer also goes to Sears. Every year, thousands of country folk visit Sears mail-order houses and are taken on a conducted tour to see at firsthand the workings of the entire mechanism. And Sears goes to the farmer not only through a host of investigators, but also through the Sears Educational Division and the Sears Agricultural Foundation. The Educational Division provides exhibits, free of all charges except transportation costs, for home-demonstration agents, county agents, and other leaders in rural economics. Well-informed advisers are retained by Sears to answer hundreds of letters from farmers asking for advice on a multitude of practical farm questions, while a home adviser answers the household questions that are sent to Sears by the farmer's wife.

Let us look at another extracurricular activity of Sears. Thousands of farmers make extra money during the winter by trapping. America, despite its industrialization, is one of the great fur-producing countries of the world. Strangely enough, the annual fur catch of the Southern state of Louisiana is more valuable than that of all Canada. But the farmer who had trapped a few mink, raccoons, or opossums was at great disadvantage when he marketed his furs. He could sell them only to a local merchant who in turn was at the mercy of the city fur dealer, or send them on consignment to city dealers and take what they pleased to give them. Sears set out to remedy this situation. Although its motive was not altruistic, that is beside the point.

A few years ago, the catalog contained a page suggesting that if farmers and trappers would consign their furs to Sears, it would, without charge, grade and market them and guarantee consignors a higher price than they could get elsewhere. Such is the confidence of its customers in Sears that thousands of shipments of furs were immediately received. The Company graded them expertly, sold them expertly, and farmers benefited.

But Sears did not stop at this point. Great money losses are caused by the fact that many farmers and trappers do not know how to prepare their skins for market in order to get premium prices. So Sears set out to teach trappers the best methods of preparing skins. Every year for the past eleven years, it has held a National Fur Show in Chicago where it exhibits the prize-winning furs that took prizes for careful pelt handling. The cash awards amount to $4,590, the first prize bringing the winner $1,000.

Sears, therefore, has an intimate knowledge of the farmer at home, in the fields, in the forests, and on the trap lines.

And back of all this, motivating it and giving it factual reality, is this statistical maxim of Sears' business: every year, year in and year out, its mail-order sales are approximately two per cent of the total farm income of the country.

The Great Divide

For about forty years—1886 to 1925—Sears was in the mail-order business exclusively. It is still in the mail-order business, but now it is also one of America's great chain-store organizations. It now has about 450 stores operating from coast to coast, rolling up annual sales in excess of $350,000,000 and overshadowing the business done by the mail-order division.

Yet Sears did not want to go into the retail business. It was forced into it.

In the early 1900's, some of America's witch doctors (synonym: economists) rattled their bones and amulets and solemnly announced that the mail-order business would soon be one with the growing of indigo. How far wide of the mark they shot is proved by Sears' (and others') lusty mail-order sales. But there was much in what they said.

By 1920, America was out of the mud and on automobile wheels. The farmer was no longer isolated. He need never again put in a stock of provisions in the fall and emerge in the spring. He had the telephone for communication and the automobile for mobility. He could go to town to sell and buy whenever he pleased. He could shop from one store to the next store, comparing goods and prices, and this particularly pleased the farmer's wife. It was obvious that, although the mail-order business would go on for years, its greatest years were behind it. Sears, therefore, was faced with this dilemma: should it continue in the mail-order business exclusively and watch its sales and profits decline, or should it go into the retail business and also retain its mail-order division? The latter course was decided upon and, in 1925, the first store was opened in the Sears Merchandise Building in Chicago.

In the furtherance of its retail plan, however, Sears undertook what was for Sears a still more radical departure—that is, it opened its largest stores in cities. This was done for the sound reason that few mail-order customers are city folk, and to open stores in cities would tap new markets. At the same time, to operate stores in agricultural communities would mean competing with its own catalog. Sears stores, therefore, are located in cities and in smaller towns which are more industrial than agricultural; for example, Gary, Indiana.

The city stores are known to the Sears organization as "A" stores. They are, in reality, department stores, but with this important exception: they lay far greater stress on hardware, refrigerators, stoves, automobile accessories, paint, washing machines, and household furnishings than does the average department store. Sears is an expert in these fields because of its long experience in selling heavy, semidurable merchandise through the catalog. The average department store, on the other hand, has tended to leave these fields to specialty stores, and content itself with more conventional department-store merchandise such as clothing, cosmetics, rugs, jewelry, and so on. Consequently, Sears readily found a market in the cities which would have been far more difficult to capture if it had made the error of attempting a frontal assault on the well-intrenched, fashion-conscious department stores.

In smaller cities, Sears has "B" stores. These are essentially stores for men. They deal in tools, men's clothes, agricultural equipment, automobile accessories, building materials, sporting goods, and, of course, household furnishings. A smaller group of smaller stores are included in the "C" division. They are, in effect, pocket-sized editions of the "B" stores.

These Sears stores are an expression of the urbanization of the United States; of the end of rural isolation and the triumph of the automobile; of the movement away from the farm and the loss of agriculture's once predominant place in the country's economic life. The fact that Sears' combined retail and mail-order sales now amount to about $600,000,-000 annually, that about $2,000,000 pours into Sears' cash registers every business day, in no way reduces the significance of the fact that when the first Sears store opened in 1925 it opened not only upon a new venture for the Company, but also upon a new day in America.

In Any Language

In endlessly changing America, some things seem to change but little. Despite the fact that the last great tide of immigration came rolling up to American shores in 1914—a quarter century ago—thousands of Sears' customers do not read or write English. It is not to be expected, however, that a firm which has found it possible to fit trusses, wigs, and artificial legs for customers whom it has never seen and will never see would be deterred from selling men simply because they do not possess a common tongue. And it is not. "WE HAVE TRANSLATORS TO READ AND WRITE ALL LANGUAGES," said the catalog of 1905. As proof of its linguistic abilities, it added:

Schreiben Sie uns Ihre Aufträge und Briefe in Deutsch.
. . .
Escriben sus pedidos y cartas en Español si quisieran. . . .
Schrifj uew bestellingen und briefen in het Hollandsch als het u past. . . .
Se Lei preferisce scrive ordine e lettere in italiano. . . .
Wysylajcie wasze ordera lub listy po polsku jerzeli wam sie podoba. . . .
Napište vaši objednávku a psani v Českém jazkyu jestli si tak přejte. . . .

Twenty-five years after this notice had appeared in the catalog, the census of 1930 was published. According to it there were over thirteen million foreign-born whites in the country nearly all of whom were adults. Only four million of this group spoke English as their native tongue. Nearly all the rest, however, convinced the Bureau of the Census that they had a workable command of the language.

Sears took these figures and conclusions, studied them, compared them with what it knew to be the facts of American life as revealed in its million-faceted contacts with flesh-and-blood people, and filed them neatly away. It did not say that the conclusions drawn by the census were erroneous. It merely inserted this notice in the catalog of 1935:

"WRITE IN ANY LANGUAGE":
Schreiben Sie uns Ihre Aufträge und Briefe in Deutsch.

. . .

Escriben sus pedidos y cartas en Español si quisieran....

Sears' insoluble language difficulty lay, however, not with men who had come from Patras, Greece; Cadiz, Spain; Lwów, Poland; Naples, Italy, or Stavern, Norway. Written communication could be established with them in their own tongues. The difficulty lay in communicating by mail with native-born whites and Negroes who live in Calico Rock, Arkansas; Hushpuckana, Mississippi; Hung Yearling Gap, North Carolina. Hundreds of thousands of this group could not read or write any language.

The catalog changes with changing America not only in the goods it offers but also in its own make-up. It is no longer the badly printed, poorly illustrated, hard-to-read book that it was in 1905. It matches in typography, readability, photography, layout, and the use of color most of the smart publications of the country. If it lags sometimes behind the fashion procession, it keeps well abreast of developments in printing and illustrating.

But basically, the catalog goes along on the principles of simplicity and honesty laid down by its makers long ago. It continues to exert a strong hold on millions of Americans and to be, in the new dress of 1940, what it was in 1905: The Farmer's Bible.

APPENDIX

AMERICANS are, in general, an articulate and garrulous people. They like to talk; the legend of the tight-lipped New Englander is overstrained. They also like to write letters, as witness the millions of letters the people send to movie and radio stars, and the thousands that daily go to newspapers and magazines. Americans, moreover, delight in reading letters written by others—a form of pleasure capitalized, for example, by *Time* magazine, which weekly prints as a feature some of the letters it receives from readers.

It is consequently understandable, therefore, that Sears should annually receive millions of letters, because it counts its customers by millions of families. All letters received are answered, whatever their contents. The majority are about business and are to the point. But what of many of the others?

The manifold reasons why men and women write letters to movie, radio, literary, stage, and other personalities would lead to an extended inquiry beyond the scope of this book. The reasons why many letters are written to Sears are clear. One is the loneliness of the writers. In this country, there are hundreds of thousands of wifeless, husbandless, childless, unloved men and women. They often live in the isolation of remote villages or farms, or in the greater isolation of cities. They write to Sears frequently because they want to assuage their loneliness; because they want to say something to somebody, and, in turn, experience the excitement of getting a letter, even though it is written by an anonymous corporation. It is not an uncommon thing, as rural postmasters will testify, for a man to ask for mail day after day and year after year, although no letter had ever come for him.

Other letters are written to Sears because customers feel a genuine affection for it, and take their troubles to the distant Company as though it were a sympathetic next-door neighbor.

The letters that follow are from Sears' files. In all cases the names of the writers and the localities in which they live, have been omitted or changed.

A Kansas gentleman, in 1936, outraged because the catalog offers dancing lessons, returns the offending page to Sears and threatens to deprive it of his patronage unless it reforms:

> GENTLEMEN: I hereby register my protest to such sales features as are displayed in your recent catalogue. I refer to the glaring, captivating way in which you play up the dance, before boys and girls. Possibly you are unaware of the fact that the dance is one of the most debasing, degrading, and damnable institutions existing today. You may say that what you have played up is the tap dance. But we know that tap dancing oftentimes is only the beginning of the social dance, the parlor dance, and the general public dance. Here in your catalogue, you have so featured it before the eyes of innocent boys and girls, as the "big" thing, the popular thing.
>
> It seems to me that there could be someway another form of appeal than to encourage boys and girls to dance. I am sending you an order today; but if this type of popular appeal is made to the youth of the country, I feel it will be necessary for me to make my merchandise purchases elsewhere.

A gentleman gardener, sojourning in Florida during the winter, inquires about flower beds, and, in asking that the catalog be sent him, assures Sears that it will not be put to profane use:

> Will you kindly advise me of the width of spaces at bottom of your Flower Bed Borders #32 EM5393?

I would also be pleased to receive your catalogue next year. . . . I have read *The Specialist* but assure you I will not put your catalogue to a more lasting use than he gives credence to.

An old-fashioned gentleman, living in Alaska, thanks Sears for procuring some old-fashioned wearing apparel for him, and takes the opportunity to air his views on modern society:

> This is to thank you for the unusual trouble to which you went in procuring the linen cuffs I wanted. I suppose I ought to fall in line with the customs of the current period, but as I feel uncomfortable and undressed in the absence of cuffs, and have not yet been convinced that such a sacrifice of my own comfort would be justified by my duty to society, I shall continue to wear cuffs until my reformation is more advanced than at present.
>
> Having drifted into an age when homes are merely sleeping places, common gentility in bad taste, and even ladies wear pants, are become experts in profanity, liquor and nicotine addiction and other forms of vulgarity, I feel I am still out of place, but there is nothing I can do about it except regret. I suppose this is what they meant when they promised me that woman suffrage would cure all the ills of society. . . .

A New Jersey justice of the peace, engaged upon the sad mission of retrieving some Sears' merchandise which had not been paid for, reports the result of his mission:

> . . . This court reconvened at the home of ———— at 8:00 P.M., 7th, inst., for the purpose of salvaging the sewing machine in the case. Court was equipped with a Ford, thirty-odd feet of clothes-line and two blankets.
>
> Court upon entering house found Mrs. ———— nursing an infant, presumably a female, and a grouch. Upon cross-examination (in this instance by the Court) of Mrs. ————, Court extracted the information that the husband of the said Mrs. ———— was attending a religious meeting at some place unknown to said Mrs. ————. Court thereupon declared a recess until such time

as Mr. —— might return. The Court after swearing himself in as an expert made a careful examination of the sewing machine.

The Court slept.

At or about 10:P.M. the Court was awakened by the return of Mr. ——.

Court then again took up the case and, in the interest of his client, made Mr. —— cough up ten dollars (money he claimed he had set aside for the gasoline man today) which you will find herewith.

Collection of the balance is going to be slow but I will ride him for another fall next month. Anything I get will be to your profit (or saving) as eight of the nine children in the house have taken varied cracks at the machine.

A lonely young man in Tennessee, looking for a wife, takes his troubles to Sears:

DEAR SIR: I thought I would write you a Line as I am looking for me a wife. I want a good cook and a clean woman. I am 24 years old. I want a girl about my age. If you can Look for me a wife I will pay you for your troubel as I am lonely and would like to be married. I am just a Poor Boy. I live on a 60 acre farm. So please look & find me a wife. If you find one have her to write to me & tell her to send me her picture. Show the girl my letter & let her see it & if she wants to she can write to me & give her age. I want to get married at an early date if suited. So please find me a woman. I am well suited with most any girl. Let me hear from you in a few days. . . .

A North Carolinian, during prohibition days, makes a heartfelt complaint to Sears:

Kindly accept my thanks for the refund for the leaky keg which I purchased from you a few days ago. No one could ask for a more just settlement than that. Regarding the purchase of a new keg, I will doubtless order again from you in a short time. For the present, however, I purchased one locally, as I had to have something to keep my "mineral water" in. I intend re-ordering in a few weeks just as soon as my present container is used up. As you doubtless know, a keg is good for only two or three usings. . . .

A Mississippi victim of prohibition writes a second letter to explain his first letter:

> Yesterday while I was drunk I sent you a small order paid for by one of your own checks and finished out in regular U.S. What I am trying to say today, while tolable sober, is that I probably forgot to tell you what I wanted! Don't blame me, it was the best I could get, and @ $1.25 per gal you can't expeckt much can you? I'll say you can't! Now get busy and spend two dollars and halfs worth of time correcting something Andrew Volstead could have prevented. Viz: one small frying pan, #21J3459 @89¢ Atta boy!! —/—#$?":!. . .

The demon rum, being on the loose in the country, a temperance reformer asks Mr. L. J. Rosenwald, then Chairman of the Board, Sears, Roebuck & Company, to help him in the good fight:

> DEAR SIR: No doubt you have heard of me and my great work in the cause of temperance. For several years I have been travelling about the country, appearing on lecture platforms. Perhaps you are familiar with some of my better known talks, such as "Down with the Evil of Drink," "Rum and Rebellion," and "There is No Booze in Christianity."
>
> For the past three (3) years I have had as my constant companion a true and faithful friend, one Clarence ————————, who used to sit with me on the platform, and I would point him out to the audience as an example of the ravages of drink. Unfortunately, during the last winter, dear Clarence passed away. A mutual friend has given me your name, and I wonder if you would consent to accompany me on my summer tour, to take the place of poor Clarence.

An irate customer in Pennsylvania writes an angry letter and apologizes for his anger in the postscript:

I got the pump which i by from you, but why for God's sake you doan send me the handle. I loose to me by customer. Wats the use a pump when she doan have no handle. Shure think you doan treat me rite. I rote ten days and me customer he holler for air like hell from the pump. You know he is hot summer now and the wind he no blow the pump. She get no handle wot the hell i goan to do with it. Doan send the handle pretty quick i send her back and I goan order some pump from Black Co.

Yours,

———

Oh Hell after i rite i find the God damn handle in the box. Excuse me.

Sears annually receives a number of letters and remittances from repentant customers. The following letter, written seventeen years after the event, is typical:

DEAR SIRS: No doubt but what this letter will be as different as any you have ever received. For many years I have been intending to do this very thing but have always been "hard up" and kept putting it off, but here goes.

In the year 1918 I sent an order to Sears for a sewing machine costing $16.98. I waited a reasonable time for my order but it did not come and so I wrote to the Company. They replied, saying it had been shipped and would reach me later if it did not let them know. After several weeks I wrote again, this time they tried to trace it but could not locate it. So they returned my money. . . .

In about six weeks I had a call from the depot, saying there was some freight there for me. It proved to be my sewing machine. I took it to my home but the money I had paid for it had been spent for other things and I had none to pay for the machine.

All these seventeen years I have been intending to send the money but the pay is never big enough to reach all the way around and have any left over for this so I have continued to procrastinate. But not long ago I had a chance to make some money of my own. I did not know how much it would be, but I promised the Lord if it was as much as $16.98 I would send it to pay for the machine. Needless to say I received $17.00. So here it is.

I have a husband and four children we have had nothing but sickness and bad luck all these years, whether this unpaid bill has anything to do with the hard luck remains to be seen. But I am extremely happy to clear this from my mind. . . .

An elderly Californian, in the days before "ham-and-eggs" pension schemes for the old, reads Sears a lecture on thrift:

I note your suggestion that you would make an extra pair of pants for $8.65. I am 71 years of age. The undertaker would charge me $35.00 for a burial suit. I would get to wear that but once. You are charging me $28.75 for a suit. I am pretty sure I will get to wear that a number of times, before being buried in it, so I am saving the difference in cost (I am not Scotch). Now as to the extra pair of pants. I will not need them where I am going.

In Kansas a customer selects a grave marker but notifies Sears that he is not quite ready to use it:

I have monument catalog. My folks thought I would kick out so I selected monument I wanted as I have the plot. But they are not ready for me above yet.

A Panhandle Texan grows lyrical as he requests a copy of the Sears catalog:

Away out on the bounding, billowy, bleak, barren, baldy prairies of the Great South Plains of Texas, the winds rage with unrestricted fury, with nothing between them and the North Pole but a barbed wire fence. The line rider is dead, the hungry coyotes howl in mournful cadence, their weird, wild music falling like a funeral dirge on the listening ears of a lonely man who, after the manner of David when Absalom was slain, "Mourned and would not be comforted," longs and yearns with all his sad heart for *just one copy* of the fall and winter edition of the Great Panhandle Wishbook, alias the catalog of Sears, Roebuck & Company.

Why, for the first time in many, many moons have you sought to economize by denying me my inalienable right, that of sitting, these long winter nights, beside a cosy fire in my lonely little shack, diligently perusing said catalog and long for the things therein contained. . . .

Likewise, since you propose to cater to the wants of everybody, everywhere, have you in stock an old maid, widow, or orphan, who might be inclined to look with favor upon the idea of a lifetime companionship with a man who is real hungry for the society of one of said fair daughters of Mother Eve? . . .

Sears, if it had conducted a matrimonial bureau, might have made two of its customers happy. Shortly after the Texan's letter requesting a wife and a catalog, a letter came from an Idaho lady teacher. She sent with it a catalog illustration of a handsome man, and wrote as follows:

I am a lonely school teacher in the dismal hills of Idaho. Would you be kind enough to do your share in assisting a poor forlorn teacher in her future happiness by sending this man which you advertised in your latest edition?

If at the present time this particular man is not in stock, I leave the responsibility of choosing my future mate up to you.

From Arkansas, a customer sends a post card begging Sears to send him the shoes that he had ordered:

Boys, I have been working bare-footed all week. Haven't needed those kicks up to now, but, we ran into some grass and cockle burrs today not to mention the sandstorm that hit us, so, in justice to a pair of faithful dogs I beg you to make me the shipment. The size is a 9. Model 69D4567 (streamlined). . . .

Shoes seem to provoke complaints from customers. A male schoolteacher in South Dakota writes as follows:

A few days ago I received from you a pair of shoes. They are good shoes. . . . But they have one great fault, that is, each one has a fault of its own. They squeak terribly!

I remember when a small boy, the little girls I used to play with, were very proud if they had a pair of squeaky shoes. But it has been so many years since I have "heard" shoes that I took it for granted that "musical" footwear had passed into oblivion along with the dinosaurus and the silent drama.

Came the awakening, when I, a middle-aged school teacher, suddenly found myself walking across the floor with a pair of shoes on my feet that sent out wave lengths that would be the envy of any broadcasting station in the country.

When I walked into the classroom the other day the boys jumped and ran to the window, thinking that spring had suddenly come upon us and what they heard was an orchestra of frogs in a nearby marshland. It was with some difficulty that I restored order.

Now what am I to do? I can't return them as they have been worn. I don't like to throw them away because they are so comfortable. I can't stop their squeaking which is rather annoying. Yours for a suggestion. . . .

A gentleman of Scandinavian extraction, residing in the state of Washington, has some difficulty obtaining parcels sent him by Sears, and more difficulty in explaining why he has difficulty:

My Dear Sear Roebuck & Co:
Today my wife she gets a parcel from you. That's allright. And I think there is more coming, and before this already I send to you by my wife for a watch for my little boy that did not come yet, but maybe so it did, we must wait and see. Now you see when I send for my little boys watch by my wife & also when I send for other order by my wife I write her name Ethel Hennigson. Well now when one of her parcels come it just says E. Hennigson on it. Now maybe that's allright, but it is not fair to the Postal service because my papa Elbert Hennigson gets mail from the same postoffice and he lives 2½ miles out

in the country. So now its this way, that parcel he goes out to Elbert Hennigson. Maybe that's all right maybe but you see it stays at the postoffice all afternoon the day it arrives and goes out on route the next day already, that's allright.

Then my papa he gets it carries it home and carefully unwraps the parcel and finds out that Ma never sent for anything like that so they wrap it up good & that's allright. But you see my papa he comes down the next box the next day after the mail carrier goes by to get his mail & leaves it in the mail box for the mail man to bring in the next day & that's allright. But you see the parcel has to wait all this time to get back to the postoffice, allright then it comes back the next day about noon just after I come back from lunch, there for it has to wait till I go at home at night before my wife she finally gets this parcel.

That's allright but what I want you to know is that when I send you any more orders for my wife is that you put my wifes name on the parcel just as I write it to you & so the Postoffice can tell if its my wife Ethel or my papa Elbert. You see this letter stuff means nothing but names explain everything. But you see my papa and my wife they do not live together—yet they just visit real chummy like sometimes, say when my papa and my mama they come to town to trade & have dinner by us. That's allright & we go out there and visit too me & my wife & three kids & we visit real chummy & have a fine dinner & everybody is happy. But you see—my wife is not my papa Elbert & my papa he is not my wife Ethel, that's all. . . .

A young Georgia gentleman is hopelessly in love, but fears competition, and asks aid of Sears:

DEAR SEARS: I have a question I would like to ask you. Do you sell love powder or the liquid? I am 29 years old & I am going with a girl & I am crazy about her but there is another boy in my way. If you sell it please drop me a letter at once. . . .

An indignant Chicago lady indicts Sears on two counts: one, that it doesn't know the sex of a canary; two, that when it has made a mistake in a canary's sex, it won't make the mistake good. She mails her indictment to the president of Sears:

> DEAR SIR: I bought a bird from the Sears store in December last, priced at $2.98. I received a 21-day guarantee with it stating it was an imported *male singing canary*. I was satisfied with the bird as long as I thought I had a male bird, but it did not sing. I had hopes of it singing in due time, but last week, by chance, I found out it was a female and wanted to set. Today, I took it back and explained the matter to the head of the department, hoping for some adjustment. But after 1½ hours wait being sent first to one and then to another, they told me there was nothing could be done about it, that my 21 days was over. . . . I had no reason to doubt their sale as being other than what they stated it was—a male. . . . This bird is marked on the wing and they tried to say this was no mark of identification and that it was only a cheap bird and I could not expect it to sing right away. When I bought it they said it would sing inside of 7-10 days. I am not complaining about it not singing, what my argument is, I bought and paid for a male and what they sold me is a female. It is in perfect condition, but as long as they sell females at the store for $1.00 I am not satisfied at having paid $2.98 for this one.
>
> . . . If you care to investigate this matter I will be grateful to assist you in any way.

An ambitious young Louisiana businessman makes Sears the offer of a deal which contains the elements of another *Merchant of Venice:*

> GENTLEMEN: Could it be possible for me to borrow Five Hundred Dollars from you all, on Ten Per Cent Interest, to buy myself a truck and trailer so I can do oil field work, and within one years time the total of $550.00 will be back in the hands of Sears Roebuck & Co without fail. And IF I fail Sears Roebuck & Co, at my say so may use my heart for a Target Spot, That Is The Kind of a Guarantee I will put up. I am well known in————, La. White. Age 24. I have got to get some way to make

a living, and I wish some good man would give me a break in Life, and then if I did not make a go of it for him to have me to kill.

So please let me hear from you at once.

A lady living in the golden state of California expresses her approval of Sears' thirteen-month year, and sees hope in it for herself:

DEAR SIRS: Please send me one of your New Calendars. Thirteen months in a year appeals to me.

Believe it or not, my man pays me $4.00 per month for doing the housework, so I'm going to try to get an extra $4.00 per year out of him.

An old Sears customer, resident in Milwaukee, more in sadness than in anger, reports his troubles in getting an adjustment for defective merchandise:

GENTLEMEN: As a customer of your house for 25 years, I'm sending you a broken hinge from a white toilet seat. Silly, perhaps, but it is a parting token from me that you might want to hang on your sales chart at the point where the sales curve lags. . . .

The story of the hinge is on this wise: June 2nd, 1934, we were in your Milwaukee store and bought a toilet seat for $2.59. In the next few days, with proper ceremonies it was fittingly and duly installed in our bathroom. On August 2nd, my wife's mother, an elderly woman, told us something was wrong with our new and beautiful toilet seat. An examination . . . indicated a defective casting. This did not annoy me at all as no one can see the inside of a casting, and the fact that I was the unlucky person to get a sour casting did not upset me, for I was sure that this matter would be speedily adjusted as soon as we called it to the attention of your salesman.

On August 4th when we called to make our monthly payment on our bedroom set we looked up the salesman from whom we had bought this seat and right there our trouble started. Your salesman hunted around for one of these units and being unable to find one, asked me to go to the eighth floor, ask for Mr. Black in Dept. 42, and talk to him about it. Mr. Black said he had no spare part to fit this seat. He asked me to go back to the salesman and in due course I arrived back at the point where I started and explained to this very patient man the results of my trip to the ninth floor. He then gave me a slip of paper and told me to go to the Adjustment Bureau, ask for Mr. Snade, who would give me a refund check for 85 cents, and that I should bring the check back to him and he would order me a new hinge. I told him the hinge was all right and that I only wanted this little gadget which certainly did not cost 85¢. I further explained to him that we had an elderly woman in the house and it was dangerous for her to use this seat in its present condition. I suggested that he give me a unit from one of the seats in stock, go ahead and order the new part and when it arrived put it on the seat he robbed to fix mine. I told him he had a lot of seats not in use and we only had one hardly fit to use without a trapeze or a parachute. He said he could not do this without authority. I asked for his boss and he told me he was out to lunch, but to go to the Adjustment Desk and they said OK he would do as I asked. I went to the Adjustment Bureau and asked for Mr. Snade and was told he was out to lunch. This was about 4.45 p.m. I then told my story to the man on the desk and he promptly squelched me by stating they could not break down merchandise. I told him mine was broken down and I needed help in a hurry but I could not move him from his position. I assure you, gentlemen, if you think a toilet seat yawing all over the bathroom is not "broken down" you should have heard the squeals and scramblings in our otherwise peaceful abode in the last few days.

It may be that I'm all wrong in this matter. I make no claims of justice for writing you this letter. But please keep in mind that for many years my dealings with your house were conducted entirely differently and maybe I'm spoiled. I might have brought back the entire toilet seat and they no doubt would have given me another one, but I felt that would have been a waste as there was nothing wrong with this seat except this little jigger under discussion. I hate waste, and thought it would be better for you if they just gave me this unit and I could install it myself. Everybody I contacted was very nice about it, except they could not see the necessity for me getting this speedy, but to me, vital service.

So in conclusion (thank goodness, says you) I guess we will just have to kiss each other good by, for it seems that as far as Sears is concerned I have lost my rabbits foot. Oh, well by the time you get this I suppose we will have a new toilet seat from Gimbels. Your waste basket is on your left, but the load is off my chest.

The varied role that the catalog may play in the American home is pointed out in this letter from two eleven-year-old Arkansas girls:

GENTLEMAN: Please put feet on your ladies in your catalog so they will make nicer paper dolls. We can hardly find enough ladies with feet to finish our families. We are eleven years old. We like to cut paper dolls out of your catalog when they get old. Please don't put the prices on their legs. Please send this to Mr. Sears.

A Missouri lady, anxious to get a corset, bursts into verse:

Dear Mr. Sears and Roebuck
To me it's a great surprise
That somewhere in your book-keeping
You have not recorded my size.

Of course to forget my measure
On my part, was a mistake
Suppose when I filled out that order
I could not have been fully awake.

I sure was in a hurry for that corset
But it's my fault I'm in such a fix,
And I wish I could say, Sears and Roebuck,
That I am a perfect thirty-six.

But while my bust is only thirty-one,
As sure as you're alive,
I'll have to admit my hips are large,
They measure thirty-five.

So bear in mind these measures
And as quickly as can be
Send me corset 18W303,
Then most grateful I will be.

A gentleman resident of Santa Lucia, Philippine Islands, awaits with more than mild interest the arrival of a new catalog:

DEAR HONESTY MESSIEURS: This is the acknowledged of my praise note which you drop it in short time ago. When the mail carrier handed me your passive Post Card, is dated March 25th, 1935, your statement attached in your letter is my basis principles to have send you to let you to understand what I understood in it. But still I can not waited until this time the catalog and I don't know is what is the one months in transit between your city and ours. One more I say, I think you did not forget me. I say this, because I received it again your second letter about this matter, and you are now explaining that you have already delivered it to me the catalogue, as you requested, and you shall be glad to send me at my request, with your complete, handsome and more bigger of your new Sears Roebuck catalogue, for a wilder and more complete variety of bargains for all the family, for 1935, —and that is for you to distributed to your true buyer customers to the origin without any charge. And for them also to remain for selecting the all goods which they prefer to buy from your store.

Here is my true insperation in this matter: Upon my honor before God before you. Anyhow I am glad to inform you that God knows if I received it, your catalogue. I may entirely grieve or not lived in the garden of Paradise. I come to explained from you clearly what they say it to me that I had doned already requested to you in time had passed. In this matter, I rush at once to the Post-Office showing your note to the Postmaster and the Postman, but sorry to say for they had told me that they did not received any catalogue of mine up to this time. Therefore and this is the reason why I trace to you to write immediately again, what I stated in your company, if you are in under respectfully to everybody. Lastly, I hope you will get a very great attention in this matter what I am taking unerring over with you.

On the other side of the world, an Alabama clergyman reports the flowering of the catalog in the pleasant fields of Holy Writ:

> Here is something original and will give you joy.
> A little child in one of my church schools was asked the other day, What was the Tenth Commandment? The reply was "Thou shalt not covet." When asked what covet meant, she replied, "not to want other folks things, but to get Sears, Roebuck Catalogue and buy for yourself."

A farm woman in Wyoming, obviously intending to take all knowledge for her province, asks Sears to do the spadework:

> Would like to know which sounds the best for children to call their parents, Father, Mother, Papa, Mama or Daddy?
> I have a girl who likes to write with her left hand. Would you train her to write with the right hand? I think it looks better to write with the right hand. What would you do? Train her to use the right hand or not and why?
> What is the meaning of rhythm? What are physics? Have you a book for sale that explains how words are pronounced?
> What color of trimming looks well on wine color? And what trimming on orange color?

Sears is sometimes an accessory to love. In this case, it helped a young man in North Dakota woo a young lady in Mexico:

> I am enclosing a letter which I received from a Mexican girl and cannot read it. Will you please translate it into English or German and send it back to me?

On other occasions, however, Sears maintains that silence

which is imposed upon gentlemen under certain circumstances:

> DEAR SEARS, ROEBUCK & CO.: I am asking a special favor of you and from the nature of this letter you will know why I ask it. Is Miss——————, of this place, a customer of yours? If so, will you please let me know if she bought a man's belt about last May and the initials — — — engraved on the buckle? And did she order a pair of men's Indestructo Saranac Buckskin Gloves last September? Also did she get a man's travel kit just before this last Christmas?
>
> If these things have been ordered from you by Miss —————— will you tell me if she orders anything else from you for a man between now and this time next year? Any information you can give me in regard to these things will be kept strictly to myself. I guarantee you that.

In the American legend, the first year of marriage is the hardest. The following letter, therefore, is the perfect expression of confidence in Sears on the part of the customer:

> GENTLEMEN: I am about to become a bride and I am ordering my trousseau from you and want you to make the selection for me. I am to be married next week. Some lady in your place might do better than the men in picking out these things. Will describe myself in order that you will know just what will best suit my type; I am tall, weighing 106 lbs., and very slender; have dark complexion, brown eyes that are large and expressive, and my hair is golden yellow or auburn.
>
> Please select youthful styles for me but, not too daring, as I am no "flapper."
>
> I want to be married in a white chiffon dress with black straw hat and black slippers. Want lace slippers with low heels (size 8½). Also want a black pocketbook with some lovely initials on it.
>
> From the underwear department please send me several pairs of bloomers in yellow or purple with trimmings of other colors. Do not send any "step-ins" or "step-outs," or whatever they are called, for I am a modest woman and I wear bloomers with elastic in the legs. Also send

some ruffled petticoats and brassieres. Will order my corset later on so you need not send it now.

Please send me three pairs of stockings . . . don't have them too expensive.

Owing to the depression and the high price of house rent in the city my husband (to be) and I will not go to housekeeping here but will buy a tent and camp out this summer in the woods and green pastures. Please select some cute calico pajamas for me to wear when camping. Or do you think overalls would look cuter on me? Come to think of it, overalls may be better, but I want some handsome pajamas anyway. Say one pair of overalls and one pair of pajamas.

Have you any tin plates in stock? If so I would like a dozen of them, as the china dishes are so hard to replace.

I can't give all the numbers on these goods as I have misplaced my catalog. You know how excited you are when you are about to be married, and as this is the first time for me I am unusually nervous. We are to be married next Friday so you see it is less than a week and the suspense is terrible.

Please be good enough to make the best possible selections as I may never be married a second time and a girl always wants to look her best on such a rare occasion.

I send a check in this letter. I am just guessing at the cost of the things as I haven't the catalog here. If it is too much you will send back the difference, and if it is not enough, let me know and I will pay you.

The last letter in the collection is from a father whose daughter had eloped and married against his wishes. The young couple disappeared and the angry father wrote to Sears and asked their help in tracing the couple: "He buys things from you, and sooner or later he is certain to send in an order. Then you will please let me know where they are?"

Sears replied that it was not in the detective business. Curiosity, however, impelled an order clerk to note the young man's name, and it was attached to his card in the files with the expectation that when he sent in an order he would mention his previous address and could thus be identified.

A few months later, the mail-order Lochinvar, now far

from his parent's home, sent in an order. It was for a woman's suit, $5.98; a woman's hat, $1.29; three pairs of silk stockings at 59 cents a pair, and a machinist's toolbox, $1.49.

CUSTOMERS' PROFIT SHARING DEPARTMENT.

Any customer of ours, anyone buying goods from us, is entitled to share in the profits of this business by selecting and receiving FREE OF ANY EXTRA COST, any one, or as many of the articles shown on the following pages, as he or she may desire, subject only to the provisions and conditions hereafter explained.

WHENEVER YOU PURCHASE GOODS FROM US (amounting to $1.00 or ore) we will send you a profit sharing certificate showing the amount of your purchase in dollars and cents. These certificates should be carefully preserved by you, and when you have received certificates amounting in dollars and cents to enough to entitle you to any one or more of the articles wanted as shown on following pages, send the certificates to us, state which article or articles are wanted, and if the certificates you send us amount to enough in dollars and cents to entitle you to the article or articles wanted, these articles will be sent to you free of any cost, carefully packed and delivered on board the cars at Chicago, or factory, and you will have only the freight or express charges to pay; not one penny will you have to pay for the article or articles you select from this profit sharing list.

PLEASE NOTE THAT WE WILL NOT ISSUE A PROFIT SHARING CERTIFICATE FOR AN ORDER OF LESS THAN ONE DOLLAR.

PLEASE NOTE that the articles in the profit sharing list are furnished FREE, but we do not prepay the freight or express charges. : : : : : The customer must pay the mail, express or freight charges in all cases.

PLEASE NOTE that no article will be given and therefore no customer can share in the profits unless all the certificates received amount to $100.00 or more. Therefore in order to share in the profits it will be necessary for you to carefully preserve each certificate sent you for each purchase made until the total amount of all the certificates you receive is $100.00 or more. On the following pages you will see there are a large number of handsome and valuable articles that will be given free in exchange for profit sharing certificates amounting to $100.00 and still much more valuable articles for CERTIFICATES AMOUNTING TO MORE THAN $100.00, up to and including the most valuable article of all, A HANDSOME UPRIGHT GRAND PIANO, which will be given in exchange for profit sharing certificates amounting to $1,000.00.

WITH EVERY ORDER (amounting to $1.00 or more) you send us for the full amount of your purchase, you will receive a profit sharing certificate but after receiving the goods and the profit sharing certificate if for any reason the goods are not satisfactory and if you wish to return them to us and get your money back, you must return your profit sharing certificate also, for failure to return the profit sharing certificate with any goods you return to us to have money refunded, not only cancels the one profit sharing certificate issued for the goods you return, but

also cancels all other profit sharing certificates you may hold. UNDERSTAND, if you receive any goods from us that are not entirely satisfactory we want you to return them to us at our expense and get your money back, but the day you return your goods you must also return your profit sharing certificate; otherwise all profit sharing certificates you hold for previous purchases made will be cancelled by us and will not be accepted if presented to us in exchange for any of the goods shown in this department.

LIMITATIONS OF PROFIT SHARING CERTIFICATES.

While these certificates are not limited as to time, and you may be months or years in accumulating certificates of a sufficient amount to entitle you to the article or articles you want, and they will be accepted by us when presented, no profit sharing certificate is transferable. They are good only for the party in whose name they are drawn, and are not good if altered or defaced in any way.

HOW TO SHARE QUICKLY AND LIBERALLY IN THE PROFITS.

IF YOU ARE IN NEED of a piano, organ, sewing machine, bedroom suite or other valuable articles shown in our profit sharing list, and would like to receive it at an early date, we would suggest as a means for receiving the article wanted in the near future that, first, before buying any kind of goods from your dealer at home or elsewhere, anything that you may need in dry goods, groceries, boots, shoes, hardware, furniture, wearing apparel, or other goods, that you first refer to our big catalogue and see how much money you can save on these goods by sending to us. From time to time as you are in need of goods send to us for everything you want, remembering with each purchase you get a profit sharing certificate for the full amount of your purchase, then if you feel it would take too long a time in the purchase of only the goods you want for your own use to accumulate profit sharing certificates sufficient to entitle you to the article or articles you want, get your friends and neighbors to join with you in sending for the goods they want also. If you have friends or neighbors who are in need of wearing apparel, hardware, furniture, groceries or other goods, if you will call their attention to our prices of the goods they want, surely you have neighbors who would be glad to take advantage of our prices and make a big saving in cost on the goods they want, glad to let you order the goods they need for them. If you can get two or three of your neighbors to order together it will reduce the freight or express charges each one will have to pay, and will mean a big saving in cost to them. Of course the order will have to be sent in your name. You needn't hesitate to say to your neighbors that your object in getting them to let you send for their goods is in order that you may share in our profits by getting the article or articles you want. They will be glad to assist you by letting you send for their goods, since in the sending they save money and you in this way increase the number and amount of the profit sharing certificates that will be issued to you and can more quickly participate in our profit sharing and will be enabled to select larger and more valuable articles from our profit sharing list.

IF YOU HAVE EVER PURCHASED FROM US a buggy, sewing machine, organ, stove, furniture or other article of merchandise call your neighbor's attention to these goods you purchased from us; tell your neighbor how much you paid for the goods and how much money you saved and suggest their ordering a needed stove, vehicle, sewing machine, furniture or other needed goods. They will surely be glad to have you send the order in your name for them for it will mean a big saving in cost to them and will enable us to issue a profit sharing certificate for the amount of the purchase in your name.

THE TIME REQUIRED to accumulate sufficient certificates to allow you to participate in our profit sharing by selecting the article wanted, will depend, first, on how many goods you naturally require for your own use and on what part of these goods you purchase from us. If you buy nearly all the goods you use from us you will not only make a big saving on the cost of the goods you buy, but you will be surprised how rapidly you will accumulate our profit sharing certificates and now quickly they will amount to enough to entitle you to select the article or articles you want; but if your needs are very few your purchases would therefore be small and infrequent even though you sent to us for nearly everything you needed, you can, nevertheless, quickly share in the profits by interesting your neighbors as explained, getting them to allow you to send to us for the goods they need.

UNDERSTAND, you or your neighbors take no risk in sending to us, for if the goods we ship are not satisfactory to you or your neighbors, they can be returned to us at our expense and we will immediately return the money sent us together with any freight or express charges paid. The only condition we make is, that in returning the goods you return the profit sharing certificate that was issued for the particular goods you returned to us.

Our Liberal Profit Sharing Plan with our customers does not add one penny to the price at which we sell our goods. On the contrary, it makes for still lower prices.

OUR PRICES today on everything shown in our big catalogue are lower than ever before printed by us, lower by far than the same goods are quoted in any other catalogue published or offered for sale by any other house, and while our profit is figured very small, no doubt much smaller than any other house in the world selling merchandise to the consumer; in other words, we no doubt make a lesser number of cents net profit each dollar's worth of goods we sell than any other merchandise house in the world, nevertheless the enormous volume of business that has been produced by reason of these low prices, prices lower than any other house in the world, has built our business up until our sales on merchandise often aggregate over $150,000 per day. We know that our customers throughout United States are responsible for this enormous business, responsible for to sell goods at prices so much lower than other houses, responsible percentage of profit than any other

OUR PROFITS are already figured so low that we feel that it would be dangerous to the interests of our business and the customers we serve to reduce our net profit even a fraction of one per cent. We also believe that in this plan we will develop an interest and an economy that will make for us a still much larger volume of business, further lessen the expense of advertising and in this way permit us to still further reduce our selling prices, at the same time permitting all our customers to share liberally in the profits of our business in proportion to the extent the individual customer patronizes our house.

MANY OF OUR CUSTOMERS after dealing with us, for months or years, having purchased goods from us amounting to one hundred dollars or even hundreds of dollars, have suggested that we send them some sort of a present as a substantial recognition of our appreciation of their trade, and no doubt where one customer has suggested that we so recognize them, thousands of our customers have felt that something of this kind was due them, and we, too, have felt that something more

INDEX

Abbott, Lyman, 73, 74, 97
Academy of Music, 5
accordions, 25-26, 36
Adam's Profession (Meade), 422
Adams, Henry, 286
Adams, James Truslow, 135
Adams, Samuel Hopkins, 230
Admirable Crichton, The (Barrie), 396
adventure books, 145
Adventures in Bird Protection (Pearson), 338 *
Adventures of a Novelist (Atherton), 321
advertising, 503-509
    nudity in, 507-509
Advertising Club (New York), 47
Advertising Guide, The, 551-552
Advocate (Shawano, Wis.), 515
agricultural implements, 490
    machinery, 486-488, 490-491, 495-498
agriculture, 483-500
Agriculture, Department of, 253, 306, 387, 487, 555
aigrettes, 338-342
Ainslie, Mayor, 299
air conditioning, 415-416
alarm clocks, 176-181
alcoholism, 223-225
Alcott, Louisa May, quoted, 371-372
Alexandra, Queen of England, 268
Allen, Devere, quoted, 309-310
Allen, Edward, 514
Allen, Grant, 89-90, 92, 93
Allen, James Lane, 85, 89
American Machinist, 195
American Medical Association, 259
American Notes (Kipling), 73

American Phrenological Journal, 369
American Scholar, The (Poteat), 72 *
American Society (Towles), 452
American Tragedy, An (Dreiser), 147
Ames, Adrienne, 352
amusement, books of, 106-109
Ancient Highway, The (Curwood), 131
Ancient Landmark (Waltz), 80
Anderson, Sherwood, quoted, 66; 130, 134, 147
Andrew Jackson, An Epic in Homespun (Johnson), 431 *
Andrews, Marietta Minnigerode, quoted, xxviii
And Then Came Ford (Merz), 157, 168
Angel in the House (Norris), 144
Angle, Paul McClelland, 334 *
Anthony, Susan B., 210
apparel, men's, 461-482
    women's, 285-316
Applegate, Jesse, quoted, 13
Après-midi d'un faune, L' (Debussy), 55
Arden, Elizabeth, 278, 282, 403
Aristotle, 327
Arliss, George, quoted, 339
Around the World on a Bicycle (Stevens), 454
artificial legs, 229
Art of Thinking, The (Dimnet), 146
Art Through the Ages (Gardner), 135
Associated Press, 381
Athalie (Mendelssohn), 28
Athenaeum Club, 508